90 0204658 9

KW-242-020

MONOPOLIES AND MERGERS COMMISSION

The supply of recorded music

A report on the supply in the UK of pre-recorded compact discs, vinyl discs and tapes containing music

Presented to Parliament by the Secretary of State for Trade and Industry by Command of Her Majesty June 1994

LONDON : HMSO
£27.50 net

Cm 2599

UNIVERSITY OF PLYMOUTH
LIBRARY SERVICES

Item No.	900 2046589
Class No.	338.4778 GRE
Contl. No.	0101259921

Members of the Monopolies and Mergers Commission as at 14 April 1994

Mr G D W Odgers[1] *(Chairman)*
Mr P H Dean CBE *(Deputy Chairman)*
Mr D G Goyder[1] *(Deputy Chairman)*
Mr H H Liesner CB *(Deputy Chairman)*
Mr A G Armstrong
Mr I S Barter
Professor M E Beesley CBE[1]
Mrs C M Blight
Mr P Brenan
Mr J S Bridgeman
Mr R O Davies
Professor S Eilon
Mr J Evans[1]
Mr A Ferry MBE
Mr N H Finney OBE
Sir Archibald Forster
Sir Ronald Halstead CBE
Ms P A Hodgson
Mr M R Hoffman
Mr D J Jenkins MBE
Mr A L Kingshott
Mr G C S Mather
Mr N F Matthews
Professor J S Metcalfe CBE
Professor A P L Minford
Mr J D Montgomery
Dr D J Morris
Professor J F Pickering
Mr L Priestley
Mr M R Prosser
Dr A Robinson
Mr J K Roe
Dr L M Rouse
Mr D P Thomson[1]
Mrs C Tritton QC
Professor G Whittington

Mr A J Nieduszynski *(Secretary)*

---

[1]These members formed the group which was responsible for this report under the chairmanship of Mr Graeme Odgers.

248336 A2

Note by the Department of Trade and Industry

In accordance with section 83(3) and (3A) of the Fair Trading Act 1973, the Secretary of State has excluded from the copies of the report, as laid before Parliament and as published, certain matters, publication of which appears to the Secretary of State to be against the public interest, or which he considers would not be in the public interest to disclose and which, in his opinion, would seriously and prejudicially affect certain interests. The omissions are indicated by a note in the text.

Contents

Part I—Summary and Conclusions

Part II—Background and evidence

Appendices   (The numbering of the appendices indicates the chapters to which they relate)

Part I

Summary and Conclusions

1 Summary

1.1. The UK record industry is large and internationally important. Retail sales in the UK amount to over £1 billion per annum and UK employment associated with the industry exceeds 48,000. The industry earns considerable income from licensing its recordings overseas. UK sales represent 7 per cent of the world market, but it is estimated that a larger proportion of world sales (about 18 per cent) are recordings involving UK artists.

1.2. Our inquiry has looked at both the record companies and the retailers of recorded music in the UK.[1] On the record companies side five multinational companies, known as 'the majors', account for about 70 per cent of the market. These companies are EMI, PolyGram, Sony, Warner and BMG. We find that a complex monopoly situation exists in their favour by reason of their pricing practices, arrangements on parallel imports[2] and terms of contract with artists. The remainder of the market is made up of some 600 other companies known as independents, many of which are small and specialize in particular genres of music, eg dance or jazz. Many of these companies engage in similar practices to the majors but lack the majors' market presence both in the UK and internationally. Across the UK industry the great bulk of sales are of popular records, with classical music accounting for only 9 per cent of sales.

1.3. On the retail side W H Smith, through its own shops and through its subsidiary Our Price, supplies 26.6 per cent by value of the market. Since this amounts to more than 25 per cent, this group of companies has a scale monopoly. Other significant retailers are Woolworths (15 per cent), HMV (13.5 per cent), Virgin Retail (4.2 per cent), Boots (3 per cent) and Tower Records (2 per cent). There are also some 1,100 independent specialist record shops and a growing number of 'non-traditional' outlets such as petrol stations and supermarkets. In addition, mail order and record clubs account for some 12 per cent of the market.

1.4. Copyright is central to the operations of the record industry, both in the UK and internationally. It allows record companies to invest money and enterprise in creating commercial recordings which can be exploited in both the home and overseas markets knowing that they have legal protection against unauthorized reproduction. Copyright is also important in ensuring that the talents of successful artists and songwriters are rewarded.

1.5. The MMC inquiry was prompted by concern about the prices of compact discs (CDs), and particularly the fact that prices appeared to be significantly higher in the UK than in the USA. Much of the apparent difference relates to different tax arrangements. Sales taxes in the USA are considerably lower than the UK's 17.5 per cent rate of VAT. Moreover, record prices are displayed without sales tax in the USA, whereas shelf prices in the UK include VAT.

---

[1]The terms of reference are set out in Appendix 1.1.

[2]See the Glossary for definition.

1.6. We commissioned our own survey of comparative UK/US prices and found that the real price differentials were considerably lower than is often supposed. The survey showed that, when tax is excluded, the prices of full-price popular CDs are on average 7 to 9 per cent higher in the UK than in the USA at an exchange rate of $1.50 to the pound. The differential for full-price classical CDs is greater at about 25 per cent. However, some 55 per cent of classical CDs sold in the UK are in the mid-price or budget categories and there are strong indications that the price differentials covering the complete range of full-price, mid-price and budget CDs are on average lower than the differentials for full-price CDs.

1.7. These price comparisons are based on an exchange rate of $1.50 to the pound, which was the average for the second half of 1993. Variations in exchange rates will lead to changes in the measured US/UK price differentials. We sought to check whether record price differentials were out of line with those existing in other low- to medium-priced manufactured goods associated with leisure activities. We found that they were not. This suggests that the price differentials for CDs are not the result of circumstances specific to the record industry.

1.8. Apart from the influence of particular exchange rate levels it was argued that the much larger size of the US market (resulting in longer manufacturing runs and the ability to recover the high initial cost of a recording over a greater number of sales) and the generally lower US retailing costs (relating particularly to lower premises costs and higher labour productivity) lead to price levels being generally lower in the USA. It has not been possible to quantify the effect of these factors but we believe the arguments have force and apply both to CDs and to a wider range of manufactured products.

1.9. We also compared record prices with those in a number of other industrialized countries and found that UK prices are generally lower. Thus it appears that the UK is not experiencing systematically higher prices for recorded music.

1.10. It was suggested to us that the differential with the USA could be eliminated if the record companies' ability to control parallel imports were removed. We do not believe this would be the case. Such a move would in any event be contrary to the EC Rental Directive and could be damaging because of the increased risk of piracy and the general weakening of copyright protection, which is territorially based.

1.11. We found that the major record companies compete vigorously amongst themselves and with the independent sector. New entrants are a pronounced feature of the industry. The major record companies' strength in the market-place is balanced by powerful retailing groups. The major companies are not therefore able to exercise market power to the disadvantage of consumers and we conclude that prices are set at competitive levels in the UK market. The major record companies are not making excessive profits.

1.12. Record retailing is also a competitive market. There is no evidence that the scale monopoly of W H Smith enables it to exploit its position. Its profits on record retailing are not excessive.

1.13. The record industry is a high-risk business. The great majority of recordings do not sell enough copies to recoup their initial investment. Record prices must therefore be set so that the earnings on successful records will cover losses on the failures. It would not be sensible for the record companies to price CDs, cassettes and vinyl records strictly in relation to manufacturing costs, which make up only a small proportion of the total costs. Instead record companies have developed pricing structures for different recordings and different formats which reflect consumers' perceptions of quality and value and hence willingness to pay. Given the strong competition in the market we believe this pricing policy is justified.

1.14. During our inquiry a number of issues were raised in connection with the contracts between artists and record companies. We found that the record companies compete actively in securing the services of new and established artists. Terms of contract have generally moved in the artists' favour over the last 20 years. Artists are normally professionally advised in their commercial negotiations with the record companies about contract terms, both at the time of the initial contract negotiations and at subsequent renegotiations. Ownership and control of copyright for a significant period is essential to a record company that has made a large initial investment in recordings and in an artist's career. We see no case for any change in the contractual or copyright framework governing the relationship between artist and record company. The proper forum for the resolution of particular disputes between artists and record companies is the court.

1.15. We had some concern about the record companies' practice of giving free singles to retailers as a means of promoting new releases. However, on balance we think no change is required in connection with this practice because it forms part of the competitive process and benefits the independent retailers, who do not receive discounts and other promotional support to the same extent as large retailers.

1.16. Finally, we also felt some concern that consumers might be misled by the practice of some major retailers in displaying charts which show the retailers' predictions of future sales rather than actual sales as recorded in the national charts. Where retailers do this we consider that they should make clear the basis on which the charts have been compiled.

1.17. Although we have found two monopoly situations to exist, we have not found that they operate against the public interest.

2　Conclusions

Contents

Introduction

2.1. The Director General of Fair Trading referred the supply of recorded music to the MMC on 14 May 1993 for investigation under the monopoly provisions of the Fair Trading Act 1973.

2.2. In announcing the reference the Director General drew attention to the relatively high prices of CDs when compared with the cost of other formats and with prices in the USA. He expressed concern that the record companies' use of copyright law to restrict parallel imports of lower-priced CDs may be frustrating competition. Similar concerns had been expressed by the National Heritage

Committee of the House of Commons and by Consumers' Association. The conclusions of the National Heritage Committee's report[1] are reproduced in Appendix 2.1.

2.3. Although the price of CDs was the main focus of the inquiry, our terms of reference are not confined to this issue. They embrace the whole field of recorded music and require us to investigate and report on 'the supply in the United Kingdom of pre-recorded compact and vinyl discs and pre-recorded analogue and digital tapes on which music is reproduced without visual image'. A number of other issues were raised with us in the course of our inquiry and we record our conclusions on all of them in this chapter.

Background

2.4. The UK has a large and internationally important recorded music industry. The retail value of sales in the UK amounts to over £1 billion per annum and UK employment associated with the industry exceeds 48,000. In addition, the industry earns considerable income from licensing its recordings overseas. The structure of the industry is complex and diverse, involving many activities from the creative work of songwriters and artists to the manufacturing, distribution and promotion of the finished records.

The record companies

2.5. The core activity of a record company is creating and exploiting copyright in sound recordings. Most record companies achieve this by signing contracts with artists under which the artist usually agrees to record exclusively with that record company for a period. In exchange for this commitment the artist will usually receive an advance of royalties at the start of work on each record album and, by virtue of copyright legislation, the record company will own the copyright in the recordings. A pop artist will usually write his own songs which he will record in a studio with the help of a record producer.

2.6. When a satisfactory master recording has been made the record company will send it to the manufacturing plants where it will be reproduced on CDs, cassettes or vinyl. The most important activities of the record company will then be the marketing and promotion of the new release and its distribution to retailers. Promotion may take the form of videos and interviews on television, advertisements in the musical press and other media and personal appearances by the artist. Some promotion may be carried out jointly with particular retailers. In the case of a pop record the aim will be to get the record played on the radio and to secure a place in the record charts, which will then lead to further exposure and increased sales.

2.7. The cost of making a record, including the artists' advance and costs of a video, can be very significant (up to £1 million or more for a pop album by a superstar). Thus a large number of copies then need to be sold before the record company will recover its initial costs. How many will be sold is difficult to predict in advance, particularly as only a small proportion of the pop artists signed by a record company actually achieves success. To try to secure those successes the company will put a great deal of effort into seeking to establish (or 'break') new artists during their early careers. If an artist becomes established the record company will seek to promote the artist's career and maintain a long-term relationship. If success is not achieved, the contract will be allowed to lapse. The initial outlays comprise a major source of risk for the company.

2.8. There are five large multinational record companies operating in the UK which are known as 'the majors'; their market shares (by volume of albums sold in 1993 by the companies and their subsidiaries) are:

---

[1]*The price of compact discs*, Fifth report of the National Heritage Committee, 1992–93, HC 609.

	%
EMI Records Limited and Virgin Records Ltd (EMI)	23.8
PolyGram UK Holdings Plc (PolyGram)	21.3
Warner Music UK Limited (Warner)	10.3
Sony Music Entertainment (UK) Limited (Sony)	9.6
BMG Records (UK) Limited (BMG)	7.0

Together these five companies have a UK market share of 72 per cent.

2.9. The remaining 28 per cent of the market is supplied by some 600 independent record companies. Many of these are very small companies, some making only one or two releases a year. However, the independent companies are a very important part of the record industry since they are often at the leading edge of developments in pop music, with the ability to discover new talent and establish new fashions. They also have to face the risks inherent in developing new repertoire.

2.10. As well as supplying records in the UK, the record companies exploit their recordings overseas. Normally this is done by licensing an overseas company to supply records in a particular country. In the case of the majors this will usually be the record company's local affiliate. The independent record companies will often rely on unconnected companies to perform this function, including the majors' overseas affiliates. Licence income generated in this way is an important source of income for UK record companies and makes a significant contribution to the country's invisible earnings (see paragraph 5.222). The UK is second to the USA as a supplier of recorded music to the rest of the world: the industry's trade association (the British Phonographic Industry Ltd (BPI)) estimates that 18 per cent of world sales have a connection with the work of UK artists, while the UK's home market represents only 7 per cent of world sales.

Retailing of records

2.11. Records are sold both through shops which specialize in music and shops which sell a much wider range of products. The specialists include chains, such as HMV and Our Price, and many small independent retailers. The non-specialists include multiples such as W H Smith and Woolworths as well as an increasing number of 'non-traditional' outlets such as supermarkets and petrol stations. In addition, mail order and record clubs account for some 12 per cent of the market.

2.12. The largest retailers and their 1992 market shares are:

	%
W H Smith Group plc (W H Smith)	8.1
Our Price Limited (Our Price) (a subsidiary of W H Smith)	18.5
Woolworths plc (Woolworths)	15.0
HMV UK Limited (HMV)	13.5
Virgin Retail Limited (Virgin Retail)[1]	4.2

Together these companies make up almost 60 per cent of total retail sales.

2.13. Records reach the retailers from the record companies by a variety of routes. Some 60 per cent go direct from the record company's nominated distributor to the retailer, 28 per cent go through a wholesaler and the remaining 12 per cent reach consumers through mail order suppliers. Almost all deliveries to retailers go direct to individual shops rather than to retailers' central warehouses. For example, each of W H Smith's some 300 outlets receives deliveries direct from the major record companies and other distributors. All Woolworths' stores are supplied by the wholesaler Entertainment UK Ltd, a sister company in the Kingfisher Group.

---

[1]Virgin Retail is a joint venture owned 50 per cent by W H Smith Limited and 50 per cent by Virgin Retail Group Limited. Proposals have been announced for Virgin and Our Price to merge and form a company in which W H Smith will have a 75 per cent shareholding.

2.14. All the major record companies operate their own distribution businesses and so a retailer who orders direct from distributors will have to order stock from several sources (the five majors plus up to 20 others for independent record companies' releases). Wholesalers generally handle the releases of all record companies and so a retailer will only have to order from one wholesaler if he uses this route. The main wholesalers also offer another service known as 'rack-jobbing'. Rack-jobbing is a method of supply used by non-traditional retail outlets (such as petrol stations). A rack-jobber supplies a complete package of records and display material and is responsible for maintaining the stock, typically on a sale or exchange basis.

The importance of copyright

2.15. Copyright lies at the heart of the recorded music industry. It allows record companies to invest money and enterprise in creating commercial recordings which can be exploited in both the UK and overseas markets knowing that they have legal protection against unauthorized reproduction. Copyright is also important in ensuring that the talents of successful artists and songwriters are rewarded. The protection of copyright is therefore crucial both to the creative side of the music industry and to the businesses of the record companies. UK legislation on copyright is primarily contained in the Copyright, Designs and Patents Act 1988 (the 1988 Copyright Act).

2.16. Two principal types of copyright are involved. First, copyright exists in the music which is performed by an artist, that is in the words and music of a song and in the composition of a classical composer. Secondly, a separate copyright exists in the sound recording when a particular artist performs a musical work and it is recorded. In the UK, music copyright lasts until 50 years after the death of the composer and copyright in a sound recording lasts until 50 years after the record is released.

2.17. A songwriter or composer will normally assign the copyright in his or her music to a 'music publisher', a business set up to exploit and protect composers' works. The activities of music publishers fall outside our terms of reference since they do not supply the reference products. Although some music publishers are affiliates of record companies, many artists sign up with publishers not associated with their record companies. The music publisher will collect a royalty for the songwriter/composer for every record containing his or her composition which is sold by a record company. This is known as a 'mechanical royalty'. It is collected by the Mechanical Copyright Protection Society (MCPS) on behalf of the music publisher and composer.

2.18. Under the copyright legislation the copyright in a sound recording will normally be owned by the record company, though the copyrights can be licensed or assigned to others. As we have noted in paragraph 2.10, a UK record company will normally license overseas exploitation to a local company and in this case the UK record company will receive a licence fee for every record sold abroad. Conversely, when a UK record company is licensed by an overseas company to issue its sound recordings in the UK (typically records of an artist signed to that company) the UK record company will pay a licence fee for every record sold.

2.19. The copyright legislation grants a bundle of rights to a copyright owner which includes the exclusive right to make copies and the exclusive right to perform the work in public (including broadcasting). Thus record companies also receive licence fees every time a record is played in public (eg in clubs or pubs) or is played on the radio or television. These fees are collected by Phonographic Performance Limited (PPL) on behalf of the record companies.

2.20. Finally, the copyright legislation gives a copyright holder the right to control imports. This derives from the territorial nature of copyright, under which UK legislation gives certain rights in the UK and other countries give rights in their territories. These may differ from country to country but generally conform to international conventions under which most countries have agreed on reciprocal arrangements for a minimum level of copyright protection. Generally, records can only be imported into the UK with the permission both of the owner of the UK copyright in the music and the owner of the UK copyright in the sound recordings.

2.21. The provisions of the EEC Treaty provide an exception. Where a record has been lawfully put on the market in one member state, by the copyright owner or with his consent, the record is able to enjoy free movement within the EC without the payment of licence fees or customs duties. Moreover, under an EC Directive[1] which has to be implemented by 1 July 1994, all member states will be required to provide copyright owners with the right to control imports from outside the EC (which the UK copyright legislation already does). The provisions of this Directive and other copyright legislation are discussed more fully in Chapter 4.

The monopoly situations

Record companies

2.22. A scale monopoly situation under section 6(1)*(a)* or *(b)* of the Fair Trading Act (the Act) is taken to exist when at least one-quarter of all the goods of a particular description which are supplied in the UK are supplied by or to the same person, or by or to members of the same group of interconnected bodies corporate. We find that no record company, nor any such group of interconnected companies, has a market share of 25 per cent or more.

2.23. A complex monopoly situation under section 6(1)*(c)* and (2) of the Act is taken to exist when at least one-quarter of all the goods of a particular description which are supplied in the UK are supplied by or to members of the same group consisting of two or more persons (not being a group of interconnected bodies corporate) who, whether voluntarily or not and whether by agreement or not, so conduct their respective affairs as in any way to prevent, restrict or distort competition in connection with the production or supply of goods of that description. We provisionally found that the five major record companies, with a combined share of over two-thirds of the market (see Table 5.21), all engaged in a number of practices which appeared to prevent, restrict or distort competition in connection with the supply of recorded music. The practices were:

(i)   adopting similar pricing policies to each other for the various formats (CD, music cassette and vinyl) of 'full-price' albums and singles;

(ii) declining to license imports of some sound recordings in which the company holds the copyright and licensing others only on payment of a fee under the MCPS/BPI import scheme; and

(iii) entering into recording contracts with artists which include terms that restrict the artists' ability to exploit their talent fully and restrict competition in the supply of recorded music (eg in clauses relating to the extent of copyright acquired, length of contract, exclusivity, options, obligations to exploit recordings, royalty rates, packaging and other deductions from royalties, and/or arrangements for accounting for and auditing royalties).

2.24. We wrote to BMG, EMI, PolyGram, Sony and Warner notifying them of our provisional finding that they, and their record company subsidiaries, were members of such a group since they each engaged in one or more of the practices listed in the preceding paragraph. We invited the companies' views on our provisional finding and on a number of issues which had been raised with us concerning their behaviour and its effects. The list of issues is reproduced in Appendix 2.2.

2.25. In their responses, each of the companies argued that a complex monopoly situation did not exist. We consider their main arguments in the following paragraphs.

---

[1]Directive 92/100/EEC (the 'Rental Directive'), OJ No L346/61, 27 November 1992.

Submission that other companies engage in the practices

2.26. The companies pointed out that they were not the only record companies which engaged in the three practices on which we had based our provisional finding. Since the practices were common throughout the industry, it was claimed, we should not single out the five majors as members of a group constituting a complex monopoly situation. It followed that either there was no monopoly situation at all or the members of the group should be extended to include all the companies, however small, which engaged in the practices. Precedents were cited of earlier reports of the MMC[1] where the complex monopoly had included large numbers of companies, including many with only small market shares.

2.27. We accept that in certain previous reports the MMC have included in complex monopoly situations all or virtually all the companies which engaged in the relevant practices which prevented, restricted or distorted competition. We now, however, have the guidance of the courts in *R v MMC and another ex parte Ecando Systems Ltd* (ECS).[2] In the High Court, Mr Justice Simon Brown held that the MMC had a wide discretion in applying the complex monopoly provisions of the Act. In the Court of Appeal, Lord Justice Ralph Gibson said 'there is force in the submission for the appellants that the questions at the first stage of the inquiry by the Commission, including whether a complex monopoly exists, and if it does in favour of what person it exists, are on their face primarily issues of fact'. He went on to accept that the MMC had acted properly when they carried out a considerable degree of selectivity.

2.28. We note that in ECS the Court of Appeal were inclined to classify the questions as 'primarily' issues of fact. They did not hold that they were exclusively ones of fact. We have carefully considered the judgments in ECS and have come to the view that the complex monopoly question is one both of fact and degree. We have also found of assistance the judgment of the Court of Appeal in *R v MMC and others ex parte Visa International Service Association*.[3] The Court of Appeal agreed with Mr Justice Hodgson that when the MMC apply the complex monopoly provisions 'it is permissible and necessary to give consideration to commercial realities'.

2.29. We have noted that the market share of the five major record companies in 1993 was 72 per cent of the number of albums (see Table 5.22) and that these companies have maintained a significant market share for at least the last ten years. During that period no other company, apart from Virgin which has now been taken over by EMI, has had a market share of more than 5 per cent. Not only have these companies maintained a significant market share in the UK for a sustained period but their affiliates in other countries have a significant market share internationally which gives them unrivalled access to the work of major artists throughout the world. This adds to their strength in the UK.

2.30. In addition, we observe that in evidence to us, and throughout the record industry and those who do business with it, these five companies are known as 'the majors'. The evidence of market share and the way they are regarded by others in the industry as well as outside it lead us to conclude that the commercial reality is that if these five companies were to act in a similar fashion, they could influence the practices of the whole industry. Having regard to the judgments and the commercial circumstances we have discussed above, we consider that 'the majors' should all be included in any group which may give rise to a complex monopoly situation in relation to the supply of recorded music. We consider, however, that in the circumstances it is unnecessary for us to include companies with a smaller market share than 'the majors'.

2.31. In defining the group we have given particular consideration to the position of MCA Records Ltd (MCA), the sixth largest company in 1992 when it supplied 4.1 per cent of albums in the UK. Although MCA is a multinational company, in contrast to the other five it has only recently acquired a market share of this size, having generally had a share of between 1 and 2 per cent between 1983

---

[1]*The Supply of Beer: a report on the supply of beer for retail sale in the United Kingdom*, Cm 651, March 1989; *The Supply of Petrol: a report on the supply in the United Kingdom of petrol by wholesale*, Cm 972, February 1990; *Motor car parts: a report on the wholesale supply of motor car parts within the United Kingdom*, Cm 1818, February 1992.

[2]Unreported judgments of Simon Brown J on 30 September 1991 and of the Court of Appeal on 12 November 1992.

[3][1991] CCLR 13 at 21.

248336 B

and 1990. Moreover, MCA still has few artists signed in the UK and it does not have its own distribution arrangements. We have concluded that MCA does not at present enjoy a similar position to the five largest companies and that it should not therefore be included in the complex monopoly group.

Practice (i)—similar pricing policies

2.32. The companies argue that they have not, consciously or unconsciously, followed the same pricing policies as each other. To the extent that their prices are similar, they say that this is a result of market forces rather than of any practice designed to prevent, restrict or distort competition. Furthermore, any similarity in pricing policies does not have anti-competitive consequences since competition is in fact vigorous.

2.33. We observe that there is consistency in the pricing of full-price CDs relative to full-price cassettes. For each of the companies the published prices to dealers of full-price albums on CDs, whether classical or non-classical, are around 50 per cent higher than the published dealer prices of equivalent cassettes. Table 2.1 (which is based on Tables 7.1 and 7.2) shows that the range is from 42 per cent to 54 per cent. The prices of LPs are generally the same as for cassettes.

TABLE 2.1 **Published prices to dealers for full-price albums, September 1993**

Type of record	PolyGram	EMI	Sony	Warner	BMG	Unweighted average
Non-classical, full-price						
Cassette price (£)	5.25	4.99	5.17	5.30	5.35	5.21
CD price (£)	7.59	7.56	7.59	7.96	7.59	7.66
Difference (%)	46	52	47	50	42	47
Non-classical, deluxe full-price						
Cassette price (£)	5.53	5.13	5.35	5.66	5.60	5.45
CD price (£)	8.15	7.86	8.03	8.21	8.14	8.08
Difference (%)	47	53	50	45	45	48
Classical, full-price						
Cassette price (£)	5.53	5.29	5.17	5.51	5.34	5.37
CD price (£)	8.15	8.14	7.59	7.96	7.89	7.95
Difference (%)	47	54	47	44	48	48

Source: See Tables 7.1 and 7.2.

2.34. The cost of manufacturing records is only a comparatively small part of the record companies' total costs, being on average £1.32 for CDs, £0.66 for cassettes and £0.93 for LPs (see Table 8.10). The remainder of the costs are royalties or licence fees, which are contracted to be a percentage of the selling price for each unit sold, and costs which relate to the title as a whole and are independent of the formats on which it is sold, such as recording costs, advances, marketing and promotion. The fact that the record companies' prices for CDs are about 50 per cent higher than for cassettes or LPs is not therefore the result of differences in the direct costs of producing the different formats. It is very largely a marketing decision for the record companies how they set their prices for the different formats in order to cover their costs and make a profit on their repertoire as a whole. Accordingly we consider that as the companies all make similar decisions their price setting constitutes a way in which they 'conduct their respective affairs' within the meaning of section 6(2) of the Act.

2.35. Having established that the companies' pricing policies constitute a practice, the remaining requirement of a complex monopoly situation is that the practice should prevent, restrict or distort competition in some way. We are not at this stage of our analysis required by the Act to make any judgment as to whether the effects of the conduct are good or bad, nor about the overall effects of the conduct on competition in the context of the market. Since price is an important component of competition, both at wholesale level and at retail level, we conclude that competition is restricted by the similarity of pricing policies between the companies. The process and operation of competition in the supply of recorded music would be different if the companies had adopted different pricing policies from each other and there would consequently be different opportunities for other record companies and retailers.

Practice (ii)—restrictions on imports

2.36. The companies do not deny that they sometimes decline to license imports or that they participate in the MCPS/BPI import licensing scheme through which they levy a fee when imports are licensed. However, they argue that the law gives them the right to prohibit imports, that they do so only occasionally and then for good reasons and that the MCPS/BPI scheme is designed to facilitate imports rather than impede them.

2.37. We accept that the 1988 Copyright Act[1] gives the owner of the copyright in a sound recording the right to control imports of that sound recording from outside the EC. However, the 1988 Copyright Act does not impose any obligation and it does not compel record companies to refuse import licences or to charge a fee if it grants them. A record company could decide that it would allow imports without charging a fee; it could decide to charge a different licence fee from other companies; it could decide to prohibit all imports; or it could follow a policy which varied according to whether or not an affiliated record company had produced the record which was to be imported.

2.38. That the companies all prohibit imports in certain circumstances and charge the same scale of fees when an import is not prohibited is therefore a practice capable of forming the basis of a complex monopoly situation. The fact that copyright law gives them certain rights does not prevent the way they exercise those rights being such a practice for the purpose of the Fair Trading Act.

2.39. This view is reinforced by the fact that section 144 of the 1988 Copyright Act specifically provides for the Secretary of State to vary the terms of a copyright licence or to order compulsory licences following an MMC report containing an adverse finding on the public interest.

2.40. The practice has an effect on competition compared with a situation in which imports were licensed either with no fee or with a lower fee (or indeed with a situation in which they were never licensed). This does not imply that the effects of the scheme are good or bad. The argument that the import licensing scheme is pro-competitive because it facilitates imports falls to be considered as part of our examination of the public interest.

Practice (iii)—artists' contracts

2.41. The companies have argued that the provisions in artists' contracts do not restrict competition and are in fact the way in which artists are able to exploit their talents fully. It is claimed that exclusivity and other provisions on copyright and length of contract are essential to enable the industry to function at all.

2.42. We believe these are all matters which bear on our consideration of the public interest if we conclude that a monopoly situation exists. Each of the major companies does normally include provisions in its contracts which provide that artists will give their services on an exclusive basis for a period which will, if the artist is successful, extend for several years. Clauses in the contract will also normally provide for the company to hold the copyright for its full term, describe the geographical extent to which the company is entitled to exploit the copyright and specify any obligation for the company to exploit the artists' recordings. It is clear on the face of such provisions that they restrict the artist's freedom to offer his recording services to other companies and so prevent, restrict or distort competition. This does not imply, however, that their effects are either good or bad or that the provisions operate against the public interest. We consider the consequences of the practices in paragraphs 2.128 to 2.147.

2.43. We accept that there will also be detailed provisions in the contracts, notably those relating to financial matters, which will vary widely from case to case. Nevertheless their common approach

---

[1]Section 22.

248336 B2

to the application of clauses restrictive on the artist and the marked degree of uniformity in the general contractual framework governing the relationship are such as to constitute a practice pursued by each of the five companies.

Conclusion on the record companies' complex monopoly situation

2.44. We conclude in the light of the preceding discussion that a monopoly situation exists by virtue of section 6(1)(c) and (2) of the Act (a complex monopoly situation) in that the following companies (being members of one and the same group for the purpose of these provisions) supply at least one-quarter of the recorded music supplied in the UK:

> BMG Records (UK) Limited
> EMI Records Limited and Virgin Records Ltd
> PolyGram UK Holdings Plc
> Sony Music Entertainment (UK) Limited
> Warner Music UK Limited
> and their respective record company subsidiaries

and these companies so conduct their respective affairs as to prevent, restrict or distort competition in connection with the supply of recorded music in that they each engage in one or more of the following practices:

(i) adopting similar pricing policies to each other for the various formats (CD, music cassette and vinyl) of 'full-price' albums and singles;

(ii) declining to license imports of some sound recordings in which the company holds the copyright and licensing others only on payment of a fee under the MCPS/BPI import scheme; and

(iii) entering into recording contracts with artists which include terms that restrict the artists' ability to exploit their talent fully and restrict competition in the supply of recorded music (eg in clauses relating to the extent of copyright acquired, length of contract, exclusivity, options and obligations to exploit recordings).

2.45. We conclude that this monopoly situation exists in favour of the companies mentioned in the preceding paragraph.

Retailers

2.46. In relation to retailers, we provisionally found that there were two monopoly situations.

Scale monopoly situation

2.47. A scale monopoly was provisionally found to exist in that W H Smith and Our Price, being members of the same group of interconnected companies, supply at least one-quarter of the recorded music supplied in the UK. As shown in Table 6.3, these companies supplied 26.6 per cent of the recorded music sold at retail level in 1992. We provisionally found that the monopoly situation existed in favour of the two companies and we invited their comments on our provisional finding and on the issues listed in Appendix 2.3.

2.48. W H Smith and Our Price accepted the existence of the scale monopoly and we therefore confirm our provisional finding that a monopoly situation exists by virtue of section 6(1)(b) of the Act and that it exists in their favour.

2.49. Although the companies accepted the existence of the monopoly situation, they argued that there were no facts that operated, or may be expected to operate, against the public interest. We consider this later in the chapter.

Complex monopoly situation

2.50. In addition to the scale monopoly, we also made a provisional finding of a complex monopoly situation in respect of retailers in that W H Smith, Our Price, HMV and Woolworths (in association with Entertainment UK Ltd) were members of a group whose members supplied at least one-quarter of the recorded music supplied in UK and appeared to so conduct their affairs as to prevent, restrict or distort competition in that they engaged in the following practice:

> securing discounts and promotional support from suppliers of recorded music that are larger than those made available to other retailers.

2.51. This finding was based on preliminary figures for discounts in respect of albums on the lines of those shown in Table 1 of Appendix 8.4 and on evidence we had received about the amounts the major record companies spent on co-operative promotions with the large retailers (see, for example, paragraphs 11.50 to 11.52). We believed competition might be distorted if the major retailers were able to use their market power to obtain large, non-cost-related discounts which were not available to smaller retailers.

2.52. In response to our finding the members of the group argued that they did not receive larger discounts than some of those retailers which were excluded, for example Virgin Retail, Boots, Menzies, Tower Records or Andys; that the smaller retailers received discounts in other forms, including free singles, which counterbalanced the file discounts of the larger retailers; and that much of the promotional support received by the larger retailers was directed towards advertising which promoted sales of particular records and was of benefit to all retailers.

2.53. We have examined the evidence in support of these arguments and have estimated the effective discounts for albums and singles for different retailers after taking into account file and other discounts, free goods, returns, marketing and support and differences in the distribution services provided by the record company. The results are discussed in paragraphs 8.47 to 8.58 from which it can be seen that singles are of particular importance to the independent specialist retailers and it is on singles that they achieve significantly better terms.

2.54. Precise figures cannot be calculated because of the different nature of the benefits. However, taking account of all these discounts and allowances, and including singles as well as albums, we consider that the largest retailers which we included in our provisional finding of a complex monopoly situation do not consistently receive higher benefits in the form of discounts and promotional spending than other retailers. We therefore conclude that there is no complex monopoly situation among retailers of recorded music.

The relevant issues

2.55. Having established the existence of a complex monopoly situation in favour of the five major record company groups and a scale monopoly situation in relation to retailing in favour of W H Smith and Our Price, we are required by our terms of reference to consider whether those companies are taking any steps to maintain or exploit the monopoly situations, whether any actions or omissions on their part are attributable to the monopoly situations and whether there are any facts which operate, or may be expected to operate, against the public interest. We believe the supply of recorded music as defined in our terms of reference is the relevant economic market in which to consider these questions and we have received no argument to the contrary.

2.56. When the reference was made the main area of concern was the price of CDs, particularly in comparison with other countries. The Consumers' Association had pointed to the higher prices charged for CDs in the UK compared with the USA and had attributed this to the fact that under the copyright legislation the record companies were able to control parallel imports. The National

Heritage Committee of the House of Commons in its report of May 1993[1] saw the question in the following terms:

> When the Committee decided to conduct this inquiry, it was looking for an answer to what seemed a very simple question. Why do compact discs cost quite a lot more in the United Kingdom than they do in the United States?

In its conclusions, which are reproduced in Appendix 2.1, the Committee also attached importance to the question of parallel imports and called for price reductions by the record companies and the retailers.

2.57. We consider these issues first. We then look at the other issues that have been raised with us in the course of our inquiry, including the relationship between artists and record companies, the extent of the companies' spending on marketing and promotion, the reduced availability of vinyl LPs and singles, the activities of relevant collecting societies and some issues relating to the record charts.

International price differentials

Comparisons with the USA

Popular perceptions

2.58. A popular perception of many international travellers is that a record costs the same number of dollars in the USA as it costs pounds in the UK. Thus a full-price CD which is on display at £14.99 in London might be seen in a shop in New York at a price of $14.99 which, at an exchange rate of £1.50 to the pound, implies that records are 50 per cent more expensive in the UK.

2.59. We need to look more closely at these perceptions to see if they are soundly based and are representative of the generality of record albums.

2.60. The first step is to examine the effect of different tax arrangements. There are two aspects to this. First, tax rates vary between the countries. In the UK VAT is levied at 17.5 per cent on records while in the USA sales tax is lower, varying between cities and States but generally from around 3 to 8.5 per cent. Secondly, one needs to make comparisons on a like-for-like basis so that tax is either excluded in both cases or included in both cases. In the UK the prices displayed in the shops include VAT; in the USA the displayed price excludes tax, which is added to the total bill at the till. The effect of this is that the purchaser of a CD which is priced at $14.99 in New York will actually pay $16.23 when 8.25 per cent sales tax has been added.

2.61. In order to make useful comparisons we need to eliminate the effect of these tax differences. We therefore use prices exclusive of tax in the remainder of this chapter. On a without-tax basis the purchaser will pay £12.76 in London and $14.99 in New York (equivalent to £9.99 at an exchange rate of $1.50 = £1, which was the average rate between July 1993 and December 1993).

2.62. Thus a retail price which at first sight appeared to be 50 per cent higher in the UK is actually only 28 per cent higher if tax is taken off in both cases. These figures only hold good at an exchange rate of $1.50 to the pound. If the dollar strengthens against sterling then the price differential will narrow: if the dollar weakens the differential will widen. These perceptions are all crucially influenced by the prevailing exchange rate.

---

[1]See footnote to paragraph 2.2.

Differences in retail prices

2.63. In order to establish a more soundly based understanding of the extent of differences in the prices of records between the UK and the USA we carried out a number of studies. These studies were more comprehensive than previous studies we have seen. We also had the benefit of a number of detailed price comparisons prepared by the record companies as part of their evidence to us. Throughout the discussion of the studies we use prices without tax and convert US dollars to sterling at an exchange rate of $1.50 to £1.

Full-price pop albums

2.64. We engaged a market research company (BMRB International) to carry out a survey of the prices of full-price pop albums in the UK, USA, Denmark, France and Germany. A full description of the survey is provided in paragraphs 7.51 to 7.56 and Appendix 7.2. Briefly, the survey looked at the retail prices in each country of eight popular titles by artists with international appeal selected from the repertoire of the five major record companies. However, national tastes differ and to allow for the fact that these titles did not reach the same chart positions in each of the countries and also for the possibility that they were at different stages in their life cycles, the survey also covered the records which were at particular positions in the national charts of each country. The prices were recorded of the albums which were numbers 1, 5 and 10 in the charts of each country at the time the survey was carried out.

2.65. The survey concentrated on full-priced popular albums because these are by far the largest selling group of records. Full-price albums represented 80 per cent by value of all UK album sales in 1992 and popular titles represented over three-quarters of all albums sold in that year. Chart records are particularly important because they make up a high proportion of these sales.

2.66. We found a fair degree of variability between the prices of the different pre-selected titles but more consistency in the prices of the three records in chart positions 1, 5 and 10. We found that the prices of the pre-selected albums on CD were on average between £10.06 and £11.78 in the UK while in the USA the prices of the same CDs were between £9.45 and £10.53. For each title the price in the UK was higher than in the USA, on average by 8.7 per cent. For the CDs that were at numbers 1, 5 and 10 in the album charts in their respective countries, the average prices were slightly lower and prices in the UK were only 7.3 per cent higher than in the USA.

2.67. From this evidence it appears that the prices of full-price pop CDs are on average about 7 to 9 per cent higher in the UK at an exchange rate of $1.50 to the pound.

2.68. The survey also showed that on cassette these albums were on average 14.8 per cent more expensive in the UK for the same titles and 8.8 per cent more expensive for the same chart positions.

Full-price classical albums

2.69. We carried out a separate study of the prices of full-price classical albums. It was not possible to do this in the same way as for the survey of pop records because of the lower availability of classical titles in the shops, classical representing 9 per cent of UK album sales but only 4 per cent of US sales, and because of the more variable pricing of classical records—where a higher proportion are available in the mid-price and budget price categories. Instead we asked five major retailers to provide the retail prices for selected titles, again selected from the repertoires of the five major record companies, in their UK stores and in the stores operated by their affiliates in the USA. Although this is narrower than the survey of full-price pop records we believe it is adequate to give a broad indication of price differentials. The study is described in more detail in paragraphs 7.67 to 7.70 and Appendix 7.4.

2.70. The study indicated that in the UK the average retail price of full-price classical CDs is higher than pop CDs, but in the USA this is not the case. The result is that the differential between the countries is wider for full-price classical CDs with prices on average about 26 per cent higher in the

UK than in the USA. Our survey found that in many cases the popular perception of pound:dollar equivalence was correct as a CD which cost £14.99 in the UK (including VAT) was often priced on the shelf at $14.99 (excluding sales tax) in the USA. The effect of mid-price and budget items on the average price of classical albums is discussed in paragraph 2.73.

Average prices

2.71. The discussion so far has dealt only with full-price CDs. In order to gain a complete picture we need to take account of all price ranges and to look at the buying habits in the two countries.

2.72. As discussed in paragraph 7.105, UK purchasers appear to buy a higher proportion of mid-price and budget CDs than US purchasers. Although our own surveys did not look at mid-price or budget CDs, other evidence (see paragraphs 7.95 to 7.105) indicates that the prices received by the record companies (ie the net dealer prices) of these categories are lower on average in the UK than the USA. This suggests that, when all price categories are taken into account, the average price differential will be lower than we found in our surveys of full-price records.

2.73. In the classical record field, although full-price records showed a price differential of about 26 per cent, some 55 per cent of classical albums sold in the UK are in the mid-price or budget categories (see Table 5.14). Sony's retail price comparisons for its classical albums (full-price and mid-price) showed that the average price in the UK is only 7.6 per cent higher than in the USA (see paragraphs 7.71 to 7.74 and Appendix 7.5). The broader range of classical prices in the UK may be a reflection of the different demand here for classical records. As already noted, classical makes up 9 per cent of UK album sales but only 4 per cent of US sales.

2.74. The Sony retail study covered popular as well as classical albums. On the pop record side the price differential was 6.1 per cent. It should be noted that Sony does not produce any pop CDs at budget price in either country.

2.75. We conclude from this that while full-price pop CDs are on average about 7 to 9 per cent more expensive in the UK and full-price classical CDs are 26 per cent more expensive, the differentials covering all price categories are somewhat lower.

International price comparisons and the exchange rate

2.76. When comparing prices of recorded music in different countries, an exchange rate is chosen to convert those prices into a common currency. The comparisons described above used an exchange rate of £1 = $1.50, the average market exchange rate in the second half of 1993.

2.77. Local prices of recorded music are set at intervals and are not changed in line with every change in exchange rates. However, in a period of floating exchange rates, those rates can fluctuate frequently and so it is difficult to know which rate to use for making price comparisons. If market rates are used, a price comparison on one date may give apparently quite different results from a comparison on another date. Thus if we had used £1 = $1.75 (around the average exchange rate for 1992) in making the price comparisons we would have concluded that the prices of full-price pop CDs were some 25 to 27 per cent higher on average in the UK rather than the 7 to 9 per cent described above. Alternatively, if the exchange rate used had been £1 = $1.25, UK prices would have been *lower* than US prices, by 9 to 11 per cent. (In the first quarter of 1985 the exchange rate reached a low point of £1 = $1.12.)

2.78. Under a system of floating exchange rates differences in the rates of inflation between countries may be expected over a number of years to be reflected in the movements of exchange rates: the latter in effect to compensate for the former. Similarly over a number of years exchange rates can be expected to adjust to other factors, such as differing economic policies. But at any point in time it is impossible to know whether the current exchange rate is approaching a sustainable long-term rate between two currencies. We have attempted to overcome this problem by using the average £/$ rate for the second half of 1993. A six-month average will eliminate short-term fluctuations in the exchange rate. The figure we have used (£1 = $1.50) is in fact very near the average for the whole of 1993.

2.79. Some record companies argued that sterling is overvalued at £1 = $1.50 relative to the US dollar. They suggested to us that international price comparisons should be based on purchasing power parities (PPPs). We have considered the relevance of PPPs. In effect, use of PPPs stands the exchange rate problem on its head. Instead of trying to estimate the 'sustainable long term rate' from observations of market exchange rates, it compares directly what consumers can buy with their money in different countries. This suggests what the exchange rate should be. Thus the PPP between two countries is the 'exchange rate' at which the price of a basket of goods would be the same in the two countries. Estimates of PPPs between the UK and the USA have for the last few years been below the market exchange rate, indicating that price comparisons using market exchange rates will show that goods are more expensive in the UK. Even if PPPs were used, there would still be a difficulty in choosing the appropriate rate to use since no generally accepted PPP exchange rates are available. Different estimates of the PPP can lead to widely differing estimates of the relative prices of goods in the USA and the UK.

2.80. While remaining sceptical about the value of evidence which relies on PPPs, we recognize the problems involved in making price comparisons using market exchange rates. We therefore decided to concentrate on the question whether recorded music was exceptional in the consumers' experience in each country. Accordingly we have carried out a survey of the prices of a wide range of consumer goods at £1 = $1.50 (described below) to see how the relative price of recorded music between the USA and the UK compared with the relative prices of other goods in those countries.

2.81. In order to match circumstances as closely as possible we chose mainly products which were manufactured goods relating to leisure activities and which had a UK retail price of less than £30. The survey is described in detail in paragraphs 7.85 and 7.86 and Appendix 7.6. We found that in almost all product groups average prices were higher in the UK than the USA, the majority of differentials lying in the range 8 to 16 per cent and the weighted average being 9 per cent. Figure 2.1 summarizes the results, together with our estimate of the differential for full-price pop CDs.

FIGURE 2.1

Price differentials (UK/US) for various product groups

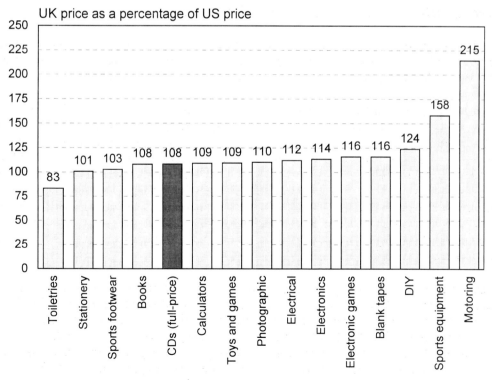

Source: Management Horizons survey (see Appendix 7.6).

2.82. This evidence confirms that for a wide range of broadly comparable goods there is a systematic difference in the purchasing power of consumers in each country which is favourable to the USA. The survey also shows that retail price differences for recorded music between the UK and the USA are not out of line with a range of other goods. We examine the factors which might explain the particular position of recorded music in the next section.

Factors affecting the prices of recorded music in the USA and UK

2.83. In addition to the exchange rate applying at any particular time, there are a variety of other factors which will affect the supply and demand conditions for goods and hence their prices. To the extent that these factors differ between countries so will the prices ruling in each market. Here we look at factors which may affect the supply and demand for recorded music. The record companies told us that demand and willingness to pay for recorded music differ between the USA and UK because of differences in income levels, tastes and the range available and relative prices of alternative leisure products. This must be true, particularly for classical records where the scale and range of demand is reflected in a broader range of price categories, but it is difficult to link these factors directly to differences in prices between the two countries. It is possible to be a little more definite on the supply side.

2.84. The price which the consumer pays is composed of three main elements:

(a) the prices, net of all discounts, charged by the record companies to the retailers;

(b) the mark-up retailers add to this price to allow for their costs and profits; and

(c) sales taxes.

The effect of differences in sales taxes between the USA and the UK has been discussed in paragraphs 2.60 to 2.62. We look now at the prices charged by the record companies and then at the retailers' gross margins.

2.85. The record companies provided us with a number of reasons why the prices charged to retailers may be lower in the USA than those in the UK. The first concerned the higher level of service they provided to retailers in the UK. Most importantly, in the UK the record companies were in general responsible for delivery to individual retail outlets whereas in the USA large retailers tended to handle their own distribution. This and other elements of higher level of service, such as a faster turnround of orders, meant that the record companies' distribution costs were higher in the UK. Second, the royalty rates paid to artists and composers were higher in the UK so increasing record companies' costs in the UK relative to those in the USA. The third set of reasons related to the relative size of the two markets. The US market for recorded music was over four times as large as the UK market and this enabled US companies to reap the benefits of economies of scale which lowered the cost and risks of supply. Manufacturing costs were reduced by longer production runs and fixed costs, such as Artist & Repertoire (A&R), could be spread over wider volumes. Top-selling records in their respective markets sold many more copies in the USA than in the UK. This meant that the rewards of the big hit would go further in the USA to offset the losses incurred in both countries as a result of the many failures inevitably associated with the policy of originating a wide range of different kinds of music. It has not been possible to quantify these supply side advantages enjoyed by record companies in the USA, but we believe the arguments set out above have force.

2.86. UK record companies claim that the power of the major retailers enables them to claim larger discounts than their counterparts in the USA. We have not been able to find any reliable evidence on differences between the USA and the UK in the mark-ups that record retailers apply to the prices they pay to record companies. The conventional wisdom is that the costs of retailing are lower in the USA. This arises primarily from the greater availability of good retail sites at significantly lower rentals and to greater labour productivity. Many of these factors would be expected to influence not just the price of records but also the prices of a wider range of retail products and this would be consistent with our findings that price differentials for CDs are not generally out of line with other products.

Comparisons with other countries

2.87. To get a broader picture of UK prices in an international context we also included France, Germany and Denmark in our study of the retail prices of full-priced CDs and cassettes (which is described in paragraph 2.64). The average retail prices without tax which we found are shown in the graph at Figure 2.2. It will be seen that, while UK prices are generally higher than those in the USA, they are lower than in each of the other countries. Prices of CDs were found to be 2 per cent higher in Germany, 16 per cent higher in France and 6 per cent higher in Denmark.

FIGURE 2.2

Retail prices of full-price CDs and cassettes in different countries

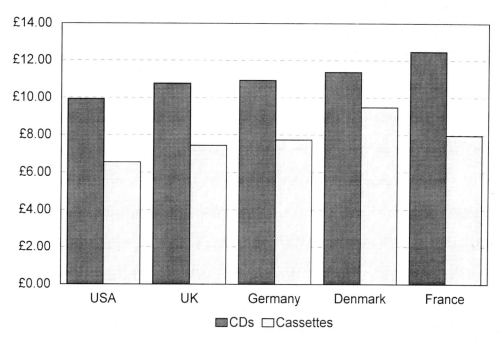

Source: BMRB Survey (see Appendix 7.2).

2.88. Because our study did not include the mid-price and budget categories it does not provide us with information on the differences in the average prices paid in these countries. We have, however, looked at other evidence, which is discussed in more detail in paragraphs 7.93 to 7.105. The material covers a wide range of countries including Japan and Canada as well as European and Scandinavian countries. Much of it is based on record company data but we see no reason to doubt the reliability of the data and since the companies are large suppliers with consistent recording systems around the world we believe it gives a fair reflection of those companies' relative prices. Although much of the evidence is based on wholesale prices, the relativities of these prices between countries can be expected to give some indication of relative retail prices.

2.89. The conclusion that emerges from these international comparisons is that, although prices of CDs are higher in the UK than in the USA, in general the UK has lower prices for CDs than most other countries. We recognize that changes in circumstances, for example currency fluctuations, will alter the position of particular countries from time to time but such individual cases do not alter the general conclusion that prices in the UK are not systematically higher than those in other countries.

Parallel imports

2.90. The Consumers' Association has argued that the price differentials between the UK and the USA are only sustainable because of the right to control parallel imports which is conferred on a copyright owner by the 1988 Copyright Act. Its reasoning is that if retailers were free to import records from the USA they would do so and this would force the UK record companies to lower their prices so that they were closer to US levels. We now examine the evidence for this in the context of the legal basis for copyright described in Chapter 4.

2.91. We have already established that the price differentials between the UK and USA for recorded music are not significantly different from those for a wide range of other products. Most of these products are not subject to copyright constraints. Parallel imports can take place. Nevertheless price differentials remain. This suggests that the similar differential for recorded music is not due to copyright. Other factors, apart from copyright, inhibit such trade. No doubt these include the costs of transport and import duties which would also affect trade in recorded music (where import duty of 5 per cent is payable). It therefore seems unlikely that allowing parallel imports would be effective in reducing the price of recorded music at the present exchange rate.

2.92. This view is supported by the level of price differentials for recorded music between the UK and other European countries. Under the provisions of the Treaty of Rome copyright cannot generally be used to restrict the free movement of records within the EC once they have been lawfully put on the market in one member state by the owner of the copyright or with his consent. Parallel imports can therefore take place. However, despite the comparatively low transport costs and the absence of customs duties within the EC, this freedom has not led to the elimination of price differentials, some of which are higher than between the UK and USA. We also note from Tables 7.12 to 7.14 and those in Appendix 7.7 that prices in Japan, France and Denmark are higher than in the UK as are those of the Scandinavian countries (with the exception of Sweden) and yet these are all countries which at the time had no law prohibiting parallel imports from the USA.

2.93. The reasons for this reluctance to import records from abroad on any significant scale probably stem from the retailers' need for the type of service provided by their regular sources of supply. Retailers need to have the particular records on their shelves which customers want to buy at a particular time. Yet it is difficult to predict demand and so retailers rely on being able to acquire stocks at short notice from their suppliers. This is not the sort of service that can be obtained by shopping around for the cheapest supplies in other countries: it depends on maintaining a good long-term relationship with local distributors or a local wholesaler. Such a relationship also brings with it the opportunity to participate in joint promotions and some rights to return stock which a retailer is not able to sell. Sources of parallel imports would not allow returns and so the retailer's stockholding risk would be increased. We believe that these reasons, combined with the added costs of transport and duty, explain the lack of parallel imports where they are not prohibited. However, the incentives could well be different if differentials widened significantly, perhaps as a result of substantial movements in exchange rates. Even in this case it seems likely that only chart releases by superstars would be imported since these are the items where a high level of sales can reasonably be predicted. Entrepreneurs are unlikely to be interested in importing catalogue items such as classical CDs, where the low level and unpredictability of demand for a particular title would not make the risks worthwhile.

2.94. Although the provisions which enable copyright owners to restrict imports are contained in the UK's national legislation, our freedom to change this situation would be constrained by any requirements of EC law and of international conventions to which the UK is a party. The UK is a party to the Berne Convention. This convention does not explicitly require member countries to give copyright owners the right to control imports although experts in the World International Property Organisation (WIPO) argue that such a requirement is implicit in its provisions. A proposed protocol to the Berne Convention is under discussion in WIPO which would have the effect of making such a requirement explicit (see paragraph 4.48) but it is not clear whether it will be adopted.

2.95. Of more central relevance is the adoption of the EC Rental Directive.[1] It is generally accepted that this will require all member states to provide the individual owner of copyright in a sound recording with the right to prevent or control imports from outside the EC from July 1994. From this date not only will the UK be unable to relax the existing provisions to this effect in the 1988

[1]See paragraph 2.21.

Copyright Act but other member states, such as Denmark, which do not currently have such provisions will have to introduce them. We conclude, therefore, that not only would it be unlawful with effect from 1 July to alter the present statutory position under the 1988 Copyright Act by removing the present right of a copyright owner to block parallel imports but to do so would go against the whole trend of international developments in the protection of intellectual property.

2.96. Moreover even if it were lawful for the UK to withdraw the right to control imports, we have been told that there would be serious consequences for the record industry. The basis of copyright is that it is territorial. There can be different licensees in different countries who will plan their exploitation in the light of local circumstances and will also have negotiated their licence payments on this basis. Any departure from this principle of territoriality would cause loss to the industry. This can happen in a number of ways. Where a parallel import displaced a sale in the UK of a record by a UK-signed artist, the UK record company would receive less revenue in licence fees and so would the music publisher. Moreover there would be a significant delay in payment. Where the artist was signed to a different record company overseas (known as 'dual-signing') the UK record company would receive no revenue at all from the sale, despite having invested in advances and promotional costs. The record companies also explained how the impact of their marketing plans, which are sometimes timed to coincide with an event such as an artist's tour, could be diminished by parallel imports. It is not only the record companies and music publishers that would lose revenue as a result of such imports; the royalties paid to artists and songwriters would also be reduced. Finally, lack of control over parallel imports would mean that it would become more difficult to control piracy which we have been told already causes serious losses of income to copyright owners.

2.97. We believe that a change in the UK's position would not only be contrary to EC requirements, but it would bring few benefits to consumers since any arbitrage would be likely to affect only a few titles and would almost certainly not affect the prices of the highest priced catalogue items which have been the focus of consumer complaints, including classical records.

2.98. We conclude that there is no case for altering either the right to control imports currently provided by the 1988 Copyright Act nor the MCPS/BPI import licensing scheme. We recognize that the scheme facilitates the ready import of records that are not available on the UK market while ensuring that the holders of UK rights are not deprived of a reasonable income. We have received no evidence that the price of the stamp under the import scheme (at £1.25 per CD) is set at too high a level, nor do we believe this to be the case.

Competition in the record industry

2.99. For at least the last ten years the five major record companies have held a combined market share of at least 60 per cent by volume of albums sold. Currently their market share is at a high point of 72 per cent. Within this total the share held by each of the major companies has fluctuated as they have competed to meet the demands of the record-buying public. Competition is vigorous to find and retain successful artists, market and promote their products to the public and to persuade retailers to stock and display them. The increased concentration in retailing has meant that the strong position of the major record companies is now mirrored by large and powerful retailers. This countervailing power gives rise to intense competition between record companies, first to get their products stocked and, second, to ensure prominence in the outlet. Special discounts, payments for co-operative advertising, returns allowances and other financial incentives are negotiated between the retailers and record companies to obtain these benefits.

2.100. In addition to competition amongst themselves, the position of the major record companies is also challenged by the many independent record companies which make up the remaining 30 to 40 per cent of the market and by new entrants. Over the last ten years new companies have entered the market and some have left. This constantly changing picture is shown in Table 5.22. The majority of those that have entered have remained relatively small or have disappeared. But the diverse and volatile nature of demand creates continuing opportunities for the smaller companies to achieve considerable success. While the market share of each of the independents is less than 5 per cent, Virgin before its acquisition by EMI had a market share throughout the period of around 6 to 8 per cent. MCA now has the Matsushita Corporation of Japan behind it and this could influence its long-term future growth. In the 12 months to September 1993 the independents were responsible for 15 per cent of the albums entering the Top 40 charts. Taking a longer view, of the new artists who have become established in the UK since 1981, defined as those who have achieved sales of over 100,000 with at least one album, over one-third (more than 100 artists) were signed to companies other than the majors.

2.101. The independent record companies are noted for their variety and dynamism. The strength of this independent sector is widely seen as one of the characteristics of the UK music industry which keeps it second only to the USA as a supplier of recorded music to the world. As Table 5.23 shows, concentration is higher in almost all other countries in the world, including the USA. It is comparatively simple to set up business as a record company. The essential requirement is to have a source of repertoire, either in the form of a contract for an artist to produce recordings in the future or in the form of a catalogue of copyrights in existing recordings. It is not necessary to own a recording studio, manufacturing facilities or a distribution network since all of these can be hired on the open market when required. Thus barriers to entry are low.

2.102. The risks for a small company are considerable at the initial stages if it is investing in new artists; that is, it must sink costs which may not be recouped. But it may be successful; there is evidence that many independents are willing to make the attempt. The majors tell us that only one in ten of the pop artists with whom they sign contracts turns out to be successful. Of course the majors can cope with this situation by spreading the risk over a number of artists. Similarly, they can spread their risks for particular records they release because, although they do not know in advance whether a particular title will sell a few hundred or several million copies, they have enough titles covering every genre of music to ensure that they receive a reasonably predictable flow of income. The small company, sometimes with only one artist, is not able to spread its risks in this way. Nevertheless, there are several hundred small record companies and a constant supply of hopeful artists seeking to sign with them or one of the majors. Some of the successful independents work in particular niches, where the majors do not compete so strongly, and many concentrate on innovative or 'alternative' music which sometimes leads to the establishment of a new fashion in musical taste which the majors are then anxious to emulate.

2.103. All this leads us to the conclusion that the UK record industry continues to be highly competitive with the potential for new companies to enter the market.

2.104. The economics of competition in the record industry are different from most areas of manufacturing because each recording is unique and, through the copyright system, can be marketed only by the owner of the rights or his licensee. However, as we discuss in paragraph 2.102, because the record company does not know which releases will sell in large numbers, it is forced to price its products under broad price categories. The company's profit depends on its skill in spotting successful artists in an industry where demand is governed by rapidly changing fashions. If it does this successfully its sales in the UK and its net licence fees from abroad will exceed the advances and other costs which it invested in order to secure the artist's services and make the initial recording.

2.105. How does this competition translate into price competition? Initially there was only one format, the 78 rpm record. Subsequently this was replaced by more durable vinyl singles and albums (LPs). Later the cassette was established which competed primarily on its portability and recordability rather than any improvement in sound quality and, more recently, we have seen the establishment of the CD which is now the highest selling format. The advent of the CD brought a step change in quality with its better sound from digital recording and its greater durability than earlier formats.

2.106. Figure 7.1 and Table 7.6 show movements in the prices of the different formats over the years. We can see from this how each new format enters at a high price and then falls as it becomes the leading format. The graph shows clearly that CD prices are conforming to this pattern.

2.107. Prices are also forced down by competition from independent record companies which choose to compete in particular niches. For example, Naxos has specialized in classical music by lesser known orchestras. Its lower CD prices, possible because of its lower costs in making recordings, have forced the majors to respond by introducing their own ranges of classical CDs at mid-price. Similarly in more popular genres of music Tring International Plc (Tring) has introduced CDs selling at a retail price as low as £2.99 mainly in non-traditional outlets such as petrol stations. It has done this mainly by acquiring copyrights which do not involve a major investment in A&R and selling its CDs in large quantities. More recently Tring has signed an agreement with the Royal Philharmonic Orchestra for recordings of its performances which are expected to retail at £4.99. The majors have responded to competition from companies like Tring by introducing their own ranges of budget-priced CDs.

2.108. We conclude that despite the established position of the majors competition is vigorous among the record companies and that the majors are unlikely to be able to exercise market power to the disadvantage of consumers, either in respect of their acquisition of artists or in their pricing policies.

Profitability of the record companies

2.109. Profitability is normally measured either as a return on turnover or a return on capital employed. In the case of the record companies, the capital employed in each of the last five years is either negative or very small, making return on capital employed an unsatisfactory measure of profitability. Return on turnover (or 'revenue') is therefore the only practicable measure of profitability that can be derived from the accounts of the major record companies. Table 2.2 shows that in the last five years the aggregate returns on revenue of the recorded music businesses of the five major record companies have varied from a high of 7.1 per cent in 1989 to a low of 2.8 per cent in 1992.

TABLE 2.2   **Aggregate results of the core recorded music businesses of the five major record companies, 1989 to 1993**

	1989	1990	1991	1992	1993 estimated
Revenue (£m)	564	645	691	817	843
Profit before interest and tax (£m)	40	31	28	23	49
Return on revenue (%)	7.1	4.8	4.0	2.8	5.9

Source: Table 8.3.

2.110. Results for different companies have varied over the years. In the last five years some have made negative returns and on only two occasions has a company made a return on revenue of more than 10 per cent. We conclude from this that the companies' accounts prepared in accordance with generally accepted accounting standards do not reveal any evidence of excessive profits, indeed the profits are not high for a high-risk industry.

2.111. Although the profits shown in the accounts of the record companies are prepared in accordance with generally accepted accounting standards, it has been put to us that profits may be understated in that the accounts do not reflect any build-up over time in the value of the catalogue of copyrights. We have sought advice in an attempt to quantify the effect on the accounts of the copyright value. A study carried out for us by KPMG Peat Marwick, which is described in paragraphs 8.36 to 8.43, suggested that after adjusting for notional copyright value the companies' profitability, averaged over the last three financial years, would have increased by 1.7 percentage points on turnover.

2.112. The method used by KPMG to make these calculations suffers from significant limitations, as was made clear by the consultants themselves (see Appendix 8.2). We do not believe therefore that much weight should be placed on these notional adjustments. The adjusted results even if accepted do not suggest that the record companies' profitability is excessive. Moreover, the value of the copyrights would only be realized on the sale of the catalogue. Additional cash flow is not available from unrealized gains. If the catalogue is not sold, its value, if any, will materialize in due course from future record sales or from licence income. In this event there will be royalty payments to artists and composers and the additional revenue will be reflected in the financial results for the company.

Price structures

2.113. In describing their pricing policies to us, the major record companies argued that the level and structure of prices had developed as a result of competition between themselves, other record companies, new entrants and the buying power of the major record retailers. It was the result of a competitive market and did not reflect any dominance of the major record companies or collusion between them. We look first at the pricing of new releases and then at the pricing of different formats.

2.114. The record companies told us that when reviewing the overall level of prices they took account of overall economic conditions, the change in their costs, changes in competitors' prices, the rate of inflation and the prices their products sold for in other countries. When pricing a new release, they faced the problem that the level of demand for each recording was highly uncertain at the time it was released. The record company incurred substantial costs prior to the release of each new record—in supporting the artist, making the recording and in marketing and promoting it. However, the unpredictability of demand meant that in practice it was not possible to price records on a cost plus basis. Even if it were, it would not make sense to charge a higher price for a less successful record to cover its higher unit costs and a low price for a successful record because its fixed costs could be spread over a larger number of sales. Successful records helped to recover the costs of unsuccessful records. Moreover, given that some 200 new recordings were issued each week, it would not be feasible to price each record individually in order to attempt to maximize profits on an individual record on the basis of likely demand.

2.115. The record companies told us that at current price levels consumers did not appear to be particularly sensitive to price changes so that price changes for recorded music as a whole would only have a minor impact on sales volume. But the price charged for a particular title could affect the demand for that title. The record companies pointed out, however, that the ultimate price to the consumer was determined by the retailers. They argued that the retailers' practice of using a limited number of price points and charging higher prices for non-chart material restricted their opportunity to reduce prices to stimulate demand for particular recordings. The use of low prices to promote recordings of, for example, new artists was also constrained by the need to ensure that such recordings were not perceived as low quality products since such a public perception would be damaging to the successful development of the artist.

2.116. In practice therefore, we were told, the record companies priced each new release at one of a limited number of dealer pricing points. They concentrated on competing with other record companies' recordings through promotional campaigns and dealer-specific discounts designed to achieve sales success. Later in the life cycle of a recording, when sales tailed off, a record company may try to increase sales through lower pricing strategies, special promotional campaigns with specific retailers and re-releases of older records at mid-price.

2.117. As to the pricing of different formats (CD, cassette or vinyl), the record companies told us that they aimed to maximize the value of their copyright subject to the constraints of the competitive market. They did this by charging a higher price for CDs reflecting the consumer's greater willingness to pay for the higher sound quality, durability and user-friendliness of the CD.

2.118. Although the cost of manufacture for CDs and cassettes differed by a comparatively small sum, manufacturing costs made up only a small proportion of total costs and most costs were not related to format. The problem they faced, the record companies argued, was to set prices across formats to recover their fixed costs and maximize their returns. Setting different prices for different formats increased the total demand for recorded music by providing a range in terms of price and quality to suit different consumers' needs. This, they argued, was common practice in industries based on the exploitation of copyright. The owner of the copyright sought methods of discriminating between customers on the basis of willingness to pay. In book publishing, hardback books were generally issued before paperbacks. Similarly films were released in well established echelons or 'windows': first-run cinema, second-run cinema, video to rent, video to buy, pay-television and finally free television. In these cases, as with recorded music, the price achieved by the copyright owner depended on the demand characteristics of the market and not on the cost of physical reproduction. In the case of recorded music, different formats were issued at the same time, the different prices charged reflecting consumers' differing perceptions of quality and value and hence willingness to pay.

2.119. The record companies argued that price differentiation by format, which was practised by record companies world-wide, had resulted in greater sales, lower costs, lower prices, and a greater variety of product in the market. When the CD was first introduced its higher quality had merited a higher price. Its sales and market share had grown rapidly so that it was now the dominant format. As with other technological innovations, the real price of a CD had fallen over time as had the differential between CD and cassette prices. This, the record companies argued, reflected the normal process of supply and demand interacting over time to produce a price level and price structure in a competitive market.

2.120. We accept the record companies' analysis of the basis of their pricing policy. They clearly face restraints in pricing new releases and we have found no evidence that the level of prices reflects a lack of competition. We accept that price discrimination can increase the range of goods available in the market and the volume of goods sold. Similarly we accept that owners of copyright are justified in offering that copyright in different formats and at different times to maximize their returns from it. Problems arise, however, if such practices are employed in such a way as to abuse market power.

2.121. We do not believe this is the case here. The competitive nature of the recorded music industry, and in particular competition in the production of new titles and in the market for artists, together with the freedom of entry to the industry, leads us to conclude that the major record companies cannot abuse their position in the market. The entry of Naxos with mid-price classics and Tring with budget price CDs are examples of the challenges that they face from the independent sector. The similarity in the pricing policies of the major companies does not appear to be the result of any lack of competition. Rather it is a reflection that competitive pressures have forced them to act in broadly similar ways.

Competition in retailing

2.122. The significant reduction in the number of independent specialist retailers over the last few years and the strong position of the major retailers has led to some concern that competition in record retailing may be deficient. Here we consider the degree and vigour of this competition.

2.123. Records are sold to the public by a number of different types of retailer: specialist chains such as Our Price and HMV, non-specialist multiples such as W H Smith and Boots, independent specialists, various other types of retail outlets which have not traditionally sold records such as supermarkets, and various mail order operations of which by far the most important are the record clubs. Over recent years there has been a significant decline in the number of independent specialists but many new types of retail outlet have begun to stock recorded music. These range from major grocery chains, such as Asda, to small retail outlets in high traffic locations such as petrol stations. In part the decline of the independent specialist reflects the general trend in retailing in the UK and elsewhere away from smaller independent to larger multiple retailers. But these trends do not mean that small retailers are not viable. They can and do survive if they offer consumers something different in terms of service or specialization in particular music genres. Entry is feasible for those who wish to try and there are entrants on a more significant scale, as witness the arrival in the UK of Tower Records and Sam Goody, two major US record retailers. Of increasing importance and a further threat to the established retailers are the record clubs and mail order businesses which now account for 12 per cent of total retail sales.

2.124. Record retailers compete in a number of ways such as price, range of titles stocked, service, location and ambience and in doing so appeal to different sections of the record-buying public. Music enthusiasts are likely to be attracted to the specialists with their wide range and knowledgeable staff. More occasional buyers are more likely to buy in the non-specialist multiples or in other convenient but not traditional outlets for recorded music. We have been told that one aspect of competition between retailers, price, is particularly important. While the demand for recorded music in general may not be very sensitive to price, consumers are sensitive to price differences between retail outlets

248336 C

for the same product. Price competition is particularly intense for the most popular (ie chart) material. Most retailers discount these products and are keen to avoid getting out of line with their competitors.

2.125. In our view record retailing, in terms both of the structure of the industry and conduct in the market, is a competitive market. We do not believe that W H Smith and Our Price have market power which enables them to exploit their scale monopoly position.

Profitability of the retailers

2.126. Our view that the major record retailers could not exploit their position is borne out by their results, which show that they are making profits on their recorded music business which are modest. Tables 1 and 2 in Appendix 8.6 show that taken together W H Smith and Our Price have achieved a profit before interest and tax on recorded music of only [*] per cent of sales over the four years to 31 May 1993. [*Details omitted. See note on page iv.*
] Although the profit levels over the last three years have no doubt been adversely affected by the recession, they lead us to conclude that the two companies are not able to exploit their combined market share of 26.6 per cent by charging high prices in order to make excessive profits.

2.127. W H Smith, Our Price, HMV and Virgin Retail have all had gross margins in the range [*] to [*] per cent in the last four years. Woolworths had lower gross margins, but Table 9 of Appendix 8.6 shows that, when the additional margin which its wholesaler affiliate, Entertainment UK Ltd, earns on its purchases is included, the combined gross margin for the year ended 31 March 1993 fell within the same range. The tables in Appendix 8.6 show that the profits before interest and tax of all the companies have generally been less than [*] per cent of sales. We do not regard this as excessive.

Contracts with artists

2.128. Some artists, through their managers, claim that the terms of their contracts with record companies restrict their ability to exploit their talent (see paragraphs 10.45 to 10.65). They argue that the contracts are inequitable in their effect on artists and, by reducing competition, lead to higher prices for recorded music. The managers highlight three particular aspects of contracts which they consider most significant in this respect: the record companies' insistence on owning copyright for its full term, the standardization of contract terms and the provisions giving the record company the exclusive right to release recordings made by an artist. They believe the record companies are able to insist on these restrictive features by taking advantage of the relative weakness of the artists' negotiating position.

2.129. It is argued on behalf of the artists that record companies should be required to change the nature of their contracts so as to allow more competition for artists' services and for the copyright in their past recordings. It is claimed that this would not only give artists more equitable rewards but would reduce the control that the major record companies have over the supply of recorded music and so benefit consumers through greater choice and lower prices.

2.130. We regard it as inevitable that the record companies, in their negotiations with artists, will seek to obtain maximum control over copyrights. Equally the individual artist will seek to maximize his advances, royalties and other benefits from the record companies. Provided there is competition between the record companies to secure the services of artists, as we believe there is, and provided the new artist is advised by professionals with appropriate experience, the negotiation of contracts should lead to an equitable outcome.

---

*Figures omitted. See note on page iv.

2.131. A new artist is likely to be interested in securing the maximum advances since he may have no other source of income and he does not know whether his recording contract is going to prove successful. Of course, he will also want to sign with the record company which he considers is most likely to launch him on a successful career. This will vary according to the genre of music and for some artists it will lead them to sign with an independent record company.

2.132. At this stage a new artist may have relatively smaller interest in the details of other contract terms and, if his recording career does not prove successful, they are unlikely ever to assume significance. However, the artist will normally have the benefit of professional advice and all the major record companies told us that they would not sign a contract unless the artist was advised by a specialist lawyer. The reason for this is that the record company wants to protect its contracts from challenge in the courts on grounds of restraint of trade.

2.133. If an artist does achieve success there are in practice opportunities to renegotiate the contract and at this stage the artist will be in a stronger position. The main concern of an artist who has achieved some success is likely to be to improve his or her long-term revenues. Over the years the courts have struck down some of the more far-reaching restrictions contained in a number of artists' contracts. As a result a number of the more onerous clauses in general use in the industry have been removed or adjusted in the artists' favour. No record company will want to include clauses in a contract which in the light of such decisions may lead to the contract being declared unenforceable. Thus, in addition to competition, there are other safeguards both for the new artist and the established artist. As a result, the terms offered to and accepted by artists have improved significantly over the last 20 years with the greatly increased royalty rates and other features described in paragraph 5.139.

2.134. We consider in the following paragraphs the three particular features of contracts which were highlighted by managers.

Ownership of copyright

2.135. The artists' managers suggest that either the artist should own the copyright and license it to the record company for a period or that the period of the record company's initial ownership of the copyright should be limited so that it will pass to the artist at the end of the contract or at some earlier time, for example when all the advances have been recouped. It is argued that a shorter copyright period would have a number of benefits. It would lead to a more lively market in copyrights which would not only give the successful artist potentially greater rewards but would lead to the establishment of a market price which would allow artists and others to raise finance from sources other than the record companies so providing a better funded, more open and competitive industry. Furthermore if the record companies were forced to take a shorter-term view they would be likely to spend less on marketing and promotion, so lowering the costs of securing a hit and making it easier for independent record companies to establish their artists. This effect would be speeded up if the major record companies were also required to divest themselves of their existing catalogues of copyrights. They would then no longer be able to cross-subsidize new artists and so competition with new independent companies would be enhanced. Finally it was argued that this heightened competition would lead to greater efficiency and so lower retail prices and this would be achieved without lowering artists' income.

2.136. The record companies say that they are not as inflexible over copyright as has been suggested. They have sometimes negotiated contracts where they hold copyright only for a period but in such contracts they would expect to adjust the other terms so as to ensure that the payback period was commensurate with the period for which they owned the copyright. Although contracts in this form had been negotiated in the past, in general new artists currently preferred to secure larger advances and royalties rather than ownership of copyright. The same normally applied at the point where a contract was being renegotiated. In such cases an artist would often willingly agree to extend the term of an agreement in return for larger advances and royalties.

2.137. Record companies go on to point out that, even where successful artists have acquired control of the copyright, there is no benefit to the public interest. An artist's only avenue for protecting and exploiting his copyright is to license it to a record company and this is achieved by

248336 C2

auctioning it to the highest bidder. The consumer does not benefit because he is primarily interested in the artist and only to a limited extent in the particular label on which the recordings are published. Hence the only beneficiary is the artist, who is able to achieve a greater share of the income generated by his copyright. The effect of paying more to the artist would be either an increase in the dealer prices charged to the retailer (and hence to the consumer) or the spending of less on A&R to develop new artists. Neither of these outcomes, the companies argue, would be in the public interest. Moreover the companies do not consider that there is anything inequitable in the arrangement. Since the record company bears the initial investment risks it is entitled to the benefits when there is a success. Otherwise, it will be unable to maintain the flow of new artists because of the high level of failures amongst those signed by the record companies. Evidence for this is provided by detailed figures made available to the MMC by one of the major record companies (see paragraph 8.61). In the case of classical music, where sales of individual recordings tend to be spread out over a long period of time and are relatively small, a restriction of the period of copyright to, say, ten years would be too short a period in which to recover the investment.

2.138. Finally it was argued on behalf of the record companies that the independents would be the companies most severely affected if the period of copyright ownership were curtailed. Independent companies needed their copyrights and a reasonable length of contract in order to be able to secure licensing agreements to exploit their artists' recordings overseas. Independent record companies would also suffer in that their investment in developing an artist who turned out to be successful would be difficult to recover if the artist were able to take the copyright and transfer it to one of the major record companies as soon as he achieved success.

2.139. We have carefully considered the arguments for changing the present arrangements and the views expressed by the record companies. We have found nothing which leads us to believe that the outcome is other than the result of free bargaining between the parties or that artists do not have adequate opportunity to secure competing offers. As well as offers from the major record companies, both established artists and promising new artists have the possibility of negotiating a different type of contract with an independent record company. Under the 1988 Copyright Act the copyright would normally be owned by the record company and, unless it agrees to assign or license that copyright, the company would be entitled to exploit it for 50 years. Of course, under the terms of the contract between the company and the artist, the latter will normally receive an agreed share of the proceeds in the form of royalty payments. We do not see anything inherently inequitable in these arrangements, nor do we consider that a case has been made for interfering with the period of a record company's ownership of copyright.

2.140. In reaching this view we have taken account of the record company's need to make a profit on its successful records which is sufficient to cover its investments in new artists, many of whom will prove unsuccessful. While we can understand that successful artists would prefer that such profits accrued to them, we recognize that record companies need to seek new artists who will meet the changing fashions in popular music and will ultimately replace the present generation of successful artists. In any event, since the record companies take the risk of investing in artists when they are unknown, they should not have the rewards taken away on those occasions when their investment turns out to be successful.

Standardization of contract terms

2.141. The artists' managers criticized the similarity of terms offered by the major record companies which, in their view, reduced the ability of an artist to negotiate improved terms. They suggested that contracts always included unnecessary complexities, such as 'packaging deductions' from royalty payments, which only served to obscure the true rate of royalty. The managers suggested that such unsatisfactory features could be eliminated if a Minimum Terms Agreement were laid down as a starting point for negotiations. They also advocated the prohibition of certain provisions relating to the assignment of copyright or which had the effect of reducing royalties (see paragraphs 10.53 to 10.56).

2.142. In response to these criticisms the record companies said that it was not surprising there were superficial similarities between their contracts. A contract for recording services needed to cover certain issues and so most contracts contained clauses on the same subjects. The fact that artists used a comparatively small circle of lawyers who sought inclusion of particular clauses also added to an appearance of similarity. However, the companies said that the details of those clauses were all available for negotiation and each company had contracts containing a wide variety of different provisions which had resulted from individual negotiations with artists. Even the traditional packaging deduction was not insisted on by companies, though they found that artists usually preferred its inclusion because it enabled them to claim that they received a higher 'headline' royalty rate than would otherwise be offered. The companies also said that a degree of similarity could enhance competition because it made it easier for an artist to compare competing offers from record companies.

2.143. We accept that a well-drawn contract will always need to deal with all those issues which arise in the relationship between a record company and artist, just as one would expect to find similarities in the range of matters regulated by a lease or by a contract of employment. We examined a number of individual contracts of each of the major record companies and found that not only were there differences between the companies in the way they usually dealt with particular issues but there were wide differences in the contracts which any one company had with its individual artists. For example, the number of albums normally covered by a contract with a new artist varied from five in the case of one company to eight in the case of another. Some contracts based royalties on dealer prices, some on retail prices. And, contrary to the views of the artists' managers, we found significant variations in the details of other clauses. This leads us to conclude that there is scope for individual negotiation of all the terms of the contract and that there is competition between record companies in the terms they offer artists—in the detailed provisions as well as in the amount of advances and royalties.

Exclusivity

2.144. A particular illustration of the effects of the exclusivity provisions often included in recording contracts was provided by the evidence of BBC Audio International Limited (BBC AI) (see paragraphs 10.115 to 10.123). BBC AI said that record companies were able to use their exclusivity to prevent or delay the entry of new competitors into the market. In their case the provisions were preventing a new company from exploiting the BBC's archives which contained a valuable collection of classical recordings of historical interest. BBC AI advocated that record companies should be required to give undertakings that they would not enforce their exclusivity in respect of a performance given more than ten years previously.

2.145. The record companies involved in the dispute with BBC AI said that their concern was not to keep out competition but to protect their contractual rights and intellectual property. The exclusivity provisions in their contracts with classical artists normally prevented the artist making any recording for issue on another label during the period of the contract and also prevented the artist re-recording a title during a period after the contract ended. The latter case was known as 'title exclusivity' and was intended to protect a company's investment in the recordings made towards the end of a contract. Without title exclusivity, which typically lasts for a period of five or ten years, an artist would be free to re-record a title for release on a competing label within days of a contract ending.

2.146. In the case of the BBC the companies had particular concerns. The recordings held by the BBC were generally made for broadcasting while the artists were under contract to the record company. They were often live performances of works which were also available from the record company in a recording made in a studio. The record companies were happy to allow the BBC to broadcast the live performance but not to release it as a record, particularly since it would probably not be of the same quality. Although some at least of the recordings concerned were now quite old, the record companies were not prepared to see them released as records without proper recognition of their rights.

2.147. The exclusivity provisions are the most restrictive aspect of contracts—on the face of them such clauses restrict competition because they prevent an artist performing for a competing record label. However, we have heard evidence of the way a record company invests in developing an artist's image and career and the company would have no way of securing a return on its investment if the artist were free to make records for another company. We accept therefore that in general a degree of exclusivity is necessary. Of course, in an individual case it is possible that such provisions may be so restrictive as to be unreasonable. In such cases the law provides a remedy by way of an action for 'restraint of trade'. With this safeguard available for individual cases we do not consider it necessary for the MMC to make any finding in respect of the exclusivity provisions common to recording contracts. In the particular case of BBC AI we believe the matter is most appropriately resolved by negotiation between the parties or, failing that, through the courts.

Position of record producers

2.148. Record producers, who work with the artist in the studio while a record is being made, claim that they should be entitled to a share in the copyright of recordings they help to make (see paragraph 10.84). Under section 9(2)(a) of the 1988 Copyright Act the first owner of copyright in a sound recording is 'the person by whom the arrangements necessary to make the recording are undertaken'. Producers believe they are such a person in some, if not all, cases and that the record companies were refusing to recognize this and were depriving them of a share of PPL's income.

2.149. We have studied statements made in Parliament during the passage of the Bill which was to become the 1988 Copyright Act (see paragraph 4.15) and in our view these make it clear that section 9(2)(a) was intended to put sound recordings on the same footing as films, where the established practice was that copyright lies with the person who takes the financial risks of investing in its production.

2.150. If the producer of a sound recording, or the artist, makes the recording at their own expense rather than with advances from a record company, then the record companies recognize that person's ownership of copyright. This sometimes happens with major stars.

2.151. The 1988 Copyright Act does not appear to give the producer any claim to ownership of copyright in other circumstances. Moreover, we consider it reasonable that copyright should lie with the record company where it takes the financial risk. We do not therefore believe that the record companies are acting unreasonably, nor do we suggest any change in the law.

2.152. Interpretation of the law is a matter for the courts and, irrespective of any view expressed by the MMC, a producer who considers his rights are being denied can seek redress through the courts. It is not therefore appropriate for us to take any action on this issue.

2.153. Producers also argue that they are being denied a share of the income of PPL to which they are entitled. If a producer does own the copyright in sound recordings, which we recognize in paragraph 2.150 will sometimes be the case, then he can assign his copyrights to PPL and receive a share of its income in respect of the public performance of those sound recordings. In other circumstances the producer receives his remuneration from the record company or artist and it is a contractual matter whether the producer is remunerated by flat fee, royalties on the sale of records and/or a share of other income. We see no reason to conclude that the arrangements for remunerating record producers normally result from the unreasonable exercise of monopoly power by the record companies either in their contractual arrangements with the producers or through their influence on the way PPL distributes its income.

Promotion and marketing

2.154. It was suggested to us that the large sums spent by the record companies on promotion and marketing (including supplying free records to retailers) could have the effect of restricting actual or potential competition from independent record companies with their more limited resources. Such spending might also reduce the royalties paid to artists because royalties are not normally paid on free stock and are normally paid at half-rate for television-advertised records.

32

2.155. Marketing and promotion are the main weapons of competition between the major record companies in seeking retail sales. This is especially true of full-price records where there is only limited scope for price competition because of the system of price points used by retailers (see paragraph 7.39). Although the smaller independent record companies may not be able to spend equivalent amounts, they have other means of competing and alternative and less costly ways of promoting their products. They can compete on their reputations for particular styles of music and they have opportunities to promote their records through the music press, where we are told that the 'indie' labels are particularly well covered, and in radio programmes dedicated to particular styles of music. Some measure of the success of these alternatives can be seen in the fact that 16 per cent of singles entering the main chart in the 12 months to September 1993 were released by independent record companies. It is clear that independent record companies are able to become established and achieve success and we do not, therefore, consider that the major record companies' practices in relation to marketing and promotion are restricting their ability to compete effectively.

2.156. So far as artists' income is concerned, we have heard that, far from objecting to this spending, artists generally seek maximum promotion for their releases, including expensive television advertising, because they believe it is effective in selling more records. Moreover in at least some contracts the artist is given the right to approve or be consulted about television advertising. In any event, the terms on which royalties are paid in such cases is a matter which can be negotiated as part of the contract if artists consider it important. We do not therefore consider that artists are being exploited through any reduction in royalties that results from promotion and marketing.

Discounts to retailers

2.157. Concern was expressed that the major retailers were distorting competition with independent retailers by securing from the record companies unduly large discounts and contributions to joint promotions. It had been suggested that this was the cause of the reduction in the number of independent specialist retailers which has taken place in recent years, from around 2,200 in 1984 to just over 1,000 in 1992. As discussed in paragraphs 2.50 to 2.54, although the larger retailers obtain file discounts which are not generally available to independent retailers, the independents gain other forms of discounts and benefits with the result that the larger retailers do not consistently receive higher benefits in total. Although we concluded on this basis that there was no complex monopoly situation involving the major retailers we need to consider the position of the scale monopolists, W H Smith and Our Price.

2.158. The tables in Appendix 8.4 show that these two companies taken together do not stand out as receiving the highest discounts or promotional support and we therefore conclude that they are not exercising market power to secure excessive discounts. This is consistent with our finding that there is strong competition among retailers so that the discounts received by different groups of retailers are the result of the different opportunities they offer record companies for promoting and selling their records.

2.159. In our view, it is this competition which has caused less efficient retailers to leave the market. Those that are more efficient continue to survive as do those that have been able to distinguish their services from those of the multiples by serving niche markets or offering specialist advice to their customers. This conforms to a general trend which is being experienced in all types of retailing.

2.160. As far as consumer choice is concerned, we are encouraged by the way in which the large specialists are expanding the number and size of their stores so as to offer a wider choice of music to consumers. In addition, as we note in paragraph 2.123, significant new entrants have joined the market. We therefore conclude that the file discounts and promotional spending obtained by W H Smith and Our Price are not distorting competition.

Availability of vinyl LPs and singles

2.161. Record companies are issuing far fewer records on vinyl albums, particularly classical albums, and some retailers (including W H Smith) have ceased to stock any vinyl albums or singles. Some consumers claimed that this was being done not in response to consumer demand but in order to increase sales of the more profitable CDs.

2.162. Although W H Smith and Woolworths have now ceased to stock vinyl albums they say that they have done so only in response to declining demand. The sales figures for vinyl albums (see Table 5.8) show that there had been a very substantial reduction in sales before these two companies ceased to stock vinyl albums in December 1992 and in 1991 respectively. We conclude therefore that the retailers were responding to changing customer demand when they decided to make space available for CDs, videos and video games at the expense of vinyl albums. Despite the decline in sales of vinyl, there is still some demand which is met by specialist shops such as HMV and Virgin Retail. In the case of vinyl singles, consumers also have a wide availability in Woolworths' stores and in many independent shops.

2.163. The record companies say that they have reduced the number of new albums released on vinyl in response to the falling demand. They claim that if retailers ordered more vinyl they would supply it. The figures in Tables 5.8 and 5.9 bear this out, showing that while vinyl represented only 5 per cent of album sales in 1992 (down from 23 per cent in 1989) the annual number of titles released on vinyl has fallen by only half over the same period.

2.164. We understand that the decline of vinyl is a world-wide trend and that it is not available at all in some countries because the demand has dried up to the extent that it is no longer profitable to manufacture or retail it. In the light of the evidence in the preceding paragraphs we conclude that the policies of the record companies and W H Smith and Our Price towards the formats they supply are not the result of their respective monopoly positions.

Collecting societies

Phonographic Performance Limited

2.165. Representatives of both the smaller independent record companies and record producers felt that the major record companies effectively controlled PPL and used their position to deny them a fair share of PPL's revenues from broadcasting and other public performances of records.

2.166. PPL explained to us that while it had a total of around 1,350 members only 16 were full members, the remainder being associate members. Nine of the full members are from independent record companies. Only full members can attend and vote at PPL's annual general meetings. The day-to-day control of PPL lies with a Board of 12 members of which the majority are drawn from the major record companies. The Board has until now decided which companies will be admitted as full members. Although it would appear from this that PPL is effectively controlled by the major record companies, we were told that the Distribution Committee, which decides on the allocation of PPL's income, has a majority of members from the smaller independent companies.

2.167. Towards the end of our inquiry we were told that the Board of PPL was considering changes to its rules for admission to full membership. Under the proposed new rules, full membership would automatically be extended to a substantially greater number of companies. A rule change on these lines should help to reassure the independent companies that control of PPL will be more broadly based.

2.168. PPL is improving its distribution of income as better information becomes available so that record companies (including independent companies) and performers will receive a share of the income which is more closely related to actual playing time of their records. We are satisfied that there is no substance in the complaint that the major record companies are exploiting their monopoly position to deprive others of a fair share of PPL's income.

2.169. We have already dealt with the position of record producers in paragraph 2.153.

Video Performance Limited

2.170. MTV Europe (MTV) complained that Video Performance Limited (VPL) was the vehicle for collusive and anti-competitive behaviour by the major record companies towards its broadcasting of music videos. Although the supply of music videos does not come within our terms of reference we examined this issue since it could be that the record companies' actions in this field were attributable to the monopoly situation which we have found to exist in recorded music.

2.171. The MMC's report on *Collective licensing** examined the merits of collective licensing bodies and noted that the convenience they offer to both the owner and the user of copyright is unlikely to be matched by any other means. The report concluded that such bodies were the best available mechanism for licensing sound recordings provided they can be constrained from using their monopoly unfairly.

2.172. VPL is a collective licensing body. It licenses the use of videos by other broadcasters besides MTV and by those who give public performances (for example, clubs and public houses). It also provides a cost-effective way for record companies to license their videos and hence offers the advantages of convenience which were identified in the report on collective licensing. Moreover, for MTV it offers the added advantage of licences for the retransmission of videos in various countries of Europe. If MTV considers that VPL is using its monopoly unfairly in relation to the terms negotiated for MTV's use of videos then it can pursue its complaints through the EC and the courts, as it already is. Since these avenues are open to MTV we do not consider it necessary for us to make any finding in respect of the operation of VPL or the particular matters on which MTV is in dispute with it.

Record charts

National charts

2.173. Umbrella Organisation Ltd (Umbrella), which represents some of the smaller independent record companies, suggested to us that the major record companies distorted competition by the way they sought the inclusion of their records in the 'independent chart'. However, evidence from the major record companies satisfied us that independent companies, which were represented on the relevant BPI committee, had been the ones to decide on the criteria for inclusion in this chart. Records *distributed* by the major record companies were not eligible, whether or not the label was owned by a major. The majors did not support this rule, which they believed had no basis in logic and which disadvantaged them in competing for contracts to distribute independent labels. We could find no evidence to support a finding that the majors were using their monopoly position to disadvantage independent record companies in relation to this chart.

2.174. Our main concern with the national charts was whether they were being distorted by the record companies' practice of giving away free records to retailers. We were told that this practice was widespread for newly-released singles and its purpose was to ensure that the records were stocked by retailers and were offered for sale to customers at an attractive price. The volume of free singles distributed was considerable, sometimes reaching 50 per cent of a retailer's stock, in the first few weeks after a record was released. It is clear that the intention is to stimulate sales at an early stage

---

*Collective Licensing: a report on certain practices in the Collective Licensing of Public Performance and Broadcasting Rights in Sound Recordings, Cm 530, December 1988.

in a record's life so that it will get into the singles chart, which is the key to getting the record played on national radio, in particular on the BBC's Radio 1 FM.

2.175. The major record companies have argued that all companies engage in this practice, including independent record companies, and it is part of the means by which companies compete for sales. They regard it as a legitimate promotional tool which is equivalent to giving a discount on singles.

2.176. The main arguments against the practice are that it could create a distortion in the charts and so mislead consumers, that it might distort competition between record companies (to the disadvantage of independent record companies) and that it might distort competition between retailers (to the disadvantage of independent retailers).

2.177. On the other hand, we note that the practice does not prevent singles from independent record companies getting into the singles chart since they released 16 per cent of the chart entries in the 12 months to September 1993. Moreover we have received no complaints from independent record companies about the practice, which suggests that they are not disadvantaged by it. As far as competition between retailers is concerned, since independent retailers are the main recipients of free records, the practice can be regarded as strengthening competition since the independent retailers do not receive discounts and other promotional support to the same extent as large retailers. We also attach weight to the argument that the record companies should be free to promote singles since these are themselves such an important competitive element in stimulating sales of albums and in establishing new artists.

2.178. Although we retain some concern about a practice which is designed to influence chart positions, we consider that on balance the benefits of not interfering with the competitive process outweigh its disadvantages and that no change is required in connection with the practice. Moreover it does not appear to be connected with the existence of the major record companies' monopoly situation.

Retailers' charts

2.179. A number of the major retailers, including W H Smith and Our Price, display their own charts which are not based on the national charts compiled by Gallup.* Concern has been expressed, by the record companies and others, that these charts may mislead or confuse consumers, particularly where they are based on the retailers' predictions of future sales rather than actual sales in the previous week.

2.180. The retailers explain that the national charts do not meet their needs because they are not geared to the type of customer who buys in their particular shops. Thus W H Smith sells records which appeal to the wider public who use its shops and it has few sales of records in specialist genres, such as dance music. However, such records sometimes come high in the national charts. W H Smith does not want to promote records which its customers will not buy. We can understand this concern but believe it is unacceptable to display a chart which might well have the effect of misleading consumers into thinking that it represents the previous week's best-selling records. We were also concerned to learn that W H Smith had in the past charged record companies for inclusion in its chart.

2.181. The effect of this practice by W H Smith and Our Price is not sufficient to warrant a finding that they are exploiting a monopoly position. However, we consider that all retailers which display charts that differ from the recognized national charts, whether they are called 'charts' or some other title such as 'hit-lists', should make clear at the point of display the basis on which they have been compiled. W H Smith has now introduced such a practice and we suggest that the Director General of Fair Trading should seek to ensure that other retailers follow the same practice. We believe this is a matter which he will want to consider in the context of his consumer protection functions.

---

*By Millward Brown since February 1994.

The public interest—conclusions

2.182. The origins of our inquiry lay in the concern that the price of CDs was higher in the UK than in other countries. We have found that some retail prices, particularly of 'full-price' CDs, are higher in the UK than in the USA, after making due allowance for differences in VAT and sales tax. UK prices are lower than in most other countries. We have also found that the price differential between the UK and USA for full-price popular CDs is no higher than for a wide range of other products.

2.183. We do not ascribe the price differentials to the right of a copyright owner to control parallel imports. It seems unlikely that removing that right would lead to a reduction in the price of recorded music generally. In any event, it would be inconsistent with international developments in intellectual property, including the EC Rental Directive. Uncontrolled parallel imports could also be damaging because of the increased risk of piracy and the general weakening of copyright protection, which is territorially based.

2.184. We have found that there is strong competition both among the record companies and among the retailers. It is also clear that neither the record companies nor the retailers are making excessive profits. Since the markets are competitive it follows that, despite the monopoly situations which we have found to exist, the companies in whose favour they operate are not able to exercise market power in a way which enables them to exploit their monopoly positions. We therefore conclude that the prices for recorded music in the UK are set at levels determined by effective competition within the UK market. We have also found that the record companies compete with each other to sign both new and established artists, which gives artists adequate bargaining ability to negotiate the terms of their contracts.

2.185. We have already concluded that two monopoly situations exist in relation to recorded music. A complex monopoly situation exists in favour of the five major record companies (see paragraph 2.44) and a scale monopoly exists in favour of W H Smith and Our Price (see paragraph 2.48).

2.186. We now conclude that the companies in whose favour those monopoly situations exist are not taking any steps to maintain or exploit them. Nor are there any actions or omissions attributable to the existence of the monopoly situations. We have found no facts which operate or may be expected to operate against the public interest.

2.187. Background information on the industry, and the evidence on which our conclusions are based, can be found in Chapters 3 to 13 which form Part II of our report.

G D W ODGERS *(Chairman)*

D G GOYDER

M E BEESLEY

J EVANS

D P THOMSON

A J NIEDUSZYNSKI *(Secretary)*

14 April 1994

Part II

Background and evidence

3   Background to the reference

Contents

The recorded music industry

3.1. The music industry is primarily concerned with the discovery, development and commercial exploitation of musical talent in the shape of composers and recording artists, and the continued commercial exploitation of the works of existing composers and artists. Although the record buyer purchases a physical sound carrier (referred to as a record 'format'—see paragraphs 3.26 to 3.37), such as a CD or cassette, the 'product' which the industry is actually promoting is the artist or sound recording of the composition captured in that format. In the future, new formats and the development of electronically transmitted recordings may alter the way music is purchased and consumed, but the product will remain the same.

3.2. Various intellectual property rights attach to the recording of a musical work, and these underpin the relationships, processes, and commercial and legal arrangements in the recorded music industry. Such rights are based on the concept of copyrights; national laws define the extent of these rights and the national regimes are linked by international copyright treaties or conventions. Within this framework of copyright law and international convention, the trade in recorded music is conducted. An account of these rights, their exploitation, and the relevant UK and international laws and conventions governing the UK music industry is contained in Chapter 4.

3.3. In this chapter, we briefly describe the overall structure of the industry and recent developments both in the UK and overseas which led to the referral of the supply of recorded music in the UK to the MMC.

Structure of the industry

3.4. The recorded music industry is both complex and diverse, carrying out many interconnected activities from the creation and production of original pieces of music and the manufacture and distribution of recordings to the final sale to consumers.

3.5. The most important participants in the industry include the record companies, the composers, the artists, the publishing companies, all those individuals and companies involved in the creation of sound recordings and the music retailers. The functions of each of these participants are briefly summarized in the following paragraphs. They are discussed at greater length in subsequent chapters.

The record companies

3.6. Record companies have a wide range of functions and occupy the pivotal role in the industry. Their principal activities are: finding and developing new artists; recording music, which will involve hiring studios, sound engineers, technicians, producers and equipment; releasing recordings and marketing and promoting them in the UK and in the international market-place; obtaining licences for the repertoire of overseas companies and selling it in the UK; and making royalty payments to artists, music publishers and others out of the proceeds of record sales.

3.7. The five largest UK record companies are usually referred to as 'the majors', by virtue of their international operations and the fact that they own and operate national distribution systems, distributing their own and third-party sound recordings to retailers, wholesalers and smaller distributors. Several of the majors also own and operate their own manufacturing plants, where cassettes, CDs and vinyl records are manufactured. The five majors are BMG, EMI, PolyGram, Sony and Warner.

3.8. There are some 600 independent record companies in the UK. They carry out a more limited range of activities than the majors, centred around the production of a recording. In terms of size, they vary from significant operations such as MCA and Mute Records Ltd to very small businesses issuing only a handful of recordings a year. Independent record companies make an important contribution to the discovery and development of new talent, particularly (although by no means exclusively) in niche areas of musical taste such as dance, jazz, modern classical music or early music. They may also specialize, for example, in the licensing-in of music originated by other record companies to create compilations or in the budget end of the classical sector. Some independent record companies have become very successful, for example Virgin before its sale to EMI.

Artists

3.9. The artists involved in the recorded music industry comprise all those individuals who compose material or who perform as recording artists, or who carry out both activities. Recording artists often write their own material, particularly so far as contemporary popular music is concerned. There are also a large number of musicians who are contracted for particular recordings and who are known as 'session musicians'.

The music publishing companies

3.10. The printing and selling of sheet music is now only a very small part of a music publisher's activities. Music publishers today play an important role in developing the careers of writers (both composers and lyricists), promoting those writers' works, and administering and collecting income from exploitation of the rights in those works. Most record companies, whether majors or independents, have an associated publishing arm. In the case of the majors, these are managed independently.

Studios and others involved in the recording process

3.11. Those who run studios where material is recorded, musical and technical equipment suppliers, producers and sound engineers are all an integral part of the process of making a recording.

Manufacturers

3.12. The manufacturing of records is carried out both by independent manufacturers and by companies which are vertically integrated into the major multinational record company groups. While the manufacturing arms of the majors mainly manufacture only for their own group requirements, the independent manufacturers serve both independent record companies and the majors, particularly when the latter require extra production capacity.

Distributors

3.13. The major record companies each operate centralized distribution systems in the UK, serving both their own record labels and third parties. The recorded music market also supports independent distributors who are closely tied both to the independent record companies and to the smaller, independent retailers. Wholesalers (such as Entertainment UK Ltd (EUK) and TBD) also play an important role in this market.

Promoters

3.14. Promoters of live performances organize venues, concert halls and support services. Live performances play an important part in the marketing by the record companies of individual groups and artists.

Retailers

3.15. Music retailing can be divided into a number of categories in the UK market: specialist music chains, such as HMV, Our Price and Virgin; non-specialist chains, such as W H Smith and Woolworths; and independent specialists, either small chains or single outlets. 'Non-traditional' outlets such as supermarkets, petrol stations and convenience stores also sell a limited selection of records.

3.16. The largest record retailers in terms of overall sales of records are W H Smith, with its subsidiary, Our Price; HMV, which is owned by THORN EMI plc; and Woolworths, which is part of the Kingfisher group. W H Smith also has a 50 per cent shareholding in Virgin Retail which is a joint venture with the Virgin Retail Group Ltd.[1]

3.17. The direct mail selling of sound recordings has increased in importance in recent years. Record clubs, of which Britannia Music Company Ltd (Britannia) and BCA are the largest, supply their members from a select list of titles. Mail order companies are much smaller in terms of the volume and range of orders. Some, such as Readers' Digest, market their own compilations.

Ancillary activities

3.18. There are a number of other organizations and activities which are important to the functioning of the music industry. These include:

— radio stations, clubs, pubs and discos, which play records and generate revenues for composers, performers and record companies in the form of royalties;

— trade organizations—there are a large number involved in the music industry, including the British Phonographic Industry Ltd (BPI), which represents record companies and manufacturers, and the British Association of Record Dealers (BARD), which represents retailers;

— the Musicians' Union, which represents many performers;

— collective licensing bodies—these represent copyright holders in negotiations with licensees over royalty payments and undertake the collection and distribution of these payments. Those

---

[1]On 2 March 1994 W H Smith announced a proposed merger between Our Price and Virgin Retail to form a new company in which W H Smith will have a shareholding of 75 per cent and the Virgin Retail Group Ltd the remaining 25 per cent.

248336 D

collective licensing bodies which are important in the recorded music industry are described in Chapter 4;

— the music press; and

— a large miscellaneous services and support sector including lawyers, accountants, managers, graphic designers, public relations companies and advertising agencies.

Size of the industry

3.19. A diagram showing the constituent parts of the UK record industry is given in Figure 3.1, together with an estimate of the total numbers employed in each sector in 1992.

FIGURE 3.1

Employment in the UK record industry

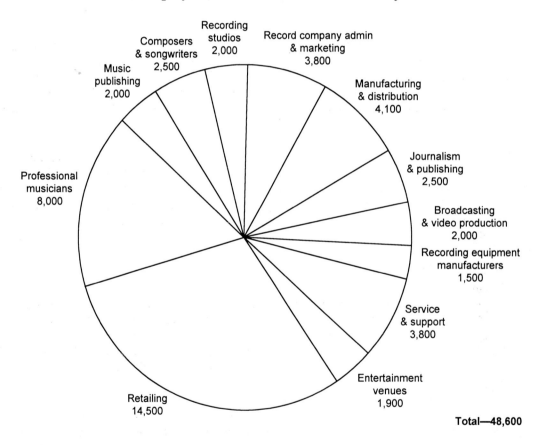

Total—48,600

Source: BPI Surveys and estimates.

The international nature of the UK music industry

3.20. Since the emergence of The Beatles in the early 1960s, music originating from UK song-writers and performers has secured a share of world music sales disproportionately larger than would be expected given the size of the UK market. The breadth and diversity of UK talent continues to be reflected in the supply of UK repertoire to the global music market. For although sales to UK consumers account for only 7 per cent of the world total, it is estimated by the BPI that a larger proportion of world sales, about 18 per cent, are from recordings involving UK artists.

3.21. UK record companies regard the international exploitation and success of their recordings as of fundamental importance, believing that many of them would not be profitable on the basis of domestic sales of their repertoire alone. The UK music industry has over the past 30 years been a significant source of export earnings and contributed to the country's balance of payments. Income to the UK from the licensing of recordings overseas exceeds £400 million per annum.

The music scene

3.22. A further characteristic of the UK music scene is its diversity. Although there is no universally accepted categorization, the BPI analyses music sales into the following categories: classical, country/folk, jazz, pop, rock, dance/soul/reggae, middle-of-the-road (MOR) and other. However, the music scene is even more diverse than this analysis would suggest, including punk, rap, heavy metal, acid-house, techno-rave, grunge and swing-beat; and new genres are constantly emerging. Accordingly, musical styles are not readily categorized.

3.23. Of the generally accepted categories mentioned above, pop and rock taken together accounted for nearly 60 per cent of album sales in 1992. Classical music accounted for a little over 9 per cent. The record companies report an accelerating trend towards fragmentation of musical genres and taste and an increased rate at which styles of music and individual releases become popular with consumers and then decline.

3.24. Certain artists and songs, however, can remain popular for many years, for example Cliff Richard or The Beatles. Classical music has enjoyed a growth in popularity in recent years. In 1982 classical music accounted for only 6.2 per cent of all albums, as measured by the BPI. In 1990 this peaked at 11.1 per cent, boosted by the popularity of such recordings as *Nessun Dorma* performed by Pavarotti and used as the theme tune for the 1990 World Cup on BBC television, but has since fallen back to 9.2 per cent in 1992.

3.25. It is the changing taste of consumers which drives the relative popularity of different types of music and this in turn has dictated the wider range of music offered by record companies. Demographic trends have also affected the demand for recorded music, particularly in terms of the volume and type of music purchased by an ageing population, while younger consumers have become increasingly attracted by alternative entertainment such as videos and computer games.

The different formats

3.26. Recordings may be physically carried on a number of different formats, a term which we use to refer both to the physical medium on to which the music has been recorded (the 'sound carrier') and to the amount of music contained on that sound carrier (ie single or album). Each sound carrier requires appropriate hardware on which it can be played, and many households will have several different items of hardware, for example the integrated stereo system, the car cassette player, the radio/cassette player and the 'Walkman'.

3.27. Over the past 25 years or so, recorded music has been available to the consumer on three principal sound carriers, the vinyl record, the music cassette (cassette) and, most recently, the CD.

Vinyl

3.28. When the pop industry took off in the 1960s, vinyl recordings dominated the market, having taken over from the brittle 78 rpm records in the late 1950s. Vinyl records were available as 7-inch singles or 12-inch long-players (LPs). Vinyl LP sales reached their high point in 1975, after which they began to decline, largely because consumers were switching to cassette. Vinyl records are generally held to produce a better sound quality than cassettes, and a small number of listeners (particularly of older jazz recordings) believe the sound reproduction on vinyl is more authentic even than that of a digital (CD) recording. But vinyl records are less easily transportable and are more easily damaged than cassettes, and the latter are very convenient for playing in cars and on personal stereo systems.

248336   D2

3.29. Since 1988, vinyl sales have declined more sharply. Demand for vinyl is now largely confined to fans of specific music genres such as heavy metal and dance, those who believe that the sound quality of analogue recordings is closer to that of a live performance than digital recordings, and those who prefer the traditional turntable to its modern replacements.

Cassette

3.30. Cassettes were introduced in 1967 but were slow to achieve popularity. As noted above, cassettes then grew at the expense of vinyl and continued to grow strongly even after the introduction of CDs in 1983. This was because their transportability and the low cost of the hardware on which they could be played offset some of the advantages of the CD, namely its durability and the fact that, unlike the cassette, the sound quality does not deteriorate over time.

3.31. One of the key characteristics of the cassette format was that for the first time consumers had the means to copy recordings, whether these were on vinyl or on pre-recorded cassette, on to a blank cassette and thus build up a music library of recordings at a fraction of the price at which recorded music was on sale.

3.32. In 1984 there was a rapid expansion of cassette sales as the result of improvements in the sound quality of tapes and the growing importance of portability in consumers' choice of formats as in-car players and personal stereos had become common. Cassette sales reached a peak in 1989. The subsequent downturn in sales from 1990 coincided with the onset of the recent recession but also reflected the increasing consumer preference for CDs.

Compact disc

3.33. The introduction of the CD in 1983 was followed by considerable investment by the industry in promoting this format which is held to offer unsurpassed sound quality and convenience to the consumer, as well as durability. The demand for CDs has steadily increased since 1983 at the expense of both vinyl and cassette. In 1992 total sales of CDs exceeded those of cassettes for the first time.

3.34. Vinyl records, cassettes and CDs are available in two formats, either 'singles' or 'albums'. Singles consist of either one title or up to 25 minutes' playing time. Albums consist of at least four tracks and, in the case of CDs, can play up to about 80 minutes of music.

New sound carriers

3.35. Two new sound carriers, the digital compact cassette (DCC) and the MiniDisc, were introduced in 1992. The DCC, developed by Philips, looks similar to a conventional cassette. It is said to combine the digital sound quality achieved by the CD with the ability to make a perfect copy of a digital recording. DCC hardware is also compatible with analogue cassettes, so that users can play their existing analogue cassette collections on their new DCC machines.

3.36. The MiniDisc, developed by the Sony Corporation, looks like a small CD in a protective cartridge. It is said to offer quick random access to tracks, high sound quality and durability. It is also available in blank form and can be used to make digital copies of pre-recorded music.

3.37. Sales of these formats have so far been low and it is not yet clear how successful they will prove to be. In the past, attempts to introduce new formats have sometimes failed. For example, after stereo LPs had become established in the late 1960s, record companies tried to introduce quadrophonic LPs but these did not develop the wide public appeal necessary to establish them in the market. Again, four- and then eight-track tape cartridges had become available in the mid to late 1960s, but although eight-track cartridges seemed at one time to be on the point of gaining wide support, their sales peaked in 1974 at just under 8 million units.

Origins of the MMC reference

3.38. In 1990 Consumers' Association (CA) had argued in its publication *Which?* that the price of CDs in the shops was too high. When they were introduced in 1983, CDs had cost £10. Since that time, CA said, full-price pop CDs had become only marginally cheaper in real terms, selling at £11 and sometimes £12. The price of classical CDs had not come down at all. Yet during this period, the cost of manufacturing a CD had more than halved and the demand for CDs had grown, so that a reduction in price would have been expected.

3.39. During 1991/92 the Office of Fair Trading (OFT) undertook an investigation into the recorded music market with particular reference to the price of CDs. The OFT's conclusions were summarized by the Minister for Corporate Affairs at the Department of Trade and Industry, in response to a written Question in May 1992. The OFT, he said, had found:

> that no producer or retailer had a market share in excess of 25 per cent ... and that there was no evidence of collusion between recorded music producers or retailers, or between producers and retailers. It concluded that prices of compact discs had settled at the level which the market was willing to bear. There was no evidence that the profits of the record producers were excessive. In the absence of any evidence of collusion or anti-competitive conduct the Director General of Fair Trading concluded that no action under the competition legislation was appropriate but the OFT proposes to keep the market under review.

3.40. The OFT continued, however, to receive representations and in July 1992 a new Director General announced that he had decided to open a further inquiry. The inquiry had three objectives:

(a) to update the information in the earlier inquiry on market structure at both the record company and the retail levels;

(b) to examine the impact upon competition in the UK market for CDs of the copyright legislation and of restrictions on the importation of CDs offered for sale in the USA; and

(c) in the light of the above, to decide whether any action would be appropriate under the Director General's competition powers.

3.41. Before the OFT had completed its further inquiry, the National Heritage Committee of the House of Commons (NHC) announced in December 1992 its intention to conduct an inquiry into the price of CDs in the UK. The NHC's report was published in May 1993.[1]

3.42. The NHC stated (paragraph 1 of its report) that when 'the Committee decided to conduct this inquiry, it was looking for an answer to what seemed a very simple question. Why do compact discs cost quite a lot more in the United Kingdom than they do in the United States?'

3.43. In its conclusions, the NHC said that it welcomed the examination by the OFT of possible restrictions on international trade represented by legislation governing parallel imports and that even if the result should not prove a reliable basis for a complex monopoly finding, the Committee believed that the operation of the 1988 Copyright Act as it related to parallel imports could work against the public interest. (The 1988 Copyright Act gives copyright owners or their licensees the right to prevent the import of records from another country, even where these records have been produced with the permission of the copyright owner in that particular country—see paragraphs 4.22 to 4.29.)

3.44. The NHC accordingly recommended that the Department of Trade and Industry re-examine current legislation on copyright with particular reference to its anti-competitive effects in the recorded music industry. It was essential, however, the NHC said, that any relaxation of the law relating to parallel imports in the UK should not be used to place the UK at a disadvantage compared with other

---

[1]See paragraph 2.2.

countries. The NHC concluded by stating that 'It is now time for consumers to show that they will no longer bear the prices currently charged for full-price compact discs'.

3.45. On 14 May 1993 the Director General of Fair Trading referred the supply of recorded music to the MMC. In the press release which accompanied the reference, the Director General said:

> Compact disc prices remain relatively high when compared with the cost of other formats and with prices in the US. I have not been satisfied by the arguments that have been put forward to explain this phenomenon. I am concerned that the record companies' use of copyright law, to restrict parallel imports of CDs at a lower cost, may be frustrating competition .... It will now be for the MMC to undertake a full study of this market and form a view as to whether or not any practices of the industry operate against the public interest. I hope they will consider in particular whether copyright, which is a reward for innovation and creativity, is being used in such a way as to restrict, distort or prevent competition.

3.46. The price of records had also been the subject of scrutiny in Australia over this period. The Prices Surveillance Authority (PSA) was asked by the Australian Government in February 1990 to conduct an inquiry into the prices of sound recordings in that country, looking at competition and efficiency, and the operation of the copyright law, as well as issues such as piracy, the health of the Australian music industry, and the introduction of new technologies. The final report[1] was published on 13 December 1990.

3.47. The PSA concluded that record prices in Australia were excessive and recommended a series of measures designed to benefit consumers, ensure recognition of the rights of Australian artists and assist the development of the Australian music industry.

3.48. The key recommendation on prices was the removal of import restrictions to promote competition in the Australian sound recordings market which was, the PSA said, dominated by the international record companies. Prices of vinyl records, cassettes and CDs had been consistently much higher than in overseas retail markets for many years, the PSA said. Record company profits had been exceptionally high, even ignoring high transfer payments to overseas parent companies. A substantial fall in prices would occur if records (except pirate records which should remain illegal) released on overseas markets could enter the country. The PSA Chairman said:

> Import restrictions effectively allow the major record companies to control imports into Australia. These companies can import from their international parent companies who own much of the copyright but this access is generally not available to other suppliers in the industry. This limits competition in the record market. Dominance of the record market's supply by a few companies, underpinned by import restrictions, keeps prices high .... The most direct and appropriate way to deal with the problem of high prices, and claims of restricted record availability, is to abolish the importation provisions of the Copyright Act regarding non-pirated recordings.

3.49. The PSA report was published some three years ago. Early in 1993 the Australian Government introduced a Bill which provided for the removal of import restrictions affecting records coming from the USA, some EC countries and New Zealand and released after 1 July 1994. That Bill lapsed following the announcement of the March 1993 Federal election. There is opposition to the proposal to remove import restrictions both from the industry itself and from some Ministers, and the whole matter is still under consideration by the Australian Government.

---

[1]*Inquiry into the Prices of Sound Recordings:* Report No 35, Prices Surveillance Authority, Canberra, December 1990.

4 The copyright system and its enforcement

Contents

The copyright system

4.1. The copyright system has been part of British statute law since the early 1700s. It is currently embodied in the comprehensive Copyright, Designs and Patents Act 1988 (the 1988 Copyright Act).

Droit d'auteur and common law systems

4.2. Throughout the world, states have their own separate copyright regimes which prevail in their own territories. These regimes reflect two different traditions. The first is the *droit d'auteur* or civil law system which applies in non-English-speaking countries and therefore throughout most of Europe. In essence, this system developed from considerations of natural justice which view the work of an author as the expression of his personality, giving him fundamental human rights both to control economic exploitation of his work and protect its integrity. The second system is the common law system of the UK and other English-speaking countries. This has as its basis the concept of safeguarding the skill, labour and investment of those responsible for the creation of works, in order to protect them from reproduction and other uses of the material which they have not authorized. Copyright under the common law system might therefore be characterized as a right to prevent people from dealing with others' intellectual property without rightful authority. However, despite these differences in philosophical approach between the civil and common law systems, the kinds of materials protected under both systems are essentially the same, as are the forms of exploitation of these materials which are protected.

4.3. Whatever the system in each jurisdiction, it is subject to the international obligations of the state concerned. Most countries belong to international conventions on copyright and so are under at least some international law obligations on copyright. In paragraphs 4.45 to 4.53 we discuss relevant aspects of the international conventions. First, however, we discuss the UK copyright system.

The UK statutory framework

4.4. In its original form under the Copyright Act 1709, copyright was a single right giving the author of a literary work the right to control the copying of that work. That of course reflected the fact that the only way in which an author's work could be widely distributed was in printed form. Throughout the last three centuries there has been a continuous process of evolution brought about through fresh legislation, leading to the 1988 Copyright Act. Parliament has amended copyright law in the UK on several occasions so that it was able to address the impact of new technologies. Copyright law has proved a flexible piece of legal machinery. Today the copyright system embraces a wide range of products involving human creativity, such as musical and artistic works, sound recordings (records, tapes, cassettes, CDs etc), films and broadcasts. It is still developing as new types of electronic and other data are developed. Accordingly, copyright is no longer a single right to authorize or prohibit copying, but comprises a bundle of individual rights giving the copyright owner the right to control the various ways in which his property can be exploited.

4.5. First, copyright is a property right. Section 1(1) of the 1988 Copyright Act so describes it. It can be dealt with in the same way as other forms of property. It can be sold, its use can be licensed, it can be given away or it can be bequeathed. The right, however, is intangible. It is not the same as the physical object, eg the book, the disc or the picture. The holder of the right may protect the right in various ways, and in the last resort through legal proceedings.

4.6. Secondly, copyright is not an indefinite right. The 1988 Copyright Act provides that copyright in a musical work expires at the end of 50 years from the end of the calendar year in which the author dies.[1] It further provides that copyright in a sound recording expires at the end of the period of 50 years from the end of the calendar year in which it is made, or if it is released before the end of that period, 50 years from the end of the calendar year in which it is released. Whilst these rights are of limited duration, we note that they are longer than the duration of certain other intellectual property rights. For example, the maximum term of a patent grant is 20 years from the filing date. However, it is the fundamental differences between different forms of intellectual property which have resulted in different terms of protection. For example, a patent gives exclusive rights exercisable against a person who subsequently makes the same invention, even independently, whereas copyright is only exercisable against a person who has demonstrably dealt with the original work and used it as his starting point. In addition copyright does not protect ideas, merely the way in which they are expressed. A patent by contrast can protect the basic concept underlying an invention, albeit only when that concept has been embodied in something which has industrial application.

4.7. Thirdly, rights under copyright are generally exclusive rights. For example, the copyright owner is the only person entitled to reproduce the work; third parties need the copyright owner's authority to do so.

4.8. Finally, a given product may embody several copyrights whose original owners are different. Thus, for example, on a record there exist rights in the sound recording, usually owned by the record company, as well as rights in the music and lyrics, owned by the composer or songwriter initially and usually assigned to his music publisher.

---

[1]See, however, paragraph 4.44 below.

The copyright system and sound recordings

4.9. The copyright system provides the legal and commercial basis for the recorded music industry. The complex web of business relationships in the industry depends on the system.

4.10. The rights incorporated or subsisting in a sound recording are generally of the following kind:

(a) copyright in the musical, literary and/or dramatic work (for example, in the case of a song, in both the music and the words) (see paragraph 4.11);

(b) copyright in the sound recording itself (see paragraphs 4.12 to 4.18);

(c) rights of performers whose performances are embodied on the recording (see paragraphs 4.19 to 4.21); and

(d) rights of persons having exclusive recording rights in the recording of artists' performances (see paragraphs 4.19 to 4.21).

We deal with each of these in turn below. In addition, the author of literary, dramatic and musical works is given 'moral rights' to be identified as the author of his work, and the right to object to derogatory treatment of it.

Copyright in the musical, literary or dramatic work

4.11. The copyright in a sound recording is separate from the composer's copyright in the musical work. Musical works may range, for example, from an opera to a simple song. Rights in such music which the composer (ie of the music and of the lyrics) desires to exploit on a commercial basis will generally be assigned or licensed to a music publisher.

Copyright in the sound recording

4.12. Under the 1988 Copyright Act a sound recording is one of the descriptions of work in which copyright subsists (section 1). The definition in section 5(1) of the 1988 Copyright Act covers any recording of a literary, dramatic or musical work or other sounds, regardless of medium.

4.13. Section 11(1) of the 1988 Copyright Act provides that the author of a work is the first owner of any copyright in it. The 1988 Copyright Act defines the 'author' of a sound recording as the person by whom the arrangements necessary to make the recording are undertaken (section 9(2)*(a)*).

4.14. Section 9(2)*(a)* has generally been interpreted in the industry as meaning that the 'person' referred to therein is the record company. In practice the record companies take steps to ensure either that they are the first owners of the copyright or that the first owner assigns the copyright to them, for the full period of copyright protection, along with the consent of the artists, and where necessary the producers, to exploit the sound recording. In return, royalties are paid. Licences are also taken from the owner of the literary and musical works, again subject to payment of royalties.

4.15. The House of Lords debated section 9 in 1987. Lord Beaverbrook, the Minister concerned, commented on the provision by reference to the then existing law covering the positions of film producers and directors:[1]

> ... The Bill deals with copyright in sound recordings in the same way that the present law [ie the Copyright Act 1956] treats films; namely, that the first owner is the person who makes the necessary arrangements for the recording. This approach works satisfactorily for films and we believe will do so for sound recordings ... to give the director a

---

[1] Hansard H L, 30 November 1987, col 890.

copyright in the film would not be fair to the person who has made and paid for the arrangements for the film production. In making those arrangements he will of course have negotiated appropriate remuneration for the director. It would be wrong for the director to be able to claim additional remuneration on the basis of his copyright ....

4.16. A different interpretation of section 9(2)*(a)* of the 1988 Copyright Act was offered to us by Re-Pro, a group of mainly self-employed recording producers, directors and engineers (see paragraph 10.84).

4.17. The rights which are comprised in the copyright in a sound recording are the exclusive rights to:

(a) copy the recording (section 17) (this includes synchronization and dubbing rights);

(b) issue copies of the recording to the public, including the rental of copies to the public (section 18);

(c) play the recording in public (section 19); and

(d) broadcast the recording (on radio or television) or include it in a cable programme service (section 20). (However, these particular rights are only exclusive rights to authorize or prohibit if they are exercised individually by a copyright owner. Section 175 of the Broadcasting Act 1990 amended the 1988 Copyright Act to the effect that where copyright owners act collectively to exercise their rights they cannot limit the broadcasting or cable transmission of sound recordings, ie they are entitled simply to receive equitable remuneration and to impose reasonable licensing terms and conditions.)

Each set of rights can be assigned separately.

4.18. A person infringes copyright if he does any of the acts mentioned in paragraph 4.17 without the authority of the copyright owner. In relation to copyright infringement, the copyright owner (or exclusive licensee of the right infringed) can claim for civil remedies. Additionally the 1988 Copyright Act provides for criminal sanctions against persons knowingly making or dealing with infringing articles. Thus, for example, the owner of material which has been 'bootlegged' (illegally recorded at a broadcast or concert) has recourse to civil remedies or to the criminal law.

Rights of performers and persons having recording rights in performances

4.19. The 1988 Copyright Act confers the following rights on a performer:

(a) to prohibit the making or reproduction of a recording of his performance (sections 180(2) and 182(1)*(a)*);

(b) to prohibit the broadcasting, or inclusion in a cable programme service, of his live performance (or an illicit recording of his performance) (sections 182(1)*(b)* and 183*(b)*);

(c) to prohibit the showing or playing in public of an illicit recording of his performance (section 183*(a)*); and

(d) to prohibit the distribution in or importation into the UK of an illicit recording of his performance (section 184(1)).

We discuss imports which infringe copyright further in paragraphs 4.22 to 4.30.

4.20. The performer generally gives consent to the exclusive making, performing, broadcast and distribution of the recording (in return for a share of the income from these forms of exploitation). However, by virtue of their contracts with a record company, performers generally confer exclusive recording rights on the record company, so that the record company is entitled, to the exclusion of all other persons, to make one or more recordings of the performer's performances with a view to their commercial exploitation. We refer to these exclusivity contracts in paragraph 5.131.

4.21. The 1988 Copyright Act confers similar rights to those listed in paragraph 4.19 on persons who have exclusive recording contracts with performers to prohibit:

(a) the making or reproduction of a recording of the performance (section 186(1));

(b) the broadcasting, or inclusion in a cable programme service, of an illicit recording of the performance (section 187(1)*(b)*);

(c) the showing or playing in public of an illicit recording of the performance (section 187(1)*(a)*); and

(d) the distribution in or importation into the UK of an illicit recording of the performance (section 188(1)).

Imports which infringe copyright

4.22. We next discuss imports which infringe UK copyright. There are two categories. The first is where the copy has been made in another jurisdiction under a licence granted by the UK copyright owner but where the licence is limited to making in that territory alone (paragraphs 4.24 to 4.29). The second is where the copy is made entirely without the consent of the copyright owner (paragraph 4.30). In either case section 22 of the 1988 Copyright Act provides that the copyright in a work is infringed by a person who without the licence of the copyright owner imports into the UK, otherwise than for his private and domestic use, an article which is, and which he knows or has reason to believe is, an 'infringing copy'.

4.23. The owner of copyright in a sound recording may give notice to Customs and Excise that infringing copies of the work are expected to arrive in the UK at a specified time and place, and that he requests Customs and Excise to treat the copies as prohibited goods (section 111(3) of the 1988 Copyright Act). The effect of the notice is that the importation is prohibited, and that the goods are subject to forfeiture. Such a notice can be given in respect of any imports which are infringing copies of either of the two categories described above.

4.24. As regards the first category, an article is an infringing copy if it has been or is proposed to be imported into the UK, and its making in the UK would have constituted an infringement of the copyright in the work or a breach of an exclusive licence agreement relating to the work (section 27(3) of the 1988 Copyright Act). An exclusive licence means a licence from the copyright owner authorizing the licensee, to the exclusion of all other persons (including the person granting the licence), to exercise a right otherwise exercisable exclusively by the copyright owner (section 92(1) of the 1988 Copyright Act).

4.25. In most circumstances, section 27(3) gives the copyright owner, or the exclusive licensee, ability to control importation into the UK of copyright material which has been lawfully made abroad with his consent. For example, a UK copyright owner may grant licences for the making of the work abroad and not in the UK. Since articles made under such licences could not lawfully be manufactured in the UK, their importation renders them infringing copies. Thus the owner of the UK copyright or the exclusive licensee can object to their importation without his consent. As explained in paragraphs 4.35 to 4.37, the provision does not apply, however, to imports from member states of the EC (section 27(5)).

4.26. The copyright owner's power to prevent the importation of copyright articles was extended to cover breaches of exclusive licence agreements in the 1988 Copyright Act. The amendment to the law was made following the judgment in *CBS United Kingdom Ltd v Charmdale Record Distributors Ltd*[1] which held that the Copyright Act 1956 did not protect exclusive licensees from importations of copies made abroad by the owner of the UK copyright.

---

[1] [1981] 1 Ch 91.

4.27. The effect of section 27(3) of the 1988 Copyright Act is to give the copyright owner, or the exclusive licensee, power to proceed against imports of recordings lawfully produced under licence in another country for sale in that country. Such imports are known colloquially as 'parallel imports'.

4.28. The power to control 'parallel imports' relates only to imports of copies of a particular work or product. If a UK record company makes a recording of a particular composition, the copyright in that recording will enable the record company to prevent copies of that recording made under licence abroad from being imported into the UK, save with its permission. It will not empower the owner of the copyright in the sound recording to prevent importation of copies of a different recording of the same composition made in, say, the USA.

4.29. Moreover, if a UK record company had no licence arrangement with others, and itself made and distributed copies abroad, it could not prevent subsequent importation of those copies. Such copies, not being infringing copies within the meaning of the 1988 Copyright Act, would lie outside section 27.

4.30. The second category of imports which infringe UK copyright relates to recordings which have been made illegally. These are infringing copies (section 27(2) of the 1988 Copyright Act). Section 22 of the 1988 Copyright Act (see paragraph 4.22) also applies to imports of such recordings. We now discuss illegal copying.

Illegal copying

4.31. Illegal copying falls broadly into two areas: first, piracy and secondly, home taping. 'Piracy' is a generic but imprecise term used to describe the commercial exploitation of a number of different kinds of unauthorized recordings, of which bootlegging and unauthorized reproductions of legitimate commercial recordings are the most common. A pirated recording may be a compilation of recordings that have never been released in the same combination on a legitimate album.

4.32. Bootlegging is the unauthorized recording of a performance broadcast on radio or television, or of a live concert. Many bootlegs are recorded at live concerts using a portable cassette recorder, or even taped directly from the console by tapping into the concert venue's sound system. Bootlegs do not usually include the name of the performer's legitimate recording company. The sound quality is usually inferior to that of a legitimate recording.

4.33. Unauthorized reproductions of legitimate recordings fall into two categories: those which simply reproduce the sound and those which copy the product as a whole, known as 'counterfeits'. Counterfeiting is the unauthorized duplication not only of the sound but also of the original artwork, label, trade mark and packaging of legitimate recordings. Counterfeits generally contain the same material as, and are designed to be indistinguishable from, a legitimate release.

4.34. Another area, which is more controversial, is that of the home taping of recordings, ie the taping by individuals on to blank audio tapes of recorded material contained on commercial recordings or of recorded material being played on the radio. There has been a long-running debate in this country as to whether home taping causes significant prejudice to copyright owners, albeit that it is illegal in most circumstances. Indeed, this is one reason why the UK Government has remained unconvinced that it should introduce a levy on blank tapes to compensate copyright owners for the effects of home taping and why the 1988 Copyright Act legalized the recording of broadcast works when this was done solely for the purpose of enabling them to be viewed or listened to at a more convenient time. Many countries have adopted such a levy.

The EC: doctrine of 'Community-wide exhaustion of rights'

4.35. Section 27(5) of the 1988 Copyright Act provides that section 27(3) (see paragraph 4.25) does not apply to an article which may lawfully be imported into the UK by virtue of any enforceable Community right. The effect of this provision is that the copyright owner of a sound recording cannot prevent importation of copies lawfully sold or distributed in other member states of the EC.

4.36. EC law has always recognized the validity of national rights of copyright and has not regarded them as inherently anti-competitive or restrictive of inter-state trade. Article 36 of the Treaty of Rome allows for exceptions to the principle of free movement of goods, where controls on imports and exports are justified on the ground of the protection of industrial and commercial property, provided that such measures do not constitute a means of arbitrary discrimination or a disguised restriction on trade between member states.

4.37. But a principle of 'exhaustion of rights' within the EC is applied so that the application of national property laws does not create a barrier to the free movement of goods within the single market of the EC. This principle operates by treating the EC as a single market for the purposes of distribution of copies of works, and therefore regards the copyright owner's right of distribution in all member states as having been exhausted by the first sale or distribution with his consent of those copies in any single member state. Accordingly the 1988 Copyright Act provides for the principle of exhaustion of rights in the EC in section 27(5).

4.38. However, the doctrine of exhaustion of rights has not been applied rigidly to negate valid national rights and in particular the copyright owner's right to consent to first distribution. In one case, for example, sound recordings (of Cliff Richard's songs) were no longer protected in Denmark but were still protected in Germany, as the latter state gave a longer period of protection to sound recordings. The European Court of Justice held that it was permissible to prohibit the import into and sale in Germany of copies of sound recordings made in Denmark, because the copyright owner had not consented to the manufacture or sale in Denmark of those particular copies of the sound recordings.[1]

4.39. The European Commission has been working on a programme of harmonization in copyright law, not with a view to a complete harmonization of the substantive law, but concentrating on those areas where co-ordinating actions at EC level are considered necessary to prevent distortions to the internal market. Directives have been adopted on a variety of matters, including the Rental Directive and the Term of Protection Directive, which are of relevance to our inquiry.

Directive 92/100/EEC: 'the Rental Directive'

4.40. The Rental Directive is one of several Directives in the copyright field which have now been adopted by the Council of Ministers. It deals with the right to control the rental and lending of copyright works, and with the protection of performers, record producers and broadcasting organizations. In particular, Article 9 provides that member states shall make provision for record producers and performers to have the exclusive right to make recordings of their performances available to the public by sale or otherwise. Producers and performers only lose this right in respect of particular copies when those copies are first sold within the EC by the rightholder or with his consent. This 'distribution right' is not lost if the copies are issued outside the EC.

4.41. The deadline for implementation of the Directive by member states is 1 July 1994.

4.42. In an article by Jorg Reinbothe, the EC official responsible for drafting the Rental Directive, and Silke von Lewinski of the Max-Planthe Institute of Munich, they comment as follows:

> While Article 9(2) states the established rule of intra-Community exhaustion, it does not expressly address 'international exhaustion', in other words, the question of whether member states are allowed to provide for an exhaustion of the distribution right under Article 9, even if the consent to putting into circulation was given in a third country for distribution there. This question is by no means purely theoretical, as it deals in fact with the prohibition (or admission) of parallel imports into the Community.
>
> In fact, Article 9(2) has to be interpreted in such as a way that member states are prohibited from applying international exhaustion; this means that a member state may

---

[1] *EMI Electrola GmbH v Firma Patricia Im- und Export* [1989] ECR 79.

not provide that the first sale in any country outside the EC results in the exhaustion of the distribution right within its own territory, and consequently within the whole EC. The distribution right is only exhausted where an object has been first sold within the EC with the consent of the rightholder; exhaustion does not occur where an object is first sold outside the EC, be it with or without the consent of the rightholder.[1]

Although the views expressed by Reinbothe and von Lewinski are stated to be their personal opinions, the same interpretation of Article 9(2) has been given by Commission officials acting in their official capacity.

4.43. The MCPS, BPI and the International Federation of the Phonographic Industry (IFPI) have made submissions to us to the effect that for Article 9 to operate in accordance with its own terms, each member state will have to enact laws (if it has not done so already) enabling the rightsholders to prevent the importation from outside the EC of recordings in respect of which the exclusive right exists.

Directive 93/98/EEC: 'the Term of Protection Directive'

4.44. The duration of copyright in the UK in literary, dramatic, musical and artistic works will increase to the life of the author and 70 years after death, as a result of the Term of Protection Directive. The Directive harmonizes the term of protection in the EC. Member states must implement the Directive by 1 July 1995. The Directive also requires that sound recordings are protected for 50 years (as is already the case in the UK).

The Berne Convention

4.45. The UK is a party to the latest act (Paris 1971) of the Berne Convention for the Protection of Literary and Artistic Works.[2] The Convention *inter alia* prescribes minimum rights in respect of literary and artistic works, which include musical and dramatic works. The rights cover most of the ways in which such works can be commercially exploited and are in general exclusive rights of authorization (although in relation to some of them there are exceptions).

4.46. The rights are in summary those of translation, reproduction, public performance, broadcasting and communication to the public by wire, public recitation and adaptation. While the Convention covers literary, musical and other works included on a recording, it gives no rights in the recording itself. Such rights are given by the Rome Convention (see paragraph 4.53).

4.47. The Berne Convention is administered by WIPO. WIPO has been considering the question whether there can be implied into the Convention rights on the part of the author or other owner of copyright to authorize first distribution, and also oppose importation of copies of a work.

4.48. The International Bureau of WIPO has taken the view that there is good reason to believe that in addition to a general right of first distribution, a right to oppose importation can be inferred from the present text of the Convention. In 1993 the Bureau proposed a protocol to the Berne Convention stating, *inter alia*, that under the present text of Berne, it is obligatory to protect the exclusive rights of the author or other owner of copyright to authorize the first distribution and the importation (for distribution) of copies of works, as these rights, although not mentioned in the Convention, are inseparable corollaries to the right of reproduction mentioned expressly in the Convention.[3]

4.49. A WIPO Committee of experts (formed of representatives of the governments of countries belonging to the international copyright agreements) last considered the proposed protocol at their

---

[1][1993] 6 *Entertainment Law Review 169* at page 174 published by Sweet and Maxwell Limited.

[2]Cm 1212. See Appendix 4.1.

[3]WIPO paper for the Committee of Experts on a Possible Protocol to the Berne Convention, BCP/CE/2-III.

Session in June 1993. The Chairman of the session summarized the discussion on a right of importation as follows:[1]

> The proposed right of importation has limited but substantial support ... among governmental delegations, and most of the non-governmental organisations have argued in support of such a right. However, opinions are divided on this issue; many delegations reserved their position, and some delegations opposed the right of importation for various reasons. The International Bureau should study the importation right in relation to trade, competition, and consumers' rights issues, as well as the question of whether the right of importation could be ensured through an appropriate limitation on the application of the principle of exhaustion of the distribution right.

4.50. As we indicate above, the 1988 Copyright Act provides for a right to oppose importation, save in respect of imports from other member states of the EC or imports as described in paragraph 4.29. Many other countries also make such provision. We observe, however, that there are several countries which do not make provision for bans on parallel imports, for example Denmark and Sweden.

4.51. We have already mentioned the report of the Australian Prices Surveillance Authority on its inquiry into the prices of sound recordings (see paragraph 3.46). The Australian Government is still considering its position on this matter.

4.52. We are not aware of any other jurisdiction where the possibility of allowing parallel imports is being considered. If there is a trend, it is in the opposite direction. We have noted in particular that Norway has recently amended its domestic law to give the producer of a sound recording the right to prevent parallel imports of copies of his recordings into Norway.[2]

The Rome Convention

4.53. The UK is also party to the International Convention for the Protection of Performers, Producers of Phonograms and Broadcasting Organisations of 1961 (the Rome Convention).[3] The rights concerned are known as 'neighbouring rights', ie those that neighbour copyright in literary and artistic works. These neighbouring rights include rights in sound recordings. In the 1988 Copyright Act those rights are assimilated with copyright (see paragraph 4.12). The Convention prescribes minimum rights and limitations on those rights. These are less extensive than Berne but include *inter alia* exclusive reproduction rights.

The GATT agreement

4.54. The Agreement on Trade-Related Aspects of Intellectual Property Rights including Trade in Counterfeit Goods (TRIPS) does not change the international position on distribution and importation rights. Article 6 of TRIPS specifically indicates that the agreement does not address the issue of exhaustion of rights.

US federal law

4.55. The USA is a member of the Berne Convention but not of the Rome Convention. The relevant law is contained in the copyright law of the USA in Title 17 of the US Code, as amended. Section 602(a) provides that importation of sound recordings into the USA without the authorization of the copyright owner constitutes an infringement of the exclusive right of the copyright owner to distribute sound recordings. This applies equally to copies which were lawfully and unlawfully made.

---

[1]Report adopted by the Committee BCP/CE/111/3 paragraph 91.

[2]Norwegian Copyright Act of 12 May 1961 as amended up to 9 June 1993.

[3]Cmnd 2425. See Appendix 4.2.

In the case of unlawfully made sound recordings, the US Customs Service has the power to prevent importation. With respect to copies lawfully made abroad, no such authority is granted under Title 17 and redress must be sought in the courts.

The exploitation of rights in sound recordings

4.56. As already noted (paragraph 4.13), the record company will own the copyright in a sound recording by virtue of sections 9 and 11 of the 1988 Copyright Act if it has undertaken the arrangements necessary for the making of that recording; and this is usually the case. Sales of such recordings in the UK generate revenue for the record company. This revenue derives from sales of records to UK customers (eg wholesalers, rack jobbers, retailers and record clubs); licensing of the rights in sound recordings to other UK record companies (eg for use in compilation albums); and from income collected by PPL on the public performance of recordings (eg from television and radio broadcasters).

4.57. In addition to deriving revenue directly from UK customers and licensees, the record company will also obtain revenue from licensing the recording to other record companies for manufacture and sale overseas. The overseas company will receive the proceeds of sale and pay a royalty back to the licensor, ie the UK record company. Overseas sales are an important source of revenue for many UK record companies.

4.58. Where the overseas company is an associate of the UK record company, the terms of the licence and royalty agreement are usually brought together under a 'matrix agreement', which will govern all cross-licensing arrangements within the record company's group world-wide. In this situation, the UK record company will usually be responsible for paying royalties on those foreign sales to its recording artists in the UK (and possibly also to the producer and mixer). The UK composer, through the UK music publisher to which he or she is contracted, will also receive royalties on sales of the recording outside the UK; these royalties are usually paid by the record company in the country where the record is sold to a local collection society; they are then passed to the local music publisher (to whom the UK music publisher will have sub-licensed the copyright in the composition) and then by the local publisher to the UK publisher; the composer then receives his or her share of royalties from the music publisher in the manner agreed between them.

4.59. A schematic diagram showing the principal routes through which returns flow from record sales in the UK and abroad to the owners of property rights is given in Figure 4.1.

4.60. The record company for its part makes the following payments:

(a) Advances (ie advance payment of royalties) and royalties (ie on sales) are paid to the recording artist in accordance with the terms of the recording contract. So far as advances are concerned, these are never repayable by the artist to the record company, even if the amounts are not recouped by the record company out of record sales. As for royalties based on record sales, the recording artist will usually receive such royalties from the record company if, and to the extent that, his or her entitlement to them exceeds the advances that have already been paid to him or her by the record company. In many cases, the record company fails to achieve sufficient sales to recoup the advances it has made. Advances of royalties and royalties may also be payable to the producer, depending on the terms of his or her contract.

(b) Royalties of 8.5 per cent of the published dealer price of the recording to the MCPS which in turn passes this to the owner of the copyright in the musical work used in the recording. The right to reproduce the work on record is commonly known as the mechanical right, and this is one of the principal ways in which the copyright owner's exclusive right to reproduce his or her work in a material form is exercised. The MCPS is a copyright collection society which acts as agent for the party controlling the mechanical rights, whether this be music publisher or composer, in licensing record companies to manufacture records reproducing copyright musical works, and to distribute those records. The MCPS deducts commission from the royalties received, and then distributes the balance to its relevant member. Where the MCPS's member is the composer, this means that the composer gets his or her royalties direct. Where the

FIGURE 4.1

Income flows from record sales to property rights owners

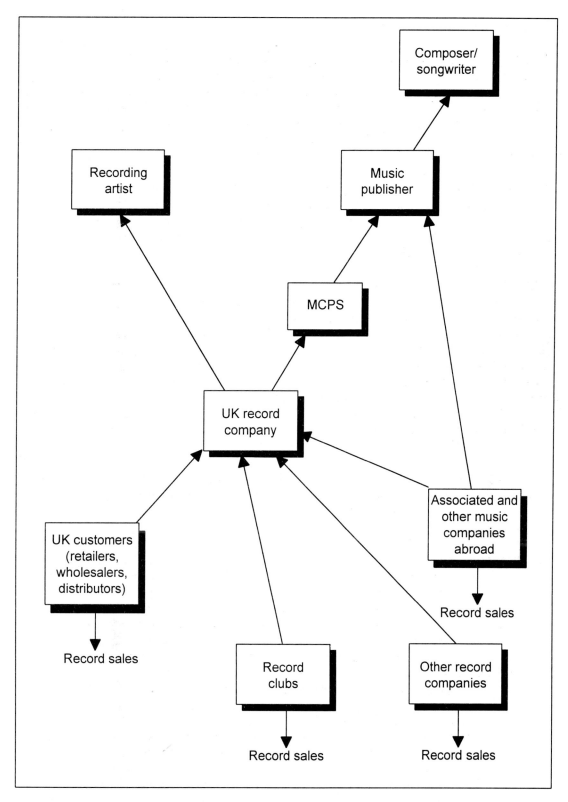

Source: MMC, based on figure supplied by Sony.

MCPS's member is the music publisher, the composer receives his or her share of royalties from the music publisher in the manner agreed between them.

Collective licensing bodies

4.61. As already noted, in addition to deriving revenue from the reproduction of music in the form of records, record companies and other rightsholders also receive income from the broadcasting, public performance, synchronization and dubbing of sound recordings. Various collective licensing bodies, acting on behalf of individual and corporate rightsholders, facilitate the licensing of rights and the collection of revenue in connection with these activities. A schematic diagram shows the revenue flows to and from the main collective licensing bodies in the UK music industry (Figure 4.2).

4.62. The principal functions of collective licensing bodies are licensing the use of copyright, determining the tariffs for that use, collecting royalties, distributing the revenue, monitoring the use of copyright material and enforcing copyright.

4.63. The role and practices of bodies in the UK concerned with the collective licensing of sound recordings for broadcasting and public performance was investigated and reported on by the MMC in 1988.[1] That report focused on the practices of PPL. The principal finding of the MMC was that collective licensing bodies were the best available mechanism for licensing sound recordings provided they could be restrained from using their monopoly unfairly.

4.64. We now consider briefly in turn each of the collecting societies which play a significant role in the recorded music industry.

The Mechanical Copyright Protection Society

4.65. The MCPS, which is owned by the Music Publishers' Association, the trade association for the UK music publishing business, is a collective licensing body representing as agent those who own, control or administer the rights in the UK to copy or to reproduce musical works and their associated lyrics which are in copyright.

4.66. The MCPS acts as agent for UK composers, writers and music publishers in relation to the vast majority of musical works which are actively exploited in the UK. The MCPS represents 4,992 composers and 3,146 music publishers. It also acts as agent in relation to works of foreign composers, writers and music publishers, either through those of its members who have sub-publishing rights in the UK, or through contracts with other mechanical rights collecting societies throughout the world.

4.67. The relationship between the MCPS and its members is now governed by an agreement under which the MCPS is mandated by a composer and/or music publisher in return for a commission to exercise certain rights on behalf of the member. The MCPS may administer these rights by operating Licensing Schemes (see section 116 of the 1988 Copyright Act).

4.68. The current rate of royalty due to MCPS members for reproduction of their works in the form of records and distribution of those records was decided in 1991 by the Copyright Tribunal (a body set up under the 1988 Copyright Act to hear and determine proceedings in respect of licensing schemes and other related matters) in a reference between BPI (the applicant) and the MCPS for variation of three standard form contracts which constituted a proposed licensing scheme to be operated by the MCPS. The Tribunal's decision[2] was that the royalty rate should be 8.5 per cent of the published dealer price.

---

[1] See footnote to paragraph 2.171.

[2] Reference No CT 7/90.

60

FIGURE 4.2

Revenue flows to and from UK collective licensing bodies

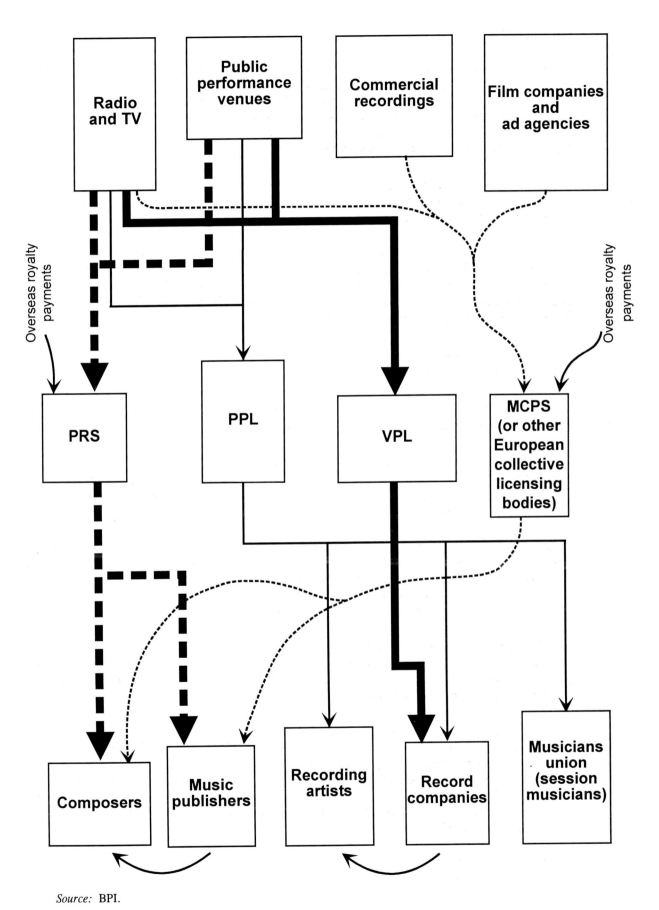

Source: BPI.

The MCPS/BPI Joint Import Scheme

4.69. As already noted, under the 1988 Copyright Act the copyright owner, or the exclusive licensee, has the ability to control importation into the UK of copyright material which has been lawfully made abroad with his consent (see paragraphs 4.25 to 4.28 above). The BPI (see paragraph 4.83) and the MCPS have set up a system to license importers of recordings from outside the EC on behalf of both the record companies and the music copyright owners (music publishers, composers or foreign societies).

4.70. This scheme, known as the MCPS/BPI Joint Import Scheme (the Scheme), is used principally in relation to specialist niche market product where the demand for the recordings comes principally from independent retailers specializing in particular genres of music. The Scheme documentation provides for:

(a) the licensing of any record lawfully manufactured outside the EC which is not, at the time of entry, in the catalogue of any BPI member company or intended for release by that company;

(b) the licensing of any special format (including any recording where the contents are different from the UK version) of a record which is in the current catalogue of a BPI member company provided that the prior written permission of that company is obtained and the MCPS is notified before importation takes place;

(c) the existence of the licence to be evidenced by the affixing of the correct denomination of stamp to the product; and

(d) copyright owners to retain their legal right to place a restriction on the importation of specific records.

The MCPS has stated that in practice the conditions under *(a)* and *(b)* above are not applied, and importers are permitted to import both catalogue and non-catalogue product unless a specific notice has otherwise been given to them.

4.71. Under the Scheme, importers (and also retailers who choose to import directly) apply to the MCPS for a licence of either the copyright in the composition or the copyright in the recording, or, more usually, both. The Scheme allows the import and sale of records without infringement of either copyright, provided that the imported product bears the appropriate royalty stamps. The royalty stamps are obtained by the importer from the MCPS prior to importation and must be affixed to the records or their sleeves within 14 days of importation, or prior to sale, whichever is the earlier. The stamps are charged at a flat rate for each format. The current rates for stamps covering both copyrights (ie in the composition and the recording) are as follows:

— 7" vinyl single—15p (plus VAT);

— 12" vinyl single—45p (plus VAT);

— cassette and vinyl albums—75p (plus VAT); and

— CD—£1.25 (plus VAT).

4.72. The revenues from stamp sales are divided equally between the BPI and the MCPS after deduction of a 15 per cent commission. Thus, 42.5 per cent is paid to the BPI for onward transmission to its members and 42.5 per cent is retained by the MCPS and distributed to its members.

Phonographic Performance Limited

4.73. As noted above (paragraph 4.17), the 1988 Copyright Act provides a copyright in the public use of sound recordings. The practical effect of this is that the companies or organizations which make sound recordings have legal protection against unauthorized public performance or broadcasting of their sound recordings.

4.74. PPL is a non-profit-making company established in 1934 by the recording industry to administer public performance and broadcasting rights centrally. Its members, of whom there are currently 1,483, have assigned these rights to PPL so that on their behalf it licenses all UK public performance users and broadcasters. At present, 21 PPL members are full members; these include all the major record companies. The remaining members have associate status. Towards the end of our inquiry, PPL informed us that it was considering changes to its membership rules, with the aim of increasing the number of full members and substantially widening the 'franchise'. All of PPL's income from licence fees (less running costs) goes back to its members and to performers and artists.

4.75. The terrestrial and satellite broadcasters licensed by PPL are the BBC (both radio and television) and the various commercial radio and commercial television companies. PPL issues licences for tens of thousands of sites for public performance, including the following types of premises and users: discotheques, night clubs, public houses, hotels, restaurants, halls, dance teachers, sports clubs, shops, theatres, cinemas, leisure centres and local authority sites.

4.76. PPL's licence gives permission to use any or all of the recordings at any time included in the repertoires of its members for the purposes stipulated on the licence. PPL has many standard tariffs covering the various different kinds of public performance users. These are often negotiated with national representative organizations. The licence usually lasts for one year.

4.77. PPL's revenues are distributed in the following proportions: 67.5 per cent to the record companies; 20 per cent to named performers; and 12.5 per cent to the Musicians' Union.

Performing Right Society

4.78. The Performing Right Society (PRS) was founded in 1914 as a non-profit-making organiza-tion, and now has over 27,000 writers and publishers in its membership. Its principal function is to derive income from and control the public performance and broadcasting and cable diffusion rights in the copyright works of these writers and publishers. Through its relationship with performing rights bodies in other countries, the PRS now represents more than 700,000 copyright owners and its income in 1993 was over £155 million.

4.79. The broadcasting of repertoire represented by the PRS takes place within blanket licences agreed with such organizations as the BBC, the independent television companies, the Association of Independent Radio Contractors and various cable and satellite television operators. In addition, more than 200,000 public performance licences are currently in force, and some 20,000 new licences are issued each year. These permit the playing of music, live or recorded, in premises as varied as pubs, hotels, concert halls and discotheques. The society operates almost 50 different tariffs, most of which are agreed with a trade association or representative body of the music users concerned.

4.80. About a third of PRS income comes from overseas use of British and Irish works, with the rest paid by UK and Irish broadcasters and public performance venues. Distribution of income takes place in April, July, October and December, after deduction of administration costs which, overall, average 18 per cent.

Video Performance Limited

4.81. VPL was set up in 1984 as a collecting society to license the UK public performance and broadcasting rights in music videos owned or controlled by its members. The music videos in question are short clips (of about four minutes) made by the record companies originally as a promotional tool. As at July 1993, VPL had a repertoire of 20,312 music videos; at the same date, it had 275 public performance licences in force and 27 broadcasting or diffusion licences.

4.82. Membership of VPL is open to anyone who owns or controls UK performance and broadcasting rights in music videos; there are currently 390 members. Of those members, around 23 are controlled by one of the five major UK record companies. The remainder are small record companies, or sometimes individual performers, on whose behalf VPL acts to ensure that they receive fair remuneration for use of their music videos by broadcasters and others. UK terrestrial broadcasters pay on the basis of a promulgated tariff. Deals are negotiated individually for satellite broadcasting and cable diffusion: MTV Europe, for example, pays fees on a scale which starts at 7.5 per cent of its net music advertising revenue up to £10 million, rising to 20 per cent on revenue in excess of £35 million, but provided that the total percentage paid is not greater than 15 per cent.

Other relevant industry bodies

British Phonographic Industry Ltd

4.83. The BPI is a UK industry trade association which represents a variety of different manufacturers, producers and sellers of all forms of records ('phonograms') including vinyl records, CDs and cassettes. It has some 150 record company members from throughout the country, which together issue the vast majority (90 per cent) of commercial records in the UK; these include the five major record companies. In addition to those members which record and issue the better known popular and classical works, BPI membership encompasses a large number of more specialized 'niche' recording companies.

4.84. The BPI is regarded in the industry as having a key role in safeguarding the interests of the industry at large. For example, the BPI's Anti-Piracy Unit, which is entirely funded by the record companies, undertakes extensive work in conjunction with the police and trading standards officers in investigating and preventing sound recording infringement. In 1992 the Unit was involved in 700 piracy actions, twice as many as in the previous year. While a good proportion of these were civil actions taken by the BPI, many of them were criminal prosecutions instigated by the police and Trading Standards Officers, in which the BPI played a central role in co-ordinating evidence, or providing back-up information. In 1993 the number of actions involving the Unit rose to between 800 and 900. The BPI is also responsible for providing much information and data on the industry via its publications.

International Federation of the Phonographic Industry

4.85. The International Federation of the Phonographic Industry (IFPI) represents the world-wide recording industry; its membership comprises 1,055 members in 72 countries. In the UK, its member companies are organized in the BPI. The IFPI is officially recognized by the United Nations as an international non-governmental organization, and participates on behalf of the recording industry in all international meetings on intellectual property.

4.86. One of the IFPI's responsibilities is to promote an effective world-wide regime of copyright protection for the recording industry, especially, but never limited entirely to, protection for producers of sound recordings. To this end, the IFPI is active in making representations to national and regional governments and official bodies such as the EC Commission, and it participates in all international meetings organized by WIPO, UNESCO, the Council of Europe and the GATT Secretariat which are concerned with intellectual property protection at the international level.

5 The record industry and the supply of recorded music

Contents

Introduction

5.1. In this chapter we describe the characteristics of the market for recorded music and examine the many different activities involved in supplying it, from the creative work of artists to the manufacture, distribution and promotion of finished records. Retailing is dealt with in the following chapter and the pricing of records in Chapter 7.

Sales of records

The industry world-wide

5.2. The industry comprises the production and sale of pre-recorded compact and vinyl discs and pre-recorded analogue and digital tapes on which music is reproduced without visual image. It is an important international industry and there is a wealth of industry statistics available relating to these products, both world-wide and by country. Table 5.1 shows estimated world retail sales, by retail value and volume, in the years from 1984 to 1992.

TABLE 5.1 **Estimated world retail sales**

	1985	1986	1987	1988	1989	1990	1991	1992
Value (US $m*)								
Total sales	12,250	14,000	17,000	20,300	21,600	24,050	26,203	28,705
% change	2%	14%	21%	19%	6%	11%	9%	10%
Volume (m)								
Singles	650	490	390	370	357	341	330	332
% change	-13%	-25%	-20%	-5%	-4%	-4%	-3%	-
Albums								
LPs	730	690	590	510	450	339	157	126
% change	-9%	-5%	-14%	-14%	-12%	-25%	-54%	-20%
Cassettes	950	970	1,150	1,390	1,540	1,446	1,599	1,552
% change	19%	2%	19%	21%	11%	-6%	11%	-3%
CDs	61	140	260	400	600	770	978	1,153
% change	205%	130%	86%	54%	50%	28%	27%	18%
Total albums	1,741	1,800	2,000	2,300	2,590	2,555	2,734	2,831
% change	7%	3%	11%	15%	13%	-1%	7%	4%

Source: IFPI.

---

*Current prices. Exchange rates used are the averages of beginning and end-year values.

5.3. Table 5.1 shows that after modest growth in 1985 the value of world sales accelerated, increasing by 134 per cent between 1985 and 1992, an annual rate of increase of about 13 per cent.

5.4. The sales success of the different record formats has varied over the period. The volume of singles fell by 56 per cent between 1984 and 1992, most of the decline occurring in the period to 1987. Sales of (vinyl) LPs fell by as much as 84 per cent between 1984 and 1992, the decline occurring throughout the period but accelerating in 1990 and, especially, 1991. Sales of cassettes grew strongly to 1989, subsequently remaining fairly flat. CD sales, starting from a negligible level, increased greatly over the whole period, more than compensating for the decline in singles and LPs. Growth in 1992, however, though still strong at 18 per cent, was modest compared with preceding years.

5.5. Table 5.2 breaks down 1992 world retail sales of records by country.

TABLE 5.2 **World retail sales by country, 1992**

	Singles (units m)	LPs (units m)	Cassettes (units m)	CDs (units m)	Retail value (US $m)*
USA	111.7	2.3	366.4	407.5	8,866.6
Japan	90.3	0.8	31.7	181.8	4,328.5
Germany	26.6	5.0	55.6	123.7	2,636.9
UK	52.9	6.7	56.4	70.5	1,998.2
France	16.8	0.3	35.5	78.5	1,935.4
Canada	2.2	-	29.5	32.9	861.7
Italy	1.1	3.1	21.2	23.6	653.8
Netherlands	4.2	0.6	1.8	33.2	647.4
Spain	1.3	9.6	21.3	20.1	586.7
Mexico	-	2.0	48.7	14.5	571.2
Australia	7.8	-	11.6	22.9	492.4
South Korea	-	25.2	45.6	6.9	471.0
Taiwan	-	-	32.7	10.4	326.3
Switzerland	1.0	0.6	3.8	13.7	321.9
Others	15.7	69.9	790.1	112.7	4,007.0
Total	331.6	126.1	1,551.9	1,152.9	28,705.0

Source: IFPI.

---

*Exchange rates used are the average of the beginning and end-year values.

66

5.6. By far the biggest market is the USA. Sales in Japan account for less than half the value of those of the USA, followed some way behind by Germany and then by the UK and France. The sales value of each of these five countries greatly exceeds that of any other country.

5.7. World LP sales are now only a small fraction of total record sales. LP sales are very small in most of the larger record markets (though still quite large in the UK and Germany), and in some markets (ie Canada, Australia and Taiwan) are negligible. However, LP sales are still relatively large (ie compared with total sales) in some smaller markets (notably South Korea).

The UK industry

5.8. The value of UK retail sales (including VAT) in 1992 was £1,199 million and the value of trade deliveries (excluding VAT) was £693 million. The value of retail sales in 1993 is not yet known but trade deliveries had risen to £786 million. The constant price (ie inflation-adjusted) indices in Table 5.3 were calculated by successively deflating the series for trade deliveries (excluding VAT) and retail prices (including VAT) by the retail price index (RPI) and then converting each resulting series into an index.

TABLE 5.3 **UK trade deliveries and retail sales of recorded music, at actual and 1992 prices (£m) RPI**

| | RPI | Trade deliveries* | | Retail sales | | |
		Current prices £m	Constant price index (1984 = 100)	Current prices Excl VAT £m	Current prices Incl VAT £m	Constant price index† (1984 = 100)
1984	100.0	329	100.0	478	549	100.0
1985	106.1	375	107.5	578	665	114.1
1986	109.7	425	117.9	646	742	123.2
1987	114.2	528	140.5	795	914	145.8
1988	119.8	612	155.4	963	1,108	168.3
1989	129.2	681	160.2	1,055	1,214	171.0
1990	141.4	678	145.8	1,029	1,183	152.3
1991	149.7	710	144.1	1,050	1,218	148.1
1992	155.3	693	135.6	1,020	1,199	140.6
1993	157.7	786	151.5	N/A	N/A	

Source: MMC, based on BPI data.

---

*Excluding VAT.
†Including VAT.
Note: VAT was 15 per cent until 31 March 1991, 17.5 per cent thereafter.

5.9. Between 1984 and 1989 trade deliveries and retail sales rose quite strongly in real terms. In 1990 and the two succeeding years, while actual values were broadly maintained, inflation-adjusted totals fell quite sharply. In the period 1989 to 1992 trade deliveries fell by 15 per cent and retail sales by 18 per cent in real terms. 1993 has seen a marked recovery, in both nominal and real terms, though the real value of trade deliveries is still well short of the 1989 figure.

Illegal copying

5.10. The sales described in Tables 5.2 and 5.3 underestimate the consumer purchases of pre-recorded music because there are some sales of illegal (or 'pirate') product (see paragraphs 4.31 to 4.34 for a description of illegal copying). The IFPI has estimated that in 1992 trade deliveries were made world-wide of some 4.1 million pirate albums with a trade value of £8.5 million. This amounts to some 3 per cent of trade deliveries by volume (1.2 per cent by value) in 1992.

5.11. Home taping also has an impact on sales of pre-recorded music. The introduction of the fully recordable cassette in the 1970s provided a simple, reliable and portable method of home taping for the first time. The BPI estimates that between 90 and 95 per cent of blank tapes purchased by consumers are used to tape copyright material. The British Market Research Bureau which has undertaken several surveys into private copying for the BPI has estimated that one in eight recordings from pre-recorded music are substituted for music sales. It also estimates that an increasing number of home tapings are made from radio broadcasts.

Formats

5.12. Till the end of the 1970s most recorded music was in the form of vinyl records—7" singles or 12" albums—though cassettes were rapidly increasing in popularity. CDs were introduced in 1983, and sales accelerated in the mid and late 1980s, virtually displacing vinyl albums and bringing the growth of cassette sales to an end. The new formats of DCC and MiniDisc were introduced in 1992, but have not yet made a significant impact on the market. Table 5.4 shows the UK retail sales value of singles and of albums by format since 1985.

TABLE 5.4 **Value of UK retail sales by format**

£ million incl VAT

Year	Singles*	Vinyl	Albums Cassettes	CDs	Album total	Total
1980	72	267	100	-	367	439
1985	138	251	243	34	528	665
1986	128	240	278	97	615	742
1987	127	257	336	195	788	915
1988	137	287	396	288	971	1,108
1989	132	223	424	435	1,083	1,214
1990	121	142	421	499	1,062	1,183
1991	122	74	404	617	1,095	1,218
1992	128	40	346	685	1,071	1,199

Source: BPI.

*All formats.
Notes:
1. The overall total for 1992 includes £0.2 million for DCC and MiniDisc.
2. Amounts may not total exactly because of rounding.

Table 5.4 shows that the share of retail sales accounted for by singles has declined since 1985. In 1985 singles accounted for 21 per cent of retail sales and albums for 79 per cent—corresponding percentages for 1992 were 11 and 89.

5.13. Figure 5.1 shows the changing volume of trade deliveries for LP, cassette and CD formats over the period 1974 to 1992. It demonstrates the decline in sales of LPs over the period, the increase in sales of cassettes to a peak in 1989, and the increase in sales of CDs from 1983. In 1992 the CD became the most popular format.

Seasonality

5.14. There is considerable seasonality in trade deliveries. BPI statistics show that, typically, about 40 per cent of albums and 30 per cent of singles are delivered by the trade in the fourth quarter of the year leading up to the Christmas season, with little difference between deliveries in the other quarters. Retail sales follow a similar seasonal pattern.

Artist nationality

5.15. The great majority of artists whose records are sold in the UK are of UK or US origin. Table 5.5 shows the breakdown of UK sales of singles and albums by artist nationality in recent years.

FIGURE 5.1

UK trade deliveries, 1974 to 1992

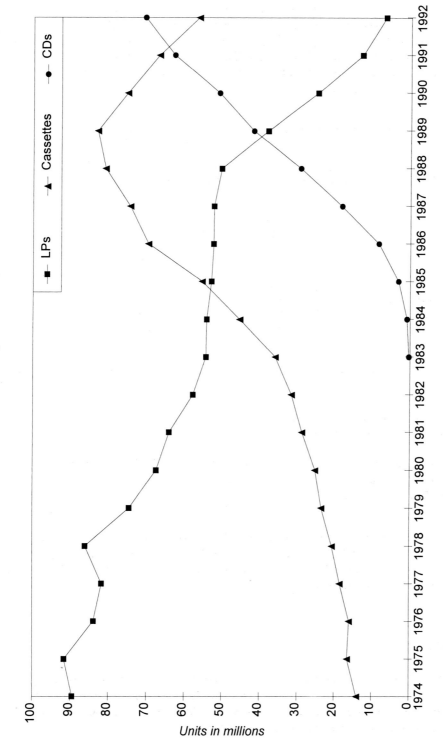

Source: MMC, based on BPI data.

Note: Trade deliveries are defined as sales of records, cassettes and CDs invoiced to dealers and distributors.

TABLE 5.5 **UK sales of records by artist nationality (volume)**

per cent

	1986	1987	1988	1989	1990	1991	1992
Albums							
UK	57.8	56.0	52.7	49.2	51.5	49.3	48.2
US	31.4	33.7	34.0	32.9	34.1	35.4	38.7
Others	10.8	10.3	13.3	17.9	14.4	15.3	13.1
Singles							
UK	55.0	54.7	54.7	49.9	52.1	59.2	54.4
US	35.0	37.3	31.4	36.0	31.8	27.3	34.6
Others	10.0	8.0	13.9	14.1	16.1	13.5	11.0

Source: BPI.

5.16. Though the percentages fluctuate from year to year, there appears to have been some tendency for the proportion of albums sold which were made by UK artists to decline and the proportion accounted for by US artists to increase. No such trend is apparent in respect of sales of singles.

Singles

Formats

5.17. Table 5.4 showed the decline of singles by value since 1985. Table 5.6 shows singles shipments by format since 1988.

TABLE 5.6 **Trade deliveries of singles by format**

million records

	1988	1989	1990	1991	1992	1993
Vinyl						
7"	40.3	37.5	28.9	21.9	12.9	7.9
12"	17.7	18.8	19.1	14.1	9.9	8.6
Cassettes	0.1	1.1	5.4	10.6	13.8	16.3
CDs	2.1	3.7	5.5	9.7	16.4	23.4
Total singles	60.1	61.1	58.9	56.3	52.9	56.3

Source: BPI.

Note: Columns may not total exactly because of rounding.

5.18. The total number of singles delivered in the UK fell by 13 per cent between 1989 and 1992, then increased by more than 6 per cent in 1993. Up to 1991 vinyl, in the form of 7" or 12" records, was the dominant format used for singles. While it is still important for singles, accounting for 29 per cent of such deliveries in 1993, this was a sharp decline from its 96 per cent share in 1988.

Categories of recorded music

5.19. Table 5.7 breaks down sales of singles by music category. The absence, with a few exceptions (for example, performances by Nigel Kennedy and Luciano Pavarotti), of classical music on singles and the predominance of pop, dance and rock music, are the main features. The table shows year-on-year fluctuations in the incidence of particular music types, reflecting the fashion element in this industry.

70

TABLE 5.7 **Singles: breakdown of sales by music category**

per cent

	1986	1987	1988	1989	1990	1991	1992
Pop	45	40	39	40	42	44	46
Dance	23	28	29	30	33	34	29
Rock	21	19	19	17	21	20	23
Folk	-	1	1	1	1	-	-
MOR*	5	4	4	3	1	-	-
Adult cont†	6	8	8	9	†	†	†
Others	-	-	-	-	2	2	2

Source: BPI based on Gallup data.

*Middle-of-the-road.

†Adult contemporary is no longer used as a classification and sales previously so classified have been reallocated to the most appropriate idiom.

Albums

Formats

5.20. Albums accounted for 89 per cent of retail sales value in 1992 (Table 5.4). Table 5.8 gives a breakdown of album sales by format in the years 1988 to 1993.

TABLE 5.8 **Albums: trade deliveries by format**

million records

	1988	1989	1990	1991	1992	1993
LPs	50.2	37.9	24.7	12.9	6.7	5.0
Cassettes	80.9	83.0	75.1	66.8	56.4	55.7
CDs	29.2	41.7	50.9	62.8	70.5	92.9
Total	160.3	162.7	150.6	142.5	133.6	153.5

Source: BPI.

Note: Columns may not total exactly because of rounding.

5.21. The number of albums sold fell by 18 per cent between 1988 and 1992, but rose by 15 per cent in 1993. As recently as 1988 vinyl accounted for almost one-third of album sales. However, since then vinyl has almost disappeared as a significant album format, accounting in 1993 for only 3 per cent of sales. The decline of vinyl albums reflects the gradual acceptance of the advantages of CDs—especially their improved sound quality and greater durability—and the increased ownership of CD players by households (up from 35 per cent in 1992 to 43 per cent in 1993, according to Gallup).

5.22. The use of vinyl for albums has been sustained to some extent by the continuing preference for this format in a number of niche markets (especially dance music) and the support of some specialist multiples and independent retailers. Cassettes continue to form a significant proportion of both singles and album sales. Their sales have been sustained by the easy portability of the format, especially for use in personal stereos and in-car cassette players.

5.23. Table 5.9 gives a breakdown of new album releases by format.

TABLE 5.9 **Albums: numbers of new releases by format**

	1989	1990	1991	1992
LPs	5,811	4,981	3,128	2,493
Cassettes	5,685	6,055	5,662	5,647
CDs	6,260	8,291	8,975	10,766
Total items (formats)	17,756	19,327	17,765	18,906
Total releases (titles)	8,752	11,021	10,141	11,988
Formats per title	2.0	1.8	1.8	1.6

Source: BPI based on Gallup data.

5.24. In spite of the decline in overall album sales, the number of new releases has grown substantially since 1989 to a weekly average in 1992 of over 200. The total number of items released did not increase correspondingly since the average number of formats on which a title was released declined from 2 to 1.6 over the period.

5.25. While the number of new album releases in vinyl has declined sharply since 1989, the decline has been less steep than that of LP sales because of the continued use of vinyl for dance music, where sales of individual titles tend to be relatively small. Numbers of new releases in cassette form have remained roughly constant while those of CDs have risen steadily.

Categories of recorded music

5.26. Table 5.10 gives a breakdown of album sales by music category, which contrasts with the breakdown of singles sales in Table 5.7. Classical appears as a significant category, with 9 per cent of 1992 sales. So is MOR, but the Dance category is much less important for albums than for singles.

TABLE 5.10 **Albums: sales by music category**

	per cent	
	1990	1992
Pop	45	35
Rock	15	24
Classical	12	9
MOR	10	9
Dance/soul/reggae	9	10
Country/folk	4	4
Jazz	1	1
Other	4	8

Source: BPI based on Gallup data.

Note: The imprecision of the boundary between pop and rock may account for some of the inter-year variation in these categories.

Price categories

5.27. Albums in each format are commonly categorized by the record industry as full-price, mid-price or budget. Each category covers a broad range of dealer prices (ie published trade prices), which may vary by format. Table 5.11 shows the breakdown of UK trade deliveries, using price ranges considered by the BPI to be appropriate for these product categories.

TABLE 5.11 **Albums: trade deliveries by price category**

	Units				Value				per cent
	1990	1991	1992	1993	1990	1991	1992	1993	
LP									
Budget	1.7	1.3	7.7	14.9	0.7	0.5	4.6	10.2	
Mid-price	18.9	13.1	11.5	6.1	13.2	8.9	8.4	4.2	
Full-price	79.4	85.6	80.8	79.0	86.1	90.6	87.0	85.6	
Total	100.0	100.0	100.0	100.0	100.0	100.0	100.0	100.0	
Cassette									
Budget	10.8	9.8	10.7	12.9	5.2	5.2	5.4	6.2	
Mid-price	17.7	20.4	20.9	16.4	12.5	14.7	15.2	11.9	
Full-price	71.5	69.8	68.4	70.7	82.3	80.1	79.4	81.8	
Total	100.0	100.0	100.0	100.0	100.0	100.0	100.0	100.0	
CD									
Budget	7.2	8.4	9.9	17.0	3.7	4.6	4.9	9.0	
Mid-price	20.0	19.1	18.8	13.6	15.7	15.6	15.3	10.3	
Full-price	72.8	72.5	71.3	69.4	80.6	79.8	79.8	80.7	
Total	100.0	100.0	100.0	100.0	100.0	100.0	100.0	100.0	
Total									
Budget	8.1	8.5	10.1	15.5	3.9	4.5	5.1	8.2	
Mid-price	18.7	19.2	19.3	14.4	14.1	14.7	15.0	10.6	
Full-price	73.2	72.3	70.6	70.1	82.0	80.8	79.9	81.2	
Total	100.0	100.0	100.0	100.0	100.0	100.0	100.0	100.0	

Source: BPI.

Notes:

1. Definitions for 1993 (dealer prices, exclusive of VAT):

	LPs and cassettes	CDs
Budget	£2.69 or less	£4.24 or less
Mid-price	£2.70 to £3.69	£4.25 to £5.99
Full-price	£3.70 or over	£6.00 or over

Price categories are adjusted from time to time to reflect current understanding of price banding.

2. Percentages may not add to 100 because of rounding.

5.28. Table 5.11 shows that by far the largest proportion of trade deliveries across all three formats is in the full-price category. The highest proportion of full-price deliveries is among LPs (especially in value terms). Taking all three formats together, full-price records have accounted for a slightly declining proportion of deliveries in volume terms, and budget for an increasing proportion. These trends are reflected in deliveries of CDs, now the dominant format.

Classical albums

5.29. Table 5.12 shows how the volume and value of classical albums as a proportion of total albums has changed in recent years.

TABLE 5.12 **Classical deliveries as a percentage of all albums**

	1985	1987	1989	1990	1991	1992
Units	7.8	8.2	8.6	11.1	10.9	9.2
Value	9.0	9.6	7.8	11.2	10.1	8.3

Source: BPI.

5.30. Table 5.12 indicates that before 1989 the share of trade deliveries of albums accounted for by classical records, about 8 or 9 per cent, was higher in value terms than in volume terms—ie classical albums were more expensive, on average, than other albums. In subsequent years this has changed, largely as a result of an increase in the proportion of classical albums accounted for by budget and mid-price records (see Table 5.14 and paragraph 5.32), so that in the most recent years the trade price of classical albums has been cheaper on average than albums in general. The overall share of classical album sales was relatively high, both in volume and value terms, in 1990 and 1991 as a result of a number of particularly successful records (for example, by Nigel Kennedy and the Three Tenors).

5.31. Table 5.13 shows how the breakdown of classical albums by format has changed in recent years.

TABLE 5.13 **Classical albums: breakdown by format**

per cent

| | LPs (vinyl) | | Cassettes | | CDs | | Total |
	Units	Value	Units	Value	Units	Value	Units/value
1985	36.0	32.0	47.0	36.0	17.0	32.0	100
1986	28.0	21.0	43.0	27.0	29.0	52.0	100
1987	18.0	12.0	43.0	27.0	39.0	61.0	100
1988	14.6	10.8	41.6	27.0	43.7	62.2	100
1989	8.0	6.6	45.6	31.1	46.4	62.3	100
1990	6.4	5.5	43.2	33.5	50.3	61.0	100
1991	2.6	2.0	36.7	28.0	60.7	70.0	100
1992	0.8	0.6	29.5	19.6	69.7	79.8	100
1993	0.4	0.2	22.6	16.3	77.0	83.5	100

Source: BPI.

Note: Percentages may not add to 100 because of rounding.

5.32. Comparison of Tables 5.13 and 5.8 shows that CDs now make up a much larger proportion of classical album sales than of albums as a whole and that this process of substitution or replacement started much earlier in the case of classical music than in other genres. The decline of vinyl sales as a proportion of total sales has also been much steeper for classical albums than for albums in general.

5.33. Table 5.14 gives a further breakdown of classical sales, by format, into standard product price categories.

TABLE 5.14 **Classical albums: trade deliveries by price category**

per cent

| | Units | | | | Value | | | |
	1990	1991	1992	1993	1990	1991	1992	1993
LP								
Budget	8.4	4.0	2.3	5.8	4.4	1.8	0.3	4.2
Mid-price	6.0	13.6	13.2	46.0	3.5	9.9	8.7	36.9
Full price	85.6	82.4	84.5	48.3	92.1	88.2	91.0	58.8
Total	100.0	100.0	100.0	100.0	100.0	100.0	100.0	100.0
Cassette								
Budget	26.7	27.0	33.8	30.1	15.6	16.1	20.5	17.3
Mid-price	21.5	28.8	29.4	28.5	15.8	23.0	28.1	24.8
Full price	51.8	44.2	36.8	41.4	68.6	60.9	51.4	57.9
Total	100.0	100.0	100.0	100.0	100.0	100.0	100.0	100.0
CD								
Budget	16.4	24.0	27.0	29.6	9.5	14.2	15.2	15.6
Mid-price	24.4	29.0	26.2	24.6	20.7	26.2	26.2	24.2
Full price	59.2	47.0	46.9	45.8	69.8	59.6	58.6	60.2
Total	100.0	100.0	100.0	100.0	100.0	100.0	100.0	100.0
Total								
Budget	20.3	24.6	28.8	29.6	11.2	14.5	16.2	15.9
Mid-price	21.9	28.5	27.0	25.6	18.1	25.0	26.5	24.3
Full price	57.8	46.9	44.2	44.8	70.7	60.5	57.3	59.8
Total	100.0	100.0	100.0	100.0	100.0	100.0	100.0	100.0

Source: BPI.

Notes:
1. Price category definitions are as for Table 5.11.
2. Percentages may not add to 100 because of rounding.

5.34. A comparison with Table 5.11 shows that the proportion of deliveries in the full-price category for classical albums (across all formats) is consistently smaller than for albums in general. The proportion of classical albums in cassette and CD format supplied at full price has declined sharply in recent years, while that of both budget and mid-price categories has increased.

Compilation albums

5.35. Table 5.15 shows the proportion of album sales taken by compilation albums (ie albums comprising tracks from previously issued recordings by various artists—the term does not apply to collections of past recordings by a single artist or group). Compilations have their own album chart and do not appear in the main chart even if they would qualify by volume of sales.

TABLE 5.15 **Compilation albums as a proportion of total album sales (volume)**

					per cent
	1988	*1989*	*1990*	*1991*	*1992*
January to July					
Multi-artist compilations	12.6	13.8	15.9	15.4	16.0
Original soundtracks	2.5	2.4	1.7	2.8	1.5
Total	15.1	16.2	17.6	18.2	17.5

Source: BPI based on Gallup data.

Consumer expenditure on records

Relation to overall spending

5.36. Figure 5.2 shows the relationship of UK retail spending on records to overall economic conditions. A simple time trend of gross domestic product (GDP)(at constant prices) was calculated for the period 1975 to 1992, and actual GDP in individual years plotted on the graph as percentage variations from that trend. On the same graph was entered annual data of consumer expenditure on records expressed as a percentage of consumer expenditure as a whole. It is not surprising to find spending on records, like other consumer spending, fluctuating in line with the economy as a whole. However, Figure 5.2 shows that spending on records has also fluctuated as a percentage of consumer expenditure, and that these fluctuations are closely correlated with cyclical movements in GDP. This strongly suggests that retail spending on records is even more sensitive than general consumer expenditure to the state of the economy. It is therefore highly cyclical and likely to have been more affected by the recent recession than other kinds of consumer spending.

Per capita consumer expenditure

5.37. Table 5.16 puts UK consumer expenditure on records into an international context. It shows that per capita expenditure on records in 1992, expressed in dollars, varies widely in a sample of major industrial countries, from $54 in Norway to $11 in Italy. UK per capita expenditure was of the same order as that in a number of other countries, namely the USA, Japan, France and Germany. Such comparisons will, of course, be affected by variations in exchange rates and individual countries' different positions on the economic cycle.

248336 F

FIGURE 5.2

Expenditure on recorded music as a proportion of consumer expenditure and GDP deviations from trend—UK

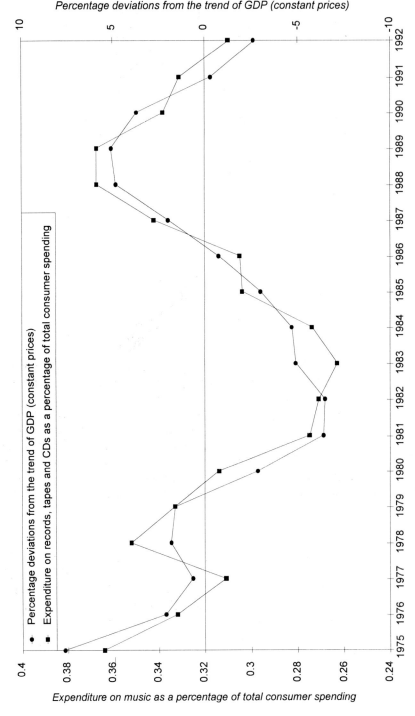

Source: BPI, and MMC calculations based on Annual Abstract of Statistics, Table 14.8, years 1994, 1990 and 1985.

Note: The deviations of GDP are from the linear equation regressing GDP at constant 1990 prices against time for the period 1975 to 1992.

TABLE 5.16 **Retail sales per capita, 1992**

	Population m	Retail sales US$m	Per capita expenditure US$
UK	57.5	1,998.2	34.75
Norway	4.3	232.5	54.07
Switzerland	6.7	321.9	48.04
Netherlands	15.0	647.4	43.16
Denmark	5.1	192.0	37.65
Austria	7.7	288.6	37.48
USA	252.0	8,866.6	35.18
Japan	124.0	4,328.5	34.91
France	56.7	1,935.4	34.13
Germany	79.6	2,636.9	33.13
Canada	26.8	861.7	32.15
Belgium	10.0	320.5	32.05
Australia	17.3	492.4	28.46
Finland	5.0	135.7	27.14
Sweden	8.6	201.8	23.47
New Zealand	3.4	54.6	16.06
Spain	39.0	586.7	15.04
Italy	57.7	653.8	11.33

Source: BPI based on IFPI data.

Influences on consumption

Taste

5.38. Consumer demand for records is affected by taste, and this can vary among consumer groups and over time. We were told that selling records can be characterized as a fashion industry in which styles come and go. When the repertoire being generated by artists is in line with the tastes of a wide range of consumers, sales are buoyant. Fashions with narrower appeal such as 'punk rock', which to an extent in its day represented a reaction against the prevailing taste, and some current forms of dance music tend to be short-lived and have limited appeal and so will be unlikely to lead to a sustained increase in sales. When consumers have become bored with a genre of music, total sales will tend to fall off until the arrival of the next genre reignites consumer interest. There are, however, some categories of music (for example, classical and main stream rock) for which demand remains relatively constant.

5.39. Social factors are also important. Where youth culture is oriented towards participation in music-making or attending music-related events (as it was to a considerable extent in the 1960s and early 1970s), it is more likely to generate both a stream of popular products and a buoyant demand for them than if there are strong alternative attractions—for instance, playing computer and video games. Peer group pressure will influence the directions in which disposable income is spent as well as on the type of record that is purchased.

Quality

5.40. The notion of 'quality' encompasses not only perceptions (closely related to 'taste') concerning the artists and the music that is being recorded and released but also more objective factors concerning the physical products themselves. The latter will include things like improvements in quality of sound reproduction, product durability and portability. The quality of repertoire is also believed in the industry to be an important determinant of sales, especially to the more discriminating older consumer, though hard evidence is not available.

77

Income and age

5.41. For most people the purchase of records is a discretionary expenditure out of disposable income. Aggregate demand for records is very sensitive to the economic cycle, there being a relatively high income elasticity of demand. We were told that one of the explanations for the youth bias of consumers, apart from questions of life-style and susceptibility to fashion movements, is the relatively high levels of disposable income in younger age groups.

5.42. With younger consumers facing an increasing choice of alternative leisure activities, the attention of the music industry may focus more in future on the older sections of the population. Demographic forecasts suggest that the middle-aged population is likely to grow significantly by the end of the decade, both in absolute terms and as a proportion of the total.[1] We were told that a real challenge facing the music industry was to continue to provide music attractive to those who constituted the 'rock and roll' generation of the 1950s and 1960s. If they can be persuaded to continue buying recorded music as they grow older, then the music industry may be able to offset, at least partly, the threat posed by the declining number of young consumers.

5.43. Table 5.17 breaks down purchases albums by the age and sex of the purchaser.

TABLE 5.17 **Demographics of album purchasers by format**

per cent

| | Population aged 16 or over | Album purchasers | | |
		LP	Cassette	CD
Sex				
Male	48	58	45	52
Female	52	42	55	48
Age				
16–24	16	39	28	30
25–34	20	25	20	29
35–44	17	17	25	21
45+	47	19	27	20
Social group				
AB	18	19	21	26
C1	24	26	26	30
C2	27	30	26	26
DE	31	24	27	18

Source: BPI based on Gallup data. Population data from OPCS.

Base: All who bought albums in the last six months.

5.44. The table shows the importance of the 16 to 24 age group to the industry. Accounting for only 16 per cent of the adult population, they account for a far higher proportion of album purchases (and even higher proportions of singles purchases). The 25 to 34 age group also accounts for a disproportionate share of purchases (though to a lesser extent). The 45+ age group, on which the industry may have to rely increasingly for sales, accounts for a disproportionately small share of record purchases.

Substitutes

5.45. Spending on records, or on equipment such as CD players that can generate a demand for records, has to compete with spending on other leisure activities, such as sporting events and video or computer games. It also has to compete more generally with ordinary household or home-making expenditure.

---

[1]According to the 1993 Annual Abstract of Statistics, the UK population is likely to grow, between 1991 and 2001, from 57.6 million to 59.2 million. Over the period the proportion of 15- to 34-year-olds will fall from 22.5 to 18.6 per cent, that of 45- to 59-year-olds will rise from 16.5 to 18.8 per cent, and that of 35- to 59-year-olds from 30.3 to 33.9 per cent.

Formats

5.46. The introduction of a new format which is perceived by consumers as having an advantage over earlier formats in terms of quality (eg the CD) or convenience (eg the cassette for personal stereos) inevitably creates extra demand for records. The new format gives those consumers with sufficient disposable income an incentive to upgrade their existing collections of favourite records. Unlike the purchase of new products, such upgrading is relatively riskless for the purchaser and, from the supplier's side, re-releases on the new format are cheaper to supply, given that they generally do not involve any new A&R costs and require a lower level of promotional expenditure.

Radio airplay

5.47. The broadcasting of records—for instance, the 'Top 40' singles or the airing of new product by popular disc jockeys—has long been an important promotional tool for new record artists and products. We were told, however, that the growing quantity of music broadcast on radio has moved towards becoming a substitute for record sales, with a consequent negative impact on such sales. Consumers who want to hear a particular kind of music are increasingly likely to be able to find a radio station that concentrates on it. This can reduce the incentive to buy records, while the growing facility for high-quality home taping may reduce the necessity for such purchases. We were told that these effects had been reinforced by the removal in 1988 of the restriction on independent radio stations which limited them to nine hours of 'needletime' per day. We have been told that this trend is likely to accelerate when high-quality digital broadcasts are introduced.

Hardware availability

5.48. The development of CD sales is closely associated with the number of CD players in the home or car. Once a CD player has been purchased, there may be a strong incentive to purchase CDs in order to benefit from purchase of the player; and many purchasers have collections of favourite records on vinyl or cassette which they wish to upgrade to the superior sound quality of the CD format. The price of CD players has fallen greatly since their introduction in 1983 as increasing sales have led to mass production and falling costs per unit. This fall in price has been a factor leading to increased sales of CD players which in turn has led to increased sales of CDs.

5.49. Gallup estimates that 43 per cent of UK households possessed a CD player in 1993. Table 5.18 gives the results of the 1994 survey into how CD penetration of households varied with the age, social group and regional location of the respondent.

TABLE 5.18 **CD player ownership, 1994**

Total: 43% of all households

	%
Age	
16-24	62
25-34	53
35-44	51
45-64	38
65+	15
Social group	
AB	51
C1	51
C2	41
DE	33
Region	
South	47
Midlands/Wales	42
North/Scotland	41

Source: BPI based on Gallup data.

Note: Some households will have more than one CD player.

5.50. Household penetration is highest with the youngest age group, though it remains fairly high even for the 45 to 64 age group. Annual increases in household penetration have been substantial in recent years and there is no indication that household penetration has yet reached a plateau.

Price

5.51. Formal studies of the effect of prices on consumer demand are not generally conducted in the record industry. However, one record company told us of a number of studies which suggested that demand for records was relatively price-inelastic. That is, at a given aggregate level of demand the effect of a general reduction (increase) in prices of records would be a less than proportionate growth (decrease) of sales. Nevertheless, price is believed to affect demand for records in a number of other ways.

5.52. Different line items,[1] whether recordings of the same title on different formats or of different titles, are in competition with one another. Such competition is most common in the field of classical music, with different recordings in the same format of the same work but in a range of prices. It helps to explain the success of record companies such as Naxos, specializing in a wide range of mid-price and budget classical music.

5.53. The phenomenon, however, is not confined to the field of classical music. While for some purchasers there may be no substitute for a particular album by a particular group, a significant proportion of all purchasers is prepared to choose between different records, and price will be one consideration. Record companies will be reluctant to raise prices to a level that will result in a reduction in sales to this group and hence in the volume of their sales. This will be less of a consideration with essentially fan-based albums—the fans will not be discouraged by the full price, and others will not buy the product at any price. However, purchasers of less fashion-driven, steadier-selling line items may well be discouraged by prices that are out of line with competing offerings. The latter are therefore the items most likely to be marketed at a certain stage in their lives as mid-priced or budget items, precisely because it is believed that the lower price will generate a worthwhile volume of sales and that at a higher price fewer or even no sales would be achieved.

5.54. Higher trade discounts (resulting in a lower price to the retailer) will help to persuade the retailer to promote products, whether at a higher retail margin or at the same or lower retail margin combined with a more competitive price to the consumer. This often leads to increased sales of the promoted item.

5.55. At the budget end of the market, price becomes a very important factor. This feature is important among consumers who are indifferent as to the relative quality of different recordings. This is particularly the case for buyers of classical music wanting to possess an acceptable range of classical repertoire without seeking to discriminate between different versions of the same piece. Such customers are catered for by a number of mid-price and budget labels.

5.56. The importance of price for different strata of the market is reflected in the conventional price structure of full-price, mid-price and budget. At successive points in a reasonably successful product's life cycle, that product will appeal to a different section of the market at each successively lower price point. We were told that the perceived value of records is of critical importance. Value is primarily related to music content but also to technical matters such as quality of reproduction, convenience and portability. Where the perceived value of the content of an album is recognized as relatively low, perhaps because it contains material which is not new, then the album may only be acceptable if offered for sale at less than full-price. Such concepts of perceived value are reflected in the industry's framework of retail prices in which records of a certain type (eg new pop CDs) tend to be sold at similar prices even if, for instance, they incorporate very different A&R costs.

---

[1]A line item is a specific recording on a particular format. For example, the same recording on LP, cassette and CD counts as three separate line items.

5.57. As we shall see when discussing retailing, competitive pricing is a very important aspect of overall inter-retailer competition and there are considerable variations in retail prices. Many retail chains are reluctant to charge prices for fast-selling products that are higher than those of competitors (eg Woolworths' Street Value scheme—paragraph 6.25(a)). Price variations at the retail level are believed to have a direct and important effect on retailer market shares.

Choice of music

5.58. The variety of products, and their relative weight in industry sales, will reflect the heterogeneity of tastes and culture, as well as the demographic composition of the population. The current music scene is extremely diverse and while there are a number of broad categories there are also numerous splinter genres, each with its own fans.[1] Table 5.19 analyses the relative buying preferences of album buyers classified by sex and age group for a number of broad categories of music.

TABLE 5.19   **Choice of music by sex and age of album purchasers**

per cent

	Classical	Country, folk	Dance, soul, reggae	Jazz	MOR	Pop	Rock	Other	Total
Total	9	4	10	1	10	35	24	7	100
Sex									
Male	8	4	10	1	8	31	30	8	100
Female	9	3	10	*	11	40	19	8	100
Age									
16–24	2	*	17	*	2	38	35	6	100
25–34	4	1	10	1	3	45	28	8	100
35–44	7	3	8	1	5	39	28	9	100
45+	21	9	4	*	26	22	9	9	100

Source: BPI based on Gallup data.

Base: All album buyers, recall of last album bought.
*Less than 0.5 per cent.

5.59. Overall, pop is by far the most popular music category, followed by rock. While pop and rock are liked best by both male and female buyers, female buyers much prefer pop music to rock while male buyers like both categories about the same. Classical music is only the fifth most popular music category, and is liked to the same degree by male and female buyers.

5.60. Musical preferences vary with age. Older age groups have a distinct preference for classical and MOR music, though they also like pop music. Dance music (not to be confused with music for ballroom dancing) has a strong appeal only for the youngest age group. Pop music retains its appeal for all generations, while rock appeals to all but the oldest age group.

5.61. Music preferences may also be expected to vary by socio-economic group because differences in taste will reflect cultural and educational differences which are reflected to some extent in these groups. Table 5.20 shows the relative preferences of album buyers from different socio-economic groups.

---

[1]A recent analysis of the dance music scene alone identified 38 specific sub-genres.

TABLE 5.20   Choice of music by social group of album purchaser

per cent

	Classical	Country, folk	Dance, soul, reggae	Jazz	MOR	Pop	Rock	Other	Total
Total	9	4	10	1	10	35	24	7	100
Social group									
AB	17	1	10	1	8	28	24	11	100
C1	8	3	9	1	10	35	25	9	100
C2	5	5	13	*	11	35	25	6	100
DE	5	5	8	*	9	41	25	7	100

Source: BPI based on Gallup data.

Base: All album buyers, recall of last album bought.
*Less than 0.5 per cent.

5.62. The principal differences between these groups revealed in Table 5.20 are the high relative preference for pop music in the DE social group compared with other groups, and the relatively high preference for classical music in the AB group.

The record companies

5.63. Traditionally record companies in the UK have been categorized into two groups: 'majors' and 'independents'.

The majors

5.64. The majors are the large international record companies, PolyGram, EMI, Sony, Warner and BMG. Each has a network of owned or affiliated companies world-wide with their own local distribution operations through which it can market local repertoire with international potential and from which it sources the bulk of its overseas licences and artists.

5.65. The majors are the local affiliates of international record companies. They are vertically integrated to varying degrees and undertake the following main activities:

(a) discovering and developing new recording artists and repertoire; developing existing artists and repertoire;

(b) recording the music—this involves hiring studios, sound engineers, technicians, producers and equipment;

(c) organizing the manufacture of each record release in the main formats (vinyl, cassette and CD);

(d) distributing the records to retailers or wholesalers;

(e) marketing and promoting each record release;

(f) selling, licensing and promoting the release of UK recordings in overseas markets;

(g) promoting the licensing of recordings for secondary exploitation (for example, in compilation albums and through record clubs); and

(h) organizing appropriate royalty payments to artists, producers, publishers and licensors arising out of record sales.

82

5.66. PolyGram is the UK holding company of the PolyGram International Group which operates in 32 countries world-wide through a network of operating subsidiaries and licensees. The group operates in the field of classical and popular recorded music as well as ancillary music activities such as music publishing and distribution of records. The ultimate holding company is PolyGram NV Holding Company, in which Philips Electronics NV holds 75 per cent of the shares. Recording activities are undertaken through a series of major international record labels such as Polydor, Phonogram, Island, A&M, Motown, Decca, Deutsche Grammophon, London and Philips. Major artists include Dire Straits, Elton John and U2 on the pop side, and Pavarotti, Kiri Te Kanawa, Bartoli, Solti, von Karajan and Carreras on the classical side.

5.67. EMI and Virgin (EMI) are UK subsidiaries of THORN EMI plc, an international company registered in England. Its main contemporary record labels are EMI, Parlophone, Chrysalis Records and Virgin Records. Classical records are sold under the EMI Classics and Music For Pleasure labels. EMI is also involved in the operation of recording studios (of which the best known is Abbey Road), music publishing (EMI Music Publishing), and the manufacture and distribution of records in the UK. EMI's best-selling artists include Cliff Richard, Paul McCartney and Queen, while Virgin Records' best-selling artists include Janet Jackson and Meatloaf. THORN EMI also owns the record retailer HMV.

5.68. Sony is ultimately owned by the Sony Corporation which purchased the CBS Records world-wide business in 1988. Sony's three principal contemporary music labels are Columbia, Epic, and S2. Classical recordings are sold under the Sony Classical label. Sony is engaged in the operation of a recording studio (The Whitfield Street Studio, formerly known as The Hit Factory), music publishing (Sony Music Publishing), the manufacture of video and audio cassettes, and the distribution of records and videos. Recording artists include Michael Jackson, Bob Dylan, Bruce Springsteen, Billy Joel, Barbra Streisand, Sade, and George Michael.

5.69. Warner is the principal company of the Time Warner Group involved in the production and marketing of records in the UK. The UK presence of the Warner Group dates from 1969. Warner releases its own-product pop music records on two principal record labels, WEA (for more established and mainstream artists) and EastWest (which has a more 'street' or 'indie' image). Its main artists include Simply Red, Enya and Chris Rea. Warner has only recently entered the market for classical records and currently markets only the recordings of its overseas affiliates.

5.70. BMG is the UK subsidiary of the Bertelsmann Music Group, which is based in New York, and whose ultimate holding company is Bertelsmann AG which is based in Germany. The principal record labels of BMG are RCA (Bertelsmann bought the music division of RCA from General Electric in 1986), Arista, and Ariola. BMG International, which is also based in New York, has responsibility for all Bertelsmann's music business outside the USA. It is also responsible for BMG Classics, the repertoire of which is licensed from the USA to affiliates world-wide, including BMG. Affiliates have no A&R function in relation to classical music. Recording artists in the UK include Annie Lennox and Take That.

The independents

5.71. In addition to the majors there are a large number of independent record companies (independents). Independents, which are generally much smaller than the majors, have widely differing characteristics but usually specialize in a certain type or style of music. Independent companies normally maintain their own A&R function and in so far as they subcontract tasks that would normally be undertaken in-house by a major, it is the non-creative rather than the creative tasks that are subcontracted. Thus they do not normally carry out their own distribution to wholesalers and retailers. Overseas exploitation of an independent's records is normally carried out by one of the majors although some independents, particularly those operating in niche areas, may license to other independents or export the finished product.

5.72. There is no agreed estimate of the number of independent companies supplying records in the UK. The BPI, the leading UK trade association for the record industry, has some 150 members of which it estimates some 100 are entirely independent of a major. 'Umbrella', a trade association for some smaller independents, has some 120 members. The BPI estimates that there are some 200 well-established, and some 400 less-established, record companies.

5.73. The independent sector includes a few large independents. These include MCA which, despite being owned by Matsushita, is not regarded as a major because it licenses repertoire to third parties in most other territories and currently does not have the international infrastructure of the majors outside the USA. In the UK, MCA had a small market share until recently and distribution of its records is carried out by BMG. An independent may grow large by developing a successful roster of artists and achieving international coverage by operating in selected territories or by licensing its recordings to overseas record companies. Companies like Virgin Records, Island, A&M and Chrysalis all started as small independents specializing in particular niche genres of music but were successful in developing into significant businesses with extensive rosters of artists covering a wide range of musical styles. Their major stars included U2 and Bob Marley (Island), Police and Sting (A&M), Boy George, Mike Oldfield and Phil Collins (Virgin) and Sinead O'Connor (Chrysalis). These companies had records suitable for global sales and achieved a prominent position in the market. They were subsequently sold to the majors. Currently, companies like PWL, Mute (Depeche Mode and Erasure), and Zomba (Billy Ocean and Stone Roses) compete with the majors in the mainstream pop sector.

5.74. Among the smaller independents some are 'fully' independent, while others are affiliated in some way to the majors. Many independents have little or no contact with a major. They use independent recording studios, manufacturers, and distributors. This may be because their current volume of sales and their growth potential are too small to interest the majors. It could be the result of the choice of niche market served or the quality of the artists. Or it might be that company finances are sufficiently stable to avoid relying on an outside agent. Company owners may be ideologically opposed to the idea of affiliating to a major. The emphasis on independent status may be a statement of principle: it may also serve as an aid to marketing its particular character in such a way as to attract artists and consumers. Some artists may prefer to sign with a particular independent even when in receipt of offers from one or more of the majors.

5.75. However, if an artist's career develops successfully, the independent may not have the financial resources to fund the promotion and marketing that the artist then requires. At this stage a major record company might be approached to help further the career of the artist both nationally and internationally. The major record company will also have an interest in signing a successful artist. There is a wide range of financial arrangements which may be entered into at this stage, including that under which the independent continues to derive a financial return from the future recordings of the artist.

5.76. Some independents are 'affiliated' to a particular major through an equity, financial or contractual relationship. Normally the major provides financial resources and marketing and distribution expertise while the independent provides A&R expertise. For example, Warner operates two joint ventures—ZTT Records (set up in 1988), and Anxious Records (1992). Both these joint ventures are with independent individuals who have well-developed A&R skills and the objective of seeking new talent. In 1991 Warner Music Group entered into an arrangement with record producer Pete Waterman, forming a new company called PWL International Limited (PWLI) which is 50 per cent owned by Warner. The world rights outside the UK in PWLI's recordings are licensed to the Warner Music Group and Warner carries out distribution for PWLI product in the UK.

5.77. Independents are often the source of innovation in the market. For instance, 'punk', 'heavy metal' and 'glam-rock' were all developed by the independent sector and then embraced by the majors. In the classical sector companies such as Hyperion, specializing in high-quality recordings, and Naxos, specializing in budget recordings, have entered the market successfully. The majors often move to compete in a new market sector by developing similar artists or products, often under new labels. Alternatively they may seek to acquire an independent and retain it as a separate label to take advantage of its reputation in the market.

UK market shares

5.78. The most reliable and widely regarded measures of the size of the UK market are the trade figures compiled annually by the BPI. Measurement based on value is more appropriate than volume when combining qualitatively different products such as singles and albums, and product available in different price bands such as budget, mid-price, and full-price. In the case of recorded music value information has to be treated with some caution since it is compiled from sales invoices to dealers and distributors, and accordingly may or may not include an amount for distribution, depending on the purchaser.

5.79. The values of the sales of individual record companies are not readily available from a published source. The major record companies were therefore asked to supply trade value figures on the same basis as the aggregate trade figures published by the BPI. Table 5.21 shows the overall market shares (singles and albums) of the majors over the last four years. In 1992, the most recent year for which figures are available to us, PolyGram had the highest share with 24.9 per cent of trade value of sales. The majors together accounted for 68.3 per cent of trade sales in 1992 compared with 57.6 per cent in 1989.

TABLE 5.21   **Market shares (singles and albums) of the major record companies, 1989 to 1992**

				per cent
	1989	1990	1991	1992
By trade value*				
PolyGram	20.0	24.4	22.6	24.9
EMI	11.9	15.9	14.8	17.5
Warner	11.7	11.0	10.7	10.7
Sony	9.2	8.6	11.4	9.8
BMG	4.8	4.9	4.6	5.4
Others	42.4	35.2	35.9	31.7
Total	100.0	100.0	100.0	100.0
Total (£'000)	680,726	678,401	709,755	692,528
By trade volume				
PolyGram	18.0	21.6	21.2	23.8
EMI	11.9	16.4	14.6	16.9
Sony	9.2	8.8	11.5	10.7
Warner	11.0	9.6	9.8	9.3
BMG	4.8	5.5	4.8	6.2
Others	45.1	38.1	38.1	33.1
Total	100.0	100.0	100.0	100.0
Total (units '000)	223,777	209,506	198,812	186,519

Source: MMC, from BPI and company information.

*Combined sales of singles and albums from record companies to dealers and distributors after discounts and before VAT.
Note: EMI's market share excludes the 1992 sales of Virgin prior to its acquisition in March.

5.80. While they may be the most accurate measure of market share, the estimates that we have made of market shares based on value do not provide a historical run of data, nor do they extend beyond the five majors. The most widely used source of market share information is that published annually by the BPI, based on Gallup retail survey estimates of the volume of album sales. It is this information which we have used as the basis for the main description of market shares and the changes through time (see Table 5.22). In 1993 EMI had a 23.8 per cent share of the album market, closely followed by PolyGram with 21.3 per cent. These two companies together accounted for 45.1 per cent of album sales in 1993. Warner, with the next largest market share, accounted for 10.3 per cent.

5.81. The market share for EMI differs between Tables 5.21 and 5.22. This is mainly because the figures EMI provided to us for Table 5.21 included the sales of Virgin only for that part of 1992 which followed its acquisition. In Table 5.22 Virgin's sales for the whole of 1992 have been combined with EMI's because that more accurately reflects the combined market power of EMI and Virgin.

TABLE 5.22 **Record company market shares (by volume of albums), 1983 to 1993**

per cent

Albums	1983	1984	1985	1986	1987	1988	1989	1990	1991	1992	1993
EMI	14.0	14.6	13.4	13.8	13.2	12.6	12.7	15.9	15.7	22.2	23.8
PolyGram	14.4	12.5	14.5	14.8	15.2	16.1	16.1	23.2	21.3	23.3	21.3
Warner	6.6	9.2	12.2	13.2	12.8	12.6	14.8	12.1	12.6	11.7	10.3
Sony	16.1	16.2	15.0	11.5	12.9	12.6	11.6	10.4	11.6	10.5	9.6
BMG	8.1	7.9	5.4	9.0	8.7	7.0	5.8	4.7	5.2	5.1	7.0
Telstar	0.8	1.7	2.0	2.1	2.3	2.5	4.3	4.4	4.2	3.5	4.5
MCA	1.2	2.0	2.0	1.4	1.3	1.5	2.9	1.2	3.8	4.1	2.9
Dino	-	-	-	-	-	-	0.1	1.0	1.9	1.6	2.7
Pickwick	1.6	2.6	2.8	2.6	1.9	1.5	1.7	2.0	1.9	2.1	2.5
Castle Communications	-	-	0.1	0.3	0.4	0.5	0.6	0.9	0.9	1.0	1.2
Music Collection	-	-	-	-	-	-	-	-	0.2	0.6	0.9
Tring International	-	-	-	-	-	-	-	-	0.1	0.3	0.7
BBC	0.8	0.5	1.3	0.8	0.5	0.4	0.5	0.8	0.7	0.7	0.7
One Little Indian	-	-	-	-	-	-	-	-	0.1	0.5	0.6
Mute	0.9	0.3	0.4	0.3	0.7	1.1	1.4	1.1	0.8	1.0	0.5
Conifer	-	-	-	-	0.1	0.3	0.2	0.2	0.3	0.5	0.5
PWL	-	-	-	-	-	1.7	2.7	0.9	0.4	0.4	0.4
Beggars Banquet	0.6	0.4	0.6	0.5	0.6	0.4	0.4	0.4	0.3	0.4	0.4
Naxos	-	-	-	-	-	-	-	-	0.2	0.3	0.4
China	-	-	-	-	-	-	-	-	-	0.2	0.3
4AD	-	-	-	-	-	-	0.1	0.3	0.2	0.2	0.3
Zomba	0.6	0.3	0.4	0.7	0.4	0.5	0.7	0.6	0.4	0.3	0.2
Arcade	-	-	-	-	-	-	-	-	0.4	0.4	0.2
Quality Productions	-	-	-	-	-	-	-	-	-	0.8	0.2
Music For Nations	-	0.1	0.1	0.2	0.3	0.2	0.2	0.3	0.2	0.2	0.2
First Night	-	-	-	-	-	-	-	-	-	0.2	0.1
Stylus	-	-	0.3	1.4	1.8	3.1	2.4	1.3	0.1	-	-
Island	2.5	5.1	3.0	2.5	4.0	3.5	0.8	-	-	-	-
A&M	3.3	1.7	2.3	3.9	3.2	2.0	1.2	-	-	-	-
Tug	-	-	-	-	-	-	-	-	-	0.7	-
K-Tel	3.7	1.8	2.3	1.6	1.4	1.0	0.8	0.4	-	-	-
Creation	-	-	-	-	-	-	-	-	0.2	0.3	-
Virgin*	7.1	7.0	8.0	7.3	7.1	7.7	8.2	7.4	6.4	-	-
Chrysalis	2.9	2.9	3.3	2.9	2.2	2.8	2.5	2.9	2.0	-	-
Others	14.8	13.2	10.6	9.2	9.0	8.4	7.3	7.6	7.9	6.9	7.6
Total market share	100.0	100.0	100.0	100.0	100.0	100.0	100.0	100.0	100.0	100.0	100.0
Majors	59.2	60.4	60.5	62.3	62.8	60.9	61.0	66.3	66.4	72.8	72.0
Independents	40.8	39.6	39.5	37.7	37.2	39.1	39.0	33.7	33.6	27.2	28.0
HHI†	836.0	876.1	898.0	880.7	895.9	877.0	914.8	1,104.4	1,066.1	1,337.6	1,293.9

Source: MMC estimates based on BPI data.

*EMI's market share for 1992 includes the sales of Virgin both before and after its acquisition in March.
†Herfindahl Hirschman Index.

5.82. The five independents that had a share of 1 per cent or greater had a combined market share of 13.8 per cent in 1993, almost half the independents' total share of the market. The remainder of the sector consists of a large number of small companies of varying character.

5.83. An overall measure of the level of concentration is the Herfindahl Hirschman Index (HHI). It is calculated as the sum of the squares of the shares of the companies in the market. The value of HHI ranges from 0 to 10,000; the higher the value, the higher the degree of market concentration. In the case of one firm supplying the whole market HHI takes the maximum value of 10,000 and in the case of many small firms each supplying only a small part of the market the value of HHI approaches zero. Table 5.22 shows that the value for HHI has increased from 836 in 1983 to 1,294 in

1993 indicating increasing concentration in the market, although it declined from the high of 1,338 in 1992. It is difficult to interpret the absolute value of this index. The Merger Guidelines used by the US authorities suggest that a value of HHI that is less than 1,000 indicates an unconcentrated market; a value of 1,000 to 1,800 indicates a moderate degree of concentration; and a value above 1,800 indicates a highly concentrated market.

International comparison of market shares

5.84. Table 5.23 shows the market shares of the overseas affiliates of the major UK record companies in a number of countries in 1992. The market share held by each company varies considerably between countries. The overall market share held by the majors in the UK is about the same as the share they hold in the USA but lower than their shares in Germany, France, Netherlands and Denmark.

TABLE 5.23 **International market shares of the majors, 1992**

per cent (volume)

Market shares	*UK*	*USA*	*Germany*	*France*	*Denmark*	*Netherlands*	*Japan*
PolyGram	23.3	11.5	22.0	32.0	24.1	24.1	12.3
EMI/Virgin	22.2	10.7	20.7	19.0	30.1	12.4	13.6
Warner	11.7	22.5	17.6	10.0	11.4	12.6	8.0
Sony	10.5	17.5	11.7	15.0	13.3	15.5	25.9
BMG	5.1	11.0	17.6	11.0	11.8	17.7	0
Majors	72.8	73.2	89.6	87.0	90.7	82.3	59.8
Independents	27.2	26.8	10.4	13.0	9.3	17.7	40.2
Total	100.0	100.0	100.0	100.0	100.0	100.0	100.0

Source: MMC from estimates provided by one of the majors.

Classical market shares

5.85. The market shares of classical sales show greater concentration than those for pop sales, with PolyGram and EMI together accounting for some 63 per cent of album sales in 1992 (see Table 5.24). Sales at the budget and mid-price levels account for a larger share of sales in the classical market than they do for albums in general (compare Tables 5.11 and 5.14). The market shares for different price categories show that while the majors tend to sell in all categories, a number of independents specialize in one price category. For example, Naxos and Tring specialize in budget product, and Hyperion and Chandos specialize in full-price product.

TABLE 5.24 **Market share of classical music albums (by volume), 1992**

per cent

Company	Mid-price/budget	Full price	Total
Polygram	31.3	47.1	38.3
EMI	24.8	24.3	24.6
Warner	-	6.8	3.0
Pickwick	11.0	0.6	6.4
Conifer	9.8	2.3	6.5
Naxos	6.4	-	3.6
BMG	4.1	2.6	3.4
Sony	3.4	5.4	4.3
Music Collection	1.4	-	0.8
Telstar	1.2	2.2	1.6
Tring International	1.0	-	0.6
Lydian	0.7	-	0.4
Castle Communications	0.7	0.6	0.7
ASV	0.6	0.6	0.6
Mainline	0.5	-	0.3
Chandos	-	1.3	0.6
Hyperion	-	1.3	0.6
Silva Productions	-	1.0	0.4
Quality Productions	-	0.6	0.3
Others	3.1	3.3	3.2
Total	100.0	100.0	100.0

Source: MMC calculations, based on BPI and Gallup data.

Note: Percentages may not add to 100 because of rounding.

Singles market shares

5.86. Market shares of singles sales broadly reflect those for album sales (see Table 5.25) but there is less diversity between the shares of the majors. The gap between the majors and the independents is more pronounced, each major accounting for more than 9 per cent of the market in 1993, and no independent accounting for more than 4 per cent. Sales of singles are more volatile than sales albums. This is reflected in the fluctuations in market share. For example, BMG nearly doubled its market share between 1991 and 1992.

TABLE 5.25 **Record company market shares for the singles market (by volume), 1988 to 1993**

per cent

	1988	1989	1990	1991	1992	1993
PolyGram	14.4	14.0	22.0	23.8	23.6	21.9
EMI	11.2	9.7	13.3	11.2	16.4	18.9
BMG	7.5	6.0	7.3	5.5	10.4	13.5
Sony	11.4	11.6	10.6	12.5	12.0	11.6
Warner	9.3	13.3	10.1	11.3	10.2	9.8
PWL	4.7	5.2	2.1	1.9	3.3	3.3
MCA	4.7	4.5	2.9	3.7	3.3	3.2
Beggars Banquet	0.5	0.7	0.6	1.2	2.0	1.0
One Little Indian	0.1	-	0.1	0.5	1.7	0.7
Mute	3.9	2.5	3.2	1.2	1.7	0.6
Kool Kat	-	-	0.1	0.5	1.7	0.3
Virgin	10.1	9.9	6.8	7.4	-	-
Others	22.2	22.6	20.9	19.3	13.7	15.2
Total	100.0	100.0	100.0	100.0	100.0	100.0
Majors	53.8	54.6	63.3	64.3	72.6	75.7
Independents	46.2	45.4	36.7	35.7	27.4	24.3

Source: MMC based on Gallup data.

Note: EMI's market share includes Virgin figures for the whole of 1992.

Changes in market share over time

5.87. The market share taken by the majors remained broadly constant between 1983 (59.2 per cent) and 1989 (61 per cent) but increased by 11 per cent between 1989 and 1993 to 72 per cent (Table 5.22). The recent increase in concentration in the market has been partly the result of the acquisition of a number of established independents by majors. Four important acquisitions have taken place in the last five years: PolyGram acquired Island Records in 1989, and A&M in 1990; and EMI acquired Chrysalis Records in 1991, and Virgin Records in 1992. (Appendix 5.1 shows the largest acquisitions made by record companies and other parties since 1985.)

5.88. Table 5.22 shows that acquisitions have had a particular impact on the market share held by the top two companies. In 1989 the top two companies (PolyGram and Warner) accounted for 30.9 per cent of album sales. In 1993 the top two companies (EMI and PolyGram) accounted for 45.1 per cent of album sales.

5.89. While the market share held by the majors together has remained fairly constant until recently, the share held by each major has fluctuated. For example, in the last ten years Warner had a low market share of 6.6 per cent in 1983, with a subsequent high of 14.8 per cent in 1989, before dropping back to 10.3 per cent in 1993; PolyGram had a low of 12.5 per cent in 1984 and a high of 23.3 per cent in 1992.

5.90. This fluctuation in market shares also partly reflects the volatility of record sales where large sales of a small number of titles can have a considerable effect. This is emphasized when market shares by label are examined. Each label tends to be associated with a particular type of music from general pop to dance and jazz. The majors and larger independents operate a number of labels. Market shares by label vary substantially year by year (see Appendix 5.2).

5.91. It has been a feature of the market that the share taken by independents has remained relatively constant over time until recently (see Table 5.22). This, however, disguises a number of market entries and exits in the independent sector. Table 5.26 identifies some current record companies which were founded since 1983, together with their major artists.

TABLE 5.26 **New entrants to the recorded music industry: some recording companies founded since 1983**

No	Name	Date founded	Major artists	Music type
1	Big Life Records	1986	Yazz De La Soul Soup Dragons	Pop
2	Castle Communications plc	1983	The Kinks Motorhead Uriah Heap	Pop, reissues, compilations
3	China Records Ltd	1984	Art of Noise The Levellers	Rock/indie
4	Conifer Records	1986	Conifer Classics	Classical, Jazz
5	The Connoisseur Collection Ltd	1986	Compilations/re-issues	Pop/Rock
6	Cooking Vinyl Ltd	1986	Bhundu Boys Oyster Band	Folk and 'Roots'
7	Creation Records Ltd	1985	Primal Scream House of Love Jesus and Mary Chain	Indie
8	FFRR Records Ltd	1986	Salt 'N' Pepa Utah Saints	Dance
9	Go! Discs Ltd	1983	Beautiful South Paul Weller	Indie
10	Kaz Records Ltd	1983	Dollar Brand	Jazz, African
12	Mute Records Ltd	1983	Depeche Mode Erasure	Pop
13	One Little Indian Ltd	1987	The Shamen The Sugarcubes	Indie
14	Peter Waterman Ltd	1983	Kylie Minogue Jason Donovan	Pop
15	Produce Record Ltd	1989	The Farm	Dance/pop
16	Quietly Confident Records	1984	Jimmy Nellis	Pop/rock
17	Rumour Records Ltd	1989	Nomad	Dance compilations
18	Silvertone Records	1988	John Lee Hooker The Stone Roses	Indie/blues
19	Today Croydon Ltd	1983	Frank Zappa Magnum	Heavy metal/rock Super budget
20	Tring International Plc	1990	Compilations/re-issues	
21	Wisepack Ltd	1988	Compilations	
22	Dino Entertainment	1988	Compilations	TV advertised
23	ZZT Records Ltd	1988	Seal 808 State	Dance/soul/rock
24	Beechwood Music Ltd	1987		Indie/dance compilations
25	Food Ltd	1984	Blur Jesus Jones	Indie

Source: Media Research Publishing, *The Record Industry, Annual Survey 1993.*

5.92.   A number of these independents have become affiliated in some way with a major record company. For example, PolyGram acquired 49 per cent of Go! Discs in 1987 and 49 per cent of Big Life Records in 1989 (and the remainder in 1993); Sony acquired 49 per cent of Creation Records in 1992.

5.93.   Table 5.27 shows some of the departures over the same period. Although the independents may have departed, the artists that they may have 'discovered' are likely to have been signed by other record companies.

TABLE 5.27 **Companies ceasing to produce in the last ten years**

No	Name	Date founded	Last accounts filed	Major successes	Music type
1	Bigwave Records Ltd	1987	1991	Jive Bunny	Pop/dance
2	Brazendown Ltd (Street Sounds)	1982	1986		Multi-artist dance compilations
3	Elcotgrange Ltd (Stiff Records)	1976	1984	Madness Elvis Costello	Punk/rock
4	Factory (Communications) Ltd	1980	1991	New Order Happy Mondays	Indie
5	FM—Revolver Records Ltd	1983	1991	Magnum	Heavy metal
6	K-Tel International (UK) Ltd	1971	1989	'Hooked on Classics'	TV advertised compilations
7	Ronco Teleproducts (UK) Ltd	1972	1983	'Disco Daze'	TV advertised compilations
8	Rough Trade Records Ltd	1979	1990	The Smiths Aztec Camera	Indie
9	Serious Records Ltd	1985	1988	'Best of House'	Dance compilations
10	Starbend Records Ltd	1984	1987	'Country Store'	Secondary marketing-country
11	Streetwave Ltd	1981	1985	Rose Royce	Soul/dance
12	Stylus Music Ltd	1984	1989	'Soft Metal' 'Pavarotti Collection'	TV marketed Compilations
13	Towerbell Records Plc	1980	1986	Shirley Bassey Chas and Dave Cilla Black	Pop

Source: Media Research Publishing, *The UK Record Industry, Annual Survey 1993.*

Barriers to entry

5.94. The evidence of market entry suggests that barriers to entry in the record industry are low. A number of independents have entered the market successfully over the last ten years. A number of artists signed to independent labels have featured in the singles and album charts. The Top 40 singles charts gained 540 new entrants in the year ending September 1993, 84 of which were from independents. The Top 40 album charts gained 272 new entries over the same period, 42 of which were from independents.

5.95. A small independent record company has few sunk costs since recording, manufacturing, distribution and marketing can all be contracted out to independent third parties. Many costs have come down in recent years. For example, recording equipment of reasonable quality can be purchased for a few hundred pounds, allowing initial recording to be done away from the studio. At the smallest end of the market a recording can be made in a home studio.

5.96. The combination of rapidly changing consumer tastes and a pool of artistic talent in the UK provides opportunities for independents. Independents can compete against the majors in the signing of new artists in a number of ways. An independent may concentrate on a particular type of music and be better placed than a major to spot new talent and make contact with an artist. Artists may be more attracted to an independent that has a good reputation in their type of music than to a major (ie they might be perceived as having more 'street cred').

5.97. There appears to be a pool of people with experience of the record business who are willing to set up record companies, for example ex-artists, producers, artists' managers or ex-employees of the majors. The reputation of these people may be sufficient to attract new artists.

5.98. The independents often develop links with the majors. For example, if a new artist is successful but the independent cannot market the artist overseas, the independent may come to an

248336 G

arrangement with a major under which the artist's recordings are licensed to the major, the artist is signed by the major, or the major takes some financial interest in the independent. Whatever the particular arrangements, there are likely to be benefits for both parties. The majors are interested in sharing in the A&R successes of the independents, while for their part the independents gain funds for further A&R. The risks to the artist of signing with an independent are reduced if this exit route is available.

5.99. The option of outright sale to a major is also open to an independent. The major may be attracted by the existing artist roster, the back catalogue, the personnel or the name of the label. The possibility of a profitable exit from the market is an incentive for a new entrant.

The artists

Introduction

5.100. Record companies make profits from their ownership of the rights in sound recordings. There are two sources of sound recordings for a record company: recordings made by artists[1] contracted to the company (ie those on its artist roster), and recordings licensed from another record company (the majority of product licensed to the majors is sourced from the companies' overseas affiliates).

5.101. A large proportion of the majors' sales in 1992 was attributable to recordings licensed from their overseas affiliates (see Table 5.28). The proportions for each company ranged from a high of 71 per cent of sales to a low of 21 per cent. UK independents that have their own artist rosters sell records almost exclusively derived from that source.

TABLE 5.28 **Source of repertoire of major record companies, 1992**

					percentage of sales
	EMI	*PolyGram*	*Warner*	*Sony*	*BMG*
Own repertoire	67.0	45.4	37.0	29.0	46.0
Licensed from own overseas affiliate	21.0	47.1	54.5	71.0	53.0
Other	12.0	7.5	8.5	0.0	1.0
Total	100.0	100.0	100.0	100.0	100.0

Source: MMC from company information.

Artist roster

5.102. A company's artist roster comprises artists contracted to the company to produce records. An artist roster can increase with the signing of new talent or the signing of artists previously with other companies. Artists can be lost from the roster by being dropped as recording artists by the company or by leaving to sign with another company. The copyright in the recordings made by the artist while under contract to the company normally remains with the company, and the recordings form part of the company's catalogue.

5.103. At the beginning of 1993 we estimate that 513 artists were contracted to the UK majors (see Table 5.29). PolyGram and EMI, the companies with the largest rosters, both gained artists (and the rights to their existing recordings) during 1989 to 1993 as a result of acquisitions: PolyGram from Island and A&M, and EMI from Virgin. Both companies subsequently reduced their rosters in 1992. The increase of 139 from 374 at the beginning of 1989 is largely accounted for by EMI's acquisition of Virgin.

---

[1]The term 'artist' is taken to include a group, band, or act.

TABLE 5.29 Artists' rosters of major record companies, 1989 to 1993

Year beginning

Record company	1989			1990			1991			1992			1993
	Total	Gain	Loss	Total	Gain	Loss	Total	Gain	Loss	Total	Gain	Loss	Total
Polygram*	191	34	46	179	94	45	228	44	42	230	24	59	195
EMI†	66	14	22	58	19	24	53	22	18	57	168	91	134
Warner	31	22	6	47	29	16	60	42	35	67	45	37	75
Sony	50	4	9	45	23	18	50	15	16	49	18	11	56
BMG	36	43	43	36	64	38	62	37	47	52	16	15	53
Total	374	117	126	365	229	141	453	160	158	455	271	213	513

Source: MMC from information provided by the record companies.

*Polygram gained artists in 1990 with the acquisition of A&M and in 1991 with the acquisition of Island.
†EMI gained artists in 1992 with the acquisition of Virgin.

248336   G2

5.104. The roster sizes of the individual companies fluctuated year by year during the period. Only Warner increased the size of its roster in each of the four years. The turnover of artists on the rosters each year was considerable. Typically the majors gained and dropped between 30 and 50 per cent of their artists each year. For example, PolyGram had some 445 different artists under contract over the period 1989 to 1992 but fewer than half that number at any one time. A major record company said that only 15 artists remained contracted to its pop labels between 1 January 1988 and 30 June 1993. We were told by one of the major record companies that its current artist roster comprised three top stars, eight steady performers, 15 new artists and 23 others who had yet to release a record or were no longer successful.

Dual signings

5.105. Exclusive audio exploitation rights in respect of repertoire recorded by a particular artist may be split between two or more record companies in different territories so that each of those companies controls the rights in its territory on an exclusive basis. This may occur in the case of an unknown artist when the record company offers smaller advances for limited territorial rights and the artist seeks a contract in another territory with a different company, or in the case of a very successful artist who considers that it is in his or her interest to be signed to different record companies in different territories.

Record company's judgment of success or failure of an artist

5.106. In simple terms, an artist's success or failure can be judged by a company according to whether or not the investment the company has made in the artist has been recovered from the sales of that artist's records. Thus the record company will seek to recoup the costs of signing the artist (ie mainly advances), recording costs, half the costs of any videos made in conjunction with recordings, and any tour support expenditure, out of royalties due to the artist and its own margin on record sales. (See also paragraphs 8.21 to 8.32.)

5.107. Success will normally mean that an artist is selling sufficient quantities of records to become an established artist who has a significant fan base, has had chart success with single and album releases, and whose records can be exploited internationally. Since 1985 at least 20 artists a year have been established in the UK market, in the sense of releasing their first 100,000 selling album. Of around 330 artists established between 1981 and 1992 on this criterion, some 38 per cent were signed to independent companies at the time of their success.

5.108. Record companies may not simply look to consistent sales growth or profit in determining the success of an artist. A company may be prepared to support an artist over a long period of time if it believes that ultimately the act will succeed or if it believes that the artist's music has great merit. For example, Island signed U2 in the early 1980s but it was not until 1988 that U2's album *The Joshua Tree* established the group as an international success. Some established artists are unable to repeat the huge success of an album with subsequent releases.

Movement of artists from one record company to another

5.109. The opportunity for an artist to move from one company to another arises in the normal course of events when his or her contract expires. A successful artist will often, however, remain with the same record company for an extended period. Some successful artists have chosen to move to another company, usually when commercial terms could not be agreed for an extension of an existing contract. An example is the move of ZZ Top from Warner to BMG. The relationship between an artist and a record company can break down and, either following litigation or simply as a result of agreement between the artist and the record company, the artist may then be able to move. Examples of this are Level 42 moving from PolyGram to BMG and Spandau Ballet moving from Chrysalis to Columbia (Sony).

5.110. An artist may be released from a contract by his or her record company. Under these circumstances, the terms of the recording agreement come to an end. Another record company may then sign the artist. A number of artists released by Virgin Records after it was acquired by EMI have subsequently signed contracts with other companies. Artists contracted to small independent record companies may wish to move to a major in order to further their careers—particularly internationally. The terms of the original contract may be terminated by agreement between the artist and the independent and the artist may sign elsewhere. For example, Rick Astley moved from PWL to BMG and Betty Boo moved from Rhythm King to Warner. When movements of this kind take place it is normally the rights in the artist's future recordings which are acquired by the next succeeding record company. Rights in the artist's previous recordings normally remain with the previous record company. However, certain major artists (eg David Bowie and The Rolling Stones) have negotiated ownership of the rights in the 'back catalogue' of their previous recordings.

5.111. Recording artists tend to contract initially with a record company in the country in which they live although at a later stage in their career they may sign with a company in the country in which they are most successful. Since this is normally the USA, there is some movement of artists' world-wide recording rights out of the UK principally to US record companies.

Artist and repertoire

5.112. While the opportunity to sign an established recording artist sometimes arises, record companies compete to discover new recording artists with talent. This aspect of the business is known as artist and repertoire (A&R) and applies to both popular and classical music. The term 'A&R' usually covers the finding of the artist, negotiating with that artist to sign him or her to the record company's label and then working with him or her to find producers and songs, provide artistic and creative guidance and organize the creation of the master recording. The majors have separate A&R departments, usually one for each label. A&R is the main business activity of most independents.

5.113. Record companies employ talent scouts to locate potential new recording artists. Talent scouts travel the country attending live performances or 'gigs' in pubs, clubs and rehearsal rooms and notify the A&R department of any potential talent. An occasional further source of talent is the unsolicited tapes that are sent to record companies. For example, Warner receives anything from 10 to 50 tapes per week. Other potential discoverers of talent are artists' managers, lawyers, disc jockeys and music publishers. An artist may seek a record label that best fits its own image. This may be based on the music type associated with a label, or the artists already signed to the label, or the reputation of the record company and its A&R personnel.

5.114. If an artist discovered in any of these ways appears to possess the necessary talent then an A&R manager will take a closer look. He will evaluate the artist on the basis of quality, originality, and commercial potential—usually after the preparation of 'demo' tapes paid for by the record company—and advise the record company as to whether the artist should be signed. It is likely that a talented artist will attract the interest of more than one record company.

5.115. Small independent record companies tend to specialize in a particular form of music such as heavy metal or dance music. They may well identify, or attract, new talent in their particular area of specialization before it is noticed by a major record company. Some artists may feel they can establish greater artistic and personal rapport with an independent, that it will be more receptive to new and developing types of music or that it will be better able to focus on developing the careers of a relatively limited number of artists.

The role of the music publisher

5.116. Music publishers perform a role for the composer (ie of the music and/or the song) comparable to that which the record companies perform for the recording artist. They seek new composers whose talents they can develop and promote. The composer normally assigns the copyright in the song or musical composition to a music publisher so that it might be commercially exploited.

The music publisher is responsible for collecting income attributable to the copyright and distributing the composer's share. Income is derived from the following principal sources:

— the use of compositions in sound recordings (collected via the MCPS);

— from licences of the performing and broadcasting rights in compositions (via the PRS) for play on television, radio and other public performances;

— from licences of the synchronization rights in compositions for use in films and television programmes; and

— from overseas publishers to whom the UK publisher has licensed the overseas copyright in the composition.

5.117. Music publishers are principally concerned with pop music because that sector is the most important in terms of overall music sales. The BPI estimates that less than 1 per cent of income received by music publishers relates to classical music. The role of the music publishers in relation to artists has changed considerably. Prior to the mid-1960s they provided a link with the record companies by suggesting that a recording star should record a cover version of a particular song. This role has changed since the 1960s with the emergence of the composer who is also a recording artist. We have been told that this has been reflected in the increased negotiating power of the composer vis-à-vis the music publisher. Traditionally, the music publisher acquired rights in the composition by taking assignment of the copyright from the composer in return for royalty payments. Increasing awareness on the part of the composer's lawyer or manager of the value of the copyright, and the increase in the number of composers performing their own material, have led to a diminished role for publishers and to their being granted only limited duration copyright licences which can be for as little as five years. At one time industry practice was to divide income attributable to the copyright 50:50 between composer and publisher. A division of 75:25 or 80:20 in favour of the composer is now more common.

5.118. The 1993 *Music Week Directory* lists 681 music publishers. The principal music publishers in the UK are listed in Table 5.30 together with approximate market shares based on a survey of the source of the top 100 singles and tracks on the top 50 albums.

TABLE 5.30 **Source of Top 100 singles and tracks on Top 50 albums**

	%
Warner Chappell Music Limited	20
EMI Music Publishing Limited	20
PolyGram Music Limited	11
MCA Music Limited	9
Carlin Music Corporation	
Sony Music Publishing	
BMG Music	
Zomba Music Publishing	20
Chrysalis Music Limited	
All Boys Music Limited	
Others	20
	100

Source: Gallup Survey published in *Music Week*, 7 August 1993.

5.119. All but one of the music publishers (Carlin Music) listed in Table 5.30 are affiliated to record companies. The record companies told us that artists generally treat their arrangements with publishers and record companies as two separate sets of negotiations. When a record company enters into a recording contract with an artist the artist will not necessarily enter into a publishing contract with the record company's music publishing affiliate. For example, a number of Warner's top stars are signed with EMI Music Publishing in their capacity as composers. Only 13 of BMG's 53 current artists are signed with BMG Music Publishing. Of the last 30 contract (re)negotiations carried out by EMI only four of the artists were signed with EMI Music Publishing.

The role of the artist's manager

5.120. The role of the artist's manager is to further the career of the artist. Apart from advising the artist on his career, he would normally represent the artist in contractual and other negotiations with a record company, organize legal and financial representation, and monitor royalty payments and other income to the artist. In the UK a manager will normally manage one main artist, in contrast to the USA where an artist may be represented by a large firm representing a number of artists.

Decision to sign

5.121. The decision to sign a new artist will normally be taken by the top management of the record company or label, taking into account the advice of the A&R manager. It is a subjective judgment as to whether a particular artist possesses the required talent, but the overriding criterion is normally whether the artist has the potential to become commercially successful.

5.122. The majors told us that they also seek to maintain the broad appeal of their rosters. There are two main reasons for this: first, a presence in a wide range of music types reduces the risk from fluctuations in demand for different types of music; secondly, it maintains the major's image as a comprehensive supplier of music to the customer and increases the likelihood that a new artist of whatever musical type will be able to identify with the company and therefore wish to sign with it.

Competition to sign artists

5.123. We have been told that any artist being considered for signing by a major record company will probably be known to other record companies. EMI estimates that at least 50 per cent of new artists it tries to sign receive competing offers from at least one other record company. There are two main reasons for this: first, the music industry is a close-knit community so that word would soon spread if a promising new artist had been found; secondly, the manager or lawyer representing the artist will often inform other record companies so as to initiate a bidding process. The advantage of being first to identify a talented artist is that it gives the A&R executive a chance to develop a rapport with the artist which may influence him to sign with that company rather than another.

5.124. For a talented artist judged to have potential earning power there is likely to be some kind of competitive bidding process between record companies. Such artists are almost invariably represented by an experienced lawyer and manager. Most record companies do not negotiate directly with the artist but with his or her representatives. The competition generally manifests itself in the terms (eg advances and royalties) which an artist is able to secure. Record companies also compete on their reputation and image. This is based on the history of the record company or label, the array of talent on the roster, and the personality and talent of the record company personnel.

5.125. Once a record company has found an artist it wishes to sign, representatives of the record company will negotiate with the artist or with his or her manager and legal representative on the commercial terms of the contract. After an artist is signed to a label, the A&R person is usually closely involved with the development of the artist's career and provides liaison between the artist and the record company.

Artist contracts

5.126. The contracts which form the basis of the arrangements between the record companies and the recording artists contain a number of common features. Individual terms will, however, vary from contract to contract as a result of negotiations with the artist. Top stars will naturally be able to secure more favourable terms than newly contracted artists. Terms also differ according to whether the contract is with a pop or a classical artist.

5.127. A number of key terms, however, commonly appear in the contracts entered into between record companies and artists. The principal common elements appearing in such contracts are as follows.

Copyright

5.128. Provisions dealing with ownership of copyright in recordings made during the term of the contract are crucial to both parties, the issue being whether copyright is to be owned by the record company outright or owned by, or licensed to, the record company for a limited period of time. While record companies generally seek to own the rights in the recordings they acquire for the whole life of the copyright, this is not always achieved and sometimes contracts have been negotiated where the record company holds the copyright only for a period. In such cases the record companies will seek adjustments to the other contract terms so that the payback period is commensurate with the period for which they hold the copyright. Currently, we were told, new artists usually prefer to secure larger advances and royalties rather than to acquire ownership of the copyright; and the same normally applies when contracts are being renegotiated.

Territory

5.129. The issue here is whether the agreement will cover the artist's recording services world-wide or for a lesser territory. It is common for record companies as a general policy to seek to sign artists for the world or for all available territories. However, for the major artists, restricted territory agreements are by no means uncommon, especially where the artist feels that the UK record company's affiliates in another territory are not best placed to exploit the recording successfully. If this is the case, the artist may sign with another record company for the territories concerned.

Term

5.130. The basic issues to be determined here are the duration of the agreement and the number of singles or albums which it is agreed that the artist will record. Typically, the agreement will provide for an initial term, during which the artist will produce a single or an album, and then separate and successive option contract periods, during which he or she will produce four or more albums. At the end of the initial and each option contract period (except for the last), the record company will have an option to elect to extend the term for a further contract period. Normally, the option has to be exercised within a certain period of time after the artist has delivered to the record company the minimum number of recordings required to be delivered during that previous period. Whether these options are taken up will depend on the success of earlier albums and the anticipated success of future work.

Exclusivity

5.131. The record company usually requires the artist to provide his or her services on an exclusive basis for the contract period. This means that the artist is prohibited from entering into recording contracts with other recording companies during the contract period. Such exclusivity is regarded as necessary by the record companies in view of the large investment they make in the artist in terms of advances and of recording, marketing, promotional, video and touring costs.

Advances and recording costs

5.132. Most recording contracts include provisions for non-returnable advances which are recoupable against artists' royalties. The advance is generally regarded by the record company as part of the consideration for the exclusive recording rights granted by the artist. It is expected to cover items such as the artist's living expenses during the contract period, the costs of producing a video in conjunction with the recording and touring costs. The level of advance varies widely from contract to contract; at the top end of the scale, established artists can command sums well in excess of £1 million; while at the bottom end of the scale a new artist may receive in the region of £30,000. In addition, the record company will usually pay the recording costs (eg session musicians' fees, studio hire, travel costs, editing costs, equipment rental, and producers' fees) but these too will be regarded as advances on royalties and therefore recoupable.

Royalties

5.133. The contract will provide for payment of royalties by the record company to the artist in respect of records sold. The royalty rate will vary depending on the bargaining power which the past or anticipated success of the artist gives him or her, and also on the territory where sales are taking place. In the UK, most record companies do not recommend retail prices and so royalties are usually calculated by reference to the Published Price to Dealers (PPD). Royalty rates range from 9 to 14 per cent for a new artist and from 15 to over 20 per cent for a top star.

5.134. However, in determining the actual remuneration due to the artist, the royalty rate is not the only factor. Once established, certain deductions are usually made from the royalty base price before royalties are calculated. These include any VAT or other tax, and a percentage deduction known as a 'packaging deduction' which has historically been taken into account when calculating the price per unit an artist receives. Packaging deductions vary from contract to contract and format to format and do not reflect the actual costs of packaging the individual recording concerned. The packaging deduction is not always insisted on by the record companies, although they find that artists usually prefer its inclusion because it enables them to claim that they receive a higher nominal royalty rate than would otherwise be offered.

5.135. Furthermore, royalties are calculated on actual records sold. This means that certain records shipped out by the record companies do not carry a royalty; these include records distributed free in order to promote sales, those given free in lieu of discounts to dealers and those returned to the record company as faulty or as part of a privileged return scheme. Most recording contracts also contain provisions for reduced royalty rates in respect of records sold through record clubs, by mail order, as compilation albums or as items used to promote the sale of other products. In addition, royalty rates are normally reduced to half rate in respect of records sold at mid- or budget price, since in this case, as in the others mentioned above, the margins to the record company are reduced. Finally, records which are supported by a substantial television advertising campaign usually attract a reduced rate royalty for a period of time. Most record company contracts provide for 'escalations' by virtue of which the royalty rate will either escalate automatically in later contract periods or will increase in respect of a particular record if a certain level of sales of that record has been achieved.

Accounting to the artist

5.136. Recording contracts also set out the mechanism for accounting for royalty payments to the artist. Typically, royalties are accounted for twice yearly (at the end of June and the end of December). All recording contracts contain audit clauses enabling the artist's representatives to inspect the record companies' books to verify the accuracy of the accountings made.

Other terms

5.137. Other common terms appearing in recording contracts cover matters such as the making of audio-visual recordings; the question of who has creative control over recording material; marketing controls which may be exerted by the artist, for example over the manner in which recordings are exploited and priced; and provisions governing the circumstances under which the record company will agree to release a recording, or not to do so.

5.138. It is common for the terms of a contract, in particular the size of the advance and the royalty rate, to be renegotiated in the artist's favour if he becomes successful.

Recent trends in recording contracts

5.139. We have been told of the following trends in contract terms over the last few years:

(a) Advances and royalty rates have increased. A record company told us that a typical royalty rate for a new act has increased over the last ten years from 9 to 13.5 per cent of the dealer price, and for a superstar from 20 to 24 per cent.

(b) The period, or number of albums for which artists are signed to record companies on an exclusive basis has fallen.

(c) Artists have been given greater involvement in approving the recording process and its costs and more control over marketing.

(d) Contracts place greater obligations on record companies to release and market artists' recordings.

(e) The outcome of a number of court cases covering restrictive clauses in artists' contracts has led to some changes in contractual terms generally in favour of artists.

5.140. We have been told that the more difficult market conditions, caused partly by the recession, have led to intensified competition to sign or retain successful artists because they can provide a more reliable source of future revenue. The trend towards shortened exclusivity periods and the tendency of artists to seek to renegotiate their terms considerably before the contract is due to expire has increased the frequency of contract negotiations.

5.141. There has also been an increase in the number and sophistication of artists' professional advisers who assist in the negotiation of contracts.

The recording

5.142. The typical events leading to the recording of a first album by a newly-signed pop artist are as follows. The artist spends the initial months writing and developing material or choosing songs written by other composers. The artist will usually make 'demo' tapes of the material to ensure that it will be satisfactory when recording begins. When the artist has written or chosen sufficient songs to make up an album, the artist and the record company's A&R team select a producer and, if required, session musicians for the recording.

5.143. Producers, who are generally self-employed, direct rehearsals and the recording process in the studio. They have different musical styles and acquire reputations for certain types of music. The A&R man and the artist will together select a producer with the appropriate skills to maximize the artistic and commercial potential of the artist. The producer normally has a contract with the record company and receives an advance (typically £20,000 to £50,000 per album) and royalties (typically at a rate of 2 to 4 per cent of the notional retail price used to calculate artists' royalties). The royalties are remuneration for work carried out and are only payable once the advance has been recouped. The artist, along with the producer and the A&R man, makes the final selection of the material, studio, amount of time to be spent in the studio and the musicians to be used.

5.144. In the recording studio the backing tracks of the rhythm sections, including drum, base, and rhythm guitar (ie those that do not include lead vocals or lead instruments), will be recorded first with the additional help of a sound engineer. The next stage is to record the vocals and add 'over-dubs' such as the lead guitar or keyboards. In the case of new artists, the A&R man will be closely involved. More experienced artists may organize much or all of the recording themselves and indeed may become producers of other artists (eg Dave Stewart of the Eurythmics). The average time spent in a recording studio to record an album is between six and eight weeks and costs may range from £80,000 to £300,000.

5.145. In the final stage all the component tracks are mixed together by a mixing engineer (who might be the producer) to give the final 'sound' and to form a master recording. The recording may be remixed several times before all the parties are satisfied. Sometimes more than one mix of a recording may be produced since, for example, a different mix will be better for the dance version than that for the main release. Up to four re-mixes may be recorded for each single. For an album with five singles this can mean 20 re-mixes.

Costs of releasing an album

5.146. The major record companies told us that the initial costs for releasing an album generally lie in the following ranges depending on the stature of the artist:

— artists' advances: £25,000 to £1,000,000;

— recording costs: £80,000 to £300,000 (including producer's advance against his royalties of £20,000 to £50,000);

— video produced in conjunction with a single: £40,000 to £150,000;

— artwork and photographic costs: £20,000 to £25,000;

— advertising, marketing (excluding losses on singles): £30,000 to £250,000; and

— tour support: £30,000 to £100,000.

The advance, the recording costs, and normally half of the video costs are recoupable from artists' royalties (should there be any) but the remaining costs are not recoupable.

Catalogue of recordings

5.147. The range of record titles available from a record company is known as the catalogue. The larger record companies publish catalogues which give details of album titles and formats. These are available to dealers and sometimes, usually for classical titles and for albums, may be available to the public. The catalogues are often organized by record label each of which usually signifies a broad 'type' of music. Singles are rarely carried in the record companies' printed catalogues because their life cycles are almost always short. *Music Week*, the industry's trade magazine, carries singles release schedules.

5.148. The catalogue consists of recent releases of singles or albums and older titles which continue to sell well enough to remain in the catalogue. These older items are variously termed in the industry 'back catalogue' or just 'catalogue' items. The dividing line between new releases and back catalogue is not a clear one. Typically a record is deemed to have become back catalogue one year after release. Most singles have been deleted by this time so back catalogue comprises mainly albums.

5.149. Table 5.31 shows shares of album sales in 1993 accounted for by records appearing each week in chart positions 1 to 200. Some 36 per cent of album sales were of records appearing in the Top 40 places in the album chart each week. For the most part the Top 40 comprises new releases.

TABLE 5.31 Album market share by chart position, 1993 averages

Album chart position	Average number of albums sold per week	Average share of total album market %	Cumulative share %
1	66,871	3.86	3.86
2	46,286	2.67	6.54
3	37,378	2.16	8.70
4	31,270	1.81	10.50
5	27,722	1.60	12.10
6	25,037	1.45	13.55
7	23,083	1.33	14.88
8	21,385	1.24	16.12
9	20,323	1.17	17.29
10	19,038	1.10	18.39
20	11,315	0.65	26.52
30	8,036	0.46	31.89
40	6,130	0.35	35.91
50	4,732	0.27	38.95
75	2,825	0.16	44.16
100	1,954	0.11	47.50
150	1,256	0.07	51.96
200	910	0.05	55.03

Source: EMI based on Gallup information.

5.150. Record companies hold the rights to many more recordings that are no longer available (or were never released) and which may be termed the 'past' catalogue. The number of titles in the past catalogue is vast. EMI told us that it is unable to give a figure for the number of titles it holds but estimates that it runs to seven figures.

Characteristics of the UK catalogue

5.151. There are a range of estimates of the size of the UK catalogue. The MCPS keeps records of sales by line item for the purposes of collecting publishing royalties. It estimates that there are some 60,000 line items in the catalogues of the UK record companies which are currently available in the UK, including singles. In contrast the BPI estimates that there are nearer 100,000 line items available. The line items range from titles that sell a few hundred and have limited availability in retail outlets to classical titles that are available in dozens of different recordings. The number of line items has been increasing over the last few years, as titles previously available on vinyl or cassette are reissued on CD, and recordings are recycled in compilations. However, the MCPS stressed the approximate nature of any estimate of catalogue size. The true number of line items available in the UK could be double its estimate because of imports.

5.152. We have been told that catalogue size in any territory is a poor indicator of choice of title available to the consumer because a retailer could probably order a copy of any title in the world catalogue of a major record company and receive it in a matter of days. To gain some impression of the 'effective catalogue' of available titles that are demanded by consumers it is useful to examine actual deliveries of records to retailers.

5.153. One major record company provided us with data of actual supplies of its albums in the UK and USA for the 12 weeks between 22 May 1993 and 13 August 1993 for every title for which there was at least one album delivered. These deliveries are shown in Table 5.32.

TABLE 5.32 **Major record company: analysis of deliveries, 22 May to 13 August 1993**

1. Number of titles delivered

     UK   2,222
     US   1,832

2. Number of titles for a given share of deliveries

	20%	30%	40%	50%	60%
UK	5	9	15	25	44
US	2	3	6	11	21

3. Share of deliveries accounted for by a given number of titles (%)

	5	10	20	50	100
UK	21%	32%	46%	63%	75%
US	39%	49%	59%	72%	81%

4. Number of titles with fewer than 12 deliveries (1 per week)

     UK   167
     US   43

Source: MMC from company information.

5.154. Table 5.32 presents four different ways of measuring and comparing the range of deliveries of records by the company in the two countries. The four measures produce a consistent picture. The UK had 21 per cent more titles delivered than the USA. In the UK 25 titles accounted for 50 per cent of deliveries—in the USA this required only 11 titles. In the UK the Top 10 accounted for 32 per cent of deliveries—in the USA they accounted for 49 per cent. In the UK the company was required to deliver one album per week for 167 titles—in the USA for 43 titles.

5.155. The evidence suggests that UK consumers demand and receive a greater range of titles than US consumers, even though the population of the USA is some five times greater than that of the UK.

5.156. The characteristics of the total catalogue of recordings available in the UK have already been described to some extent in the section on sales (eg in terms of music category, price category and format). Similar figures for numbers of titles are not readily available. Record companies tend to identify catalogue items by title and format (ie a line item) rather than title alone. Hence an album may appear three times if it is available on CD, cassette, and LP. However, one of the major record companies was able to provide figures for its catalogue by line item for the last five years (see Appendix 5.3). This demonstrates the importance of the CD format and the decline of the vinyl format particularly for classical titles. It also illustrates the increase in the number of titles available at mid-price and budget.

5.157. Since each title is likely to be available on CD the number of CD line items may be regarded as a good indicator of the number of titles. On this basis it has been possible to compile estimates of the numbers of titles currently available from four of the major companies (see Table 5.33).

	Non-classical	*Classical*
PolyGram	2,077	3,730
EMI	N/A	N/A
Sony*	944	1,128
Warner*	1,190	944
BMG*	812	1,263

Source: MMC estimates from company information.

*Based on numbers of titles offered on CD.

5.158. Typically the record companies do not categorize different types of music by genre apart from classical and non-classical. One company carried out an analysis by music genre of the titles currently in its UK catalogue (Table 5.34). Classical titles represent about half of the total number of titles available but they accounted for less than [†] of its album sales in 1992. The lower sales volumes for classical albums result in a much longer period for the recovery of the initial costs of a successful album. An analysis of the sales of all the albums released in the second half of 1992 by three of the majors showed that by six months after release the classical albums had each sold an average of only 1,125 copies compared with an average of 17,500 for the non-classical albums.

TABLE 5.34 **The catalogue of [†   ] UK by music type**

	Number of album titles in current catalogue	% of total catalogue
Pop	[	9.6
Rock		15.0
Classical		54.4
MOR		5.8
Dance, soul, reggae	†	5.9
Country, folk		1.9
Jazz		5.0
Other		2.3
Total	]	100.0

Source: [†   ]

Note: Percentages do not add to 100 because of rounding.

5.159. Comparisons of catalogues available in different countries is not a simple process. First, demand characteristics vary by country. For example, Japan, Germany, and France tend to have relatively large catalogues because, in addition to the internationally available titles from English-speaking artists from the USA and the UK, there are particular traditional and linguistic features to the markets. Secondly, titles are not always available on all formats. The decline of the vinyl format is widespread and in some countries such as the Netherlands and Japan almost all sales are of CDs. Thirdly, in some countries, the single is no longer a significant feature (France and Germany) while in others it remains significant (UK and Japan). Fourthly, markets with a relatively high interest in a wide range of genres tend to have broader catalogues available (USA, UK, Netherlands and Japan).

5.160. A major record company has provided estimates of the numbers of line items it offers currently in a number of countries (Table 5.35). Apart from Japan, it offers the largest number of line items in the UK. By contrast another estimated that it offered 5,500 titles in the USA (3,472 non-classical, 2,028 classical) compared with 2,128 in the UK (1,000 non-classical, 1,128 classical).

†Details omitted. See note on page iv.

TABLE 5.35 **Current catalogue of a major record company**

Country	Album line items	Single line items	Total line items
UK	10,135	1,187	11,322
USA	7,811	146	7,957
France	8,158	109	8,267
Netherlands	9,389	389	9,778
Germany	9,650	1,050	10,700
Japan	11,093	427	11,520
Denmark	5,120	182	5,302

Source: A major record company.

New releases

5.161. According to *Music Week* magazine 96 singles releases and 185 album releases were made on average each week in 1992. Singles are normally released as part a strategy for breaking a new artist or promoting an album release (see paragraphs 5.233 to 5.235). Singles rarely make a profit. They are a means to obtain press, radio and television exposure and trial purchases. Sales success brings the potential for increased media exposure and retailer support. There are, however, variations to this pattern. In dance music, singles remain the major format for artists. In other forms of pop music such as heavy metal, consumers are album-oriented, loyal to particular artists and not influenced by fashion. The 'alternative' music market is another example of a segment that does not always require a singles success to stimulate album sales. By contrast, classical repertoire is almost never released on singles because of the length of classical works and the general lack of demand amongst consumers. There are exceptions such as Pavarotti's performance of *Nessun Dorma* which was used as the opening music for a television sports programme.

5.162. The timing of album releases is normally driven mainly by the availability of new recordings from the artists on the record company's roster but releases may be timed to take advantage of the Christmas period or some other appropriate event. Each new release will normally be discussed by the management of the company and the artist, bearing in mind contractual commitments and wider issues concerning the marketing and promotional campaign that will accompany the release. With regard to repertoire licensed in from an overseas affiliate the release date is normally determined in conjunction with the repertoire owner. A record that is to be released internationally might have a sequence of release dates in different countries so that the artist is able to make promotional appearances.

5.163. Most releases of new pop recordings are made at full-price. Records from past or back catalogue which are re-released may be priced at mid-price. By contrast, new classical albums may be released at full-price, mid-price or budget depending on factors such as the quality of the recording and the status of the artist. It is common for there to be many versions of popular classical works, with a choice of artist, orchestra and conductor offered in different price categories.

5.164. In recent years the number of titles released has increased. There has been a trend towards a greater variety in the market as record companies issue more titles in an attempt to cover a range of music genres. EMI told us that since 1987, album releases (excluding classical releases) have more than doubled. By contrast, the BPI estimates that the album market in volume terms in 1992 was much the same size as in 1986. Figure 5.3 shows the increase in the number of titles released and the decline in sales per title. The average album sold fewer than 5,000 copies in 1992, across all formats, compared with 10,000 in 1987. Singles releases have risen 10 per cent since 1986 while average sales per release fell from 15,060 in 1986 to 10,750 in 1992.

FIGURE 5.3

Market release volumes and sales per title

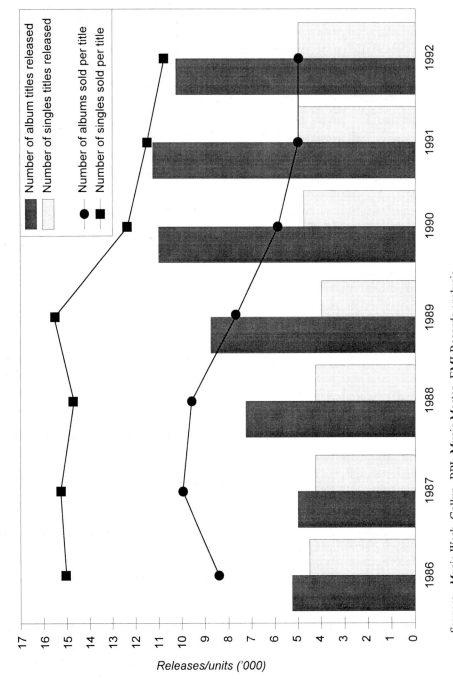

Sources: Music Week, Gallup, BPI, Music Master, EMI Records analysis.

Notes:
1. Excludes classical releases.
2. One title = one release, regardless of the number of formats.

Back catalogue

5.165. The back catalogue of pop albums consists of recordings which are no longer new releases but continue to be available. Since the initial costs of production and promotion have been recouped or written off, sales of back catalogue are particularly valuable to the record companies. Some records by established artists (such as Bob Dylan, The Beatles or Elvis Presley) have been part of the catalogue for a considerable number of years.

5.166. The record companies continually seek ways of exploiting back catalogue titles. The introduction of the CD has led to the reissue of back catalogue material on the new format, often after the original recording has been digitally remastered to enhance the quality. Consumers who already own a title on another format may wish to purchase the CD version for their collection. Sometimes a reissue can have significant sales and enter the charts (eg EMI's re-release of the Beatles' Red and Blue albums on CD in 1993). Older titles might also be re-released at mid- or budget price. Licensing tracks for use on compilation albums (eg *Greatest Hits, Love Songs, Dance*) is particularly important and such albums form a significant sector of the record market which has grown in recent years. Some compilation albums are marketed through television advertising by record companies such as Telstar and Dino Entertainment, as well as by the majors. Many old classical recordings have also been digitally remastered and offered on CD either at full price (for collectors' items) or at mid- or budget price in recognition of the lower quality of recording.

5.167. A recent development has been the introduction and success of the commercial classical music station, Classic FM. This has generated interest in classical music and led to promotional spin-offs such as a classical music chart in W H Smith. It also provides an opportunity to advertise classical music but this does not seem to have led to the expected increase in sales of classical music or attendance at live concerts.

Past catalogue

5.168. The majority of recordings in the past catalogue were commercial failures and are therefore unlikely to be released again. A small proportion of the past catalogue, however, may be released if reasonable sales are possible. Examples of circumstances that may lead to the release of past catalogue are:

— the anniversary or death of an artist may lead to the re-release of old albums or the release of new compilations;

— the revival of interest in a particular period of music, eg a 1960s revival prompted by a television series;

— the use of a particular track in a television programme or advertisement may generate demand for other recordings by the same artist; and

— third parties may request licences to re-release certain recordings, typically as part of a compilation.

5.169. Some past catalogue may be released for the first time. For example, interest in a successful artist may lead to the release of works that were recorded some years before but not released at the time. These might be tracks that were not selected for release on an album or different versions of tracks that were included on previous albums. For example, Bob Dylan released an album entitled *The bootleg series (rare & unreleased) 1961–1991*. The title was prompted by the fact that some of the tracks on the album had already found their way on to the market illegally over the years.

UK releases compared with other countries

5.170. The major record companies provided us with details of the releases they made in 1992 in a number of countries (see Appendix 5.4). The estimates suggest that more singles titles were released

248336 H

in the UK than in the other countries featured and more album titles were released in the UK than in the USA or Denmark but fewer than in the other countries. The titles released in the UK comprise many by internationally known artists, together with those released by local artists. The high number of releases in France and Germany reflects the larger number of local artists with a small following. We have been told that in Japan the same album may often be released twice in the same year.

Deletions

5.171. Singles have only a limited life span and almost all are deleted from a record company's current catalogue if they are not a success or as soon as they drop out of the singles charts, although the record company continues to hold the rights in the recording and it can be re-released. The sales of albums are reviewed regularly. Record companies may establish sales thresholds by which to assess whether a title should be deleted or not [*Details omitted. See note on page iv.*   ]. Each format is reviewed separately and the deletion of one format will not necessarily result in the deletion of other formats. Items might not be deleted if some event (such as the release of another album or a tour) might lead to an increase in demand. In the case of the classical catalogue, titles may be retained if their sales are small because it is recognized that demand is likely to remain steady for a longer period of time than for a pop title.

5.172. The evidence provided by the companies suggests that 15 to 25 per cent of album titles in their catalogues are deleted in any year. The number of titles deleted is broadly matched by the number of releases made in a year.

Manufacture of records

Formats

5.173. When the pop music industry took off in the 1960s, vinyl recordings dominated the market, having taken over from the brittle 78 rpm records in the late 1950s. Reel-to-reel tapes were available for pre-recorded music in the 1950s and 1960s but never became major sellers. In the late 1960s stereo recordings were introduced and for some time recordings were issued in both mono and stereo versions. Once stereo LPs had become established, record companies tried to introduce quadraphonic LPs but this format did not develop the wide public appeal needed to establish it as an alternative format. In addition, four- and then eight-track tape cartridges became available in the mid to late 1960s but the sales peaked at just under 6.2 million units in 1974 and then fell away sharply; the cartridges were eventually removed from the market.

5.174. Cassettes were introduced in 1967 but were slow to become successful. One of the key advantages for the consumer of the cassette format was that for the first time the consumer had the ability to copy recordings, whether from vinyl or from pre-recorded cassette, and build up a music library at a fraction of the price at which recorded music was on sale. This was, and remains, illegal in most circumstances (see paragraph 4.34). There was steady growth in the sales of this format until 1984 followed by a rapid expansion in sales arising from improvements in the sound quality of tapes and the growing importance of portability in consumers' choice of formats, as a result of the growing number of in-car players and the fashion for personal stereos. The sales peak for cassettes occurred in 1989 and there has since been a decline in the format.

5.175. The introduction of the CD in 1983 was followed by massive investment by the industry in promoting this format which offers improved sound quality, durability and convenience to the consumer. Cassettes and CDs have to a considerable extent displaced vinyl although a few listeners still prefer the latter's sound reproduction quality.

The manufacturing process

CDs

5.176. A digital master tape, containing the recording of a particular title and encoded at the studio with additional data such as track identification, timing and location, is delivered to the CD manufacturing plant. The audio signals are transferred at the plant to a glass master from which stampers are made via a galvanic process. The stampers are then used to press the CDs.

5.177. The process is broadly as follows. The CD to be used as the master disc is an optically-ground, spotlessly clean, polished glass disc which is evenly coated with a light-sensitive coating. The master tape is used to produce the CD master disc by controlling a high-powered recording laser which etches the pit-structure into the coating. The matrix process then produces the 'stamper'—the moulding tool that will be used to manufacture the disc. A layer of silver is vacuum-evaporated on to the disc's surface and the silvered glass master is electroplated to produce a nickel master (a metal negative) which is in turn used to produce a positive. This disc then becomes the original from which duplicates can be made. Another coating process produces the stampers, or positives for the pressing of CDs. Several stampers may be required to complete an order.

5.178. The stamper is mounted into an injection-moulding press and polycarbonate is injected into the cavity created on the press between the stamper and a blank placed opposite it. The output from this process is an unmetallized disc known as a substrate. The side with the pit structure is then thinly coated with aluminium (which provides the CD's reflective surface) and a protective film coating applied to prevent oxidization of the metal. The disc is then precision-centred and the centre hole punched out. Each CD which passes the factory's final quality control is a totally accurate reproduction of the original master tape. The final stages of the process are printing the face of the CD by a silk screen printing process; and putting it in its package, together with any artwork inserts, ready for despatch.

Music cassettes

5.179. The studio master tape is usually transferred to a Digital Audio Tape (DAT), which is sent to the factory. There the music is transferred on to a 1" wide 'duplication master tape', or 'running master', which contains Side One (forward play) and Side Two (reverse play).

5.180. The master tape is loaded into a master loop bin, with the ends of the master spliced together to form a continuous loop. In addition, a small section of reflective film is fixed next to the splicing tape. The loop bin machine plays the 1" running master at high speed in a continuous loop, using two replay heads. The reproduced signal from the master loop bin is transmitted to a bank of duplication machines (the number depending on the size of the order) which record the music on to ¼" cassette tape which is mounted on the machines in 'pancakes', reels of tape up to 5,500 metres long. The recording heads have capstan motors either side to ensure consistent tension during tape handling. After duplication the recorded pancake contains a number of cassette programmes, the actual quantity varying with the play-length of the original recording.

5.181. After duplication, the pancake is transferred to a winding machine which puts the programme into empty cassette shells. The machines are able to detect the beginning and end of each programme by a cue tone generated by the reflective film earlier fixed on to the duplication master tape. The complete cassette is then transferred to a finishing process where either a label or 'on-body' print is applied. Finally the cassette is put into its plastic case with a paper inlay.

Vinyl

5.182. The manufacture of vinyl discs starts with either a lacquer disc or a DMM (Direct Metal Master) made of copper, which is cut at the studio and delivered to the factory.

248336   H2

5.183. If a lacquer disc is used it is first made electro-conductive by chemically coating silver on to the surface. The silvered lacquer is then placed in an electroforming bath and plated with nickel to produce a master (negative). This is separated from the lacquer, cleaned and chemically treated and then returned to the electroforming bath and plated with nickel to produce a positive. The positive is separated from the master and is cleaned and sound tested. It is now used to produce nickel moulding tools (stampers) for record moulding. The music faces of the stampers are protected with a plastic coating until used, and the reverse side is polished. Next the stamper is optically centred and a hole accurately punched in the centre. It is then mechanically formed to fit the record press mould blocks.

5.184. DMM copper processing was introduced some ten years ago and is much simpler than lacquer processing. Since the DMM is metallic it needs no silvering before producing a master. The DMM is itself the positive for producing stampers; the master is only used in future to grow another positive if the DMM becomes damaged.

5.185. The stampers (one for the A side and one for the B side) are mounted on to the moulding press. A piece of hot, soft vinyl is squeezed between the stampers and a vinyl positive copy of the original lacquer (or copper) is formed. This is the record. It is now transferred to the trimming and bagging station. The complete cycle takes approximately 20 seconds. Numerous sets of stampers can be grown from each 'positive', and several 'positives' from each 'master'. When the 'master' eventually wears out a re-cut becomes necessary.

5.186. Seven inch records are made on a modified injection moulding press. The A side and B side stampers are inserted into the press, and the plastic injected into the gap between them. Once moulded the label area of the disc is inked, highlighting information pre-etched into the stamper, and then bagged. The bagged record is then boxed for despatch if it is a single; albums are hand packed into the outer sleeve.

Economies of scale

5.187. Economies of scale can result either from the size of the plant and the technology employed or from the length of the production run, or from both.

(a) Plant size

    (i) EMI told us that its own very slimmed down vinyl operations in the UK show that a very small operation can be just as efficient as a larger one. We were informed, nevertheless, that benefits of size do accrue as plant size increases, since management and other overheads can be spread across a larger number of units. The example we were given was that a freehold plant with a 100 million unit capacity has broadly the same fixed overhead as a 40 million unit capacity plant. The ability to spread these fixed costs over a higher number of units provides scale economies.

    (ii) A further benefit of larger-scale plants relates to service quality. With more production lines, it is easier to juggle volatile order profiles. As priorities change quickly in accordance with chart activity, it is easier for a large plant to respond to that success without jeopardizing service levels for the rest of their customers. This is even more important in the UK than in the rest of Europe because of the continuing importance of singles which are 'perishable' products, with tight turnround times (24 to 48 hours). In a facility with only two or three CD lines, all other orders might have to be delayed (or outsourced, at potentially higher cost) for the sake of supplying one or two very fast-moving lines. If all demands are to be met in a highly seasonal business, the plant may be under-utilized during the slower-selling months.

(b) Run length

There are considerable potential economies from increasing run length in CD production (for example) because of fixed costs in the areas of set-up time, process yield and paper parts. In the UK market the system of distribution allows retailers to order daily, so that manufacturing is typically against customer order than for stock. This makes for smaller production runs in the UK than are typical either in the rest of Europe, where demand is less volatile, or in the USA, where overall demand is so much greater and retailers order less frequently. We were told that the prevalence of small manufacturing runs in the UK is an important explanation for the number of small manufacturing operations which are able to remain competitive, in spite of the potential economies of larger-scale production.

(i) Set-up time: Changing the mould (stamper) on the press takes anything from 5 to 20 minutes so that with longer runs more productive use is made of the equipment. Changing the screens on a label printer takes on average 15 to 20 minutes. For a series of orders of 500 units each, it takes approximately twice as long to set up the screens for the next order as to complete the order itself. Finally, every time a new order is placed on the finishing equipment, the printed material, and sometimes the type of jewel boxes, must be changed over. This takes about 20 minutes.

(ii) Process yield is the ratio of good product obtained at the end of the production line to the number of discs pressed. When discs are pressed the moulding machine must be at a constant high temperature for good results. This is much more easily achieved with long runs than with short ones, since the temperature drops when the presses are stopped for stamper changes.

(iii) The unit cost of paper parts (CD book and inlay) drops significantly with the size of the print run.

Location

5.188. The progressive replacement of vinyl by cassettes and, later, by CDs will have greatly reduced the importance of transport costs in the economics of record supply. Cassettes and CDs are much less fragile than vinyl and have a higher value:weight ratio, both of which tend to reduce the relative unit cost of transport. Many of the larger record companies employ manufacturing facilities which are located a considerable distance away from the market being served.

5.189. Nevertheless, some companies clearly believe that for certain time-sensitive product, especially singles, it is important that the location of manufacturing should not be very far from the market to be served, in order to facilitate rapid response to perceived changes in demand for particular records. EMI, for instance, has a policy of sourcing chart product, whether singles or albums, as close to the source of demand as possible, while back catalogue may be sourced from more remote plants.

The relationship of manufacturing and record companies

5.190. Most major record companies have closed their manufacturing plants in the UK. The exceptions are EMI, which continues to produce all formats, and Sony, which manufactures music cassettes only. Apart from manufacturing their own products, EMI and Sony manufacture cassettes for third parties, and EMI does the same with vinyl. There is a flourishing and competitive independent manufacturing sector, with individual companies usually specializing in a particular format, although some (eg Damont Audio Ltd in Hayes, Middlesex and Mayking in London) manufacture multiple formats. Manufacturers compete on the basis of service (fast, consistent turnround), product quality and price.

5.191. Most of the majors obtain the bulk of their manufacturing requirements from sister companies. Apart from EMI, which manufactures CDs at Swindon and cassettes and vinyl records at Hayes, Middlesex, and to a lesser extent Sony, which manufactures cassettes at Aylesbury, these sister companies are located abroad.

5.192. The record company identifies the product and the market for it. It is responsible for producing the initial master recording and for subsequent record distribution, marketing and promotion. It decides the format in which the product will be produced and the size of the order needed to meet initial customer demand. The larger the order the better the deal obtainable from the record manufacturer but the greater the risk of having product left unsold. The lower the order the less attractive it will be to the manufacturer, who wants to spread fixed costs over longer production runs.

5.193. The independent manufacturers principally supply the requirements of independent record companies. However, a number of the major record companies regularly obtain a proportion of their requirements from the independent manufacturers. This is mainly (though not exclusively) for the supply of singles, where the flexibility and rapidity of response of local companies gives them an edge in a market where these factors are specially important. The majors may also utilize the independent manufacturers when their regular suppliers are overloaded.

5.194. We were told that supply arrangements in the independent sector tend to be governed by exchanges of letters, rather than by firm contracts. Failure to perform leads to rapid switching of custom. Record companies will sometimes confine their subcontracting to a single supplier, but some will double- and triple-source. Where record company and manufacturer are part of the same organization, as is the case with most of the majors, this does not arise to the same extent.

Prices charged by manufacturers

5.195. The price charged for record manufacture is made up of several components, some of which will be consistent across manufacturers and some of which will vary. The cost of record manufacture will include that of the plastic, vinyl or tape used for the singles or albums and the outer case. The sound carrier and its case are standard and their cost tends to be consistent across manufacturers. Singles vinyl product is cheaper than that of LPs (ie single albums). Music cassettes have a variable price structure depending on the playing time of the tape. CD singles are usually cheaper than CD albums because of the smaller amount of printed material and differences in the finish. Some manufacturers charge separately for mastering costs while others include an element of mastering in the unit price. Similarly, delivery may be included in a unit price or charged separately.

5.196. Paper parts (sleeves, booklets, etc) may be included in the unit cost or sourced from a different manufacturer. The use of extra colours, more pages, special folding, etc will increase the unit cost. Where a manufacturer is responsible for paper parts, it may agree to bear the inventory risk on these parts and this will be reflected in the price charged.

5.197. There is often a minimum order quantity (especially on initial orders) and small orders will have a higher unit price than larger orders to reflect higher unit costs. Negotiations between large record companies and manufacturers will usually be on a standard price, irrespective of order quantity, which takes account of a mix of order sizes. One-off purchases of capacity to handle one or several orders will be made at the 'spot' competitive supply price prevailing in the market at the time. Longer arrangements will be specially negotiated.

5.198. Price will reflect the time of year, especially in such a seasonal industry. Manufacturing prices will be relatively high in the peak pre-Christmas period. At other times of the year, when there is spare capacity, very keen prices, based on marginal cost, may be obtainable. We were told that record companies tend to prefer annual arrangements with manufacturers in order to preserve guaranteed access to manufacturing capacity at peak times. Negotiated prices will reflect product specifications, average order size and overall volumes, with retroactive discounts sometimes payable when target volumes are exceeded. Service specifications are very important to record companies, since they will often require many small orders to be made up at very short notice. Such requirements could not be met by relying on the spot market. Bearing in mind the variety of factors that can affect the unit manufacturing price, we were told by the record companies that unit prices charged for CDs can vary between 70p and £1.60, exclusive of inlays.

Sourcing of product by record companies

5.199. Supply arrangements for a number of the larger record companies are as follows:

(a) *EMI:* The company manufactures all the principal formats in the UK, but imports product that is not time-sensitive from its sister plant in Uden (Netherlands). Its UK vinyl manufacturing facility is used to meet EMI's European requirements. Declining demand for the vinyl format means that EMI's capacity has been enough to cover its own requirements and also those of third parties, the latter accounting for 54 per cent of EMI's vinyl output in 1992/93. While it has been building up its CD capacity, EMI has been sourcing a significant proportion of such product from third parties. By 1992/93 the in-house manufacturing percentage of such product was 74 per cent. EMI is likely to continue to source a small proportion of its requirements for cassettes from third parties.

(b) *PolyGram:* Record supply is from a variety of sources. Most CDs are obtained on a long-term contract, from the Philips factory at Blackburn which is not regarded as an in-house source. CDs are also produced by the PolyGram factories at Louviers and Hanover and are sourced through its International Supply Centre, PolyGram's central European warehousing complex at Hanover. All classical CDs are supplied from that centre. Until recently a number of independent UK sources had been used to supply cassettes. Though these sources are still used, most cassettes (including singles) are now sourced from PolyGram's factory at Amersfoort. Vinyl records are sourced from France through an agent.

(c) *Warner:* The great majority of the product sold by Warner is manufactured by the affiliated company Warner Music Manufacturing Europe (WMME) which carries out manufacturing for all the European Warner companies. However, 29 per cent of the total volume of Warner records in 1991 were supplied either by a variety of UK independents or (to a minor extent) by other UK record companies (Sony and EMI). Supply by independents was mostly of singles.

(d) *Sony:* Sony manufactures cassettes at Aylesbury, both for itself and for a number of third party customers. Supplies of CDs are obtained from a sister company in Austria and of vinyl from a sister company in the Netherlands. CD singles needed urgently are air freighted from Austria.

(e) *BMG:* All CD and cassette albums are obtained from BMG's Central Manufacturing Group, in Germany. This is a logistics organization which organizes supply for all BMG companies, mainly through Sonopress (a division of Bertelsmann), but also to some extent through UK independents (eg Nimbus and Disctronics). Vinyl albums are normally UK-sourced. All BMG's singles are sourced in the UK because of the need for a quick, flexible response. In 1992, 42 per cent of BMG's sales of CDs (by volume) were supplied by UK independent manufacturers, and 31 per cent of cassettes.

Artwork and packaging

Artwork

5.200. Major record companies may have in-house art departments to design sleeves and other display materials, though they may also employ external designers. Other record companies rely on contracting with third parties who specialize in such design and will oversee the process from photo-session to print organization. Such agencies will work to standard specifications set by the record company—eg incorporating the required size, catalogue number and product bar code. EMI told us that it uses any of about 20 different third party agencies, depending on the type of design required.

5.201. The budget for artwork will often be higher for the more established and popular recording artists. Where product is originated in the UK, artwork will also be prepared in the UK, even if actual production takes place overseas. Where product is not originated in the UK, the original artwork may be used subject to any necessary language or other changes—eg incorporation of catalogue and bar code numbers—to make it suitable for the UK market.

Packaging

5.202. Packaging refers to the cost of any booklet, jewel box, tray or shrink-wrap and excludes the cost of any incorporated artwork. It is a minor part of the total cost of an album—according to EMI, 5 to 6 per cent of the average realized dealer price of a CD. The major part of the packaging cost is the booklet containing information about the record. For a CD this is usually at least four pages long, but it can be longer, especially for classical albums.

Distribution

5.203. In the record industry the term distribution refers to the ways in which records are delivered from the record companies to the retailer (or mail order companies/record clubs). The BPI estimates that some 60 per cent of recorded music in the UK is distributed to retailers directly by the record companies' distributors, 28 per cent goes via a wholesaler and the remaining 12 per cent is supplied to mail order and record club operators. Figure 5.4 summarizes the main channels of distribution. Distributors and wholesalers are considered below. Retailers are considered in Chapter 6.

Distributors

5.204. A distributor normally acts on an exclusive basis for a record company. This means that all the finished product of a record company is bulk-shipped from the manufacturer or a central warehouse to the exclusive distributor where it is broken, picked and packed for onward distribution. Any dealer (ie wholesaler or retailer) wishing to obtain the record company's products must contact the distributor. The supply by the distributor to a dealer is deemed to be a sale by the record company. The record companies therefore bear the cost of delivery to retail outlets.

5.205. Distributors need to carry full catalogue ranges, and to hold sufficient stocks to satisfy anticipated demand. Because of frequent fluctuations in demand for individual titles and the unpredictability of sales, the distribution system has to ensure that records are delivered as quickly as possible, usually within 24 hours of receipt of an order from the retailer. Most of the major retail chains do not have central warehouses and require delivery direct to each of their stores.

5.206. Final delivery to retail outlets is carried out for distributors by contract couriers such as Securicor. Securicor picks up packages from distribution depots and transports them to its own depot where they can be sorted according to their final destination. It is therefore usual for the products of different record companies to arrive at a retail outlet in the same van.

5.207. Each of the five major record companies has its own centralized distribution operation (eg EMI at Leamington Spa, Sony at Aylesbury). A major might also act as a distributor for an independent record company; for example, Warner distributes for Beggars Banquet Records Ltd (Beggars Banquet). There are also a number of independent distributors. Pinnacle Records (Pinnacle), a division of Lambourne Productions Ltd, is the main independent distributor and acts in an exclusive capacity for many independent record companies. Pinnacle warehouses, physically distributes to, and invoices the retail trade for the product that it carries for a record company under an exclusive UK distribution contract. At the point of sale from Pinnacle to its customers the product is deemed to be purchased from the record company. Independents therefore have a choice of distributor and there is evidence that switching takes place. For example, MCA switched from PolyGram to BMG in 1990.

FIGURE 5.4

Distribution of records in the UK

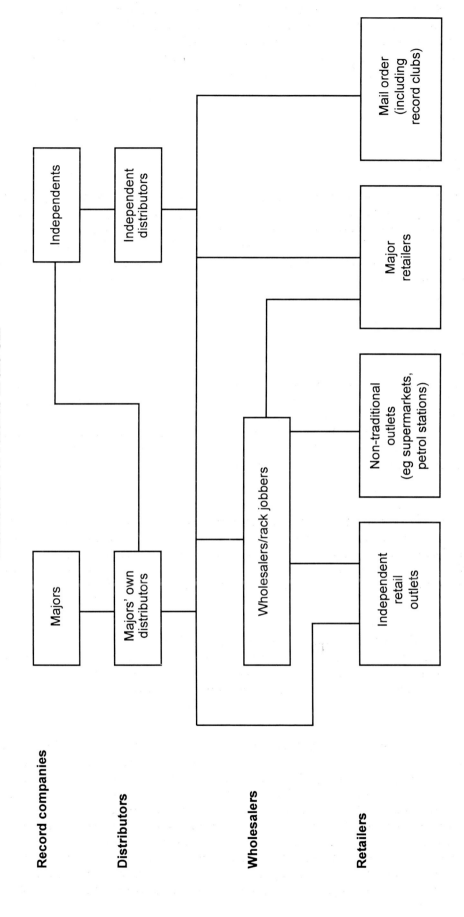

Source: MMC.

5.208. Table 5.36 shows the shares of distribution held by the nine leading distributors. Table 5.37 shows the record companies for which they act as distributor. The shares of the majors generally reflect their parent company's sales. The exception is BMG which has a larger share of the distribution market since it acts as distributor for a number of independents. Pinnacle had an 8 per cent market share (by value) in 1992.

TABLE 5.36 **Market shares of distributors (by value of album sales), 1992**

Distributor	Market share %
PolyGram	23.9
EMI*	23.1
BMG	15.8
Warner	13.1
Sony	11.0
Pinnacle	7.9
Pickwick	1.0
TBD	0.4
Conifer	0.4
Others	3.4
	100.0

Source: MMC based on information supplied by Gallup.

*Virgin product was distributed by PolyGram in 1992 and moved to EMI only in 1993 after the acquisition of Virgin Music by EMI. However, Virgin's market share has been included with EMI's in this table to reflect the current situation.

Wholesalers

5.209. Wholesalers purchase catalogue from distributors and offer a range of product, sometimes on a 'sale-or-return' basis, to accounts too small to deal directly with individual distributors. They do not stock every line item offered by the distributors but typically restrict their stock to the 'mainstream' artists. They also provide 'top-up' stocks for next day delivery for many of the multiples and independent retailers which otherwise deal directly with the main distributors. This role has diminished recently as the main distributors have reduced order response times (see paragraph 5.212). A wholesaler may also act as exclusive distributor for a small record company. The major wholesaler in the UK is TBD which is owned by John Menzies. It supplies numerous independent specialist and non-specialist accounts. Rack-jobbing is a form of wholesaling that has grown in importance in recent years. It comprises a more extensive range of services. Records are generally supplied to non-traditional music outlets such as garage forecourts, motorway service stations or supermarkets. Rack-jobbers will negotiate with the owners of such outlets to acquire display or shelf space for records. The rack-jobber will then be responsible for all aspects of stock ordering, display and maintenance for that outlet. In some cases the rack-jobber will supply the retailer on a sale-or-return basis. It is therefore normal for there to be only one rack-jobber supplying a particular retailer. The retailer will receive the sales revenue for sales of such music and pay a percentage to the rack-jobber.

5.210. The main rack-jobbers that supply non-traditional outlets in the UK are EUK, part of the Kingfisher Group, through its 'Chart Stop' offering, TBD and Pic-A-Tape, through 'Entertainment Stop'. EUK is solely responsible for the supply of records to Woolworths, which is also part of the Kingfisher Group, as well as acting for third party non-specialist customers such as Tesco and Asda. TBD is the exclusive supplier of records to John Menzies and Boots.

Recent developments in distribution

5.211. Over the last five years there has been increased concentration at both the retail and wholesale levels. This has resulted in a higher percentage of business going through fewer accounts and an increase in the bargaining power of some dealers. However, increased retail and wholesale concentration has not had any great impact on the number of delivery points the record companies have to service because most retailers do not carry out their own wholesaling.

TABLE 5.37 Distributors' market shares by company's records distributed (by value of album sales), 1992

Distributor	Source of records distributed	Share of records distributed in UK %
PolyGram	PolyGram	23.7
	Others	0.2
		23.9
EMI	EMI	14.4
	Virgin*	7.8
	Others	0.9
		23.1
BMG	BMG	5.1
	MCA	4.3
	Telstar	4.0
	TUG	0.7
	Castle Communications	0.7
	Sony	0.2
	Beechwood	0.1
	Zomba	0.1
	Others	0.4
		15.8
Warner	Warner	12.4
	Beggars Banquet	0.2
	PWL	0.4
	Others	0.1
		13.1
Sony	Sony	10.5
	Arcade	0.4
	Others	0.1
		11.0
Pinnacle	BBC	0.6
	China	0.2
	Connoisseur Collection	0.2
	Creation	0.3
	Dino	1.8
	Factory	0.1
	First Night	0.2
	Music for Nations	0.2
	Mute	1.0
	One Little Indian	0.6
	Quality Productions	0.9
	Ritz	0.2
	Zompa	0.2
	4AD	0.1
	Others	1.6
		7.9
Pickwick	Pickwick	0.9
	Others	0.1
		1.0
TBD	Music Collection	0.1
	Others	0.3
		0.4
Conifer	Conifer	0.2
	Others	0.1
		0.4
Others		3.4
Total		100.0

Source: MMC based on information supplied by Gallup.

*Virgin product was distributed by PolyGram in 1992 and moved to EMI only in 1993 after the acquisition of Virgin Music by EMI. However, Virgin's market share has been included with EMI's in this table to reflect the current situation.
Note: Percentages may not add to the totals because of rounding.

5.212. The nature of distribution in the record industry is influenced by the service required by retailers. Recently, retailers have sought to decrease the level of stock that they keep at their stores. For example, the Our Price chain has a stockholding sufficient to service an average of 70 to 75 days' sales. This policy is partly the result of the recession, partly to enable more store space to be freed for product display, and partly in response to the unpredictability of demand for individual titles. This has led to increased demands on distributors to provide a 'just-in-time' delivery service to each store. The record companies told us that it is now common for retail outlets such as Our Price, HMV and Virgin to place orders twice a week (and even every day during the Christmas peak period). In the case of Virgin's larger stores, orders for best-selling product and chart product may be placed every day. This change has been facilitated by the introduction of computer ordering of product by some stores. EMI, with PolyGram and BMG, have recently invested in an electronic ordering system known as EROS Music Systems, which enables any dealer to key orders directly into the relevant distribution centre at any time.

5.213. The effect of the 'just-in-time' service has been to increase the number of deliveries made by distributors. A major record company estimated that, between 1988 and 1992, whilst there was a decrease in the number of lines it shipped of 24 per cent and of units shipped of 24 per cent, the number of orders it processed increased by 42 per cent. But the average number of records per order fell by some 47 per cent.

5.214. The increase in the number of orders and a decrease in the number of records per order puts an upward pressure on distribution costs. Primary distributors, notably Sony and EMI, have responded by increasing automation at central distribution centres. Also, reductions in delivery times from manufacturers have enabled distributors, wholesalers and rack-jobbers to reduce stock for normal expected supply.

International trade in recorded music

Visible trade

5.215. Visible (ie physical) imports and exports of finished product are limited because most product is distributed locally by the rightsholder in a particular territory. The main categories of imports of finished product into the UK are:

(a) imports under the MCPS/BPI Import Licensing Scheme;

(b) imports from the EC; and

(c) imports of pirate product.

Imports under the MCPS/BPI licensing scheme

5.216. Under the MCPS/BPI Joint Licensing Scheme (see paragraphs 4.69 to 4.72) an importer can import finished product from outside the EC with the permission of the UK rightsholders. From the MCPS's records of royalty stamps 'sold' it can be estimated that imports under the Scheme amounted to some £6 million in 1992, representing about 0.5 per cent of retail sales. Income from sales of royalty stamps in 1992 was £566,000.

5.217. The MCPS sent 95 letters to importers in 1992 informing them that particular records could not be imported under the Scheme. Table 5.43 shows who had requested these withdrawals from the Scheme. Nearly half the letters were sent on behalf of independent record companies.

TABLE 5.38 **MCPS letters withdrawing records from the import licensing Scheme, 1992**

	7"/12"/CD and MC singles	CD/LP/MC albums	Multi-formats	Total
Multinational record company	8	31	6	45
Independent record company	13	19	8	40
Music publisher	3	3	2	8
BPI (Anti-Piracy Unit)	-	1	1	2
				95

Source: Record companies from MCPS information.

Imports from the EC

5.218. Finished product produced legally anywhere in the EC, or produced legally elsewhere and in free circulation in the EC with the consent of the copyright holders, can be imported without further permission since there is freedom of parallel trade within the EC. There are no data available for the levels of imports originating from within the EC.

Imports of pirate product

5.219. Piracy consists of illegal copying for commercial gain. It includes counterfeiting (the unauthorized duplication of a sound recording, designed to sound and look as much like the original as possible), and bootlegging (the unauthorized recording or duplication of a live performance or concert). The BPI estimated that the value of total UK retail sales of pirate product in 1992 was some £17 million. The estimated retail value of imports of pirate product was £2.75 million for the same year. Current unpublished BPI estimates suggest that sales of pirate product increased markedly in 1993. The BPI operates an Anti-Piracy Unit which, among its other activities, issues notices to UK importers and distributors of product, alerting them to the likelihood of a particular counterfeit or bootleg product being offered to them. For example, in March 1992 it issued a notice in relation to substantial quantities of counterfeit CD albums of recordings by some top stars (including REM and Simply Red) manufactured in Singapore and Taiwan and shipped to Europe for distribution.

Invisible trade

5.220. Invisible exports consist of royalty and other earnings by UK owners of the rights in recordings which are licensed to overseas record companies. Records in respect of which invisible earnings accrue are manufactured, distributed and marketed by the overseas company.

Trade statistics

5.221. Official figures for UK imports and exports collected by Customs and Excise and reported in the BPI Handbook 1993 give a value of £140 million for total visible imports and £211.6 million for visible exports in 1992. However, the figures may be an overestimate of the trade in finished product because they include intra-industry transfers of unfinished product.

5.222. The BPI estimates that the value of invisible exports from the UK was some £500 million in 1991. This takes into account all sales and other royalties directly associated with the exploitation of sound recordings. We have been unable to obtain any estimates of invisible imports. The BPI provides no estimate of invisible imports and the CSO does not collect separate information on invisible trade in music.[1] However, our examination of the financial data of the five major record companies, which is discussed in Chapter 8, shows that the amount of the licence fees they receive greatly exceeds the amount that they pay out.

---

[1]The CSO, the BPI and British Invisibles have recently set up a working party to examine ways of improving the collection of information on invisible imports and exports.

119

Marketing and promotion

5.223. Record companies use marketing and promotion to help ensure that an individual artist is established in the consumer's mind and that there is the maximum exposure of each record release. The ultimate aim is to ensure the sales of albums. The returns from marketing and promotion may take time to accrue. For example, a campaign to raise the profile of an artist may not only boost sales of the current album but all future albums.

5.224. The sales success of a new release is dependent on consumers being able to hear the recording. The record companies estimate that fewer than 10 per cent of albums are bought by consumers who have not heard the music before. However, in order to achieve playing time in the first place and in order to exploit any playing time that is achieved, it is also necessary to promote the recording. It must be promoted to retailers, to persuade them to stock it, to the media, to draw the recording to the public's attention, and directly to consumers. The process is complex and mixes various elements in different degrees depending on the characteristics of each artist and recording. These elements include: media exposure in the form of airplay and comment on radio, television and in the press; live performances and touring; personal appearances in dance clubs; advertising in the press, on radio and television, and on posters; in-store promotion and retail co-operative advertising; and direct mail.

Media exposure

5.225. Radio airplay is a very important medium for record promotion. BBC Radio One, Capital, Virgin 1215, and some 50 independent local radio stations are usually supplied with free samples of records prior to release. Deregulation of radio in the UK has led to an increasing number of new radio stations (both regional and national), some of which target a particular musical taste (eg Kiss FM, Jazz FM, Classic FM). About 200 albums and 100 singles releases are made each week in the UK. Pop radio stations add some 20 titles to their playlists each week. The inclusion of a record on a playlist can make the difference between success or failure.

5.226. The record company devotes considerable effort to securing mention of a recording in the general press and specialist music press, and on radio and television, and to ensuring that the record is played on the radio and in clubs and discos. Television exposure is also a significant factor. This may involve the artist's live performance, or the showing of video clips on BBC's *Top of the Pops* and ITV's *The Chart Show*, on more general shows such as Des O'Connor, or on breakfast television. The record company usually books and delivers artists and videos for the available slots. Pop acts are generally promoted in this way. Record companies often make a video of an artist performing the single that has just been released. If the single is a success and the video is considered good quality it can receive extensive airplay in television programmes that are devoted to pop music or otherwise (eg children's programmes), thereby generating performance income for the record company. In a typical record deal, 50 per cent of the cost of a video will be expressed as recoupable from the artist's record royalties. Videos may also be made to accompany albums (both pop and classical) and sold to the consumer.

5.227. Press coverage divides into two areas: specialist and general. The UK has a tradition of specialist music papers such as *New Musical Express* and *Melody Maker*. New magazines such as *Q* and *Vox* also feature music. This area of the press reviews new releases of singles and albums, and carries news, features and interviews on artists and on the music scene generally. The releases of the independent record companies in particular are featured in the specialist music press. The general press is also important for music coverage.

Live performances

5.228. Tours and performances are normally arranged by the artist's manager. They will be co-ordinated with new releases and record companies are usually expected to contribute towards the costs. Most tours make a loss on ticket sales although some major artists make a profit. Promotional appearances in clubs may also be important particularly when co-ordinated with the release of a single. New artists may build up a fan base by performing at a number of small venues in a region.

Advertising

5.229. All forms of advertising media are used, ranging from radio and television to outdoor posters. Advertising is normally funded by the record company, although co-operative activity with retailers and concert promoters is common.

Retailers

5.230. Retailers are notified in advance of new releases and in the period leading up to the release date the record company will seek advance orders from the retailer to ensure that the records are in stock in stores on that date. Some form of co-operative marketing may be agreed between the record company and the retailer to accompany the release.

5.231. Campaigns in conjunction with retailers can take various forms. Television and press advertising, posters and other material advertising the retailer may feature particular recordings. Depending on the status of the recording artist, such a campaign may be initiated by the retailer. The costs of such 'co-operative' advertising are normally borne by the record company. The record companies also pay for in-store advertising material in the form of posters, carrier bags, etc, bearing the image of the artist or reproducing the cover of the record, and for space in the window display of the store. Retailers and record companies may co-operate to mount back catalogue campaigns whereby the retailer offers a reduced price to the consumer and receives a discounted price from the record company for stocks to be included in those campaigns.

5.232. As part of the promotional strategy for a particular recording a record company may offer retailers additional discounts to have stocks on display on the release date. Further discounts may be available to a retailer that stocks a record as part of an in-store campaign or to tie in with a tour by the artist.

The role of singles and charts

5.233. Release of singles is the most common and most effective means of promoting a pop album. It is success in the singles chart which is particularly important because the Top 40 is the basis for playlists on radio and for pop programmes on television, and which generates demand from consumers and retailers (see paragraphs 6.55 to 6.60).

5.234. Singles are usually not a profitable format for the record companies in themselves; they usually have a catalogue life of less than six months from release to deletion and most do not generate enough sales to cover all the costs of the promotional activity and manufacturing. However, they play an important role in establishing an artist and improving or maintaining his or her popularity. For a new artist the release of the first single generally precedes the release of the album. The main function of the single is to attract media attention to the artist by focusing on a specific song. If the single is successful and enters the charts this will generate more media interest which in turn increases the amount of exposure the record receives.

5.235. The album may be released after the first or second single and there is a definite correlation, although not a hard and fast one, between the chart position attained by the single and the sales of the album. For example, the sales of Tasmin Archer's album *Great Expectations* reflected the impact of the success of singles drawn from it. The debut single (*Sleeping Satellite*) reached No 1 in the singles chart in the week prior to the release of the album. The debut album was an immediate hit, reaching No 8 in the album charts. To revive falling sales, subsequent singles were released; each time the high point of that single in the singles chart coincided with, or just preceded, a 'peak' in the album chart (see Appendix 5.5).

Free records

5.236. The singles charts in the UK are based on sales of records through a range of retail outlets. In general only the specialist multiples and the independent retailers are willing to stock a wide range of singles. The generalist chains and multiples are generally only willing to stock singles which are already in the Top 40 or 60 of the singles charts. However, given the volatility of singles sales and competition for display and storage space, the specialist multiples and the independents require some incentive to stock a particular singles title. The supply of free singles constitutes such an incentive. By supplying free copies to retailers, record companies seek to raise the public's awareness of an artist's music and to achieve retail sales sufficient to secure a place in the singles chart (which is based on retail sales). If a retailer has the single in stock at a higher margin than average there is an incentive to try to sell the recording.

Classical music

5.237. Most of the features of marketing and promotion discussed so far apply particularly to non-classical records. Marketing and promotion of classical records has many of the same features: promoting and developing the artist, advertising new releases, in-store promotions. Popular works performed by well-known artists (such as Nigel Kennedy, Luciano Pavarotti or Kiri Te Kanawa) may be advertised on television, in the press and on radio (such as Classic FM).

5.238. An important part of the promotion of classical records which is different from that of pop recordings and partly reflects the longer life of classical catalogue items is development of the 'brand' image of the label. The label may be associated with works of critical acclaim (eg EMI Classics, Deutsche Grammophon, Hyperion) or with budget product (Naxos, Music For Pleasure). Record companies may seek to associate themselves with classical events or institutions (eg Glyndebourne, the Royal Opera House and the South Bank Centre).

Expenditure on marketing and promotion

5.239. According to the BPI, total advertising expenditure by record companies and retailers increased from £42.1 million in 1991 to £47.7 million in the following year. Marketing expenditure by the majors increased from 14.7 per cent of gross sales (17.8 per cent of net sales) in 1989 to 17.7 per cent of gross sales (22.3 per cent of net sales) in 1992 (see Table 8.6). This was partly in response to the decline in sales over this period. The estimate for 1993 shows a decline to 15.9 per cent of gross sales (19.9 per cent of net sales). The majors told us that over 80 per cent of their marketing and promotion expenditure is on new releases.

Future developments

5.240. The record companies told us that the main developments likely to affect the industry in the next ten years are related to technological developments in the supply of home entertainment.

5.241. In the shorter term it is likely that the record industry in the UK will follow the developments that have already been taking place in countries such as Japan and the USA. The CD is becoming, and may continue to be, the principal carrier, not only for music, but also for video, games and information. The introduction of two new audio-only digital carriers—Philips' DCC and Sony's MiniDisc system—represents the attempts by these companies to introduce alternative digital carriers to consumers. One of these may succeed as there appears to be a requirement for a portable digital format to replace the analogue cassette.

5.242. The traditional core business of the record companies, the production and sale of copies of recordings, may begin to be replaced by other means of distributing music. For example, digital broadcasting by satellite or cable is currently under development. The ability to 'compress' multiple signals to be carried by fibre optic cables will mean that households will be able to receive a wide range of specialist radio and television stations, catering for a variety of musical tastes. For example, a service called Digital Cable Audio Services which can deliver more than 30 channels of digital audio transmissions of original sound recordings through the consumer's hi-fi system is already operating in the USA and Time Warner Entertainment is developing a 'Super Highway' project in the USA where fibre optic cables carry 500 channels of digital home entertainment services. Consumers may even be able to select the specific recordings they wish to hear. They may substitute listening to radio broadcasts for the purchase of records or make home recordings of broadcasts. There are implications for the flow of income to rightsholders, the incidence of piracy, and the role of the retail sector.

5.243. New technologies are likely to allow delivery of music as part of multimedia (ie film, video, music, information, communication) in a physical format such as the CD or via broadcast media. There are currently in various stages of development at least 12 multimedia 'platforms', including CD-I and CD-ROM, for which music programming will be an integral part of the software offering.

5.244. The ownership structure of the major record companies means that links are growing between the music, entertainment, media, communications, information technology and consumer electronics industries. Apart from EMI all the large companies in the music industry are parts of international corporations with extensive interests in one or more of these sectors.

5.245. The record companies told us that it is extremely unlikely that in the next ten years the physical distribution of product will disappear completely, given the perceived consumer benefits associated with the packaging and tactile qualities of the object (portability, durability, and convenience). Nevertheless it seems likely that the balance between physical and non-physical distribution will change and that direct access via satellite and cable systems will assume a much greater importance.

248336 I

6 The retail market

Contents

Background

6.1. The expansion of the UK music industry in the late 1970s and early 1980s was reflected in a growing retail trade, which almost doubled in value between 1985 and 1989 (see Table 5.3). This was followed by a recession in the industry which was more marked than the general economic recession (see paragraphs 5.8, 5.9 and 5.36). The retailing of recorded music in the UK has become increasingly concentrated in recent years. By 1992 some 55 per cent of retail sales were made by four businesses (W H Smith, Our Price, Woolworths and HMV), the first two of which were under common control. As far as we are aware, this is a higher level of concentration than occurs in any other major country (see paragraphs 6.72 to 6.80 for a comparison with other countries).

Types of outlet

6.2. Recorded music is now sold in many different kinds of retail outlets—often as part of an entertainment section which also includes videos and computer games. These outlets range from specialist 'superstores' offering more than 100,000 items of CDs, cassettes and vinyl product to petrol stations with one or two racks of cassettes and CDs. The products are sold both over the counter and via direct mail businesses such as record clubs (often referred to as music clubs) and mail order catalogues.

6.3. Retail outlets in this market may be classified as follows:

(a) specialist multiples;

(b) non-specialist multiples;

124

(c) independent specialists (mainly single units, but including some chains);

(d) non-traditional outlets; and

(e) mail order/record clubs.

Table 6.1 gives estimates of the number of outlets in categories *(a)* to *(c)* (ie outlets selling over the counter (OTC)) for 1984, 1988 and 1992. It has not been possible to estimate accurately the total number of outlets in category *(d)*, but it is almost certainly significantly greater than the total number of outlets in categories *(a)* to *(c)* combined.

TABLE 6.1 **Numbers of retail outlets selling records**

Retailer type	1984 (Nov)	1988 (Mar)	1992 (Aug)	Percentage changes		
				1984–1988	1988–1992	1984–1992
Specialist multiples						
HMV	37	58	84	+57	+45	+127
Our Price	93	203*	335*	+118	+65	+260
Virgin Retail	37	100*	13*	+170	-87	-65
Total specialist multiples	167	361	432	+116	+20	+159
Non-specialist multiples						
W H Smith Retail	260	277	297†	+7	+7	+14
Woolworths	896	803	781	-10	-3	-13
J Menzies	110	112	170	+2	+52	+55
Boots	275	263	251	-4	-5	-9
Other multiples‡	316	319	319	+1	0	+1
Total non-specialist multiples	1,857	1,774	1,818	-4	+2	-2
Independent specialists§						
Large¶	375	437	126	+17	-71	-66
Medium¶	673	792	347	+18	-56	-48
Small¶	1,159	763	648	-34	-15	-44
Total independent specialists	2,207	1,992	1,121	-10	-44	-49
Other outlets¤	N/A	N/A	N/A	N/A	N/A	N/A

Source: BPI Handbook compiled from Gallup data, and information from suppliers.

---

*70 smaller stores, shown above as belonging to Virgin Retail in 1988, were acquired by Our Price in that year.
†336 according to BPI, but 39 of these do not sell reference products.
‡Includes Littlewoods department stores, Asda and Tesco supermarkets, Martins and Forbuoys newsagents, and EUK's Chart Stop outlets.
§Includes some chains, eg Tower Records, Sam Goody, Andys.
¶Large = 1,000+ units per week; medium = 500 to 1,000 units per week; small = 100 to 500 units per week.
¤There are a large number of 'non-traditional' outlets, eg petrol stations, newsagents, convenience stores, ethnic shops, most selling fewer than 100 units per week. This sector is understood to have expanded in recent years. Its size is uncertain but has been estimated by some in the industry to contain as many as 10,000 outlets.

6.4. Changes over time in the numbers of outlets selling records, as shown in Table 6.1, are only a rough guide to developments in the range of choice facing consumers. In recent years most chains have tended to increase the average size of their music stores or the space in their stores that is devoted to records. For example, HMV's average store size increased by almost two-fifths between 1988 and 1993.

Specialist multiples

6.5. This segment of the market currently comprises HMV, Our Price and Virgin Retail, the first of these being part of the THORN EMI group. Our Price is owned by W H Smith, which, through a joint venture, is also a 50 per cent shareholder in Virgin Retail (but see footnote to paragraph 3.16). For these businesses, recorded music is the principal product sold, though video cassettes are increasingly important, together with other entertainment products, especially computer games.

125

6.6. The number of outlets belonging to these chains has greatly increased since 1984, with most of the increase occurring in the period to 1988. We have been told that 1985 was a particularly important year for the music market, with music retailers starting to move to prime high street locations, and with major expansion begun by HMV and Virgin Retail. In 1988 many of the smaller Virgin stores were acquired by Our Price. Specialist stores vary greatly in size and therefore in the range of records which they can offer for sale. Most Virgin outlets are superstores. HMV's outlets range very widely in size from its flagship store in Oxford Street to much smaller outlets, although all of HMV's newer stores are large. Our Price stores are smaller on average than those of HMV and Virgin Retail and offer a narrower range of records.

6.7. Only the superstores are able to accommodate most of the record companies' very large product range. There is therefore considerable competition among record companies to place products in the smaller high street stores. We have been told that products receiving promotional support from record companies, including co-operative advertising between record company and retailer, stand a higher chance of being stocked and prominently displayed, reflecting the anticipated effect on demand of promotion and advertising.

Non-specialist multiples

6.8. The growing importance in recent years of high street multiple retailers in recorded music is similar to other retail markets. The main non-specialist chains are W H Smith, Woolworths, John Menzies and Boots. W H Smith and John Menzies have substantially increased the numbers of their outlets selling records since 1984. The number of Woolworths stores selling records has declined since 1984 but the prominence given by Woolworths stores to this business and the space devoted to it have increased. Other multiples selling records include newsagents such as Martins and Forbuoys, and supermarkets (a fast-growing sector) such as Tesco and Asda. While sales of recorded music through multiples account for a major share of total sales of recorded music, they usually account for only a fraction of the total range of goods available in these retail outlets. The range of recorded music offered depends more on the floorspace devoted to music than on the size of the store. For many of the non-specialist chains (including Boots and Menzies) recorded music is not regarded as a core product, and is only sold in the larger branches.

6.9. The range of reference products offered by the non-specialist multiples is significantly narrower than that of the specialist chains. Both Woolworths and W H Smith stores tend to have a relatively narrow range, even when compared with the average Our Price store. Table 6.2 shows how outlets of the different chains vary in terms of the numbers of line items stocked.

TABLE 6.2 **Estimated range of reference product line items stocked by retailers**

Retailer	Line items
HMV	10,000–160,000
Virgin Retail	50,000–100,000
Tower	50,000–100,000
Our Price	10,000– 30,000
Woolworths	1,000– 4,000
W H Smith	5,000– 20,000

Source: Retailers.

6.10. Offerings tend to be concentrated on fast-moving titles, typically chart items and compilations and, increasingly, budget-priced items, the range being adjusted by each business to its perceived customer profile. Some concern has been expressed by record companies that further concentration of record retailing in such non-specialist stores could limit consumers' ability to choose from the full repertoire of record company catalogues.

Independent specialists

6.11. Record companies have emphasized to us the importance of independent specialists for the breaking of new artists. However, the expansion of chains (specialist and non-specialist) in recent years has been at the expense of independent specialist retailers, who usually occupy locations less favourable than those of the chain-owned stores and do not have their buying power.

6.12. The number of independent specialists fell by almost half between 1984 and 1992. The pattern of reductions, however, has changed over the period. Between 1984 and 1988 the number of large and medium specialist retailers rose quite strongly, though this was offset by an even greater fall in the number of small specialists. During 1988 to 1992, however, for much of which period the UK economy was in recession, there were very large falls in the numbers of large and medium-sized specialists (especially the former, which faced the most direct competition from the chains, both in terms of price and breadth of offerings). Numbers of small specialists fell much less in this later period. We were told that this was because they tend to occupy market niches, specializing in particular music genres (dance, hard rock, classical etc) in which they are less vulnerable to competition from the chains.

6.13. Although the number of independent specialists has declined in recent years, some new ones have entered the market. Interesting developments include the entry in 1990 of Musicland (the largest US retailer) with its Sam Goody brand of record stores, with ten outlets. It is too early to judge how the US retailing formula of the Sam Goody stores, which compete particularly against Our Price, will fare in the UK. Another major US retailer, Tower Records, entered the UK market in 1985 and currently has four superstores. Tower, which is a direct competitor to Virgin Retail and HMV, now seems firmly established and continues to expand, if slowly.

Non-traditional outlets

6.14. Recorded music is also sold in a wide variety of outlets regarded by the industry as 'non-traditional'. These include convenience stores, corner shops, airports, ferries, motorway service stations and petrol stations. We were told by several parties that the number of such outlets, and the importance of sales through them, has increased considerably in importance in recent years. The principal suppliers to such outlets, usually on a rack-jobbing basis, are EUK and Pic-a-Tape, though there are many small suppliers. Because this segment of the market is so fragmented, there are few statistics available for it. However, our discussions with suppliers suggest that there might be up to 10,000 individual outlets, a large proportion of which would be very small, selling fewer than ten items per week.

Mail order and record clubs

6.15. Direct mail has increased its share of the recorded music market in recent years. Within this segment, we were told, mail order business has been flat, while that of record clubs, accounting for the majority of direct mail selling, has grown quite strongly.

6.16. Record clubs, of which Britannia Music is by far the largest operator, followed by BCA's Music Direct, recruit members as customers and supply them from a select list of titles. Items supplied are usually popular mainstream albums obtained from leading record companies, usually after an agreed interval following the initial release date. This is generally six months, though it can be a longer or shorter period. If, for instance, a record company wishes to run a special sales campaign for a record it may well wish to delay its release to a record club.

6.17. Record clubs' marketing strategy is to persuade their members, by attractive initial offerings, to commit to a minimum level of purchases. We were told that the average record club customer tends to be somewhat older, and from a higher socio-economic category, than the average OTC record purchaser.

6.18. Unlike retail shops, the whole of the country is the catchment area for a record club. Advertising is national and a proportion of a record club's custom will be from purchasers who are either unable, or do not find it convenient, to buy from local shops.

6.19. Conventional mail order companies tend to be much smaller operations. Some companies, such as Reader's Digest, market their own compilations, not available OTC. Others offer customers their expertise in obtaining out-of-stock or rare titles.

Market shares

6.20. The OTC retail sector for recorded music is currently estimated to account for 88 per cent of total retail sales of recorded music. Of OTC sales, 59 per cent are currently accounted for by five businesses. Of these, W H Smith and Our Price are members of the same group.

6.21. The rest of the retail sector consists of mail order businesses and record clubs. Sales through mail order and clubs are more concentrated, 63 per cent of this segment being accounted for by a single company, Britannia Records. Table 6.3 gives estimates of retail market shares in 1991 and 1992.

TABLE 6.3 **Retail market shares (by value)**

		per cent
Retailer	1991	1992
W H Smith	8.3	8.1
Our price	19.0	18.5
Virgin	2.7	4.2
HMV	11.8	13.5
Woolworths	14.1	15.0
Boots	3.1	3.0
Menzies	2.0	1.9
Tower	1.9	2.1
Other OTC retailers	26.4	21.5
Britannia music	7.0	7.7
Other mail order/clubs	3.7	4.5
UK total	100.0	100.0
UK total (£ million)	1,036.5*	1,020.5*

Source: MMC, based on BPI and company information.

*Excluding VAT.

6.22. The total size of the national retail market is estimated by BPI based on information from various sources. Market shares of individual retail businesses were calculated by relating their estimates of their own sales to the BPI total market estimate. On this basis it appears that W H Smith and Our Price, taken together, had a little over a quarter of the UK retail market in 1992.

6.23. Other major shares were held by Woolworths (15 per cent), HMV (13 per cent) and Britannia Music (8 per cent). A large share of the sector is accounted for by 'other OTC retailers', comprising a mixture of smaller multiples, independent specialists and non-traditional outlets.

6.24. We have not attempted to estimate market shares on a regional basis, although there are significant regional variations in market shares. John Menzies, for instance, is relatively more important in Scotland and the North of England than on a national basis, and W H Smith has a larger share in the South than in the North of England. On an even more local basis, consumer choice of retail outlet may be more limited in smaller towns where the large specialist stores do not operate.

How retailers compete

6.25. There are a number of ways in which retailers compete with one another, and we have been told that there are important differences in how they concentrate their efforts:

(a) *Price.* Records tend to be discretionary purchases, which are sensitive to changes in consumer income. However, a number of retailers said that demand for records is fairly insensitive to price, in that a general price reduction would not result in a large increase in demand. They also believed that consumers are sensitive to price differences between retail outlets for the same product. This has led to a high level of retail price competition, which has intensified during the past three years, especially for popular records. Chart products are usually sold at prices £1 or more lower than those of catalogue items, and retailers continually monitor local competition to ensure that they can respond quickly to price cuts by competitors. An example of such competition is Woolworths' 'Street Value' scheme which guarantees to refund differences in price on chart products bought more cheaply elsewhere. While price competition is most evident for records in the charts ('chart product'), many retailers conduct periodic price campaigns, often supported by record companies. Multiples such as Woolworths, Our Price and W H Smith Retail lay particular emphasis on their price competitiveness, though some small independents also do so, relying on low operating costs to make this an affordable strategy. Non-traditional outlets often emphasize price in a different way, by selling a small selection of chart or 'greater hits' product and catering for impulse buyers.

(b) *Wide range of stock.* This is a strategy pursued by specialists like HMV and Virgin Retail, and large independents such as Tower. Breadth of stock nowadays extends to videos and computer games, in addition to records. Among records, by far the greatest space is devoted to rock and pop music, although there is usually also a classical section. A version of this strategy is pursued by many small independent retailers who specialize in particular music genres, such as dance, jazz or classical, or in a particular format such as vinyl. Such specialization makes possible a considerable depth of choice for the consumer favouring the specialism on offer.

(c) *Quality of service.* Both large and small specialists employ trained staff with detailed product knowledge, an advantage not easily available to retailers for whom music is only one of many products or whose range is relatively narrow. Retailers such as HMV and Virgin Retail invest heavily in staff training.

(d) *Location.* The outlets of the leading retail groups tend to have prime high street locations, while other retailers (typically smaller independents) tend to be less favourably located. Such locations will, of course, have a relatively high cost.

(e) *Ambience.* Much effort is expended on making stores attractive to the browser. Many large stores have multiple video screens, up-to-date racking, display posters and listening pillars, where customers can sample selected records. Smaller independents can be at a disadvantage in this dimension of competition.

Formats

6.26. Paragraph 5.21 referred to the decline of vinyl records, especially albums. The main reason for this decline has been the reduced attractiveness to consumers of vinyl compared with cassettes and CDs. Vinyl records have also become harder to find, as a consequence of two separate trends. The first has been the declining proportion of albums released on vinyl (13 per cent in 1992, compared with 33 per cent in 1989). The second has been the commercial decision by major retailers, following reduced demand for the format, either to cease stocking vinyl (eg W H Smith, Woolworths and John Menzies) or to cut back on the retail space given to it (HMV, Our Price, Virgin Retail). Table 6.4 shows the distribution of sales of singles and albums by all formats and by type of retailer in 1992.

TABLE 6.4 **Sales of singles and albums by format and retailer type, 1992**

Volume of sales by retailer, per cent

	Specialist multiples	Non-specialist multiples	Independent specialists	Total
Singles				
7" singles	20.8	23.3	55.9	100
12" singles	23.2	3.6	73.2	100
Cassette singles	38.6	33.4	28.0	100
CD singles	28.9	21.5	49.6	100
Total singles	28.1	20.9	51.0	100
Albums				
LPs	37.8	5.4	56.8	100
Cassettes	34.6	48.3	17.2	100
CDs	40.8	35.8	23.5	100
Full-price	38.8	37.8	23.4	100
Mid-price	41.2	35.0	23.8	100
Budget	22.0	64.4	13.6	100
Total albums	37.7	39.6	22.7	100

Specialist chains: HMV, Virgin, Our Price.
Non-specialist multiples: Menzies, W H Smith, Boots, Woolworths.

Source: BPI Handbook: Gallup data.

Notes:
1. This table does not include sales made through non-traditional outlets.
2. Percentages may not total to 100 because of rounding.

6.27. Table 6.4 indicates the importance of independent specialist retailers in the sale of singles (in all formats except cassette) and their much smaller role in the sale of albums. Among multiples, the specialist multiples sell many more singles, and fewer albums, than do the general multiples. These figures reflect the importance of specialist retailers, whether independents or chains, but especially the former, for the introduction of new product to the market. Independent specialists are particularly important for launching new dance records, but they are also important for rock and pop. Table 6.4 also shows the disproportionate importance of independent specialists in the sale of vinyl albums and the negligible album sales of this format made through general multiples.

Access to retail outlets for record companies

6.28. In order to sell their products, record companies must be able to place them before the public. Although in principle this could be done by direct marketing (and, in fact, this is the method chosen by large companies such as Reader's Digest or Time Life for their special compilations), the essential requirement is access to retail outlets. We have been told that non-specialist outlets are more concerned with stocking records whose sales are assured (either as a result of past success or because of current promotional expenditure by record companies) than with taking risks with unknown artists or products. We were told that the growth in importance of non-specialist multiples could therefore make it more difficult for small record companies to promote unknown artists by arranging wide distribution on a speculative basis. Even with specialist chains, the narrower range stocked by smaller stores—for instance Our Price—means that stocking will be highly selective.

6.29. Superstores, and, in general, the outlets of specialist multiples, will normally try to hold a very wide range of product and thus provide many small independent producers with a shop window. Even they, however, make buying judgments on individual releases, both at Head Office (in placing a record on the stock guideline list) and at the local store buyer level. There are also many specialist stores willing to try out new product, with individual stores often specializing in a particular music genre, so that it will normally be possible for a small company at least to reach a niche audience with a new product.

130

6.30. For companies trying to reach a mass market, however, it is necessary to achieve chart entry. Apart from products which manage to catch the public's attention without major promotion by the record company (perhaps when a prominent disc jockey gives them a lot of airtime), considerable marketing expenditure may well be necessary, as well as widespread retail distribution. Small record companies advertise their products in the trade press (eg *Music Week*) and consumer press (eg *Melody Maker* and *New Musical Express*) and can place product in specialist stores. However, they are unlikely to be able to afford co-operative advertising or to have the associated relatively easy access to shelf space in non-specialist retailers. In practice these difficulties have not prevented independents from continuing to survive in the market and accounting for a substantial proportion of successful new product.

Relationship between retailer and supplier

6.31. The business of the supplier (usually the distribution department of a record company but sometimes an intermediary) is to supply each retailer with the range of stock which the retailer believes will meet his customers' requirements. Such stock must also be supplied only in the quantities demanded by the retailer and only at the time that it is required.

6.32. Most retailers, whether independents or chains, deal with a number of suppliers, each responsible for processing orders for the products of one or more record companies. Actual delivery to stores has been delegated by major record companies to Securicor—see paragraph 5.206. With each of these suppliers the retailer will have negotiated a contract, indicating the normal terms of business, including any discounts and allowances for returns. Extra discounts may be negotiated on a case-by-case basis at the request of the retailer. There will also be arrangements for normal and special deliveries, arrangements for ordering and reordering stock, and agreed response times.

6.33. Record companies will generally provide information on the range of products available, new releases and special promotions, while the retailer will be responsible for deciding the size and frequency of orders. Some retail businesses which lack expertise in the recorded music business hand over some of these functions to a wholesaler, or a rack-jobber. Woolworths is exclusively supplied by EUK,[1] which also services other multiple retailers (eg Asda) and a large number of non-traditional outlets.

6.34. Stores are generally supplied on an individual basis by distributors—that is, the responsibility for warehousing and breaking bulk is undertaken by the distributor, even in the case of multiple chains (by contrast with other retail sectors, such as grocery, where final distribution is generally undertaken centrally from the chain's warehouse). Though ordering and reordering is done by individual stores, which usually communicate directly with the record companies, decisions concerning the products to be stocked, and their pricing in the store, are usually taken centrally in the case of non-specialist multiples. Specialist multiples generally allow local stores full discretion on stocking and some discretion on pricing. The wholesaler TBD is commonly used as a supplier of last resort in cases where the regular distributor is unable to meet the retailer's needs in the time required.

Promotion

6.35. Both record companies and retailers engage in promotional activity, using all kinds of advertising media. Record companies need to inform the public about the excellence and range of their back catalogue and about current releases. Retailers want to advertise the availability in their stores of a wide range of products from many record companies, but also wish to promote themselves to the public.

6.36. There is a large category of co-operative promotional activity conducted jointly by retailers and record companies, through which a record, or range of records, connected with a particular record company are advertised along with the name of the retail store where they can be purchased.

---

[1] A fellow-subsidiary of Kingfisher plc.

Advertising may take the form of television, radio, specialist press or poster campaigns. Co-operative advertising may take place within the stores themselves, using point of sale advertisements, special racking or window displays supplied by the record company. Campaigns of this nature usually involve advance purchases of additional stock by the retailer in order to meet the enhanced customer demand expected to result from the campaign.

6.37. We have been told that although major co-operative promotional campaigns are more difficult to organize for independent retailers than for chains with many branches, such campaigns, involving groups of independent retailers, do take place, usually through print advertisements.

6.38. Record companies told us that promotional expenditure which used to be shared with retailers is now largely borne by themselves. They often have to pay the retailer for privileged in-store display and for window displays, previously usually supplied free.

6.39. Table 6.5 shows the promotional costs incurred in 1992/93 by one large retailer, and the amount by which they were defrayed by supplier contributions.

TABLE 6.5 **A large retailer's promotional costs and supplier contributions**

	1990/91	1991/92	1992/93
UK promotional costs (£m)	[	Figures omitted.	
Supplier contributions (£m)		See note on page iv.	]
(%)	36	76	85

Source: A UK retailer.

6.40. This retailer told us that it was not necessarily bearing a smaller proportion of co-operative promotion costs than the supplier, since in the earlier years a much larger proportion of total promotion costs had consisted of solus promotion by the retailer. There had been a change in the marketing mix towards co-operative television advertising, and the figures reflected the retailer's success against other retailers in attracting suppliers' limited promotional funds. Whatever the explanation, it is clear in this case that a progressively increasing share of the retailer's total promotion costs (including both solus and co-operative) has been paid for by record companies.

6.41. Retailers also emphasized that such promotions helped all retailers who stocked the records being promoted. Consumers seeing an advertisement would often make their purchases of the records advertised from a retailer other than the one featured in the advertisement.

The balance of power between retailers and record companies

6.42. Record companies and retailers have different roles in the distribution chain, but both have essentially the same goal: to profit from consumers' demand for recorded music. The balance of power between them will help to determine how the profits from recorded music are divided. Record companies told us that the growing concentration of retailing has tilted the balance of power in favour of the retail chains. If increased retail concentration means that a record company knows it has to persuade a small number of chains to stock its product in order to achieve adequate sales, then it is in a weak position to resist demands—for extra discounts or promotional support—from any one of those chains.

6.43. Retailers, on the other hand, stressed to us the implausibility of this scenario. Records, they said, are not commodities, but unique products. There is a non-substitutable demand for a high proportion of them. When such products are in demand, retailers have no choice but to offer them for sale.

6.44. Discounts to the larger retailers do appear to have risen (see paragraph 7.29), together with allowances for returns. On the other hand, W H Smith and Our Price do not co-ordinate their buying arrangements, even though this might be expected to increase their bargaining power. Indeed, we were told that when W H Smith took over Our Price in 1986, some record companies initially reduced the level of price discount given to Our Price to that being given to W H Smith.

6.45. Record companies also pointed to the growing share of co-operative advertising borne by them (see paragraph 6.38) as evidence of the increasing power of retailers. Retailers, however, denied this interpretation. They tended to point out the value to record companies of such promotions and claimed that it was more cost-effective for them to promote records by paying retailers than by undertaking the promotion themselves. Retailers also referred to the risks they take in pre-buying television and press advertising space.

6.46. We were told that record companies tend to have a closer relationship with specialists (including smaller independents) than with non-specialists. A number of record companies have expressed concern about the decline in the number of independent specialist outlets because of what is seen as their crucial role in breaking new artists and launching non-mainstream products. The relationship between record companies and independents is largely conducted on a personal basis by the record companies' field sales representatives, who negotiate one-off deals, supply free stock and point of sales material and keep the retailer in touch with developments, especially new issues. As a result of retailer policy, record company representation with certain multiples—notably Woolworths, W H Smith and Our Price—is normally at headquarters level rather than through the field sales force.

Order processing

6.47. Ordering of records by retail stores is still typically made by telephone. However, orders are increasingly made via computer links (eg EROS, a computer-based reordering system, which is a joint venture by BMG, PolyGram and EMI). A number of respondents have told us that record supply has increasingly gone on to a just-in-time basis, with smaller and more frequent orders being made and retailers taking reduced responsibility for stockholding. We were told that this had led to an increase in record companies' distribution costs. The spread of electronic point of sale (EPOS) systems in chain stores has increased efficiency of ordering and somewhat reduced the risk of retail overstocking.

Imports

6.48. Where there is demand for records which are not available in the UK, Virgin Retail obtains its requirements from the USA and Japan directly and from EC countries through specialist importers. HMV imports directly from the USA and uses specialist importers for its other requirements. The other major retailers obtain all their foreign record requirements from such specialist importers. As for parallel imports (see paragraphs 4.25 to 4.28), W H Smith pointed out the difficulties that would exist if it were to rely on such imports while otherwise operating on a 48-hour ordering cycle. Moreover, such a practice would make for a difficult trading relationship with the UK supplier.

Seasonality of retailing

6.49. Due to the popularity of records as gifts, sales are much higher before Christmas, especially for albums. According to BPI statistics, around 40 per cent of albums (30 per cent of singles) are retailed in the fourth quarter of the year, compared with about 20 per cent (24 per cent) in each of the other quarters. A major retailer informed us that December accounted for almost 21 per cent of annual sales.

6.50. Weekday retail sales are concentrated on Friday (16 per cent of sales) and Saturday (34 per cent).

Product life cycles

6.51. Most releases of new pop recordings by record companies are made at the full-price level (though we have been told of examples of first issues at a mid-price level). Many pop records are deleted a few weeks after issue, if there is only a limited demand for them. However, others are longer lasting, and after some months will become part of the record company's back catalogue, generally priced at the full-price level. Periodically the record company will conclude that there is a significant market for some of its back catalogue at a lower price, and decide to re-release these products, at a mid-price or budget level.

6.52. A number of companies, such as Pickwick and Castle Communications, license back catalogue items from major record companies and reissue them, often as budget-price compilations. Many of these products are sold through non-traditional outlets. Alternatively, record companies may themselves reissue records from their back catalogue at budget prices—for instance, EMI, through its Music for Pleasure brand. In the classical area many new titles are now released at mid-price or budget.

6.53. We were told that product life cycles have less significance for retailers than for producers. Some generalizations are possible, however, for broad groups of records. Singles tend to be demanded (and hence stocked) for a very short period; pop albums can have a longer, but still highly peaked, life cycle; classical records tend to be more consistent sellers. However, within each of these categories there are large variations.

6.54. Retailers try to carry as little excess stock as possible. However, there will always be some stock that cannot be sold at the expected price. From time to time retailers will clear such stock by selling it at sharply reduced prices. Periodic sales will also be held of regular stock, often (though not always) purchased at special campaign rates of discount from record companies. When record companies delete a record, stocks will either be returned to the company (according to agreements on returns) or sold by the retailer at a knockdown price. Some retailers purchase deleted lines for special sale.

Charts

6.55. A number of charts are produced weekly for the UK market. They allow producers and retailers to monitor the degree of sales success being achieved by particular records and inform consumers about which records are currently most popular. Inclusion in a chart can also promote a record or an artist among consumers, resulting in greater sales for the record company and retailers. This role is most important for music with mass appeal, and so the charts are most important for pop music, though we were told that classical charts also have a strong impact on consumers. BMG told us that [*] per cent of the [*] full-price albums it issued in 1993 reached the Gallup Top 100 and that its three top-selling albums accounted for over [*] per cent of its album sales in 1992/93. Sony told us that [*] per cent of its total sales in 1993 were from albums that entered the Gallup Top 75 Album Chart.

6.56. The main charts are as follows:

(a) *The Official Charts.* Based on sales data supplied by a large sample of record outlets,[1] these are regarded as having most credibility in the industry. Separate charts for the Top 75 singles and the Top 75 albums are published in *Music Week* and are widely publicized in the media. Until recently they were compiled by Gallup[2] under a contract from Chart Information Network (CIN), a joint venture between the BPI and a subsidiary of United Newspapers, the publisher of *Music Week*. The album chart is split into an individual artist chart and a

---

*Figures omitted. See note on page iv.

[1]Analysis is based on sample data from 1,500 to 1,600 retail outlets. Data concerning sales of records for the full week are obtained using Epson machines or EPOS terminals which transmit direct to the collection agency.

[2]Since February 1994 the charts previously compiled by Gallup (referred to in paragraph 6.56*(a)*, *(b)* *(c)* and *(f)*) have been compiled by Millward Brown.

compilation chart, the latter containing multi-artist compilation releases. Between January 1993 and February 1994, when it was discontinued, there was a 'Breakers Chart', identifying singles currently outside the Top 40 whose sales had been increasing relatively fast. Some concern was expressed to the MMC about the scope for distortion of the charts, especially by major record companies distributing free records to retail outlets whose sales are taken into account in compiling the charts. The majors denied that it was possible to distort the charts on a consistent basis, and pointed, as evidence, to the success of independent companies' records in the singles charts.

(b) *The Independent Charts* (singles and albums). These are compiled under similar arrangements to the Official Charts, but include only records that have been distributed by distributors other than those of the major record companies (ie mainly Pinnacle). We have been told that major record companies sometimes arrange for those of their own records which they believe would benefit from inclusion in the independent chart to be distributed through Pinnacle.

(c) *Classic FM chart*. This is produced by Millward Brown (previously by Gallup) under CIN auspices and promoted by the radio station Classic FM, whose Chart show is sponsored by W H Smith. The chart is based on national retail sales of classical CDs.

(d) *Network chart*. This is compiled by ERA on behalf of independent radio and is broadcast on Sunday evenings by a number of independent radio stations. The Top 10 is identical to the official singles chart, but selection of numbers 11 to 40 takes account of both retail sales and independent radio airplay.

(e) *Retailers' own charts*. Most major retailers now produce and display their own record charts (or 'hit lists') for albums, and sometimes also for singles. Table 6.6 shows which large retailers display in-house charts (see Appendix 6.1 for examples).

TABLE 6.6 **Type of charts displayed by major retailers**

Retailer	In-house charts		Official charts	
	Singles	Albums	Singles	Albums
W H Smith Retail	Yes	Yes	No	No
Woolworths	Yes	Yes	No	No
Our Price	No	Yes	Yes	No
HMV	No	Yes	Yes	No
Virgin Retail	No	Yes	Yes	No

Source: Retailers.

In-house charts differ from the official charts. Most importantly, unlike the official charts, in-house charts are not exclusively based on actual sales performance. This is not usually pointed out[1] or otherwise made clear to the consumer. In-house charts purport also to reflect the retailer's own forecasts of sales in its own stores. Such charts are likely to include new releases, which would not qualify for an appearance in the official CIN chart since they have no sales record. These charts may also be based on the previous week's sales performance in the retailer's own outlets rather than national sales performance, and thus reflect the customer profile of the retailer in question rather than of the market as a whole. We have also been told that promotional expenditure by a record company can qualify a record for entry to some retailers' charts, or for an improved position on them. There have been cases in the past where record companies have been charged for inclusion of a record in a retailer's in-house chart. We understand, however, that this practice has been discontinued.

(f) There are many other charts compiled for the industry, many (though not all) from Gallup data. Some of these charts (often for particular music genres) may be important in specific niches, but are not considered to rival the official charts as indicators of success.

[1] However, W H Smith's singles and albums charts now indicate that chart positions reflect sales in W H Smith stores or, in the case of new releases, expected sales through those stores.

6.57. The official singles chart is considered in the industry to be of considerable importance. It is the principal focus of the buying public's interest, and inclusion in it serves to increase the public profile of an artist through virtually guaranteed airtime on radio and television and press attention. Retailers are likely to stock and promote chart records ahead of other records, displaying them in the most prominent position with special racking and point of sale advertising.

6.58. Although the official singles chart remains important, its significance is said by some in the industry to have declined in recent years. This may be partly attributed to the overall fall in sales of singles, although the decline was reversed in 1993. A further explanation is the shorter life of chart records—42 per cent of releases reaching the Top 40 of the Singles Chart in 1992 remained there for no more than two weeks compared with 11 per cent in 1988. This has been said to reflect the greater incidence in the charts of dance music, the popularity of which tends to be ephemeral.

6.59. Though singles account for a relatively small proportion of sales (paragraph 5.12), inclusion in the singles chart is often the key to driving album sales. From the viewpoint of the record company, success in the singles chart enhances the company image, increases media interest, increases its ability to attract new artists and helps sales representatives to obtain retail support for new releases. It will also help to direct the company's policy towards album releases.

6.60. In spite of the relative importance of album sales, the official album charts are considered in the industry to have much less importance than the official singles charts. The major retailers place much greater emphasis on their own album charts. Nevertheless, the official album charts retain some importance because of their impact on support, both in the media and the retail sector, for newly-issued singles taken from previously-issued albums. Success in album charts is useful as advertising copy for such subsequent singles (eg 'Taken from Top 10 album'). It can also lead to increased radio exposure and increased retail support (eg priority racking).

Dealer prices, discounts and retail prices

6.61. The prices charged to retailers by record companies for the supply of records, the discounts retailers may be able to negotiate, and retail prices are described in paragraphs 7.4 to 7.44.

International comparisons of retailing

Retail concentration

6.62. We were told that concentration of music retailing in the UK is the highest of any developed country, especially if W H Smith and Our Price are counted as one retailer. Three UK retailers (Woolworths, HMV and Our Price) accounted in 1992 for 47 per cent[1] of the market. We were told that in a small number of markets a single retail buyer (eg FNAC in France and Fona in Denmark) accounted for over 20 per cent of the market, but in such cases the next two largest buyers were much smaller. In the USA, no individual retailer accounts for as much as 10 per cent of the national market, though regional concentration can be much higher.

6.63. One major international record company supplied an international comparison of the share of its sales taken by its top five customers (including wholesalers) in 1993, as follows:

	%
UK	61
Denmark	57
France	50
Japan	49
Germany	37
USA	36
Netherlands	35

---

[1]The largest three buyers in the UK would account for a larger percentage, since EUK, which buys on behalf of Woolworths, also has other customers.

Information supplied by other record companies was broadly consistent with this picture, and certainly with the conclusion that retail concentration in the UK is high by present international standards.

UK and US retailing compared

6.64. The UK and USA are both highly developed markets for recorded music, encompassing a wide range of types of outlet—small independents, multiple chains, and a growing number of large music stores—and including many direct sales channels.

6.65. The US market is very much larger than that of the UK. Unlike the UK, it has a relatively small number of national retailers, many retail chains confining themselves to particular regions. On average, individual specialist music stores in the USA have a narrower product range than in the UK—8,000 line items as against at least 10,000 in the UK.

6.66. In contrast to the UK situation, where primary distribution is generally direct to store, nearly all large US retailers undertake their own final distribution to individual stores, primary distributors supplying product in bulk to the retailer's central warehouse. Intermediate distributors also play a larger role in the US market than in the UK. The result is that individual orders to record companies are on average for a much larger number of units in the USA than in the UK. Reflecting this fact, in the USA (but not in the UK) an extra charge is levied by the primary distributor for delivering product in less than box-lot quantities (25 units per order line).

6.67. The Robinson Patman Act in the USA prevents suppliers differentiating between customers of the same class in the terms on which they will supply them. This is designed to eliminate the exercise of buying power in trading terms, and the kind of individual negotiations over the level of dealer discounts, co-operative advertising, credit days or returns, that occur in the UK could not legally take place in the USA.[1] This has not, however, prevented the multiple chains (either in this or other product markets) from progressively increasing their market share at the expense of independent retailers.

6.68. We were told that, relative to the UK, US retailers benefit from a number of structural advantages: cheaper, more flexible and more productive staff; greater availability of attractive retail space; cheaper and highly flexible property terms.

6.69. The US system of distribution is characterized as 'push-through' compared with a 'pull-through' system in the UK. That is, in the USA initial shipments from record companies of new release stock are very large (up to eight weeks' supply), and retail buyers are given both very long credit (80 to 100 days) and sale-or-return terms (with returns of up to 18 per cent incurring no penalty). By contrast, in the UK, record companies usually aim to supply only two to four weeks of retailers' requirements prior to a major record release,[2] on less generous credit terms (30 days) and with limited returns allowances. Distribution to store is much quicker in the UK, however, so that retailers can get rapid replenishment of stocks for new releases that prove successful.

6.70. In the USA the numbers of purchasers in each segment are much greater than in the UK, and there is also a much greater availability of targeted media in the USA (eg MTV and genre-related local radio stations), so that a narrowly-defined target audience can be addressed relatively cheaply.

6.71. Free stock is a major part of trading terms in the USA with all kinds of retailer and to a greater extent than in the UK.

---

[1]Retailers performing their own distribution might be regarded as a different class from those supplied direct and thus offered distinct terms. The retailer who pointed this out, however, does not itself make such a distinction in its US operations.

[2]If retail sales are good, reordering occurs.

Music retailing in other countries

6.72. While each national retail market has its own peculiarities, we have been told that all have experienced stagnation of music sales. Small independent retailers are losing share to multiple chains and superstores (where planning regulations permit) as well as to other retailers (eg supermarkets), diversifying away from their traditional product business. This decline in numbers of small independents has in most cases (with the USA and Japan as exceptions) been accompanied by a fall in total numbers of outlets. Another common feature is a growing tendency for a number of major retailers, such as Virgin, HMV and Tower Records, to expand their activities beyond their national boundaries and to enter foreign markets. Some characteristics of individual national markets are mentioned below.

Japan

6.73. The special feature of this market is said to be its highly restrictive retailing laws, including the retention of resale price maintenance (RPM) for domestically-sourced product up to two years old (RPM does not apply to imports). This has resulted in the retention by small retailers of an unusually high share of the market. 36 per cent of all outlets are served by the same wholesaler.

Germany

6.74. There has been a severe decline in the number of music outlets—from 15,000 in West Germany in 1975 to 7,000 in Germany as a whole in 1993. The largest single music retailer is Karstadt, a department store. The independent sector is said to be quite strong, with little dominance exerted by major chains. Specialist stores and superstores are slowly making gains. Some German retailers (large specialist chains, department stores and supermarkets) operate central distribution operations for music. We have been told that the larger specialist chains and the superstores stock parallel imports.

France

6.75. Following the transformation of French retailing by the advent of hypermarkets and the rise of specialist superstores there has been a very sharp fall in the number of specialist music outlets. There are now estimated to be around 610 independent retailers in France, compared with some 2,000 in 1978. Specialist superstores account for the largest share of sales of any European territory (30 per cent, against 20 per cent in the UK).

6.76. The largest multiple retailer is FNAC, said to account for almost one-quarter of French music sales, whose large stores stock an average of 80,000 line items. It competes with hypermarkets such as Carrefour and Auchan on new releases, but much less on back catalogue, which hypermarkets do not stock in large quantities. The proximity of Virgin and FNAC stores in Paris has led to intensive price competition.

6.77. In the recession music retailers have become more price competitive. Hypermarkets are the main parallel importers, obtaining chart product from the Netherlands and the UK.

Netherlands

6.78. Record retailing in the Netherlands is quite different from that in the UK, with specialist shops, including independents and chains, accounting for a relatively low proportion of sales (46 per cent in 1992). Record clubs are relatively important, their 19 per cent market share largely accruing to one company, ECI, which is owned by Bertelsmann. This company is said to exert considerable market power. There are approximately 1,000 outlets of sufficient size to be supplied direct by distributors. Very small retail outlets and general shops selling music are supplied by wholesalers.

138

Music is also sold through the music sections of department stores. There is only one superstore (Virgin), located in Amsterdam.

6.79. Virtually all marketing and promotion of artists and releases is done directly by the record companies. There is very little co-operative advertising.

Denmark

6.80. The Danish retailing market is underdeveloped compared with the rest of Europe. There are no music superstores. The market is dominated by electrical goods retailers who also stock music. There are just two specialist chains, accounting for about 10 per cent of the market, an unusually low proportion. There are signs of development in the market, especially from supermarkets, which account for 17 per cent of the market and are increasingly stocking chart product at discounted prices to generate custom. Most music departments and retail outlets are too small to have space for spare stock. The distribution system operates on very quick turnround, with small retailers making very small and frequent orders.

248336   K

7 Prices

Contents

Introduction

7.1. Concern over the prices of CDs was an important factor leading to this inquiry and in this chapter we examine in detail the prices of recorded music in all its formats. We begin by looking at prices in the UK and then compare these with prices in other countries, examining in particular the differential between the UK and the USA since this has been the particular focus of consumer concern about CD prices.

7.2. The final price a consumer pays for a record is made up of the following components:

(a) The price charged by the record company to supply the record to the retailer (or wholesaler). This is based on a list price, known as the *published dealer price*, from which individual retailers are given various discounts and allowances to arrive at a *realized dealer price*.

(b) The margin added by the retailer to arrive at the *retail price* without tax.

(c) Value added tax (VAT).

7.3. We follow this order in examining the prices of records in the UK, beginning with published dealer prices and realized dealer prices before moving on to retail prices. VAT is charged at the standard rate of 17.5 per cent on all records sold in the UK.

Published dealer prices in the UK

7.4. The published dealer price is the wholesale price at which the record company offers to supply retail outlets (there is usually no extra charge for delivery, except in the case of very small orders). It is also the starting point from which any negotiated discounts will be calculated. Prices are specific to particular products, but individual products will normally be priced in a range relating to the type of product.

7.5. These price ranges are defined in terms of the format (single or album; CD, cassette or vinyl) and the price position relative to other items of that format.

7.6. The published dealer price of singles will normally depend only on the format in which it has been produced. However, each album release is placed in a price category (eg full-price, mid-price, budget) for each format. Tables 7.1 and 7.2 show certain recent published dealer prices for the five major record companies for non-classical and classical records respectively, for the main price categories and for each product format.

TABLE 7.1 **Published dealer prices for non-classical records,* September 1993**

£

Albums		Polygram	EMI	Sony	Warner†	BMG	Unweighted average
LP	Mid-price	3.07	3.19	2.97	-	-	3.08
	Full-price‡	5.25	5.13	5.17	5.61	-	5.29
	Deluxe full-price	5.53	5.29	5.35	6.22	5.60	5.60
MC	Mid-price	3.07	3.19	2.97	-	3.35	3.15
	Full-price‡	5.25	4.99	5.17	5.30	5.35	5.21
	Deluxe full-price	5.53	5.13	5.35	5.66	5.60	5.45
CD	Mid-price	5.25	5.04	5.05	-	5.24	5.21
	Full-price‡	7.59	7.56	7.59	7.96	7.59	7.66
	Deluxe full-price	8.15	7.86	8.03	8.21	8.14	8.08
Singles							
LP	7"	1.36	1.20	1.21	1.35	1.35	1.29
	12"	2.49	2.27	2.15	2.50	2.49	2.38
MC		1.36	1.20	1.29	1.35	1.35	1.31
CD		2.59	2.15	2.15	2.59	2.59	2.41

Source: MMC from information supplied by the companies.

*The table shows the main price categories. Some record companies also have a Budget price category.
†Warner increased its prices on 27 September 1993. The table shows the increased prices.
‡Full-price is sometimes called 'standard' price.

248336   K2

£

Albums		Polygram	EMI	Sony	Warner*	BMG	Unweighted average
LP	Budget	2.37	-	-	-	-	2.37
	Mid-price	3.07	3.19	-	-	-	3.13
	Full-price	5.53	5.29	5.17	-	-	5.33
MC	Budget	2.37	-	2.12	2.75	-	2.41
	Mid-price	3.07	3.19	2.97	3.42	3.27	3.18
	Full-price	5.53	5.29	5.17	5.51	5.34	5.37
CD	Budget	3.75	-	3.57	3.93	3.24	3.53
	Mid-price	5.53	5.40	5.05	5.36	4.99	5.27
	Full-price	8.15	8.14	7.59	7.96	7.89	7.95

Source: MMC from information supplied by the companies.

*Warner increased its prices on 27 September 1993. The table shows the increased prices.

Price categories

7.7. The broad groupings shown in Tables 7.1 and 7.2 are those generally acknowledged in the industry.

7.8. *Full-price*, sometimes called 'standard' price, is the bench-mark against which the other categories are defined. Products priced in this category are normally new releases and older recordings which continue to sell well and are perceived as premium products. Products by top stars may be priced in a premium price category known as 'deluxe' full-price which is higher than full-price. Records that are heavily promoted on television might also be released at a premium price known as 'TV' which might be the same as deluxe.

7.9. *Mid-price* is usually set around 60 to 70 per cent of full-price. This category is used principally for older, slower-selling products. These products will normally have been re-released at this price having been deleted from the full-price category, since there was believed to be a residual demand at the lower price. The category might be used for a new release where it is judged that the release would be unlikely to succeed at full-price.

7.10. *Budget-price* is normally around 50 per cent of full-price. Several types of product can fall into this category. New compilations of existing solo artists' repertoire or concept albums with a relatively low brand image which are likely to be sold through non-traditional outlets are often sold as budget items. Some old works by big name artists and less popular works may also be sold as budget items. Many classical recordings, including new releases, sold through all types of outlets also fall into this category. The entry of companies like Tring, specializing in product that attracts minimal royalties, has resulted in prices well below the normal 'budget' level, sometimes referred to as 'super budget'.

7.11. Special pricing arrangements apply to mail order, the bulk of which relates to record clubs. Usually, a distinction is made between the manufacturing price, payable to the supplying record company for goods delivered, and royalties for each unit sold by the record club. The latter are paid quarterly in arrears, to the record company for the copyright in the sound recording and (through the MCPS) to the owner of the music copyright. Prices to record clubs are significantly below ordinary dealer prices to reflect the special conditions of supply to this market segment (see paragraph 6.16).

Variation in price of a recording over time (ie the product life cycle)

7.12. The price of the same recording can change over time as its position in the market-place changes. This is known as the product life cycle (see also paragraphs 6.51 to 6.53). A release at full-price will normally be aimed at the existing fans or purchasers of the current 'fashion'. The product may continue to be successful and sell at full-price for some time. Eventually sales will fall and the record company will then have to decide whether to delete the product from its catalogue or re-release it at a lower price in the hope of achieving further sales.

Variation in dealer prices between companies

7.13. The published dealer prices shown in Tables 7.1 and 7.2 show a degree of variation between companies for each price category. If in each category the dealer price of the company with the lowest price is taken as 100, the most expensive published dealer price in that category is shown in Table 7.3.

TABLE 7.3 **Highest published dealer prices for each price category***

	Full-price	Mid-price	Budget
Cassettes	111	115	130
CD	108	111	121

Source: MMC from information provided by the companies.

*Lowest price for each category = 100, based on Tables 7.1 and 7.2.

7.14. We have described the main price categories. The record companies have told us that they have a considerable array of published dealer prices for each format which partly reflect special characteristics of the recording such as double or triple albums. Some of these prices are shown in Appendix 7.1.

Reasons for price categories

7.15. The price categories reflect a clustering of prices around price points. We were told by the record companies that these price categories have developed over time, through competition between record companies, and through interaction between record companies, on the one hand, and retailers on the other, to become the 'standard' form of pricing in the industry in the UK and in other countries.

7.16. We were told that new releases were priced according to price categories because the demand for individual recordings is highly uncertain. The sales success of a new release cannot be known in advance and in the result varies from album to album for both new and established artists. This uncertainty about likely sales levels, coupled with the great number of new releases, means that it is difficult if not impossible to price each record individually in order to attempt to maximize net revenues in respect of individual albums on the basis of likely demand.

7.17. In addition, records cannot be priced on the basis of costs incurred in the production of an individual recording. There are production costs associated with the manufacture of each unit. Some A&R, marketing and general overhead costs are associated with each recording, but many cannot be. To allocate these costs on a per unit basis would necessitate knowing in advance the likely level of unit sales that the recording will achieve. Even if these could be estimated within reasonable limits it would not make sense to charge a less successful record at a higher price to cover its high unit costs and a successful record at a very low price because its fixed costs could be spread over a larger number of sales. In practice, because sales of individual records are so difficult to predict, successful records have to help recover the costs of unsuccessful records, so the object is to make a return over the company's catalogue taken as a whole.

7.18. The record companies told us that it would also be impractical for the industry to operate a perfect price continuum. It would be costly at wholesale and retail levels and would be confusing for the consumer. In practice record companies price each new release at one of a number of list pricing points and concentrate on competing with other record companies through promotional campaigns and the discounts that they offer on specific releases in order to achieve sales.

Other constraints on pricing

7.19. The record companies told us of a number of factors relating to retailing and consumer behaviour that constrain their pricing decisions and reinforce the price categories described above. For instance, retailers use price bands that reflect dealer price categories. A dealer price reduction within the same price band by a record company is unlikely to result in a lower retail price (see paragraph 7.41).

7.20. A further factor influencing a record company's pricing strategy for new releases is the perception of the public, the retailer, and the artist, that a low price indicates that a recording is a low-quality product, in the sense that the artist is unsuccessful or the recording an old one. The ability of a record company to use low prices as a means of promoting a particular recording is constrained by the need to ensure that the recording is not perceived as a low-quality product since such a public perception would be fatal to the successful development of the artist. Often more established artists secure some contractual control over the pricing of their releases such as a requirement to issue only at full-price.

Format prices

7.21. The same recording will be priced differently according to the format on which it is released. A recording will be offered at broadly the same price on the analogue formats (LP and cassette) but at a higher price on the digital format (CD). On the basis of the prices in Tables 7.1 and 7.2 the published dealer prices of full-price CD albums, whether classical or non-classical, are around 50 per cent higher than the published dealer prices of cassettes or LPs.

7.22. Figure 7.1 shows the UK trade (ie dealer) prices (at 1992 prices) for LP, cassette and CD since 1974. In 1974 the average price of the new format, the cassette, was higher than the average price of the established format, the LP. By 1979 the cassette price had fallen to the same as the LP and since then the prices of the two formats have remained broadly the same.

7.23. When a new format, the CD, was introduced in 1983, its price was above those of the other formats. The record companies told us that this price reflected the costs of production and the judgment that market penetration would be low and confined to classical music 'buffs' who placed a premium on high sound quality. The record companies told us that the prices for analogue formats were extremely low at the time, as a result in part of the fear of increased home taping if prices were seen by consumers as being too high. The average trade price of a CD has been falling in real terms since 1986. The record companies attribute this fall in relative price partly to the fall in manufacturing costs, and partly to the more widespread use of the format for products in lower price categories.

7.24. When the CD was introduced in 1983 its price at wholesale was 2.13 times that of the cassette and LP (see Figure 7.2). The disparity in prices increased to a peak of 3.08 in 1986. However, the ratio has declined from that point and now appears to have levelled out at 1.47. That is to say, CDs are on average 47 per cent more expensive than cassettes.

Reasons for price differences for each format

7.25. The record companies told us about their pricing policies for different formats. The policies of most companies have the objective of maximizing their returns on the copyrights they own. These policies are the same as those operated by record companies generally around the world.

7.26. The manufacturing costs are only a relatively small proportion of the price of each format and most other costs are not format-related. The record companies told us that they price different formats according to the consumers' willingness to pay. The higher price they charge for a recording on CD, relative to the price of the same recording on cassette or LP, reflects the consumers' perception that the CD is a higher-quality product.

144

FIGURE 7.1

UK average trade prices, 1974 to 1992,* LPs, cassettes and CDs

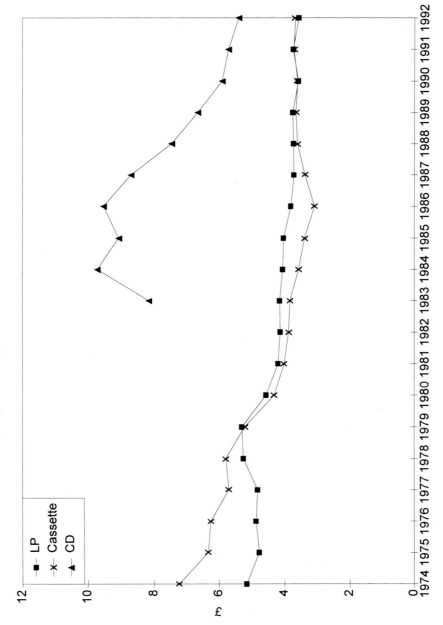

Source: MMC calculations based on BPI data.

*Trade deliveries are defined as sales of records, cassettes and CDs invoiced to dealers and distributors. Values are at 1992 wholesale, do not include VAT and are net of returns and discounts.

FIGURE 7.2

Ratio of CD prices to cassette prices (1992 trade prices*) for years 1983 to 1992

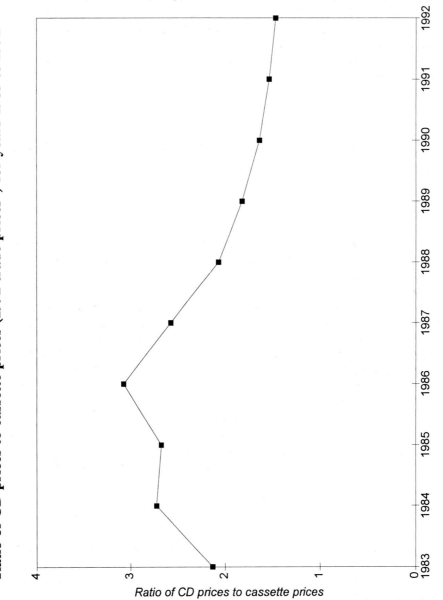

Source: MMC calculations based on BPI Surveys data.

*Trade deliveries are defined as sales of CDs and cassettes invoiced to dealers and distributors. Values are at wholesale, do not include VAT and are net of returns and discounts.

7.27. It is by means of this price discrimination that the record companies aim to maximize their returns, subject to the constraints of the market. They regard the initial high price of the CD in real terms, and relative to the other formats, over the past few years (see Figures 7.1 and 7.2) as normal for a successful technical innovation in a competitive market. Some of the record companies pointed out that price discrimination—setting prices according to the consumers' willingness to pay rather than according to the costs of production—was common practice in industries based on the exploitation of copyright.

7.28. In such industries, price discrimination takes place mainly on the basis of the timing of the 'release' of the product in a different form. For example, book publishers generally publish hardback books before the paperback version; films are screened at cinemas before they are released on video or appear on television. In the case of records, all formats are released at the same time. The record companies argued that price discrimination by format had increased the total demand for recorded music by providing simultaneously a range of price and quality to suit different consumers' requirements. This had resulted in greater sales, lower unit costs, and therefore lower prices, and a greater variety of products.

Realized dealer prices (ie prices to retailers and wholesalers after discounts)

Discounts

7.29. Prices paid to the record companies by retailers and wholesalers will depend on any discounts to published dealer prices which may be negotiated by individual retailers and wholesalers. The main types of discount are as follows:

(a) *File discounts.* These are discounts which apply to all purchases made by a customer. They sometimes vary by format, and sometimes between albums and singles, but they do not vary from one recording to another. They depend on the bargaining power of the individual retailer and therefore, generally speaking (though not usually in any formal sense), on the amount of business in question. They are principally obtained by the retail chains—to a smaller extent by the independent retailers—and are mostly in the region of 6 to 8 per cent. File discounts have risen in recent years. [
Details omitted. See note on page iv.
] CDs used to attract a lower rate of file discount, but there has been a tendency to equalize the rate given to all formats. This equalization process has taken the form of a small fall in the discount for LPs and cassettes with a larger rise in that for CDs.

(b) *Incentive discounts.* Small additional discounts, usually paid retrospectively against the achievement by the retailer of particular sales targets, are sometimes offered.

(c) *Campaign.* Record company distributors conduct special sale campaigns, for instance prior to the Christmas season. Extra discounts of 15 per cent and upwards are offered to all customers on all product, including back catalogue, to encourage retail stocking. Similar discounts may be offered from time to time on specific product lines selected for promotion.

(d) *Discounts* may be offered for new releases, both singles and albums. This is a major source of discounts for independent retailers, reflecting their important role in breaking new artists, and also recognizes the fact that they do not generally receive file discounts. It is usual to offer greater inducements to retailers to stock a new artist's album than a release from a major artist. Discounts will greatly vary between products, depending on the record company's view as to how much particular records need to be 'pushed'.

(e) Wholesalers will normally receive a special discount in recognition of the work which they save the principal distributors in terms of breaking bulk and serving individual retailers.

7.30. Table 7.4 gives a matrix of the percentage value of average discounts on albums given by major record companies to their principal customers in 1992/93.

TABLE 7.4 **Average discounts on sales of albums, 1992/93**

per cent

	BMG	EMI	PolyGram	Sony	Warner
W H Smith	[				
Our Price					
Virgin Retail					
HMV					
Average					
Other multiple retailers	*Figures omitted. See note on page iv.*				
Other retailers					
All retailers					
EUK					
TBD					
Other wholesalers					
All wholesalers				]	

Source: Record companies.

[*Details omitted. See note on page iv.*]

7.31. [

Details omitted. See note on page iv.

]

7.32. We have been told by both retailers and record companies that the benefits obtained by independent retailers in the form of free stock and one-off discounts on new releases are of the same order as those obtained by the larger retail chains. Indeed, one major record company calculated that in a recent year benefits given by it to major retailers,[1] as discounts, free stock, returns allowances and promotion contributions, came to the equivalent of a 13.7 per cent discount from dealer prices, compared with 14.2 per cent for independent retailers, in a similar calculation.

Returns

7.33. All record companies allow retailers full credit on the return of faulty products or those which have been wrongly delivered. On occasion, at the record company's discretion, it may allow a retailer to return product that has been accidentally overstocked. In addition, special 'privilege' returns allowances are individually negotiated. These may allow the retailer to return certain percentages of the value of stock of particular formats, or different percentages of turnover of albums and singles, or a certain percentage of overall turnover. Record companies inform retailers each quarter of their current privilege entitlement.

7.34. Stock sold in the course of a particular record company's campaign may attract a higher percentage of allowed returns. In the case of products merchandised through a television campaign, the record company may allow sale-or-return conditions on initial orders in order to encourage retailer stocking. In the case of retailers supplied by rack-jobbers, all product is supplied either on a sale-or-return or a sale-or-exchange basis.

---

[1]Excluding Woolworths, because of the special distribution arrangements of that business.

7.35. We were told that the system of privilege returns is expensive for record companies. The product returned is often unfit for resale, and has to be laboriously checked in order to ascertain whether this is the case. Thus, from the record company's viewpoint the privilege returns allowance is as expensive as an ordinary discount (though it has the compensating commercial advantage to the record company of persuading the retailer to accept a higher level of stocks than it might otherwise take). From the retailer's viewpoint it reduces the risk of overstocking. While it is difficult to judge the monetary value to the retailer of this, we were told by one record company that W H Smith had negotiated away its privilege return entitlement in exchange for an increase in its file discount.

Free records

7.36. Part of record companies' discounts, especially on singles, are given in the form of free stock to retailers. This can take a variety of forms ranging from simply the supply of records for no charge to allowing an extra record for every ten bought. Free copies of new releases are distributed widely, as part of promotional activities, especially when the record company is trying to break a new artist. In view of the importance of getting new issues into the charts, record companies usually try to supply free singles (and, to a much smaller extent, albums) to those outlets that are willing to stock single records that are not in the charts and whose sales qualify for inclusion in the totals from which the charts are compiled. This is an important source of dealer price discounting to independents. W H Smith, J Menzies and Woolworths told us that they do not allow their outlets to accept free stock, because the practice distorts sales and stock records. Our Price said that it discourages its outlets from doing so, but that some of its stores are forced to participate in order to compete with local independents who can price singles keenly because they receive free stock.

Retail prices in the UK

7.37. Retailers purchase records at realized dealer prices and add their retail margin and VAT to arrive at the retail price charged to consumers.

7.38. As with dealer prices, retail prices are often categorized by certain retailers as 'full', 'mid' and 'budget'. There is usually also a special 'chart' price category and some retailers have a 'campaign' category used periodically for promotions. For an individual retailer each of these categories usually covers a range of prices, and different retailers appear to recognize different ranges. Table 7.5 compares the ranges currently recognized by different retailers.

TABLE 7.5 **Some retailer price ranges**

£

	W H Smith	Our Price	Woolworths	Virgin
Chart				
CD	11.99–13.99	10.99–13.99	10.99–13.49	11.99–12.99
Cassette	7.99– 9.99	7.99– 8.99	6.99– 8.49	8.49
Full-price				
CD	12.99–14.99	10+	9.49–14.99	13.49
Cassette	8.99–10.99	6+	6.49– 9.99	9.49
Mid-price				
CD	7.99–9.99	4–9.99	6.99–8.99	8.99–9.49
Cassette	4.99–6.99	3–5.99	5.49–5.99	5.99
Budget				
CD	3.99–5.99	to 3.99	4.99–5.99	3.99
Cassette	2.99–3.99	to 2.99	2.99–3.99	-

Source: Individual retailers.

7.39. Retailers told us that the prices that they charge are largely based on the dealer price structure. Typically, we were told, retailers work on a required percentage gross margin and apply this to the average realized dealer price, with the result being rounded to the nearest pricing point.[1] The required margin depends on various factors, including the product format, whether the product is chart or catalogue material, and whether the product is being specially promoted, for instance via a campaign. Retailers' gross margins on recorded music in 1992 ranged from 29 to 36 per cent (see Table 8.17).

7.40. Retailers usually offer records that are currently in the charts to customers at discounted prices (usually at least £1 to £2 lower than the normal 'full' price). We were told that this was mainly because a retailer who did not do the same would lose business to others. One retailer told us that it had tried to sell chart product at the full price but had lost too many customers to justify continuing the policy. We were also told that a reduction in retail price does not always increase sales volume sufficiently to maintain the retailer's gross margin. Later, often when the record leaves the charts, the retailer raises the price to the undiscounted full-price, until such time as the record is either deleted or re-released by the record company as a mid-price or budget recording.

7.41. Retailers said that record companies were aware of how published dealer prices were translated into retail prices; where record companies had a view on the desirable retail price for a product, they would set their dealer price at a level that would generate that retail price. The method by which retailers set prices also acts as a constraint on price-setting by the supplier since it discourages small price reductions which will not be translated into retail price reductions. For example, a retailer might resell all CDs bought in at between £7.58 and £7.85 at £13.99, or resell all those bought in at between £7.90 and £8.20 at £14.99. Consequently, a record company that reduces its price to the retailer risks finding itself at the bottom of the same price band as before with the result that the retail price will be unchanged. By the same token, a record company may increase its dealer price and find that the retail price remains the same. Therefore the record company has little incentive to make price reductions within the same price band.

Retail price movements

7.42. Table 7.6 shows the movement in the 'typical' price of full-price record albums, by format, since 1987, compared with the movement of the RPI over the same period. These typical prices have been estimated by the BPI.

TABLE 7.6 **Typical retail prices* of full-price albums with adjustments for inflation**

	LPs/cassettes			CDs		
		Price indices			Price indices	
	Typical retail price	*Current prices*	*Adjusted for inflation†*	*Typical retail price*	*Current prices*	*Adjusted for inflation†*
	£			*£*		
1987	6.49	100.0	100.0	10.99	100.0	100.0
1988	6.99	107.7	102.6	11.49	104.5	99.7
1989	7.99	123.1	108.8	11.99	109.1	96.5
1990	8.49	130.8	105.7	11.99	109.1	88.1
1991	8.99	138.5	105.7	12.49	113.6	86.7
1992	9.49	146.2	107.6	12.99	118.2	87.0

Source: Derived by MMC from BPI data.

*Not average prices. 'Typical' prices are estimated by the BPI, on the basis of knowledge and information supplied from its members.
†For RPI, see Table 5.3.

[1]Usually £x.49 and £x.99, though £x.29 and £x.79 are also sometimes used (as is the case with HMV).

150

7.43. Table 7.6 indicates that typical retail prices of full-price albums in vinyl and cassette formats have been identical since 1987, increasing on average about 1.5 percentage points per annum faster than general inflation over the period to 1992. Much of the increase occurred in 1989, at the height of the consumer spending boom, when the 'typical' album price is judged by the BPI to have leapfrogged a major price point (rising from £6.99 to £7.99 in one year). Typical prices of CDs, which Table 5.4 shows have progressively accounted for a rapidly increasing share of total sales, fell quite steeply over the period. Between 1988 and 1991 in particular, the typical price of a full-price CD fell by 13 per cent in real terms. In 1987 the cost of a typical full-price CD album was over two-thirds higher than that of the same album in one of the other formats; by 1992 it was little more than one-third higher.

Record club pricing

7.44. Record clubs normally sell products which are regarded in the industry as full-price products; only occasionally are lower-price recordings featured. Prices quoted to record club members are comparable with OTC retail prices for catalogue product, and OTC retail prices are monitored for this purpose. The clubs' method of marketing (for example, an initial offer of five items for the price of one, with subsequent half-price or free offers once a contracted minimum number of full-price items has been purchased) means that average prices paid by club members are relatively low.

International comparisons of retail prices

7.45. In this section we examine the difference in the retail prices of recorded music between the UK and other countries. Unless otherwise specified we have converted prices into pounds sterling using the average exchange rate for the period 1 July 1993 to 31 December 1993 (£1=$1.50).

7.46. Public concern about CD prices in the UK was an important factor leading to this inquiry. A Report of the National Heritage Committee of the House of Commons in May 1993[1] concluded that CD prices in the UK were too high. This conclusion seemed to rest in part on evidence from Consumers' Association, and in part on the NHC's own examination of prices, which indicated a significant difference between the price of CDs in the UK and the price of CDs in the USA.

7.47. The Consumers' Association, in its evidence to the NHC, reported a survey it had carried out of the retail prices of five titles in five shops in London and in eight shops in New York in January 1993. It concluded that at the then current exchange rate (February 1993: £1=$1.45) CD prices in the USA were 70 per cent of those in the UK (ie UK prices were 43 per cent higher than those in the USA). No allowance was made for differences in sales taxes between the UK and the USA (paragraph 3, page 22, NHC Report).

7.48. The NHC was aware of the importance of allowing for sales tax differences but no survey of retail prices was carried out. The price information presented in its report was based on the dealer list prices charged by record companies and their suggested retail prices (Tables 1 and 2, page viii, NHC Report).

7.49. With the 'Full-Line' category treated as the standard, this evidence showed that a CD was selling at a suggested retail price of $13.99 in the USA (£8.91 at the current exchange rate (May 1993: £1=$1.57)) and a suggested retail price of £11.74 in the UK. Our understanding is that these prices did not include sales taxes in either country. On this basis CD prices in the USA were 76 per cent of those in the UK (ie US prices were 24 per cent lower than those in the UK).

7.50. This evidence provides a very limited basis on which to draw conclusions about comparative prices. We have therefore sought to establish the extent of price differences between the UK, the USA and other countries for ourselves. We commissioned BMRB International to undertake a survey

---

[1]See footnote to paragraph 2.2.

of retail prices in a number of countries. Our intention was to carry out as full a survey as possible within the limits of the time and resources available to us. We wished to include a greater number of titles and retail outlets than were covered in the NHC Report.

The BMRB survey of international prices

7.51. The survey that BMRB carried out for the MMC is described in Appendix 7.2. In the following section we briefly consider the method used before we turn to the results of the survey.

The method of surveying retail outlets

7.52. In its survey, BMRB compared the retail prices of pre-selected full-price album titles, for both CD and cassette formats, across five countries (UK, USA, Germany, France and Denmark) in September 1993. A follow-up survey of the same titles covering the UK and the USA was carried out in November 1993 as a check on the main survey (see Appendix 7.3).

7.53. Information was collected from a sample of retail outlets in each country (250 in the UK and the USA, 100 in each of the other countries) covering three types of full-price sales, namely *(a)* eight specified pop titles, *(b)* chart titles in the various national album pop charts, and *(c)* three specified classical titles. Mid-price and budget titles were not included in the survey for the following reasons. First, full-price titles, including both chart and catalogue, account for most sales. In the UK, sales of full-price album titles accounted for about 80 per cent of sales by trade value in 1993 (see Table 5.11). Secondly, we considered that any anti-competitive activity might well affect full-price sales rather than mid-price or budget sales. Thirdly, the definitions of price categories vary between countries and records may be released in different categories in different countries. We also had to take into account the costs we could reasonably incur in an exercise of this kind.

7.54. Since artists vary widely in their international appeal, each of the eight pop titles was by an artist with an international following. They were drawn from short-lists provided by the major record companies. However, national tastes differ and the selected artists' records may not have achieved the same popularity in each country. Nor, at the time of the survey, were the selected artists' records necessarily at the same point in their life cycle. In order to overcome these problems, three chart titles were also selected: those in positions 1, 5 and 10 in the various national charts at the time of the survey. Titles in the charts account for a significant proportion of sales. Titles appearing in the UK Top 40 in 1992 accounted for about 36 per cent of sales (paragraph 5.149).

7.55. As explained in Appendix 7.2, there were problems with collecting prices for the classical titles and no results are presented below. With the help of the major record companies and a number of major retailers we carried out a further exercise to provide some comparison of prices of classical titles in the UK and the USA (see paragraphs 7.68 to 7.70).

7.56. The major record companies were invited to comment on the survey method. They had three main reservations. First, the number of titles in the sample was too small to provide a representative picture of the relative prices of full-price titles. Secondly, a comparison based on weighted average prices between countries might be more meaningful than a comparison based on full-price titles only. Thirdly, the geographical coverage of the survey in the USA focused on large urban locations and excluded smaller urban locations and rural areas in which a considerable proportion of the US population lives (see paragraphs 12.51 to 12.63).

Sales taxes and exchange rates

7.57. In presenting the results we have recognized two important factors that affect a comparison of prices between countries but are outside the control of companies selling goods—sales taxes and exchange rates.

7.58. Sales taxes vary between countries and affect the retail price. In order to ensure that the results are presented on a comparable basis any sales taxes included in the retail prices obtained in the survey have been removed. All results are presented on a without-tax basis.

7.59. Exchange rates fluctuate over time for a number of reasons. It is important to ensure that the exchange rates used to convert prices to a common currency are not the result of a short-term fluctuation. The exchange rates used in the conversion of prices in local currencies to pounds sterling are the average of rates from July to December 1993 (see Appendix 7.2, paragraph 53).

7.60. The results of the BMRB survey are presented below along with other relevant evidence. Given the importance of this aspect of our study, prices in the UK and the USA are considered first. We then turn to the comparison of prices in the UK and other European countries.

Price comparisons between the UK and the USA

Evidence from the BMRB survey

CDs

7.61. The average prices for the selected full-price pop CD titles without tax and adjusted to pound sterling equivalents in each country covered in the survey are presented in Table 7.7. For ease of comparison the results are presented as indices in Table 7.8. For the average of all the pop CD titles, US prices were lower than the UK by 8 per cent and the average prices in the other countries were higher than those in the UK. The US price is lower than the UK price for each title, with the difference varying from 13.3 to 0.3 per cent.

TABLE 7.7 **Average price of full-price popular CDs***

£

	UK	USA	France	Germany	Denmark
Pre-selected titles					
Diva—Annie Lennox	11.78	10.21	13.03	11.23	11.38
Soul Dancing—Taylor Dayne	11.25	9.83	12.87	11.19	11.58
Zooropa—U2	10.22	9.85	11.88	10.72	11.33
Keep the Faith—Bon Jovi	10.56	10.53	12.81	10.89	11.50
River of Dreams—Billy Joel	10.33	9.45	11.74	10.75	11.28
Timeless—Michael Bolton	11.26	10.45	12.41	11.00	11.28
Tubular Bells II—Mike Oldfield	11.71	10.21	12.71	10.92	11.25
What's Love Got To Do With It?—					
Tina Turner	10.06	9.67	13.12	11.15	11.44
Column average (pre-selected titles)	10.90	10.03	12.57	10.98	11.38
Chart titles					
Number 1	10.34	9.69	11.89	10.82	11.34
Number 5	10.15	9.49	12.48	10.59	11.24
Number 10	10.43	9.65	12.04	10.81	11.49
Column average (chart titles)	10.31	9.61	12.14	10.74	11.36

Source: BMRB survey.

*Prices are without taxes.

†Exchange rates used for conversion to pounds sterling are the average of those prevailing between 1 July and 31 December 1993.

153

TABLE 7.8 **Indices of average prices of full-price popular CDs**

	UK	USA	France	Germany	Denmark
Pre-selected titles					
Diva—Annie Lennox	100.0	86.7	110.6	95.3	98.6
Soul Dancing—Taylor Dayne	100.0	87.4	114.4	99.5	102.9
Zooropa—U2	100.0	96.4	116.2	104.9	110.9
Keep the Faith—Bon Jovi	100.0	99.7	121.3	103.1	108.9
River of Dreams—Billy Joel	100.0	91.5	113.6	104.1	109.2
Timeless—Michael Bolton	100.0	92.8	110.2	97.7	100.2
Tubular Bells II—Mike Oldfield	100.0	87.2	108.5	93.3	96.1
What's Love Got To Do With It?—Tina Turner	100.0	96.1	130.4	110.8	113.7
Average (pre-selected titles)	100.0	92.0	115.4	100.8	104.4
Chart titles					
Number 1	100.0	93.7	115.0	104.6	109.7
Number 5	100.0	93.5	123.0	104.3	110.7
Number 10	100.0	92.5	115.4	103.6	110.2
Average (chart titles)	100.0	93.2	117.8	104.2	110.2

Source: BMRB survey.

7.62. The average prices for chart titles are shown in Table 7.7 and are expressed in index form in Table 7.8. Chart titles are normally the subject of promotions and discounts. This accounts for the generally lower level of prices for chart titles than for catalogue titles. The results for the chart titles show the same pattern of price differences as those for the pop titles although the average price difference between the USA and the UK is slightly less (6.8 per cent). Figure 7.3 shows the variation in average prices for pre-selected and chart CD titles for the UK and the USA.

Cassettes

7.63. As regards cassette prices the general pattern is similar to that for CDs (see Tables 7.9 and 7.10). However, the price differences between UK and the USA are generally greater for cassettes than for CDs (12.9 per cent lower in the USA for pre-selected titles, 8.1 per cent lower for chart titles).

TABLE 7.9 **Average price of pre-selected full-price popular cassettes***

	UK	USA	France	Germany	Denmark
Pre-selected titles					
Diva—Annie Lennox	8.11	6.79	7.62	7.62	9.21
Soul Dancing—Taylor Dayne	7.91	6.67	7.55	7.79	9.33
Zooropa—U2	7.07	6.39	7.62	7.77	9.28
Keep the Faith—Bon Jovi	7.30	6.80	7.83	7.85	9.48
River of Dreams—Billy Joel	7.12	6.17	7.32	7.71	9.30
Timeless—Michael Bolton	7.76	6.79	7.77	7.72	9.29
Tubular Bells II—Mike Oldfield	8.13	6.80	7.91	7.72	9.27
What's Love Got To Do With It?—Tina Turner	7.24	6.42	8.58	7.96	9.33
Column average (pre-selected titles)	7.58	6.60	7.78	7.77	9.31
Chart titles					
Number 1	7.03	6.31	10.47	7.75	11.41
Number 5	6.56	6.34	7.74	·7.60	9.28
Number 10	7.27	6.51	7.65	7.61	9.32
Column average (chart titles)	6.95	6.39	8.62	7.65	10.00

Source: BMRB survey.

*Prices are without taxes.

†Exchange rates used for conversion to pounds sterling are the average of those prevailing between 1 July and 31 December 1993.

FIGURE 7.3

Average retail prices* of CDs, September 1993

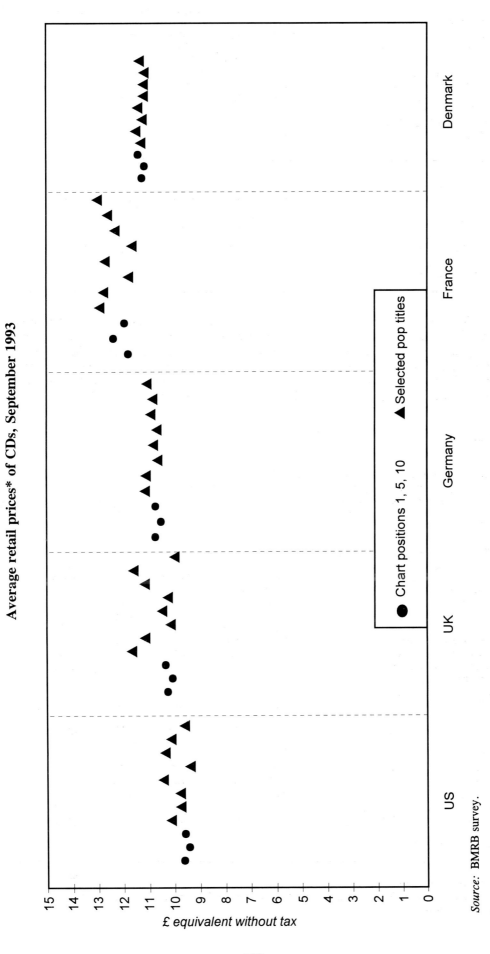

Source: BMRB survey.

*Unweighted average of retail prices without tax.

155

248336   L

TABLE 7.10 Indices of average prices of full-price popular cassettes

	UK	USA	France	Germany	Denmark
Pre-selected titles					
Diva—Annie Lennox	100.0	83.7	94.0	96.4	113.6
Soul Dancing—Taylor Dayne	100.0	84.3	95.4	98.5	118.0
Zooropa—U2	100.0	90.4	107.8	109.9	131.3
Keep the Faith—Bon Jovi	100.0	93.2	107.3	107.5	129.9
River of Dreams—Billy Joel	100.0	86.7	102.8	108.3	130.6
Timeless—Michael Bolton	100.0	87.5	100.1	99.5	119.7
Tubular Bells II—Mike Oldfield	100.0	83.6	97.0	95.0	114.0
What's Love Got To Do With It?—					
Tina Turner	100.0	88.7	118.5	109.9	128.9
Average (pre-selected titles)	100.0	87.1	102.6	102.8	122.8
Chart titles					
Number 1	100.0	89.8	148.9	110.2	162.3
Number 5	100.0	96.6	118.0	115.9	141.5
Number 10	100.0	89.5	105.2	104.7	128.2
Average (chart titles)	100.0	91.9	124.0	110.3	114.0

Source: BMRB survey.

7.64. The result of taking a simple average of all the pre-selected and chart titles shown in Tables 7.7 and 7.9 is that full-price pop CD prices in the USA were 7.7 per cent lower than in the UK and cassette prices were 11.7 per cent lower.

7.65. The follow-up survey of the same titles, which was carried out for a more limited number of retail outlets in the UK and USA in November 1993, confirmed the evidence of the first survey (see Appendix 7.3).

Other evidence

7.66. This section concentrates on the full-price category to provide a comparison with the results of the BMRB survey. To allow comparability, all prices are without tax and converted to pounds sterling at the exchange rates used for the BMRB results.

Classical prices

7.67. In order to obtain detailed information on pricing of classical recordings on sale in CD format in the full-price range, we carried out a small survey of pricing among five major retailing groups covering sales of 53 selected classical titles in December 1993. Titles were selected from lists of classical recordings provided to us by each of the five major record companies.

7.68. After eliminating observations for recordings which were no longer selling in the full-price range in the UK or in the USA, it was possible to compare the prices for 53 separate recordings (see Appendix 7.4). In the case of 27 of these, identical recordings were on sale in at least two of the store groups in both the UK and the USA, while the other 26 provided examples of price quotations for recordings of similar status which were available in one or other country but not both.

7.69. Using an exchange rate of £1 = $1.50, the average price in the UK without tax came to £12.32 for the 27 items available in both countries, while the corresponding average US price was £9.74. Averaging over all the recordings in the survey which were available in either or both countries produced little change to this picture, with corresponding figures of £12.37 and £9.71 respectively.

7.70. On average US prices for full-price classical recordings available in both countries were 20.9 per cent lower than those of the UK on a without-tax basis. One price marking, which was very common in particular stores in the US section of the survey, was $14.99 dollars (without tax)—

equivalent to £9.99 (without tax). In the UK two price markings were frequently noted, and these were £14.99 (including tax) and £14.49 (including tax), equivalent to £12.76 (without tax) and £12.33 (without tax) respectively.

Sony retail price survey

7.71. Sony carried out a survey of the prices of a sample of its own pop and classical titles in the UK and the USA (see Appendix 7.5). On the basis of weighted average prices of full-price titles, prices in the USA were 5.8 per cent lower than in the UK for CDs and 11.0 per cent lower than in the UK for cassettes. These price differences are of the same order as those found in the BMRB survey.

7.72. On the basis of weighted average prices of all the Sony pop CD titles surveyed (ie both full-price and mid-price), the price in the USA was 5.6 per cent lower on average than that in the UK. On a similar basis, the prices of Sony's pop cassette titles in the USA were 10.9 per cent lower on average than those in the UK.

7.73. As regards Sony's classical titles, the average price of full-price CDs was 12.9 per cent lower in the USA compared with the UK and the average price of full-price cassettes was 18.3 per cent lower. For all classical CD titles, on average US prices were found to be 7.0 per cent lower than the UK prices, and for all classical cassette titles average US prices were 14 per cent lower.

7.74. Since this survey was confined to the titles of a single company, the results may not be representative of the overall price differences between the USA and the UK.

Summary of UK/US retail price comparisons

7.75. Table 7.11 brings together the evidence of retail prices in the UK and the USA from the BMRB survey, the MMC's survey of classical titles, and Sony's survey. The Sony evidence supports the findings of the BMRB survey that the prices of full-price pop CDs and cassettes are lower in the USA than in the UK and that the difference in price is greater for cassettes than for CDs. As regards classical titles, the findings of the Sony survey of average prices for full-price titles support the findings of the MMC's classical survey that the prices of full-price titles are lower in the USA than in the UK.

TABLE 7.11 **Percentage by which US retail prices are lower than those of the UK**

Study	Full-price				All prices categories			
	Non-classical		Classical		Non-classical		Classical	
	CD	Cassette	CD	Cassette	CD	Cassette	CD	Cassette
BMRB	7.6	11.6	-	-	-	-	-	-
MMC (classical)	-	-	20.1	-	-	-	-	-
Sony	5.8	11.0	12.9	18.3	5.6	10.9	7.0	14.0

Source: MMC from market research survey and company information.

Possible reasons for the difference in the prices of recorded music in the USA and the UK

7.76. A variety of factors will affect the supply and demand conditions for goods and hence their prices. To the extent that these factors differ between countries so will the prices ruling in each market. On the demand side, the record companies told us that willingness to pay for recorded music differs between the USA and UK because of differences in income levels, and tastes, and the available range and relative prices of alternative leisure products.

248336 L2

7.77. On the supply side the record companies provided us with a number of reasons why the prices they charged retailers may be lower in the USA than in the UK (see paragraphs 12.64 to 12.69). These concerned differences in the services provided to retailers, in the level of royalties, and in the relative size of the markets which led to economies of scale in the USA that reduced the cost and risk of supply. As for the retail margin, record retailers and others directed our attention to various comparisons of retail prices in the USA and the UK such as the report by McKinsey & Co.[1] A number of reasons have been suggested why the cost of retailing may be lower in the USA. These include lower property costs and higher staff productivity.

7.78. All these speculations are prompted by the perceived differences in prices between the USA and the UK. They hinge on the exchange rate selected. We now turn to the problems this poses.

International price comparisons and the exchange rates

7.79. When comparing prices of recorded music in different countries, an exchange rate must be chosen to convert those prices into a common currency. The difficulty of choosing any one exchange rate for price comparisons in a period of floating exchange rates is that the exchange rate fluctuates frequently over time. Local prices of recorded music are set at intervals to reflect conditions in the national market, so changes in exchange rates do not affect them. Hence, merely because of exchange rate fluctuations, a price comparison on one date may give apparently quite different results from one on another date. Thus if the exchange rate used in comparing the prices identified in the BMRB study was £1 = $1.75, we would have concluded that the prices of full-price pop CDs were some 20 to 22 per cent lower on average in the USA. Alternatively, if the exchange rate we had used was £1 = $1.25, US prices would be 10 to 12 per cent higher than UK prices.

7.80. The importance of the choice of the exchange rate used in making price comparisons is clearly demonstrated in the examples given above. The difficulty of settling on any one rate is shown by Figure 7.4 which presents the sterling/dollar exchange rate since 1983. Sterling depreciated to a low of £1 = $1.12 in the first quarter of 1985 and subsequently rose to a high of £1 = $1.94 in the fourth quarter of 1990. Following its exit from the ERM in September 1992, sterling depreciated against the dollar, though the rate in 1993 was fairly stable around £1 = $1.50.

7.81. Under a system of floating exchange rates, differences in the rates of inflation between countries may be expected, over a number of years, to be reflected in the movements of exchange rates, the latter in effect to compensate for the former. Similarly, over a number of years exchange rates can be expected to adjust to other factors, such as differing monetary and fiscal policies, which also cause them to fluctuate. But at any point in time it is impossible to know whether the current exchange rate is approaching a sustainable long-term rate between two currencies. We have attempted to overcome this as far as possible by using the average £/$ rate for the second half of 1993. A six-month average will eliminate short-term fluctuations in the exchange rate and would be a reasonable rate for use by those contemplating the importation of goods.

7.82. Some record companies suggested to us that, given the difficulties of using market exchange rates, we should use purchasing power parities (PPPs) in making international price comparisons. The PPP between two countries is the 'exchange rate' at which the expenditure weighted price of a basket of goods would be the same in the two countries. In effect, use of PPPs stands the exchange rate problem on its head. Instead of trying to choose an appropriate rate for international price comparisons from observations of market exchange rates, it compares directly what consumers can buy with their money in different countries. The exchange rate which equalizes the prices of the same basket of goods in each country can then be used for making international price comparisons. As estimates of PPPs between the UK and the USA have for the last few years been consistently below the market exchange rate, making price comparisons using market exchange rates inevitably leads to the conclusion that goods are more expensive in the UK.

7.83. There are no generally accepted PPP exchange rates available. There are various different estimates of PPPs, each of which provides different results. EMI suggested to us three alternative PPP

---

[1]See *Financial Times*, 28 June 1993, page 7.

FIGURE 7.4

UK/US exchange rate, 1983 to 1993

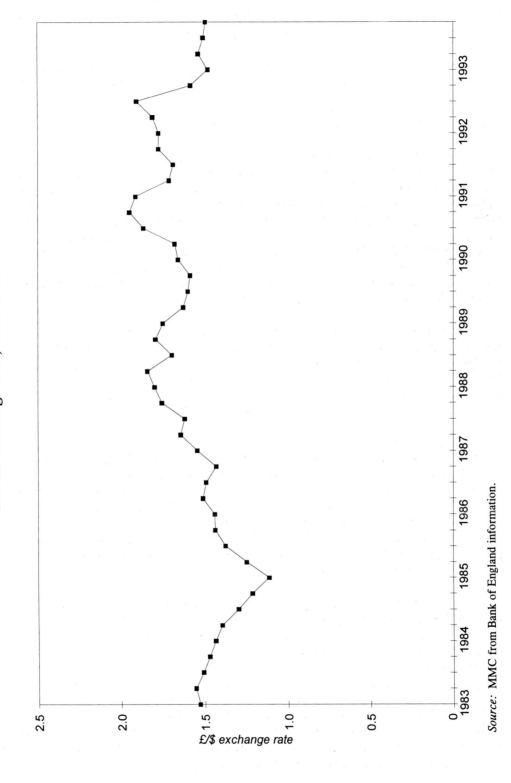

Source: MMC from Bank of England information.

measures: the purchasing power parity estimate made by Goldman Sachs in June 1993 (£1 = $1.32), the estimates made by Credit Suisse First Boston in the quarter to September 1993 (£1 = $1.21), and the rate derived from the *Economist* newspaper's 'Big Mac' index in April 1993 (£1 = $1.27). The first two of these estimates build on the work of the Organization for Economic Co-Operation and Development (OECD) which provide measures of PPPs, derived by directly comparing the domestic price of a homogenous basket of goods and services in each country, for particular bench-mark years. The OECD figures are adjusted to exclude non-tradeable goods and services and extrapolated forward using price index data in each country. The 'Big Mac' index is based on the local price of the McDonalds Big Mac hamburger around the world. The Big Mac is often described as the perfect universal commodity, produced locally in over 50 countries. As such it is said to reflect local labour and space costs and the general price level of consumer goods around it.

7.84. Clearly, using the PPP exchange rates rather than market exchange rates would provide a very different picture of the relative prices of recorded music in the UK and USA. For example, if we use the Goldman Sachs estimate of the PPP (£1 = $1.32) then for the eight pre-selected pop titles in the BMRB survey, the average price in the USA is some 4.6 per cent higher than the price in the UK. This compares with the US prices being some 8 per cent lower if the average of the market exchange rate of the second half of 1993 (£1 = $1.50) is used.

The Management Horizons study of price differentials for other products

7.85. In order to assess whether the relative pricing of recorded music in the UK compared with the USA was out of line with the relative prices of other products on sale in those countries we arranged for a survey to be carried out by the specialist retail consultancy, Management Horizons. It carried out a price audit on a predefined carefully matched basket of manufactured leisure goods, sold in similar price ranges to recorded music, in late November and early December 1993. An account of the Management Horizons survey is included in Appendix 7.6.

7.86. On average, US prices (without tax and using the same exchange rate as the BMRB survey) across the items in the survey were 8 per cent lower than the corresponding goods in the USA. For ten of the fourteen product groups covered in the survey, on average US prices were between 3 and 14 per cent lower than the UK.

Comparisons between the UK and other European countries

7.87. We turn now to consider the evidence provided by the BMRB survey of retail price differences between the UK and other European countries.

CDs

7.88. The results of the BMRB survey show that for full-price pop CDs, average retail prices were higher in each European country (see Tables 7.7 and 7.8). The prices of the pre-selected titles were on average 0.8 per cent higher in Germany than in the UK, 4.4 per cent higher in Denmark, and 15.4 per cent higher in France. As regards individual pop titles, the UK price was lower than the price in France for each title, but the UK had higher prices for four titles compared with those in Germany and higher prices for two titles compared with those in Denmark.

7.89. The results for chart CD titles show the same pattern but the price differences were greater. Prices were 4.2 per cent higher in Germany, 10.2 per cent higher in Denmark, and 17.8 per cent higher in France.

Cassettes

7.90. As regards full-price pop cassette prices, compared with the UK prices were higher in France, Germany and Denmark (see Tables 7.9 and 7.10). While the difference in average cassette prices between the UK and Germany is similar to that for CD prices, the difference between the UK and France is narrower (2.6 per cent), and between the UK and Denmark, wider (22.8 per cent).

7.91. There was a similar pattern for average chart prices but the differences between the UK and the other countries were greater. The average cassette price for chart titles in Denmark was 43.9 per cent higher than in the UK.

Comparison of format prices

7.92. A comparison of average CD prices and average cassette prices for each country shows that in the UK the average CD price is about 44 per cent higher than the average cassette price. In the USA the average CD price is 52 per cent higher than the average cassette price (see Table 7.12). Of all the countries in the survey France had the greatest difference (62 per cent) and Denmark the lowest (22 per cent).

TABLE 7.12 **Comparison of average CD and cassette prices (all pre-selected popular titles)**

	UK	USA	France	Germany	Denmark	Total
Average CD price (£)	10.90	10.03	12.57	10.98	11.38	11.17
Average cassette price (£)	7.58	6.60	7.78	7.77	9.31	7.81
Percentage by which average CD price is greater than average cassette price	43.8%	52.0%	61.6%	41.3%	22.2%	43.0%

Source: MMC from BMRB survey.

International comparisons of dealer prices

7.93. Here we look at the prices that record companies charge retailers for the supply of records. We did not carry out a study of realized dealer prices but we obtained information from a number of sources. This information is described below. To facilitate comparison, all prices have been converted into pounds sterling using the average exchange rate for the period 1 July to 31 December 1993.

Information from Understanding and Solutions

7.94. Understanding and Solutions (USS), a market research consultancy specializing in media and entertainment, has provided us with estimates of weighted average realized dealer prices charged by record companies for CDs in a number of countries. It estimated that in 1992 average prices were lower in the UK than in the USA and the other major European countries apart from Spain (see Table 7.13).

TABLE 7.13 **Understanding and Solutions, estimates of average realized dealer prices, 1992**

In pounds		Indices (UK = 100)	Total
UK	5.52	UK	100
USA	6.09	USA	110
France	7.55	France	136
Germany	6.30	Germany	115
Denmark	7.22	Denmark	130
Sweden	6.24	Sweden	113
Norway	6.50	Norway	117
Italy	6.48	Italy	117
Spain	4.99	Spain	90

Source: MMC, using information provided by USS.

Note: Calculations are based on average exchange rates from July to December 1992.

Information from PolyGram

7.95. PolyGram calculated its average realized dealer CD prices for 20 countries for the year ending September 1993. It also calculated average realized prices by price category (ie full-price, mid-price and budget). The results are set out in Appendix 7.7.

7.96. In respect of all price categories for both popular and classical CDs, the average realized dealer price in the USA was 12 per cent higher than that in the UK. The UK had the third lowest average price (after Sweden and Germany) of all the countries covered in the study. Japan had the highest average price (Table 7.14).

7.97. Taking all popular CDs, the average price was 12.0 per cent higher in the USA compared with the UK, and for classical CDs the average US price was 13.0 per cent higher compared with the UK.

7.98. Taking each price category separately, price differences between the USA and the UK show considerable variation. For full-price popular CDs, the average realized dealer price in the USA was 7 per cent lower than that in the UK. For full-price classical CDs, the US price was 5 per cent higher than that in the UK. At mid-price, prices for popular and classical CDs were higher in the USA than the UK by 10 per cent and 5 per cent respectively. Differences were greatest in the budget category where US prices for popular CDs and classical CDs were some 250 per cent and some 25 per cent greater respectively than those in the UK.

7.99. Relative to all the countries in the study, PolyGram's average realized dealer prices in the UK were amongst the lowest in the full-price and mid-price categories and were the lowest in the budget category.

7.100. PolyGram acknowledges that its results may not be representative of the market as a whole because of differences in the proportions of records sold by PolyGram in each price category compared with the overall market in each country. In the UK PolyGram sells an average of 38 per cent of units below full-price while the other majors only sell an average of 22 per cent in this way.

Information from EMI

7.101. EMI calculated average realized dealer CD prices for its total sales in the countries covered by the BMRB survey, and also in the Netherlands and Japan, in the year ending 31 March 1993. The UK had the lowest average realized dealer price for CDs.

7.102. As regards the UK and the USA, the average realized dealer price of CDs in the UK was 12.2 per cent lower than in the USA. This finding is broadly in line with that of PolyGram (paragraph 7.96) and may again reflect the greater number of budget sales in the UK compared with the USA. EMI did not provide results by price category.

Summary of evidence

7.103. Table 7.14 summarizes the information on the overall realized dealer prices of CDs from USS, PolyGram and EMI. It shows that on the basis of these estimates, the average realized dealer price in the UK was lower than that in the USA and most other countries.

TABLE 7.14 **Average realized dealer prices* of CDs**

Source		UK	USA	France	Germany	Denmark	Japan	Sweden
USS	Average price (£ sterling)	5.51	6.09	7.54	6.35	7.22	-	6.24
	Indices (UK = 100)	100	110	136	115	130	-	113
PolyGram	Average price (£ sterling)	5.37	6.06	6.82	5.23	6.01	9.56	4.83
	Indices (UK = 100)	100	112	127	97	111	178	89
EMI	Average price (£ sterling)	5.34	6.08	7.54	6.98	6.85	8.81	-
	Indices (UK = 100)	100	114	141	131	128	165	-

Source: MMC, based on information supplied by USS, PolyGram and EMI.

*Based on average sterling exchange rates for the period July to December 1993.

7.104. The other major record companies also provided some information on their realized dealer prices in different countries. This showed a similar pattern of price differences between countries.

7.105. While the use of dealer price information from individual record companies allows some international comparison of dealer prices, it suffers from a number of drawbacks. First, the pattern of sales of one company might not be representative of the pattern for the overall market in a country. Secondly, differences in average realized dealer prices between countries partly reflect the different mixes of full-price, mid-price and budget-price records sold in each country. The proportions of albums sold at full-price, mid-price and budget-price in the UK in 1993 were 70 per cent, 14 per cent and 16 per cent respectively (Table 5.11). For classical records the proportion of mid-price and budget albums was 55 per cent (Table 5.14). We do not have the comparable percentages for the USA but we understand from the record companies that the percentages for mid-price and budget categories taken together are lower than in the UK. This is supported by the US/UK figures in Table 7.14 which show lower average prices for the UK.

8 The financial performance of the principal suppliers of recorded music

Contents

Introduction

8.1. In this chapter we summarize the financial information we obtained from the principal companies involved in the supply of recorded music in the UK. These companies are:

   (a) the five major UK record companies—BMG, EMI, PolyGram, Sony and Warner (the majors);

   (b) four leading independents—MCA, Telstar, Pickwick and Beggars Banquet—and some of the smaller independent companies;

   (c) certain large retailers—W H Smith, Our Price, Virgin Retail, Kingfisher (including EUK) and HMV; and

   (d) the largest record clubs—Britannia, BCA and Reader's Digest.

The five major recorded music companies

8.2. The majors (and MCA, the largest independent) are also the main participants in the international recorded music business. BMG, PolyGram, Sony and Warner are all subsidiaries of overseas companies. EMI's ultimate parent company is located in the UK, but its recorded music business in this country is controlled through the EMI Music headquarters (EMI Music HQ) which is located in New York.

8.3. The businesses of the majors in the UK consist of a number of diverse functions, already described in Chapter 5. Typically these companies finance new recordings and supply and distribute recorded music products in this country. They also license their rights in recordings to other companies both in the UK and overseas. Connected companies manufacture recorded music products or run substantial music publishing businesses. Some of the majors (EMI, Polygram and Sony)

164

distribute some or all of their recordings through separate self-accounting distribution businesses. In addition to the results of the recorded music companies, we obtained separate information on the results of their manufacturing affiliates in the UK.

8.4. All record companies refer to the money they spend on developing new recordings and on advances to artists as A&R (Artist and Repertoire) expenditure. When records are sold or royalty and licence income is received, the A&R costs that are recoupable from artists are either charged against the income arising on the sale of recorded music products or set off against the companies' gross royalty income receipts. Unrecouped or abortive A&R is written off or provided for in the companies' accounts as it is incurred[1] but some of the A&R (net of provisions) may be carried forward in the companies' balance sheets. As well as selling recordings which they have financed (own repertoire), the companies also sell recordings manufactured in the UK but licensed-in from other (usually connected overseas) companies (licensed-in repertoire).

8.5. The UK recorded music companies export very small amounts of finished recorded music products. In order to simplify the information provided, the companies have included these exports and their related costs and profits with the sales of recorded music products sold in the UK. In 1992/93 BMG's direct exports, as a percentage of gross sales, were 0.8 per cent; PolyGram's 3.5 per cent; and Sony's 1.7 per cent. Warner's exports were negligible. EMI's direct exports (excluding Virgin) were 1.9 per cent of net sales. In addition, some of EMI's sales to independent third party customers were exported overseas. For EMI, excluding Virgin, these exports were estimated at 6.8 per cent of gross UK sales of recorded music products.

8.6. The income of the recorded music companies consists of:

(a) sales of own-repertoire records and records of artists of overseas affiliates;

(b) royalties and licence fees from allowing these records to be used for broadcasting and public performances domestically; and

(c) royalties and licence fees from the sales of own-repertoire records mostly by their foreign affiliates.

The main items of expenditure include:

(d) A&R expenditure (dealt with in more detail from paragraph 8.21 onwards);

(e) royalties to artists and holders of copyrights in the music for own-repertoire records;

(f) licence fees to affiliates abroad for the use of their copyrights; and

(g) the general expenses of manufacturing, distributing and promoting records domestically.

8.7. Each of the majors has provided us with information on its inter- and intra-group transfer pricing policies. In this chapter we refer only to those policies that bear most directly upon the results of recorded music companies, ie usually those that apply between the companies and their manufacturing affiliates.

8.8. To simplify our analysis of the results of the recorded music companies, we have divided their activities into three separate categories. These are:

(a) their core business activities;

(b) their non-core activities; and

(c) their non-recorded music business activities.

---

[1] In the tables in this chapter, unless indicated otherwise, both the amounts written off or provided for are shown or referred to together.

Where we deal with the companies' core and non-core activities together, we call these two categories combined the companies' total recorded music business.

8.9. In our core business category are the sale of recorded music in the UK and income from royalties and licence fees less A&R expenditure written off in the accounts. In the non-core activities are recorded music joint ventures; the distribution of recorded music labels other than the companies' own labels (which are part of the core business); joint venture labels in which the company is a participant; and other recorded music activities such as operating recording studios. The non-recorded music business category is any activity such as music publishing which is dealt with in the statutory accounts of the recorded music companies but which lies outside the core business and the non-core activities.

8.10. In their statutory accounts, three of the majors (BMG, EMI and PolyGram) include in turnover their net sales of recorded music products (and other products) and gross royalties and licence fees. Net sales are shown after the deduction of discounts and returns. The other two majors (Sony and Warner) only include net sales of recorded music products (and other products) as turnover. Royalty and licence fee income is dealt with as a separate item under other operating income. Out of the royalty and licence fee income (the gross income) received by the companies, there are amounts due to artists. In their statutory accounts Sony and Warner report this income as a net figure; with sums due to artists being set off against the gross income received. In this report we show royalty and licence fee income gross, with sums due to the artists included in costs. We have adopted this presentation so as to show the full amounts received by the companies and also to present these figures on a uniform basis. We report both net sales and gross royalties and licence fees together under revenue. For the core business we then go on to show the profit before interest and tax (PBIT) as a percentage of total revenue (return on revenue—ROR). Total revenue is the income arising from net sales and gross royalties and licence fees; and PBIT is the sum of the contributions from recorded music products and royalties and licence fees less the A&R written off.

8.11. The companies themselves told us that their preferred measures of profitability are calculated from their profit and loss accounts and the operating statements in their management accounts, as the companies' balance sheets show low or negative capital employed. Consequently return on capital employed (ROCE) calculated from the companies' financial and management accounts is not a relevant indicator of their overall performance. These low or negative figures are shown in Table 8.1 which summarizes the aggregate year-end capital employed of the five majors' recorded music businesses. The reason for these low figures is the very high level of creditors in relation to tangible fixed and current assets. These creditors include the amounts due to artists in respect of royalties. The balance sheets do not include any amounts that reflect the value of the companies' copyrights (see paragraphs 8.33 to 8.43).

TABLE 8.1 **Capital employed in the recorded music businesses of the five majors, 1989 to 1993**

£ million

	1989	1990	1991	1992	1993 estimated
Tangible fixed assets					
Land and buildings	12.6	13.9	13.4	23.8	22.2
Plant and machinery	13.0	16.8	15.0	14.0	17.7
Other	8.4	10.9	10.2	19.4	17.8
Total (A)	34.0	41.6	38.7	57.2	57.7
Current assets					
Investment in artists	46.6	63.5	74.7	105.5	100.1
Stock	11.8	12.0	10.8	10.7	9.0
Debtors	251.0	229.9	192.4	239.3	202.1
Total (B)	309.4	305.4	277.9	355.5	311.2
Less creditors (other than borrowings) (C)	(351.3)	(330.9)	(345.7)	(527.7)	(432.6)
Year-end capital employed (A + B - C)	(7.9)	16.1	(29.1)	(115.0)	(63.7)
Average capital employed*†	(7.9)	4.1	(6.5)	(76.8)‡	(89.4)

Source: MMC from companies' data.

*For 1989, year-end only.
†Chrysalis and Virgin are included for the first time in 1992.
‡Average of opening and closing balance, £72.1 million, plus an adjustment for the Chrysalis and Virgin opening net balances amounting to £4.7 million.
Note: Amounts may not total exactly because of rounding.

8.12. In this section, where aggregate figures are shown for the majors, the years relate to those calendar years in which most of a company's financial year falls. All figures for 1993 are estimated, except for BMG which was able to provide us with actual figures for its year ending in 1993 in response to our request for information.

Aggregate results

8.13. The aggregate results of the five major record companies' total recorded music business are set out in Table 8.2. This table shows that ROR has declined each year from 8.0 per cent in 1989 to 3.4 per cent in 1992. This is the outcome of an average annual increase in revenue of 12.4 per cent and an average annual decrease in PBIT of 16.0 per cent over the period. The companies estimate a recovery in 1993 to an ROR of 6.2 per cent with a PBIT almost doubled from 1992, and turnover increasing by 3.3 per cent in the same period.

TABLE 8.2 **Aggregate results of the total recorded music businesses of the five major record companies, 1989 to 1993**

£ million

	1989	1990	1991	1992	1993 estimated
Revenue:					
Net sales of records	382	441	455	471	498
Gross royalties	182	204	236	347	345
Other	48	49	38	50	55
Total (A)	612	695	729	868	898
PBIT (B)	49	41	33	29	56
Average capital employed*†	(8)	4	(7)	(77)	(89)
ROR (B/A) (%)	8.0	5.9	4.5	3.4	6.2

Source: MMC from companies' data.

*For 1989, year-end only.
†See paragraph 8.11.
Note: Amounts may not total exactly because of rounding.

8.14. Set out in Table 8.3 are the aggregate results of the major record companies' core businesses from 1989 to 1993. Despite the overall growth in income, partly because of acquisitions, the aggregate PBIT of the five companies' core business has declined on average by 17 per cent annually up to 1992 but is forecast to more than double in 1993. The ROR has declined each year from 7.1 per cent in 1989 to 2.8 per cent in 1992 with an estimated 5.9 per cent in 1993. The results of the core business of each company from 1989 to 1993 are set out in Table 8.4.

TABLE 8.3 **Aggregate summarized results of the core recorded music businesses of the five major record companies, 1989 to 1993**

£ million

	1989	1990	1991	1992	1993 estimated
Revenue:					
Net sales of records	382	441	455	471	498
Gross royalties	182	204	236	346	345
Total (A)	564	645	691	817	843
PBIT (B)	40	31	28	23	49
Average capital employed*†	(10)	3	(6)	(74)	(91)
ROR (B/A) (%)	7.1	4.8	4.0	2.8	5.9

Source: MMC from companies' data.

*For 1989, year-end only.
†See paragraph 8.11.
Note: Amounts may not total exactly because of rounding.

TABLE 8.4 **Aggregate results for the core recorded music business of each major, 1989 to 1993**

£ million

	1989	1990	1991	1992	1993 estimated
Revenue (net sales plus gross royalties)					
BMG	[				
EMI					
PolyGram					
Sony					
Warner					
Total					
			Figures omitted. See note on page iv.		
PBIT					
BMG					
EMI					
PolyGram					
Sony					
Warner					
Total					]

per cent

	1989	1990	1991	1992	1993 estimated
ROR (PBIT/revenue)					
BMG	[				
EMI					
PolyGram					
Sony		Figures omitted. See note on page iv.			
Warner					
Total					]

Source: MMC from companies' data.

Note: Amounts may not total exactly because of rounding.

168

8.15. The aggregate results of the core businesses of the five majors for 1989 to 1993 are set out in greater detail in Table 8.5. The results of each company's core business is summarized in Appendix 8.1. In Table 8.5:

1. 'Gross sales of records' is the total of sales of records at published dealer prices in all formats in the UK.

2. 'Returns' is the value of records at published dealer prices returned to the record companies.

3. 'Discounts' are the deductions from published dealer prices allowed by the record companies to their customers.

4. 'Net sales of records' is the amount received by the record company for records sold after deducting returns and discounts.

5. 'Recording' is included as part of A&R cost. This is because recording costs are generally recoupable from artists' royalties. This aspect of A&R is dealt with more fully in paragraphs 8.21 to 8.32.

6. 'Manufacturing' is the purchase or manufacturing costs of the products (ie the records in all formats) and includes packaging, paper parts, duty etc.

7. 'Artists' royalties' are amounts payable to artists on the record companies' rosters arising in respect of sales of records in the UK, and are shown gross before any recoupments.

8. 'Mechanical royalties' are amounts payable to the MCPS, which collects such sums on behalf of music publishers (which own, control or administer the copyright in the music as distinct from the copyright in the recorded work).

9. 'Licence fees' are fees payable to third party and intercompany licensors who own, control or administer the copyright in the recorded work.

10. 'Distribution' is the cost of distributing product from warehouse to purchaser (retailer or wholesaler) and includes distribution fees and warehousing costs.

11. 'Marketing' includes costs of advertising, promotion, public relations, cost of free goods (whether or not intended for resale), staff costs and the non-recoupable cost of music videos (less any net profit in the UK from the sale of videos). The recoupable part of video costs is a part of gross A&R expenditure.

12. 'Selling, general and administrative' includes costs of the departments responsible for sales, finance, systems, personnel, administration, and legal and general management. It also includes bad debts and trade body subscriptions.

13. 'Gross royalties etc received' is income received by the record companies comprising licence fees for use of copyrights by affiliated companies overseas and third parties in the UK and abroad, including fees for track licensing and synchronization, and PPL and VPL fees.

14. 'Matching royalties and other costs' includes royalties payable to artists in respect of the use of copyrights for which royalties etc are received by the record companies, together with associated marketing and selling, general and administrative costs.

15. 'A&R written off' comprises A&R costs (which include advances to artists, recording costs, video costs, costs of A&R staff, management costs and related expenditure and tour support) not expected to be recouped, and written off to profit and loss account.

TABLE 8.5 **Aggregate detailed results of the core recorded music businesses of the five major record companies, 1989 to 1993**

£ million

	1989	1990	1991	1992	1993 estimated
1. Gross sales of records	465	543	564	594	622
2. Returns	(31)	(44)	(37)	(42)	(39)
3. Discounts	(52)	(57)	(72)	(81)	(85)
4. Net sales of records	382	441	455	471	498
Direct costs:					
5. Recording	-	-	-	-	-
6. Manufacturing	(88)	(108)	(108)	(113)	(114)
7. Artists' royalties	(41)	(46)	(51)	(54)	(61)
8. Mechanical royalties	(32)	(41)	(38)	(42)	(45)
9. Licence fees	(31)	(41)	(45)	(44)	(50)
Other	(4)	(5)	(3)	(1)	(2)
Total	(195)	(242)	(245)	(254)	(272)
Gross profit on sales of records	187	200	209	217	226
Indirect costs:					
10. Distribution	(21)	(27)	(28)	(28)	(30)
11. Marketing	(68)	(83)	(87)	(105)	(99)
12. Selling, general and administrative	(54)	(69)	(66)	(81)	(88)
Other	(2)	1	(2)	(10)	(8)
Total	(145)	(178)	(183)	(224)	(225)
Contribution from records before A&R costs (A)	42	22	26	(7)	1
Royalties and other fee income:					
13. Gross royalties etc received	182	204	236	346	345
14. Matching royalties and other costs	(113)	(114)	(145)	(207)	(201)
Net royalty income (B)	69	90	91	139	144
Contribution from records plus net royalty income (A+B)	111	112	117	132	145
15. A&R written off (C)	(71)	(81)	(89)	(109)	(95)
PBIT (A+B - C)	40	31	28	23	49

Source: MMC from companies' data.

Note: Amounts may not total exactly because of rounding.

8.16. The results in Table 8.5 are shown again in Table 8.6 with all items expressed as percentages of gross sales in each year. These percentages are used solely to facilitate a comparison of one item of income and expenditure with another. In particular, the figures for PBIT in this table, which are expressed as percentages of gross sales, should not be confused with the actual percentage returns on the combined net sales and gross royalties which are set out in Table 8.3.

8.17. Although discounts given to record retailers and wholesalers dropped in 1990 to 10.5 per cent from 11.2 per cent, they rose to 13.7 per cent in 1992 and are predicted to stay at that level in 1993. Manufacturing costs remained at around 19 per cent of gross sales from 1989 to 1992 and are predicted to fall slightly in 1993 to 18.3 per cent. Artists' royalties have grown steadily as a percentage of gross record sales since 1990 and both mechanical royalties and licence fees have grown since 1989 but not steadily over the period. Marketing costs have remained in the range between 15 and 16 per cent, except for 1992 when they rose to just under 18 per cent of gross sales. A&R cost write-offs showed similar characteristics, staying in a range of around 15 to 16 per cent of gross sales but reaching just over 18 per cent of gross sales in 1992.

8.18. An indication of the net overseas earnings of the five majors' core businesses can be obtained from item 13 in Table 8.5 (gross royalties etc received, which are largely received from outside the UK) less item 9 in Table 8.5 (cost of licence fees, which are largely paid overseas) and the payments to connected companies overseas shown in Table 8.13.

8.19. Summarizing these results over the period, the salient features are:

(a) the increases, as percentages of gross sales, in discounts, artists' and mechanical royalties and licence fees paid out; and

(b) the relative stability of manufacturing and marketing costs and A&R write-offs as a percentage of gross sales.

TABLE 8.6 **Aggregate detailed results of the core recorded music businesses of the five major record companies, 1989 to 1993**

per cent

	1989	1990	1991	1992	1993 estimated
Gross sales of records	100.0	100.0	100.0	100.0	100.0
Returns	(6.7)	(8.1)	(6.6)	(7.0)	(6.3)
Discounts	(11.2)	(10.5)	(12.9)	(13.7)	(13.6)
Net sales of records	82.1	81.4	80.5	79.3	80.1
Direct costs:					
Recording	-	-	-	-	-
Manufacturing	(18.9)	(19.9)	(19.1)	(19.0)	(18.3)
Artists' royalties	(8.7)	(8.5)	(9.0)	(9.1)	(9.8)
Mechanical royalties	(6.8)	(7.6)	(6.8)	(7.1)	(7.3)
Licence fees	(6.6)	(7.6)	(8.0)	(7.5)	(8.0)
Other	(0.9)	(1.0)	(0.5)	(0.1)	(0.4)
Total	(41.9)	(44.6)	(43.4)	(42.8)	(43.8)
Gross profit on sales of records	40.2	36.8	37.1	36.5	36.3
Indirect costs:					
Distribution	(4.6)	(5.1)	(4.9)	(4.8)	(4.8)
Marketing	(14.7)	(15.3)	(15.3)	(17.7)	(15.9)
Selling, general and administrative	(11.6)	(12.7)	(11.7)	(13.5)	(14.1)
Other	(0.4)	0.3	(0.6)	(1.7)	(1.3)
Total	(31.3)	(32.8)	(32.5)	(37.7)	(36.2)
Contribution from records before A&R costs (A)	8.9	4.0	4.6	(1.2)	0.1
Royalties and other fee income:					
Gross royalties etc received	39.1	37.7	41.8	58.3	55.4
Matching royalties and other costs	(24.3)	(21.1)	(25.7)	(34.9)	(32.2)
Net royalty income (B)	14.9	16.6	16.1	23.4	23.2
A&R written off (C)	(15.2)	(14.9)	(15.8)	(18.3)	(15.4)
PBIT as a percentage of gross sales (A + B - C)	8.6	5.7	4.9	3.9	7.9

Source: MMC from companies' data.

Note: Percentages may not total exactly because of rounding.

8.20. The non-core income of the major companies is summarized in Table 8.7. Here there is no consistent pattern since 1989 and PBIT, although increasing by 12 per cent in 1990, declined by 50 per cent in 1991 and has grown slightly since then. Annual non-core revenue is less than 9 per cent of core revenue over the review period.

TABLE 8.7 **Aggregate results of the non-core recorded music businesses of the five major record companies, 1989 to 1993**

£ million

	1989	1990	1991	1992	1993 estimated
Revenue (A)	48	49	38	50	56
PBIT (B)	9	10	5	6	6
Average capital employed*†	2	1	0	2	2
Return on revenue (B/A) (%)	18.5	20.2	14.0	12.1	11.7

Source: MMC from companies' data.

*For 1989, year end only.
†See paragraph 8.11.
Note: Percentages may not correspond exactly to the figures shown because of rounding.

248336 M

The companies' A&R expenditure and its accounting treatment

8.21. A&R expenditure is incurred to develop a record company's own repertoire, and can be divided into recoupable and non-recoupable parts. The extent to which expenditure is recoupable varies between artists, depending on the specific terms of their contracts, but the classification of expenditures between these two categories usually follows similar lines.

8.22. Non-recoupable expenditure consists mostly of the costs of the A&R department, such as salaries, management costs and related expenses, and the costs of the business affairs department.

8.23. Recoupable expenditure usually includes advances to artists (often the largest single cost), recording and (usually) half the video costs. In return for incurring this expenditure, the company retains the artist's share of royalties and licence fees until all this expenditure has been recovered. In many instances the artist's share of royalties and licence fees will be insufficient to cover recoupable A&R expenditure, and any shortfall has to be borne by the record company. In this way part of the company's gross A&R expenditure is paid by its artists through recoupment, but a larger proportion is finally met by the company. Terms and conditions of classical contracts are usually different; generally advances to artists are very low and recording costs may not be recoupable.

8.24. A&R expenditure covers a mixture of successful and unsuccessful projects. On those which are successful, all recoupable expenditure is recouped. On those which are unsuccessful, there will be recoupable A&R expenditure which is not in fact recouped. This unrecouped A&R expenditure and the company's non-recoupable expenditure together make up its net A&R expense.

8.25. A record which has not fully recouped its A&R expenditure may not necessarily be a loss-making project for the record company. The record company receives all proceeds from the sale of records, and after paying for the direct costs of manufacturing, marketing and distribution, retains the remaining contribution. It also benefits from its entitlement to any royalties and licence fees.

8.26. For recoupable expenditure the prospects of full recovery will be greater for an established artist than for one who is unknown. A substantial part of recoupable A&R is either written off or provided for as incurred. But some of the companies carry forward part of this expenditure which is then recouped or written off in subsequent years. The main reason for writing off A&R expenditure is because it is prudent to do so; and this practice accords with the relevant accounting standards in the UK and the USA, under which the amount recoverable from each artist is considered separately. The A&R costs that are carried forward are typically those expended on major successful artists, where there is the best prospect of recoupment from the royalties that will become due to them.

8.27. The A&R expenditure that is carried forward in the companies' balance sheets is normally called 'investment in artists' and classified as a current asset. The amount carried forward for each artist will be reduced or eliminated as records are sold and other income arises. Unrecouped amounts are written off once it becomes clear that they will not be recovered from future income.

8.28. Except for classical recordings, most recoupments from artists arise in the months immediately following a new release, with any remaining amounts (the recoupable tail) being collected over a much longer period. Advances paid in the year relate to activities in that year and in succeeding years; recoupments will relate to activities in that year and in preceding years. The pattern of sales (which is one element from which a part of the recoupments arise) is illustrated in Table 8.11 in the section on income and expenditure over time.

8.29. In each accounting period the A&R that is written off in the companies' profit and loss accounts is a combination of:

(a) non-recoupable A&R; and

(b) (i) recoupable A&R write-offs and provisions; less

(ii) any recoupment of A&R costs that have been written off or provided for in prior periods.

8.30. Set out in Table 8.8 is the aggregate A&R expenditure for the five major record companies. As a proportion of A&R gross expenditure, advances comprised between 54 and 60 per cent over the period. The other major A&R cost component was recording and origination costs which consisted of between 19 and 32 per cent of gross expenditure. Between 50 and 56 per cent of gross A&R expenditure was written off annually. Recoupments from artists as a percentage of advances varied between 66 per cent (in 1990) and 93 per cent (estimated for 1993). In comparing royalty etc income and A&R expenditure, there is a degree of mismatching, in that the recoupments in a given year do not all relate to advances made in that year.

TABLE 8.8 **Five major record companies: aggregate A&R expenditure and movements on A&R account, 1989 to 1993***

£ million

	1989	*1990*	*1991*	*1992*	*1993 estimated*
Opening balances (net of provisions)	39	48	66	86†	107
Expenditure incurred	127	157	163	218	183
Recouped from artists	(46)	(58)	(64)	(85)	(93)
A&R borne by company (written off)*	(71)	(81)	(89)	(112)	(96)
Closing balances (net of provisions)‡	48	66	76†	107	101
Expenditure incurred					
Advances	66	88	95	128	99
Recording and origination costs	41	43	37	42	40
Video costs	6	7	7	10	9
Tour support	3	4	4	3	2
Staff	9	12	14	15	15
Others	2	3	6	20	18
Total	127	157	163	218	183
A&R borne by company (written off)*					
Movement on provisions	(29)	(31)	(39)	(52)	(43)
Artists balances written off	(14)	(19)	(17)	(23)	(17)
Non-recoupable expenditure	(28)	(31)	(33)	(37)	(36)
Total	(71)	(81)	(89)	(112)	(96)

Source: MMC from companies' data.

*The figures for A&R costs written off ('A&R borne by companies (written off)') in 1992 and 1993 are £3.4 million more and £0.7 million more respectively than the A&R costs written off shown in Table 8.5 and the tables relating to individual record companies. This is because two companies treated some items of A&R costs differently as between their A&R analysis and their summarized reported results.

†The difference between the 1991 closing balance and the 1992 opening balance relates to acquisitions.

‡Differences between the closing balances shown in this table and 'investments in artists' shown in Table 8.1 arise from differences in the results reported to us for each table by two companies.

Note: Amounts may not total exactly because of rounding.

8.31. The companies' sales of *(a)* own-repertoire records and *(b)* royalties and licence fees are joint sources of income (joint products) arising from new releases and reissues from the back catalogue. While the amounts recoupable from artists can be allocated to sales or to royalty and licence income, the companies do not apportion the A&R costs that are written off or provided for in their accounts between them; and there is no generally accepted accounting method for doing so. Though the financial performance of the companies from *(a)* the sale of records and *(b)* royalties and licence fees may be measured and considered separately, the financial results arising from these two income streams have at some point to be judged together after deducting the costs of A&R written off in the companies' accounts.

8.32. The companies' expenditure on A&R creates, maintains and develops their inventory of copyright in recorded works, the exploitation of which is their essential business. As already noted, the core business exploits copyrights in two ways, ie by:

(a) making and selling records in the UK; and

248336 M2

(b) licensing someone else either to make records overseas (usually an associated company) or to use the records in another way (eg for broadcasting).

This aspect of record company activity is described in Chapter 5. In accounting terms, the copyright inventory is an unrecorded intangible asset and its value is only recognized on the sale or flotation of a company or when the copyrights themselves are sold. It is, however, through undertaking the arrangements necessary for the recording, which entails expenditure on A&R, that the copyright in recorded music generally becomes the property of the company. By virtue of the contract between the artist and the record company A&R costs are agreed to be expended by the company. Thus, not only are A&R costs the costs of creating the master tape of a record, they are also the investment which creates and develops the company's inventory of copyrights.

Alternative measures of profitability

8.33. The financial performance of the major record companies, set out in the preceding sections of this chapter, is based on their financial and management accounts. These accounts are drawn up in accordance with accounting standards, which require the companies to take a prudent view of the recoverability of all A&R expenditure and to write most of it off as incurred rather than capitalize and amortize it.

8.34. No intangible assets reflecting their catalogues of copyrights are capitalized in the balance sheets of the companies, either at historical cost less amortization or at a valuation. The balance sheets (see Table 8.1) are characterized by very large debtors and creditors which result in the companies having either low or negative capital employed. As a result, ROCE based on the financial accounts is not a relevant indicator of the companies' overall performance.

8.35. The International Managers Forum (IMF) told us that in its opinion the true profitability of the record companies is understated in their published accounts because of their conservative methods of accounting for copyrights (see paragraph 10.57). The IMF's view is that the copyright catalogues of the record companies are their most valuable asset but neither their cost nor their value appear in the companies' balance sheets. Most of the costs relating to the creation and build-up of value of copyrights (such as advances, recording costs, advertising and promotion) are written off against profits in the year in which they are incurred, although the companies may continue to earn income from exploiting these copyrights for many years. The effect of the companies' conservative accounting policies is that their capital employed is understated by the value of their copyrights and their results are similarly understated by the amount of any increase in their value.

8.36. We believe that, from an economic viewpoint, the major record companies' catalogues of copyrights can be valuable assets and increases in the value of these assets contribute to profitability. Since increases in this value are not specifically accounted for in the reported accounting profits, we agree that the accounting profits may understate economic profitability. In order to examine this question more fully we engaged consultants, KPMG Peat Marwick, to advise us whether there was a way in which the companies' accounts could be adjusted to give us an insight into this.

8.37. It should be emphasized that 'profits' relating to the build-up of uncapitalized copyright value would only be realized on the sale of the business or of the copyrights themselves. No additional funds are available to make payments from these unrealized gains. The cash flows of the record companies remain unchanged from those shown in their audited accounts as they are not affected by unrealized gains and losses. If the catalogue value is not realized through the disposal of the catalogue, the values will materialize in due course through future record sales or licence income and the resulting cash flow will lead to the payment of royalties to artists and composers and will be reflected in the financial results.

8.38. Recognizing these limitations, we asked our consultants (KPMG Peat Marwick) to undertake a broadly-based desk exercise, with the aim of producing a report that would:

(a) advise us on possible methods for valuing the economic profits and intangible assets in the form of copyrights not shown in the accounts; and *(b)* apply these methods to provide us with:

    (i)   a rough gauge estimate of the underlying value that is currently not reflected in the balance sheets of the five major record companies;

    (ii)   a rough gauge set of corresponding adjustments over time to each company's operating results; and

    (iii)   calculations of the return on turnover and ROCE which reflect these adjustments, together with any qualifications on their usefulness as indicators of the underlying profitability of the companies.

8.39. Our consultants' report is reproduced in Appendix 8.2. We have excluded the individual companies' results and certain other material, as noted in the appendix.

8.40. The consultants concluded that the most appropriate way to value the business of the record companies in a 'desk-top' exercise was to apply a multiple to the previous year's turnover. To derive this multiple, 15 of the largest acquisitions in the music industry from 1986 to 1993 were reviewed. For each acquisition, the ratio of the purchase consideration to turnover was calculated; this ratio was then adjusted to allow for the bid premium included in the purchase consideration (25 per cent) and for trade marks and other factors (10 per cent). A simple average of these adjusted turnover multiples gave a figure of 1.20 as the appropriate multiple.

8.41. This multiple was then applied to the actual turnover of each of the majors for the most recent four years and to the forecast turnover for the current year to obtain the total economic value of their businesses. The change in this valuation from year to year, after adjustments for acquisitions and changes of financial year-end, was taken as the economic profit.

8.42. After setting out the difference between the financial PBIT[1] and the economic profit, our consultants calculated revised rates of return on revenues and capital employed. However, they advised us that the ROCE was not meaningful because the method of calculation involved a circularity (ie the capital employed grew in proportion to the profitability). In Table 8.9 we set out the revised performance of the five majors, including RORs.

TABLE 8.9 **Five major record companies: aggregated performance, 1991 to 1993**

				£ million
	1991	*1992*	*1993*	*Average*
Revenues	728.9	868.2	897.9	831.7
Financial PBIT (Table 8.2)	32.9	29.3	55.9	39.4
Adjustment	23.4	(13.9)	32.3	13.9
Economic profit	56.3	15.4	88.2	53.3
				per cent
	1991	*1992*	*1993*	*Average*
RORs				
Financial returns (Table 8.2)	4.5	3.4	6.2	4.7
Economic returns	7.7	1.8	9.8	6.4

Source: KPMG/MMC.

8.43. We asked the five majors for their views on this exercise and these are summarized from paragraph 12.120 onwards.

Results by format

8.44. In Table 8.10 we set out aggregate information for all the majors on individual formats. In their management accounts the majors do not generally apportion costs by format below gross margin.

---

[1]Taken from their audited accounts (see Table 8.2).

The allocation of indirect costs to format was carried out by the companies specifically for our inquiry. The majority of the companies allocated the main part of their indirect costs (including marketing, and selling, general and administrative expenses) in proportion to the value of gross sales less returns or net sales. As the unit prices of CDs are higher than those of cassettes, the amounts allocated to cassettes would be higher and the amounts allocated to CDs would be lower if another basis (such as units sold) had been adopted consistently. A reconciliation of the results in Table 8.10 with the aggregate results for 1992 in Table 8.5 is set out in Appendix 8.3.

8.45. Nowadays singles usually produce losses for the companies, which is consistent with the companies' views of the single as a promotional format for the album and the artist. Of the other formats, vinyl is consistently the worst performer in terms of net margin per unit and CDs produce the highest net margin per unit.

TABLE 8.10 **Aggregate results of the majors by format, 1992/93***

£'000

	Singles all formats	Vinyl	Tape	CD	Other	Total
Gross sales	74,281	13,646	153,061	305,289	9,129	555,406
Less discounts	(15,295)	(1,548)	(17,635)	(40,867)	(1,262)	(76,607)
returns	(5,197)	(2,039)	(12,655)	(17,675)	(527)	(38,093)
Net sales	53,789	10,059	122,771	246,747	7,340	440,706
Direct costs:						
Manufacturing	(25,408)	(2,159)	(20,291)	(55,651)	(2,240)	(105,749)
Other	(17,481)	(3,584)	(39,245)	(72,029)	(2,204)	(134,543)
Total	(42,889)	(5,743)	(59,536)	(127,680)	(4,444)	(240,292)
Gross margin	10,900	4,316	63,235	119,067	2,896	200,414
Indirect costs	(35,375)	(3,900)	(50,370)	(94,112)	(1,934)	(185,691)
Net margin†	(24,475)	416	12,865	24,955	962	14,723
						per cent
Gross margin‡	20.3	42.9	51.5	48.3	§	§
Net margin‡	(45.5)	4.1	10.5	10.1	§	§
						£
Unit results						
Net realized price per unit	1.44	4.36	4.02	5.86	§	§
Manufacturing costs per unit	0.68	0.93	0.66	1.32	§	§
Gross margin per unit	0.29	1.87	2.07	2.83	§	§
Net margin per unit	(0.66)	0.18	0.42	0.59	§	§

Source: MMC from company data.

*(i) Results are summarized from the results of the following financial years for the companies: BMG to 30 June 1993, EMI to 31 March 1993, PolyGram to 31 December 1992, Sony to 31 March 1993 and Warner to 30 November 1992.
(ii) In the case of one company, these results exclude (a) special exports and (b) repertoire centre costs with no corresponding sales.
(iii)In the case of EMI, the aggregates do not include figures for Virgin or Chrysalis (see Appendix 8.1).
(iv)Sony was unable to provide us with separate data on vinyl. Sony's vinyl results are included with cassette.
†Net margin is before A&R write-offs and net royalty income.
‡As a percentage of net sales.
§Not calculated.

8.46. Based on the information in Tables 8.5 and 8.10, we have attempted below to build up the cost structure for a 'typical' full-price CD priced at retail at £12.99:

	%
Price to retail customer (£12.99)	100
of which:	
VAT at 17.5% represents	15
Retailers' gross margin	30
Leaving realized price to record company of	55
of which approximately:	
Manufacturing costs	10
Mechanical royalties and artists' royalties/licence fees	15
Total direct costs	25
Balance remaining	30

The record companies' non-direct costs, including unrecouped A&R, distribution, marketing and administrative costs, have to be covered out of the balance (30 per cent) plus net royalty income, mainly earned from overseas. After full allocation of costs and income, profits relating to any individual CD will vary enormously, with the bulk of recordings being in loss and a small number making large profits.

Discounts and other allowances from record companies to their customers

8.47. The record companies set a published dealer price for each record, but this differs from the actual net proceeds that are finally received from the wholesalers and retailers which are their customers. First, the dealer price may be reduced by various types of discount. Secondly, customers may be allowed to return for credit a proportion of the records which they have purchased. Thirdly, some retailers benefit from marketing expenditure of the record companies, including direct expenditure on joint marketing programmes. Finally, retailers benefit from supplies of free records, usually singles. In this section we examine how these discounts and allowances vary from one customer or group of customers to another.

8.48. We asked the five major record companies to analyse their sales for their most recently completed financial year by trade channel, and within each channel by major customer. Gross sales were to be shown at published dealer price with separate deductions for discounts and returns. The companies were also asked to identify any direct marketing or promotional costs attributable to each channel or major customer, including supplies of free records. Separate analyses were requested for albums and singles, because we had been told that singles were used as a means of promoting sales of albums and therefore attracted higher rates of discounts and other allowances. We also asked for unit information so that we could calculate average selling prices. We asked the companies to include not only the discounts and allowances specified in contracts with their customers but any additional allowances and expenditure given for promotional purposes. Detailed tables of discounts and other allowances have been included in Appendix 8.4. In the tables EUK has been treated as a wholesaler, although about 80 per cent of its purchases are resold to Woolworths.

8.49. The record companies have not been able to provide information on a completely uniform basis. It is therefore not possible to make comparisons between the discounts and other allowances given by one record company and another (by comparing columns in the tables in Appendix 8.4). However, the information for each record company is internally consistent so that it is broadly possible to see any differences between the business terms applied by each record company to its various customers.

Discounts

8.50. The various types of discount are described in paragraph 7.29. Discounts may take the form of reductions in unit prices or the supply of additional goods, for example ten for the price of nine. These free goods discounts have been treated as discounts in the tables and, where information was available, dealt with separately from issues of free records for promotional purposes (see paragraph 8.55).

8.51. Discounts granted on albums and singles for the companies' most recently completed financial year are set out in Tables 1 and 2 of Appendix 8.4. [*] enjoys significantly higher discounts from most of its suppliers than the other major retailers for both albums and singles. The record companies usually give higher discounts on singles than on albums to all their customers. While the major retailers generally receive higher discounts on albums than the independent retailers, the position is reversed for singles where the independents generally receive much higher discounts than the majors. Wholesalers generally receive higher discounts than retailers on albums but not on singles.

---

*Detail omitted. See note on page iv.

Returns

8.52. As well as returning faulty products and those which have been wrongly delivered, wholesalers and retailers are allowed to return unsold records up to an agreed proportion of their purchases, which reduces their risk of stockholding losses. These 'privilege' return allowances are described in paragraphs 7.33 to 7.35.

8.53. Returns of albums and singles are set out in Tables 3 and 4 of Appendix 8.4. Returns have been calculated as a percentage of sales at dealer price, so that they are stated in value rather than in volume terms. Returns of albums from wholesalers, particularly EUK, are significantly higher than those from retailers. Our Price returns a higher than average percentage of its purchases of albums compared with the other major retailers and for singles, for which it is the second largest retailer after Woolworths, it has by far the highest returns, significantly greater than its returns of albums. With the exception of Our Price, the returns of the major retailers are not out of line with those of the independents.

Promotional support

8.54. Both record companies and retailers engage in promotional activity, much of it organized on a co-operative basis. The promotional activities of the retailers are described in paragraphs 6.35 to 6.41.

8.55. In Table 5 of Appendix 8.4 we set out the value of expenditure by the record companies on joint promotion schemes as a percentage of net sales. We have not prepared separate tables for singles and albums, since promotional expenditure cannot easily be allocated between them. The major retailers generally receive considerably more support than the independent retailers, with [*] receiving significantly higher promotional support than the other major retailers.

Free issues

8.56. Record companies generally give some free copies of singles to retailers for promotional purposes. Some retailers do not take free goods, but for others it is an important form of promotional support. In Table 6 of Appendix 8.4 we show the volumes of free singles as a percentage of all singles delivered. We also asked the record companies to value free issues at dealer prices less all normal discounts, and in Table 7 we show them as a percentage of net sales of singles and albums. The independent retailers are by far the largest beneficiaries of free singles, which are of particular benefit to them since, as Table 6.4 shows, independents accounted for 51.0 per cent of retail sales of singles in 1992, but only 22.7 per cent of albums. Finally, in Table 8 we have combined the promotional expenditure in Table 5 with the value of free issues in Table 7, to show the total value of all promotional support as a percentage of singles and albums. This table shows that the independent retailers receive much the same level of support as the major retailers, with [*] still enjoying higher levels of support than the other major retailers.

Transaction costs

8.57. Transaction and administrative costs vary widely between customers. A small retailer who uses telesales support, has visits from sales representatives and places small orders will be far more expensive to serve than a large wholesaler. Kingfisher estimated the cost savings to a record company of delivering to EUK rather than to individual retail outlets as equivalent to 6 to 7 per cent of dealer price. One of the record companies supplied figures to us in which it had treated these differential costs and savings as an adjustment to sales proceeds. Calculated in this way, its effective selling prices were lower for the independent retailers than for the large wholesalers, suggesting that the additional discounts received by the wholesalers do not fully cover the savings arising from dealing with them rather than with other channels.

---

*Details omitted. See note on page iv.

Overall levels of discounts

8.58. We do not believe that it is possible to combine the values of these various forms of discount and other allowances in order to arrive at a single overall figure showing the effective rate of discount from published dealer prices enjoyed by each retailer. However, the figures in Appendix 8.4 do not indicate that any one retailer or group of retailers is consistently receiving better terms than the others.

Income and expenditure over time

8.59. To illustrate the flows of income and expenditure over time on individual own-repertoire recordings, we asked the companies to provide us with detailed information on these recordings for a small number of albums and singles from 1990 onwards. This information was provided separately for a range of albums and singles and has given us an insight into the pattern of the income and costs of these recordings. But this material is difficult to summarize because one company was able only to provide us with information for calendar years, rather than the financial years requested, and for all the companies the albums and singles were released at different times in 1989, 1990 and 1991. The companies also attached certain qualifications to some of the data (eg the results were atypical or recoupable A&R costs could not be analysed to particular recordings). However, in Table 8.11 we summarize that data we obtained on net sales which conformed to our requirements. The number of sales is very small but it illustrates that the bulk occur in the period immediately following the release of these recordings.

TABLE 8.11   **Own-repertoire recorded music products in their first year and next two years following their release (Year 1 = 100)***

	Year 1	Year 2	Year 3	Total	Total net sales of the sample £m
15 best-selling pop albums†	100.0	22.0	6.0	128.0	58.3
15 best-selling singles	100.0	0.8	0.0	100.8	5.5
5 moderately successful albums	100.0	1.5	0.7	102.2	2.2
5 unsuccessful albums	100.0	5.9	1.3	107.2	0.9
					66.9

Source: MMC from the companies' data.

*For each company we asked for the three best-selling pop albums and singles and one moderately successful album and one unsuccessful album.
†These results include one double album.

In the table we have not included the information we obtained on classical recordings because the numbers of such recordings sold was not significant. But the income from these recordings is spread over a longer period.

8.60. In Table 8.12 we show the sales in the first accounting year in which the best-selling recordings were released as a percentage of each company's net sales included in the 1990 net sales figure shown in Table 8.5. In relation to their total catalogues, Table 8.12 indicates the importance of their best-selling own-repertoire albums to the overall results of the companies.

TABLE 8.12   **Best-selling own-repertoire pop albums and singles as a percentage of 1990 net sales***

					per cent
	Company A	Company B	Company C†	Company D	Company E
Percentage of 1990 net sales:					
3 best-selling own-repertoire pop albums	19.8	13.0	10.3	7.4	6.8
3 best-selling own-repertoire pop singles	5.4	0.6	0.7	0.9	1.1

Source: MMC from the companies' data.

*1990 net sales for each company are as included in the total of £441 million shown in Table 8.5. The basis of aggregation of individual company net sales is as set out in paragraph 8.12.
†This company's three best-selling pop albums includes a double album.

8.61. One company provided us with a far more extensive analysis of its own. This study tracked artists' income and expenditure flows (from 1985 to 1992) rather than individual recordings. We have extracted data relating to the [*] artists signed from [*] to [*] in the study to show the recoupable A&R for each artist and the company's estimate of its profit and loss on the artist to [*]. The results are set out in Figure 8.1. This shows that of the [*] artists 16 were estimated to be profitable.[1] These profits arose after taking account of all income received after up to [*] years for artists first signed in [*], and going back each year, for up to [*] years, for artists first signed in [*]. Sums in excess of £[*] million were spent on [*] artists over the period; and this expenditure represented [*] per cent of the total recoupable A&R. Of these nine artists, five were profitable and four were loss-making over this period.

FIGURE 8.1

Results for each of the [*] artists signed by a major pop label between [*] and [*]

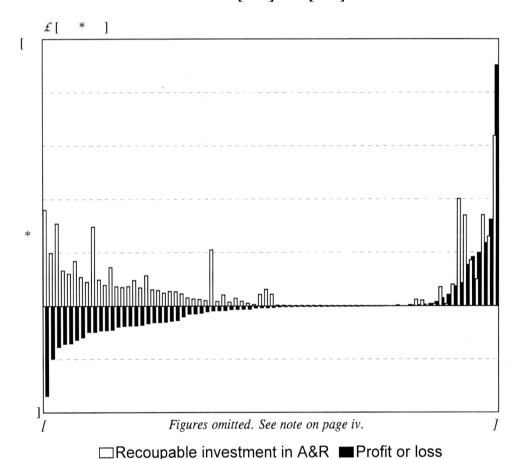

Figures omitted. See note on page iv.

☐Recoupable investment in A&R ■Profit or loss

Source: MMC from company data.

Notes:
1. Cases are shown in ascending order of net profit/loss, ie the greatest loss is on the left-hand side and the greatest profit on the right.
2. Cases [*] to [*] each had a profit or loss of less than £15,000 and recoupable investment of less that £22,000.

---

*Details omitted. See note on page iv.

[1]This is before taking into account the time value of money which would make some of the profitable artists unprofitable.

Products and services bought in from connected companies and divisions

8.62. In addition to royalty payments to connected companies overseas for licensed-in repertoire, all the majors' recorded music businesses buy in cassettes, CDs or products in other formats from connected companies or divisions. Also, in some cases, distribution is undertaken by connected self-accounting units. In Table 8.13 we summarize the majors' expenditure on bought-in products and services from connected companies and divisions in the UK and overseas, together with the profits (or losses) on this business reported to us by the principal connected companies and divisions in the UK. Also shown is all this expenditure as a percentage of the total costs of the recorded music businesses before A&R write-offs. In 1992, for example, this percentage was 23.5 per cent. For the connected business (£67.1 million) for which we obtained information the reported losses were £2.0 million.

TABLE 8.13 **Products and services bought in by the core businesses of the majors from connected companies and divisions, 1989 to 1993**

£ million

	1989	1990	1991	1992	1993 estimated
Connected businesses in the UK:					
Manufacturing	26.8	33.4	33.7	43.3	39.8
Distribution	19.4	26.3	25.1	23.8	25.6
Other	1.2	1.1	1.1	1.5	1.3
Total	47.4	60.8	59.9	68.6	66.7
Connected businesses outside the UK					
Manufacturing*	31.5	34.0	40.5	41.0	43.1
Other	2.4	2.8	3.3	2.8	2.8
Total	33.9	36.8	43.8	43.8	45.9
Total from all connected businesses	81.3	97.6	103.7	112.4	112.6
Recorded music business total expenditure before A&R write-offs†	309.8	382.3	428.3	478.5	496.9
Total from all connected companies and divisions as a percentage of the costs of recorded music business before A&R write-offs (%)	26.2	25.5	24.2	23.5	22.7
Total connected costs in respect of principal companies and divisions in the UK on which we have obtained profitability information:					
Manufacturing‡	25.6	33.4	33.7	43.3	39.8
Distribution	19.4	26.3	25.1	23.8	25.6
Total	45.0	59.7	58.8	67.1	65.4
Profits/(losses) of the principal companies and divisions in the UK on which we have obtained profitability information:					
Manufacturing‡	0.3	0.3	0.6	1.1	0.6
Distribution§	(3.5)	0.2	0.8	(3.1)	(1.0)
Total	(3.2)	0.5	1.4	(2.0)	(0.4)

Source: MMC from companies' data.

---

*One company was unable to supply figures for its transactions with connected companies for 1989 and 1990. All this company's transactions were for manufacturing outside the UK.

†From Table 8.5. But for 1989 and 1990 excludes costs for the company that was unable to provide us with the details of its transactions with connected companies in these two years.

‡One company connected to a major which supplies the major's recorded music business with CDs was unable to provide us with information for 1989.

§One major's connected distribution company receives fees for the products it distributes for the recorded music business. In its recorded music business results, the major reported its connected company's actual costs of distribution rather than the fees paid to it. Accordingly, neither profits nor losses arise in the figures reported to us for distribution through this division.

8.63. Additional information on the results of the principal connected companies and divisions in the UK, together with the basis of transfer pricing, is set out in Appendix 8.5.

Results of the four leading independents and the smaller independent companies

8.64. We obtained financial information from the four leading major independents (MCA, Telstar, Pickwick and Beggars Banquet) for their last three completed financial years. Their core businesses showed varying results. For the two companies that made profits in each year (ranging from £2.8 million to £0.2 million), the PBIT on revenue ranged from 14.1 to 2.6 per cent. The third company reported losses in two of the three years; and the fourth losses in all three years. In the case of the fourth company, the main reason for these losses was that the company was building up its own roster of artists in the UK and the majority of the recordings that were released were not successful.

8.65. We asked just over 100 smaller independent companies to provide us with a brief summary of their financial results. The results of those companies that provided us with information showed no clear pattern. Reported profitability was varied, with both profits and losses being shown.

Financial results of the major retailers

8.66. We requested financial information from the five largest retailers of recorded music (listed in Table 6.3) for their four most recent financial years. The information which we received from them is based on their management accounts, which have been reconciled to their statutory accounts. We also requested various analyses of sales and margins, and a calculation of average capital employed. In many of these analyses, costs, expenses and assets had to be apportioned between the companies' recorded music businesses and their other retail businesses. Some of these apportionments were taken from the management accounts of the companies but, more often, they were the results of special analyses carried out by the companies specifically for our inquiry.

8.67. We did not receive all the analyses which we had requested because the companies' information systems did not hold the necessary information. There was little information relating to unit sales, so that we are unable to calculate average selling prices. There was an increase in the information available towards the end of the four-year review period because of improvements to information systems, including the installation of EPOS terminals in some stores.

8.68. From each of these retailers we have obtained calculations of the overall gross profit, PBIT and, except for Kingfisher, ROCE of its recorded music business for the last four completed business years. We have also obtained calculations of gross profit by format from each of the retailers except W H Smith. This information is shown in detailed tables in Appendix 8.6.

W H Smith

8.69. In June 1993 W H Smith operated in England and Wales from 399 high street shops, 59 bookstalls (located at 47 stations) and 37 airport shops (located in 8 airports). Of these 495 outlets, 317 sold recorded music.

8.70. W H Smith's retail shops are operated as a division of W H Smith Ltd (a wholly-owned subsidiary of W H Smith Group plc) and the division (W H Smith Retail) does not have separate statutory accounts. It told us that in its management accounts, it calculates gross profit for each of its main merchandise groups, which include news, books, stationery and recorded music. Operating costs and head office costs are not allocated to merchandise groups in W H Smith's management accounts. However, it carried out a special exercise for us. Head office costs were allocated to its merchandise groups in proportion to turnover. Fixed assets were apportioned to reflect the amount of selling space actually occupied by recorded music in W H Smith branches, and stocks were taken from the management accounts. The results for recorded music from 1989 to 1993 are set out in Table 1 of Appendix 8.6.

8.71. W H Smith's information systems do not provide any analysis of sales, gross profit and operating expense by price category (full-price, mid-price and budget); similarly, there is no analysis by chart, catalogue, special promotions, etc. Also, it was the only one of the major retailers which was unable to provide us with an analysis of gross profit by format.

8.72. W H Smith Retail's sales and gross profits for each of its merchandise groups are shown in Table 8.14.

TABLE 8.14 **W H Smith Retail: sales and gross profits, 1993**

	Sales excl VAT £'000	Gross profit £'000	Gross profit %
Books	[		
News			
Stationery	Figures omitted. See note on page iv.		]
Recorded music	[	]	29.6
Video	[		
Cards	Figures omitted. See note on page iv.		
Other*			]

Source: W H Smith.

*Includes sound accessories, personal computing, calculators and typewriters, photography and games and toys.

The gross profit of 29.6 per cent for recorded music is almost [*] percentage points below that for the whole of W H Smith Retail. Commenting on this, W H Smith told us that it did not see music as one of the big cash or profit contributors to its business. Its role was much more about adding to the character and feel of the whole W H Smith brand.

Our Price

8.73. Our Price, which was acquired by W H Smith in 1986, is a specialist chain operating 336 stores. It has the same financial year as its parent company but, as an independent operation, has its own system of management accounts. This differs from that of W H Smith Retail, and Our Price has been able to provide us with information on its gross profit by format, which is included in Table 3 of Appendix 8.6. Its financial results for the four years ended 31 May 1993 are set out in Table 2. [

Details omitted. See note on page iv.

] Recorded music has accounted for 87 to 90 per cent of Our Price's sales during each of the last four years.

8.74. Our Price told us about the power of the record companies in negotiating discounts. For example, after W H Smith bought Our Price in 1986, the major record companies, rather than giving increased discounts to reflect the combined volumes of the two businesses, had reduced the Our Price terms to those of the W H Smith business.

Virgin Retail

8.75. Virgin Retail sells recorded music through 21 megastores. W H Smith acquired 50 per cent of its share capital in September 1991 from Virgin Retail Group Ltd (Virgin Retail Group), and it has since been operated as a 'deadlock joint venture', with each parent company having equal representation on the Board of Directors. Virgin Retail's financial year was changed from 31 July to 31 May in 1992 and, as a result, the accounting period which ended on 31 May 1992 was a ten-month period. In 1988 Virgin Retail sold 74 of its smaller stores to Our Price.

8.76. The joint venture agreement contains a put option, giving Virgin Retail Group the right to require W H Smith to purchase all, but not some only, of its shares in and loan notes due from the

---

*Figure omitted. See note on page iv.

joint venture after 31 May 1994; W H Smith has a call option exercisable after 31 May 1997. The agreement also contains a non-competition clause governing the number of Virgin Retail and Our Price outlets in 36 towns and how new retail sites in these towns should be allocated between Virgin Retail and Our Price.

8.77. Virgin Retail is managed separately from W H Smith's other businesses, so that the system of management accounts differs from those operated by W H Smith and Our Price. The financial results of Virgin Retail are set out in Table 4 of Appendix 8.6.

8.78. Sales and gross profit by format are set out in Table 5. Virgin Retail told us that there are no costs which vary disproportionately between formats. The other analyses of sales and gross profit which we had requested were not available. It does not record sales and costs by price category. Sales are analysed by music type, but the related cost of sales and unit information is not held.

8.79. On 2 March 1994 W H Smith announced that Virgin Retail's UK and Irish operations would be combined with those of Our Price. W H Smith would hold 75 per cent of the enlarged business and Virgin Retail Group would hold the remaining 25 per cent. Until regulatory approval was received, Our Price and Virgin Retail would continue to be managed as separate businesses.

Kingfisher

8.80. Kingfisher sells recorded music through 785 Woolworths stores in Great Britain and Northern Ireland. All of Woolworths' recorded music is sourced from EUK, another Kingfisher subsidiary, which was acquired in 1987 from EMI and PolyGram. Kingfisher also sells recorded music through its Titles Video subsidiary, but the amounts are very small and have not been included in the tables below nor in those in Appendix 8.6.

8.81. EUK is the largest wholesaler of recorded music, but the Woolworths business has consistently accounted for around 80 per cent of EUK's turnover. In 1993 EUK's non-Woolworths turnover was £28.1 million, so that TBD with a turnover of £[*   ] is the largest independent wholesaler of recorded music in terms of third-party sales.

8.82. Woolworths divides its operations for management purposes into divisions, the largest of which is the Entertainment Division, comprising several departments. Some of these departments (records and cassettes; CDs; singles) are concerned with recorded music. The results of Woolworths for recorded music are shown for only three years in Table 6 of Appendix 8.6 because, for the year ended 31 January 1990, there is no separate analysis of sales and profitability by department, nor any calculation of the trading profit of the Entertainment Division. For the years ended 31 January 1991 and 1992 the allocation of store-related expenses between recorded music and other departments has been estimated by us.

8.83. Table 7 of Appendix 8.6 shows Woolworths' sales and gross profits by format. Sales and gross profit by format for EUK are set out in Table 8. EUK separates the sales of vinyl LPs from sales of cassettes in its management accounts; Woolworths no longer sells vinyl LPs.

8.84. The sales and gross profit of Woolworths' Entertainment Division for the year ended 31 January 1993 are set out in Table 8.15.

TABLE 8.15 **Woolworths: sales and gross profit of Entertainment Division, 1992/93**

	Sales excl VAT £m	Gross profit £m	Gross profit %
Recorded music	[		
Other entertainment		Figures omitted. See note on page iv.	
Entertainment Division			]

Source: Kingfisher.

*Details omitted. See note on page iv.

8.85. Table 8.15 shows a gross profit accruing to Woolworths on recorded music which is significantly lower than that for other retailers. It does not include the further profit on these sales which arose within EUK. Kingfisher therefore prepared a consolidated profit and loss account for EUK's recorded music sold through Woolworths for the year to 31 January 1993, broken down by format. This analysis, which includes the sales, expenses and profits of both Woolworths and EUK, is included as Table 9 in Appendix 8.6 and shows gross profits for each format which are similar to those of other retailers, except that the gross profit on singles is reduced because Woolworths aims to have the lowest prices on chart products. A similar analysis showed that for products other than recorded music (mostly videos and games) the Entertainment Division had a gross profit of [†] per cent and a net profit of [†] per cent; these margins are a little better than those achieved on CDs and much higher than those on cassettes and singles.

8.86. Table 9 also shows a consolidated PBIT of £[†] on Woolworths' sales of £[†]. In addition EUK had a PBIT of £[†] from its business with third parties, so that the total PBIT of Kingfisher's recorded music business was £[†]. Kingfisher has not prepared a consolidated balance sheet for the recorded music businesses of EUK and Woolworths, so it is not possible to calculate its ROCE.

HMV

8.87. HMV, a division of THORN EMI Home Electronics (UK) Ltd, is a multiple retailer specializing in music. It has 94 stores with a total trading area of 393,000 square feet.

8.88. The results of HMV for the four financial years ending 31 March 1993 are set out in Table 10 of Appendix 8.6.

8.89. HMV told us that it recorded turnover by merchandise group, format and main product category, but that cost information was not recorded in this way and had been estimated on the basis of the margins at which the company sold different products and product categories. An estimated analysis of sales and gross profit by format for the year to 31 March 1993 is included as Table 11 in Appendix 8.6.

Comparative performance of the retailers

8.90. Because the retailers have different financial year ends, we have taken the results for their most recently completed year in the tables below. For W H Smith, Our Price and Virgin Retail the most recent financial year ended on 31 May 1993; for Kingfisher on 31 January 1993; and for HMV on 31 March 1993.

Gross profit by format

8.91. Table 8.16 shows the gross profit by format for all the major retailers except for W H Smith Retail, which was unable to provide us with this information.

TABLE 8.16   **Major retailers: comparative gross profit by format, 1992/93**

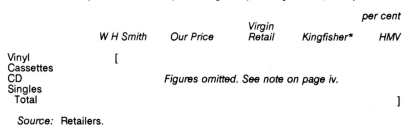

	W H Smith	Our Price	Virgin Retail	Kingfisher*	per cent HMV
Vinyl	[				
Cassettes					
CD		Figures omitted. See note on page iv.			
Singles					
Total					]

Source: Retailers.

*The gross profit for Kingfisher is the consolidated gross profit of Woolworths and EUK arising from Woolworths' sales after deduction of distribution costs.

†Details omitted. See note on page iv.

For each retailer there is little variation in gross margin between formats. [

Details omitted. See note on page iv.

]

Profitability and ROCE

8.92. Table 8.17 shows the sales, contribution and ROCE of the five major retailers for the financial year nearest 31 December 1992.

TABLE 8.17 **Major retailers: comparative sales, contribution and ROCE from recorded music, 1992/93**

	W H Smith	Our Price	Virgin Retail	Kingfisher	HMV	£'000 Total
Sales excl VAT	[					613,315
Cost of goods sold						410,401
Gross profit						202,914
Direct costs						25,105
Contribution			*Figures omitted. See note on page iv.*			177,809
Allocated overheads						
Store-related expenses						149,610
Head/regional office expenses						27,766
Marketing adjustment						(4,910)
PBIT						5,343
Average capital employed					]	
						per cent
Gross profit:sales	[					33.1
Contribution:sales						29.0
PBIT:sales			*Figures omitted. See note on page iv.*			0.9
ROCE					]	N/A

Source: Retailers.

Kingfisher undertakes its own distribution and the cost of £[*   ] (almost [*   ]) has been included in cost of goods sold so that its results are comparable with those of the other retailers.

8.93. Overheads have had to be allocated to the recorded music business for each of the companies, and these varied from [*Details omitted.* *See note on page iv.*

]

Financial results of the major record clubs

Britannia

8.94. Britannia Music Company Ltd is part of the PolyGram International Group. It is by far the largest of the record clubs, and estimates that during the last five years it has increased its share of the total market for recorded music from 4 to 8 per cent.

8.95. Unlike the retailers, Britannia does not buy a finished product from the record companies at a discount from a dealer price. Instead, each item purchased has three separate elements of cost:

(a) a 'manufacturing' cost on each item delivered;

---

*Details omitted. See note on page iv.

(b) a royalty payable to the record company on each item sold; and

(c) a mechanical royalty payable to the holder of the copyright in the music.

In most cases royalties are paid directly by Britannia to the appropriate record company or copyright owner quarterly in arrears, although, on occasions, advances are paid.

8.96. In Table 8.18 we set out the results of Britannia for the three years to 31 December 1992.

TABLE 8.18 Britannia: sales, gross profit and PBIT from recorded music

£'000

| | *Years ended 31 December* | | |
	1990	*1991*	*1992*
Sales excl VAT	[		
Cost of sales		*Figures omitted.*	
Gross		*See note on page iv.*	
Indirect expenses			
PBIT			]

per cent

Gross profit:sales	[	*Figures omitted.*	
PBIT:sales		*See note on page iv.*	]

Source: Britannia.

8.97. [*Details omitted. See note on page iv.*

]

Other record clubs

8.98. Reader's Digest supplies only its own compilations which are sold in packages. A typical package consists of four double-play cassettes, six CDs or eight LPs. Reader's Digest licenses tracks from many record companies, majors and independents, as well as recording some repertoire itself. It uses independent studios to compile the sets from masters supplied by the record companies, and it manufactures with a range of suppliers including the majors and independent manufacturing companies. Its recordings all carry the Reader's Digest label.

8.99. Reader's Digest's management accounts for 1992 showed that recorded music accounted for £[*   ] out of group sales of £[*   ], on which there was a trading profit of £[*   ].

8.100. BCA (formerly Book Club Associates) is a partnership between Reed International Books Ltd and Bertelsmann Books & Magazines Ltd. BCA purchases all its products from the record companies in the same way as Britannia. Its terms are at no time expressed as a discount from dealer price or any other price. BCA does not supply its own compilations.

8.101. The management accounts of BCA's music division show turnover for the year to 30 June 1993 of £[
Details omitted. See note on page iv.
] As a partnership, BCA neither files its audited accounts at Companies House nor does it otherwise publish them.

*Details omitted. See note on page iv.

248336 N

9 Views of interested organizations and members of the public

Contents

9.1. During the inquiry the MMC received letters from a number of organizations representing consumers and others not directly involved in the supply of recorded music. The views of these organizations and a number of members of the public who wrote to the MMC are summarized below.

Consumers' Association

9.2. The Consumers' Association (CA) submitted to the MMC a copy of the evidence which it had presented to the NHC, and attended a hearing.

9.3. CA, the publisher of *Which?* magazine, said that it had taken a close interest in the CD prices issue for some years, ever since it had first produced a report in *Which?* on the subject, in January 1990, together with an accompanying policy report which set out the arguments in detail. In that report CA had, in particular, drawn attention to:

(a) the continuing high prices of CDs since their introduction to the UK market in the early part of 1983: the failure of CD prices to fall had stood in marked contrast to the price of CD players, which had more than halved since their introduction;

(b) the falling cost of producing CDs, by then little more than the cost of producing LPs which nevertheless were selling for far less in the shops; and

(c) the CA survey of the general public in August 1989 which had shown widespread dissatisfaction with CD prices, and remarkably low levels of CD ownership among people who had bought music systems which included a CD facility.

9.4. Since publishing the 1990 report CA said that there had been widespread interest in the subject and a number of organizations had carried out reviews. CA said that perhaps the most interesting development in the last couple of years had been the PSA's report on record pricing, published on 13 December 1990. That report recommended some important changes to the market protection afforded to the recording industry by Australian copyright legislation (see paragraphs 3.46 to 3.49.)

9.5. CA noted that a full-price CD in UK shops now cost up to £15. CA gave some examples from a recent survey it had carried out, which showed substantial variations from shop to shop, and that some special offers had pushed the price down to below the £10 mark. There had also been a substantial increase in the number of budget and mid-priced recordings at around £5 to £7 and £8 to £10 respectively. But the absolute level of full-price recordings was extremely high, and indeed had risen considerably, in the two years since the January 1990 *Which?* report.

9.6. CA said that what was instructive about these figures was no longer how they compared with vinyl LPs—which had now been discontinued by some record companies and retailers—but how they compared with the price of the same CDs bought through retailers in the USA. CA gave comparative prices for the USA in respect of the sample recordings which it had looked at in the UK. Thus, the Welsh National Opera recording of *The Mikado*, retailing in W H Smith at £14.49, could be obtained at prices ranging from $13.99 to $14.99 in the USA. Similarly, Pink Floyd's *Dark Side of the Moon* on sale at £13.99 or £14.99 in the UK ranged from $10.99 to $15.99 in the USA. CA argued that it was possible to conclude from these prices that CDs broadly cost the same number of dollars in the USA as they did pounds in the UK; and, even with the pound's relatively weak exchange rate of around $1.45 (as at early February 1993), this implied that US prices—for exactly the same product—were only around 70 per cent of those in the UK.

9.7. CA gave us a summary of a survey which had been carried out in June and July 1992 by the Bureau of European Consumer Unions (BEUC). CA said that this was a little more difficult to interpret, because it had been carried out before 'Black Wednesday' on 16 September 1992, since when the value of sterling had fallen by some 20 per cent. The figures broadly suggested that, prior to 'Black Wednesday', UK shop prices, including VAT, were around 18 to 20 per cent higher than those in Germany, the cheapest country in the survey; excluding VAT, the margin was around 13 to 15 per cent. Although CA did not have any more recent figures readily available, it was fair to assume that the price differential between the UK and Germany had more or less disappeared since 'Black Wednesday' and that UK CD prices were now more or less equal to, if not cheaper than, those elsewhere in the EC. CA said that in many respects this approximate equalization of CD prices across the EC ought not to be particularly surprising, given that trade barriers had been removed within the EC, and parallel imports were allowed. Any retailer who could see bargains to be struck in another EC country could get supplies sourced from that country, and pass any savings on to consumers. Far more disturbing, however, was the persistent gap between prices in the EC and in the USA, given that these prices related to an identical product.

9.8. CA said that it was very hard to pinpoint the underlying reasons for the discrepancy between EC and US prices. Given its persistency over the years, and the fact that it continued even at very weak sterling exchange rates, it could not possibly be due to exchange rate changes alone.

9.9. Equally, CA did not think that the price differential could be attributed to differences in production costs or levels of royalties, given that these applied to exactly the same product, produced by the same artists, for the same recording company. The most likely explanation was quite simply that the record companies saw the EC as a relatively low-volume but high-profitability market as compared with the low-profitability mass market that existed in the USA. CA thought that this interpretation was to some extent borne out by the continuing low level of CD player ownership in the UK: the most recent figures available showed that 27 per cent of households had CD players, up from 21 per cent in 1990; broadly comparable figures suggested that the UK was roughly in line with Germany (24 per cent), France (23 per cent) and Denmark (20 per cent) in this respect, though well below the position in the Netherlands (43 per cent) and Switzerland (39 per cent), and well above the position in Italy (9 per cent).

9.10. CA said that, in theory, it would be possible for EC consumers to take advantage of at least some of the lower prices in North America. A number of US companies offered mail order. However, there were obvious limitations to this; in addition to postage and packaging, where charged, import duty was payable at EC borders at a rate of 4.9 per cent of total costs, and 17.5 per cent VAT had to be added to that. In addition, many consumers would need to take account of the (not insignificant) cost of a telephone call or fax across the Atlantic. CA believed that considerations of this kind, together with the inconvenience and risk of ordering from another country, ruled this option out for

248336 N2

all but the most enthusiastic, and more or less eradicated the prospect of EC retail prices being forced down by competition from personal imports from the USA.

9.11. Nevertheless, CA considered that if import agents, UK distributors and retail chains were allowed to import direct from wholesalers in the USA they could circumvent the obvious practical problems faced by private buyers. This was effectively barred, however, by UK copyright law—the 1988 Copyright Act—which provided that copyright owners or their licensees had the right to prevent the importation of records from another country, even where those records had been reproduced with the permission of the copyright owner in that particular country. In other words, the right of the copyright holder to prohibit imports extended to what would otherwise have been legitimate parallel imports, as well as to pirate recordings. Imports were sometimes permitted under licence, although they would normally be labelled as such, and were often sold in a special section of the shop concerned. CA said it understood that such specially licensed imported recordings were normally of material for which there was a very limited domestic market.

9.12. CA considered that the net result of import restrictions was the ability of copyright owners to segment the world market according to what price they thought different sections would bear. Arbitrage was impossible and competition from non-EC imports non-existent.

9.13. CA set out its response to each of the main arguments which might be put in favour of the current restrictions:

(a) *Copyright restrictions were needed to prevent piracy*. CA said that this was true. However, it was not a justification for preventing parallel imports from countries that had signed up to the various intellectual property conventions and enforced them properly. CA said that these conventions were specifically designed to ensure that copyright holders, among other rights-holders, would get a fair reward for their creative effort, and be well protected from counterfeiting and piracy. Provided copyright was being respected in the country of origin, it ought not to be any concern of the copyright holder if recordings were being exported and sold in another country. CA observed that international intellectual property conventions did not explicitly require member states to control parallel imports of recordings that had been legitimately produced and sold. Such restrictions would, after all, be incompatible with the freedom for parallel imports now enjoyed within the EC; moreover, Sweden had no restriction on parallel imports in its copyright legislation. It might even be argued that the lower prices that would result from a removal of controls over parallel imports would reduce the incentive to import pirated recordings.

(b) *Freedom of parallel imports would damage the UK music industry*. CA said that the argument could be made that high CD prices in the UK helped to keep our own music industry profit-able so that profits could be invested in recordings by UK artists. However, that argument was in CA's view misconceived. It was wrong to think of the prices paid by UK consumers as a kind of local subsidy for artists whose works would otherwise be unprofitable: if they were unprofitable, the artistic works concerned should either be subsidized by the state on clear public interest grounds, or they should not be produced. CA said that record companies invested in UK artists with the expectation that they could make a profit out of that investment which was, in this sense, simply risk capital. Inevitably there were considerable risks, since many works failed, but the rewards from success were great, especially if recordings sold well in overseas markets, including the USA with its low retail prices.

(c) *Imports would be 'free riders' on domestic investment in advertising and promotion*. CA argued that this could in theory be a problem for a UK producer without any overseas affiliates which had licensed the sale of its recordings to an overseas company, say in the USA, with which it had no direct links. In such circumstances, the UK company would probably be forced to charge a higher licence fee to the US company to cover its UK promotional efforts (the US company should have a sufficient incentive to accept this because of the prospect of UK exports). Otherwise, however, international music companies or companies that had major overseas affiliates should face no real problem: freedom of parallel importing would not reduce overall sales, merely sales through the UK arms of the companies.

190

9.14. CA noted that arguments of this kind had been considered in great detail by the Australian PSA (see paragraphs 3.46 to 3.49); CA said that the PSA report deserved careful study, as many of its conclusions applied directly to the UK.

9.15. CA said it was clear that copyright restrictions lay at the heart of the extreme and unfavourable price comparisons between the USA and the UK (and, for that matter, the rest of the EC). Such restrictions gave the record industry a degree of control over prices charged in different sections of the world market which very few other sectors of industry enjoyed. CA said that reform of these controls over parallel imports offered by far the best way of removing artificial barriers to genuine price competition in the UK market for sound recordings, thereby helping to secure a fairer deal for the public. CDs suffered from a 'market failure' which kept prices unjustifiably high, and that was due to a lack of clarity about what the copyright restrictions were for. Copyright was supposed to give artists an incentive to compose and perform their works without fear that others could copy them and take the gain. This should be entirely a matter for the production phase of the industry. Once a recording was put on the market there was no such market failure to be corrected and no reason to put obstacles in the way of international trade.

9.16. During the inquiry we invited CA to comment on the surveys conducted for the MMC by BMRB and Management Horizons Europe. In its comments, CA said that to a considerable extent these surveys underlined what it and many other critics of the record industry had alleged for some time, namely that prices were far higher in the UK and the rest of the EC than in the USA, and for no good reason. The precise percentage differences were slightly lower than in previous comparative exercises of this kind, but this was by no means unexpected given the recent substantial decline in the sterling/$ exchange rate. CA said that in assessing these developments, it was important that the MMC should take a long-term view—much as it had done with its comparisons of new car prices across the EC—before reaching a final verdict on the public detriment arising from the current situation. CA, however, did not consider that the BMRB survey on its own was sufficiently wide-ranging; the sample of titles assessed was far too small, particularly on the classical side.

9.17. In relation to the Management Horizons Survey, CA said that it was essential for the MMC to deal firmly and decisively with the arguments that adverse price differentials for other products justified adverse price differentials for recorded music; and that open parallel importing regimes had not eliminated price differences between other markets. CA considered that both of these arguments were spurious; they had nothing to do with the fundamental question of whether copyright holders should have a right to restrain parallel imports in the interests of market segmentation. CA remained strongly of the view that they should not.

British Copyright Council

9.18. The British Copyright Council (BCC) explained that it represented the interests of the copyright owners of virtually all the categories of works and products eligible for protection under the copyright law of the UK, save for sound recordings (represented by the BPI), films (represented by the British Film and Television Producers' Association) and the rights of broadcasters. The members of the BCC are the individual organizations which represent the various sectors of the copyright industry; currently there are 30 members.

9.19. The main points made by the BCC were:

(a) It was in the public interest for a copyright owner to be able to control the importation of all copies of his works or products made in another country without his authorization, including copies made in a country where there was no protection and hence no need for authorization; and the need for copyright owners to have this protection was recognized, and required, by the Berne Convention.

(b) Potential 'parallel imports' were copies of a protected work made with the direct or indirect authorization of the person who was the copyright owner in the country of manufacture. It was also in the public interest that a copyright owner should be able to control the importation of such copies.

191

(c) Copyright depended entirely upon statute; national laws did not have extra-territorial effect, and hence the copyright system internationally comprised a set of national systems defining and regulating national markets; and within each national intellectual property market the economic, commercial and legal characteristics were separate and distinct.

(d) Intellectual property had therefore been marketed on an individual market basis; copyright owners of national works and products needed to protect their investment from unfair competition by importations of copies of those works and products.

(e) Those who sought to bring in parallel imports made no contribution to the development of national production, nor to the publishing, printing and production industries, nor to the earning power of authors.

(f) Those who sought to bring in parallel imports were engaging, in effect, in unfair competition by capitalizing on the expenditure of the national copyright owners in developing the public demand for the works whose copies they sought to import; they did not stimulate competition or develop markets, but simply distorted legitimate trade.

(g) Those who sought to bring in parallel imports did not usually pass on the benefit of any cost differential between the imported copies and the copyright owner's supplies.

(h) Because of the availability of today's high technology to pirates, pirated copies were often almost indistinguishable from other copies. This meant that a power to control only the import of pirated copies would be unworkable in practice.

(i) There was no evidence that the existence of the power to control parallel imports, for example in the USA or Germany, had resulted in excessively high prices. There was also no evidence that in a country which had withdrawn the power prices had fallen; for example, prices of books in Australia.

9.20. The BCC noted that the EC Rental Directive required member states to make legislative provision for the power to control the importation of copies of protected works into the EC (ie not moving from one Community state to another, but into the EC). That Directive had to be implemented by 1 July 1994. The BCC said that similar discussions were being pursued in the WIPO meetings.

Trademarks Patents and Designs Federation

9.21. The Trademarks Patents and Designs Federation (TMPDF) explained that it represented the interests of owners of intellectual property (patents, trade marks, designs and copyright) over a wide spectrum, and included members who were owners of copyright sound recordings, computer programs1 and video recordings.

9.22. The TMPDF considered that the protection afforded by intellectual property rights had allowed important and creative segments of the market to develop without being undermined by piracy. The right to control the licensing of intellectual property rights was fundamental to the ownership of those rights. Licence rights must include the ability to control the distribution of the protected goods, including the right to license importation of goods into a territory. The reason for this was the straightforward need to ensure an orderly supply of goods on to the market, thereby avoiding sporadic local supply or unsatisfactory supply from a single source at a remote location. Any recommendation on the pricing of recorded music should allow for a continuation of the right to license the distribution of goods. This was a right which the TMPDF considered to be critical to success in a number of industries, not just that of sound recording.

9.23. The TMPDF noted that WIPO had held meetings of Government experts in June and July 1993 to discuss a possible protocol to the Berne Copyright Convention. The question of distribution rights was on the agenda of that meeting with an endorsement from WIPO in support of the right of copyright owners to control importation and distribution of copyright works. The TMPDF had supported the WIPO endorsement and had advised the UK Government representative of its support.

9.24. During the MMC inquiry the Uruguay round of the GATT agreement was completed. The TMPDF noted that a part of that agreement concerned intellectual property in what was referred to as the agreement on Trade Related Intellectual Properties (TRIPS). Within the TRIPS agreement there was a Part II which addressed copyright and specifically provided in Article 14 that producers of records should enjoy the right to authorize or prohibit the direct or indirect reproduction of their records. The TMPDF hoped that any MMC recommendations on the pricing of recorded music would accord with the fundamental principles of intellectual property law, including TRIPS.

National Music Council of Great Britain

9.25. The National Music Council of Great Britain (NMC) submitted written evidence. It is a member of the International Music Council, and has 37 member organizations in Great Britain, including the BPI, the MPA, the MCPS, and the Musicians' Union (MU). The NMC said that its submission had been prepared independently of any member organization and was submitted on behalf of its constituent members.

9.26. The NMC said it recognized that the reference related to whether or not a monopoly existed, and that it had been made against the background of the NHC's inquiry into CD prices. That inquiry had led to press and other comment that CD pricing in the UK could be dealt with by amendments to the 1988 Copyright Act, by removing from a copyright owner the ability to prevent parallel imports. The NMC said that such amendments to copyright legislation could have unforeseen adverse results.

9.27. The music industry relied on the legal rights which existed at different levels. These levels interacted, and any action to restrict the operation of any one element might adversely affect other rights. If imports were allowed from the USA, and volume became significant, three consequences would follow. First, the UK publisher of the musical work would not receive royalties on the imported product; secondly, a British composer of works contained on such records would ultimately receive a royalty from the USA, but only after some time, and at the US rate, which was lower than the UK or European rate; and thirdly, such product, once imported into the UK, would be able to circulate freely within the EC, influencing price levels, and hence the profitability of record companies and publishers, as well as the income of composers.

9.28. A significant inflow of product from the USA, resulting from a lifting of the import restrictions, could have a serious effect on the royalty earnings of composers and publishers per unit shipped. Composers and publishers would have no say in the price of a record, and in the UK they were not protected by a minimum royalty which would take effect when the price dropped below a certain level.

9.29. The NMC did not represent record retailers, but noted that if import restrictions were lifted, the most likely beneficiaries would be the large retail chains such as W H Smith and HMV. It said that these operations already controlled a large percentage of the market, and retail competition was unlikely to increase if import restrictions were lifted. Indeed any such move would probably have an adverse effect on independent record retailers, who tended to stock a wider range of product.

9.30. The NMC considered that protection against parallel imports was covered in the EC Rental Directive, and noted that one country, Norway, had recently passed an amendment to its Copyright Act effectively outlawing parallel imports. The USA already did so under section 602 of the US Copyright Act. It was unlikely to change its policy, and would no doubt welcome any relaxation by the UK.

Department of Trade and Industry

9.31. The Textiles and Retailing Division of the Department of Trade and Industry (DTI) submitted written evidence. The DTI stressed that its note was limited to certain economic issues and had not been seen by any DTI Ministers involved in competition matters.

9.32. The DTI observed that the record industry made an important contribution to the national economy; that its performance had compared favourably with that of the whole of UK manufacturing in recent years; that it was a sector in which the UK had absolute and comparative competitive strengths which should be exploited for the maximum advantage of the national economy; and that these competitive strengths should be allowed due scope for their expression. The DTI submitted some comparative statistics which highlighted the main facets of the record industry's recent performance.

9.33. The industry needed to earn sufficient revenues to enable it to invest not only in the most up-to-date plant and equipment, but also, and of particular significance, in the finding and development of new artistic talent. This multifaceted nature of 'investment' in the record industry meant that comparisons with other sectors required particular care; nevertheless, the DTI observed that the 20 per cent or so of turnover devoted to expenditure on A&R, together with expenditure on fixed capital formation, compared well with the 2.2 per cent of the value of sales spent on R&D in manufacturing industry generally and the 10.2 per cent in the electronics sector.

9.34. The DTI noted that the UK domestic market accounted for some 7 per cent of world record sales. The UK had one of the largest and best developed music industries in the world. Domestic product accounted for some 49 per cent of the UK record industry's sales value in 1992, against 39 per cent home production in France and 24 per cent in Germany. A buoyant, competitive and appropriately profitable domestic market was likely to remain a major factor in the UK record industry's ability to invest in the development of new artistic resources and in the growth, whether through direct export or royalty earnings, of its external business.

Media Research Publishing Ltd

9.35. *Mr Cliff Dane*, the author of the 1993 annual survey of the UK record industry for *Media Research Publishing Ltd*, a research and publishing company concerned primarily with the UK media sector, gave the MMC an overview of his general conclusions about the UK record industry which he had reached in the course of that survey. Mr Dane explained how his general approach had been to look in detail at the published accounts of all significant UK record companies, drawing on his personal knowledge of the industry.

9.36. Mr Dane said that, in analyzing the accounts of the largest record companies, there did not appear to be significant *prima facie* evidence of 'super-profits' either in absolute terms or by comparison with the recent past. This, he said, was certainly the case with PolyGram, BMG, Sony, Virgin, Warner and EMI.

9.37. However, the overall profitability of these companies might not give a true representation of their results from music products alone. The majors' UK subsidiaries often included video interests and distribution and manufacturing activities, which might or might not benefit from overseas income from direct sales or royalty income from licensing. Mr Dane believed that the MMC might be in a position to separate out the results of such different activities.

9.38. One of the keys to analyzing the underlying profitability of the majors was to look at their treatment of A&R costs, ie all those costs involved in the production and exploitation of new recordings. Theoretically, if there was a 'conspiracy' to remove super-profits from the main UK limited companies, this could be effected by paying onerous royalty rates on recordings originating outside the UK, and licensing out to other territories at a rate which subsidized the real costs. However, Mr Dane had no information in this area, and in view of the present UK tax regime, multinationals would be likely to want to increase rather than reduce their UK profits.

9.39. Nor did smaller, independent companies which had been considered 'successful' in the industry, such as Mute Records, Creation Records and Go! Discs, appear to have been making significant profits, or indeed yielding excessive management remuneration.

9.40. Two factors which Mr Dane considered had been significant in stopping what appeared to be high CD prices from generating excess profits had been the much higher returns enjoyed by artists than in the past, and the increasing costs of artist development such as promotional videos, recording costs and tour support. Moreover, the industry appeared to be taking a much more stringent approach to costs and overheads than hitherto, becoming increasingly dominated by accountants.

9.41. One area where the industry certainly did spend substantial sums was in investing in bands which were never successful. Mr Dane said that the majors could give numerous examples of this. He said that a low 'hit' rate was a key factor in high overall prices, and although the record companies obviously would not go out of their way to lose money on new artists, they in fact often did so.

9.42. Mr Dane considered that the exploitation of back catalogue and the success of a few major artists probably subsidized a large amount of unsuccessful A&R activity. Where companies were able to avoid originating new material, and instead to license in recordings from primary sources, they were often able to generate some of the more impressive profit figures in the industry, particularly in the mid- and budget-price markets. For example, the survey had included Tring, the super-budget specialist, and Music Collection International.

9.43. Mr Dane said that a feature of the industry in the last 20 years had been the growth of secondary marketing companies such as Pickwick, Castle, Demon, Ace and See for Miles.

9.44. Another factor in the debate over excessive profit, which Mr Dane believed could be overlooked, was the number of companies that had failed over the last decade. It was generally possible to salvage a company containing substantial copyrights, but there were many examples of failed companies which had relied on licensed rights, such as Stylus, K-Tel and Ronco (all of these in the television advertised market).

9.45. Mr Dane considered that other significant factors were:

(a) *Ease of, and barriers to, entry.* The music industry was relatively easy to enter and historically, small new companies had often developed major new talent, even if their artists subsequently moved on to the majors. In the last 20 years there had been significant new independents such as Chrysalis and Virgin; more recently Telstar, Castle and Mute had emerged in different sectors of the market, while in distribution Pinnacle had become a significant threat to the majors.

(b) *The relationship of the independents and majors.* Mr Dane thought that the NHC had appeared to adopt an 'independents are good' and 'majors are bad' stance. However, he noted that a feature of the industry was the multi-faceted links between majors and independents which included:

   (i)   majors linking with A&R-based independents (PWL, Big Life, ZTT, Go! Discs) in jointly-owned companies;

   (ii) independents licensing acts or labels to majors (Food);

   (iii) majors distributing independents' records (Beggars Banquet, Castle, Telstar);

   (iv) independents developing bands which then moved on to majors; and

   (v)   independents linking with majors for international sales.

Simkins Partnership of Solicitors

9.46. The Simkins Partnership of Solicitors (Simkins), a legal practice specializing in the media and entertainment sector, submitted written evidence. It said that the UK music industry in its present form operated in the public interest, generating a significant level of employment and export earnings, sustaining cultural dynamism, and producing a large number of internationally respected British cultural ambassadors at a corporate and individual level. Any amendment to legislation which was likely to have a harmful effect on such an important sector of UK industry should be considered as contrary to the public interest. Simkins considered that the removal of the current restriction on parallel imports would have such an effect.

9.47. Simkins said that the current system was designed to remunerate the UK artist, composer, record company and publisher on the basis that record manufacture took place within the UK or EC. The result of allowing into the UK market records manufactured outside the EC would be a massive distortion and inequitable distribution of reward, in which the creative contributors to the industry, the artists, composers and individual producers, would be likely to suffer most.

9.48. Simkins said that, notwithstanding the market share held between the majors, the independent record companies were responsible for a significant proportion of the market. Established artists often tended to gravitate to majors after starting their careers with independents. The independents ranged from one person with sufficient capital to press 1,000 records, up to sophisticated operations such as Beggar's Banquet and Mute Records which sold millions of records each year. The independents were also very important in the classical music field, where companies such as Conifer, Hyperion, Chandos and ASV supplied much innovative material.

9.49. If import restrictions were lifted, the effects would be as follows:

(a) First, a significant part of a UK music publisher's income was currently generated by the levying of a mechanical royalty in relation to each CD manufactured in the EC and sold in the UK. This was collected locally by the UK publisher and then divided between it and the UK composer. Simkins considered that it would be very harmful to UK publishers if that mechanical royalty were paid to the local sub-publisher in a country outside the EC and remitted to the UK publisher by its local sub-publisher for the following reasons:

   (i)   The UK publisher's receipts would be reduced by its sub-publisher's retention, which could be between 10 and 50 per cent. Thus UK publishers would earn significantly less. Where the UK publisher was a major, overseas retentions would benefit the multinational but not its UK operating company. Thus, even in the case of a major, the UK operating company would have its margins reduced.

   (ii) The rate of mechanical royalties payable by record companies to publishers outside the EC was significantly lower than in the UK, and elsewhere in the EC it was higher than in the UK. In the USA, for instance, royalties were calculated at a rate which was effectively 30 to 50 per cent lower than in the UK. The US rate was greatly reduced by the operation of what were termed 'controlled composition' clauses in the recording contracts entered into with artists. These typically provided for a ceiling on the level of mechanical royalties payable to publishers. That ceiling was usually set at 75 per cent of the rate recommended by the US Copyright Royalty Tribunal.

   (iii) The UK publisher would have to rely on the efficiency and accuracy of the accounting practices of its sub-publisher. This was probably not such a concern for the majors, but for independent publishers, relying on the veracity of accounts submitted from distant parts of the world with cheap labour costs (and therefore cheap CD manufacturing costs), there was bound to be a significant loss of revenue.

   Simkins argued that the combined effect of these three factors could well reduce the margin of UK publishers by 25 per cent and possibly by more than double that figure. This would seriously damage the UK publishing business which made a major contribution to the success of the industry.

(b) Secondly, Simkins said that the margins that UK record companies earned on UK CDs which they had manufactured in the UK or the EC were significantly higher than the margins earned from royalties paid in respect of sales of CDs manufactured outside the EC. Simkins estimated that the return would be between four and six times as great on domestically manufactured CDs as on royalties paid by licensees outside the EC in respect of locally manufactured CDs. Again, problems regarding the ineffectiveness of audit rights and the veracity of accounts would apply. Simkins considered that if the proposed copyright changes were implemented, UK record companies would undoubtedly suffer from a significant level of 'leakage' of product from overseas into the domestic market. This would reduce the sales of their own domestically manufactured CDs upon which they received the margins which underpinned their investment in new talent, promotion and marketing costs. The majors would suffer less than the independents because any profits foregone in the UK would be made by the multinational through its overseas affiliates and thus kept within the organization. But the importance and influence of the majors' UK operating companies would be significantly reduced.

(c) Thirdly, UK recording artists generally received their remuneration in the form of royalties and advances from UK record companies. Simkins said that the UK record companies' profits would be significantly reduced by the lifting of import controls under the 1988 Copyright Act, and inevitably the artist would suffer. Fewer artists would be engaged by record companies and those who were would receive lower royalties and advances.

(d) Fourthly, in the case of much contemporary popular music, the recording artist was often also the composer of the musical works he or she recorded. Simkins said that in the early stages of his or her career, it was frequently the advance received from a publishing company that provided the means by which the artist or composer could develop his or her talent. Without such support from the publisher, creative talent would be deprived of a vital source of support at a critical stage of its development. Simkins argued that the specific disadvantages that would occur for a composer if import restrictions were lifted were as follows:

    (i)   The composer typically received a share of the publisher's income from the exploitation of publishing rights. This would range from 50 to 80 per cent of the publisher's receipts. Accordingly, if the UK publisher's return from mechanical royalties was reduced by 25 per cent to 50 per cent in the case of imported CDs, then there would be the same diminution in the composer's remuneration from this important source.

    (ii)   The problems regarding royalty collection supervision and audit rights that had been mentioned above would apply equally to UK composers.

(e) Finally, any manufacturing or duplication outside the UK that would previously have taken place within the UK would detrimentally affect this area of the business. The lifting of import restrictions would inevitably have such an effect. The result would be lay-offs and ultimately a reduction in capacity. This would diminish the service that the manufacturing sector of the industry could supply to the record companies, which required speed and flexibility of response in a fast moving retail market.

9.50. Simkins noted that WIPO was proposing a Protocol to the Berne Convention on authors' rights which would improve copyright protection, rather than reduce it. It said that one of the four proposals which had been included for discussion was the introduction of a general right to control the import of sound carriers. Sections 22 and 27 of the 1988 Copyright Act already did that for the UK, and Simkins considered that it was illogical to remove a level of protection at national level that was being proposed at the international level.

9.51. Furthermore, the unilateral removal of a level of protection that was enjoyed by music industries in other advanced countries would inevitably put the UK industry at a competitive disadvantage. Such changes had to be made on a world-wide basis to have an equitable effect.

9.52. Simkins said that, in any case, it was not at all sure that allowing parallel imports would result in generally lower UK prices. If allowing parallel imports did bring down prices, such reductions

197

would only apply to the most popular recordings. It doubted that there would be sufficient volume to justify wholesalers in the UK importing records for artists who were not in, say, the top 10 or 20 positions in the *Music Week* albums chart. Damage to the industry would be caused because of the narrowing of margins in relation to the most commercially successful material. This would have the knock-on effect of reducing the funds available for investment in less commercially successful sectors or in nurturing new talent.

9.53. Simkins said that if the Norwegian experience (prior to the change in Norwegian law) was relevant, then imports were likely to remain at a high level. 20 per cent of the CD market in Norway consisted of parallel imports, mostly from the USA; furthermore, the emphasis was on best-selling albums.

9.54. Nor was Simkins convinced that any lowering of prices would lead to increased sales. Many UK record companies had demonstrated a level of success that would be the envy of large sections of British industry. If those record companies thought they could increase the number of units sold and thereby their return by lowering prices then Simkins was sure that one or other of them would have done so. It therefore doubted very much whether any increase in sales would outweigh the reduction in income per unit.

9.55. Simkins considered that the effect of parallel imports on independent record companies would be particularly damaging. Independents might well be able to command premium prices for some of their releases, but they would have great difficulty doing so in relation to their best-selling albums if these were competing with parallel imports. For example, a group which released their records through an independent in the UK and through a major in the USA would find that the UK dealer price applied by the independent would be significantly undercut by parallel imports from the USA.

9.56. Independents lived off their most successful albums. If they were unable to retain their margins on those very successful acts, they would be in no position to release many of their less commercial records. The question whether those less commercial records could command premium prices or not would therefore be academic since the independents would be unable to sustain the cost of recording and releasing the numbers of records that currently made their way into the market.

9.57. Simkins said that the irony of the proposed change was that arguably the least harmful effects would be felt by the major multinational companies who would be able to take their profits through overseas affiliates. It was the independents who would be put out of business first by the change. Ownership and control of the industry would be concentrated into fewer, increasingly foreign hands, often interested more in short-term profits than in nurturing indigenous talent. Thus, far from serving the public interest, the lifting of import restrictions would strengthen the monopolistic position of the small number of multinational record companies that controlled the global market.

Members of the public

9.58. The main points made in the letters from members of the public were that prices were higher in the UK than the USA, Hong Kong, or Europe; that the larger retail chains such as W H Smith and HMV charged higher prices than some smaller retailers even though they must be obtaining larger discounts; that record companies were charging 'full price' on 'back catologue' CDs; that small retailers experienced difficulties in obtaining supplies from the large record companies and were forced to purchase through distributors; that the public was being forced to purchase CDs because vinyl records were being eliminated (and cassettes did not offer comparable quality); that availability of some CD recordings was a problem; that there should be some relationship between price and playing time rather than an arbitrary divide between mid-price and full-price—many CDs ran only for 50 to 60 minutes although they had been promoted as offering up to 80 minutes' playing time. The view was also expressed that since the inquiry had been announced, CD prices had fallen, but no doubt they would rise again if the MMC made no pricing recommendations. Other comments are summarized in the following paragraphs.

9.59. One member of the public submitted a petition. One hundred and two people had signed it, also stating at what price 'they would buy more than twice as many CDs'. The prices cited ranged from £4.99 up to £9.99.

9.60. *A songwriter* and music fan, who had been a performer and had worked in artist management and record production, made a submission.

9.61. He said that since the mid-1960s, British popular music had enjoyed great success throughout the world. Overseas sales of British music had contributed greatly to the country's economy as markets such as the USA, Japan and Germany have looked to the UK as a major talent source. The British record chart was a shop window and UK chart success was often a springboard to international sales. However, in recent years Britain's position had weakened, as its music industry had failed to sustain the launch and development of world-beating musical talent. Whilst many music industry executives chose to regard this problem as short-lived, it was hard to imagine Britain regaining its former pre-eminence by the end of the decade. There were two main reasons for this: first, the nature of music broadcasting, and secondly, the high price of CDs.

9.62. He observed that in the UK there existed a massive audience for song-based rock music; this sold albums, filled concert halls, created worthwhile music copyrights, built careers and, unlike 'dance', 'novelty' and 'lightweight pop' music, was capable of making an impression in the international market. In his view both the BBC and independent radio (and television) had failed to cater properly for this audience and had therefore lessened the incentive for record companies to sign and develop the sort of acts that might otherwise have achieved international success.

9.63. On the pricing question, he argued that the music industry's only consideration seemed to be the short-term goal of satisfying corporate demands, ie as unit sales declined, profits could only be maintained by increasing prices. The short-sighted policy of pushing the retail price of CDs beyond £14, when there was clearly justification for a significant price reduction, was seriously damaging the domestic market and the future for British music around the world. He observed that in defending this policy, record companies had stated that the signing of new talent would be compromised by lowering prices, but this did not ring true. How could the record labels be taken seriously in this respect when CDs of new acts were selling for the same high prices as CDs by established names? What was the point of signing new talent and pricing it beyond the reach of the average record buyer?

9.64. He said that in order to maintain the illusion that CDs were fairly priced at £12 to £13, the record companies had artificially inflated the price of other formats to flatter CDs. In the case of vinyl, the format was slowly being killed off. At the same time, there was gross wastage of money in A&R, promotion and marketing.

9.65. By gradually raising dealer prices, the record companies had put the onus to sell units more and more on to the retail sector. But there was also a degree of hypocrisy from the high street. The biggest retailers' profiteering could not have gone unnoticed by the record companies' account managers and had perhaps added to the atmosphere of mistrust between the two factions.

9.66. There had, however, been one significant development since the NHC inquiry and that was the proliferation of CD special offers in the high street. Whilst record companies would have preferred to maintain the illusion that CDs were fairly priced at £14 (and therefore an absolute bargain at £9.99), they were clearly being forced to offer them at considerably less than that. As each month passed, the major companies, co-operating with the retail chains, took turns in offering 'selected releases' at £9.99. The following month they 'all swapped places'. Retailers and record companies were unlikely to publish the results of these price-cutting campaigns, but it was understood in the industry that sales often increased dramatically.

9.67. Finally, he said that any proposal to change copyright law, which was extremely complex, would be an inappropriate response, but if that were to happen, the industry would be responsible.

9.68. *Mr C E Barrans* said that one of the advantages of CDs was the available playing time of up to about 78 minutes, more than the equivalent of two whole 12-track LPs, yet there very few CDs which featured the contents of two complete LPs. He noted that some CDs had less than 30 minutes of music on them. He considered that there should be some relationship between price and playing time.

9.69. Another unfair practice adopted by recorded music manufacturers and retailers was their use of the manufacturers' 'special price' stickers. Often the customer would in fact be charged full-price at the counter. Mr Barrans said that his queries about this practice had met with rather feeble excuses from the manufacturers and retailers concerned. Mr Barrans also queried why some productions were sold at mid-price and others at full-price, whereas there had been no price difference when these productions had been available in LP and cassette formats. He also did not understand why megastores charged between 50p and £1 more for CDs than the usual price in other stores such as W H Smith. Finally, Mr Barrans said that there had been further price increases in recent months with mid-price CDs costing nearly £10 and full-price CDs costing nearly £15.

9.70. *Mr M Hodgson* said that in comparing the various retail prices within the UK it should be borne in mind that the megastores and chains had much more buying power than an independent retailer such as his employer, Covent Garden Records (CGR). He said that there seemed little justification for the megastores' higher prices. Overheads might be high in the central London megastores, but the provincial branches of the same shops generally charged the same prices.

9.71. Mr Hodgson also considered that average retail margins in the UK were higher than in the USA, but said that US record shops had much of their stock on a sale-or-return basis, which meant they did not have to pay for it until sold, and could return any 'over-buys'. He pointed out that small companies such as CGR generally had to reduce prices to clear stock. Furthermore, he understood that UK mail order companies generally carried little or no stock and obtained discs only to meet specific customer orders, thereby avoiding the retailers' heavy investment in stocks. He said that US stores were also used to having the record companies' representatives coming in and counting the stock for them prior to taking an order, with considerable savings for them in staff time and salaries.

9.72. He considered that the economies of scale in a market the size of the USA were considerable compared with the UK. Both because of this discrepancy, and the greater productivity of US workers, most consumer goods were cheaper in the USA. He therefore wondered why CDs were being investigated. They were after all a luxury, whereas food was a necessity. Mr Hodgson observed in any case that CDs in the UK were around £5 cheaper than in France or Germany, which he considered a more relevant comparison than the USA with its very different economies of scale.

9.73. He nevertheless concluded that there was one aspect of the record companies' pricing policy which did warrant investigation. There were two rival systems ready to replace the analogue cassette— the DCC and the MiniDisc. Both offered recordability, and both were digital, but the specification was not as high as for CD. Yet the pre-recorded software cost the same as a top price CD. There seemed to be no justification for this, and even less for the policy of bringing out new titles on DCC and MiniDisc (for which there was hardly any market yet) but not on analogue cassette. It seemed to him to be a cynical attempt to force the consumer to invest in yet another format.

9.74. Finally, Mr Hodgson said that he hoped the MMC would bear in mind that any attempt to force UK retailers to reduce prices generally would force some out of business and would certainly have a detrimental effect on their staff in the present recession—none of the staff at CGR, for example, had had a pay rise for nearly two years, despite there having been redundancies.

9.75. *Mr P Howat* said that like many people who had commented on the high price of CDs, he had seen and bought CDs in the USA, and had wondered why they were relatively so much cheaper there than here. Similarly, he had observed that they were even more expensive in other European countries, albeit that the sterling equivalent price of CDs bought in other countries depended on prevailing exchange rates. However, as a *Gramophone* reader he was aware that many discounts were available on CDs sold in the UK. Indeed he said that it was extremely rare for him to pay the full price. He argued that presumably the advertisers in *Gramophone* (and other magazines) were able to support the smaller mark-up over the wholesale price by the greater volume of sales that their lower prices achieved. This suggested that the price elasticity significantly exceeded minus one. On the other hand he assumed that these mail order companies might not have the high cost of retail premises.

9.76. He was aware of the argument that it was necessary for the wholesale price of CDs to be high to enable the manufacturers to cross-subsidize, ie pay for losses on poor sellers, with the profits from good sellers. He was prepared to accept this. He said that on scanning *Gramophone* he was always surprised at the number of new CDs that were issued each month. He noted that some of these issues were of music that was very rarely heard, and the existence of such recordings was a boon. He believed that the industry could and should regulate itself; a company whose product failed to satisfy its market would, after all, go out of business.

9.77. He concluded that, while he would welcome cheaper CDs, he himself rarely paid more than 80 per cent of the full price. He was prepared to accept that the present wholesale price structure supported the recording industry well, enabling it to be innovative. Record buyers had the choice of high shop prices or lower mail order prices. On balance he considered that the price of CDs was satisfactory and a wide choice was available to the consumer.

9.78. *Mr R A Kempster* hoped that the inquiry would obtain satisfactory answers to the following questions:

(a) Why was it apparently essential that all full-priced CDs cost virtually the same price? The production costs for an opera must be appreciably more than those for a solo piano recital.

(b) Why was it invariably the case that a two, three, or four CD set cost two, three, or four times the single CD price? Surely the production, packaging and retailing costs were not in this proportion?

(c) Why were cassettes and LPs sold at appreciably lower prices than CDs, when the actual manufacturing costs had now become similar?

(d) Why did recordings from small specialist labels have to cost the same as those from major international companies? In other branches of publishing this was not the case—the stock of a major bookshop would reflect a diversity of prices as well as subject matter.

9.79. Mr Kempster did not consider that prices of CDs were necessarily too high, but did believe that some of the manufacturers' practices needed investigation and explanation, and that the behaviour of the major retailers, who had an apparent stranglehold on the market, should also be reviewed. He concluded that there was a suspicion of a monopoly which partially worked to the benefit of the consumer, but which mainly benefited the large manufacturers and retailers, and that it should be investigated.

9.80. *Mr J R A Lilley* raised the following points for consideration by the MMC:

(a) Should a small number of companies, one of which had developed the CD format at great cost at a time when the technology was already dated, be allowed to force out other formats by simply using their dominant position and by not issuing recordings in those formats? He noted that one often heard or saw 'CD only' or 'no cassettes'. Thus it seemed that people were being forced to buy the high profit margin CDs to the benefit of the record companies and retailers.

(b) Why limit comparison of the sales price of CDs in the UK with that of CDs in other countries? Why not make a comparison of the recording, manufacturing and distribution costs of CDs, LPs and cassettes, as well as their sales price? In this respect Mr Lilley noted that in quality terms it was difficult to distinguish between CDs and digitally recorded LPs.

9.81. *Mr G O'Neill* said that he had built up a collection of some 800 CDs covering a range of music from opera to rock and pop over the past four years. They were largely replacements for his existing vinyl record collection. A number of these recordings had been imported from the USA, Europe and Japan.

9.82. Mr O'Neill had observed that prices in the retail chains such as Woolworths or Boots tended to be near the top of the range. Those in the specialist chains such as Our Price, HMV and Tower varied; many records were at full price, but sales were held on a regular basis in these outlets and typically £2 or £3 might be deducted from the nominal price. It was in the independent record shops that prices were often lower, as such outlets had to compete with the chains. Here, price reductions might be made in niche repertoire as an inducement to regular customers; these stores also typically competed on the specialist knowledge of their staff and their willingness to order records either from within the UK or from abroad.

9.83. Mr O'Neill said that imported CDs were available, but at a higher price than UK product and in much smaller quantities. It was sometimes possible to obtain such imports before the release date in the UK but the major record companies tended to use their oligopolistic position to prevent the importation of such parallel product. Often, customers who had been willing to pay a premium for imported records found that the record companies reissued these at mid-price at a later date; this tactic tended to act as a disincentive to collectors purchasing imported CDs and enabled the major record companies to control the CD market. Mr O'Neill considered that the import licensing rules should be relaxed in order to encourage importers to bring product into the UK and increase competition.

9.84. In Mr O'Neill's view, the major record companies constituted an oligopoly in the international music industry. Their multinational operations allowed them to achieve economies of scale, for example in marketing, and to segment the market, thus enabling discriminatory pricing to occur. Their relationship with the independents was parasitic; while the latter discovered new talent, the longer-term gains from its exploitation were enjoyed by the majors. The latter also benefited from their long-term contractual relationships with artists. The majors had also effectively killed off the vinyl record, forcing consumers to purchase the more profitable CD.

9.85. *Dr M C Steele* said that, as recent contributors to the *Gramophone* magazine had pointed out, a blanket assertion that CDs were being overpriced by the companies that produced them considerably oversimplified the issue. He considered that there certainly was overpricing, but that the case had to be established fully, with examples.

9.86. Dr Steele said that that the present full price for a CD of £14 to £15 was certainly too high—even allowing for inflation—and was inhibiting the type of expansion in sales that had occurred with the LP in the 1950s and 1960s. He hoped that a long-term study of production costs, clearly distinguishing technical costs (which one would expect to fall) and labour costs (which one would expect to rise in line with the RPI), would be made. He observed that the record collector would need to be satisfied that the second category was now the chief determinant—ie that the increasing price of the CD was not simply going into the pockets of the record industry at whatever level.

9.87. Dr Steele said that with a few minor exceptions, the industry had served the classical collector reasonably well so far as mid-price CDs were concerned. However:

(a) The current high street price of £9.99 for EMI and PolyGram CDs—ie over 65 per cent of the full price—could not be termed 'mid-price'. This niche was filled by Classics for Pleasure and IMP, termed 'budget' price. He believed that the spirit, if not the letter, of trades description legislation should be applied to ensure the correct nomenclature.

(b) Even allowing for VAT increases last year ('very smartly passed on to the consumer by most high street retailers!'), the mid-price CD had increased in price from £7.99 to £9.99 over the past two years—an increase proportionately higher than that of full-price CDs over the same period.

(c) Regular perusal of *Gramophone* suggested that the listings of mid-price releases by the major companies had declined in number over the past two to three years. If these impressions were correct, he suggested that any inquiry into CD pricing would need to take this into account.

9.88. Dr Steele welcomed the arrival of the budget-priced Naxos recordings to the UK market and noted similarly that collectors had benefited from other, smaller producers such as IMP, which used British as well as Croatian and Hungarian orchestras, and had managed to maintain reasonable price levels, although he noted that such recordings were often poorly represented on the shelves of larger retailers.

9.89. He noted that in the late 1980s some companies—notably Olympia, Hyperion and Bis—had maintained price levels some £1.50 to £3.00 below those of the majors. Such price differences seemed to have narrowed since then. He said that while retailers might be responsible, CD purchasers needed to be reassured that it was not the result of a trend towards price setting at a uniformly high rate, and the end of free competition between independents and majors.

9.90. However, Dr Steele considered that the industry should be congratulated for giving the classical consumer value for money most of the time—ie providing over 65 minutes of music on each CD. Nevertheless, it still occasionally tried to sell CDs with 37 minutes of music on them at full price. Similarly, he noted that the industry had profited on works just over 80 minutes in length, usually spreading them over two full-price CDs—eg the *Nutcracker* ballet and *Salome*—although recently there had been signs that the industry had responded to criticism of this practice.

9.91. Dr Steele said he was surprised that the high street retailing arm of EMI (HMV) sold full-price EMI CDs at prices not greatly different from its competitors. He said that he knew the argument was that EMI did not want to compete unfairly with its high street rivals by exploiting its role of record producer and retailer: on the other hand he considered that this really amounted to a price-fixing understanding at the expense of the customer. In any case, it was commercially anomalous that a major recording company should also be a retailer.

9.92. In his view the recording industry had not helped itself by investing in new vehicles such as DCC and MiniDisc. The collector was having to subsidize technical developments that he or she might not want, and which were commercially inappropriate in the present climate of economic recession. Dr Steele argued that it made more sense to cut costs for existing well-established delivery systems (the cassette and the CD), rather than to spend vast amounts on research and development to devise yet more systems for which there was no mass market.

9.93. *Mr R Westcott* made representations on behalf of Analogue Addicts (Analogue), a national voluntary organization of which he was a member. Analogue had been formed in 1988 with the aim of saving vinyl LPs from disappearing.

9.94. Mr Westcott said that he appreciated that pricing might be the principal concern of the inquiry, but he hoped that the MMC would not fail to address the matter of the unfair treatment of the vinyl LP format. He considered that the media had failed to recognize the minority concern about the record companies' deliberate policy to eliminate vinyl LPs, in the interests of greater profits, and against public demand, by the 'forced' substitution of CDs. In Mr Westcott's view, LPs were good value for money (costing no more than £10.00 an album); they were the most collectable format with the best packaging; and most importantly, they offered musical superiority. The British specialist hi-fi industry had recognized vinyl LPs as having the best sound quality of any format.

9.95. Analogue considered that recent consumer surveys had indicated sufficient demand for vinyl LPs to warrant a renewal of sales from high street stores. However, it was clear that the record companies, which formed a cartel, wanted to control format supply to maximize profitability irrespective of the public's wishes. Analogue said that this was wrong. People deserved the freedom to choose, and vinyl deserved fair treatment.

248336 O

10   Views of industry bodies

Contents

Collective licensing bodies

Mechanical Copyright Protection Society Limited

10.1. The MCPS is a member of the BCC, and a society representing as agent those who own, control or administer the rights in the UK to copy or to reproduce those musical works and their associated lyrics which are in copyright. The MCPS submitted written evidence to the MMC and attended a joint hearing with its parent body the Music Publishers' Association Limited (MPA). The MCPS has been owned since 1976 by the MPA (for the MPA's views see paragraphs 10.89 to 10.105). The MCPS's role and activities are described in Chapter 4.

10.2. The MCPS said that copyright was in essence a territorial right. Apart from the International Conventions (Rome and Berne) and the Treaty of Rome, it was subject to the national laws of each country. The aim of both the International Conventions and of domestic copyright legislation was to protect the original creative works of the composer and author. Copyright safeguarded the need for a composer as the creator of an original musical work to receive a fair reward for its exploitation by those who used it for their own commercial gain. That reward could only be derived from the royalties payable by users. This right of a composer to receive equitable remuneration was recognized in the revision to the Berne Copyright Convention signed at Stockholm in 1967.

10.3. Copyright owners of musical works could not in practice license and administer the inclusion of those works in sound recordings on an individual basis. Collective licensing on standard terms, including the royalties payable, recognized this reality.

10.4. It was important to clarify the position regarding the importation of records into the UK from third countries outside the EC and in particular from the USA. CA had suggested that the same open-borders policy should apply to imports of pre-recorded music from the USA as applied within the EC. In view of the purported lower cost of pre-priced recorded music in the USA, it had been argued that these lower-priced goods would act as a stimulus to competition in the UK market, and result in lower prices for the consumer.

10.5. The MCPS drew attention to recent evidence given to the NHC by W H Smith, a major retailer with a high percentage of the UK retail market for recorded music. W H Smith had pointed to many practical difficulties in the way of importing US products, quite apart from issues of copyright law. It would be necessary to import in bulk in order to get discounts; moreover, the attendant costs of stockholding and distribution would considerably erode any price advantage which could be passed down to the consumer.

10.6. Copyright owners had to be sure that imports of pirate material produced without any copyright licence were banned from entry into the UK. The MCPS stressed the importance of current copyright protection, in particular the right of the copyright owner to control importation under section 27 of the 1988 Copyright Act, in helping to control piracy. Any erosion of this right would undermine the basic principles of copyright law and make the control of piracy more difficult.

10.7. The MCPS said that the scale of imports of pre-recorded product from outside the EC under the MCPS/BPI Import Scheme had over the years been cyclical, depending in part on exchange rates, particularly the exchange rate between the US dollar and pound sterling. For example, if the US dollar was too high, imports of records made in the USA declined because their price to the consumer was above that of locally-produced products. The reverse was also true.

10.8. The MCPS noted that the NHC had recognized in its report that section 602 of the US Copyright Act:

> prevents the importation into the USA from the UK of any CDs, tapes or LPs containing copyright material owned, controlled or licensed to American producers or publishers and that as a result of this trade barrier the UK's share of the American market had diminished from 34 per cent in 1985 to 14 per cent currently.

This legislation was much stronger than the comparable UK provisions. In addition, most US licences were for distribution within the USA. Exports in breach of such licences could not be totally prevented.

10.9. The MCPS stressed the potentially adverse effect of any relaxation of the law relating to parallel imports from the USA, if this was not matched by a similar relaxation in US law. The MCPS considered that the concept of reducing copyright protection to the lowest common denominator would damage the UK's creative abilities and would reduce its foreign earnings.

10.10. Unlike the UK, which had abolished its compulsory licensing procedure, the USA still had a compulsory licence, and record companies were able to force the low statutory royalties payable in the USA even further down by the operation of controlled composition clauses. If parallel import provisions were removed in the UK, the effect of the US statutory provisions and the controlled composition clauses would spread to the UK. The MCPS submitted that this would be a breach of the Berne Convention which provided that compulsory licence provisions only applied in the country in which they were imposed.

10.11. Finally, the MCPS said that the MMC should not consider only the roles of retailers and record companies, balanced against the interests of consumers. Composers were also an intrinsic and essential part of the music industry. Decisions which were taken regarding the production and distribution end of the industry should be considered in the context of the effects they would have on the composers and on the music publishers who represented them. The MCPS said that no erosion of copyright law and protection must take place. If it were to do so, that could be to the detriment of the creative parties, and also, ultimately, to the consumer.

248336 O2

Phonographic Performance Limited

10.12. PPL submitted written evidence and attended a hearing. Since 1934, PPL has licensed the UK Performance Copyrights in records, namely the right for third parties to broadcast and play recordings in public, on behalf of record companies (see paragraphs 4.73 to 4.77).

10.13. Commenting on the recommendations made by the MMC in their 1988 report,[1] PPL said that only two had not yet been implemented. The first was that all performers should receive equitable remuneration paid directly by PPL. PPL's revenues were distributed as follows: 67.5 per cent to the record companies, 20 per cent to named performers and 12.5 per cent to the MU for its session musicians. PPL said that in respect of the payments to the MU, negotiations were at an advanced stage, and PPL hoped that the question as to how the 12.5 per cent would now be distributed to session artists would be resolved. The moneys were being held on account. PPL said that it expected a settlement soon.

10.14. The second recommendation which had not yet been carried out related to the distribution of payments to named performers. PPL explained how matters had moved on since the 1988 recommendations were made. It was presently considering a new method of distribution based on more comprehensive sampling of Independent Local Radio broadcasts. PPL said that distribution relating to public performance was the least satisfactory part of its operation. At the moment the vast bulk of the money which was distributed was on the basis of Radio 1 and 2 broadcasting returns. PPL was now considering basing its distribution of public performance revenue principally on usage returns from relevant licensees.

10.15. PPL confirmed that all member companies and artists, whether in specialized repertoire or popular, whether large or small, famous or unknown, would get the same rate of remuneration per second or per minute of playing time if their record was shown on a broadcasting usage return.

10.16. PPL told the MMC that it was currently considering proposals to change the 'Rules of Admissibility' to full membership of the organization. At present, of the 1,483 members, 21 were full members; the remainder had associate status. The intention was to increase the number of full members of the organization and substantially widen the 'franchise'.

10.17. No decision about changes to PPL's membership rules had been made by the time our inquiry was completed.

Performing Right Society Limited

10.18. The PRS has 2,453 publisher members and 24,602 composer members. It administers the performing rights of composers, authors and publishers (see paragraphs 4.78 to 4.80). The PRS said that it associated itself fully with the views expressed by the MCPS (see paragraphs 10.1 to 10.11). Any erosion in copyright protection would be harmful to its members. Moreover, since the copyright regime existed in order to provide economic incentives to creators, if those incentives were to be diminished, so too would be the output of those creators, and this would be to the detriment of society generally.

Video Performance Limited

10.19. VPL submitted written evidence and attended a hearing. VPL originated in 1984 as a collecting society to license the UK public performance and broadcasting rights in music videos owned or controlled by its members (see paragraphs 4.81 and 4.82).

---

[1]*Collective Licensing: a report on certain practices in the Collective Licensing of Public Performance and Broadcasting Rights in Sound Recordings*, Cmnd 530, December 1988.

10.20. Referring to the EC complaint and UK court case brought against it by MTVE (see paragraph 10.138), PPL said that it had made clear in its various submissions to the EC Commission that it had little doubt that MTVE's objective in seeking to negotiate rates individually with the record companies for use of their music videos was to create for itself in Europe the same dominant position as its sister company, MTV, already enjoyed in the USA. If, as a result of pressure from MTVE through its various legal actions, collective licensing of music videos through VPL were no longer possible, it would be the smaller VPL members who would suffer even more than the majors. The majors enjoyed a sufficient degree of bargaining power to ensure that they would still receive payment for use of their videos. Smaller companies, on the other hand, would be likely to find that they received little or no payment. Once the principle of 'pay for play' was undermined in this way, the whole value of copyright in recorded music (including music videos) would also be undermined, with potentially very serious consequences for the whole music industry.

10.21. VPL explained that it received moneys from the broadcasters over the year and then distributed those moneys to its members, after deduction of expenses, on the basis of the actual usage made of each member's videos. Distributions were made annually with two payments on account during the year. VPL estimated that between 75 and 80 per cent of the titles it licensed were produced by the major record companies.

10.22. VPL said that any move away from a single negotiation by VPL on behalf of its members to a situation where each record company had to arrange fees itself with broadcasters would be a potentially very serious problem for independents.

Representative bodies in the industry

International Federation of the Phonographic Industry

10.23. The IFPI submitted written evidence and attended a hearing. It represents the world-wide recording industry with a membership of 1,055 members in 72 countries; in the UK its member companies are organized in the BPI (see paragraphs 4.85 and 4.86).

10.24. The IFPI said that there was a wide diversity of economic, commercial and legal infrastructures across the different countries having copyright laws. These shaped decisions about when and where, and on what terms, records were manufactured and distributed. International copyright and neighbouring rights protection of sound recordings varied so widely that new recordings were likely always to find themselves completely unprotected in several countries and subject to limited protection in many others. In so basic a matter as duration of copyright protection, for example, national laws were still far from uniform. To deprive authors, performers and producers of the ability to protect the rights they enjoyed in states with strong copyright laws from exports originating in states that failed to respect their interests would be generally harmful. But, of equal concern to the public interest, it allowed the indifference to authors, performers and producers reflected in one country's laws to thwart the cultural and economic policies of other countries that vigorously promoted creativity through generous copyright systems.

10.25. In a world characterized by sharply uneven levels of intellectual property protection accorded to record producers, the role of importation rights had become critical. The IFPI believed that the importance of importation rights was becoming more widely recognized—in national laws, in the negotiation of new treaties and other international agreements and in the developing rules of the EC.

10.26. The IFPI said that there was an absolute need for a right to authorize or prohibit the importation of sound recordings and any reduction of the importation right now provided in the 1988 Copyright Act would be contrary to the international trend to recognize such a right in national legislations and would raise conflicts with obligations existing under EC law.

10.27. The right to authorize or prohibit importation served the public interest, because parallel imports tended to have an unfavourable effect on national art and culture. The consequences of parallel imports for national cultural heritage included a smaller range of recorded music available to the general public and a limitation on the funds for the promotion of national arts and artists.

Depriving intellectual property owners of a specific importation right would mean acting against a prosperous national cultural heritage, and it would also have a negative influence on the fight against piracy, given the difficulties in distinguishing legitimate from illegal copies.

10.28. The IFPI concluded that this was why the majority of countries provided a right to authorize or prohibit the importation of copies of works. Some of these rights had been introduced fairly recently and it seemed that more countries were set to follow these examples. In the member states of the EC such a right was required under the terms of the EC Rental Directive, which had to be implemented by member states by 1 July 1994.

British Phonographic Industry Limited

10.29. The BPI held meetings with MMC staff, commented on draft MMC questionnaires and surveys, and submitted written evidence, including a submission representing the views of the BPI independent record company membership, and an economic study commissioned by the BPI and carried out by National Economic Research Associates (NERA), which addressed the question of how the independent sector could be affected by a significant reduction in the prices of CDs. The BPI also attended a hearing.

10.30. The BPI is a trade association which represents a variety of different manufacturers, producers and sellers of all forms of phonograms, including vinyl discs, CDs and audio cassettes (see paragraphs 4.83 and 4.84). The BPI explained that its membership was open, on an entirely transparent and non-discriminatory basis, to any UK company which was engaged in the production of records or audio-visual recordings, or which was engaged in the business of selling records under its own label or trade mark. The BPI emphasized the importance of the role played by the independent company representatives on BPI committees and the BPI Council. There was currently a majority of independent Council representatives.

10.31. The BPI said that the MCPS/BPI Joint Licensing Scheme (the Scheme) facilitated rather than frustrated the importation of sound recordings into the UK and was of positive assistance in the licensing of imported copyright works into the UK. It said that the Scheme enabled unnecessary anti-piracy actions to be avoided and it preserved the integrity of domestic copyright protection. We were told that, prior to the BPI's involvement in the Scheme, the MCPS was only able to license to importers the copyright in a musical work and therefore an importer had to approach each record company individually for a separate licence in respect of the sound recording. This had caused many problems for importers, who had often thought, incorrectly, that they were licensed both in respect of the musical work and the sound recording, whilst in fact they were only licensed for the copyright in the musical work.

10.32. The BPI explained that it received, for distribution to its members, half of the royalties received under the Scheme after deduction of the MCPS's commission. This payment was not intended to be compensatory, but was recognition of the fact that, in the absence of the UK copyright owner's consent, importation into the UK would be unlicensed and would represent a copyright infringement.

10.33. It would be wrong to assume that there was an essential contradiction between competition policy on the one hand and the protection offered by copyright legislation on the other hand. One of the primary objectives of competition policy was to promote short-run, allocative efficiencies with a view to driving prices towards marginal costs and thereby maximizing output. While the potentially exclusionary nature of copyright protection might appear to be in conflict with that principle, this was not necessarily the case. While the BPI accepted that copyright had a zero marginal cost of use and could be used by an infinite number of people simultaneously without exhausting the information, there were, in the BPI's view, compelling consumer welfare arguments to justify the current position.

10.34. The BPI believed that the distribution right inherent in UK copyright protection and now introduced across the EC by the Rental Directive was consistent with increased productive efficiency. Equally, parallel imports were inconsistent with such productive efficiency since they might reduce efficiency to the detriment of consumers by denying them qualities for which they were prepared to pay, such as, for example, consistently high standards in pre-sales and after-sales service and a reduction in the level of innovation. Such imports might also have the effect of raising the cost of supplying consumers as a result of disruption to record companies' investment planning and general distribution policies.

10.35. The reality of this situation had been recognized by the European Commission when, in 1991, it published its initial proposal for what later became the EC Rental Directive:

> With regard to the economic rights, the above applies similarly to the organizational, technical and economic achievements of phonogram producers, film producers and broadcasting organizations. Their large-scale investments have to be protected, not least to enable them to contribute to the protection of authors and performing artists. Only if such investment is protected will producers *et al* be able to invest not only in productions which are oriented towards pure commercial success and which would therefore guarantee a certain income, but also in such productions which are novel, particularly demanding or unusual in any respect and therefore less likely to be financially rewarding, but which still represent a necessary contribution to the increasingly threatened diversity of culture. Finally, a sufficient protection is a pre-condition for a situation in which producers may risk investing in recordings with still unknown, young performing artists, or in works of unknown composers, or in compositions which are important from a cultural point of view, but which are not very popular.

10.36. The BPI noted that Norway had recently introduced into its legislation a prohibition of unlicensed parallel imports. The proposal for the introduction of this prohibition had emphasized the following:

(a) the unfavourable impact of parallel imported products on national culture;

(b) the loss of finance for popular products which required financing for their maintenance on the market;

(c) the effect of parallel imports on the success of Norwegian recorded works abroad; and

(d) the introduction of the EC Rental Directive into Norwegian legislation under the EEA Agreement.

10.37. Similar arguments applied in the UK:

(a) the current import control provisions enabled UK artists to have a significant impact on the domestic market; currently they commanded about a 50 per cent share of this market;

(b) the British record industry was a significant exporter, with invisible earnings running at about £500 million a year; this international success had led to other cultural and economic advantages for the British economy by encouraging a predisposition on the part of foreign consumers towards other British goods and services;

(c) British music had a high level of penetration in overseas markets; this ranged from between 15 and 25 per cent over recent years and currently accounts for 18 per cent of the world market; and

(d) the EC Rental Directive would become effective in the UK after 1 July 1994.

In short, therefore, not only was UK current legislation on parallel importation consistent with the existence of a distribution right as part of a coherent system of protection of copyright, but it was particularly striking that the economic and cultural rationale for the existence of such legal protection clearly existed in the UK market.

10.38. The BPI said that opponents of the parallel import restrictions had argued that the effect of those provisions had been higher prices for recorded music in the UK. The BPI believed it was not disputed that any industry dependent on R&D and innovation, and justifying intellectual property protection for this purpose, required adequate opportunity for profits in order that such investment could continue. The need to reward innovation implied that the innovator should be allowed to price that innovation higher than its marginal cost. However, apart from this fundamental principle, there was no evidence to suggest that the existence of parallel import restrictions was in any sense synonymous with higher prices: indeed, the contrary appeared to be the case.

10.39. The need for copyright legislation as a source of economic wealth and creativity and the dynamic productive efficiency which it created had been recognized in recent years by the UK Parliament, the European Commission, the OECD and by the legislatures of a rapidly increasing number of countries. The underlying trend in recent years had been increasingly for the rights of importation or first public distribution to become an integral part of national copyright protection. In most cases where copyright legislation had recently been introduced or amended (for example, in Eastern Europe, Greece, Norway and Taiwan) the importance of parallel import protection had necessitated the inclusion of specific importation rights.

10.40. The BPI said that it would be unlawful and a breach of Article 9 of the Rental Directive to remove the current importation rights in section 27 of the 1988 Copyright Act. It would also, the BPI maintained, fly in the face of all recent developments at both national and international level for the importation right to be removed. At a time when the movement in the EC and internationally was for greater convergence of national copyright laws, it would be very striking if the UK were to move in the opposite direction.

10.41. The UK independent music sector was vibrant, dynamic, diverse and a source of great strength to the UK record industry as a whole. The advancement and success of this sector of the industry was of great importance to the BPI and its members. The removal of the parallel import restrictions would result not only in a decline in UK prices, but also to these independents losing a significant proportion of their UK domestic record sales as a result of the UK market being flooded by parallel imports. Independents would then have the stark choice of either terminating their existing licensing arrangements for their repertoire in other countries, so as to prevent licensed works being available for importation into the UK, with the consequential loss of licensing income, or alternatively suffering the loss of what might be a significant proportion of their UK domestic sales to parallel imports. In some cases the impact of the removal of parallel import restrictions would be fatal.

10.42. The NERA study (see paragraph 10.29) also concluded that there was sufficient evidence to support a prediction that a reduction of £2 in the prices of CDs would threaten the financial viability of a large percentage of independent record companies.

10.43. Commenting on the BMRB Survey results (see Appendix 7.2), the BPI said that it was not surprised by BMRB's findings. The BPI would have expected retail prices to be lower in the USA than in the UK, but it would also have expected prices in the UK to be the lowest in the EC. However, the BPI considered that BMRB's survey was inadequate in a number of respects. In particular, because of the limited range of products included in the sample, the survey did not reveal the much wider range of pricing structures available in the UK and in particular the extensive mid- and budget-price ranges available. The BPI also considered that it was not possible to ascertain from the survey the greater range, and therefore wider consumer choice, available in the UK as compared with the USA. The BPI noted that, notwithstanding the relatively weak or non-existent controls on parallel imports in Denmark and France, the survey showed that retail prices in these countries were amongst the highest recorded in the survey.

10.44. Finally, commenting on the UK music charts, the BPI said that the official Chart had been effectively policed by Gallup and this would continue when it was controlled by Millward Brown. The BPI submitted to the MMC a memorandum describing how the Charts operated and were effectively policed, and provided details of the BPI's own Code of Conduct for the Charts, which specifically forbade any actions which were likely to distort chart positions.

10.45. The IMF gave written evidence and attended a hearing. The IMF was founded in September 1992 as a forum for discussion and concerted action among managers of popular music artists and producers. It has over 650 members, including managers of some of the most successful artists and producers in popular music, and also managers of artists who do not currently have any recording agreement.

10.46. The IMF said that it welcomed the MMC inquiry, in particular because the MMC's terms of reference extended beyond a consideration of retail prices to encompass a consideration of all aspects of the supply of recorded music.

10.47. In the opinion of the IMF, it was in the acquisition and retention of the services of recording artists (and especially the treatment of copyright in the recordings which those artists produced) that the anti-competitive character of record companies (in particular the major record companies) could most clearly be seen. In the insistence on record company ownership of copyright, in the standard-ization of the principal terms of artists' contracts, and in their exclusivity, record companies had taken advantage of the relative bargaining weakness of individual artists. No matter how successful he might become, an individual artist could never hope to overturn many of the terms which record companies regarded as 'standard'. Though some artists might negotiate improvements in their terms, these new terms rarely, if ever, became incorporated as standard terms in other artists' agreements.

10.48. The IMF noted that there had been numerous court cases between artists and their record companies alleging undue influence, restraint of trade, and more recently (in the case brought by George Michael against his record company Sony) breach of Article 85 of the Treaty of Rome, on the ground that his recording agreement had as its object or effect the distortion of competition in the EC.

10.49. The IMF considered that if record companies were precluded from holding copyrights for the full term of copyright and had to return them to the artists at least, say, every ten years, a very lively market in the licensing of these copyrights would develop. In general, if the companies were forced to take a shorter-term view, it was probable that their more excessive advances and marketing programmes would be curtailed. This would be to everyone's advantage. Above all it would be easier for new companies to grow and develop, as they would be able to compete on fairer terms for back catalogue. The majors would have to be more cautious about predatory marketing practices, since they would not be able to cross-subsidize their new product from their catalogue sales, as they did now.

10.50. If restrictions on copyright ownership were introduced, the IMF said, it might be argued that the majors would have to reduce their investment in new artists. The IMF thought this concern was probably groundless; even if a reduction in such investment materialized, that would not necessarily be detrimental to the consumer, especially if it helped new companies to grow. Perhaps the greatest benefit would be that with an open market in copyrights their value would become easier to establish. In a short space of time copyrights would become useful securities or assets for all those small firms, individuals and artists who at the moment found it hard to obtain capital from anywhere other than the major record and publishing companies, and then only on very disadvantageous terms. This factor alone could be enormously beneficial both to the industry and the public in providing a better funded, more open and competitive industry.

10.51. The IMF was aware that such a course would take the UK record industry into uncharted waters, but it believed there was no evidence that the general improvement in copyright terms for writers had caused any long-term problems for music publishers. Nor was there any evidence that the more equitable terms given to writers by book publishers had led to the decline of book publishing. Whatever the risks from this course it would be a British or European problem to solve and the principle of intellectual property protection would have been upheld. Above all, from the IMF's point of view, as artists' managers, the position of the weakest participants in the industry—the artists and their families—would have been strengthened, especially in their later years, when many now suffered so badly.

10.52. The more genuinely competitive environment that would follow from these changes would, the IMF concluded, also lead to lower prices to the consumer, due to the greater efficiency that would ensue from this heightened level of competition.

10.53. The IMF advocated the adoption of industry-wide Minimum Terms Agreements (MTAs) which would permit artists greater freedom of movement between record companies and more equitable rewards for their creative endeavours. The IMF considered that whatever steps were taken to improve competition in the record industry, unless there was increased competition in the acquisition of artists' services and in particular in the way that artists' copyrights were dealt with, the major record companies would increase their control over the supply of recorded music in the UK and elsewhere, to the detriment of the consumer both in terms of choice and price.

10.54. Three core provisions of MTAs should be as follows:

(a) Ownership of copyright should either remain with the artist (subject to a limited licence to the record company) or revert to the artist on the happening of one or more of the following events:

(i) recoupment of recording costs; or

(ii) a given number of years after either release or recoupment; or

(iii) on the artist leaving the record label; or

(iv) on the record label becoming insolvent.

(b) All artists' contracts should include a statement of Real Royalty Rate (RRR) in relation to each format, analogous to the APR which banks and other lenders had to declare. The RRR should have a statutory definition and should be the sum an artist would actually receive by way of royalties expressed as a percentage of a notional retail price (eg PPD less VAT (but no dealer discounts or other deductions) uplifted by 130 per cent). Contracts might still contain packaging deductions and provisions that royalties were payable on only 90 per cent of sales, for example, but artists and managers would have a clear method of comparing the terms offered by different companies. The RRR would be a significant disincentive to the use of artificial means of reducing effective royalty rates and would greatly simplify auditing and accounting calculations. The RRR should also be quoted to each and every artist to whom royalties were paid, irrespective of when his or her agreement with the record company was concluded, either on every royalty statement or in a separate document sent with each royalty statement.

(c) Artists should be given greatly increased audit rights, including rights to audit records of the manufacture of sound carriers and the books of foreign licensees (especially where licensees were affiliated to the record or publishing company concerned). In particular, artists should be given collective audit rights so that the costs of audits could be shared among an unlimited number of artists. At present artists were prevented from employing an accountant to audit a record company's accounts if that accountant was (or, in some cases, had recently been) engaged in an audit of the company on behalf of another artist. There was no justification for such a term other than to inconvenience artists and their advisers, and discourage them from undertaking audits.

10.55. The IMF also suggested the following further terms for inclusion in an MTA:

(a) Ownership of copyright in artwork, videos and other visual and audio-visual works should also vest in the recording artist rather than the record company, provided that an assignment from the designer, photographer or director could be obtained.

(b) After an initial period of, say, three albums, options should operate by mutual agreement, ie a company should only be able to exercise its option with the artist's consent (this would not give the artist a right to require the company to release a further album if the company did

not wish to exercise its options). Once an artist had fulfilled his minimum commitment and it had been released, and provided that he had recouped all outstanding advances, he should be free to leave the record company if he wished to do so, subject, perhaps, to granting his record company the right to retain his services if they chose, by matching the best offer he might receive from another company.

(c) Record companies could absorb all recording costs themselves and pay the artist a lower royalty on all sales until recoupment. This would solve one of the major problems afflicting 'average' artists who at present received no income if they were unrecouped.

(d) Recording and publishing agreements should be exclusive only for relatively short periods of time (possibly to be measured by reference to recoupment). In particular, artists should be given ownership of and freedom to release any recordings rejected by the record company currently entitled to their services, and record companies should themselves pay wholly or partly for the cost of making any rejected recordings.

(e) Artists should be free to place their recordings with another company in any territory in which the work concerned had not been released within, say, three months of its initial release in the home territory or another major territory. Similarly an artist should be free to release his works through another company on any format (eg vinyl) on which his company refused to release his works.

10.56. The IMF also proposed that the MMC should give consideration to whether the following practices should be made unlawful or otherwise proscribed:

(a) requiring of an outright assignment of copyright in sound recordings (with no realistic prospect of reversion to the artist) as a pre-condition of entering into a recording agreement;

(b) requiring of an outright assignment of copyright in sound recordings as a pre-condition of entering into a publishing agreement;

(c) requiring an artist to enter into a publishing agreement with an affiliated company, as a pre-condition of entering into a recording agreement, or vice versa;

(d) distributing so-called 'promotional' records to dealers for the purposes of retail sale. There might, for example, be a limit on promotional distribution of 10 per cent of records manufactured. An artist should, in the IMF's view, receive full royalties on any records so distributed;

(e) requiring the artist in certain circumstances to grant licences for the mechanical reproduction of his songs at below the statutory rate, by means of so-called 'controlled composition clauses'; and

(f) giving so-called 'file discounts' whereby major retailers obtain goods from record companies at substantially cheaper rates than smaller independent retailers, simply as a result of their bulk purchasing power.

10.57. Turning to the question of the profitability of the record companies, the IMF told us that in its opinion the true profitability of those companies was understated in their published accounts because of the inappropriate methods used for accounting for copyrights. The IMF drew a distinction between record companies' income and expenditure on a current account basis, and their acquisitions and disposals on a capital account basis. Copyright catalogues were the record companies' most valuable asset. Accordingly, the acquisition and disposal of copyrights should be accounted for on a capital account basis. Record companies almost never made a capital payment to the artist in return for the company's acquisition of copyrights. As a result, neither the cost nor the value of those copyrights appeared in the companies' balance sheets. Current accounting rules and practices enabled record companies effectively to disguise the value of the rights they acquired from artists. And while the companies' level of profitability on turnover might appear to be moderate, their profit expressed as a proportion of capital employed was much higher.

10.58. The IMF also stressed the significance of the arrival of Direct Digital Broadcasting, which would allow whole albums to be broadcast in perfect digital sound quality without interruption directly into consumers' homes, whether by cable or satellite. It was widely thought that such broadcasting would eventually replace physical sound carriers as the means of delivery of sound recordings. The implications for the retail and distribution side of the industry were very significant, particularly for artists, in view of the fact that the record companies owned copyrights for the full length of the copyright term. The experience of the introduction of CDs had indicated that record companies might abuse the introduction of new technology as a means of reducing the share of income paid to artists. The record companies controlled PPL, and they could treat this new form of transmission as just another type of broadcast no different in principle from the present system. The recent introduction in an EC Directive of a right to an equitable remuneration for performers when their sound recordings were broadcast further highlighted the importance of this aspect of record companies' relationship with their artists.

10.59. Thus the question of who owned the copyright in the recording had, the IMF said, become an even more crucial question for the future. The constant development of new technology was always running ahead of contractual provisions and this, combined with the long life of pop music (far longer than anyone would have predicted 20 years ago), made ownership of copyright a vital issue for the future health and structure of the UK music business.

10.60. The IMF considered that the issue of 'promotional copies' was contentious. A distinction should be drawn between records distributed to disc jockeys, magazines and newspapers for the purposes of criticism and publicity, and copies given away to retailers as a form of disguised discount. There was usually no limit on the number of promotional records which could be given away, so a record company could deprive an artist of royalties on records given away 'free' to dealers, thereby effectively subsidizing a large proportion of the discount from the artists' pocket. Indeed this was an area which the IMF considered as being open to serious abuse.

10.61. Turning to the question of parallel imports, the IMF said it did not believe that the rather simplistic solution suggested by CA, and others, of abandoning parallel import controls would result in any benefit to consumers. It would, on the contrary, almost certainly lead to increased piracy, and ultimately to an overall increase in the cost of recorded music. In addition, it would cause damage to artists out of all proportion to any conceivable benefit which might accrue to consumers. It would deprive copyright owners of a fair reward for their innovation and creativity. In particular, new artists and smaller independent record labels who were unable to pursue importers of pirate material would find it especially difficult to become established. The IMF said that in particular:

(a) Attacking copyright protection in this way risked undermining all forms of intellectual property, including patents, copyrights and trade marks. Abandoning parallel import controls might superficially appear to benefit some consumers in the short term, but the implications were enormous and the results were highly unpredictable.

(b) The vast increase in imports of records that could occur would inevitably lead to an increase in the importation of pirate records, for the simple administrative reason that it would be impossible to ascertain in many cases which imports were legitimate and which were pirated. Customs and Excise was underfunded and undermanned and so could not take on the additional task of differentiating between pirate and genuine products on such a scale.

(c) The majors would have an advantage over the independents by being able to source from the cheapest market in the world, namely the USA. A range of pressing costs was available to all, but through their subsidiaries the majors could source from countries which paid lower artist and mechanical royalties. In addition, by choosing to source product in countries with high rates of inflation, and where payment was slow, royalties to artists could be very severely reduced. As artists had neither the right nor the resources to conduct world-wide audits, this would raise huge problems for the artists.

(d) The present relationship between artist and record company, and hence the whole UK music industry, relied, in effect, on investment in copyright. That was the key security for UK and overseas industries lending into the market. Without a clear knowledge that the benefit from investment would return to them, UK companies and UK divisions of the multinationals would find it hard to invest. It was hard to see how a successful industry could survive in this country if it were opened to imports from markets which had no effective system of copyright enforcement (however strict the laws against infringement might be). Imports from countries with similar levels of mechanical copyright payments presented a lesser problem, though the difficulties of conducting audits meant that artists would be significantly disadvantaged.

10.62. The IMF considered that the prices charged to the consumer in the UK (and Western Europe) for CDs were too high. CD prices had fallen markedly on average since the NHC hearings on CD pricing, though full-price CDs were still highly priced, particularly in comparison with videos. The IMF argued that its suggested restrictions on record companies owning artists' copyrights in perpetuity might help to achieve the same ends as parallel imports but in a far less dangerous and unpredictable manner.

10.63. The IMF also emphasized that as the retail trade had become more and more corporate, decisions about stocking records increasingly became decisions about sales per square foot and less and less about music.

10.64. Finally, the IMF noted that in a further attempt to maximize profits, some record companies had recently attempted to control or share in the merchandising income of their artists. Their justification for this had been that the artist owed his success to the record company's efforts and should share with them his income from the association of his name and image with sales of merchandise (other than records and videos). The IMF did not agree with this approach. The artist's name and image were plainly the artist's intellectual property, to be exploited for his benefit. The record company should be paying the artist for the use it made of this property, not the other way round.

10.65. To demand that the artist give up his merchandising income, as well as granting a royalty-free licence to use his name and image for the promotion of records, was a clear abuse of the record company's negotiating strength, and an attempt to control aspects of the artist's career which were not the legitimate concern of a record company. In its view, 'brand association' was a significant factor in the valuation of the copyright of all artists and one for which artists currently received no income or compensation whatsoever. The IMF suggested that artists should either receive a royalty from record companies for the use of their name and image, or that this 'brand association' factor should be incorporated into regular capital revaluations of the artists' copyrights, a proportion of which should be paid to the artist.

Association of Professional Recording Services Ltd

10.66. The Association of Professional Recording Services Ltd (APRS) made representations and attended a hearing. The APRS was founded in 1947. It is the trade association for the professional sound industry of the UK. Its members include recording studios, post-production facilities, manufacturers, suppliers of products and services, record producers, recording engineers, duplicating and pressing facilities, audio equipment hire firms, consultants and other businesses and individuals professionally involved in the sound recording industry.

10.67. The APRS said that the health of the recording industry which it represented was dependent on customers' continuing to buy recorded music. But those customers had freedom to choose. Recorded music was not an essential purchase. If it was too costly, few would buy it.

10.68. Over the last two decades, the studio industry had greatly enhanced the facilities and standards of excellence demanded by its clients by continuous reinvestment in equipment. Yet studio hire rates had not risen to recover the costs of technical improvements, let alone to match inflation. Indeed, as a result of improved efficiency and greater competitiveness, none of the prices charged by APRS members had been raised in real terms for at least the past two years, and some had even fallen.

10.69. The availability to the consumer of reasonably-priced, high-quality playing equipment in the last few years had made it necessary for all parties in the production of recorded music, from the studios and record producers to the post-production and duplicating facilities, to improve their quality standards, which involved even greater investment in time and care as well as equipment.

10.70. The APRS said that it was for other parties, particularly the record companies and the record retailers, to explain how they established and justified retail price levels. Theirs was the commercial judgment which determined the price at which each record must sell, to cover the costs of manufacture and overheads of promotion and distribution while leaving a surplus for necessary profit and for the speculative investment in new talent, which was undoubtedly a major expense.

10.71. From its understanding of record company operations the APRS believed the essential surplus of these companies was in fact under pressure. The days had gone when listening to records was a major leisure activity. An increasing array of alternatives, from computer games and videos to sport of every sort (much of it publicly subsidized), was now competing for the consumer's interest. In these circumstances the APRS considered that campaigns such as that to cap the price of CDs, or moves to legitimize parallel importing, and so unnecessarily limit the record companies' room to manoeuvre in their pricing strategy, were misguided and dangerous.

10.72. The danger was that any reduction in the current levels of profitability of the record companies would have grave implications for most APRS members; some had already been forced to shut down, and more would have to do so. The record companies were the principal users of studio time, they were the hirers of the record producer, and it was they who contracted with pressing and duplicating facilities for the manufacture of cassettes, vinyl and CDs.

10.73. The APRS observed that it was an unfortunate feature of the system that when record companies were obliged to cut costs, they traditionally did so—because the rates were negotiable—by reducing what they would pay the studio, the record producer or the duplicator.

10.74. The actual or prospective reduction in revenue from the record companies would produce many knock-on effects, both immediate and long-term. Among the most important of these would be a decline in the profitability of studios, leading to static or even declining staffing levels. The result of this would be that the pool of competent studio engineers—the talent which should sustain the future of UK recording studios—would become ever smaller. Low profitability of studios would also mean less investment in new equipment. Up to 80 per cent (in value) of the equipment in a typical UK commercial studio was made in this country.

10.75. The success of the UK in consistently maintaining its place among the international leaders in professional recording had underpinned the development by several British manufacturers of advanced mixing consoles highly tuned to the specific requirements of recording studios. This was one of the reasons why the UK had become the leading world supplier of such equipment. If UK studios lost their skilled staff and fell behind in their investment in new equipment, they would attract fewer and fewer recording projects from overseas. At the level of major recording artists, the business was entirely international. In the past, mostly foreign artists (particularly from the USA) readily came to record in this country because of their faith in the skills of our staff and the excellence of the equipment available. The UK was still regarded, with New York and Los Angeles, as among the greatest recording centres of the world. The UK should do everything to preserve this reputation.

10.76. Less speculative investment in new artists meant fewer projects on which record producers could be engaged. Because their skills could be applied in many countries, some of the more highly talented producers been forced to look for work elsewhere (mainly in the USA, and, to a lesser extent, in Europe). The overseas studios in which they then worked gained invaluable experience, while British studios stood empty. As record companies strove harder and harder for the lowest price in the manufacture of cassettes, CDs or vinyls, the pressers and duplicators faced diminished profitability, which again was leading to job losses and closures. The temptation for the record industry to shift its cassette and CD production to other countries, where surplus capacity was ready and waiting, might become irresistible. Another cornerstone of the UK recording industry would have crumbled. Once a customer had decided to have his duplication carried out by an overseas supplier, the decision also to place the whole recording, mixing and post-production process in overseas recording facilities was likely to follow.

10.77. The *Commercial Recording Studio* (CRS) arm of the APRS said that the monopoly position of the MU was a matter of concern. Its complaints were that: session musicians had to be members of the MU; the Union had a list of approved studios which indirectly discriminated against other ones; the Union placed constraints on the use of music; and exclusive Union agreements existed with the BBC and effectively with the BPI, since the BBC only used BPI members.

10.78. The *Pressers and Duplicators Group (PAD) of the APRS* made the following points:

(a) Some duplicator (cassette) companies were now moving towards the manufacture of both CDs and cassettes, in order to remain viable. This called for a very heavy investment, with consequent high financial risks, in view of the difficulty of winning new orders.

(b) The manufacturing cost of all formats was very low compared with the retail price, and this in turn meant that the profit per unit to the manufacturer was also low.

(c) In order to safeguard order books, levels of service and quality needed to be of the highest standard, which in turn meant a continual investment in applied technology.

(d) PAD's concern was that if the record companies, wholesalers and retailers attempted to apply a significant price cut, they would be driven to source their manufacturing outside the UK (and even outside the EC), where although manufacturing equipment cost the same, wage rates and other overheads were considerably lower. Even so, this would be unlikely to reduce the unit cost by more than around 15p; yet the damage to the UK industry would be irreparable.

(e) As to parallel importing, PAD said that it was self-evident that UK pressing and duplicating plants would suffer if there were a reduction in the demand for their products, directly proportionate to the volume of vinyl, cassette or CD recordings which entered the UK market from abroad; if those products were cheap because they were manufactured without regard to due copyright payments, that would amount to unfair competition and should not to be countenanced.

10.79. The *Suppliers Group (Manufacturers and Distributors) (SGMD) of the APRS* represents numerous equipment manufacturers, component suppliers, distributors, dealers and technical consultancy companies operating in disparate fields of the professional audio industry.

10.80. The SGMD said that the manufacturers' position was under severe threat from increasing competition from the Far East and other European countries, and from some revival in the USA. This had recently resulted in many acquisitions, mergers and take-overs. In all too many cases, the buyers had been foreign. The jobs might remain in the UK, but, ultimately, the profit would not.

10.81. There was no clear evidence to suggest that the consumer would significantly increase his purchase of CDs if they were reduced in price by a modest amount. However, there was certainly evidence to suggest that a reduction in profit would have a detrimental effect on jobs, exports, quality and consumer choice.

Re-Pro

10.82. Re-Pro, which is the working name of the Guild of Recording Producers, Directors and Engineers and a division of the APRS, also gave written evidence and attended a hearing. It has some 140 members who are actively involved in the audio recording industry—professional record producers, directors and sound engineers.

10.83. Commenting on CD pricing, Re-Pro said, first, that it was imperative to maintain the profitability of the industry not only for the good of those working within it, but also for the consumers of the product, namely the general public; secondly, the question of CD pricing was a commercial matter which should rest with the record companies; and thirdly, the proposal to lift import restrictions to allow products manufactured outside the EC to be imported into the UK should be resisted.

10.84. Referring to producers' performance income, Re-Pro said that the position enjoyed by the major record companies allowed them to adopt certain uncompetitive practices in their dealings with record producers, and these operated against the public interest. Re-Pro considered that PPL was dominated by the major record companies (thus, Polygram and EMI between them accounted for 9 out of 13 full members) which did not accept that section 9(2)(a) of the 1988 Copyright Act applied to producers. Re-Pro argued that this section of the 1988 Copyright Act should be considered to confer at least joint ownership of the copyright in the sound recording on the producers. Re-Pro submitted a copy of Counsel's opinion in support of this view. PPL had refused to discuss the matter with Re-Pro since 1989. Re-Pro therefore urged the MMC to seek undertakings from the principal record companies that they would modify producer contracts to ensure that record producers received an equitable share of performance income from PPL, and use their control of PPL to ensure comprehensive and accurate logging of sound recording usage so that performance income could be distributed correctly to each individual contributor.

10.85. Re-Pro said that the method of supplying recorded music to the consumer in the UK was likely to change radically in the future. It therefore asked the MMC to examine the question of how income derived from future methods of supply, such as digital diffusion, could be distributed equitably between the various contributors; and to seek undertakings from the major record companies that every digital transmission would be accurately logged and that the revenue derived was collected and distributed accurately and fairly. Re-Pro said that the current methods of licensing, collecting and distributing performance and broadcast income undertaken by PPL were untenable.

10.86. Re-Pro contrasted the position of PPL with that of the PRS. Whereas PPL was owned and controlled by the majors and was only obliged to serve their interests, it was clear to Re-Pro that the PRS was an accountable and democratic organization which was organized to fulfil its aim of providing regular and accurate distributions to a vast number of writer and publisher members. But even the PRS needed to guard against corporate complacency.

10.87. Re-Pro hoped that its views might contribute to the development of an accurate, transparent and accountable system to handle the collection and distribution of performance revenues, so that all those, including creative record producers, who were entitled to a share in them received that share.

10.88. In particular, Re-Pro urged the MMC to recommend changes in UK legislation which would ensure that the role of the record producer would be deemed to fall within the definitions of either 'record producer' or 'performer' referred to in international conventions and EC Directives.

Music Publishers' Association Ltd

10.89. The MPA also made representations. It is a member of the BCC, and the trade organization which represents music publishers in the UK. One of its functions is to protect and enhance the law relating to the copyright in music. The MPA currently has 175 members plus their associate and subsidiary companies.

10.90. The MPA said that it was independent of record companies and of retailers. It did not deal directly with the licensing of mechanical rights, and was not the main negotiating body with the record industry. Both these roles were carried out by the MCPS. However, it did issue guidelines on the use of 'grand right' works, such as operas and stage productions, and negotiated fees with broadcasters.

10.91. The majority of composers delegated the promotion of their work to music publishers. The creative role of music publishers was to find and develop new composers and new works, as well as to promote their existing catalogue of musical works.

10.92. The MPA said that music publishers, particularly those who specialized in classical music and in the educational market, continued to publish printed music. However, leaving aside performing rights income, the great majority of their income was derived from royalties from records. Royalty income from this source formed the main income stream for both music publishers and composers.

10.93. Commenting on record prices, the MPA said that CDs had traditionally been more expensive than vinyl records or cassettes. This, in part at least, reflected the higher quality of the product. CDs had a better sound quality, were more durable, allowed for pre-programming of tracks, and had longer playing time.

10.94. Any decision which might be taken by the MMC over CD pricing had to take into account the music industry as a whole, including the royalty income of music publishers and the composers whom they represented. Undue pressure on prices would have the adverse effect of reducing royalties. An enforced reduction in the price of CDs in the UK would be detrimental to the interests of music publishers, composers, songwriters and lyricists for whom royalties from records were their mainstream income.

10.95. The prices of records were not dissimilar throughout the EC, but the royalty rate payable was lower in the UK than in continental Europe. In 1991 the Copyright Tribunal had set the royalty rate as a percentage of 'published price to dealer' (PPD) which meant that, if the PPD were to be reduced, then UK composers and their publishers would be further disadvantaged as compared with their continental colleagues.

10.96. The MPA noted that when in 1928 the price of the product had fallen, the statutory rate of royalty had been increased. It wished to avoid a further expensive and time-consuming review in order to readjust the appropriate royalty rate upwards.

10.97. If the price of CDs at the higher end of the spectrum for recorded music were reduced, there was a considerable danger that music publishers would suffer a disproportionate burden of the fall in price. The MPA did not accept the premise that any lowering of CD prices was bound to be financially beneficial to music publishers because they would receive royalties on increased sales. When record companies had varied their prices in the past there had not been any noticeable change in sales levels. In the classical field, for example, a new symphony, the Gorecki Symphony No 3, had recently by far and away outsold any other classical record. This was in a market in which one could buy at prices ranging from £2 to £15 and yet this biggest-selling record was at full price. This was the case despite the fact that two other, cheaper, versions of the symphony were on sale during the same period, and one of those (the Koch version) had been recommended by *Gramophone* as representing better value overall.

10.98. The MPA also considered that the price structure in the UK was important for the industry which had a great number and variety of independents; in a sense these independents operated under the umbrella of a relatively high full price, and therefore a drop of £2 on CD prices could drive many of them out of business since their profit margins were known not to be high. In this context, the MPA noted that the variety of product available to the UK consumer was probably wider than anywhere else and feared that a loss of choice would be the logical consequence of an imposed £2 price reduction.

10.99. The UK music market was amongst the most successful in the world. That had happened through investment by music publishers in composers on the basis of an expected level of return, and on the basis that British composers had been extremely successful in the past in being able to sell their music outside the UK. If the income of the UK music publishers were effectively to be lowered, this would affect the ability of the UK music publishers to invest in talent, and that in turn would have an effect on the industry's ability to export its product to the USA or elsewhere. Foreign earnings coming back into this country would fall.

10.100. Again, any lowering of the barriers to cheaper US imports would be extremely harmful to the interests of music publishers in the UK. Music publishers had no power to determine the wholesale price of records, but would suffer doubly from an erosion of royalty income from reduced prices, and from an erosion of copyright protection. Any relaxation of the UK law relating to importation would inevitably curtail the financial benefit music publishers in the UK gained from 'sub-publishing'. Music publishers and the composers whom they represented would lose this source of

248336 P

their income. The music publisher in the UK, acting as a sub-publisher (for example, for a copyright owner in the USA), would continue to be responsible for promoting the musical work in the UK, but might well not be paid a royalty on UK sales. The benefit might well accrue solely to the copyright owner in the USA.

10.101. The MPA said that there was a constant need for copyright owners of musical works to be diligent in order to prevent the importation of records, particularly CDs, made without licence in their country of origin, for example in Taiwan and Korea. The piracy problem was widespread.

10.102. In view of the considerable difficulties in detecting whether products were pirated, the MPA thought that the administrative burden would be greatly increased if an open-borders approach was taken for products from outside the EC. The provisions of the 1988 Copyright Act relating to importation of infringing copies of musical works (section 111(1), (2) and (4) and section 112) only related to printed goods, and therefore did not assist music copyright owners in controlling the input of unlicensed records.

10.103. The MPA also expressed concern that parallel imported records might not have borne royalties even in the country of origin, a matter that was difficult to establish. So far as the USA was concerned, it said that as the owner of rights within that territory, it had no evidence or knowledge in particular cases of whether royalties had been paid in the USA. The licence issued in the USA was for the sale of those records there and would not cover export. The MPA added that if imports were allowed from markets (such as South-East Asia) which were not properly organized, it was doubtful whether royalties would filter back to the UK.

10.104. The MPA submitted that there was a fundamental difference between the removal of parallel import provisions in the EC and removing them in total. The EC market had worked well for the UK industry. However, the USA had import barriers in position.

10.105. Finally, the MPA said that music publishers were in a high-risk industry which demanded considerable investment with uncertain returns. Market forces should be left to determine the price of records to the consumer. Any decision to the contrary had to take into account not only the interests of retailers, record companies and consumers, but also the needs of music publishers and the composers whom they represented.

Musicians' Union

10.106. The MU made representations and attended a hearing. It said that it was the representative organization for all musicians in the UK and had some 37,000 musicians in membership. It was the second largest musicians' organization in the world, second only to the American Federation of Musicians. The Union recruits and represents musicians across all areas of the music profession and maintains a collective agreement with the BPI in relation to popular music recordings and symphonic/chamber ensembles.

10.107. The MU considered that if the existing copyright law governing parallel imports was amended, it was by no means certain that CD prices in the UK would fall. Indeed, the price of original recordings in countries without such a restriction, such as the Irish Republic, Denmark, France and Japan, was without exception higher than in the UK. None of these countries had the same international reputation as the British recording industry, and none compared with the UK in terms of the diversity of its music product.

10.108. The abolition of the parallel imports rule would certainly have repercussions within the UK recording industry, and would allow the US record industry to provide cut-price products directly to the UK. It was significant that the USA currently operated parallel import controls.

10.109. Furthermore, the MU considered that if such imports were allowed, major retail record chains would buy in bulk but might not pass on such reduced prices to the consumer. Such cheaper product would result in the UK record companies having to reduce their prices and therefore their profit margins. The success of the British recording industry, second only to the USA, was based on the ability of companies to invest in failure; in other words, to record and sign up musical talent which might or might not be successful in either artistic or monetary terms. As a result of the general profitability of the British recording industry, such risks had been taken many times in the past and would, it was to be hoped, continue; such investment had the direct result of making the industry as diverse as it was.

10.110. The MU expressed particular concern about the future of classical music recordings which, as a result of the number of musicians involved and the need for high-class product, were more expensive to produce, and said that if profit margins were further squeezed then reissues of existing recordings or more recordings from eastern bloc countries would result, with a consequent loss of recording engagements that formed an important element of work for UK orchestras. The British record industry was a major invisible earner for the UK.

10.111. In the view of the MU there was no monopoly situation existing in this industry; the public interest was best served by maintaining the status quo.

10.112. The Union was concerned that in the investigation the MMC should be sensitive to the principles of intellectual property law, and in particular to the internationally recognized principle of licensing and distribution of copyright works. Performers had a fundamental interest in ensuring that their rights were protected and adequately remunerated, and to this end, as a result of the European Community Directive 92/100 (the Rental Right and Neighbouring Right Directive), they were involved in discussions with the record industry in an attempt to agree jointly recommendations to the Government as to how the new Directive should be implemented. Implementation of the measures recommended in the MMC report into PPL's licensing policies formed part of those discussions.

10.113. In that connection, PPL had withheld all payments of moneys owed to Union members since the allocation period ending on 31 May 1989. The moneys owed were significant, at the rate of 12.5 per cent per recording. Negotiations directly with PPL and indirectly through the BPI had failed, but the Union considered that the EC Rental Directive would solve the difficulties, since performers would have a statutory right to payment.

10.114. The MU also criticized the majors for paying low wages and arranging poor living conditions for foreign acts and orchestras, particularly those of eastern bloc origin.

Other bodies

BBC Audio International

10.115. BBC AI submitted written evidence and attended a hearing. BBC AI is a joint venture between BBC Enterprises (a wholly-owned subsidiary of the BBC) and Monty Lewis Associates Ltd. The objective of the company is to enable the BBC's archive of classical music recordings to be released commercially on record through the licensing of the BBC sound recordings to record companies for duplication, distribution and sale in the world market. However, BBC AI said that it had met with resistance from certain record companies, which had relied on the exclusivity provisions in their contracts (with the artists performing in the BBC recordings) to prevent BBC AI from concluding agreements with these artists.

10.116. BBC AI considered that the structure of the record industry had been firmly set by the majors through a dominance that they had established over decades by amassing a roster of artists protected by exclusive agreements; this industry practice of exclusivity was encountered by any company wishing to enter the market.

10.117. BBC AI was concerned about the part played by the BPI and took the view that in August 1991 the BPI was mobilized by the majors, in particular PolyGram, whose Chairman had just been appointed as Chairman of the BPI. BBC AI believed that, in turn, the BPI had mobilized its members to deter artists' agents from dealing with BBC AI, primarily by drawing their attention to the exclusivity provisions of their artists' contracts: this ensured that BBC AI was both denied a supply of product and frustrated in its attempt to enter the market.

248336 P2

10.118. BBC AI said that the efforts of the record industry had effectively delayed its entry into the market and might have caused BBC AI irreparable damage.

10.119. BBC AI still did not have product on the market; but in June 1993, after having initiated court proceedings, BBC AI considered it had reached agreement with EMI which removed the restraints previously imposed. It was now bringing proceedings against Decca Records of the PolyGram Group.

10.120. Since BBC AI's formation in 1991, both EMI and PolyGram had launched budget or mid-price labels which featured recordings by famous and well-established artists. BBC AI considered that a comparison between the artists offered by these labels and those from a typical independent demonstrated not only the importance to the majors of their exclusive agreements with artists, but also how those agreements reinforced their dominance.

10.121. BBC AI said that the majors saw it as a direct threat to them because it had a large back catalogue of prominent artists and performances; it had the financial backing of BBC Enterprises and the expertise of Monty Lewis (previously Chairman of Pickwick Records); and it had entered a sector of the market (mid-price/budget) which had been previously under-exploited by the majors and which was becoming rapidly more profitable.

10.122. BBC AI considered that the following matters were at issue:

(a) the BBC Archive Recordings were historical documents belonging to the nation (many were unique first performances or performances of artists only recorded by the BBC) and the public should be able to buy them;

(b) the entry of these recordings into the market-place would introduce an element of competition in an area controlled by two major companies;

(c) the entry of the BBC into the market-place would generate an income from the BBC's Sound Archive assets in accordance with the Heritage Secretary's expectations; and

(d) through BBC AI, those independent record companies that had been unable to enter the market-place because of the limited supplies of archival recordings would now have a source of product that was not controlled by the majors.

10.123. BBC AI recommended that, if the MMC were to make an adverse finding on this issue, the OFT should look into the behaviour of the record companies and the BPI under the provisions of the Competition Act or the Restrictive Trade Practices Act; and that an undertaking should be sought by the Secretary of State from the major record companies and in particular from the PolyGram Group that they would not seek to exercise the exclusivity provisions in their artists' contracts, in respect of BBC recordings, beyond a period of ten years from the date of any particular performance by an artist who was under contract at the time of performance.

Chart Information Network Company Limited

10.124. CIN wrote to the MMC explaining its role in the music industry. It said that it was the company which commissioned and was the copyright holder in the official UK Music and Video Charts. It did not have any direct involvement in the monitoring of retail record prices, although it tracked official dealer prices for the purposes of chart eligibility and carried out price band analyses.

10.125. The CIN Chart survey currently monitored the official dealer price for each title and format released, as registered by record companies with Gallup at the time when release information was first available. These prices were used to classify all product for the purposes of chart analysis (eg full, mid and budget category albums), and in the case of singles, to set a dealer price threshold for a single to be eligible for the Chart. Historically, the price threshold was introduced at a time when the integrity of the charts was being compromised by the release of extremely cheap singles; retailers were then selling large volumes of these singles at artificially low prices. The price thresholds for eligibility were in no way a requirement for record companies to set their prices at a particular level. It was perfectly acceptable for prices to be below this threshold; it was simply that the product would not then form part of The Chart. The dealer price threshold in no way precluded retailers from selling singles at lower prices.

10.126. CIN said it understood that it was not uncommon for special promotions to be made available to retailers when purchasing singles, although it had no reason to dispute the comments of EMI to the NHC that these promotions were available to all retailers. Gallup (and now Millward Brown) was required to devote adequate resources to ensuring that ineligible singles did not enter the charts, and CIN was satisfied that they had done this well, and in line with good market research practice. It was not feasible for Gallup to assess individual promotions across all chart and non-chart outlets to guarantee that a balance existed.

10.127. Commenting on the existence of retailers' own charts for both singles and, more often, albums, CIN said that they had effectively diluted the impact of the national CIN Chart in the eyes of consumers. It was confusing to hear 'number one' on BBC Radio 1 FM on Sunday only to find another title at 'number one' in the local record store. However, CIN said that its own Chart remained the industry's bench-mark, not only because it was the only accurate sales monitor of all UK record sales—a nationally representative poll—but also because its wide media exposure, especially on BBC, ensured its 'bench-mark' status. Its function was to 'photograph' the market each week, reflecting the 'average taste' across disparate styles of music. Although the top 40 Chart was no longer a homogeneous collection of 'pop songs', it still represented the 40 best-selling singles in order of popularity.

10.128. CIN observed that with the increasing segmentation of the music retail market, each chain considered that it had to appeal to its own customer profile by reflecting purchasing patterns and taste within its own stores. The retailer's objective in promoting its 'exclusive' own-brand charts was to draw a particular type of customer to the store and to encourage loyalty. Such charts allowed retail chains to differentiate themselves from others, and to establish an image associated with the range of music they promoted.

10.129. In CIN's opinion the effect of these charts on record companies could be both positive and negative. High chart placings for new releases offered them an opportunity for tailor-made in-store promotions (eg window displays and co-operative press advertising), while the dilution and confusion created among some chart-watchers could diminish the title's chances of a high placing in the Official CIN Chart, if consumers were not clear of its chart status.

Gallup Chart Services

10.130. Gallup Chart Services (Gallup) submitted information about how its charts were compiled, in particular summarizing the security measures which it employed to ensure the fairness and accuracy of its charts. Gallup also attended a hearing and gave a presentation at its premises to members of the Group and staff conducting the inquiry.

10.131. Gallup explained that all retailers who supplied information for use in its charts (the 'panel') were obliged to sign a Code of Conduct. Gallup would not consider using shops for chart compilation unless they signed the Code and abided by its terms. Where breaches had been discovered, shops had been removed from the panel. BPI members also signed a code which outlawed any activity which might distort the charts. That code was currently under review.

10.132. Gallup also drew attention to some press and trade articles which were commenting on the singles chart since Millward Brown had taken over the role of compiling the weekly pop charts at the beginning of 1994. The two major complaints in the articles concerned, first, the speed with which singles were now entering and leaving the chart, and secondly the ousting of independent music from the chart, because under the new arrangements with Millward Brown, a number of independent retailers had lost their chart return status.

10.133. MTVE submitted written evidence and attended a hearing. MTVE had since 1987 operated a satellite-delivered television service which transmits programming across Europe 24 hours a day. MTVE's programming centres on music videos which are produced by record companies primarily for the purpose of promoting new releases and increasing the sales of CDs, records and tapes. More than 80 per cent of the music videos aired on MTVE are supplied by the five major record companies.

10.134. MTVE's views focused on what it regarded as the collusive and anti-competitive behaviour of record companies in relation to promotional music videos. The price demanded by record companies for licensing the dubbing, broadcasting and cable transmission of these videos was far higher in the UK and elsewhere in Europe than it was in the USA.

10.135. MTVE considered that it was the victim of collusive practices by the record companies in the UK, especially the five majors. It said that these collusive practices related to the licensing of broadcast and cable transmission of promotional music videos, products which fell outside the definition of 'reference products' but which nonetheless clearly fell within the remit of the MMC's terms of reference. MTVE said that the practices constituted steps being taken to exploit the joint monopolistic position of the record companies downstream but were intimately linked to the production of recordings in their various forms. Furthermore, the downstream behaviour of the record companies in relation to promotional music videos constituted important evidence of their upstream joint monopolistic position, and as such was of immediate relevance to the MMC's inquiry.

10.136. MTVE argued that it would not make sense economically or commercially to examine vinyls, CDs and cassettes without also examining videos, which were after all produced for the precise purpose of marketing audio products. Videos were clearly in a distinct category from the use of music as background to films and television programmes, and the motivation of record companies in producing and using them was driven by their commercial strategy in relation to the marketing of recordings.

10.137. MTVE said that the record companies were acting collusively through the collective licensing body VPL. MTVE had made a complaint to the European Commission on the anti-competitive activities of VPL and the record companies.

10.138. MTVE explained how its programming format had originated in the USA in the early 1980s. It had observed that two markedly different schemes had developed in the USA and Europe for licensing rights from the record companies to play promotional videos. In the USA each record company separately licensed its music videos directly to MTV for inclusion in the US service, and each had done so since the inception of the music video programming concept by MTV. The situation in the UK (and Europe generally) was quite different. Here, in MTVE's view, the record companies were determined not to repeat the practice of separate, open market negotiations of licence fees between each major and MTV (as in the USA), and had created a mechanism to exact higher licence fees from MTVE (and other users of music videos). Led by the five majors, the record companies had created VPL as the exclusive entity through which music video rights could be obtained by any potential user. Thus, MTVE (and other users of music videos) could not negotiate directly for UK rights with the same record companies with which they negotiated directly, and separately, for US rights.

10.139. As a result of this price collusion, users in Europe, including MTVE, were paying higher licence fees than in the USA, where in general such videos were provided free of charge in consideration of their promotional value. MTVE said that the record companies had used VPL as a veil for their collusive and anti-competitive refusal to negotiate, and the exploitation of their monopolistic position in relation to promotional music videos.

10.140. MTVE alleged that more than 80 per cent of the licensing by VPL was on behalf of the five majors; that the record companies had abused their dominant position by using VPL to apply excessive royalty rates which took a substantial proportion of 'pre-royalty profit'; and that neither independent record companies nor recording artists had any representation on VPL. MTVE said that the majors should be precluded from using VPL, and should be forced to negotiate with MTVE individually.

10.141. MTVE noted that since the MMC inquiry had been in progress, four of the major record companies had launched 'VIVA', a 24-hour music video cable channel in Germany. MTVE had no objection to competitors entering the market. It was concerned, however, that VIVA was a joint venture between four horizontal competitors who collectively accounted for 70 to 75 per cent of the supply of pop music videos and who also controlled VPL (and the IFPI in respect of the licensing of the rights in their products to MTVE) with which they now competed.

10.142. MTVE explained that it had filed a complaint with the European Commission in respect of VIVA on 25 November 1993. It observed that in late January 1994 all five major record companies had announced their intention to launch a 24-hour music television network world-wide and that this was a further exploitation of their oligopolistic position. It also threw doubt on their claim that the investigations by the MMC and the European Commission were being taken seriously by them.

Careful Arts

10.143. Careful Arts, a company which manages acts, particularly 'development' acts (the industry label for those which have yet to achieve any significant commercial success), made a submission.

10.144. It supported the position of the IMF, particularly about the ownership of copyright and parallel imports (see paragraphs 10.47 to 10.61), and criticized the length and restrictive nature of the majority of the agreements in the industry between record companies and artists. It noted that they included many examples of unfair royalty breaks and packaging deductions.

10.145. Careful Arts observed that many of the problems which affected development acts arose from the massively superior bargaining power of the record companies at the time of contract negotiations, and their resources for protecting and enforcing those contracts. Such acts represented more than 95 per cent of those seeking careers in the business.

10.146. Careful Arts proposed that a voluntary code of practice be introduced to cover contracts, and that an effective and binding independent arbitration service be available when the code of practice proved insufficient to facilitate agreement. These measures would greatly reduce the costs to acts who might not have the resources to go to law.

11 Views of independent record companies

Contents

Introduction

11.1. We sent a questionnaire to four of the largest independent record companies, MCA, Pickwick, Beggars Banquet and Telstar, and a rather shorter questionnaire to a sample of other independents. The questionnaires sought information about these record companies' businesses and invited any views they wanted the MMC to take into account. In this chapter we record the views expressed by the four large independents, and by nearly 60 other independent companies which responded to our questionnaire or which separately wrote to us. These companies are listed in Appendix 11.1. Many independent companies, as well as the majors, are represented by the BPI but a number of others are represented by Umbrella, a separate association recently set up to represent their interests. Umbrella made written representations and attended a hearing.

11.2. This chapter records the views of all these parties. The independent record companies generally took a position which was not dissimilar to that of the majors. Umbrella, and one of the companies, Tring International Plc, however, took rather different positions from the other independents and their evidence is dealt with separately at the end of the chapter.

MCA Records Ltd

11.3. MCA, whose ultimate parent is Matsushita of Japan, said that it saw itself as a relatively small player in the UK market and was a price follower rather than a price setter. It had its own quite modest repertoire of UK artists and acted as the UK licensee of its US parent. It was reliant upon one of the majors, BMG, for the manufacture and distribution of its product in the UK.

11.4. MCA said that the UK music business was highly competitive, with vigorous competition from the majors and the independents. MCA priced its products with a view to increasing sales; in view of its size and the nature of its repertoire, it did not have sufficient market power to set prices. MCA considered it very important that copyright protection for recorded music was maintained at its current level.

11.5. MCA said that it faced competition from other record companies in the UK at three main levels: the acquisition of contracts with recording artists, the promotion and marketing of its artists and the sale of its records to retailers. First, as to competition for artists, MCA told us that it took a significant risk when it signed an artist, in view of the unknown chances of the success of a recording, even for an artist with an established reputation. The terms on which it offered a recording contract represented a balance between that level of advance necessary to persuade the artist to accept the offer in preference to a rival record company, and a prudent maximum, given the unpredictability of an artist's reception in the market. There was keen competition to sign up artists, and in negotiations artists and their managers tended to play off one record company against another in order to maximize the terms of an offer.

11.6. Secondly, MCA faced fierce competition for media exposure and retail promotion of its records from both major and independent companies. In MCA's experience, entry to the charts compiled by retailers and displayed at the point of sale depended upon whether those retailers were prepared to promote the product and what a record company was prepared to pay to have the recording featured in retailers' chart lists in their outlets.

11.7. Thirdly, there was intense competition for sales to retailers, and this was compounded by the considerable market power exercised by the large retail chains. That power was reflected in aggressive, permanent discount purchasing from MCA. In addition, major retailers almost always sought a marketing contribution from MCA.

11.8. Turning to the question of parallel importation of records, MCA said that the 20 or so cases in which it had exercised its right to prevent parallel imports in the last three years had generally related to instances where the release date of the record in the USA had been earlier than that scheduled for the UK. MCA had had a legitimate interest in seeking to protect its marketing campaign in respect of those records in the UK. It accordingly endorsed the arguments which had been submitted by the BPI and the IFPI to the MMC in support of the current restriction on parallel imports into the UK.

11.9. MCA considered that the UK music industry made a major contribution to the British economy in terms of the level of turnover generated, the employment created and the consumer demand that was satisfied. It also stimulated developments in a wide variety of related markets such as fashion, publishing and radio and television broadcasting; these in turn created a favourable response to British cultural products on world markets. The music business was almost unique amongst cultural sectors in the UK (such as opera, film and theatre) in that it received no Government subsidy whatsoever. Nor did it receive any indirect support comparable to the pricing support enjoyed by the book publishing industry under the Net Book Agreement.

Pickwick Group Ltd

11.10. Pickwick Group Ltd (Pickwick), a subsidiary of Carlton Communications plc, told us that the majority of its records were retailed at budget prices; they were sold in traditional record outlets and also in supermarkets, garage forecourts and airports, and by mail order. Pickwick's main competitors were other budget labels, such as those produced by PolyGram and EMI and by independents such as Tring and Castle.

Beggars Banquet Records Ltd

11.11. Beggars Banquet told us that its records were sold primarily in independent retail outlets; however, the more successful records were also available in the multiple retail stores. Beggars Banquet said that it competed with all other record companies, including the majors, on a range of industry activities including signing artists, promotion, marketing and price, and believed the market was intensely competitive. It kept its dealer prices a little lower than those of the majors for similar products and was prepared to experiment with pricing, for example by offering a major release at a reduced price to gain initial orders. The problem was that this reduction in dealer price might not be reflected in the retail price, since retailers tended to operate price categories.

11.12. Beggars Banquet said that it also ran some retail shops and from its perspective both as record company and retailer said that to its knowledge neither sector made unreasonably high profits.

As to copyright law in the recorded music area, any lessening of the current protection would be disastrous for the industry.

Telstar Records plc

11.13. Telstar Records plc (Telstar) said that it licensed product from repertoire owners and sold its records in high street retailers, multiple chains and specialist stores. Its records were marketed largely through television advertising. Because of the high costs of such promotion, most of its records were sold at full price. Telstar said that it was in direct competition with the major record companies; moreover, competition from non-music products such as videos and computer games was increasing.

11.14. Telstar told us that, from its experience both in Europe and the USA, the UK market was the most competitive and the one where it was most difficult to succeed. The recent concentration in power of the retail chains was having an increasing effect on dealer prices and as the market share of the chains increased, so Telstar's margins decreased. These retailers achieved large discounts off the dealer price and exercised complete control over the retail price of records.

Other independent record companies

11.15. While individual companies generally commented on only one or two aspects of our inquiry, many made the same points and in this section we summarize the main points made by one or more of the companies listed in Appendix 11.1.

Need for the inquiry

11.16. A number of the companies thought that the industry should not have been referred to the MMC for investigation. Some took the view that the continuing adverse publicity could only damage a successful industry with good export earnings. Others said that it was wrong for the MMC to be asked to investigate the prices of luxury products like CDs which involved discretionary spending by consumers. Many of the necessities of life were supplied by highly profitable monopolists and these were more appropriate areas for investigation.

The price of CDs

11.17. Many companies claimed that the price of CDs was not high by international standards; indeed, records were more expensive in virtually every major market in the world than in the UK. It was true that records were generally cheaper in the USA, but so were most other products. This was because the USA had a totally different economic, political and social structure, with lower operating and manufacturing costs than the UK and other European markets. Retail margins were generally higher on UK than US goods; in particular, the major UK record chains demanded high levels of discount, which kept UK dealer prices high. A comparison of UK prices with those of other European countries was more appropriate, and this showed that UK prices were generally lower.

11.18. The companies said that it was important to remember, in comparing the price of products as between the UK and other countries such as the USA, that the level of the exchange rate at any particular time could affect the relative prices considerably. Thus, the data which the NHC had published about the prices of records in the USA had been collected at a time when the exchange rate was approaching $2:£1. After 'Black Wednesday' the rate had moved to $1.50:£1, a rate at which UK prices, although still higher than US prices, had moved considerably closer to their US counterparts.

11.19. One classical record company said that it was also important to remember, in looking at comparative CD prices in the UK and the USA, that consumers often failed to take into account the VAT which was charged on records in the UK. Prices in the USA were always quoted ex-sales tax and this gave a misleading impression of the price actually paid by the customer at the till. This company pointed out that there were strong parallels between the classical record industry and the publishing industry, and that consideration was being given in Europe to a joint VAT level for publishing and classical CDs—5.5 per cent in the case of France. A lower VAT level of, say, 8 per cent on both classical CDs and print might be a solution which would contribute to Treasury revenues but would be seen as giving back something to the consumer and to an unfairly vilified industry. It would also make US and UK prices broadly comparable.

11.20. Some companies said that there was no evidence that cheaper records would lead to an overall increase in record sales. Moreover, there was at present a wide variety of different prices for consumers to choose from within each format.

11.21. One company pointed to the fact that it had to pay royalty rates for licensed-in US repertoire that were at least double those paid by its competitors in the USA; those had to be covered in the prices it charged. Another said that any lowering of CD prices without a corresponding reduction in manufacturing costs could have the effect of damaging many independent labels. These had been very successful in the UK, many occupying niche markets. The independent classical sector had done particularly well in the UK.

11.22. Moreover, in real terms, CD prices had come down over the years. By the end of the 1970s, inflation had left vinyl LP prices far below their true level and the record industry was having difficulty in surviving in view of the inadequate returns. Since that time, record prices had not kept pace with inflation and were now in reality too low. At the same time, artists and collecting societies acting on behalf of rights owners had been pressing for, and often obtaining, higher royalty rates, and this had put an extra burden on the independent sector.

11.23. One company told us that it had tried, without success, to release CDs containing recordings by some of its best-known artists at budget prices in the hope of stimulating increased sales. This company considered that the budget area of the market had been swamped by pirate CDs imported from the EC; these provided their importers, distributors and retailers with margins that legitimate record companies could not match.

Value for money of CDs

11.24. Many companies expressed surprise that a high-quality product such as a CD should be expected to cost no more than the inferior formats which had preceded it. Just as a hardback book commanded a higher price than a paperback, so CDs justified higher prices than vinyls or cassettes. They offered a considerably higher sound quality than either or those formats, a total playing time of up to nearly 80 minutes, and a virtually indestructible format. To that extent, a CD offered better value than many more ephemeral forms of entertainment. Consumers were willing to pay for a quality product. On the classical music side in particular, consumers were abandoning cassettes in favour of CDs because of the superior sound quality of the newer format.

11.25. One of the classical record companies told us that, while it was true that the manufacturing costs of CDs had fallen over the past few years, the savings in manufacture were more than outweighed by the extra costs involved in producing a longer and technically more sophisticated product. Typically, half a dozen sessions would be required in order to take full advantage of the format, and further costs were involved in editing. Another classical record company said that it cost about twice as much to record a CD, typically 70 minutes long, as a 40-minute vinyl LP. The consumer was routinely receiving twice as much music on the CD format and it would therefore be fairer to start from the assumption that a classical CD should cost the same as two LPs.

Profitability

11.26. The 20 or so companies which directly addressed the question of profitability in the independent sector said that it was clear that they were not making large profits. Some stressed the precariousness of the record business and said that they barely succeeded in remaining in a profit-making position. Such companies typically survived only by finding a niche audience, exploiting it skilfully and keeping overheads to a minimum. Sometimes a small company did produce a record with mass appeal, and it might then become profitable for a time, but such success was usually short-lived. A significant number of independent record companies went out of business each year, mainly because they had had a run of loss-making releases, a position that could not be sustained indefinitely. Because of the higher costs of manufacturing CDs, as opposed to other formats, the losses which occurred when a recording failed to achieve sales were correspondingly all the greater.

11.27. A number of these companies said that a price reduction of £2 on a record would have very serious implications for their businesses and might force them to close. The effects on the industry would also be serious: the smaller companies were the creative seedbed for the industry in terms of new talent and if they did not survive, the overall music scene would be impoverished and the public offered a far narrower range of music than was currently the case. There would also be serious employment implications throughout the industry, already affected by the recession.

11.28. Several companies stressed the vitally important role which the independent companies played in fostering contemporary classical composers and artists. The costs of producing contemporary classical orchestral or operatic repertoire were high and were sometimes only made possible by public funding, and yet the numbers of records sold were often tiny. In these circumstances, and at a time when further subsidies were threatened, a reduction in the current dealer price would have serious implications for the future of such companies.

Research and development

11.29. A number of the companies stressed the vital importance of being able to continue investing in new artists. Investment was needed to sustain the creative cycle, developing new, successful artists who would produce recordings ultimately forming part of a company's back catalogue, which would in turn generate the money to fund the next round of new artists. It was only by being able to control the pricing of their records that companies could generate sufficient funds to invest in this way. Any measures that threatened this capacity to invest would have the effect of upsetting the whole cycle of development of new music and artists.

11.30. Many of the companies also pointed to the high risks associated with the record business. To achieve chart success, it was necessary only to sell a few thousand records, and so there was intense competition for such success. It was much more difficult and risky for an independent label to promote and market its products than for one of the majors. Rapidly changing consumer tastes also made success less predictable. In effect, the business was akin to gambling, and those companies survived which were able to control and limit the number of loss-making records which they released. It was necessary to have an acute sense of the developments taking place in consumer fashions and how well particular music was selling. While the majors could employ large numbers of people to fulfil these functions, and in any case had their vast back catalogues to sustain any losses, the smaller companies had to rely on becoming familiar with niche genres and markets.

Contribution of record industry to UK economy

11.31. Several companies stressed the major contribution which the independent sector had made and was continuing to make to the UK's balance of payments and to the international standing of the UK in the music field. The industry had also used the power and influence of popular music to make an important contribution to charity work, through such initiatives as Live Aid. Outside interference in a self-sufficient and successful industry was both unnecessary and undesirable.

The pop and classical music sectors

11.32. Several companies stressed the very different economics of running a pop record company on the one hand and a classical label on the other. One company, in the classical field, said that while there would never be as large an audience for classical as for pop music, classical music would always be relatively more expensive to record, not only because of the artists who had to be paid for their skilled services, but because of the immense care and expensive equipment needed at every stage of a modern digital recording. The pop industry was able to recoup its costs with potentially enormous sales, sometimes in the millions; the classical side had to do so with sales typically around one-hundredth of this volume or less. Moreover, while pop artists were frequently paid in the form of royalties which, by definition, diminished if a recording was unsuccessful, classical choirs, orchestras and producers had to be paid in full at the time a recording was made irrespective of its subsequent commercial success or failure.

11.33. By contrast, a company in the pop sector said that it bore all the risks of one of the major record companies, but, unlike the classical company which might be acquiring very cheaply the rights to an old recording or making a recording itself with no artist royalty and without copyright liability, it had to survive on the sales performance of new acts alone and could not escape copyright.

11.34. Another classical independent said that it specialized in world première recordings, and that its costs, which mostly involved major orchestras, more than justified its present prices. A further classical specialist said that it offered an enterprising and diverse range of excellent recordings at a reasonable price and it was one among a number of highly respected labels which had proved that quality and dedication could be more than a match for the economic might of the majors' labels. The real or imagined misdeeds of the majors could hardly be applied to small labels such as these.

Parallel imports

11.35. Several companies expressed concern about the possibility of UK copyright legislation being amended to remove the current restriction on parallel imports. In their view, such a change would pose a real threat to the UK music industry. The UK represented around 7 per cent of the world market and was responsible for nurturing the talent that was responsible for more of the music sold around the world than any other country except possibly the USA.

11.36. Allowing unlimited parallel imports into the UK market was an invitation to companies with a much lower cost base in other countries to flood the UK market with product which was deliberately priced to undercut the UK record companies but which was only viable for such overseas companies because they were not incurring the marketing expenses or other costs involved in developing the products. The additional sales were a bonus to such overseas companies. But the effect in the UK would be to undermine the viability of the record industry here and to threaten its very existence. The only UK beneficiaries would be the major retailers who would set up distribution hubs to deal with the bulk quantities of product which would be needed to offset the shipping costs. This would threaten the independent retailers and further reduce competition in the high street.

11.37. More particularly, UK record companies would suffer at the hands of non-UK licensees, who had the benefit of manufacturing under licence for their local market, at low cost, and without the attendant expense of long-term artist development and recording costs.

Trade barriers in the USA

11.38. One company said that until 1985/86 the UK industry had been responsible for one-third of US domestic sales. It believed the USA had, since then, systematically created disincentives to UK distributors (and in return to UK business) in the USA by erecting trade barriers. Behind this protection, the USA had been able to develop new labels, artists and repertoire for sale to export markets, hitting UK companies in the rest of the world.

Retailers

11.39. A number of companies criticized the role of the major retailers in the industry. One referred to comments made to the NHC by the former Chairman of W H Smith to the effect that W H Smith was in favour of reducing CD prices but was thwarted by the high dealer prices charged by the record companies and their distributors. This company said that such comments could only appear hypocritical, since W H Smith's prices for classical recordings were among the highest charged by any retailer, yet the market power of that company allowed it to demand and obtain dealer prices that were among the lowest paid by any retailer. Moreover, W H Smith's staff appeared to have very little knowledge of classical music, which was regarded as just another commodity like pens or envelopes. Of all the record retailers, W H Smith could most benefit from better informed staff and a less predictable and limited range of classical recordings.

11.40. Another company said that the major retailers were seeking lower prices as a desperate short-term measure to improve store traffic. If the UK music industry contracted as a consequence of reduced CD prices, such retailers would readily switch their floor space to computer games if that produced the requisite margin. The UK would then be left with an ever-diminishing music retail sector, concentrated in fewer hands.

11.41. A classical record label said that its trade price had in recent years risen much less than the retail price of its records. In the 1980s its trade price had been £7.29 and the retail price £10.99 to £11.99. In the succeeding years, its trade price had risen to the current level of £7.79, whereas retail prices now ranged from £12.99 to £14.99. It wondered how such retail mark-ups could be justified.

11.42. Another company said that it was concerned about the levels of concentration in the retail market, with too much power in the hands of one group, W H Smith. This retailer extracted large discounts from suppliers and was achieving large profits, even though it took no risks (since it could return product to the suppliers) and was doing no more than passively displaying the product.

11.43. Other companies also referred to the substantial margins achieved by the major retailers, and doubted whether these were really justified in order to cover the overheads and staff costs involved in selling recorded music.

11.44. Finally, one company pointed to the importance of distributors to independent record labels. Artists appearing on smaller labels relied on distributors being prepared to supply their releases to retail outlets, both in the UK and the USA.

Other points

11.45. One company said that national radio and television airplay was still dominated by the majors who could spend significant sums on promotional activities. Referring to the difficulty of getting radio airplay, it said that it had the impression of being shut out from a 'very exclusive club'.

Umbrella Organisation Ltd

11.46. Umbrella, an association of independent record labels with independent distribution, said that its members represented 20 per cent of the value of UK recorded music sales in 1992.

11.47. Umbrella explained that it had originally started as a pressure group to keep the independent charts as free from interference by the majors as possible, but had developed into a more general lobbying body. It hoped that its role would develop further to enable it to influence policy at government level with respect to the industry, not only in the present case, but in the case of the proposed EC-wide blank tape levy and more general copyright harmonization.

11.48. Umbrella did not make a collective submission on behalf of its whole membership, but several individual members submitted views to us separately and we held a hearing with them. One member put the following points to us:

 (a) the price of CDs for major popular artists was probably too high;

 (b) CD prices were kept high by the retailers; attempts by one of the majors (Warner) to start a discounting policy had failed because the retailers failed to pass on the discount to the customer;

(c) the major record companies and the major retail chains had an affinity of interest to maintain CD prices at their current levels;

(d) vinyl record prices were too low;

(e) it was in the interests of major international record companies to force vinyl as a music carrier out of the market, and keeping vinyl prices (and hence margins) low helped achieve that; and

(f) parallel importing would cause problems for independent record companies. This was because most independents were forced to license to majors in the USA, and at today's prices US exports to the UK would undercut UK independent record companies and further squeeze their margins. In addition, overstocks could be dumped on the UK market and have the effect of distorting the UK record industry.

11.49. He suggested the following action to make the market more competitive:

(a) the majors should be made to divest themselves of record company acquisitions of past years and to demerge the different labels they operated in order to reduce their dominance of the market and allow more competition;

(b) the majors should be made to divest themselves of ancillary interests in the music industry including music publishing and record distribution;

(c) collective licensing bodies such as PPL and VPL should be made more independent of the control and influence of the majors by the restructuring and opening up of their governing bodies to representatives of recording artists, consumers and smaller record companies;

(d) the majors should not be allowed to own more than 20 per cent of any engineering, technological or manufacturing concern which was directly concerned with the reproduction of sound recordings; and

(e) the major retailers should be broken up to remove their dominance of the market and to encourage more price competition.

11.50. Another member of Umbrella said that in his view, pricing in the industry was led by the larger record companies and the larger retailers, and in the absence of retail price maintenance the smaller companies had to follow the lead or they would simply pass their profits to the large retailers. There was a degree of implicit collusion between the large retailers and the large record companies. Record companies wanted to sell as many units as possible in as short a time as possible in order to obtain a high chart position and benefit from the resulting media exposure. To maximize sales, the record company needed its recordings to be prominently displayed in the large retail outlets.

11.51. This put the large retailers in a commanding position. They could demand large discounts off dealer price, sale-or-return deals, and that advertising and promotion must be paid for by the record company. These retailers could then choose either to pass the discounts on to the public by undercutting smaller rivals or taking the extra profit. This had the effect of squeezing the record company's margins, especially on titles which did not sell well, with the result that they in turn set dealer prices as high as the market would bear in order to maximize their profit.

11.52. Smaller retailers were unable to compete with the larger chains in this situation and were forced to concentrate on selling non-chart, niche items and to seek trade through their greater knowledge of the industry and personal customer service. Similarly, the smaller record companies could not secure the sort of promotion of their records which the majors were able to purchase and in their turn concentrated on selling into the independent specialist shops.

11.53. The power of the large retailers had been most apparent in the rapid loss of sales experienced by the vinyl format. These retailers could stock larger quantities of CDs and sell them at a higher price than their vinyl equivalents, so they had simply stopped stocking vinyl. Once this happened, it became uneconomic for the record companies to manufacture vinyl and it declined, notwithstanding that 90 per cent of households still had a turntable and did not want to be forced to purchase a CD player.

11.54. The final point made by this Umbrella member was that very careful thought should be given to any proposal to amend the current copyright law. The protection afforded by UK copyright legislation was vital, not least for the thousands of unsuccessful artists and musicians in the industry who were unlikely ever to become highly successful.

Tring International Plc

11.55. Tring said that its marketing approach was very different from that of the majors and most of the independents. It was cost-based, and aimed to provide very low-priced CDs and cassettes. Price was the determining factor. Tring thought it could sell any product at the right price and in the right outlets.

11.56. Tring said that it did not seek to record new acts; in fact it very rarely signed new artists. When it did take on new acts or artists, it signed them up for one-off productions rather than attempting to form a long-term relationship with them. Tring said that it had a large current catalogue of products, larger even than was typical of the major record companies. It had some 800 lines available at the moment.

11.57. Explaining its cost structures, Tring said that these allowed it profitably to sell good-quality CDs and cassettes to the market at £2.99 and £1.99 respectively.

11.58. Tring said that it had an excellent relationship with the MCPS. Since it was very much involved with signing acts for the purpose of re-recording material which had already been recorded in the past, it had to be particularly careful that copyright was not infringed. Tring had found that marketable catalogue was tending increasingly to return to the artist's ownership; ie that rights were reverting from the record companies or management to artists.

11.59. An important aspect of Tring's philosophy was to give value for money. It therefore tried, so far as possible, to market CDs which contained the maximum playing time. This was good business sense, since it cost the same to manufacture 73 minutes of music as it did 7 minutes.

11.60. Tring was confident that the BPI handbook considerably understated its market share; no doubt this was also true of other companies which sold other than through traditional outlets. Tring said that it did not supply Boots, John Menzies, W H Smith or Woolworths, ie the very outlets from which the BPI predominantly collected its data.

11.61. Unlike the majors, Tring was not selling predominantly to a 15- to 24-year-old market. Its target market was mainly the 30 to 55 age group, ie a market not only with a larger disposable income, but one which tended to appreciate more than the young market the repertoire which Tring produced. The majors had traditionally relied on the chart market, which appealed mainly to the younger age group, to establish an artist. Tring considered that the majors could only make profits on their album sales, not on their singles, which were being sold to an ever-diminishing youth market.

12 Views of the major record companies

Contents

Introduction

12.1. In this chapter, we summarize the views of the five major record companies, BMG, EMI, PolyGram, Sony and Warner (together referred to in this chapter as 'the companies').

12.2. In a letter dated 26 November 1993, we informed the companies of our provisional finding that they (and their subsidiaries in the UK) were members of a complex monopoly group, within the meaning of the Fair Trading Act, which engaged in one or more of the following practices:

(a) adopting similar pricing policies to each other for the various formats (CD, music cassette and vinyl) of 'full-price' albums and singles;

(b) declining to license imports of some sound recordings in which the company holds the copyright and licensing others only on payment of a fee under the MCPS/BPI import scheme; and

(c) entering into contracts with artists which include terms that restrict the artists' ability to exploit their talent fully and restrict competition in the supply of recorded music (eg in clauses relating to the extent of copyright acquired, length of contract, exclusivity, options, obligations to exploit recordings, royalty rates, packaging and other deductions from royalties, and/or arrangements for accounting for and auditing royalties).

12.3. We invited the companies to comment on our provisional finding, and on a number of issues arising out of that finding. A summary of their views is set out below.

The competitiveness of the UK recorded music industry

12.4. All the companies maintained that the recorded music industry in the UK was both highly successful and very competitive.

248336   Q

12.5. BMG said that the industry was a British success story in international terms, with about one-sixth of albums sold world-wide coming from the UK. In 1992 the industry had domestic earnings of about £1.2 billion at retail level and overseas earnings of around £800 million. Given fair conditions of international competition, the industry would continue to prosper to the benefit of the British economy as a whole.

12.6. At the same time, it was a complex and finely balanced industry and externally imposed changes could easily upset that delicate balance. In particular, artists and record companies were in partnership together, but their relationship could only flourish with a fair allocation between them of the risks and rewards involved in developing, making and selling records. Thus, for example, if restrictions were imposed on record companies in the UK as to the terms on which they could contract with their artists, such that they could no longer expect a fair return on their investments, recording contracts in future would simply by signed elsewhere in the world, most notably in the USA.

12.7. BMG stressed the importance of copyright, which it said was the foundation upon which the music industry was built. It was essential that the value of its copyrights was preserved. Intellectual property rights protected both the industry and consumers from the distortions which resulted from piracy and home taping, and would become even more important to the health of the industry in the future in the new environment of multimedia and with the spread of digitalization which offered new means to deliver music.

12.8. As to the price of recordings, consumers were buying the experience of the music, not a commodity. Therefore, the process of pricing a record was determined by its perceived value to the public, not by the cost of the plastic. The price of a particular recording reflected what people were willing to pay for that perceived value in relation to the prices of substitute forms of entertainment. It was significant that there had been a considerable growth in the unit sales of CDs since 1988. The prices of records to consumers were, however, fixed by retailers not by record companies.

12.9. EMI said that record companies operated in a highly competitive environment, with intense competition on signing and retaining artists, on price, on marketing and promotion and on obtaining shelf-space for their recordings. They faced a constant threat from new entrants and were squeezed between powerful suppliers, in the shape of artists, supported by expert managers and lawyers, and powerful buyers, in the form of large retail chains. They had responded to this competitive pressure by offering consumers choice, quality and innovation at reasonable prices.

12.10. As a consequence of the competitive nature of the market, and in view of the considerable investment in the music industry, UK prices for recorded music were not high, either in absolute terms or by comparison with those in many other countries.

12.11. EMI maintained that the UK recorded music industry served its customers in the UK extremely well and that the high quality and popularity of UK artists contributed to the UK's relatively large share of the world market. Regulatory intervention in this market was unnecessary and could both damage the interests of consumers and undermine the UK's position as a leading exporter. The market forces which operated so powerfully in the industry today should be allowed free play.

12.12. PolyGram said it was strange that, given the success of the record industry and its contribution to the national economy, it should have become such a focus of concern in recent years. It was an industry in which internationally the UK had absolute and comparative competitor strength. The UK domestic market accounted for some 7 per cent of world sales. The industry's international success could be measured by comparing this domestic base with UK penetration of world sales; these were currently around 18 per cent, according to the BPI.

12.13. The industry was competitive, according to the usual criteria by which competitiveness was assessed. First, profitability was modest. Secondly, concentration in the market was also modest, particularly by comparison with the USA or France. Thirdly, all the evidence pointed to relatively low barriers to market entry; there was a vibrant and dynamic independent record sector which competed actively and very successfully with the major record companies.

12.14. PolyGram also stressed the importance of copyright protection in the operation of the UK market for recorded music. The scope of copyright protection (both temporal and in terms of the rights which it gave) in the general operation of the market for recorded music was designed to encourage efficient investment and overall economic efficiency. The consequence was that innovation had to be priced higher than at its short-run marginal costs. The copyright legislation had rightly recognized that limiting imitation and encouraging investment was in the best long-term interests of consumers.

12.15. Sony said that a number of factors were important in understanding the nature of competition in the UK market for recorded music. There was the investment required in new artists, a highly risky business since artists failed more often than they succeeded. Only by having the security of long-term contracts with artists were Sony and the other record companies able to take a long-term view of their investment in an artist. The imposition of shorter-term contracts would only benefit the small number of existing successful artists while aspiring new artists and independent record companies would suffer and the industry overall would risk stagnation from lack of investment in new artists and new music genres.

12.16. The record companies needed an adequate incentive in the form of prospective revenue to enable them to continue to take the risks inherent in investing in new artists. Sony's profits from the sale of copyrighted works did result in significant investments in the creation of new artistic works. Whether the market as a whole achieved the socially optimal level of investment was less easy to determine. But it would be dangerous to tamper with the current balance between risk and reward without clear evidence of excessive investment and rewards in the industry.

12.17. Sony said that the activities of the UK record companies in investing in new artists not only provided a cultural platform for the UK abroad but also generated employment and the development of skills and expertise in the UK in the extensive infrastructure of recording studios, musicians, sound engineers, producers, designers, managers and promoters who were involved in the UK record industry.

12.18. Warner pointed to benefits which the record buying public enjoyed as a result of the way in which the UK record industry currently operated; among these were the wide range of recordings placed on the market by the record companies and their signing of UK songwriters and artists; the continued technological development of the recordings supplied by the record companies, of which the MiniDisc and the DCC were the latest examples; the strength of competition in the industry, which had ensured that prices were reasonable in relation to the costs of the record companies and to prices elsewhere in Europe; and the international success of the industry, with the licensing of copyrights of UK-originated product overseas providing a substantial flow of income into the UK.

12.19. Certain aspects of the industry had been, and were, essential, Warner said, if these benefits were to continue. They were the maintenance of current levels of profitability, which were currently entirely reasonable; the continued protection of record company copyrights which were exercised reasonably and responsibly by record companies of all sizes; the maintenance of a balanced relationship with the other parties involved in the production of the recording, in particular the artist; and the continued existence of a wide range of retail outlets stocking a variety of music and formats.

The complex monopoly situations

12.20. BMG, EMI, PolyGram and Warner challenged the jurisdictional basis of the MMC's provisional finding of a complex monopoly in favour only of the five major record companies. They maintained that there was no material difference between the conduct of the majors in relation to the three grounds identified by the MMC and the conduct of record companies of whatever size. First, there was no evidence to support a contention that the prices charged by the independent record companies were significantly different from those of the majors. Secondly, the members of the BPI who operated the import licensing scheme included not only the majors but a large number of smaller record companies as well, who derived particular benefit from the practice in question; moreover, the same royalty terms applied to them as applied to the majors. Thirdly, many of the features of artist recording contracts referred to by the MMC were also likely to be found in the contracts offered to artists by independent record companies.

12.21. BMG said that it seemed wholly arbitrary for the MMC to have provisionally found that, with a market share in 1992 of 5.4 per cent by value and 5.1 per cent by volume, it was part of a complex monopoly while not coming to the same provisional finding with respect to MCA, a company which also engaged in the three specified practices and which had a market share in the same year of 4.1 per cent. EMI added that a number of companies not in this complex monopoly group were subsidiaries of large, amply resourced corporations, based in the UK or overseas, for example MCA (Matsushita); Echo (Chrysalis 75 per cent and Fujisankei 25 per cent); and Pickwick (Carlton).

12.22. EMI also said that, so far as it could see, the only feature which distinguished the companies identified as group members from other record companies was that the five engaged in record distribution in the UK and in many other territories. This fact appeared to EMI to be wholly irrelevant in the context of the reference, in particular given the nature of the practices that were provisionally found to give rise to a complex monopoly situation.

12.23. BMG, PolyGram and Warner took the view that the MMC were required by the terms of the Fair Trading Act 1973 to determine 'in favour of what person or persons that monopoly situation exists'. That required the MMC to determine *all* those persons in whose favour the monopoly situation existed. It was not, in their view, open to the MMC arbitrarily to select certain persons in whose favour they believed the monopoly practice might or might not exist and omit others without a fully reasoned analysis demonstrating how the complex monopoly group was distinguished from other members of the industry; on the contrary, there must be a rational, objective and fully verified basis upon which to conclude that they had identified all those parties that operated some or all of the identified practices.

12.24. PolyGram said that it distinguished the provisional finding of the complex monopoly situation in this case from that identified by the MMC in the Ecando case. In that case, in recognizing that only the hall owners and their tied contractors constituted participants in the complex monopoly, the MMC were rightly distinguishing between two separately identifiable groups, which carried on different functions. But the MMC had not identified any proper reason for distinguishing the activity or conduct of the majors from the other record companies in the case of recorded music. Warner said that it did not interpret the Ecando judgment as giving the MMC a general discretion as to which of the companies to include as persons in whose favour the complex monopoly situation existed.

12.25. The MMC had apparently limited the group to the five majors on the grounds that those companies held some 72 per cent of the UK market and that they also had a significant market share at the international level. This, the MMC had said, had led them to the view that 'the practices of the five companies effectively determine the practices of the UK industry as a whole'. In the companies' submission, this was an irrelevant consideration upon which to base a provisional finding and had not been substantiated by any evidence presented to the companies. Moreover, it represented a significant and unwarranted departure from previous MMC practice. In their previous reports on the supply of petrol, beer and motor cars, the MMC had included in the respective complex monopoly groups not only the largest players whose market shares accounted for the greater part of the market in question, but also smaller suppliers. Those smaller suppliers had also been found to be persons 'in whose favour' the monopoly situation existed and the MMC had not thought it relevant in that regard to consider whether their conduct was influenced or dictated by the conduct of the major players.

12.26. EMI said that the commercial reality of the music industry was that the persons whom the MMC had excluded from the group, and who had accounted over a 20-year period for 30 to 40 per cent of the market, were a significant factor in the overall competitive equation. Only those companies which had not been in existence for an appreciable time when the inquiry started or who had not been active in the market could properly be omitted on the grounds of commercial reality. EMI also said that it did not understand what the MMC meant when they said that the companies 'effectively determined' the practices of the industry as a whole. The latter was driven by competitive forces, not by the companies.

Prices

The pricing practice

12.27. The companies said that the provisional finding that they adopted similar pricing policies to each other for the various formats (CD, music cassette and vinyl) of full-price albums and singles could not be sustained, however the alleged practice was interpreted.

12.28. BMG said that so far as the relative prices charged for different formats as between the companies was concerned, CDs were now the standard carrier for audio products, and offered, through the quality of their reproduction, their extended playing time and their virtually indestructible format, considerable value to consumers. Consumers were not willing to pay the same price for the older analogue formats which did not offer the same value. As a result, record companies had no choice but to price CDs at a higher level than their vinyl and cassette equivalents.

12.29. But having a piece of music available in two or three formats at different prices was, if anything, pro-competitive; and it was likely that, if the price differential between the digital and analogue formats were to be eroded completely, prices for analogue formats would increase, while those for CDs might only be reduced only a little, if at all. Once the analogue formats no longer had a price advantage over CDs, they would be likely to disappear quite quickly, depriving consumers of choice.

12.30. EMI said that it was certainly a common feature of pricing by record companies generally, and not just by the majors, that where a new popular title was released on CD and also on cassette (or cassette and vinyl), the CD would generally (although there were many exceptions) be marketed at a higher price than the cassette (and vinyl, if any). This feature was not confined to full-price lines and EMI did not understand why the MMC had so confined the alleged practice.

12.31. EMI said it strongly resisted any conclusion that a higher price of CDs relative to other formats prevented, restricted or distorted competition, or was a manifestation of any lack of competition. On the contrary, this was the normal response by record companies to free market forces and, in particular, to the differing price elasticities of demand for CDs, on the one hand, and cassettes and vinyl, on the other. The record companies were operating in an environment in which various forces—competition from industry competitors, competition from new entrants, the bargaining power of suppliers (in the shape of artists) and of buyers (particularly the large retailers), and the threat from substitute products—forced them to make the right judgment about the price of CDs relative to other formats. If the price of CDs was set too high relative to those formats, that left room for competitors, including new entrants, to obtain greater sales and a higher return by setting a lower differential. Recent successful new entrants who had done just that included Naxos and other budget classical labels.

12.32. EMI noted that CDs were generally priced higher than cassettes in all markets around the world (where both were available), despite the different market structures and demand conditions.

12.33. EMI said that the structure of costs in the industry was also very important. The industry incurred appreciable fixed costs in producing the first copy of a new title, and the marginal cost of production was therefore very much less than the average cost. If prices were set equal to marginal cost, record companies would make a loss and go out of business. Marginal cost pricing was therefore unrealistic. Any interference with the ability of the record companies to price above marginal cost would lead them initially to reduce the number of titles they produced, with a view to reducing average costs, and later to their losing money and quitting the business. This would reduce consumer choice and competition and operate against the public interest. EMI also pointed out that its average percentage margin on CDs was very similar to that on cassettes.

12.34. Moreover, since record companies did not make excess profits, any forced reduction in the absolute or relative price of CDs might result in a rise in the price of cassettes, all other things being equal. This might well have the effect of reducing the range of titles and prices of recorded music available to consumers.

12.35. PolyGram said that the MMC's own data suggested that there was significant variation in the list prices pursued by the major record companies for their full-price products of all formats, and therefore the provisional finding that the companies all had the same differential for their full-price CDs, cassettes and vinyl products could not be sustained. On the contrary, each record company appeared to be pursuing its own pricing policy according to the precise marketing mix which it wished to follow for its individual products.

12.36. Not only were there considerable differences in the individual price categories between individual companies, but also differences in these companies' discount structures. It was highly unlikely that discounts and returns offered by the majors on full-priced formats would be similar. Indeed, it would be an extraordinary outcome, given the wide variety of discounts made available by PolyGram and other record companies, and the highly competitive nature of discounts offered by the record companies in this regard.

12.37. Sony said that, by focusing on the relationship between dealer list prices for CDs and cassettes, the MMC had disregarded a significant number of other factors which, both individually and collectively, had considerably greater impact on the level of competition between the record companies. Sony concentrated its efforts on competing with other record companies through the promotional campaigns and dealer-specific discounting that it offered to retailers. Any assessment of the impact of record companies' pricing policies on competition should therefore take into account the effect of these promotional arrangements and discounts.

12.38. The pricing policies which Sony adopted were a response to the competition that it faced from the records of other record companies, to the strong purchasing power of the retailers and to the control that retailers exercised over the price to the consumer. It was therefore inappropriate to reach a conclusion about the effect of a particular element of a record company's pricing policy on competition without taking into account how that element formed part of the wider pricing policy and looking at the overall effect of that policy.

12.39. Warner said that the MMC had not identified the way in which the practice was alleged to prevent, restrict or distort competition or how levels of prices would be different in the absence of any such practice. Warner's published dealer price for CDs had been significantly lower than that of any other major record company from mid-1988 until September 1990. In introducing this price reduction, the purpose of which had been to bring its records into a lower retail price band and thus securing it a considerable competitive advantage at the retail level, Warner had clearly not adopted a pricing policy similar to that of the other majors. It was clear from the MMC's reports on *Flour and Bread*[1] and *Insulated Electric Wire and Cables*[2] that the MMC had to look at realized prices after the discount had been given, and not simply at the PPD, when considering whether there was really a coincidence of pricing.

12.40. The price of cassettes was strongly influenced by the fact that the customer had the opportunity to create an almost identical product for himself from a blank cassette at a fraction of the price. This had artificially deflated the price of pre-recorded cassettes over the years and was a factor felt equally by all the record companies.

12.41. Warner said that the MMC's assertion that the difference in price between CDs and cassettes for full-price albums and singles bore no relationship to the costs of producing the different formats was of doubtful validity, at least in its case. Warner did not allocate costs to different formats; the actual costs of manufacture made up only a small element in the overall costs of the business and the major elements of costs in terms of A&R spend or marketing and publicity were not format-related. One could not therefore expect the difference in price to be attributable to an identifiable difference in cost.

---

[1]*Flour and Bread: a report on the supply in the United Kingdom of wheat flour and of bread made from wheat flour*, HC 412, July 1977.

[2]*Insulated Electric Wires and Cables: a report on the supply in the United Kingdom and the export from the United Kingdom of insulated electric wire and cables*, HC 243, March 1979.

Whether the alleged pricing practice results in higher prices than would otherwise be the case

12.42. We asked the companies whether the alleged practices (set out in paragraph 12.2) resulted in higher prices for recorded music in the UK than would otherwise be the case. The companies said that none of the practices had this effect. In respect of the pricing practice, their reasons are set out below. (Their responses in relation to the other two practices are summarized in paragraphs 12.70 and 12.96 respectively.)

12.43. With respect first to the pricing practice, the companies said that the use of multiple formats at different price levels was characteristic of record companies generally (and companies in other industries), both in the UK and world-wide, and was a rational, economic response to ownership of intellectual property rights.

12.44. BMG said that, so far as dealer prices were concerned, it was clear from the MMC's market information that the dealer list prices charged by each of the companies for different formats varied quite widely; realized prices probably differed to an even greater extent. The only pricing policy which the companies had in common was that, for full-price albums and singles, prices for CDs were higher than prices for other formats, and that was simply a reflection of the greater value offered to consumers by CDs as compared with other formats.

12.45. EMI said that price differentiation by format resulted in greater sales, lower costs and lower prices and/or greater variety for the consumer, for the reasons given in paragraphs 12.30 to 12.32. This alleged practice did not affect the choice of price band or the price within a band at which records were marketed or the incidence of shifting albums from one price band into a lower band in the course of their life. The alleged practice had not prevented a massive growth in the sale of CDs in the UK and world-wide, nor had it inhibited EMI from releasing a large number of records at mid-price or budget price. Moreover, the alleged practice had not prevented CDs from rapidly gaining market share from other formats, nor had it prevented a large fall in the real average realized dealer price of CDs over the past decade.

12.46. PolyGram stressed that the initial full-price release was invariably the critical release, for unless the record was successful at this stage, its chances of achieving success later were limited. For this reason, most of PolyGram's promotional spend went on new releases. A copyright owner had to be able to anticipate receiving a sufficient return on his investment within the often short-term commercial life of the innovation and that implied that he should be allowed to price the innovative copyright work higher than its short-run marginal cost. At the same time, retailer power (as a result of which increasingly high discounts were negotiated by retailers) accompanied by the increasing levels of concentration at the retail level, ensured that there was no scope for record companies to charge higher prices for recorded music than would otherwise be possible.

12.47. Sony said that a number of factors affected its pricing decisions. First, variations existed even between the list prices of the companies' full-price albums and these variations were greater if mid-price and budget price records were taken into account. The differences would be greater still if record companies' realized prices were compared. Secondly, at retail level, prices were set by the retailers and record companies had little opportunity to price records individually. Thirdly, Sony had a limited number of pricing points for new releases, in respect of which it sought to achieve sales through dealer-specific discounts and promotional campaigns. Fourthly, the importance of chart success to the overall sales success of a record, and the fact that retailers and consumers tended to view records in the charts almost as commodity items, meant that there was little or no opportunity to premium price chart successes. Fifthly, any attempt to promote new records through a low-price strategy needed to be combined with a wider campaign involving retailers in order to overcome the consumer perception of low-price products as low-quality products and to ensure that retailers passed on the lower price to consumers. Finally, although the opportunities for pricing strategies to be implemented at the time of release were limited, there were opportunities, which Sony used, to implement price strategies later in the life-cycle of a recording in order to promote sales.

12.48. Warner said that it had at all times pursued its own pricing policy, which was designed to maximize the range and volume of its recordings stocked and displayed by retail outlets and to enable the retailers to offer the consumer particular promotional deals both on new releases and on back catalogue material. It was also clear that the pricing policies of the record companies were not the only factor affecting the price at which recorded mucic was sold in the UK. In Warner's experience, the decisions of the retailers as to the appropriate retail margin were more important in determining the level of prices than either the dealer price or the level of discounts and rebates offered by the record company. Thus the willingness of the retail side of the industry to respond to the introduction by the record companies of mid-price and budget categories, and the popularity among retailers of offering shorter-term price reductions and special offers, had to be set against the effects of price banding by retailers and the reluctance, particularly on the part of the specialist chains of retailers, to pass on overall price reductions by the record companies.

Relative prices charged for CDs, cassettes and vinyl records

12.49. As to the question whether they were exploiting the monopoly situation by the relative prices they charged for CDs, cassettes and vinyl records, the companies said that their pricing policies were exactly what would be expected in a competitive market. The use of multiple formats at different price levels was a rational economic response to the structure and development of the market for recorded music, the structure of demand for that music and the ownership of intellectual property rights in that market. The enormous success of the CD format in the last few years demonstrated clearly that consumers valued the qualities which it offered, and were prepared to pay a higher price for it than for the cassette or vinyl record formats. There were many examples of consumers paying different prices for what was essentially the 'same' product with somewhat different characteristics: for example, hardback and paperback editions of the same book; business and economy class tickets for the same flight; and differently-priced seats for the same concert. Similarly, differential pricing in the case of recordings was beneficial to consumers, artists and record companies alike, since it widened the range of goods available in the market-place, increased the volume of goods sold and was evidence of a competitive market. By contrast with other sectors dominated by intellectual property, such as books and films, music formats were not marketed by withholding one format now and releasing another at a later stage. Record companies did, however, charge different prices for those formats which they considered were of the highest quality and for which consumers were prepared to pay.

12.50. Quite apart from differently-priced formats for the same recording, within each format different recordings were available at a huge range of different prices, as was shown by the MMC's own market information. Moreover, mid- and budget-priced recordings were taking up an increased share of album sales. As for the price of CDs, these had followed the usual pattern with new technologies, and there had been a significant reduction in the real price of CDs over the period 1983 to 1992 as they had become the most popular format. Any pricing which aimed to decrease the differential between cassettes and CDs in order to encourage the sale of CDs would risk destroying the market for cassettes without causing a corresponding shift of purchases to CDs. All these factors created a situation which was wholly inconsistent with the notion that the companies collectively were following any particular policy with regard to the relative prices of the different formats or that a monopoly situation was being exploited.

Price differences between the UK and other countries

12.51. We asked the companies what was the extent of the price differences between the UK and other countries and the explanation for these differences. In responding to these questions, the companies referred to the survey of retail prices commissioned by us and carried out by BMRB and to individual dealer price company surveys which they themselves had carried out in the course of the inquiry.

12.52. BMG said that it was not in a position to comment in detail on the extent of the price differences between the UK and other countries. It noted with interest, however, the findings of the BMRB survey of international retail prices, which had found that the USA was the cheapest, no matter what the genre or format or whether with or without tax, and that Britain and Germany were generally the next cheapest for both CDs and cassettes, with France and then Denmark as the most expensive. That survey also showed that the average price differential was very much smaller than was popularly supposed, being only 11.7 per cent without tax for a full-price CD; with actual differentials ranging between 3.1 and 18.6 per cent.

12.53. It was also very important, BMG said, to note that the BMRB survey covered only full-price recordings and did not deal with budget or mid-price product. It pointed to research by BIS Strategic Decisions which showed that on the basis of a weighted average across the price range, prices in the UK ($12.6) were in fact lower than prices in the USA ($13.9), and substantially lower than elsewhere in Europe where they ranged from $21.4 in Denmark to $15.6 in Switzerland.

12.54. Both of these studies had been based on an examination of retail prices. BMG said that decisions on the level of retail prices in the UK were made by the retailers and not by the record companies. An examination of overall dealer prices from data supplied by the BPI and Record Industry Association of America showed the average differential between the UK and the USA to be very much smaller than the average differential in retail prices, ie only 2.5 per cent.

12.55. Commenting on the principal conclusions to be drawn from the BMRB survey of retail price comparisons, EMI said it broadly accepted the MMC's finding that full-price pop records in the USA were priced between 10 and 12 per cent higher in the UK than in the USA at an exchange rate of £1:$1.54. However, EMI had a number of reservations about the BMRB survey, the main one being that the sample was restricted to only 14 titles. The survey was therefore statistically insignificant.

12.56. EMI had conducted its own study to investigate the extent of EMI dealer, rather than retail, price differences between the UK and other countries. That study was designed to strip out the effects of local retail conditions. It had involved three price comparisons: gross dealer price comparisons for 100 titles across nine countries; gross dealer price comparisons between the UK and USA for 200 titles; and average realized price comparisons across seven countries. The study had shown that price differences as between the UK and other countries surveyed were generally in favour of the UK consumer. UK prices compared favourably with those in countries such as Japan, Germany, France and most of the rest of Western Europe, and only in the USA could prices sometimes be said to be lower. In particular, while the results of the UK/US gross dealer price comparisons varied from an unfavourable to a favourable outcome, depending on the exchange rate used to translate dollars into sterling, the results of the CD average realized dealer price comparison did not; the UK was cheaper than the USA regardless of which exchange rate was used. If classical recordings were separated out from EMI's sample survey of gross and realized dealer prices, the differential between UK and US prices, at an exchange rate of $1.49, was in the range of 2.5 to 10.5 per cent in favour of the USA.

12.57. PolyGram said that, for its own products, the average wholesale price for all CDs was lower in the UK than in any country other than Sweden. When all CD albums were considered together, the average realized price was lower in the UK even than the USA. Therefore, while both the BMRB's retail survey and PolyGram's assessment of its own dealer prices confirmed that full-price albums were cheaper in the USA, when mid-price and budget albums were also considered, average prices were lower in the UK. So far as the average wholesale prices for all PolyGram classical CDs were concerned, its analysis showed that the UK ranked eighth in terms of cheap classical CDs, some 10 per cent cheaper than the USA but marginally more expensive than Northern Europe and Scandinavia, Australia and Canada.

12.58. At retail level, the BMRB survey confirmed PolyGram's belief that UK prices for full-priced products were lower than in most other European countries. PolyGram was also pleased to note that the survey confirmed higher levels of availability in the UK than in most other EC countries. While the survey also confirmed that prices in the USA were lower than in the UK, this differential did not exceed 10.5 per cent. PolyGram said, however, that it had a number of reservations about the methodology of the BMRB study which made it difficult to draw definitive conclusions from the results.

12.59. Sony said that it was necessary to consider separately the price at which record companies supplied their customers (dealer or wholesale price) and the retail price. As to the prices charged by record companies, a comparison of Sony's own dealer prices after average discounts for a range of formats in the UK, Germany, France, the Netherlands and Denmark showed prices in April 1993 in the UK being the lowest across the range of formats. Differences in price, however, depended to a great extent on the exchange rate used. The dramatic effect of exchange rate fluctuations on relative prices between markets could be seen from a comparison of Sony's average net wholesale price for CDs in 1992 with those of its US counterpart. Based on an exchange rate for 1992 of £1:$1.754, the UK price was 79p higher than in the USA. In the first six months of 1993, when the exchange rate averaged a lower £1:$1.509, the UK price was 91p lower than that in the USA.

12.60. Turning to retail price differences, Sony said that it had not undertaken any detailed analysis of retail prices in Europe. The BMRB survey, however, although limited in the number of titles and therefore not wholly representative, indicated that retail prices in the UK were generally below those in other European countries.

12.61. As for retail price differences between the UK and USA, Sony said that it had carried out its own survey in these countries, covering a wide range of titles from its current UK catalogue, 85 in all, and including chart, non-chart and a range of specialist records. The same 85 titles were used in the US survey. Mid-price as well as full-price records were chosen. Sony said that the results of its survey showed pre-tax price differences which were significantly less than those found by the MMC. Non-classical CDs in the UK were on average only 58p more expensive than in the USA; for cassettes, the difference was 77p. For classical CDs, it was more difficult to obtain comparable titles in both countries, but for CDs where 15 titles could be compared, the UK prices were 73p higher on average than in the USA; and for eight comparable titles on cassette, the difference was 95p.

12.62. Sony said that its own survey, because of its broader coverage and Sony's additional information on sales, provided some additional insights into the nature of price competition in the two markets. First, the selection of popular titles had a strong influence on the results of any price comparison. In the Sony survey, five titles alone made up over 55 per cent of sales in the samples in both countries. The pre-tax price differences on these titles varied considerably from title to title and prices were heavily discounted in both countries. Secondly, there was a high frequency of titles for which the UK price was lower than the US price—19 in the non-classical survey. Thirdly, the Sony survey showed that in the UK there was a greater dispersion of prices across titles than in the USA; the maximum price was always higher in the UK but the minimum price was often lower. Fourthly, there appeared to be as much variation in the pre-tax prices within the USA as between the UK and USA; widely differing retail prices could therefore occur within a single market.

12.63. Warner said that the BMRB study broadly confirmed its view that the prices in the UK were lower than elsewhere in Europe but higher than those in the USA. Warner considered, however, that far from disclosing 'some very strong and consistent patterns' in the prices of pre-selected recordings in the different territories, the BMRB report had in fact demonstrated very little consistency in the relativities between the different countries. Warner took the view, therefore, that had a different range of albums been selected for the survey, a very different picture might have emerged. A further factor suggesting that there was in fact no strong or consistent pattern in pricing across the countries surveyed was the difference in price relativities between CDs and cassettes. For example, while France had consistently the highest prices for CDs without tax across all titles, this was not the case for cassettes, where in two cases it was cheaper even than the USA; and while Denmark had the highest cassette prices both before and after tax, for CDs it lay in fourth place in the pre-tax prices. Warner added that it was important to recognize that the process of averaging the prices charged in the BMRB survey masked the practice of retailers of setting their own retail prices in clearly defined bands, for example £8.99, £10.99 or £13.99 for CDs and £4.99, £5.99 and £7.99 for cassettes.

12.64. In the companies' view, there were a number of reasons for variations in gross and realized dealer prices as between different countries, including the size and competitiveness of the local market, differing manufacturing and distribution costs, the degree of retail power and concentration, the role of intermediaries, different legal regimes, the local cost of living, differences in musical tastes and the local levels of disposable income.

12.65. So far as differences specifically between the UK and USA were concerned, 'structural' differences, including higher sales tax and property costs and lower labour productivity and economies of scale in the UK, were also likely to be key drivers of higher retail prices here. Factors particularly affecting different dealer prices in the two countries were: the huge disparity in the sizes of the two markets; the different distribution patterns; the higher level of retail concentration in the UK which gave record companies' customers considerable power in negotiating discounts and other favourable terms; the longer manufacturing runs in the USA which led to substantial savings in manufacturing costs in that country; and the lower per unit cost of the A&R departments in the USA because of the size of that market in terms of volume sales. This volume difference meant that in the USA the costs and risks were allocated over a wider base, resulting in a lower unit cost and hence lower prices. The policy of originating a wide range of different kinds of music was a much less risky policy in the USA than the UK since a record was likely to generate the number of sales needed to recover the costs even if it was not a major hit. Accordingly, a higher proportion of albums released in the USA was profitable compared with the UK.

12.66. Another important difference between the two markets which affected the relative costs and risks was the higher level of advances and royalties paid to UK artists than US artists. Record companies in the USA paid lower average artist royalties than their counterparts in the UK and, as a result, lower advances. Another factor which helped to keep US advances below the level of those in the UK was that the competition for finding and signing new talent was less fierce in the USA than the UK, since the wider geographical dispersal of potential artists in the USA meant that US A&R departments were less likely than those in the UK to be bidding against rival record companies in particular cases.

12.67. EMI said that the UK/US differential was typical of the generality of other goods and services at present rates of exchange, but had hitherto been exaggerated by partial (in both senses of the word) investigations that had told more about exchange rates than about competition or lack of it in the UK music industry.

12.68. Sony believed that the general perception among the public of retail price differences in the USA and the UK might well be distorted by a failure to take account of US sales tax. Whereas VAT in the UK was incorporated into the shelf price of a record, US sales tax was not, and its effect on the price of a record only became apparent at the store cash till. Further, Sony thought that public perception had been affected by a lack of awareness of the dramatic differences between the levels of US sales tax and VAT.

12.69. PolyGram added that willingness to pay was certainly higher in the UK than the USA, despite higher US incomes. This might be due to the greater range of leisure activities available to US customers and to the lower prices of these other leisure activities. All in all, the US consumer had more alternatives competing for a share of leisure spend and the prices of these alternatives were relatively low, so it was not surprising that UK consumers were willing to pay more than their US counterparts for recorded music.

MCPS/BPI Import Licensing Scheme

The import practice

12.70. The companies emphasized the fact that the right to decline the licensing of imports derived not from the MCPS/BPI Import Licensing Scheme (the Scheme), but from UK law (section 27(3) of the 1988 Copyright Act). They also pointed out that this position under UK domestic law was consistent with the EC's Rental Directive, which had to be incorporated into the laws of all member states by 1 July 1994. Their policy on licensing was accordingly a normal and legitimate exercise of their intellectual property rights, and it was well settled under both EC and UK competition law that a party did not prevent, restrict or distort competition simply because it declined to license third parties to use its property. It was also relevant to note that UK copyright law was an integral part of an international network of historical and current Conventions, which were recognized internationally as providing an appropriate balance between the interests of consumers, creators and risk-takers.

12.71. Far from acting as an impediment to importation, the Scheme facilitated imports and thus enhanced competition in the UK. Without the Scheme, such importation would be largely impracticable because of administrative problems associated with the obtaining and granting of licences from and by the rights-owner concerned. In any case, the companies said that they exercised their ability under the Scheme to stop imports of particular records very sparingly, and only for legitimate marketing reasons or for the prevention of piracy.

12.72. EMI said that there was no reason to suppose that abolition of the Scheme would by itself make importing any easier. Indeed, many independent record companies were not members of the Scheme and it was very difficult, if not impossible, to get permission to import their records. By contrast, members of the Scheme operated a liberal regime whereby there was a general open licence subject to a right to withdraw that licence. The right had been exercised infrequently by EMI, although it was likely that independent record companies belonging to the Scheme exercised such rights rather more frequently. It therefore appeared paradoxical to single out the Scheme and the majors participating in it for criticism, whilst ignoring the conduct of those who were responsible for the majority of licence withdrawal under the Scheme, or of those who did not participate in it. Any distortion of competition would seem to be due rather to those latter groups.

12.73. Referring to the licensing of imports only on payment of a fee under the Scheme, EMI said that if the alleged practice at issue was the charging of a royalty in itself, rather than the level of that royalty, then it was not open to the MMC to make a provisional finding, since again, EMI was simply exercising a property right derived from UK and EC law. If on the other hand it was the level of the royalty rates that was considered to prevent, restrict or distort competition, then EMI did not know what lower rates could be thought not to do so. The present royalty rates had been held constant in money terms for six years, ie since the introduction of the Scheme in 1988, and had therefore fallen in real terms by over a quarter. The royalties were shared between the record company and the music publisher. EMI's total annual receipts under the Scheme had been economically insignificant. If the Scheme were brought to an end, the royalty rates that EMI would itself charge, were it willing individually to administer import licences, would certainly be no less and would almost certainly be greater than its half share of the Scheme royalties.

12.74. PolyGram said that it had no specific corporate policy in relation to the licensing of parallel imports and each individual case was considered on its own merits. Sony said that the only 'conduct' in which it had engaged had been to permit imports through the Scheme except in what the MMC had itself admitted was a limited number of cases each year. Warner said that it understood from the BPI that in 1992 a total of 95 import bans had been issued under the Scheme, 45 of those by the majors and 40 by independent record companies. Warner itself had not issued any bans in that year.

12.75. Warner said that the levying of a fee under the Scheme could not amount to conduct of a kind contemplated by section 6 of the Fair Trading Act. It could not be suggested that a complex monopoly existed in any industry where the suppliers all chose to charge for their product instead of giving it away free. The Scheme obviated the need for the importer to negotiate a licence fee for each particular recording; a flat rate was applied to all recordings, regardless of the status of the artist. This enabled the importer to know the level of fee in advance and to determine on that basis whether importing was commercially attractive.

Effect on prices of the Scheme

12.76. Turning to the effect on prices of the alleged practice regarding the Scheme, BMG said that it was clear from the MMC's own research on international retail prices that the ability to control imports had no effect on prices. That research showed that the lowest prices for recorded music were generally to be found in the UK and the USA, and that the highest prices were generally to be found in France and Denmark. In both the UK and the USA copyright owners had the right to control imports; in France and Denmark they did not. It was also highly questionable whether imported products were necessarily cheaper than domestically-produced ones, once the costs of importation were taken into account. In fact, it was not uncommon to find that imported recordings were more expensive. There was the further consideration that if controls on imports were removed unilaterally by the UK, other countries, particularly the USA, might retaliate; this was a danger which even the NHC had recognised.

12.77. Referring to the question whether the statutory rights conferred by the 1988 Copyright Act, rather than the Scheme itself, resulted in higher prices than would otherwise prevail, EMI said that the answer was complicated. In the absence of such rights, parallel importers could bring in non-pirate recordings from any third country without paying any royalty. However, the opportunities for profitable importing were limited and even where they arose, the main benefit might accrue to the importer rather than to the consumer. Moreover, EMI said that there appeared to be no correlation between the general level of prices for records in a country and the degree of protection, if any, against parallel importation enjoyed by rightsholders in that country; for example, the USA, which excluded parallel imports, was a relatively low price territory, whereas Denmark and the Netherlands, which had not so far afforded protection against parallel imports, were relatively high-price territories. It was therefore to be doubted whether, if unrestricted parallel importation were possible, it would appreciably affect the price level in the UK.

12.78. To the extent that abolition of the rights in question were to lead to any significant increase in parallel imports from third countries, the titles likely to be affected would be the 'best-sellers'—certainly, the evidence from other countries with lower levels of protection from parallel importation suggested that that would be so. But it was precisely those titles that were most likely to be the subject of split rights, so that there would be no certainty of the UK rightsholder's loss being compensated for by a gain on the part of one of its overseas associates. The overseas supplier and the export-import agency would therefore be in the classic position of free-riders. Even in the absence of split rights, parallel importation of large numbers of best-selling records would play havoc with the UK rightsholder's marketing, promotion and manufacturing plans and consequently with its financial results.

12.79. PolyGram said that its own research on cross-country comparisons showed that there was no evidence that licensing controls led to higher prices; or that removing controls on parallel imports led to lower prices to the consumer. Parallel importation was a free-rider activity which involved no local investment or commitment to productive activity in the UK. The continued existence of copyright protection against imports safeguarded both record companies and artists; its removal would have a number of adverse consequences, including a decline in investment in new artists, who would be more likely to sign overseas where record companies retained the means and incentive to invest; an increase in the extent to which existing catalogue was recycled; an increase in investment in broken, established artists, resulting in less innovative music; and an increase in the amount of US (and other foreign) music in UK record shops.

12.80. Sony said that for parallel imports to lead to lower prices for recorded music in the UK, a number of conditions had to be met. First, the wholesale price for the product had to be sufficiently lower in other major markets than in the UK to cover the transport and other costs involved in importing into the UK and supplying retailers and wholesalers. However, at least so far as Sony was concerned, comparison of the average wholesale prices in the UK and the USA for 1992 and the first six months of 1993 did not indicate significant differences at present. In these conditions, the necessary price differential for parallel imports to occur was only likely to arise where there were further significant exchange rate fluctuations—and here, imports were likely to be opportunistic imports of large quantities—or where the importer was able to achieve significant discounts off the average US wholesale price by placing individual large orders for a single title.

12.81. Secondly, the parallel imports had to be available at a time and in quantities to meet UK retailers' and wholesalers' requirements. Because retailers received a number of service benefits from the distribution operations of UK record companies (for example, rapid delivery of small orders, promotional support) which parallel importers would be unable or unwilling to match, parallel importing would not occur across the full range of titles currently supplied by the UK record companies. Consequently, Sony believed that, even if the existing legislation were changed, imports would only occur in two circumstances, namely niche demand for records not available from UK record companies and volume imports of selected titles, typically major stars and chart successes.

12.82. The third condition necessary for parallel imports to lead to lower prices was that retailers had to pass on the lower wholesale prices to the consumer. In the case of niche recordings, there was no incentive for the retailer to pass any cost savings on to the consumer, while in the case of volume imports, there was no guarantee that retailers would do so. As to chart successes, these tended currently to be sold at lower prices by retailers. It was therefore doubtful whether they would be prepared to offer further discounts if they parallel imported this material.

12.83. Warner considered that, in so far as the Scheme had any effect on prices, it operated to reduce the level of prices in the UK. The charging of the current fee of £1.25 for a CD could not possibly be regarded as excessive; it was not designed to bring the price of the imported product up to the price of the locally-marketed product, nor did it do so in practice. It would not be in the public interest to deprive the record companies of their right to license their copyright for a fee. In any case, half of the £1.25 fee was given to the MCPS for distribution to its members and the record company therefore only received 62.5p. The public interest lay not simply in obtaining cheap product but in ensuring that the creative skill of the record company and the holders of the other copyrights in the record were adequately rewarded.

12.84. The operation of a flat fee for all recordings also served to reduce the price level of the product, because it encouraged importers to take advantage of any price discrepancies that existed across the whole repertoire of the record companies. Whether or not consumers received the benefit of the lower prices charged to the retailers by the importers of product would depend on the pricing decisions of those retail outlets. Warner's experience of the industry did not lead it to believe that cost savings made by retailers from buying in imported product would necessarily be passed on to the consumer. Warner noted that the MMC's survey of prices in different countries had shown that Denmark's before-tax prices were generally much higher than those in the UK, despite the absence of any national provisions restricting parallel imports into Denmark.

Contribution of the Scheme to the prevention or detection of piracy and to the success of the UK recorded music industry

12.85. We asked the companies whether the right to control imports and the operation of the Scheme contributed to the control of piracy and to the success of the UK industry.

12.86. The companies said that record piracy was a complex, global problem which had been increasing dramatically in recent years. The right to control imports and the existence of the Scheme undoubtedly contributed both to the prevention and the detection of piracy. By having a scheme in place which controlled flows of imports from countries outside the European Union by the fixing of stickers on to incoming commercial product, illegitimate products were the more readily detectable, whether pirated or unauthorized imports. It was often extremely difficult to distinguish pirated from legitimate product and to do so required co-operation not only within the recorded music industry under the Scheme, but also from UK Trading Standards Officers and Customs and Excise. The Scheme also fostered co-operation between importers and the record industry, and importers were regularly able to provide information about suspected pirate imports.

12.87. If imports could take place free of copyright restrictions, the industry would then have much less involvement in imports by third parties, and it would be much more difficult for customs officials on their own to distinguish between a pirate recording and a legitimate one. There appeared to be a link between levels of sales of pirate records and the ability to use local laws to control importation of copyright-protected products. The UK had one of the lowest levels of piracy in the world, and one of the highest levels of piracy seizures in the European Union, while levels of piracy in countries with significantly lower levels of protection against imports appeared to be higher. The IFPI, for example, reported in its 1992 Review that pirated product was estimated to account for 9 per cent of total unit sales in the Netherlands.

12.88. Turning to the question of the contribution which the right to control imports and the Scheme made to the success of the UK record industry, the companies said that the right to control the distribution and exploitation of a copyright work was vital to such success. In and of itself, the Scheme was of no great significance and generated only a tiny income for the record companies. Nevertheless, it was a manifestation of the rights of copyright owners and embodied principles which ensured that competition between the UK and its international competitors was fair. Effective copyright protection was at the very heart of the success of the UK music industry.

12.89. The right to control imports protected record companies' ability to earn a return on the small percentage of releases which were successful, and which were vital to record companies' profitability. The evidence from other markets with lower levels of protection against imports was that it was precisely those titles on which parallel traders were most likely to concentrate their activities. It was also those titles which were most likely to be the subject of split territory deals, particularly in the case of independent record companies but also very frequently in the case of the majors. If record companies lost the right to control imports from North America of those albums to which they held only non-North American rights, their own UK sales of those albums would be reduced, perhaps significantly. That in turn would affect their ability to reinvest in new repertoire, and would also impinge on the artists' rights to grant copyrights for individual territories as he or she thought fit. Over time, the UK's continuing position as a major source of international and domestic repertoire would undoubtedly be affected by a withdrawal of the right to control imports, with serious consequences for all elements of the industry.

12.90. Parallel imports into the UK effectively 'free-rode' on the marketing and promotion expenditure of UK record companies and loss of revenue from units it would otherwise have sold would further prejudice the UK record companies' capacity to invest in new artists; such investment was vital to the UK as one of the two major sources of international repertoire. Artists, too, would be damaged by unrestricted importation, as it would be more difficult for the artist to track royalties and ensure proper payment; moreover, exports would increase from countries in which the artists' royalty was lower than in the country of importation. Music publishers also had a major interest in protecting their investment in the relevant UK rights in sound recordings.

12.91. More immediately, the ability of record companies to place a ban on recordings, particularly from the USA, before the record was released in the UK was a vital element in securing the effectiveness of a UK record company's launch campaign. The infiltration of products from the USA in such circumstances would undermine the impact of the promotional campaign and diminish the chances of the recording achieving a chart position on the basis of the initial sales figures. It was also likely to be more difficult to persuade retailers both to stock and promote the recording. Ultimately, the possibility of imports reaching the UK market ahead of the UK release date might result in reduced total UK sales of the recording, to the detriment of record companies, artists and writers.

12.92. BMG noted that the Australian Government had recently reversed its decision to accept a recommendation by the PSA that copyright restrictions on parallel imports into that country be removed. A report which it had commissioned on the implications for the industry of such a move showed that there was disquiet and loss of confidence within the Australian record industry at the prospect of the removal of protection, which was thought likely to have a major adverse effect on investment, to lead to an increase in the level of piracy in Australia, and to act as a constraint on the industry's capacity to grow and develop.

Independent record companies and the Scheme

12.93. We asked the companies whether certain independent record companies, in particular those represented by Umbrella, were being excluded from the Scheme in order to restrict their ability to compete in the UK.

12.94. The companies said that the only reason why an independent record company was excluded from the Scheme was because it was not a member of the BPI. There was nothing to prevent any member of Umbrella joining the BPI and the fee was nominal. By joining the BPI, an independent could then benefit from the Scheme, as well as all the other services offered by that body. PolyGram said it noted that Umbrella's Memorandum of Association specifically prohibited any major record company from joining that organization.

12.95. In any case, it was difficult to see on what possible basis an independent record company's ability to compete could be jeopardized by the operation of the Scheme, since it was open to any such company simply to allow importation of recorded works of which they were copyright owners in the UK or, alternatively, to exercise their rights to refuse to license such importation. Moreover, the core business of many of these companies was making records in the UK for sale in the UK and although in a few cases overseas rights might be licensed, this occurred on a very limited scale for the kind of companies represented by Umbrella. EMI suggested to us that it would be possible to design an industry-wide import scheme open to all record companies.

Artists' contracts

The practice

12.96. The companies said that all recording companies—majors and independents alike—included, to a greater or lesser extent, terms such as the MMC had identified in their contracts with artists (the term of the copyright, the length of the contract, options, obligations to exploit recordings, royalty rates, packaging and other deductions from royalties, and/or arrangements for accounting for and auditing royalties). It was hard to see how there could be a recording contract at all if it did not deal with such matters or how record companies could carry on their business without such contracts. Nor did these contracts constitute a general practice which restricted either party, since both parties were creating new rights and were assuming obligations which they did not previously have.

12.97. There was no such thing as a 'standard form' recording contract. All recording contracts were actively negotiated on an individual basis, often in circumstances where a number of companies were competing fiercely with each other to sign a particular artist. The negotiating process could take anything from six weeks to three months. Artists were almost invariably represented in the negotiations by lawyers and managers whose job it was to ensure that the terms finally agreed were the best that could be obtained. Not only were there very wide variations in the terms offered by each company, but each of them might well have a very different approach to the relationship with its artists. Moreover, it was quite wrong to suggest that the companies regarded many of their terms as non-negotiable; record companies were responsive to requests to renegotiate contracts, particularly, but by no means exclusively, in the case of successful artists.

12.98. PolyGram added that there might be circumstances where the enforcement of (but not the entering into) a contract might operate in restraint of trade and it was precisely for that reason that the common law doctrine of restraint of trade had developed. However, in reaching any determination as to whether enforcement of such a contract did operate in restraint of trade, there was no hard and fast rule and it depended ultimately on the facts of each case, taking into account a number of relatively general legal principles.

12.99. The companies said that contracts with artists accomplished a variety of pro-competitive rather than anti-competitive goals. They operated to enable the record companies to maximize sales, to increase product quality, to enhance productive efficiency and to take the very significant risks in investing in new artists. Without such recording contracts, another company would be able to sign an artist after the first company had heavily invested in the development and promotion of that artist and would thus be able to free-ride on that development and promotion. If that occurred, record companies would find it considerably less attractive to invest in new artists. They had to be able to count on artists who succeeded to cover the costs of those who failed, thereby spreading their risk across many artists. It was only by concluding contracts which embodied such terms as retention of copyright, exclusivity and a reasonable length of contract term that the companies could reap the necessary long-term benefits for those few artists who succeeded and that the artists who succeeded could reap the long-term benefits in their development and career.

Exploitation of the monopoly situation

12.100. We asked the companies whether the terms of their contracts with artists amounted to an exploitation of the monopoly situation.

12.101. The companies said that the contracts they had with artists did not reflect any lack of competition between record companies to secure and retain those artists' services; although there were similarities in the legal structure of contracts, the key terms, including advances, royalties and term, were all vigorously negotiated in each case. There was nothing to suggest that the potential rewards were insufficient to attract an adequate supply of recording artists and indeed the size of advances and royalties had increased substantially in recent years, reflecting a shift in the balance of power in favour of the artist at the expense of the record company. In this sense, therefore, there was no market failure. At any one time, there was active competition for the services not only of new artists but also of established and superstar artists. The terms of artists' contracts did not, therefore, present an obstacle to expansion by established record companies or to new entry by companies currently outside the industry. While it was true that the opportunities for buying-in established and superstar artists would be enhanced if the duration of artists' contracts were shortened, such a development would result in a shift by established companies from their well-tried policy of developing their own artists. Moreover, only the larger record companies with deep pockets would be able to take advantage of such opportunities.

12.102. As to retention of copyright, there was no benefit to the public interest in a successful artist acquiring control of the copyright in his recordings. An artist's only avenue for protecting and exploiting his copyright was to license it to a record company and this was achieved by auctioning it to the highest bidder. The consumer did not benefit because he was primarily interested in the artist and only to a limited extent in the particular label on which the recordings were released. There was a public interest in freedom of contract as well as in freedom of trade and in so far as the artist accepted contractual obligations, he or she received consideration for so doing in the shape of greater remuneration or remuneration on a more attractive basis than if those obligations had not been accepted. Where freedom of contract was abused, the law provided redress. But the expenditure by a record company on an artist represented an investment risk which would benefit both the artist and the record company if the risk paid off; if it did not, the record company would lose its money, whereas the artist would not only lose nothing but would also have received substantial advances on royalties which he or she would be under no obligation to repay to the record company. Investment in nine out of ten artists was not fully recouped.

12.103. Far from restricting artists' ability to exploit their talent fully, artists' recording contracts were precisely the means by which they were able to exploit that talent. A recording contract gave an artist not merely the opportunity of a recording career, but also the chance to earn significant income from touring, publishing, merchandising deals and public appearances. The artist could also exploit his or her talent by taking on session work, producing, remixing and soundtracks; the record company received no income from these activities, yet without the initial investment by the record company, these opportunities would not become available. If material modifications were made to the key provisions in recording contracts, dealing in particular with the extent of copyright acquired by the record company, the length of the contract and the exclusivity provisions imposed on the artist, then the companies would be forced to take a much more short-term view of their relationship with artists, which would not only be detrimental to the long-term development of those artists, but which would inevitably mean that the companies would not be able to invest as widely in new UK artists as they did at present. This would have the wider effect of reducing the numbers of artists who signed with UK record companies, to the detriment of UK artists and the industry alike. PolyGram added that the record industry could not be viewed in pure risk reward terms because, first, the services supplied by artists were not homogeneous and the industry was characterized by extremely high rewards for a few stars; secondly, the star artist was in an extremely strong bargaining position; and thirdly, other than in relation to star artists, there was an endemic oversupply of talent in the industry.

Effect on prices of the companies' contracts with artists

12.104. So far as the effect on prices of the terms of the companies' contracts with artists was concerned, the companies took the view that those contract terms generally operated to keep prices down. Record companies took very considerable risks in signing new artists. They were able to continue to justify investment in new artists at present levels only because they were able to generate sufficient sales revenue (both in the UK and from overseas sales) from those artists that were successful to offset the losses that they made on the majority of their signings. Changes to recording contracts which had the effect of materially limiting the companies' ability to benefit from their initial investment would, on the basis of current levels of profitability, mean either that record prices would have to rise or that investment in new artists would have to be curtailed, all other things being equal.

12.105. By having contracts which lasted for a reasonable period of time, the companies were able to take a longer-term view of the likely returns. By exercising a limited number of options to continue the term of the contract, record companies had the opportunity to reinvest in situations where the commercial potential had not been fully realized. Exclusivity served to protect the investment made by a record company in a particular artist; in the absence of exclusivity, other record companies could

251

free-ride on that company's investment; the resulting impact on its ability to earn profits from its successful albums could only lead to increased prices at the time of release. Further, the removal of exclusivity would result in a greater proportion of the record companies' budgets being devoted to bidding for the 'stars', to the detriment of new artists with minority appeal. If contract terms were shortened, the record company would seek to earn a return over a shorter period of time. Again, this would be likely to result in higher prices. The same considerations would apply to any enforced curtailment of the companies' interest in copyright.

Producers' rights

12.106. We asked the companies whether they were exploiting the monopoly situation by not recognizing any rights of producers as first holders of copyright in the sound recordings they produced.

12.107. The companies said that the role of the record producer varied considerably so far as his or her involvement in the production of a sound recording was concerned. Although often making a significant creative contribution, the producer by no means always did so. A very small number of record producers, such as Pete Waterman, took the risks in funding and undertaking all the arrangements for records they produced; but in most cases, the producer took no risk. In practice, the role of the record company was closer to that of a film producer in relation to the making of a sound recording: the film producer took a financial risk, obtained the rights in the work to be filmed, arranged the financing, supervised the making of the film and delivered it to the distributor.

12.108. It was clear that, in drafting the relevant provisions of the 1988 Copyright Act dealing with the grant of copyright in sound recordings, Parliament had intended that the record company should be the holder of that right, since it was the record company which generally made the necessary arrangements for the making of the recording, including the provision of the necessary finance. There was authority as to the meaning of 'the person by whom the arrangements ... are undertaken' in relation to films. The courts had held that the word 'undertake' meant 'be responsible for', especially in the financial sense but also generally. It could therefore be assumed that in using the same formula for sound recordings as for films in the 1988 Copyright Act, Parliament had intended that copyright should vest in the person who had undertaken the financial responsibility for making the recording. The ownership of that copyright was the reward for the risk they had undertaken. The 1988 Copyright Act was entirely consistent with the Rental Directive, which made it clear that the producer of a film or record was intended to refer to the person by virtue of whose investment a recording or film came into being. There was no question, therefore, of record companies 'not recognising any rights of producers as first holders of copyright in the sound recordings they produce' as had been suggested by some producers. Rather, those rights did not subsist at all.

12.109. The companies considered that record producers operated in a highly competitive market and were already more than adequately remunerated (often in the shape of a sizeable advance and a share of royalties), especially considering that they did not contribute to the investment in an artist made by the record company or bear any part of the risk inherent in making a new recording. Moreover, where the producer was entitled to royalties on the sale of the record, he generally received payment more quickly than the artist because only the advance had to be recouped. But in any case, in the companies' submission, this was not an issue which raised any public interest concerns.

Effect of the terms of artists' contracts on competition

12.110. We asked the companies whether competition between them, or between them and independent companies (including BBC AI), was adversely affected by the terms of artists' contracts.

12.111. The companies said that, for the reasons already given above, artists' contracts did not adversely affect competition between them and other record companies, of whatever size. As between themselves, contract terms varied significantly and artists could and did move from one company to another. Competition between the companies to sign artists was intense.

12.112. Competition between the companies and independents was also intense. All record companies were able to offer packages which would appeal to different artists. Competition for artists had tended to increase the level of advances offered to new artists, but there was no evidence that this had put new artists beyond the reach of smaller, independent companies. There were a number of reasons why artists might prefer to sign with an independent company: for example, such companies were often specialists in a particular musical genre and could offer expertise in that area; they were often prepared to be more flexible and innovative in their approach because of the smaller scale of their operations; they could often give more individual attention to artists in a business where personal contact was crucial; and they were often 'closer to the ground' than larger companies and were in a position to offer a contract to an unknown artist before he or she had come to the attention of such companies. The existing commercial arrangements assisted the smaller record companies by giving them the security of being able to retain their successful stars rather than losing them to the larger companies in more frequent bidding wars or, if they wished, by 'selling' their stars to larger record companies for significantly large sums of money. Independent companies needed their copyrights and a reasonable length of contract in order to be able to secure licensing agreements to exploit their artists' recordings overseas. They would find it difficult to recover their investment in a successful artist if that artist were able to take the copyright and transfer it to one of the major record companies as soon as he achieved success.

12.113. As for BBC AI, the companies maintained that it could not be equated with ordinary independent record companies. Indeed, it was in a unique position, possessing an archive of recordings of famous classical artists originally made by the BBC for the purpose of broadcasting only, at a time when it had a monopoly of broadcasting in the UK and when the artists in question were under exclusive recording contracts with a number of record companies. The artists concerned knew very well the contractual basis upon which permission to broadcast was granted at the time they contracted with the BBC and both parties had until now always accepted the conditions involved. It might be that the consequences of the operation of artist and title exclusivity and the terms of the Broadcasting Permission were not now commercially convenient for the BBC. But artist and title exclusivity were no more than was reasonably necessary to protect the legitimate commercial interests of all record companies to ensure a reasonable return on their significant investments in classical (and indeed other) repertoire; many classical recordings were unsuccessful and many more could take many years to recoup the initial investment undertaken. The classical repertoire was of very considerable cultural and public interest and if the BBC were allowed to free-ride on the back of that investment to release public performances which were made on the basis of a clear recognition of the record companies' need to protect their investment, the continuation of such investment in classical artists by record companies would be seriously undermined.

12.114. PolyGram added the following points. First, it was the wish of artists that recordings of performances made for broadcast purposes should not be issued to the public otherwise than by broadcast, so that the artistic integrity of the work and its reputation for quality might be preserved. Secondly, artist exclusivity was also essential to enable a record company to identify itself with the totality of an artist's work and thereby to provide and maintain a nexus between the reputation of the artist at a particular point in his or her career and the image and reputation which attached to the particular record company. Thirdly, in addition to artist exclusivity, the object of title exclusivity was to prevent record companies' investment in an artist being undermined by that artist recording, a relatively short time after the expiry of a contract with another record company, the same work as had been recorded by that artist with that record company. Fourthly, BBC Enterprises Limited, of which BBC AI was a subsidiary, was a major economic operator in, *inter alia*, the market for recorded music. It was not correct for BBC AI to maintain that it represented the first attempt by the BBC to enter the record industry; BBC Enterprises had consistently released a wide variety of sound recordings of the BBC's broadcast activities and indeed the BBC had figured prominently in the BPI's own table of record industry market shares over the past ten years; fifthly, the issues identified in relation to BBC AI applied equally in the field of pop music and to all broadcasters of pop music, whether on radio or television, and artist and title exclusivity equally protected the record companies' investments against release of those archive recordings. Finally, if the MMC were to limit the scope of, or prohibit altogether, title and artist exclusivity, this would put the UK out of line with practice in the rest of the world and place all the record companies at a significant competitive disadvantage.

248336   R2

Profitability

12.115. We asked the companies whether their underlying profitability was excessive in relation to sales and capital employed. We also asked them to comment on the suggestion that their profitability was effectively understated as a result of the present accounting treatment of their investment in A&R and copyright material. On this second point, we had commissioned a study into the business valuation of the companies by KPMG Peat Marwick (KPMG), and a summary of this report is at Appendix 8.2. Thirdly, we asked them whether they were choosing the formats on which they released recordings in a way which was designed to increase their profits rather than meet consumers' requirements.

Levels of profitability

12.116. The companies maintained that levels of profitability in the UK market for recorded music over the past five years had been low, particularly within the context of the high degree of risk to which record companies were exposed and the volatile return on investment in this market. The companies did not consider that ROCE was a meaningful measure of profitability for the recorded music industry which had a large service element and a small requirement for capital; return on sales, although it had certain limitations as a measure of profitability, was the more appropriate. If returns were compared with those achieved in various other sectors which had certain characteristics in common with the recorded music industry, such as the leisure industry, the pharmaceutical industry, publishing, broadcasting and software companies, it was clear that the underlying profitability of the companies was in line with profitability in those comparable sectors and that it was not excessive in relation to sales. In any case, profitability did not provide a reliable guide to the nature or extent of effective competition in the market for recorded music.

Accounting treatment of A&R and copyrights

12.117. The companies said that their accounts were prepared fully in accordance with UK accounting standards and the profits shown in those accounts were fairly stated. Their policy was also consistent with the fundamental accounting concept of prudence, which dictated that A&R costs should be provided for as they were incurred unless there was a reasonable expectation of recoupment from future revenues. It was common practice among UK companies not to include on their balance sheets the value of their intangible assets and the companies were following UK accounting practice in this respect.

12.118. BMG said that the part of its A&R investment which represented prepayment of royalties to artists was recoverable only from artists' future royalty earnings. Because there was a risk of non-recovery in respect of those advances, dependent upon the success or otherwise of the individual artists, provisions were made as appropriate on an artist by artist basis to reflect this risk and to reduce the value of the 'investments' to recoverable amounts. The level of such provisions was reviewed on an annual basis, and as it was applied consistently year-on-year, there should be no material impact on profitability.

12.119. Internally generated copyrights, such as rights to exploit future recordings by artists under contract to BMG, were not carried as intangible assets on BMG's balance sheet, because the carrying of internally-generated intangibles on the balance sheet did not comply with either UK accounting standards or group accounting policy and because of the high degree of subjectivity involved in their valuation, as a result of which the values ascribed to copyright might vary significantly year-on-year. Any impact of internally generated copyrights on the company's balance sheet would only occur when the value of those copyrights was realized on a sale.

12.120. Commenting on the KPMG report, BMG said that it disagreed fundamentally with the methodology adopted, the data used in preparing the analysis and the usefulness of the results obtained. In its view, the methodology was so flawed as to provide no useful insight even at the aggregated level. The turnover multiple was used because it was the least flawed of the methods considered and because a discounted cash flow analysis was not feasible. However, even the least flawed method was insufficient to produce a useful contribution and the number of key unjustified assumptions fatally undermined the results of this analysis. While valuations of individual companies would clearly be necessary in a bid situation, and could be generated with sufficient understanding and expert knowledge of the value of the different assets of the company (tangible and intangible), KPMG had not demonstrated the expertise to provide a sensible valuation for the industry as a whole.

12.121. BMG accepted that the valuation of a target company's catalogue was a major factor in mergers and acquisitions transactions in the music industry; but it was only one among many key factors in assessing the attractiveness of a target, and was as difficult to estimate in money terms as the quality of management. This problem had become worse as the markets had fragmented and consumer tastes were changing at an increasing rate. Any estimate would be a guess based on knowledge of the catalogue and the market. The uncertainty of the business meant that the valuation would be a high-risk endeavour, and would often be determined by the broader range of factors.

12.122. EMI said that the proper way to arrive at an economic return, as opposed to an accounting return, was to value the intangible assets and include the increase or decrease in the overall return. However, it was very difficult to measure either the value of the additions to the intangibles during the year or the changes (upwards or downwards) in the value of the existing intangibles. Even if it were possible to arrive at reasonable estimates of value, based on projections of future revenues, the circularity involved would render them of no use to the MMC in considering whether or not excessive profits were being made. The KPMG exercise had not overcome these difficulties and consequently EMI did not believe it was helpful in considering whether or not excessive profits were being made. EMI also had a number of more specific concerns about the KPMG turnover methodology. For example, EMI did not believe that a standard multiple applied to turnover could produce an accurate valuation of intangibles, since it took no account of differences in profit margins between companies. Moreover, use of acquisition values to estimate the multiple could be misleading because in some cases copyright had represented the main value to the acquirer, while in others potential cost savings had been the main benefit.

12.123. The stock market rating of THORN EMI suggested that EMI's intangibles did have a substantial value but did not suggest that the market considered that THORN EMI's accounting practices understated its underlying economic profitability to a greater extent than other public companies. The evidence from the acquisitions by THORN EMI of Chrysalis and Virgin suggested that the greater part of the acquisition prices was based on EMI's ability to achieve cost savings and the lesser part on the value of the intangibles in Chrysalis and Virgin. In both cases, the current artist roster was considered by THORN EMI to be more important than the back catalogue.

12.124. PolyGram said that it was generally accepted accounting practice in the UK that assets should only be carried at a valuation if the value could be measured with reasonable certainty. The uncertainties and subjectivity inherent in endeavouring to project future earnings on albums not yet released or even recorded, and the general problems of valuing artists who had unique economic and commercial characteristics and potential, were such that any valuation of back catalogue or its artists' roster would not be verifiable under the accounting guidelines. While recognizing that value had been created in the back catalogue and artists' roster through A&R activities, this value only became quantifiable with reasonable certainty on disposal.

12.125. PolyGram said that it had asked Ernst & Young to explore alternative means by which measurements of ROCE could be achieved to include the company's intangible assets. Ernst & Young had concluded that if the artists' roster and back catalogue were recalculated and restated at an independently determined valuation, any such valuation would normally be based on a forecast of net earnings from the artist and back catalogue using a normal ROCE. The result would be entirely circular, since actual earnings were likely to be different from forecast earnings. Therefore, any differences in actual ROCE from the 'normal' ROCE would merely reflect the inaccuracy of the original forecast earnings and, as a consequence, the inaccuracy of the valuation.

12.126. If, alternatively, a revised capital base were calculated by restating the balance sheet and profit and loss account as if A&R investment had been capitalized and amortized rather than written off in accordance with current policy, the only difference with PolyGram's current accounting policies would be one of timing. Under the capitalization method, expenditure would be spread over the estimated economic life of the catalogue, say 10 or 20 years. Under the method used by PolyGram, costs were written off against royalties recouped or written off as soon as non-recoupment was foreseen. The capitalization method produced a 'mismatch' between the 10 or 20 years over which the advance was written off as against the actual time when an advance would be recouped which, in the case of a successful artist, was likely to be much more quickly through royalties. The net assets on the balance sheet therefore merely represented historical costs that had been capitalized and amortized in an arbitrary manner, reflecting neither the value of the catalogue and artists to the business, nor accepted accounting policies. An ROCE based on a capitalization method was accordingly flawed, potentially misleading and largely meaningless.

12.127. Sony said that its accounting policy for A&R costs, which had been adopted consistently over recent years, was to capitalize only significant advances where it was reasonably certain that they would be recouped from future royalties. In practice that meant that only advances to established artists were capitalized. Most advance payments were written off, a practice which simply reflected the nature of the business: the vast majority of releases were not successful and hence most advances were not recovered. Where a recording did not sell immediately after its release, it was highly unlikely to fare any better in subsequent years.

12.128. It was possible to consider alternative accounting treatments of A&R costs. Even if these were acceptable in terms of the fundamental accounting concepts of prudence and matching, their adoption would not affect the long-term profitability of Sony's UK business. This was because, in a mature business, changing the accounting policy would tend to have a one-off effect on the profit of the company, with a permanent adjustment on the balance sheet.

12.129. Commenting on the KPMG report, Sony said that there were a number of flaws in the methodology adopted which undermined the validity of the 1.2 turnover multiple used in KPMG's calculations and made it inappropriate for the MMC to rely on the KPMG calculations. In particular, they had failed to give proper weight to a number of factors which significantly affected the purchase price paid for a business and had also failed to take proper account of the differences between the various transactions considered. For example, the value of a trade mark of a record company had been taken to represent of the order of 10 per cent of the purchase price required to acquire the company, yet no explanation had been given of the basis for that figure. A blanket 10 per cent deduction gave insufficient weight to the large number of factors other than the copyright valuation that affected the price paid for a record company, and failed to take adequate account of the differences between the various businesses acquired and the differing factors affecting the price paid in each case, such as the infrastructure of the business and the current management team. Other factors which KPMG failed to take into account were, for example, the fact that almost all the acquired businesses considered by KPMG included a range of business activities, not just core record company activities; the businesses covered ranged from purely national concerns to multinational operations; no allowance was made for macroeconomic factors over the period during which the transactions took place; no allowance was made for the price being driven up by competitive factors; and no allowance was made for the effect on price of potential synergies and cost savings which the purchaser could achieve. In addition, Sony questioned the validity of applying a turnover multiple of 1.2 to the major record companies' figures when it was apparent from the KPMG study that there was very considerable price variation in the turnover multiples calculated in the various individual transactions and that 1.2 was merely a simple average.

12.130. Warner said that it believed its accounting treatment of A&R spend and copyright material was the most appropriate in accordance with prudent accounting practice, taking into account the risks inherent in the recorded music industry.

12.131. Warner had asked Ernst & Young to review the KPMG study. Ernst & Young took the view that the methodology did not lead to useful measures of economic profitability, for the following reasons. First, there was inevitably a problem of circularity associated with market-based valuations of intangible assets, although KPMG had overcome this difficulty to some extent by focusing on changes in the value of intangibles during the period in question. However, secondly, if the resulting rate of return measures were to have any useful meaning, increases in asset valuations should be attributed to the appropriate period in which the expectation of higher future earnings, and hence the notional increase in the 'value' of the back catalogue, first arose; the KPMG method seemed unlikely to do this. Thirdly, the KPMG method made little or no allowance for the success or lack of success of individual record companies in creating intangible assets with an enduring earning power. Fourthly, an economic profit approach could increase the profit attributed within a finite period but it could not increase the overall quantum of profit. And finally, even if it were applicable to the global operations of a record company, the KPMG method could not yield a realistic measure of the capital employed by a UK record company with significant income derived from the international licensing of repertoire.

Profitability in relation to record formats

12.132. We asked the companies whether the formats on which they chose to release recordings were designed to increase their profits rather than meet the requirements of consumers, thus reducing consumer choice.

12.133. The companies said that the formats on which they released their recordings were determined by consumer demand; in that way, they maximized their profits by anticipating and meeting consumers' needs at the prices consumers were willing to pay. Purchasers of recorded music had a far wider choice than was offered to consumers in other sectors in which intellectual property rights were fundamental, such as books and films. In the case of books, for example, publishers generally issued the more expensive hardback version of a book first and the cheaper paperback version some considerable time later. The companies continued to offer all three formats—vinyl records, cassettes and CDs—to their customers at the time the recording was released on to the market, notwithstanding the decline in demand for the vinyl record format.

12.134. The trend among consumers was towards the newer formats at the expense of vinyl records. Consumers who were prepared to pay more for a higher-quality product had increasingly chosen CDs over both vinyl records and cassettes. There had been increased CD player penetration over the past ten years and CD prices had fallen in real terms over the period from 1983 to 1992. At the lower end of the market, consumers had increasingly chosen cassette over vinyl because of its greater durability, convenience and flexibility. Moreover, retailers had shown an increasing reluctance to stock the vinyl record because, although it sold at the same price as cassette, it was heavier, more fragile and required more shelf space than cassette or CD and was therefore a less attractive format for retailers to stock.

12.135. BMG said that it had continued to release a significant number of titles on vinyl until 1991, by which time there had been a dramatic collapse in demand, and it still offered the vinyl format in areas where demand was still strong, namely dance music, pop singles and 'alternative' albums.

12.136. EMI said that it still released virtually all new pop records—ie both singles and albums—on CD, cassette and vinyl, even though sales of vinyl pop albums now accounted for only 5 per cent of total UK album sales. Demand for classical music on vinyl had now fallen away and although EMI had continued to supply classical recordings on vinyl until 1991, it had now generally discontinued doing so. EMI considered that the days of vinyl records were numbered and their decline would soon reach the point at which any remaining demand would be too small to enable them to be marketed at commercially acceptable prices, except perhaps in the case of pop singles.

12.137. PolyGram said that, far from being limited in the choice of formats with respect to its recordings, consumers were able to obtain these in all formats, including vinyl, even though demand for vinyl had fallen to very low levels, particularly since 1990. It was PolyGram's policy, however, to continue to release recordings on vinyl and to continue to market this format and make it available for distribution for as long as this was commercially possible, and although this was usually at a considerable loss to the company.

12.138. Until 1991 Sony had released all albums on cassette, CD and vinyl. Vinyl had been manufactured at its own pressing plant at Aylesbury. In 1991 Sony had decided that the plant was no longer commercially viable and was closed; vinyl was now manufactured for Sony by a sister company in the Netherlands. Sony said that it usually released singles on 12" vinyl, cassette and CD; although it continued to release vinyl albums, sales had continued to decline sharply.

12.139. Warner said that at present most of its singles were released on vinyl, cassette and CD; so far as its albums were concerned, they were released at least on CD, and the decision whether to release on vinyl (or DCC, MiniDisc etc) was taken in relation to every recording. In any case, since many retailers (for example, W H Smith) had now stopped stocking vinyl, there was little point in the record companies continuing to produce it.

Phonographic Performance Limited

12.140. We asked the companies whether they were taking steps to maintain or exploit the monopoly situation by the way in which they controlled PPL so that *(a)* some independent record companies did not receive a fair share of PPL's income and *(b)* no part of PPL's income was paid to producers.

12.141. The companies denied that they in any way controlled PPL. PPL had a broad membership of some 1,440 member companies which controlled over 5,000 labels between them. Any person who owned or was entitled to the performing right in a sound recording was eligible to become a member and there was no fee or charge for membership. The companies could in no sense be said to dominate the committee structure of PPL and indeed, of the three PPL Distribution Committee members, two were from independent record companies and the third was from EMI. The rules which governed PPL were entirely transparent and non-discriminatory and did not confer any benefit on the companies as against the independent record sector.

12.142. PPL's three main revenue sources were the BBC, Independent Local Radio (ILR) and public performance. Distribution of BBC revenue was in accordance with returns from virtually every service of the BBC and independent record companies received their right and proper share of this revenue. PPL was currently in the process of improving the distribution system for ILR revenue by increasing the number of local radio stations used as the basis for returns; this would benefit smaller companies whose specialist repertoire was played by specialist stations which did not at present analyse the playing of records in detail. The most difficult area was public performance, since full or even large sample returns were not practicable from more than 100,000 different locations. PPL was, however, understood to be considering proposals for a substantial change of approach here aimed at more accurately measuring actual usage.

12.143. To the extent that there were imperfections in the current distribution arrangements, these were not attributable to any action on the part of the companies, nor were they likely to discriminate against independents and favour the companies. The companies fully supported the moves being taken to improve the system. Any remaining unfairness would be the result of operational and administrative difficulties, and there was a balance to be struck between the amounts of money involved in improving usage measurement and the complexity of the analysis of fair play returns required for splitting the income equitably. The companies believed PPL had largely succeeded in achieving a fair system.

12.144. As to the question of any part of PPL's income being paid to producers, the companies said that since producers had no copyright interest in the sound recordings which they produced, they correspondingly had no performance rights in those sound recordings (see paragraphs 12.106 to 12.109). There was therefore no reason why record producers should expect to receive any part of PPL income.

Video Performance Limited

12.145. We asked the companies whether collective negotiation through VPL of licence fees for the broadcasting of music videos was justified or whether it constituted a step taken for the purpose of exploiting the monopoly situation.

12.146. The companies said that although music videos were part of the package of methods used to promote certain artists and types of music, they were also now primarily products in their own right, involving considerable creative effort and expenditure on the part of the record company. They were offered for sale as an additional format in which consumers could enjoy the music of a particular artist. Music videos had now become an important source of programming for an increasing number of broadcasters. Broadcasting organizations also benefited from the availability of music videos by increasing their advertising revenue and enhancing their market position.

12.147. VPL had been set up in 1984 in order to facilitate the grant of licences in music videos. The MMC's 1988 report on *Collective Licensing* had set out very clearly the rationale and justification for such a body as VPL which, like any other collective licensing body, carried out a range of functions, including licensing the use of copyright, determining tariffs for that use, collecting royalties, distributing the revenue, monitoring the collective use of copyright material and enforcing copyright. Its convenience both to users and rights owners was particularly applicable to music videos, which were short, song-length pieces, each of which might be licensed to a number of different broadcasters and shown several times in a single day and many times during a week. In practice, all VPL's activities were interrelated, so that if it were to be prevented from negotiating royalties with broadcasters, it would cease to play any part at all in relation to those particular licences. This would significantly undermine its value to members.

12.148. VPL currently had around 390 members, the vast majority of whom were independent of the companies. Revenue received from users was distributed strictly in accordance with the use made of each member's videos. If VPL were to be prevented from negotiating on a collective basis, then it was likely that most broadcasters would only wish to negotiate on an individual basis with the major groups. The smaller companies would then find that their videos were not played at all or that they were played without payment. Very few of the smaller companies would have the resources to negotiate effectively with major broadcasting organizations, and the very considerable power which such organizations already enjoyed would be further enhanced. Nor would smaller companies have the resources to take action individually to control unlicensed use of their videos. The benefits of collective licensing through VPL also included a reduction in the number of transactions that would otherwise be necessary, the maximization of music video broadcasting output, and the avoidance of duplication in such matters as negotiation, monitoring of use, granting licences, collecting fees and enforcing rights. It therefore avoided the need for broadcasters to seek separate licences in each jurisdiction in which it operated.

12.149. If the royalties required by VPL were unreasonable, it was open to a broadcaster under the 1988 Copyright Act to refer the issue to the Copyright Tribunal for determination. It was notable that MTVE, which had alleged that the companies were abusing their monopoly position in relation to VPL, had not chosen to put its case to the Copyright Tribunal on the question of royalty rates.

12.150. PolyGram made a number of additional points in response to the complaints made by MTVE to the MMC. First, it was incorrect for MTVE to state that it could not negotiate directly for UK rights. The rights in the relevant music videos which members of VPL had assigned to VPL were terminable on six months' notice and it had therefore always been open to PolyGram to seek to license MTVE direct; indeed, PolyGram had undertaken extensive negotiations with MTVE prior to the expiry of the original five-year agreement between VPL and MTVE. Secondly, MTVE had failed to note in its submission to the MMC that it was the only dedicated 24-hour broadcaster of music videos and that it was therefore in the position of a monopsonist in its negotiations with VPL. Thirdly, MTVE's bare assertions of the record companies' anti-competitive intentions were untenable; they implied certain motivations and intentions on the part of PolyGram and the other majors acting through VPL but had produced absolutely no evidence in support of any of those assertions. Fourthly, MTVE had chosen to ignore all of the benefits offered by the VPL/IFPI collective licensing arrangements because it wished to seek a change in the UK market structure with the sole, unrealistic objective of reducing the royalty payments to VPL to a level which it considered to be appropriate in order to further boost its already substantial profits. PolyGram submitted that in any event, individual licensing would result in higher and not lower royalty payments by MTVE. Fifthly, MTVE appeared to be arguing that copyright owners such as PolyGram must market their copyrights in a form convenient to MTVE. In order to achieve this, MTVE was seeking to substitute the market conditions in the EC by those prevailing in the USA. But the legal, cultural and historical background to the licensing of music videos in the UK and the EC was fundamentally different to that prevailing in the USA. Record companies were entitled to seek fair and reasonable remuneration in respect of their intellectual property rights in music videos and it was quite wrong for MTVE to consider that such videos should be provided free of charge 'in consideration of their promotional value'. The record companies provided MTVE with cheap programming with a proven appeal to consumers and advertisers for which they were entitled to reasonable remuneration. Finally, PolyGram pointed out that the various benefits to MTVE, to the copyright owners and to consumers offered by collective licensing in general applied even more to the IFPI/VPL pan-European licensing arrangements. The pan-European licensing arrangement offered the only legal and practical means of obtaining a pan-European licence, given the different legal positions prevailing in EC member states and the legal position in EC law following the judgment of the Court of Justice in *Coditel v Ciné-Vog*.[1] Moreover, the benefits of collective negotiations through a 'one-stop shop' had recently been recognized by the European Commission.

Independent record companies

12.151. We put to the companies a number of issues relating to various aspects of their relationship with independent record companies; these covered the music charts, the companies' spending on promotion and marketing and the role of the BPI.

The music charts

12.152. We asked the companies whether they were seeking to exploit the record charts in a way that restricted or distorted competition with independent record companies, eg by the inclusion in the 'independent chart' of records released by the companies in which they had an interest or with which they had a business relationship.

12.153. The companies said that this issue appeared to reflect a basic misunderstanding of the operation of the independent charts. These were intended to reflect the success of a particular genre of music, loosely described as 'alternative' music. The original criterion for inclusion in these charts had been independent distribution, but in 1992 a second criterion was added, namely that the record must be within the 'indie' music genre; the purpose of this second criterion was to eliminate from the independent chart any mainstream artists who were independently distributed but whose music was not part of the 'indie' music scene. The genre criterion was, however, subsequently abandoned and the independent charts reverted to a single rule, namely independent distribution through music specialist panel stores.

12.154. The companies said that, to the extent that the independent charts operated unfairly, they did so in respect of them rather than the independents. The application of the distribution criterion had the effect of excluding from the independent charts some recordings which consumers would consider 'indie' music even though it was distributed by one of the majors. By the same token, some 'indie' recordings of the independent record companies were excluded from these charts because they chose to have their product distributed by one of the companies. The current arrangements also operated to the companies' disadvantage because they acted as a disincentive to independent record companies to enter into distribution agreements with them, even though the independents and the record-buying public might be better served by the lower prices and greater efficiency of such arrangements.

12.155. But in any event, the companies denied that the practice of having a small number of releases distributed by independent, and often more costly, distributors could be thought to restrict or distort competition. On the contrary, it was a feature of the intense competition and the wide range of choice available to consumers. If the chart compilers thought it was somehow wrong for these releases to be eligible for the independent charts, it was open to them to redraw the qualification criteria to exclude them.

---

[1]Case 262/81 [1982] ECR 3381.

Promotion and marketing

12.156. We asked the companies whether the practices of spending large sums on promotion and marketing and supplying free copies to retailers constituted uncompetitive practices which had the effect of restricting actual or potential competition with independent record companies and/or reducing the amount of the royalties paid to artists.

12.157. The companies said that the UK recorded music market was highly competitive, being driven by the availability of substitutes, the power of retailers, the power of artists and media costs. In those circumstances, it was inevitable that companies would be forced to invest heavily in promotion and marketing in order to differentiate their products from their competitors', to develop a distinct identity for their artists and to introduce consumers to new music which they might otherwise be unwilling to buy. Promotional expenditure was in addition to and not a substitute for price competition, as evidenced by the size and the nature of discounts. Although the independent record companies did not always have the resources to match the marketing and promotional expenditure of the companies, this did not mean that actual or potential competition from independents was restricted. Independents simply competed in different ways, for example by concentrating on niche products, exploiting their flexibility, speed of response and proximity to customers, taking advantage of a generally lower cost base, obtaining additional funding by licensing overseas rights or selling out contracts with particular artists, and entering into strategic alliances with the majors in order to take advantage of the wider range of skills which they possessed. Moreover, the most important promotional medium, radio, was free and open to access by all record companies. The specialist press was not only also free but tended to prefer featuring independent artists.

12.158. It was in any event difficult to see how the normal commercial activity of spending large sums on promotion and marketing could, in and of itself, amount to an uncompetitive practice. In a market where loyalty was shown to the artist rather than to the record label, small record companies were at no disadvantage in marketing and promotional terms. Nor was there any evidence that independents were being squeezed out of the market; their historically stable share of the market overall, their ability to break new artists and the inroads which had been made by niche specialists in classical music proved that they were competing fairly and effectively.

12.159. In general, the level of promotional and marketing spend did not reduce the amount of royalty paid to the artist since such expenditure was not treated as recoupable against royalties. On the contrary, the aim of such expenditure was to increase the volume of sales, from which the artist derived benefit by virtue of the increased accrual of royalties. Artists and their managers tended therefore to press for more marketing and promotional spend rather than less in order to boost record sales and, consequently, royalties received. It was true that the costs of some marketing and promotional activities, particularly television advertising, were treated as wholly or partially recoupable. However, such arrangements were made to reflect the high cost of television advertising and the mutual benefit it brought to artist and record company alike.

12.160. As for free copies, these were primarily new releases of singles and were provided largely to independent retailers as part of the normal promotional discount terms to this retail sector. The practice was intended to encourage independent retail outlets to display larger quantities of the particular recording in order to encourage sales and help the record to achieve chart success, and it appeared to be just as widespread, if not more common, among the independent record companies. The success of independent record companies in the singles chart indicated that the practice did not have the effect of excluding them from the charts.

12.161. With regard to the effect of free goods on the royalties payable to artists, artists' royalties were paid on sales, so the artist would benefit in the longer term from the larger overall volumes of sales of that recording generated by the free issues. Since the majority of artists were in any case unrecouped, it was irrelevant that those artists did not receive royalties on free goods.

12.162. The companies were asked whether they were exercising effective control over the BPI in a way that distorted competition with independent record companies.

12.163. The companies denied that they exercised actual or effective control over the BPI. They pointed to the fact that the BPI currently had 147 members, of whom 102 were fully independent and 18 were associate members. The balance of 27 comprised the companies and entities connected to the companies; in voting terms the companies held only 21 per cent of the votes and did not, therefore, hold actual control. Of the 14 elected members of the Council, six were representatives of the companies. The companies had no influence over the activities of the BPI outside of the votes which could be cast at general meetings.

12.164. The BPI operated through its Council and any full member or employee of a full member was eligible for election to the Council. The various BPI committees operated in a fully transparent fashion and frequently included representatives from independent record companies. In a recent instance where there was a divergence of views between the companies and some of the independent record companies over the independent charts, the Council put in place the decision which these independents favoured, notwithstanding the opposition of the companies and many other independents. Subscriptions were based on turnover, so that the companies paid considerably more than the independents. The independent BPI members nevertheless derived the same benefits from membership, for example over measures to combat piracy, in lobbying over copyright matters, in collective dealings with broadcasters and in many other ways. To the extent that staff from the companies took an active role in BPI affairs, they did so on behalf of the industry as a whole.

Complaints from third parties

12.165. We had put to the companies for comment, by way of an annex to the issues letter, a number of complaints from individual members of the public, CA, industry bodies and other interested parties. We have recorded the companies' response to many of these points in the course of dealing with the issues set out above. Summaries of the companies' comments on some of the complaints from consumers are set out below.

12.166. EMI said that it was not true, as alleged, that small retailers experienced difficulties in obtaining supplies from the large record companies and were forced to purchase through distributors. EMI maintained a much more liberal policy with regard to the size of customer accounts than did, for instance, its US sister company. As a result of its UK policy, EMI's distributor costs represented a higher percentage of its turnover than the equivalent costs in the USA. PolyGram too said that this criticism was unfounded. It was very much in PolyGram's interest that small, independent retailers had full access to the totality of PolyGram's repertoire, and indeed independent retailers had a pivotal role to play in the competitive process. The development of new electronic ordering systems such as EROS was clear evidence that record companies wished to improve and develop facilities for direct ordering by all record retailers from record companies in order to maximize sales, rather than the reverse. Warner too stressed that it did not discriminate against small retailers in any way and in fact provided an excellent service to all sizes whatever their requirements. Its distribution centre currently serviced over 2,200 retail accounts, of which over half were accounts with small retailers which were not part of a national chain. The centre had no minimum order requirement in respect of new releases and, as far as product already released was concerned, made a charge of £3 only if the order value was less than £50.

12.167. In response to the criticism that many CDs ran for only 50 or 60 minutes, Warner said that the criticism ignored the fact that a recording was a creative work and any attempt by a record company to require extra tracks to extend the length of an album would be viewed by the artist as an unjustified interference with his or her artistic control over the album. Most CDs stated the playing time of the different tracks or the total playing time on the back of the CD. EMI added that it had no policy of marketing CDs as offering any particular playing time. PolyGram said that the economics of the record industry were such that it was inappropriate and not economically rational for record companies to charge a different price according to the running time of a particular product. Sony said that no one had forced consumers to purchase CDs; they did so because they wanted the higher quality which CDs offered and record companies had simply responded to the demand.

12.168. As regarded the criticism that all CDs were priced more or less the same, despite the different production costs which must be attached to different kinds of recording, EMI said that the impact of production costs on total unit cost was highly dependent on the length of the production run. There was no direct relationship between the cost of a recording and its dealer price; this was because demand, and hence unit cost, was almost impossible to forecast, particularly with new releases. Overall, EMI attempted to price its recordings so as to sustain its business. PolyGram said that, as with all high-risk, research-intensive industries, the record industry must look at its total costs of production and must take into account its overall total risk in deciding how to price its products. The use of multiple formats at different price levels was the rational economic response to the structure and development of the market for recorded music, the structure of demand in that music and the role and importance of ownership of intellectual property rights in that music. Warner pointed to the enormous range of prices for classical CDs and to the availability of different versions at widely differing prices. The production costs for a full-length opera were indeed significantly greater than those for a solo piano recital and this was reflected in the dealer price of the two types of recording.

12.169. With respect to the price of CD sets, EMI said that it had a vast range of recordings at different prices. It was possible to buy two-CD sets for less than the price of a full-price individual CD. PolyGram said that its earlier comments about production costs applied equally here. Warner said that the economies of production, packaging and retailing for multiple sets of CDs were in fact minimal; since each disc in the pack did, of course, contain different music, there was no particular saving in producing the discs; and although there was some saving in the packing, many boxed sets had a higher standard of insert with more substantial booklets, some, for example, containing an opera libretto or programme notes, which counterbalanced that saving.

12.170. In response to the allegation that consumers were subsidizing, through high prices for CDs, the investment being made in new music carriers such as DCC and MiniDisc, which moreover they did not want, having only just spent large sums on acquiring a CD collection, the companies said that in the first place CD prices were not too high, as explained elsewhere in their responses. But the bulk of investment on DCC and MiniDisc had been incurred by the hardware manufacturers. Such investment could hardly be recouped by record companies raising CD prices, since the benefit would then go to the record companies rather than the hardware manufacturers. There was no evidence that CD prices had been affected by these new formats. EMI said that its own investment in releasing music on these new formats had been modest to date. It was clear that consumers were not rushing to acquire the new hardware necessary to play these formats and that was their prerogative. But for those consumers who had, or were intending to acquire, such systems, it was helpful to have a range of titles available to play on their systems. PolyGram and Sony said that consumer sovereignty would prevail and if new delivery systems were not wanted by consumers, this would be reflected in the lack of demand for those formats. Warner noted that one unusual feature of the music industry had been the ability of different formats at different prices to maintain their place in the market at the same time, although lower-quality formats did in time become obsolete.

The retail sector

12.171. We invited the companies to comment on the retailing of recorded music in the light of the provisional retailers' complex monopoly practice which we had identified, namely that W H Smith, Our Price, HMV and Woolworths (in association with EUK) (the retailers) were securing discounts and promotional support from suppliers of recorded music that were larger than those made available to other retailers. The companies' comments are briefly summarized below.

12.172. Commenting on the role of the retailers in the supply chain, BMG said that the price which the consumer finally paid for a record was a function of the retailer's margin, which the retailer was able to take as a result of the concentration of retail power in the market-place. BMG said that its own published dealer prices had dropped substantially in real terms, particularly for full-price CDs, and in terms of its realized prices, over the past four years. At the same time, its marketing costs had risen considerably during that period and a significant part of those costs was represented by co-operative and marketing support with retailers. This trend of increased marketing and promotional spend had developed during the 1980s and had led to a heavier cost base than BMG considered appropriate. In BMG's view, this situation had resulted from retailer power and was now irreversible.

12.173. BMG thought that the retail market was competitive. It took the view that Our Price had adopted the strategy in the late 1980s of spreading geographically throughout the country and setting up in the smaller high street locations close to independent retailers, with a view to competing directly against them. The strategy had achieved considerable success.

12.174. BMG also said that the pricing points at which records were sold by retailers were determined by the retailers. As a record company, BMG had found that there was little point in pricing below one of these price points because the retailer simply priced at the higher price point and took the difference in extra margin.

12.175. EMI said that increased concentration was a common feature of retailing of a wide range of goods and services in the UK and abroad. As with the trend towards larger stores, it appeared to be driven by a broad range of factors and to be quite independent of the level of discounts or promotions. EMI pointed to the Robinson-Patman Act in the USA which severely restricted the granting of volume-related discounts, yet in that country retailer concentration in many sectors, including music, was proceeding apace. EMI believed that there would always be a place for the independent retailing sector, although it might be smaller than in the past. Such diminished importance would not represent a threat to the UK music industry since artist and record labels, whether large or small, would find a way of launching releases and breaking acts. In this connection, EMI stressed the important role which HMV played, as well as the independent sector. It was generally accepted that barriers to entry in retailing of music were very low, as evidenced by the huge increase in outlets which now stocked music in the UK.

12.176. PolyGram said that each retailer sought and negotiated its own discounts and promotional mix according to its own business requirements. Quantity-related discounts obtained by large buyers were part and parcel of competitive selling terms and were a natural part of the buying power of large customers. Over the past five years, there had been, first, a significant increase in the level of discounts and other financial support given to major retailers, and secondly, a consolidation in ownership which had been accompanied by an increase in the general level of retail margins. PolyGram had found that levels of retail concentration and retail margins were higher in the UK than in the other countries under consideration by the MMC; that average independent retailers' CD prices were shown by the MMC's study to be lower than prices for the equivalent products both in multiples and specialists; and that it was not common for retailers to pass a dealer price decrease to consumers. The major record retailers had a degree of countervailing market power which could be used to their advantage in securing discounts from PolyGram and other record companies.

12.177. PolyGram had no evidence to suggest that, other than in terms of the diminution in numbers of retailers as a result of increasing concentration, there had been any reduction in choice for consumers in the availability of recorded music. If the increasing discounts offered by PolyGram and, it was assumed, the other record companies were passed on to consumers by all retailers, independent and multiple alike, consumers should benefit from lower retail prices. However, this did not appear to be happening in practice and the BMRB analysis strongly suggested that average retail prices were lower amongst independent retailers than the large multiples.

12.178. Sony said that it could not rely on retailers to pass on to the consumer the benefits which they had received from Sony in the shape of reduced dealer prices. The large retailers had considerable power to extract large discounts, together with the marketing and promotional expenditure required to launch new releases. Sony also expressed concern about increased concentration in the retail market and the effect which that might have on the continuing development of talent in the UK. Sony said that six customers now accounted for 85 per cent of retail sales, and that put Sony in a vulnerable position, since retailers such as W H Smith and Woolworths might not continue to sell recorded music indefinitely. To them, it was just another product, whereas to the independent specialist, it was their sole livelihood. It was true that the large specialists such as HMV, Virgin and Tower had expanded their floor and shelf space so that they were able to accommodate both music and the other forms of entertainment such as video games. In these specialist multiples,

Sony considered that its catalogue was still very well represented; but in the general retailers, it was under-represented. Sony did not think that there was much room for further concentration at the retail level. In the meantime, it was doing what it could to encourage and increase the strength of the independent retailers, which were willing to stock a much larger range of singles than the multiples and large specialists (who tended only to stock chart successes) and which were therefore needed to break new artists.

12.179. Warner said that it believed the continued survival of the independent record stores was important for the health of the industry, and to this end it sought to offer them special deals and promotional help so far as their limited floor space and low volume of sales permitted. These shops had an important role to play in breaking new talent, given the increasingly conservative stocking policies operated by the multiples. Although Warner wished to continue to produce a broad range of music going beyond the mainstream hits, it was reliant on the retailers to provide an outlet for these recordings. In the absence of a significant number of record shops prepared to offer a more adventurous range of music, there was little point in the record companies investing in signing and promoting those artists who, despite great musical talent, were unlikely ever to reach or appeal to a mass audience.

13 Views of retailers, distributors and record clubs

Contents

Introduction

13.1. In this chapter we summarize, first, the views of the principal retailers of recorded music in the UK, secondly, those of two leading wholesalers, TBD and Pinnacle, and finally those of the principal record clubs. We begin with W H Smith, in respect of which we had provisionally found that a scale monopoly situation existed in relation to the supply of recorded music, and then summarize the views of the three companies in respect of which we had provisionally found that a complex monopoly situation so existed, namely W H Smith, HMV and Kingfisher (which we together refer to as 'the companies'). We then move briefly to other retailers who sell recorded music, to the distributors and finally to the record clubs.

W H Smith scale monopoly

13.2. W H Smith said it accepted that a scale monopoly situation existed in respect of W H Smith and Our Price. Were the proposed transaction for the restructuring of Our Price and Virgin Retail into a single company to proceed,[1] then it also accepted that Virgin Retail would form part of the scale monopoly. W H Smith said that it in no way exploited its scale monopoly position and none of its actions operated against the public interest.

---

[1]See footnote to paragraph 3.16.

The retailers' complex monopoly situation

13.3. We had provisionally found that a complex monopoly situation existed in relation to the supply of recorded music in the UK at the retail level, in that the companies engaged in the following practice: 'securing discounts and promotional support from suppliers of recorded music that are larger than those made available to other retailers'; and that this practice had the effect of preventing, restricting or distorting competition in that supply. We invited the companies to comment on our provisional finding, and on a number of issues arising out of that finding.

The composition of the 'group'

13.4. HMV said that it did not know how the MMC had arrived at the membership of the complex monopoly group. The group included one retailer, Woolworths, which to HMV's knowledge did not deal direct with record companies and was therefore not in a position to engage in the practice identified. On the other hand, other retailers who presumably did engage in the practice had been excluded. The choice of persons included in the group therefore appeared to HMV, at least *prima facie*, to lack a rational foundation. Moreover, this irrationality extended to the exclusion of non-retailers. Wholesalers, record clubs and mail order houses which might also be expected to secure discounts or promotional support from record companies had also been excluded. If the securing of special terms by retailers was believed by the MMC to prevent, restrict or distort competition, HMV could not understand why the securing of such terms by other intermediaries was not thought to do so.

13.5. So far as HMV was aware, the MMC had not in the past singled out particular members of a group for identification as persons in whose favour a complex monopoly situation was held to exist. In the reports on beer and motor cars, for example, the group had included not only the largest suppliers, but also companies with very small market shares indeed. To single out particular undertakings in the way the MMC had done in this case was objectionable both as a matter of law and of fact, and gave the misleading impression that the major operators comprised a monopolistic group rather than that, like everyone else in the industry, they engaged in certain industry-wide practices.

The alleged practice

13.6. The companies did not accept either that a complex monopoly situation as provisionally identified existed or that they conducted their affairs in any way which operated to prevent, restrict or distort competition in connection with the supply of recorded music in the UK.

13.7. HMV said that discounts were quite different from promotional allowances, which were linked to particular activities on the part of retailers who received those allowances. Dealing first with discounts, HMV pointed to the treatment of differential discounts by the MMC in their earlier reports, in particular in *Discounts to Retailers* (1981) and *Carbonated Drinks* (1991). In the first of those cases, the MMC had concluded that the practice of granting discriminatory discounts was widespread; the only line of business in which the practice was found to be insignificant was the cigarette trade which was characterized by high concentration on the supply side and very low concentration on the retail side, with many sales made by a plethora of small outlets. Nor had the Government apparently felt inclined to ban or regulate differential discounts generally. Accordingly each case had to be approached on its own facts.

13.8. HMV also pointed to what it considered were important parallels between the carbonated drinks market and that for recorded music, which showed that the allowance of special discounts was not operating anti-competitively in the recorded music market. First, differential discounts were the norm in trades where large multiple retailers accounted for a significant proportion of total turnover. There was therefore nothing abnormal about the practice, and HMV had no reason to believe that the amount of the discounts was abnormal either. Secondly, it was vital to record companies, even more than to suppliers of carbonated drinks, that their products were on sale in prime outlets. Special discounts made an important contribution to the typically higher costs of operating from prime retail

248336 S

sites which were sought after not only by major retailers of records but also by major retailers in other lines of trade, who, in turn, generally secured preferential discounts from their suppliers. Thirdly, HMV was not aware of the existence in the recorded music market of 'a degree of market power [such as] may be used in an anti-competitive way' of the kind referred to in *Carbonated Drinks*; in particular, it was not aware of special discounts being related to exclusivity, or of such discounts being granted with predatory intent, in the recorded music market. Fourthly, net trade price differentials had not caused market shares to stabilize at either the supplier or retailer level in the record market and had, indeed, assisted dynamic retailers to expand rapidly. Equally, there was no evidence that the practice had hindered 'the development of new brands' (to use the MMC's words in *Carbonated Drinks*) by independent record companies. Finally, there was nothing in the evidence presented by the MMC to suggest that the allowance of special discounts was operating anti-competitively in the recorded music market in any other way.

13.9. Turning to differential promotional allowances, HMV said that not only did such allowances not operate anti-competitively in the recorded music market, but rather they performed their own valuable and pro-competitive function in that market. Promotional allowances essentially recompensed retailers for the cost of specific promotional activity. It was often more cost-effective for the retailer than the record company to undertake the promotion but the main benefit gained was often to the record company, since many promotions led consumers to purchase the promoted records not only at the outlets running the promotion but also from other retailers. The fact that record companies generally bore most of the costs of such promotions confirmed that it was they who received the main benefits.

13.10. HMV said that without discounts, its retail prices would have to rise significantly or else it would have to reduce its costs by, for example, moving to inferior premises in inferior locations, reducing its stock range or employing less knowledgeable staff. The securing of discounts therefore helped to keep prices lower and to maintain overall value for money than would otherwise be the case, all of which was to the benefit of the consumer.

13.11. Kingfisher said that it did not believe the MMC had supplied the factual material to support its provisional finding that the companies were securing discounts and promotional support from suppliers of recorded music that were larger than those made available to other retailers. So far as differential discounts were concerned, Kingfisher said, first, that the information supplied to it in the issues letter overstated the discounts negotiated by EUK with the record companies. Secondly, the record companies achieved a substantial saving in distribution costs by delivering to EUK's warehouse rather than to the hundreds of different outlets serviced by EUK. Any comparison of the discount accorded to EUK with that accorded to other retailers should be calculated on a like-for-like basis. Thirdly, the level of discount was in part a reflection of the distribution costs involved in delivering different quantities of product to different outlets at particular frequencies with particular service obligations. None of this was reflected in the information supplied by the MMC as the basis for the provisional complex monopoly finding. As for the level of promotional support, Kingfisher said that it had not seen any material which supported the provisional finding.

13.12. W H Smith made the following points. First, differential discounts and promotional support were granted by suppliers to their trade customers in the case of almost every class of branded consumer goods, not only in the supply of recorded music. Secondly, the practice reflected competition among suppliers; the absence of such differential terms could indicate the absence of such competition. Thirdly, it was the record companies which individually determined the discounts and promotional support granted to their various trade customers; as the only sources of supply for retailers, it was taken for granted that they should decide their discount policies and implement them in a manner designed to promote their own business objectives. Fourthly, when discussing discounts and terms with a record company, W H Smith did not know the terms which were being granted to their competitors. Fifthly, it would be inconceivable for a trade customer to refuse the offer of a discount simply because it believed some of its competitors were being granted inferior terms. Sixthly, there was no suggestion that the companies had acted together to secure larger discounts or greater promotional support; on the contrary, competition between such companies made such a course of action wholly impractical. Finally, and in consequence, any differences in discounts and promotional support between the companies and other retailers were the result of the operation of market forces in a competitive market.

13.13. W H Smith said that no steps, actions or omissions had been taken by W H Smith, Our Price or Virgin Retail, collectively or individually, for the purpose of exploiting or maintaining the alleged monopoly situations; nor had any of them acted in any way which was against the public interest or likely to become so.

Issues

13.14. We put to the companies a number of issues arising out of the provisional complex monopoly finding. The companies' responses to these issues are set out below.

Competition

13.15. We asked the companies whether competition between them and independent retailers was being distorted by virtue of their securing unduly large discounts from record companies or through joint promotions with them; and whether this resulted in a lack of choice for consumers as independent retailers closed their outlets.

13.16. HMV said that it was important to remember the following points: first, there had been a demand-led restructuring of record retailing in the UK which had reflected much more widespread trends in UK retailing; secondly, the total number of recorded music outlets had, however, increased rather than fallen; thirdly, there had been a trend for some smaller record stores, whatever their ownership, to close and be replaced by larger, better located stores which could better meet changing consumer requirements; fourthly, there had been an increase in total record retailing square footage since 1984; and finally, these trends had contributed to vigorous competition between specialist chains, multiples, independents and newer forms of outlets and to considerable widening of consumer choice.

13.17. HMV said that these trends had resulted from a need to meet consumer requirements for larger stores offering greater choice and an improved, more informed service. In particular, the specialist chains had increased the average size of their record retailing outlets, moved them into prime high street locations, expanded their product range and improved greatly the quality of service and standard of presentation in new and existing stores. HMV's own stores, which had recently increased in number from 90 to 94, provided excellent examples of such developments.

13.18. Competition between retailers was vigorous, as shown by the 2,000 independent outlets which existed alongside the specialist chains and multiples, the significant new entry into UK record retailing of new types of outlets, in particular of US retailers such as Sam Goody and Tower. Price competition was fierce, as was manifested by a variety of pricing initiatives, and non-price competition was also very significant, with different strategies being adopted by the various kinds of outlets; and there was local as well as national competition in the shape of varying product ranges and prices. Overall, competition among record retailers could be regarded as more vigorous than in the past and resulted in an extremely wide choice of products and prices for consumers.

13.19. HMV also stressed that it was not only, or even primarily, the independent retailers who were responsible for breaking new acts. The breaking of new acts involved a number of parties and methods, including media coverage and artist contact with the public. One of the ways in which HMV contributed to this process was by co-operative promotion of new artists and releases, including the personal appearance of, or live performance by, the artist in HMV stores. HMV also encouraged direct contact between local store managers and record label marketing staff, and other distributors.

13.20. Kingfisher said that it did not secure unduly large discounts from record companies. The record companies set the dealer prices from which file discounts were taken. File discounts were granted to EUK, which negotiated with the record companies to improve its trading terms, but changes to the file discount were infrequent. It was important to remember that the record companies were the monopoly suppliers of each product. The prices and terms for all EUK's retailers, including connected retailers, were commercially negotiated and reflected both the size of the business and the supply criteria and service requirements specified by the customer.

248336   S2

13.21. In comparing discounts secured by EUK and independent retailers, it was important to remember that the record companies only had to make one delivery to EUK, send it one invoice and arrange for one representative to contact it, rather than each of the hundreds of retail outlets which it serviced. EUK had, moreover, contributed to increasing both the number of outlets for recorded music and the volume sales of recorded music. It was always endeavouring to further increase the size of the market. For example, it had introduced 'CHART STOP' which serviced the impulse market. EUK's success in this respect meant that consumers now had a larger choice of where to shop.

13.22. Kingfisher said that Woolworths was an important retailer of chart product for all record companies. It would only promote new releases when it was setting the lowest price in the high street. Promotions might take one of two forms: first, the promotion might be integrated with the record company's own media schedule; secondly, Woolworths might decide to promote a new release where a record company was not undertaking any equivalent promotion. In each case the promotion was planned in conjunction and in co-operation with the record company. Again, if Woolworths tradition- ally had a low market share for a particular artist, it might set a low price for a new product from that artist as part of its own price promotion, in order to generate increased sales and traffic through the entertainment area.

13.23. In contrast to the joint funding of promotions between record companies and Woolworths, many independent retailers received free promotional stock, particularly in respect of new artists. This could partly be explained by the fact that the independent retailers' customer base consisted largely of consumers seeking to purchase new trends in music. Once established, these trends were then typically followed by the more general market. Because many independent retailers received free promotional products from record companies, they were able to compete on very different terms from Woolworths on promotions.

13.24. W H Smith said that, in the first place, it did not believe that its stores were granted 'unduly large' discounts, whether viewed in isolation or in contrast to the discounts achieved by independent retailers. In themselves, the discounts could not be regarded as unduly large in view of the volumes involved, the substantial stock which specialist record shops had to carry and the costs involved in the provision of the service and in-store ambience which their customers expected. When the discounts were contrasted with the discounts achieved by independent retailers, account had to be taken of the following factors: first, independents sold between 100 and 1,000 units per week, and the larger ones were sizeable operations not dissimilar from the major retailers in their presentation, location and range of products; secondly, the file discounts believed to be granted to the large independents (such as Andys and 4 Play) were broadly the same as those received by W H Smith, Our Price and Virgin Retail; thirdly, the independents received other benefits not granted to the major specialist retailers, such as supply of free stock, favourable payment terms, 'car' stocks and product which was relatively cheap because it had been deleted or was not at the height of its popularity; and fourthly, the major retailers had to sustain higher costs in terms of rents, rates, stock size and range, shop fittings and promotional costs than the independent retailers.

13.25. Two other matters reinforced W H Smith's view that the discounts which their competitors received enabled them to be competitive. First, the difference between a large discount and no discount at all was not of such significance that it would, in any event, distort competition either among the major specialists or between all record retailers. Secondly, independent retailers were as a matter of fact able to offer product for sale at prices which were lower than those offered by specialist record retailers. Rival Records and Spinadisc were but two examples.

13.26. When all the above considerations were taken into account, it was clear that independent record retailers did not receive less support from the record companies, nor did they routinely price at higher levels than the major retailers. Moreover, joint promotions with the companies were of benefit to all record retailers, not just those involved in the promotion, because they promoted the advertised product generally.

13.27. As to the decrease in the number of independent record retailers, W H Smith said that to the extent that these had occurred, they were the result of changes in consumer attitude to the purchase of recorded music. This had been happening particularly since the development of large specialist record retailers. Consumers had different demands and expectations. Music enthusiasts wanted a wide range of product in a specialist environment, together with specialist staff and service. Such consumers gravitated towards the specialist retailer. Occasional record buyers, on the other hand, were content with a narrower range and less expertise and were catered for by any number of outlets, including garages, food supermarkets and other non-specialist outlets. Many independent record retailers had adapted to this market development by either operating in a niche to serve particular customer interests (for example, vinyl shops, specialist jazz, dance or classical shops) or alternatively by lowering their cost base and offering low prices (for example, Rival Records, Spinadisc and 4 Play). Those retailers which had not adapted to this market pattern had in many cases been forced to close.

13.28. All these developments had resulted in the widest possible choice for consumers. To the extent that record retailers had closed, this was due to the operation of market forces, and not to any action on the part of the companies.

Prices

13.29. We asked the companies whether the alleged practice resulted in higher prices for recorded music in the UK than would otherwise be the case.

13.30. HMV said that the position was the very reverse of that postulated by the MMC. Retailers competed with each other to secure discounts and support from record companies and where these were obtained, they helped to keep retail prices lower. So far as discounts from suppliers were concerned, it was clear that these had significantly exceeded HMV's operating profits in each of the last three years. The securing of discounts thus acted to the benefit of consumers by helping to keep prices lower, and product and service quality higher, than would otherwise have been the case.

13.31. As for promotions, as already noted, the majority of promotional costs were currently met by record companies, for whom they were much more cost-effective than for retailers. Retailers such as HMV took the risk of committing to media advertising spend and were then in competition with other retailers to secure record companies' finite promotional support resources. Without supplier contributions, levels of promotional activity would fall. This would lead to reduced sales and would put upward pressure on costs and prices because fixed costs would be spread across a smaller volume.

13.32. HMV said that it was important to bear in mind here the strength and variety of the price competition which kept retail prices of recorded music low. National price competition (particularly in the form of discounting of chart product) and local price competition were strong, permanent features of the market. Price campaigns were run by retailers to cover the product of particular artists, sets of artists, record labels or genres. They had become particularly widespread as a further focus for price competition during the 1990s.

13.33. Kingfisher said that the large retailers in the recorded music business competed for market growth on price. Chart products in particular were heavily discounted. In the case of Woolworths, its 'Street Value' strategy was that of always being the lowest retailer or as low as any other retailer on any entertainment products, whether chart or catalogue. In terms of chart product, Woolworths monitored the prices of all the other major retailers weekly and adjusted its prices as necessary. This strategy was supported by the Woolworths price promise which meant that if any customer could demonstrate that another retailer was selling the product at a lower price, Woolworths would immediately refund the difference to that customer.

13.34. Kingfisher said that Woolworths' strategy had the effect of holding prices down while increasing sales volume. It had been Woolworths' decision to bring the overall prices of chart material down and over the past five years this had resulted in approximate real reductions in the price of cassettes and CDs of 50p and £1 respectively.

13.35. W H Smith said that retail prices for recorded music were, for all practical purposes, determined by the dealer prices established by the record companies which knew, first, the margin required by the retailer to cover its costs, and secondly, the competitive pressures that would require the retailer to have regard to the proximate 'price point'. The material provided by W H Smith to the MMC showed that the retail margin was virtually exhausted by its costs; neither W H Smith nor Our

Price generated acceptable, let alone substantial, profits. Further, from their net margins, it was clear that a decrease in retail prices was not viable unless accompanied by a reduction in the dealer price.

13.36. In fact, W H Smith and Our Price had tried to persuade record companies and distributors of recorded music to reduce their dealer prices. They had arranged meetings with them and argued that a reduction in retail prices would lead to an increase in sales of recorded music, improved economies of scale and, consequently, increased profitability for record companies, distributors and retailers. Despite these discussions, none of the record companies or distributors approached had been prepared to reduce its dealer prices; on the contrary, the record companies had increased them. That most record retailers had continued to resist an increase in retail prices was demonstrated by the fact that, despite the increases in dealer prices by numerous record companies in autumn 1993, retail prices were not increased as a result. All the above factors demonstrated that prices for recorded music in the UK were no higher than would have been the case in the absence of any alleged monopoly situation.

Price differences between the UK and other countries

13.37. We asked the companies what the extent of the price differences was between the UK and other countries, and what was the explanation for these differences.

13.38. HMV said that it was very difficult to comment on the extent of any differences in retail prices for recorded music as between the UK and other countries and so far as it was aware, there was no reliable evidence on this issue. But because each national market was quite distinct, no comparison would have any real commercial meaning or relevance. The MMC's own survey, carried out by BMRB, was not reliable, mainly because the sample was small and only full-price records were selected. A different choice of even one title in a survey of this size would have substantially affected the average price differential.

13.39. There were a number of reasons why, in general, retail prices would be expected to differ between countries. These would include the levels of demand for different types of repertoire, major differences in terms of trade between record companies and retailers in different countries, cost differences (particularly in relation to property and staff), differences in sales tax rates and applications, the nature and level of competition and national regulations affecting such matters as prices and copyright.

13.40. Kingfisher said that it was not involved in retailing recorded music outside the UK and could not comment on pricing in other countries. It noted, however, that the BMRB survey had shown the UK to be among the cheapest countries for both CDs and cassettes after the USA, and that multiples tended to be cheaper than independents or specialists.

13.41. W H Smith said that while it was impossible to establish precisely the price differences between the UK and other countries, it accepted the ranking of countries produced by the BMRB survey, in particular the finding that prices for recorded music on the Continent were generally higher than those in the UK and the USA. Commenting on the BMRB survey, however, W H Smith said, first, that the number of titles chosen was very small, particularly in the context of the 100,000 or so titles currently available. Secondly, the survey had not taken sufficient account of discounts in the UK and the different ways in which these were communicated to customers. In the UK, it was usual to reduce the price below that at which it would otherwise have been sold and then promote the record at that lower price but without expressly advertising the discount or its extent.

13.42. With reference to the Management Horizons survey, W H Smith said that it was significant that when the products which had the same characteristics as recorded music, such as electronic games, were singled out from the other products, the differential was greater than the average; in the case of electronic games, prices were some 19 to 20 per cent higher in the UK. More generally the finding of a 12 per cent differential between the UK and the USA contrasted with the results of other surveys, possibly of a broader sample of products, where the differential was generally accepted to be greater, for example the 1993 McKinsey Survey and the 1993 BICOL Indices, both of which showed prices in the UK to be of the order of 30 per cent above those in the USA.

Profitability

13.43. HMV said that it had used Extel's MicroEXTAT to look at the returns achieved by other major retailers and compare them with its own. These calculations had been submitted to the MMC. HMV had found that its returns were not out of line with those achieved by other major retailers, either on a return on sales or ROCE basis. HMV could not, therefore, be regarded as making excessive profits either in relation to sales or in relation to capital employed.

13.44. Kingfisher said that the figures which it had submitted to the MMC showed that it did not make excessive profits. A product group with a low stock turnover, such as resulted from a policy of stocking back catalogue product, would expect to produce relatively high gross margins; Woolworths was reducing its back catalogue stock, since its strategy was to offer chart material, not specialist repertoire. On the other hand, a product group with a high stock turnover, such as was represented by chart products, would expect to have a lower gross margin. However, retailers had to hold substantial stocks of chart material if they were to satisfy the demand from customers, and because stockholding costs were high for chart products, Woolworths' margins were lower than they would otherwise be. Kingfisher said that recorded music produced the lowest gross margins within the Entertainment Division of Woolworths and within Woolworths as a whole.

13.45. W H Smith said it did not consider that, however viewed, the profits of W H Smith or Our Price could be regarded as excessive, whether in relation to the costs of acquiring and selling recorded music or in relation to the capital employed. On the contrary, the figures it had submitted to the MMC showed that these retailers had struggled to make any profits at all in the years to 1991, 1992 and 1993. Furthermore, their ROCE had been low by any normal criteria.

Formats

13.46. We asked the companies whether they were choosing the formats of recorded music which they stocked in a way which was designed to increase their profits rather than meet the requirements of consumers, thus reducing consumer choice.

13.47. HMV said that retailers must meet rather than ignore the requirements of consumers if their profits were to increase or be maintained. Furthermore, the practice described could hardly apply to HMV, whose strategy was to appeal to the committed music purchaser and one of the ways it did this was to stock the widest possible range of products (across genres and formats) in its stores. It had also increased the average size of its stores to accommodate wider product ranges. Thus HMV stocked all available sound carriers (vinyl, cassette, CD, MiniDisc, DCC and LaserDisc) subject to the availability of space store-by-store. This was in spite of poor sales performance of the newer formats, DCC and MiniDisc; however, provided that this remained a commercially viable proposition, HMV would continue to stock them in order to provide customers with a full range of formats. HMV also stocked vinyl to a much greater extent than was justified by sales of vinyl units but its stocking policy would continue to be the same as that for the newest formats.

13.48. Overall, there was a considerable availability of all formats in the UK and the availability of non-CD formats was also almost certainly higher in the UK than in any other country. Consumers of recorded music thus had been and still were able to exercise their changing tastes for recorded music formats and hence determine the pattern of sales across formats.

13.49. Kingfisher said that Woolworths would stock any format of recorded music for which there was a market. Consumers' buying habits were monitored by periodic customer surveys and if consumers demonstrated their requirement for a particular format, it was Woolworths' strategy to stock that format. Woolworths had been the last major multiple generalist retailer to stop stocking vinyl LPs, over a period of seven to eight months in 1991 and 1992, and aimed to be the last such retailer to stop stocking vinyl singles.

13.50. Since Woolworths aimed to be *the* retailer for chart material, it had to offer consumers chart titles in all formats; for this reason, it continued to stock vinyl singles even though it made a net trading loss on them. Woolworths had no return rights for vinyl singles with EUK and had to destroy those it did not sell, which amounted to approximately half its vinyl singles stocks. Woolworths believed that if it stopped selling vinyl singles, the record companies would no longer produce this format. As sales of vinyl dwindled, there would come a point where there would be no risk to Woolworths' consumer base if the format were withdrawn; this point had not yet been reached. But by no longer stocking vinyl LPs, Woolworths was now able to stock a larger range of recorded music and improve its stock depth. Improved stock resources meant that consumers were more likely to be able to purchase the album they wanted, when they wanted it.

13.51. If Woolworths were to charge any less for CDs without any reduction in dealer prices, its margins would be eroded completely and it would have to stop selling CDs. That would significantly restrict consumer choice.

13.52. W H Smith pointed to the steady decrease in the number of full-price mainstream releases in vinyl since the early 1980s, which had led to a reduction in demand for that format. Over the same period, there had been a trend towards 'entertainment' stores catering for the video and computer games market. These had put pressure on retailers to reallocate the space formerly dedicated to music to those products which were in demand. These two factors had contributed to the demise of the vinyl format. W H Smith had finally removed all vinyl records from its shops in December 1992; in doing so, it had simply been reacting to trends.

13.53. Our Price's policy had been to continue to stock vinyl records unless and until it became uneconomical to do so. In line with that policy, certain Our Price stores continued to stock vinyl. So far as Virgin Retail was concerned, vinyl records had constituted the major part of its core business until 1988 and, until 1991, sales of such records remained material in sales terms. After that, volumes of sales began to fall and record companies reduced discounts in respect of vinyl records while increasing them for CDs. Virgin Retail nevertheless continued to stock vinyl records despite the ever-declining sales.

13.54. It was clear that the decline in vinyl sales had not been caused by any conduct by companies in the W H Smith group. Rather, the decline was predicted by the record companies and had been caused by the withdrawal of classical vinyl records by PolyGram in 1991, a steady reduction in the number of new releases in the vinyl format between 1989 and 1992, and a decline in consumer demand, caused mainly by the emergence of the CD format. The record companies had a key role to play in the demise of vinyl because they had a vested interest in the promotion of CDs, they were in a position to determine the particular format which new releases took and they were able to set the relative prices of the different formats.

Retailers' record charts

13.55. We asked the companies whether consumers were confused or misled by the display of record charts based on a particular retailer's estimate of future sales, rather than the generally accepted charts produced by Gallup and based on record sales throughout the UK. We also asked them whether such charts distorted competition between record companies and retailers.

13.56. HMV said that this issue only applied to its 'HMV Top 60 album chart'; with respect to singles, HMV displayed the Gallup chart in its shops. It was important, HMV said, to recognize the highly promotional role of the charts in the music industry; customers used them as a means of finding out what was new or popular and the retailers used them to provide information and to give priority to the merchandising of different product. In addition, HMV believed, first, that only 8 per cent of consumers would buy an album without having heard one of more of its tracks; and secondly, that the wide availability of alternative charts militated against retailer album charts misleading consumers.

13.57. Nor did HMV believe that competition was distorted by the use of its album charts. They were simply another form of promotion, essentially no different from other forms of music promotion such as in-store displays, or from other forms of promotion generally. That they were non-distortionary could be demonstrated by the fact that 59 of the 60 titles in the HMV chart for the week beginning 25 October 1993 achieved positions 1 to 59 in the actual sales of the week in question. Only one title failed to make it to the actual top 60. HMV told us that it did not wish to mislead any consumer, whether or not charts really contributed to consumer purchases, and it was accordingly considering alternative names for its album chart.

13.58. Kingfisher said that Woolworths' charts were based on a number of criteria: Gallup sales data relating to the previous week, Woolworths' sales data applying to the previous week and historical information on artists (indicating how well a particular product was likely to sell). These charts did not confuse or mislead consumers, but on the contrary were of positive benefit to them. As the Gallup singles chart was only released each Sunday night, if Woolworths' own chart were not available, consumers would have to wait until Tuesday to have a chart offer available. Woolworths' chart ensured that consumers had a chart offer available on Monday morning. In the case of albums, there was no widely accepted chart available and so Woolworths produced its own as a guide for the public.

13.59. Kingfisher said that Woolworths' own charts were of benefit to the consumer, because they could be used to locate products within the stores and they ensured high levels of record availability—as units were sold, they were automatically reordered for next day delivery. Moreover, there was little difference between Gallup's and Woolworths' own charts; the important point was that Woolworths had a chart available on Monday morning.

13.60. W H Smith pointed to the different policies adopted by W H Smith, Our Price and Virgin Retail with respect to in-store charts. So far as W H Smith was concerned, because it was catering for the occasional record buyer for whom the charts were generally of little interest, it produced its own album 'Hit Lists' based partly on the Gallup charts, partly on the expected sales of new releases and partly on the tastes and preferences of customers. New entries on the lists were clearly identified as being based on expected sales through W H Smith stores. Consequently, there ought to be no confusion in the minds of customers that the store compiled its own album hit lists or that they were not solely based on previous weeks' sales.

13.61. Our Price displayed the Gallup singles chart in its stores and in addition compiled and displayed its own in-store 'Top 40' album chart based on an analysis of its own customer profile. Virgin Retail also displayed a printed version of the Gallup singles chart in all its outlets and also displayed its own album chart, compiled by reference to its stores' sales for the previous week and therefore directly reflecting the tastes of its customers.

13.62. W H Smith said it understood that all the major retailers produced their own in-store album charts and it did not believe such charts confused or misled the customer. In the case of W H Smith and Our Price, the album charts were in a distinct format and bore the relevant company's logo; there was no reference to Gallup; and they had a different title or designation to the Gallup charts. In any case, the Gallup album chart was not widely published and was not well recognized by the public. Finally, as promotional tools, the in-store charts stimulated competition between retailers.

Complaints

13.63. We had put to the companies a number of complaints from consumers and small independent record companies. To the extent that the matters raised by these complaints have not already been covered above, the companies' responses are summarized below.

Consumers

13.64. Responding to the charge that the larger retail chains such as W H Smith and HMV charged higher prices than some smaller retailers, even though they must be obtaining larger discounts, HMV said that it was not aware of any research which substantiated this claim. Overall, prices varied too much for any such conclusion to be drawn. On high-volume chart product, however, HMV believed the major chains were always at the forefront of discounting.

13.65. As to the question whether HMV should be able to offer the consumer some of the benefits of its vertical integration with EMI, HMV said that while both HMV and EMI had the same ultimate parent, trade between them was conducted entirely on an arm's length basis. It was THORN EMI's view that neither company would benefit from operating on another basis. There were accordingly no special savings available to be passed on to consumers.

13.66. Kingfisher did not accept that the large retail chains charged higher prices while failing to pass on larger discounts to customers. This had been shown by the MMC's own BMRB survey, where a high proportion of the pre-selected titles on CD were found to be retailing by specialists at higher average prices than those charged by multiples. Moreover, many independent retailers received free singles from record companies which they could then sell at whatever price they chose, sometimes at prices as low as 99p, at other times at full price. As described above, Woolworths' 'Street Value' strategy was always to be the lowest or as low as any other retailer.

13.67. W H Smith said it did not accept that the larger retail chains must be failing to pass on larger discounts to customers. The economics of the larger retail chains gave rise to higher costs compared with those borne by smaller retailers and these had to be taken into account when the relevant store or company set its retail prices. Such costs included those arising from a larger range and volume of stock, the increased rent and rates of prime location retail space and its associated fittings, and the additional facilities expected by customers.

13.68. Responding to the charge that Sony 'Nice Price' CDs should be cheaper than the £9.99 charged in Our Price stores, W H Smith said that the £9.99 price was neither surprising nor controversial, since each retailer had to decide the prices which were appropriate for each product title and those in respect of which a higher or lower margin would be made.

Small independent record companies

13.69. In response to the charge that the major retail stores dominated the market and should be broken up in order to remove their dominance and encourage price competition, the companies maintained that price competition was as fierce in the UK as it was in other, less concentrated, markets. Since retail prices were higher in many markets where concentration was lower, there was no obvious connection between concentration and price levels. HMV pointed to the low barriers to entry into record retailing, both by traditional outlets and by foreign music retailers. W H Smith said that the major retailers did not dominate the record retail market; that market, and in particular the price of recorded music, was predominantly influenced by the record companies. Price competition existed at all levels amongst retailers, and major retailers and independents were equally keen and well placed to compete on prices.

13.70. In response to the allegation that the retailers' insistence on substantial margins had sometimes led to a conflict of interest between the small record company and the retailer, HMV said that it stocked a wide range of back catalogue which was offered to it by record companies at a vast range of dealer prices. Its selling prices were always set on the dealer price, taking account of file, and additional, discounts. The complaint was therefore not applicable to HMV. Kingfisher said that Woolworths always passed on all discounts it received from record companies in promotions to its customers. The low stock turnover of catalogue product meant that the associated stocking costs were high.

13.71. The companies responded to a complaint that discounting policies inaugurated by record companies had generally proved unsuccessful because the discount was not passed on by the major retailers to the customers—an example had been Warner's discounting campaign some years ago. HMV said that the Warner campaign had been some time ago. These days, customers always benefited from discounts. HMV had increased the frequency of its price campaigns and sales in the last several years precisely because such discounting campaigns were successful. Kingfisher said that EUK always endeavoured to encourage suppliers to reduce cost prices to enable EUK ultimately to pass those savings on, to the benefit of EUK's customers and the market as a whole. W H Smith said that downward structural changes in dealer prices had rarely been introduced by record companies. Furthermore, where increased discounts had been adopted on particular titles, its group companies had passed on all the benefit to the customer. So far as the Warner initiative was concerned, those companies had followed Warner by reducing their retail prices accordingly. However, when other retailers did not do so, Warner had increased its dealer prices again, returning them to their earlier levels.

13.72. Finally, the companies responded to the charge of collusion between themselves and the large record companies, to the detriment of small record companies and small retailers. The companies said that in their experience no such state of affairs existed. HMV said that it was legitimate and to be expected that record companies and retailers should have the common objective of selling recordings to customers. But the process of negotiation of trade terms was a wholly adversarial one, in which each party sought to maximize its negotiating position. It was in the companies' interests to have as many strong suppliers as possible and the modest profitability at both record company and retailer level was an indication that a balance was being struck. Kingfisher said that Woolworths co-operated with record companies on advertising and promotions, but did not, as many independent retailers did, receive free promotional goods. W H Smith said that the large retailers did not have a commanding position and could not insist on being granted large discounts and other benefits. On the contrary, it was the record companies which determined the terms. Moreover, they did not make sufficient profit to be able to choose whether or not to pass on discounts. Smaller retailers received benefits which enabled them to compete effectively, particularly having regard to their lower cost base.

Other retailers

13.73. Responding to a questionnaire we had sent it, Boots The Chemists Ltd (BTC) said that it did not agree with the public perception that the recorded music industry was highly profitable. From a retail perspective margins were typically low. Probably only in the buoyant 1980s had there been sufficient volume to make up for the low margins, and in that period the market was relatively profitable.

13.74. BTC considered that the only way in which the recorded music market could become more profitable was through greater efficiency, ie creating more sales through more effective artist development.

13.75. Music Discount Centre, an independent classical music specialist retailer with six shops, all in London, said that it failed to understand why the music industry had been singled out for investigation by the NHC, particularly since the perfume industry had been given 'a clean bill of health' by the MMC.

13.76. T R Services Inc (Tower) made two general observations. First, the fee charged by the MCPS for importation of parallel recordings, to account for royalties, was unnecessary, as royalties were paid at source. Secondly, the negotiation of price on purchase volume allowed record companies to force smaller retailers out of business by selling at a price which they could not match.

Distributors

13.77. The TBD Division of John Menzies (UK) Limited (TBD), which formerly traded under the name Terry Blood Distribution, responded to our Intermediaries questionnaire.

13.78. TBD said that a number of changes had occurred in the recorded music industry during the last five years:

(a) The market shares and financial muscle of the major record companies had increased substantially due to acquisitions and the purchase of two major record companies by Japanese consumer electronic giants (Sony and Matsushita). One of the five majors, PolyGram, was already 75 per cent owned at the start of the five-year period by Philips, the Dutch electronics conglomerate. This meant that three out of the five majors had become controlled by powerful hardware producers which had thus obtained a dominant influence, not only over sales of music product, but also over the format in which it was sold.

(b) A corresponding increase had occurred in the dominance of the chains in the retail market, with a growth of 20 per cent in the number of outlets owned by specialist chains and a decline of 28 per cent in the number of independent specialist outlets. BPI figures showed that a dominant market share of 56 per cent was now held by W H Smith, Our Price and Woolworths.

(c) The BPI statistics showed that the total number of retail outlets selling recorded music had declined by 13 per cent.

(d) There had been a substantial growth, which was difficult to quantify, in the sales of mail order houses, a significant number of which were controlled by record companies.

(e) The majors had expanded their own operations as prime distributors, in which capacity they offered significantly more favourable terms to the high street chains.

13.79. EMI was vertically integrated through its HMV chain which, according to BPI figures, had expanded its outlets within the last five years by 45 per cent, having previously acquired the Midland-based Revolver chain. Consumers were being offered less choice, because retail sales were increasingly channelled through a limited number of specialist and multiple chains. TBD said that a retailer had the choice of buying recorded music through one of two distribution routes: either direct from a prime distributor or via an independent intermediary. Competition in record distribution had become more intense between, than within, these two channels, and this competition had been active at both price and non-price levels.

13.80. There were clear reasons for the relatively low level of competition within these two distribution channels. The prime distributors were each dealing, by definition, with their own unique products. The independent wholesalers, since they operated on low margins, had little room for price competition amongst themselves. Indeed, due to developments in the distribution sector, there were few independent wholesalers remaining and, largely for historical reasons, they tended to focus on different sectors of the retail market. EUK, for instance, had been set up to service the Woolworths account and this remained its major customer. TBD said that it was in fact the only significant independent wholesaler remaining which serviced the independent specialist retailer.

13.81. TBD suggested that there were grounds for concluding that a complex monopoly situation existed as a result of the major record companies' common approach to: terms of supply, including concentration on sales of largely chart-based product to the chains and amendment of their terms of supply to the disadvantage of the independent wholesalers; pricing policies; and the control of parallel imports.

13.82. TBD considered that:

(a) The policy of the record companies in supporting the chains in preference to the independent specialists had resulted in a restriction in the choice of product. Any retail chain (including John Menzies) would confirm that its interest was in achieving a high turnover in current chart-based titles supported by a high level of record company-backed promotional activity. The decline of the independent specialist, combined with the reduction in the number of smaller record companies and independent wholesalers, meant that it would become increasingly difficult for the public to obtain specialist and back catalogue recordings.

(b) The decline of the independent specialists also resulted in a reduction of choice in recorded music. The BPI figures showed that there had been a fall in the total number of outlets selling recorded music over the past five years of 13 per cent. This principally affected members of the public located outside the larger towns where the chains predominated.

(c) The high prevailing prices for recorded music were clearly against the public interest.

278

13.83. Pinnacle, a division of Lambourne Productions Ltd, said that it acted as an independent distribution company on behalf of a large number of independent labels in the UK. It observed that, as the five major record companies distributed their own records, there was little competition between them and the independent distribution companies except for third party labels. Pinnacle thought that whilst overall UK record sales might not show further dramatic growth, new entertainment products and new formats would ensure that the public continued to view music as an exciting and important entertainment medium, and that the influence of independent artists and labels would continue to grow.

Record clubs

13.84. BCA (a partnership owned as to 50 per cent by Bertelsmann Books and Magazines Ltd, and as to the other 50 per cent by Reed International Books Ltd) said that it operated a club called Music Direct. It considered that record (or, as it preferred to term them, music) clubs were complementary to the retail music business, by providing an in-house service for those customers who either did not have a convenient music retail outlet or found the environment of music retailers uncomfortable. Some clubs also offered products which often were not available in their local retail outlets.

13.85. Britannia is owned by Polygram. It said that during the past 25 years it had pioneered the development of record clubs in the highly diversified, competitive and dynamic UK market for recorded music. Competition in this market operated at a number of different levels, all of which had a symbiotic relationship with one another, and which ranged from book clubs, record clubs and direct marketing sales through to more traditional retail outlets.

13.86. Britannia considered that the level of activity of the traditional catalogue mail order houses in selling music had probably remained fairly constant, as had that of 'own compilation' specialists such as Reader's Digest. Clearly, the fastest growing and most competitive area in direct mail sales was to be found in record clubs. Britannia had doubled its market share during the last five years from 4 to 8 per cent of the total market. In addition, BCA had launched its own music clubs; Odhams and Barclaycard had launched a CD club; and a number of smaller players such as Crescent Direct had also appeared. In 1993 two new big players had appeared on the scene: Great Universal Stores (GUS) under the name of Entertainment Direct, and EUK (owned by Kingfisher plc) under the name of Titles Direct. Both were already considerable players in the industry, EUK mainly as a supplier to Woolworths and GUS through its mail order catalogues.

13.87. Britannia said it was clear that many customers found direct mail a convenient service, particularly those who were too busy, or who were not inclined, to shop, and those who appreciated the guidance on repertoire that direct marketers were able to make by recommending products. The majority of direct mail operators also offered credit terms to their customers which allowed them to satisfy themselves that the product met their expectations before they made payment. Britannia expected an even more competitive market to emerge in the next five years, not just between record clubs and other providers of recorded music but between them and other entertainment and leisure suppliers.

13.88. Britannia also noted the emergence of at least three new formats: CD-I, DCC and Mini-Disc. Exploitation of new technology by record clubs, however, was only possible some years after the launch of new formats, as these required a 'critical mass' in home ownership of the requisite hardware to develop before they could become economic.

13.89. Reader's Digest said that direct mail sales in the UK recorded music market appealed to people who typically were older than the regular purchaser through record stores, or who did not generally purchase through such outlets. People belonged to record clubs because they were attracted by the selection of music they offered and by their convenience.

APPENDIX 1.1
(referred to in paragraph 1.2)

Conduct of the inquiry

1. On 14 May 1993 the Director General of Fair Trading sent to the MMC the following reference:

> The Director General of Fair Trading in exercise of his powers under sections 47(1), 49(1) and 50(1) of the Fair Trading Act hereby refers to the Monopolies and Mergers Commission the matter of the existence or the possible existence of a monopoly situation in relation to the supply in the United Kingdom of pre-recorded compact and vinyl discs and pre-recorded analogue and digital tapes on which music is reproduced without visual image.
>
> The Commission shall investigate and report on the questions whether a monopoly situation exists and, if so:
>
>   *(a)* by virtue of which provisions of sections 6 to 8 of the said Act that monopoly situation is to be taken to exist;
>
>   *(b)* in favour of what person or persons that monopoly situation exists;
>
>   *(c)* whether any steps (by way of uncompetitive practices or otherwise) are being taken by that person or those persons for the purpose of exploiting or maintaining the monopoly situation and, if so, by what uncompetitive practices or in what other way;
>
>   *(d)* whether any action or omission on the part of that person or those persons is attributable to the existence of that monopoly situation, and if so, what action or omission and in what way it is so attributable; and
>
>   *(e)* whether any facts found by the Commission in the pursuance of their investigations under the preceding provisions of this paragraph operate, or may be expected to operate, against the public interest.
>
> The Commission shall report upon this reference within a period ending on 31 March 1994.

(Signed) BRYAN CARSBERG
Director General of Fair Trading

14 May 1993

2. The Secretary of State for Trade and Industry subsequently directed that the period for reporting on the reference should be extended to 14 April 1994.

3. The questions asked in the reference are answered in the following paragraphs of the report:

whether a monopoly situation exists: paragraphs 2.44, 2.48 and 2.54;

(a) paragraphs 2.44 and 2.48;

(b) paragraphs 2.45 and 2.48;

(c) paragraph 2.186;

(d) paragraph 2.186; and

(e) paragraph 2.186.

4. The composition of the group of members responsible for the inquiry and report is indicated in the list of members in the preface. Mrs Doreen Miller MBE JP was originally appointed as a member of the group but, following her elevation to the House of Lords, Mr J Evans was appointed in her place on 15 September 1993. The Baroness Miller of Hendon subsequently resigned as a member of the MMC.

5. Notices inviting evidence were placed in the *Daily Mail, Gramophone* and *Q*.

6. Written evidence was provided by record companies, distributors, retailers, record clubs, trade associations, CA, the BPI, the IFPI, artists' managers, the MPA and MCPS, the MU, Umbrella, VPL, PPL, other industry bodies, and a number of individual consumers. We held a total of 27 hearings, including two with EMI, PolyGram, W H Smith, Our Price and Virgin Retail, and one each with BMG, Sony, Warner, HMV and Kingfisher.

7. Members and staff of the MMC visited EMI's Abbey Road recording studio in London, its manufacturing plant at Swindon, Sony's manufacturing and distribution plant at Aylesbury, Gallup and a number of retail stores in London. In addition, two members made a short visit to the USA where meetings were held at the headquarters of EMI Music and with an independent US record company, and visits were made to a variety of retail locations.

8. A comparative study of recorded music prices in the USA and Great Britain was carried out for the MMC by BMRB International, and a comparative study of the UK/US prices of other goods was carried out by Management Horizons Europe. A study to value the businesses of the major record companies was carried out for the MMC by KPMG Peat Marwick.

9. In November 1993 we informed the five major record companies (EMI, PolyGram, Warner, Sony and BMG) and a number of retailers (Kingfisher, W H Smith, Our Price and HMV) of our provisional findings that monopoly situations existed in their favour in relation to the supply of recorded music in the UK. Each of these parties submitted written views addressing the issues we raised with them as well as attending a hearing. Their views are summarized in Chapters 12 and 13.

10. Some of the evidence obtained during the course of our inquiry was commercially confidential and our report contains only such information as we consider necessary for a proper understanding of our conclusions.

11. We should like to record our thanks to all those who helped with our inquiry, particularly the companies principally involved and also the Intellectual Property Policy Directorate of the DTI for its help with the description of the national and international copyright system recorded in Chapter 4.

Extract from the Report of the National Heritage Committee

CONCLUSION

40.   The Consumers' Association placed much of the blame for the unfavourable price comparisons between the United States and the United Kingdom on copyright restrictions. While acknowledging the absolute necessity for legislation to protect against piracy and counterfeiting the Association did not believe that the legislation should also be used to prevent parallel imports from countries that had signed the various intellectual property conventions and enforced them properly. The OFT is currently examining such restrictions on international trade to consider whether they might be the basis for a complex monopoly finding. The Committee welcomes this examination and re-emphasises the importance it attaches to the question of parallel imports. Even if the result should not prove a reliable basis for a complex monopoly finding, the Committee believes that the operation of the Copyright, Designs and Patents Act 1988 as it relates to parallel imports could work against the public interest. **The Committee recommends accordingly that the Department of Trade and Industry re-examine current legislation on copyright with particular reference to its anti-competitive effects in the recorded music industry.**

41.   It is essential, however, that any relaxation of the law relating to parallel imports in the UK should not be used to place the UK at a disadvantage compared with other countries. The Committee was told that section 602 of the United States Copyright Act prevents the importation into the USA from the UK of any CDs, tapes or LPs containing copyright owned, controlled or licensed to American producers or publishers and that as a result of the trade barrier the UK's share of the American market had diminished from 34% in 1985 to 14% currently. It appears that the effect of existing international copyright agreements is that the record music industry has been able to segment the world market to enable it to charge different prices to its own advantage and to the detriment of the consumer. **The Committee recommends that the Government should seek ways of lowering or removing this barrier.**

42.   The Committee condemns most strongly the pricing practices of the major record companies. Sir Malcolm Field of W H Smith advocated in evidence to the Committee a reduction of £2 in the dealer price of full-price CDs. This Committee believes that such a reduction is the minimum that is required. The difference between the dealer price of full-price CDs and full-price cassettes is more than enough to accommodate such a reduction. Instead, however, the record companies are seeking to reduce this difference not by cutting the price of CDs but by raising the price of cassettes. The Committee also believes that the major retailers can and should play their own part in securing price reductions both by exerting pressure on the major record companies and by making their own price reductions.

43.   It is now time for consumers to show that they will no longer bear the prices currently charged for full-price compact discs. In the United States 'the consumer is king': it is high time that the customer insisted on a similar status in the United Kingdom.

List of issues for discussion with major record companies

(a) Do the practices listed at paragraph 3 of the covering letter result in higher prices for recorded music in the UK than would otherwise be the case?

(b) What is the extent of the price differences between the UK and other countries? What is the explanation for these differences?

(c) Is the underlying profitability of the major record companies excessive in relation to sales and capital employed?

(d) Is the profitability of the companies effectively understated as a result of the present accounting treatment of the value of their investment in A&R and copyright material?

(e) Are the companies choosing the formats on which they release recordings in a way which is designed to increase their profits rather than meet the requirements of consumers, thus reducing consumer choice?

(f) Is the monopoly situation being exploited by the relative prices charged for compact discs, music cassettes and vinyl records?

(g) Do the terms of the companies' contracts with artists amount to an exploitation of a monopoly situation?

(h) Is competition among the major record companies, and between them and independent companies (including BBC Audio International Ltd), adversely affected by the terms of the artists' contracts?

(i) Are the companies exploiting a monopoly situation in not recognising any rights of producers as first holders of copyright in the sound recordings they produce?

(j) Are the companies taking steps to maintain or exploit the monopoly situation by the way they control PPL so that:

    (i) some independent record companies do not receive a fair share of PPL's income, and

    (ii) no part of PPL's income is paid to producers?

(k) Is the collective negotiation through Video Performance Ltd of licence fees for the broadcasting of music videos justified or does it constitute a step taken for the purpose of exploiting the monopoly situation?

(l) Are the companies seeking to exploit the record charts in a way that restricts or distorts competition with independent record companies, eg by the inclusion in the 'independent chart' of records released by companies in which they have an interest or with which they have a business relationship?

(m) Do the practices of spending large sums on promotion and marketing and supplying free copies to retailers constitute uncompetitive practices which have the effect of (i) restricting actual or potential competition from independent record companies and/or (ii) reducing the amount of the royalties paid to artists?

(n) Is the MCPS/BPI import licensing scheme operated with a view to maintaining high prices for recorded music?

(o) Are the independent record companies (represented by Umbrella) being excluded from the import licensing scheme in order to restrict their ability to compete in the UK?

(p) To what extent do the right to control imports and the MCPS/BPI import licensing scheme contribute to:

(i) the prevention or detection of piracy, and

(ii) the success of the recorded music industry in the UK?

(q) Are the major record companies exercising effective control over the British Phonographic Industry Limited in a way that distorts competition with independent record companies?

APPENDIX 2.3
(referred to in paragraph 2.47)

List of issues for discussion with major retailers

(a) Are the major retail companies distorting competition with independent retailers by securing unduly large discounts from record companies or through joint promotions with them? Does this result in a lack of choice for consumers as independent retailers close their outlets?

(b) Does the existence of the monopoly situations result in higher prices for recorded music in the UK than would otherwise be the case?

(c) What is the extent of the price differences between the UK and other countries? What is the explanation for these differences?

(d) Are the companies making excessive profits in relation to the costs involved in acquiring recorded music and selling it at retail level? Or in relation to the capital employed in these activities?

(e) Are the companies choosing the formats of recorded music which they stock in a way which is designed to increase their profits rather than meet the requirements of consumers, thus reducing consumer choice?

(f) Are consumers confused or misled by the display of record charts based partly on a particular retailer's estimate of future sales, rather than the generally accepted charts produced by Gallup and based on record sales throughout the UK? Does the use of such charts distort competition between record companies and/or retailers?

248336 T2

APPENDIX 4.1
(referred to in paragraph 4.45)

Signatories to the Berne Convention

The following 95 States were party to the Berne Convention for the Protection of Literary and Artistic Works on 7 March 1993:

Argentina, Australia, Austria, Bahamas, Barbados, Belgium, Benin, Brazil, Bulgaria, Burkina Faso, Cameroon, Canada, Central African Republic, Chad, Chile, China, Colombia, Congo, Costa Rica, Côte d'Ivoire, Croatia, Cyprus, Czech Republic, Denmark, Ecuador, Egypt, Fiji, Finland, France, Gabon, Gambia, Germany, Ghana, Greece, Guinea, Guinea-Bissau, Holy See, Honduras, Hungary, Iceland, India, Ireland, Israel, Italy, Japan, Lebanon, Lesotho, Liberia, Libya, Liechtenstein, Luxembourg, Madagascar, Malawi, Malaysia, Mali, Malta, Mauritania, Mauritius, Mexico, Monaco, Morocco, Netherlands, New Zealand, Niger, Norway, Pakistan, Paraguay, Peru, Philippines, Poland, Portugal, Romania, Rwanda, Senegal, Slovakia, Slovenia, South Africa, Spain, Sri Lanka, Suriname, Sweden, Switzerland, Thailand, Togo, Trinidad and Tobago, Tunisia, Turkey, United Kingdom, United States of America, Uruguay, Venezuela, Yugoslavia, Zaire, Zambia, Zimbabwe.

The Convention, concluded in 1886, was revised at Paris in 1896, at Berlin in 1908, completed at Berne in 1914, and revised at Rome in 1928, at Brussels in 1948, at Stockholm in 1967, and at Paris in 1971, and was amended in 1979.

The Convention is open to all States. Instruments of ratification or accession must be deposited with the Director General of WIPO.

Signatories to the Rome Convention

The following 40 States were party to the Rome Convention for the Protection of Performers, Producers of Phonograms and Broadcasting Organisations on 6 January 1993:

Argentina, Australia, Austria, Barbados, Brazil, Burkina Faso, Chile, Colombia, Congo, Costa Rica, Czech Republic, Denmark, Dominican Republic, Ecuador, El Salvador, Fiji, Finland, France, Germany, Greece, Guatemala, Honduras, Ireland, Italy, Japan, Lesotho, Luxembourg, Mexico, Monaco, Niger, Norway, Panama, Paraguay, Peru, Philippines, Slovenia, Spain, Sweden, United Kingdom, Uruguay.

The Convention is open to States party to the Berne Convention or to the Universal Copyright Convention. Instruments of ratification or accession must be deposited with the Secretary-General of the United Nations. States may make reservations with regard to the application of certain provisions.

The Rome Convention, which was concluded in 1961, secures protection in performances of performers, in phonograms of producers of phonograms and in broadcasts of broadcasting organizations.

Some large acquisitions by record companies, 1983 to 1993

1985

Acquisition of Charisma Records Limited by Virgin in June for £0.1 million.

Acquisition of 75 per cent of Lasgo Exports Limited by Chrysalis in December (remaining 25 per cent also acquired in 1988 and 1989)

1986

Acquisition of RCA Records by Bertelsmann Group

1987

Acquisition of 49 per cent of Go! Discs Limited by PolyGram UK Limited in June for £0.75 million

1988

Acquisition of CBS Records by Sony Corporation in January for $2 billion

Acquisition of Magnet Records Limited by Warner Music UK Limited

1989

Acquisition of Island Records/Island Music by PolyGram UK Group in July for £272 million

Acquisition of 50 per cent of Chrysalis Records by THORN EMI in August for £54 million

Acquisition of 49 cent of Big Life Records Limited by PolyGram Record Operations Limited for £1.05 million

1990

Acquisition of A&M Records Limited by PolyGram International Group in January for $460 million

Acquisition of Warner Communications Inc by Time-Life in January for $14 billion creating Time-Warner Inc

Acquisition of Geffen Records by MCA Inc in March for $545 million

Acquisition of IRS Records Limited by EMI Records in July for £2.25 million

Acquisition of MCA Inc by Matsushita in December for $6.1 billion

1991

Acquisition of 30 per cent of Really Useful Holdings Limited by PolyGram International Group for an initial payment of £70 million and deferred payments based on performance

Acquisition of EG Records by Virgin in May for £3 million

Acquisition of remaining 50 per cent of Chrysalis by THORN EMI in December for £35 million

1992

Acquisition of Pickwick by Carlton Communications in January for £71 million

Acquisition of Virgin Music Group by THORN EMI in March for £593 million

Acquisition of 76 per cent of Conifer Record's immediate holding company Embaro Limited by Zomba Records Limited in July

Acquisition of 49 per cent of Creation Records by Sony Music Entertainment in August

1993

Acquisition of outstanding 51 per cent of Big Life Records Limited by PolyGram in June

Acquisition of Motown by PolyGram International Group in August for $301 million

Source: PolyGram.

Label market share

Singles	1988	1989	1990	1991	1992
Arista	2.2	1.9	2.8	1.7	6.1
CBS/Columbia	6.5	6.1	5.6	5.4	5.3
Epic	3.5	4.5	4.1	5.2	5.0
London	4.8	4.0	2.7	4.1	4.2
A&M	1.5	1.8	2.5	5.9	3.5
Capitol	0.8	1.6	3.1	1.6	3.4
RCA	3.8	2.1	1.3	1.4	2.7
EMI	5.4	2.5	3.7	2.6	2.7
Virgin	5.1	3.8	2.6	3.7	2.7
East West	-	-	0.6	1.4	2.1
PWL International	4.7	5.2	2.1	1.1	2.0
Motown	1.0	0.3	0.4	0.2	1.9
Parlophone	2.6	2.9	2.4	3.7	1.8
Polydor	1.1	1.1	1.3	2.0	1.8
MCA	4.5	4.5	2.5	2.2	1.7
Network	-	-	0.1	0.5	1.7
Mercury	2.4	1.6	1.8	1.3	1.7
One Little Indian	0.1	-	0.1	0.5	1.6
XL Recording	-	-	-	0.9	1.5
Mute	1.5	1.3	1.5	1.0	1.4
Geffen	0.7	1.6	0.5	1.8	1.1
PWL Continental	-	-	-	0.8	1.1
Cooltempo	1.0	1.8	1.3	1.3	1.1
Island	1.4	0.9	0.5	1.0	1.0
Warner Bros	1.6	3.1	1.4	2.0	1.0
Fontana	0.3	0.8	0.7	1.2	1.0
WEA	2.4	2.4	0.4	0.3	1.0
Others	41.1	44.2	54.0	45.2	37.9
Total	100.0	100.0	100.0	100.0	100.0
Albums					
CBS/Columbia	6.3	5.2	5.7	6.2	5.8
Virgin	4.4	4.2	4.0	3.3	4.5
THORN EMI	4.3	4.2	5.8	4.4	3.6
Telstar	3.3	5.0	4.7	4.3	3.6
Epic	3.7	4.1	3.0	4.0	3.3
Parlophone	2.0	1.7	1.5	3.3	2.6
East West	-	-	0.7	2.2	2.6
Polydor	2.7	2.9	3.1	2.9	2.6
'Now' Series	2.7	2.1	2.0	1.4	2.4
A&M	1.9	2.0	2.6	2.6	2.4
RCA	3.6	3.0	1.5	2.5	2.3
Warner Bros	3.7	3.0	2.5	2.7	2.1
Geffen	0.6	1.5	1.0	2.0	2.0
Capitol	1.2	1.6	2.1	2.1	2.0
Arista	1.2	1.0	1.6	1.2	1.9
Motown	0.9	0.6	0.4	0.3	1.6
Dino	-	-	1.0	1.8	1.6
MCA	1.4	2.8	1.1	1.5	1.3
PRO-TV/PolyGram TV	0.5	0.3	-	-	1.3
WEA	1.8	2.3	0.5	0.8	1.3
MFP	0.9	1.0	1.2	1.1	1.3
Mercury	2.2	1.5	1.5	1.7	1.3
Island	2.7	1.2	1.2	1.2	1.3
London	1.9	1.9	1.6	1.0	1.2
Decca	0.4	0.5	2.6	2.1	1.2
Fontana	-	0.6	0.4	0.5	1.0
Vertigo	2.3	1.2	1.7	1.9	1.0
Mute	0.9	1.2	0.8	0.6	1.0
Others	42.5	43.4	44.2	40.4	39.9
Total	100.0	100.0	100.0	100.0	100.0

Source: BPI Handbook: Gallup data.

Note: Market share attributed to joint ventures has not been included in the share of the respective labels. Qualifying criterion 1 per cent or more in 1992.

(referred to in paragraph 5.156)

Changes in catalogue for one major record company between 1987 and 1992

		Catalogue at 31 December 1987	Additions	Deletions	Catalogue at 31 December 1988	Additions	Deletions	Catalogue at 31 December 1989	Additions	Deletions	Catalogue at 31 December 1990	Additions	Deletions	Catalogue at 31 December 1991	Additions	Deletions	Catalogue at 31 December 1992
Pop																	
Singles	7"	335	264	233	366	219	295	290	235	274	251	234	235	250	171	283	138
	12"	221	210	203	228	210	232	206	221	229	198	236	221	213	116	247	82
	MC	11	12	11	12	41	16	37	68	50	55	122	81	96	92	115	73
	CD	14	64	8	70	173	67	176	174	207	143	187	143	187	164	238	113
Albums	LP full-price	321	120	139	302	163	94	371	164	137	398	88	222	264	44	152	156
	LP mid-price	461	75	94	442	66	184	324	88	67	345	29	124	250	10	149	111
	LP budget	2	0	0	2	0	0	2	0	0	2	0	0	2	0	0	2
	MC full-price	288	97	124	261	160	92	329	161	107	383	111	176	318	74	151	241
	MC mid-price	427	70	118	379	77	114	342	108	73	377	59	105	331	54	139	246
	MC budget	18	0	4	14	0	0	14	20	0	34	12	2	44	56	13	87
	CD full-price	279	125	122	282	162	95	349	145	99	395	122	94	423	112	185	350
	CD mid-price	53	168	6	215	137	16	336	128	36	428	109	60	477	85	218	344
	CD budget	0	27	1	26	0	0	26	41	14	53	11	17	47	84	13	118
	DCC	0	0	0	0	0	0	0	0	0	0	0	0	3	16	0	16
Classical																	
Singles	7"	2	0	1	1	0	1	0	0	0	0	0	0	0	2	1	1
	12"	0	0	0	0	0	0	0	0	0	0	0	0	0	0	0	0
	MC	0	0	0	0	0	0	0	0	0	0	0	0	0	2	1	1
	CD	0	2	1	1	2	1	2	0	0	2	1	3	0	1	0	1
Albums	LP full-price	81	46	49	78	10	10	78	15	60	33	3	29	7	0	2	5
	LP mid-price	132	59	86	105	8	1	112	4	89	27	0	26	1	0	0	1
	LP budget	1	0	0	1	0	0	1	0	0	1	0	0	1	0	0	1
	MC full-price	75	57	31	101	89	17	173	75	49	199	44	160	83	14	9	88
	MC mid-price	147	98	56	189	109	38	260	151	61	350	65	273	142	29	32	139
	MC budget	0	24	0	24	28	1	51	30	15	66	40	37	69	12	6	75
	CD full-price	200	296	101	395	109	120	384	110	139	355	135	102	388	115	35	468
	CD mid-price	48	93	3	138	139	35	242	214	41	415	141	54	502	139	42	599
	CD budget	0	44	0	44	30	3	71	33	15	89	154	62	181	15	0	196
	DCC	0	0	0	0	0	0	0	0	0	0	0	0	0	10	0	10
Total		3,116	1,951	1,391	3,676	1,932	1,432	4,176	2,185	1,762	4,599	1,903	2,226	4,276	1,417	2,031	3,662

Source: MMC from company information.

Note: This pattern is not necessarily typical of all the majors.

Number of titles released by the major record companies in various countries

		UK	USA	Germany	France	Netherlands	Denmark	Number Japan
EMI*	Albums	1,140	828	1,495	1,022	921	579	1,684
(including Virgin)	Singles	303	270	352	276	427	88	239
	Total	1,443	1,098	1,847	1,298	1,348	667	1,923
Warner	Albums	801	644	491	761	330	485	1,200
	Singles	944	967	314	403	200	-	150
	Total	1,745	1,611	805	1,164	530	485	1,350
Sony	Albums	626	725	424	971	668	-	1,220
	Singles	253	199	239	106	58	-	311
	Total	879	924	663	1,077	726	-	1,531
PolyGram	Albums	1,393	916	1,850	1,630	2,205†	-	2,679
	Singles	504	161	550	307	480†	-	151
	Total	1,897	1,077	2,400	1,937	2,685	-	2,830
BMG	Albums	550	888	842	2,257	1,335	480	769
	Singles	165	64	170	285	268	150	160
	Total	715	952	1,012	2,542	1,603	630	929
Grand total	Albums	4,510	4,001	5,102	6,641	5,459	1,544	7,552
	Singles	2,169	1,661	1,625	1,377	1,433	238	1,011
	Total	6,679	5,662	6,727	8,018	6,892	1,782	8,563
								Indices (UK = 100)
EMI*	Albums	100	80	131	90	81	51	148
(including Virgin)	Singles	100	91	116	91	141	29	79
	Total	100	83	128	90	93	46	133
Warner	Albums	100	80	61	95	41	61	150
	Singles	100	102	33	43	21	-	16
	Total	100	92	46	67	30	28	77
Sony	Albums	100	116	68	155	107	-	195
	Singles	100	79	94	42	23	-	123
	Total	100	105	75	123	83	-	174
PolyGram	Albums	100	66	133	117	158†	-	192
	Singles	100	32	109	61	95†	-	30
	Total	100	57	127	102	142	-	149
BMG	Albums	100	161	153	410	243	87	140
	Singles	100	39	103	173	162	91	97
	Total	100	133	142	356	224	88	130
Grand total	Albums	100	89	113	147	121	34	167
	Singles	100	77	75	63	66	11	47
	Total	100	85	101	120	103	27	128

Source: MMC, based on company information.

*The figures for EMI are line items.
†These figures included 'double counting' of albums released on both cassette and CD.
Notes:
1. The information in this table relates to 1992.
2. Figures are based on the assumption that all new titles issued are at least in the CD format.

Sales profile in the Top 200 of Tasmin Archer's album *Great Expectations*

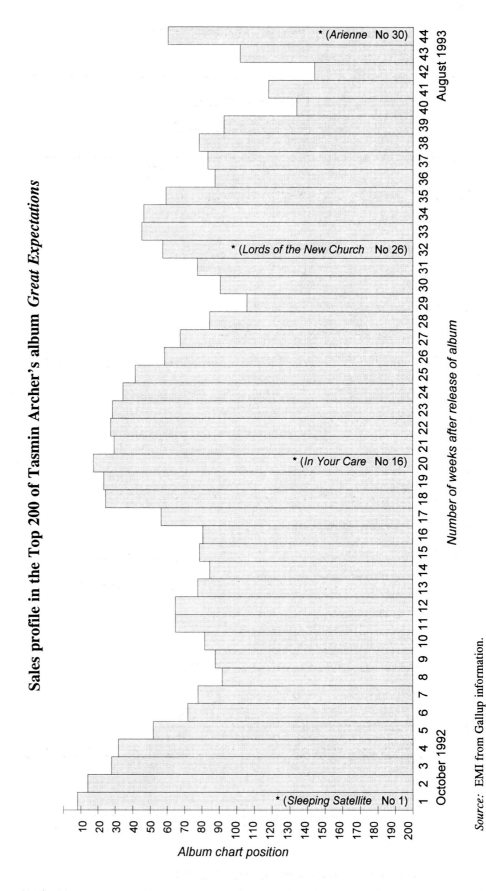

Source: EMI from Gallup information.

*Single released from album and the highest place it reached in the singles chart.

Examples of retailers' charts

W H Smith
Singles Hit List

---

1. MARIAH CAREY—Without You.

2. TONI BRAXTON—Breathe Again.

3. D:REAM—Things Can Only Get Better.

4. ENIGMA—Return To Innocence.

5. CAPELLA—Move On Baby.

6. ARETHA FRANKLIN—A Deeper Love.

7. **ELTON JOHN & RU PAUL—Don't Go Breaking My Heart.**
   `NEW`

8. CELINE DION—The Power of Love.

9. WENDY MOTON—Come In Out Of The Rain.

10. SUEDE—Stay Together. `NEW`

11. ADAMS/STEWART/STING—All For Love.

12. CROWDED HOUSE—Locked Out.

13. 2 UNLIMITED—Let The Beat Control Your Body.

14. MEATLOAF—Rock 'n' Roll Dreams Come Through.

15. **LEVEL 42—Forever Now.** `NEW`

16. K7—Come Baby Come.

17. STING—Nothing 'Bout Me. `NEW`

18. N.K.O.T.B.—Dirty Dawg.

19. PROCLAIMERS—Let's Get Married.

20. SINEAD O'CONNOR—You Made Me The Thief Of Your Heart.

Chart positions for new releases are based on expected sales through W H Smith stores.

Singles of the week—week commencing 14/2/94

W H Smith albums hit list

Album of the week: *You Must Remember This*

Monday 14th February	Cassette Price	CD Price
1. GARTH BROOKS: In Pieces _____W H SMITH PRICE	**£7.99**	**£11.99**
2. ENIGMA: The Cross Of Changes _____	£7.99	£12.99
3. TORI AMOS: Under The Pink _____	£7.99	£12.99
4. CHAKA DEMUS & PLIERS: Tease Me (New Version) _____	£8.99	£12.99
5. RICHARD MARX: Paid Vacation _____	£7.99	£12.49
6. DANCE TO THE MAX: Various Artists _____NEW	£8.99	£12.99
7. NOW DANCE '94: Various Artists _____	£8.99	£12.99
8. MOVIES GREATEST LOVE SONGS: Various Artists _____	£7.99	£12.99
9. YOU MUST REMEMBER THIS: Various Artists _____	£5.99	£9.99
10. ROBERTA FLACK: The Best Of—Softly With These Songs _____	£7.99	£12.99
11. DIANA ROSS: One Woman _____	£8.99	£12.99
12. BRYAN ADAMS: So Far So Good—Greatest Hits _____W H SMITH PRICE	**£7.99**	**£11.99**
13. D:REAM: On Vol 1 _____	£8.99	£12.99
14. PHIL COLLINS: Both Sides _____	£8.49	£12.49
15. THE BRIT AWARDS 94: Various Artists _____	£10.49	£18.99
16. STING: Ten Summoners Tales _____RE-ENTRY W H SMITH PRICE	**£7.99**	**£11.99**
17. LOVE OVER GOLD: Various Artists _____	£9.49	£18.49
18. DANCE DIVAS: Various Artists _____	£7.99	£12.99
19. SWEET SOUL HARMONIES: Various Artists _____	£8.99	£12.99
20. ZZ TOP: Antenna _____	£8.99	£13.99

	Cassette Price	CD Price
21. VAN MORRISON: Best of Vol.1 _____RE-ENTRY	£8.99	£12.99
22. DINA CARROLL: So Close _____	£7.99	£11.99
23. DANCE HITS 94: Various Artists _____	£8.49	£12.99
24. M PEOPLE: Elegant Slumming _____	£7.99	£11.99
25. BJORK: Debut _____	£8.99	£12.99
26. 100% REGGAE: Various Artists _____	£8.49	£12.49
27. SOUL MATE: Various Artists _____	£7.99	£11.99
28. CHICAGO: The Heart Of _____	£7.99	£12.49
29. NOW 26: Various Artists _____	£9.99	£18.99
30. TONI BRAXTON: Toni Braxton _____W H SMITH PRICE	**£7.99**	**£11.99**
31. ETERNAL: Always & Forever _____W H SMITH PRICE	**£7.99**	**£11.99**
32. MEATLOAF: Bat Out Of Hell II—Back Into Hell _____	£8.99	£12.99
33. TAKE THAT: Everything Changes _____RE-ENTRY W H SMITH PRICE	**£7.99**	**£10.99**
34. PET SHOPS BOYS: Very _____RE-ENTRY W H SMITH PRICE	**£7.99**	**£11.99**
35. GABRIELLE: Gabrielle _____W H SMITH PRICE	**£7.99**	**£11.99**
36. SHIRLEY BASSEY: Sings Andrew Lloyd Webber _____	£7.99	£9.99
37. CROWDED HOUSE: Together Alone _____	£7.99	£11.99
38. PAULINE HENRY: Pauline _____	£7.99	£12.99
39. MARIAH CAREY: Music Box _____	£8.99	£12.99
40. ELTON JOHN: Duets _____W H SMITH PRICE	**£7.99**	**£11.99**

Chart positions for new releases are based on expected sales through W H Smith stores.

	VIRGIN TOP 40 ALBUM CHART	
	DATE W/C 7TH FEBRUARY 1994	
NO	ARTIST	TITLE
1	TORI AMOS	UNDER THE PINK
2	ALICE IN CHAINS	JAR OF FLIES/SAP
3	GARTH BROOKS	IN PIECES
4	BJORK	DEBUT
5	KRISTIN HERSH	HIPS AND MAKERS
6	CHAKA DEMUS & PLIERS	TEASE ME
7	D:REAM	D:REAM ON VOL. 1
8	ZZ TOP	ANTENNA
9	M PEOPLE	ELEGANT SLUMMING
10	MARIAH CAREY	MUSIC BOX
11	UNDERWORLD	DUB NO BASS WITH MY HEAD MAN
12	DIANA ROSS	ONE WOMAN – ULTIMATE COLLECTION
13	BRYAN ADAMS	SO FAR SO GOOD
14	K.D. LANG	INGENUE
15	CULTURE BEAT	SERENITY
16	CYPRESS HILL	BLACK SUNDAY
17	SOUL ASYLUM	GRAVE DANCERS UNION
18	TONI BRAXTON	TONI BRAXTON
19	DINA CARROLL	SO CLOSE
20	MICHAEL BOLTON	ONE THING
21	STING	TEN SUMMONERS TALES
22	LISA STANSFIELD	SO NATURAL
23	ELTON JOHN	DUETS
24	MEAT LOAF	BAT OUT OF HELL II – BACK INTO HELL...
25	K7	SWING BATTA SWING
26	PHIL COLLINS	BOTH SIDES
27	PEARL JAM	VS.
28	RICHARD THOMPSON	MIRROR BLUE
29	ROLLING STONES	JUMP BACK – BEST OF
30	KENNY G.	BREATHLESS
31	UB40	PROMISES & LIES
32	ETERNAL	ALWAYS AND FOREVER
33	JAMIROQUAI	EMERGENCY ON PLANET EARTH
34	R.E.M	AUTOMATIC FOR THE PEOPLE
35	KATE BUSH	RED SHOES
36	TOM PETTY & THE HEARTBREAKERS	GREATEST HITS
37	WAYNE'S WORLD 2	OST
38	NIRVANA	IN UTERO
39	WET WET WET	END OF PART I (GREATEST HITS)
40	CROWDED HOUSE	TOGETHER ALONE

	VIRGIN TOP 10 COMPILATIONS	
NO	TITLE	
1	SWEET SOUL HARMONIES	
2	NOW DANCE '94 VOL 1	
3	DUB HOUSE DISCO 3	
4	CREAM OF UNDERGROUND HOUSE 3	
5	NOW 26	
6	100% REGGAE	
7	SOUND OF KISS FM	
8	BEST DANCE ALBUM IN THE WORLD EVER VOL 2	
9	RAVE GENERATION 2	
10	BLUES BROTHER/SOUL SISTER	

Our Price album chart

				cass.	cd's
1	Enigma	The Cross of Changes	new	7.99	11.99
2	Therapy?	Troublegum		7.99	11.99
3	Chaka Demus & Pliers	Tease Me		7.99	11.99
4	Richard Marx	Paid Vacation	new	7.99	11.99
5	Garth Brooks	In Pieces		8.49	12.49
6	Tori Amos	Under The Pink		8.49	12.49
7	Dance Hits '94	Various Artists	new	7.99	12.49
8	Diana Ross	One Woman—The Ultimate Collection		8.99	11.99
9	Sweet Soul Harmonies	Various Artists		8.49	11.99
10	Now Dance '94 Vol 1	Various Artists		7.99	11.99
11	Dina Carroll	So Close	price zap	7.99	**10.99**
12	Bjork	Debut	price zap	8.49	**10.99**
13	Bryan Adams	So Far So Good		7.99	11.99
14	Toni Braxton	Toni Braxton		8.49	12.49
15	Movies Greatest Love Songs	Various Artists	new	7.99	11.99
16	D:Ream	D:Ream On Vol 1		7.99	11.99
17	Mariah Carey	Music Box	price zap	8.49	**9.99**
18	Phil Collins	Both Sides	price zap	**6.99**	**10.99**
19	M-People	Elegant Slumming		8.49	11.99
20	Take That	Everything Changes		7.99	11.99
21	ZZ Top	Antenna		8.99	12.99
22	UB40	Promises And Lies		8.49	12.49
23	Dance Divas	Various Artists	new	8.49	12.49
24	Eternal	Always And Forever		7.99	11.99
25	Elton John	Duets	price zap	8.49	**10.99**
26	KD Lang	Ingenue		8.49	12.49
27	Culture Beat	Serenity		8.49	12.49
28	Wet Wet Wet	End Of Part One (Their Greatest Hits)		8.49	11.99
29	Meatloaf	Bat Out Of Hell II— Back Into Hell		8.49	11.99
30	100% Reggae	Various Artists		8.49	12.49
31	Bee Gees	Size Isn't Everything		8.99	12.99
32	Kristen Hersh	Hips & Makers	price zap	**6.99**	**10.99**
33	Cypress Hill	Black Sunday		8.99	12.99
34	Meatloaf	Bat Out Of Hell		8.49	12.49
35	Michael Bolton	The One Thing		8.99	12.99
36	Now 26	Various Artists		9.99	18.49
37	Bodyguard	Original Soundtrack		8.49	12.49
38	Sound of Kiss FM	Various Artists		9.99	16.99
39	Ce Ce Peniston	Thought Ya Knew		8.49	12.49
40	Rave Generation 2	Various Artists		8.99	13.99

HMV album chart, 7 February

THIS WEEK	LAST WEEK			
1	NEW	THERAPY	TROUBLEGUM	
2	NEW	ENIGMA	THE CROSS OF CHANGES	
3	2	TORI AMOS	UNDER THE PINK	
4	1	GARTH BROOKS	IN PIECES	
5	12	DIANA ROSS	ONE WOMAN: THE ULTIMATE COLLECTION	VIDEO
6	8	NOW DANCE 94 VOLUME 1	VARIOUS ARTISTS	
7	7	CHAKA DEMUS & PLIERS	TEASE ME	
8	37	BRYAN ADAMS	SO FAR SO GOOD	
9	55	PHIL COLLINS	BOTH SIDES	
10	20	DINA CARROLL	SO CLOSE	
11	NEW	RICHARD MARX	PAID VACATION	
12	NEW	MARILLION	BRAVE	
13	16	M-PEOPLE	ELEGANT SLUMMING	VIDEO
14	NEW	SOUL MATE	VARIOUS ARTISTS	
15	6	ZZ TOP	ANTENNA	
16	NEW	PAULINE HENRY	PAULINE	VIDEO
17	NEW	BITTY MCLEAN	JUST TO LET YOU KNOW	
18	3	D:REAM	D:REAM ON VOL 1	
19	NEW	BRIAN MAY	LIVE AT BRIXTON ACADEMY	
20	NEW	BRIT AWARDS	VARIOUS ARTISTS	VIDEO
21	NEW	CHICAGO	THE HEART OF CHICAGO	
22	NEW	DANCE HITS 94	VARIOUS ARTISTS	
23	60	REM	AUTOMATIC FOR THE PEOPLE	
24	11	SWEET SOUL HARMONIES	VARIOUS ARTISTS	
25	42	UB40	PROMISES AND LIES	
26	NEW	ROBERTA FLACK	THE BEST OF ROBERTA FLACK	
27	48	TAKE THAT	EVERYTHING CHANGES	
28	NEW	THE MISSION	SUM AND SUBSTANCE	
29	62	NOW 26	VARIOUS ARTISTS	
30	NEW	LOVE OVER GOLD	VARIOUS ARTISTS	
31	NEW	DANCE DIVAS	VARIOUS ARTISTS	
32	13	ETERNAL	ALWAYS AND FOREVER	
33	19	MARIAH CAREY	MUSIC BOX	
34	4	ALICE IN CHAINS	JAR OF FLIES SAP	
35	64	BODYGUARD	ORIGINAL SOUNDTRACK	
36	NEW	THE MOVIES GREATEST LOVE SONGS	VARIOUS ARTISTS	
37	18	THE SOUND OF KISS FM	VARIOUS ARTISTS	
38	10	BJORK	DEBUT	
39	50	MEATLOAF	BAT OUT OF HELL II—BACK INTO HELL	
40	24	WET WET WET	END OF PART ONE (THEIR GREATEST HITS)	
41	NEW	CLASSIC MELLOW MASTERCUTS 3	VARIOUS ARTISTS	VIDEO
42	30	TONI BRAXTON	TONI BRAXTON	
43	34	100% REGGAE	VARIOUS ARTISTS	
44	29	ELTON JOHN	DUETS	
45	14	K.D. LANG	INGENUE	
46	23	THE VERY BEST OF THAT LOVING FEELING	VARIOUS ARTISTS	
47	5	KRISTIN HERSH	HIPS & MAKERS	
48	45	BEE GEES	SIZE ISN'T EVERYTHING	
49	36	MEATLOAF	BAT OUT OF HELL	
50	32	MICHAEL BOLTON	THE ONE THING	
51	65	EAST 17	WALTHAMSTOW	
52	62	GABRIELLE	FIND OUR WAY	VIDEO
53	38	PAVAROTTI	MY HEART'S DELIGHT	
54	92	GIN BLOSSOMS	NEW MISERABLE EXPERIENCE	VIDEO
55	17	CROWDED HOUSE	TOGETHER ALONE	
56	33	CYPRESS HILL	BLACK SUNDAY	
57	47	JODECI	DIARY OF A MAD BAND	
58	72	SHARA NELSON	WHAT SILENCE KNOWS	
59	28	SECRET LOVERS	VARIOUS ARTISTS	
60	NEW	WYNONNA	TELL ME WHY	

WOOLWORTHS
Album Chart
Top 75

1		ONE WOMAN/ULTIMATE COLLECTION DIANA ROSS

#		Title / Artist	#		Title / Artist
2		DANCE HITS 94 VARIOUS	39		SECRET LOVERS VARIOUS
3		BRIT AWARDS 1994 VARIOUS	40	NEW	THE BEST OF... VAN MORRISON
4		THE CROSS OF CHANGES ENIGMA	41		END OF PART ONE (GREATEST HITS) WET WET WET
5		IN PIECES GARTH BROOKS	42		ANTENNA ZZ TOP
6		UNDER THE PINK TORI AMOS	43		LESLEY GARRETT — THE ALBUM LESLEY GARRETT
7		PAID VACATION RICHARD MARX	44		WHAT SILENCE KNOWS SHARA NELSON
8		LOVE OVER GOLD VARIOUS	45		ALWAYS AND FOREVER ETERNAL
9		SO CLOSE DINA CARROLL	46	▲	A GIFT OF LOVE BILL TARNEY
10		TEASE ME CHAKA DEMUS & PLIERS	47	▲	VERY PET SHOP BOYS
11	▲	MUSIC BOX MARIAH CAREY	48		NOW 26 VARIOUS
12		SOUL MATE VARIOUS	49	▲	TEN SUMMONERS TALES STING
13	▲	BAT OUT OF HELL II MEATLOAF	50		THE HEART OF CHICAGO CHICAGO
14		THE MOVIES GREATEST LOVE SONGS VARIOUS	51	NEW	CROOKED RAIN PAVEMENT
15		SO FAR SO GOOD (THE BEST OF) BRYAN ADAMS	52		MY HEART'S DELIGHT LUCIANO PAVAROTTI
16		NOW DANCE 94 VOLUME 1 VARIOUS	53		BAT OUT OF HELL (RE-VAMPED) MEATLOAF
17		ELEGANT SLUMMING M-PEOPLE	54		ARE YOU GONNA GO MY WAY LENNY KRAVITZ
18		DANCE DIVAS VARIOUS	55		INGENUE KD LANG
19		BOTH SIDES PHIL COLLINS	56		THE VERY BEST OF THAT LOVING FEELING VARIOUS
20		SWEET SOUL HARMONIES VARIOUS	57		THE BODYGUARD VARIOUS
21		THE BEST OF... ROBERTA FLACK	58		AUTOMATIC FOR THE PEOPLE REM
22	NEW	DEEP FOREST DEEP FOREST	59		HADDAWAY — THE ALBUM HADDAWAY
23		TONI BRAXTON TONI BRAXTON	60		JANET JANET JACKSON
24		TROUBLEGUM THERAPY	61		THE RED SHOES KATE BUSH
25		BRAVE MARILLION	62		BREATHLESS KENNY G
26		D:REAM ON VOLUME 1 D:REAM	63		SIZE ISN'T EVERYTHING THE BEE GEES
27	▲	TOGETHER ALONE CROWDED HOUSE	64	▲	FIND YOUR WAY GABRIELLE
28		PAULINE PAULINE HENRY	65	RE	WOODFACE CROWDED HOUSE
29	▲	DUETS ELTON JOHN	66		WALTHAMSTOW EAST 17
30		EVERYTHING CHANGES TAKE THAT	67	RE	THE BEST OF...VOLUME 2 VAN MORRISON
31		LIVE AT THE BRIXTON ACADEMY BRIAN MAY	68		SO NATURAL LISA STANSFIELD
32	NEW	DANCE TO THE MAX VARIOUS	69		RAVE GENERATION 2 VARIOUS
33		SERENITY CULTURE BEAT	70		GOLD HEART LOVE SONGS VARIOUS
34		DEBUT BJORK	71		JAR OF FLIES/SAP ALICE IN CHAINS
35		PROMISES AND LIES UB40	72		SWING BATTA SWING K7
36	▲	JUST TO LET YOU KNOW BITTY MCLEAN	73		ALADDIN SOUNDTRACK
37		THE ONE THING MICHAEL BOLTON	74		THE SOUND OF KISS FM VARIOUS
38		100% REGGAE VARIOUS	75	NEW	SUM AND SUBSTANCE MISSION

▲ = Chart increases of 5 or more places over last week

WEEK COMMENCING 14 FEBRUARY 1994

WOOLWORTHS
Singles Chart
Top 50

1	**8**	**WITHOUT YOU** — MARIAH CAREY			

Pos	LW	Title / Artist	Pos	LW	Title / Artist
2	1	THINGS CAN ONLY GET BETTER — D:REAM	27	27	DIRTY DAWG — NKOTB
3	3	BREATHE AGAIN — TONI BRAXTON	28	16	FOR WHOM THE BELL TOLLS — BEE GEES
4	4	RETURN TO INNOCENCE — ENIGMA	29	26	I LOVE MUSIC — ROZALLA
5	2	ALL FOR LOVE — ADAMS, STEWART & STING	30	NEW	FOREVER NOW — LEVEL 42
6	14 ▲	MOVE ON BABY — CAPPELLA	31	NEW	STAY TOGETHER — SUEDE
7	12 ▲	THE POWER OF LOVE — CELINE DION	32	25	A WHOLE NEW WORLD — PEABO BRYSON/REGINA BELLE
8	22 ▲	COME IN OUT OF THE RAIN — WENDY MOTEN	33	19	THE RED STROKES — GARTH BROOKS
9	NEW	DON'T GO BREAKING MY HEART — ELTON JOHN/RU PAUL	34	34	LOCKED OUT — CROWDED HOUSE
10	10	A DEEPER LOVE — ARETHA FRANKLIN	35	35	LOVER — JOE ROBERTS
11	7	COME BABY COME — K7	36	NEW	SOUL OF MY SOUL — MICHAEL BOLTON
12	21 ▲	I LIKE TO MOVE IT — REEL 2 REAL	37	NEW	THE SIGN — ACE OF BASE
13	18 ▲	LET THE BEAT CONTROL YOUR BODY — 2 UNLIMITED	38	38	WHY? — D MOB WITH CATHY DENNIS
14	5	TWIST AND SHOUT — CHAKA DEMUS & PLIERS	39	39	UPTIGHT — SHARA NELSON
15	11	I MISS YOU — HADDAWAY	40	40	CAN'T WAIT TO BE WITH YOU — JAZZY JEFF AND FRESH PRINCE
16	6	CORNFLAKE GIRL — TORI AMOS	41	NEW	TWO TRIBES — FRANKIE GOES TO HOLLYWOOD
17	17	ROCK AND ROLL DREAMS COME THROUGH — MEATLOAF	42	48	LET'S GET MARRIED — PROCLAIMERS
18	9	ANYTHING — CULTURE BEAT	43	NEW	DOWNTOWN — SWV
19	13	NOW AND FOREVER — RICHARD MARX	44	NEW	INSANE IN THE BRAIN — CYPRESS HILL
20	20	PERPETUAL DAWN — ORB	45	36	LIFE BECOMING A LANDSLIDE — MANIC STREET PREACHERS
21	31 ▲	LINGER — CRANBERRIES	46	37	IMPOSSIBLE — CAPITAIN HOLLYWOOD PROJECT
22	42 ▲	SAIL AWAY — URBAN COOKIE COLLECTIVE	47	47	YOU MADE ME THE THIEF OF YOUR HEART — SINEAD O'CONNOR
23	23	SWEET LULLABY — DEEP FOREST	48	NEW	RUSH — FREAK POWER
24	24	WIND BENEATH MY WINGS — BILL TARNEY	49	49	STAY WITH ME BABY — RUBY TURNER
25	NEW	BECAUSE OF YOU — GABRIELLE	50	50	PALE MOVIES — ST ETIENNE
26	15	IT'S ALRIGHT — EAST 17	▲		= Chart increases of 5 or more places over last week

WEEK COMMENCING 14 FEBRUARY 1994

248336   U

Published dealer prices of the major record companies*
for non-classical recordings, September 1993

£

		Polygram	EMI	Sony	Warner†	BMG
Albums						
LP	Mid-price	3.07	3.19	2.97	-	-
	Deluxe mid-price	-	-	3.49	-	-
	Mid-price double	-	-	4.86	-	-
	Full-price	5.25	5.13	5.17	5.61	-
	Full-price special	-	6.08	-	-	-
	Full-price double	-	6.40	7.29	8.16	-
	Deluxe full-price	5.53	5.29	5.35	6.22	5.60
	Deluxe double	-	6.75	-	-	-
	Superstar	-	5.40	-	-	-
	TV/superstar/premium	5.53	5.65	5.35	-	-
Cassette	Mid-price	3.07	3.19	2.97	-	3.35
	Deluxe mid-price	-	-	3.49	-	-
	Mid-price double	-	-	4.86	-	-
	Full-price	5.25	4.99	5.17	5.30	5.35
	Full-price special	-	5.91	-	-	-
	Full-price double	-	6.25	7.29	7.65	-
	Deluxe full-price	5.53	5.13	5.35	5.66	5.60
	Deluxe double	-	6.50	-	-	-
	Superstar	-	5.29	-	-	-
	TV/superstar/premium	5.53	5.50	5.35	-	-
CD	Budget	-	3.64	-	-	3.57
	Mid-price	5.25	5.04	5.05	-	5.24
	Deluxe mid-price	-	-	5.36	-	-
	Mid-price double	-	-	7.59	-	-
	Full-price	7.59	7.56	7.59	7.96	7.59
	Full-price double	-	14.69	12.49	12.95	-
	Deluxe	8.15	7.86	8.03	8.21	8.14
	TV/superstar/premium	8.15	8.14	8.03	-	-
	TV double	-	11.82	-	-	-
Singles	7" standard	1.36	1.20	1.21	1.35	1.35
	EPs	-	1.40	-	-	-
	12" standard	2.49	2.27	2.15	2.50	2.49
	12" special	-	1.60	-	-	-
	CD	2.59	2.15	2.15	2.59	2.59
	CD in a jewel box	-	2.45	-	-	-
	Cassette	1.36	1.20	1.29	1.35	1.35

Source: MMC, based on company information.

---

*The record companies may have other prices which are not included here.
†Warner increased its prices on 27 September 1993. The table shows the increased prices.

BMRB International survey of retail prices, September 1993

Introduction

Background

1. As part of the inquiry, the MMC commissioned BMRB International to carry out a survey of retail prices of recorded music in different countries. The countries selected include both those where comparisons with UK prices are often made (eg the USA), and those of interest in relation to parallel imports and protection of copyright. Thus the countries selected were: Great Britain, USA, France, Germany and Denmark.

2. Two measures were taken, the first between 6 and 19 September 1993 in all five countries, the second between 17 and 23 November 1993 in Great Britain and the USA only.

3. The objective of the research was to provide up-to-date information on prices of pre-recorded music with and without tax in a range of different countries.

4. The first section of this appendix concentrates on the British survey.

The sample

5. The sample of 250 outlets was drawn from *Yellow Pages*. A representative sample of 75 local expenditure zones (LEZs) was picked and within each a cluster of three to four outlets was selected.

6. The sample used is representative of urban, suburban and regional retail locations. However, different types of retailer were represented equally, and thus the sample is not fully representative of the total market.

7. Interviewers were provided with specific outlets and addresses at which to record prices, so that the structure of the sample might be maintained. In Great Britain the principal retailer types are:

Specialist — chains specializing in music (eg HMV, Our Price, Virgin);
Independent — specializing in music, but not part of a chain; and
Multiple — non-specialist in music (eg W H Smith, Woolworths).

Data were collected from 86 specialists, 74 independents and 89 multiples.

8. The survey also covered a sample of 250 outlets in the USA, with smaller samples of 100 outlets in each of France, Germany and Denmark. Details of sampling and fieldwork abroad are given in paragraphs 53 to 65.

Method

9. Fieldwork was conducted between 6 and 19 September 1993. Interviewers visited the outlets selected and recorded the prices of 14 titles on both CD and cassette. Of the 14 titles, 11 were pre-selected by the MMC with the other 3 being numbers 1, 5 and 10 in the national album chart in each country. Of the 11 pre-selected recordings, 3 were classical titles. In view of survey problems particularly affecting two of the latter, details of this part of the survey have been omitted from the analysis.

10. All interviewers were provided with letters from both the MMC and BMRB detailing the legitimacy of the survey and providing telephone numbers which could be called to check on this.

11. If interviewers were unable to find the price of a title they were instructed to ask the price of the title if it was to be ordered.

12. Interviewers were given precise written instructions and all fieldwork was conducted in accordance with the Code of Conduct of the Market Research Society.

13. Details of the titles researched in each country, including the Top 10 popular album chart titles at the time of the survey from which the chart position selections were made, are given in paragraph 50. For the purpose of comparing prices across different countries we have used the average exchange rates for the period July to December 1993 as set out in paragraph 51.

Results

Pre-selected popular titles

14. As detailed above, prices were collected for a total of 14 titles. For each title, the price was recorded for both CD and cassette formats. The 14 titles may be broken down into the following classifications:

— 8 pre-selected popular titles;
— 3 pre-selected classical titles; and
— 3 chart titles (positions 1, 5, 10).

15. All pre-selected titles were chosen by the MMC from short-lists provided by the major record companies. This section covers the eight pre-selected popular titles. We begin by commenting on the availability of each title.

Availability of pre-selected popular titles

16. One of the criteria on which pre-selected titles were chosen was that they were widely available in the countries surveyed. Although this was largely the case, there were still instances where a title was often not available, and it was rare for a title to be available at every store surveyed. If a title was not on the shelves, interviewers were instructed to ask store staff whether the title was in stock or, if not, whether it could be ordered. This gives us three measures of availability:

(a) available from stock;

(b) available to order; and

(c) not available.

17. Table 1 lists the overall availability (ie *(a)* or *(b)*) of each pre-selected popular title in each of the five countries surveyed, with an average, total measure.

302

TABLE 1 Availability of pre-selected popular titles, September 1993

Base: All stores

	Total	Great Britain	USA	France	Germany	Denmark
Number of stores in sample	807	249	250	97	111	100
						per cent
Diva—Annie Lennox						
CD	88	96	78	84	93	93
Cassette	85	96	81	80	79	78
Soul Dancing—Taylor Dayne						
CD	81	76	85	53	94	92
Cassette	77	75	86	52	79	76
Zooropa—U2						
CD	96	98	90	94	98	100
Cassette	92	97	91	91	84	84
Keep the Faith—Bon Jovi						
CD	92	98	88	82	100	94
Cassette	87	98	86	76	84	78
River of Dreams—Billy Joel						
CD	94	99	91	85	99	97
Cassette	89	98	89	84	81	81
Timeless—Michael Bolton						
CD	92	98	89	86	91	91
Cassette	88	97	88	83	80	78
Tubular Bells II—Mike Oldfield						
CD	83	97	60	88	96	90
Cassette	78	96	56	83	83	76
What's Love Got To Do With It?—Tina Turner						
CD	96	98	90	96	99	100
Cassette	90	98	87	92	84	83

Source: BMRB survey.

18. Overall, most titles were widely available, to be found in at least four-fifths of the stores included in the research. The exceptions to this are the availability of *Soul Dancing* by Taylor Dayne in France, and the cassette version of *Tubular Bells II* in the USA. *Soul Dancing* was available from only half of the stores surveyed in France, either in CD or cassette format. For both formats the title was mainly available to order, and not actually stocked.

19. Generally, the CD version of a title was slightly more likely to be available than the cassette version. This difference was more marked in Germany and Denmark, where we understand cassettes are becoming increasingly difficult to find.

20. In terms of whether titles were available from stock or to order, there are a few divergences, but generally the pattern of availability is consistent and so we have not tabulated the data here. Certainly overall, where titles were available, they were largely available from stock. It is more likely that cassettes were only available to order. This is driven primarily by the poorer availability of cassettes in Germany and Denmark. In Denmark, most titles were at least equally likely to be only available to order as they were to be in stock. In quite a few cases, it is more likely that the title needed to be ordered.

Prices of pre-selected popular titles

21. Table 2 shows the average price obtained for each of the pre-selected popular titles on both CD and cassette format. This figure is based on the number of stores where a price was obtained. The base therefore excludes stores where the title was unavailable. However, it varied from store to store as to whether store staff could give a price for a title that was only available to order. Therefore this has also depressed some base sizes. This appeared to be a particular problem in France.

TABLE 2 **Average price of pre-selected popular titles**

Base: All stores where obtained a price

£ sterling

	Great Britain		USA		France		Germany		Denmark		Total	
	Without tax	With tax	Without tax	With tax	Without tax	With tax	Without tax	With tax	Without tax	With tax	Without tax	With tax
Diva—Annie Lennox												
CD	11.78	13.85	10.21	10.83	13.03	15.45	11.23	12.91	11.38	16.07	11.53	13.82
Cassette	8.11	9.53	6.79	7.19	7.62	9.04	7.82	9.00	9.21	11.51	7.91	9.25
Soul Dancing—Taylor Dayne												
CD	11.25	13.23	9.83	10.42	12.87	15.26	11.19	12.87	11.58	16.36	11.34	13.63
Cassette	7.91	9.29	6.67	7.06	7.55	8.95	7.79	8.95	9.33	11.66	7.85	9.18
Zooropa—U2												
CD	10.22	12.02	9.85	10.44	11.88	14.09	10.72	12.33	11.33	16.00	10.80	12.98
Cassette	7.07	8.31	6.39	6.77	7.62	9.04	7.77	8.94	9.28	11.60	7.63	8.93
Keep the Faith—Bon Jovi												
CD	10.56	12.42	10.53	11.15	12.81	15.19	10.89	12.53	11.50	16.25	11.26	13.51
Cassette	7.30	8.58	6.80	7.21	7.83	9.29	7.85	9.03	9.48	11.85	7.85	9.19
River of Dreams—Billy Joel												
CD	10.33	12.14	9.45	10.01	11.74	13.92	10.75	12.36	11.28	15.93	10.71	12.87
Cassette	7.12	8.37	6.17	6.53	7.32	8.68	7.71	8.87	9.30	11.63	7.52	8.82
Timeless—Michael Bolton												
CD	11.26	13.23	10.45	11.07	12.41	14.72	11.00	12.65	11.28	15.93	11.28	13.52
Cassette	7.76	9.13	6.79	7.19	7.77	9.21	7.72	8.88	9.29	11.61	7.87	9.20
Tubular Bells II—Mike Oldfield												
CD	11.71	13.76	10.21	10.81	12.71	15.08	10.92	12.56	11.25	15.90	11.36	13.62
Cassette	8.13	9.56	6.80	7.20	7.91	9.38	7.72	8.88	9.27	11.59	7.97	9.32
What's Love Got To Do With It?—Tina Turner												
CD	10.06	11.83	9.67	10.25	13.12	15.56	11.15	12.83	11.44	16.16	11.09	13.33
Cassette	7.24	8.51	6.42	6.80	8.58	10.18	7.96	9.16	9.33	11.66	7.91	9.26

Source: BMRB survey.

22. The tables show prices with and without tax for each country. The varying tax levels are detailed in paragraph 52. Each pair of prices (ie with and without tax) is calculated on individual bases, which vary as described above. All prices in Table 2 are shown in £ sterling equivalent based on average exchange rates for the period July to September 1993, as shown in paragraph 51.

23. Overall, the average price of these titles on CD across the countries covered in the survey tends to range between about £13 and £14 with tax. Without tax, average prices for CDs range between £10.50 and £11.50. On cassette the titles average between £8.08 and £9.30 after tax. Without tax prices range from £7.50 to £8.

24. When we compare prices between countries some very strong and consistent patterns emerge. In terms of the price paid by the consumer, the USA is consistently the cheapest country for all eight titles. Average prices for the selected CDs range from £10.01 to £11.15. Great Britain and Germany vie for second place in terms of the price paid by the consumer. Some titles are cheaper in Great Britain, and some are cheaper in Germany. Average prices for the eight pre-selected CDs range from £11.83 to £13.85 and £12.33 to £12.91 respectively in these two countries.

25. France and Denmark tend to be significantly more expensive for CDs. They are the most expensive countries for all eight titles, with Denmark consistently more expensive than France. Average prices in France range from £13.92 to £15.56. In Denmark prices range from £15.90 to £16.36, thus making it noticeably more expensive than France.

26. The various local taxes have a marked effect upon the relative average prices between countries. This can be seen by inspecting prices without tax. These figures show a weaker, and to some extent different, pattern from those which relate to prices with tax. The USA is again the cheapest country. Britain and Germany again tend to share second place in terms of having the cheapest CDs without tax, although this pattern does vary very slightly, in contrast to shelf prices.

27. The biggest discrepancies between taxed and untaxed prices occur in France and Denmark. The basic, average price of CDs in France without tax is consistently the highest across all eight titles. Denmark is thus not the most expensive country without tax, but tends to lie in second place. This illustrates the impact of the heavy taxes attracted by CDs in Denmark. These data also mark France out as having relatively expensive prices for CDs on a without-tax basis.

28. Cassette prices tend to tell a similar story, but with some interesting divergences. The USA is clearly cheaper than any of the other countries for all of the eight titles, with and without tax. With tax average US prices are generally £1.50 to £2 cheaper than elsewhere. Following the USA, Britain, Germany and France are fairly closely grouped as the countries least expensive for cassettes, based on average prices with tax. Denmark is clearly the most expensive for all eight titles on cassette with tax, as it is for CD.

29. As noted above, the USA is cheaper on average for all cassette titles on a without-tax basis. Britain, Germany and France follow, the order varying by title, but with relatively little discrimination in terms of value in most cases. In fact Germany tends to be relatively more expensive than Britain and France in terms of without-tax cassette prices compared with with tax prices. Denmark is seen to have the most expensive cassette prices both without and with tax. This is partly due to the relatively lower cost of cassettes in France, despite the lower tax applied to cassettes in Denmark compared with CDs.

30. A final consideration here is whether a title was in a sale or on special offer. On the questionnaire there was an option for each title on each format to record whether it was in a sale or on special offer. For most titles, and in most countries, this was not a significant factor, accounting for less than a tenth of prices collected. However, discounting appears to have been more common in the USA than elsewhere for the eight pre-selected popular titles. The following proportions of prices collected were discounted in the USA by 10 per cent or more in one or other format:

		%
Soul Dancing	CD	19
	Cassette	15
Zooropa	CD	39
	Cassette	40
River of Dreams	CD	52
	Cassette	49
Timeless	CD	10
	Cassette	8
What's Love Got To Do With It?	CD	29
	Cassette	29

31. Although this undoubtedly contributes to the cheaper prices recorded in the USA, it is also true that it remains the cheapest country even for titles where discounting was not widespread. France appears, for the titles surveyed at least, to be the only other country where discounting is common. The following proportions of prices collected were in a sale or on special offer in France:

		%
Zooropa	CD	22
	Cassette	15
River of Dreams	CD	16
	Cassette	13
What's Love Got To Do With It?	CD	12
	Cassette	5

32. The only other significant incidence of discounts was also for *What's Love Got To Do With It?*, for which the CD was in a sale or on special offer for 17 per cent of prices recorded in Britain. The fact that this was the most commonly discounted in Britain is likely to be driven by promotions linked to the film of the same name.

Price of pre-selected popular titles by retailer types

33. In Britain and the USA enough stores were surveyed to allow some basic breakdowns by retailer type. There are three principal retailer types in each country: specialists, independents and multiples. These store types are defined in detail in the introduction and the individual country details beginning at paragraph 53. Table 3 gives the average price for each title on CD and cassette format, for each retailer type in Britain and the USA.

34. Overall there is little discrimination by retailer type in Britain. Individual titles tend to dictate which type of retailer is the most expensive or the cheapest. However, there seems to be a greater tendency for multiples to be cheaper than specialists or independents, or at least not to be the most expensive. Overall the pattern is similar for both CD and cassette formats

35. In the USA there is greater discrimination by retailer type, with a more discernible pattern to the list of prices. Independent retailers in the USA are more expensive than their multiple and specialist counterparts for most of the eight pre-selected titles, be they on CD or cassette. It is

generally true to say that multiples are the next most expensive retailers, with specialists tending to be the cheapest. There is little variation in this pattern by format.

TABLE 3 **Average price of pre-selected popular titles by retailer type with tax**

Base: All British/USA stores

£ sterling

	Great Britain			USA		
	Specialist	Independent	Multiple	Specialist	Independent	Multiple
Diva—Annie Lennox						
CD	14.66	12.85	13.83	10.49	11.32	10.44
Cassette	9.99	9.00	9.49	6.70	7.56	7.21
Soul Dancing—Taylor Dayne						
CD	13.78	12.68	12.80	9.84	10.97	10.39
Cassette	9.82	8.87	8.56	6.54	7.35	7.24
Zooropa—U2						
CD	11.93	12.17	11.99	10.16	10.93	10.12
Cassette	8.41	8.41	8.13	6.57	6.93	6.77
Keep the Faith—Bon Jovi						
CD	11.93	12.47	12.84	10.54	11.75	11.05
Cassette	8.42	8.76	8.60	6.78	7.54	7.19
River of Dreams—Billy Joel						
CD	12.29	12.28	11.89	9.93	10.16	9.92
Cassette	8.38	8.65	8.14	6.48	6.51	6.59
Timeless—Michael Bolton						
CD	14.14	12.53	12.92	10.52	11.58	11.05
Cassette	9.89	8.76	8.64	6.78	7.51	7.19
Tubular Bells II—Mike Oldfield						
CD	14.20	12.74	14.10	10.39	11.17	10.85
Cassette	9.94	8.94	9.68	6.74	7.47	7.55
What's Love Got To Do With It?—Tina Turner						
CD	10.95	12.19	12.38	10.03	10.57	10.09
Cassette	8.74	8.56	8.26	6.52	6.90	6.97

Source: BMRB survey.

The chart titles

36. This section covers the three titles taken from the album chart in each country. It was decided to select numbers 1, 5 and 10 from the chart unless one of the pre-selected titles occupied one of these positions. In this eventuality the next position down was used. Full details of the titles selected are given at the end of this section.

Availability of the chart titles

37. As would be expected for chart titles, availability was high with all titles being available in at least eight out of ten stores and most in nine out of ten with some almost reaching 100 per cent. Table 4 illustrates the availability of the three chart titles.

TABLE 4 Availability of chart titles

Base: All stores

	Total	Great Britain	USA	France	Germany	Denmark
Number of stores	807	249	250	97	111	100
						per cent
Number 1						
CD	95	99	90	94	95	98
Cassette	90	98	87	90	85	81
Number 5						
CD	87	83	80	96	96	97
Cassette	82	81	77	97	80	81
Number 10						
CD	96	99	92	95	96	98
Cassette	91	98	90	92	84	80

Source: BMRB survey.

38. In all but one case (number 5 in France) CDs were slightly more likely to be available than cassettes. CDs were also more likely than cassettes to be available from stock in all cases. This is particularly true in Germany and Denmark where use of the cassette format is dropping. However, stocking levels remained higher than for the eight pre-selected popular titles.

Prices of the chart titles

39. This section deals with the prices of widely demanded music in each of the countries represented in this research. Demand patterns for the pre-selected titles vary from country to country, while it is known that demand for the chart titles is high in each country. These data should be less title-sensitive. Table 5 shows the average price obtained for each of the chart titles. Looking firstly at the prices with tax a clear pattern emerges for both formats. The following ranking of countries by price on a with-tax basis can be applied for all titles.

Most expensive:	1. Denmark	CD	£15.88–£16.02 with tax
		Cassette	£11.60–£14.27 " "
	2. France	CD	£14.10–£14.81 " "
		Cassette	£9.07–£12.42 " "
	3. Germany	CD	£12.18–£12.44 " "
		Cassette	£8.73–£8.92 " "
	4. Great Britain	CD	£11.93–£12.26 " "
		Cassette	£7.72–£8.54 " "
Cheapest:	5. USA	CD	£10.06–£10.27 " "
		Cassette	£6.68–£6.89 " "

40. It is interesting to note the presence of special offers and sales in the different countries. In the USA, for both formats around three in ten stores offered a special offer or sale price for numbers 5 and 10, this figure rising to 43 per cent for the number 1 title.

41. Sales and special offers also seem common in France with at least 11 per cent of stores offering a discount on each title rising to 20 per cent for the number 1 CD. In Germany, Denmark and Great Britain it appears that sales and special offers did not form such an important part of the chart market with less than 10 per cent of stores offering such discounts in all cases. However, it may be that discounting is less conspicuous in these countries.

TABLE 5 Average price of chart titles

Base: All stores where obtained a price

	Great Britain		USA		France		Germany		Denmark		Total	
	Without tax	With tax	Without tax	With tax	Without tax	With tax	Without tax	With tax	Without tax	With tax	Without tax	With tax
Number 1												
CD	10.34	12.15	9.69	10.27	11.89	14.10	10.82	12.44	11.34	16.02	10.82	13.00
Cassette	7.03	8.27	6.31	6.68	10.47	12.42	7.75	8.92	11.41	14.27	8.59	10.11
Number 5												
CD	10.15	11.93	9.49	10.06	12.48	14.81	10.59	12.18	11.24	15.88	10.79	12.97
Cassette	6.56	7.72	6.34	6.72	7.74	9.18	7.60	8.73	9.28	11.60	7.50	8.79
Number 10												
CD	10.43	12.26	9.65	10.22	12.04	14.28	10.81	12.43	11.49	16.23	10.88	13.08
Cassette	7.27	8.54	6.51	6.89	7.65	9.07	7.61	8.75	9.32	11.65	7.67	8.98

Source: BMRB survey.

309

42. It should also be pointed out that while the same proportion of stores in the USA offer discounts on CDs as they do on cassettes, in France, Germany and Denmark cassettes were less likely to be discounted than CDs. This further indicates the declining importance of the cassette in these countries.

43. Looking at prices without tax, again patterns emerge although these differ between formats. The following ranking of countries by price can be applied for the CD chart titles:

Most expensive:	1. France	£11.89–£12.48 without tax
	2. Denmark	£11.24–£11.49 " "
	3. Germany	£10.59–£10.82 " "
	4. Great Britain	£10.15–£10.43 " "
Cheapest:	5. USA	£9.49–£9.69 " "

44. Here we see again that the pre-selected titles are relatively expensive in France, cheapest in the USA and that it is the level of taxation that makes CDs in Denmark the most expensive among the countries selected.

45. Looking at cassettes, the pattern is slightly less clear. The following ranking may generally be applied although Germany and France swap positions for the number 10 cassette:

Most expensive:	1. Denmark	£9.28–£11.41 with tax
	2. France	£7.65–£10.47 " "
	3. Germany	£7.60–£7.75 " "
	4. Great Britain	£6.56–£7.27 " "
Cheapest:	5. USA	£6.31–£6.51 " "

As noted for the pre-selected titles, the average price of cassettes in Denmark is higher than in the other countries researched, both with and without tax. The USA continues to have the lowest average prices and those collected in Great Britain also remain at the lower end of the scale.

46. Looking at Great Britain it would appear that the average price of pre-recorded music in the Top 10 is lower than in all of the countries researched except the USA.

Prices of the chart titles by retailer type

47. Table 6 shows the average price of each of the chart titles by different retailer types.

TABLE 6 **Average price of chart titles by retailer type with tax (sterling)**

Base: All stores where price obtained

£ sterling

	Great Britain			USA		
	Specialist	Independent	Multiple	Specialist	Independent	Multiple
Number 1						
CD	12.30	12.29	11.91	10.31	10.63	9.79
Cassette	8.44	8.55	7.89	6.73	6.77	6.53
Number 5						
CD	12.01	11.90	11.78	9.65	10.39	10.11
Cassette	7.83	7.86	7.18	6.41	6.92	6.79
Number 10						
CD	12.21	12.39	12.23	10.42	10.73	9.39
Cassette	8.63	8.83	8.27	6.78	7.25	6.60

Source: BMRB survey.

48. Looking first at CDs, in both Great Britain and the USA 'multiples' (ranging from £11.78 to £12.23 in Great Britain and £9.39 to £10.11 in the USA) tend to be cheaper than 'independents' (Great Britain £11.90 to £12.39, USA £10.39 to £10.73) and 'specialists' (Great Britain £12.01 to £12.30, USA £9.65 to £10.42), on two out of three titles in both cases. Higher average prices are to be found in 'specialists' in Great Britain (two out of three titles) and 'independents' in the USA for all titles.

49. For cassettes, in Great Britain the average price is highest for all titles in 'independents' (Great Britain £7.86 to £8.83, USA £6.77 to £7.25) followed by 'specialists' (Great Britain £7.83 to £8.63, USA £6.41 to £6.78) and 'multiples' (Great Britain £7.89 to £8.27, USA £6.53 to £6.79). The same tends to be true in the USA, although the average price in 'multiples' is higher than 'specialists' for title number 5.

Background information on the survey

Pre-selected titles (popular music)

50. The eight pre-selected titles were as follows:

1. *Diva* by Annie Lennox (BMG).
2. *Soul Dancing* by Taylor Dayne (BMG).
3. *Zooropa* by U2 (PolyGram).
4. *Keep the Faith* by Bon Jovi (PolyGram).
5. *River of Dreams* by Billy Joel (Sony).
6. *Timeless* by Michael Bolton (Sony).
7. *Tubular Bells II* by Mike Oldfield (Warner).
8. *What's Love Go To Do With It?* by Tina Turner (EMI).

The three chart titles (popular music)

51. Prices were collected for the albums positioned at numbers 1, 5 and 10 in the album chart of each of the countries. Details of the titles are as follows:

UK
No 1 *Music Box* by Mariah Carey.
No 5 *Last Splash* by The Breeders.
No 10 *Ant Music—The Very Best of Adam Ant* by Adam Ant.[1]

[1]This was in fact number 9 in the charts and was selected because *Keep The Faith* by Bon Jovi, one of the pre-selected titles, was at number 10.

USA

No 1 *Sleepless in Seattle*—Soundtrack.[1]
No 5 *Blind Melon* by Blind Melon.
No 10 *The Bodyguard*—Soundtrack.[1]

France

No 1 *Au Parc des Princes* by Johnny Hallyday.
No 5 *Promises and Lies* by UB40.
No 10 *Carcassonne* by Stephan Eicher.

Germany

No 1 *Bigger, Better, Faster, More!* by 4 Non Blondes.
No 5 *Seiltänzertraum* by Pur.
No 10 *Serenity* by Culture Beat.

Denmark

No 1 *Absolute Music 3*—Various artists.
No 5 *The Bodyguard*—Soundtrack.
No 10 *Sunshine Dance*—Various artists.

The charts

52. The following lists show the Top 10 in the national album chart of the respective countries at the time of fieldwork in September 1993:

UK

1. *Music Box* by Mariah Carey.
2. *Promises and Lies* by UB40.
3. *Levellers* by Levellers.
4. *Pocket Full Of Kryptonite* by Spin Doctors.
5. *Last Splash* by The Breeders.
6. *River Of Dreams* by Billy Joel.
7. *Automatic For The People* by REM.
8. *Zooropa* by U2.
9. *Ant Music—The Very Best Of Adam Ant* by Adam Ant.
10. *Keep The Faith* by Bon Jovi.

USA

1. *River Of Dreams* by Billy Joel.
2. *Sleepless in Seattle*—Soundtrack.
3. *Black Sunday* by Cypress Hill.
4. *Janet* by Janet Jackson.
5. *Blind Melon* by Blind Melon.
6. *Core* by Stone Temple Pilots.
7. *The World Is Yours* by Scarface.
8. *Promises and Lies* by UB40.
9. *The Bodyguard*—Soundtrack.
10. *Zooropa* by U2.

France

1. *Au Parc des Princes* by Johnny Halliday.
2. *Zooropa* by U2.
3. *Je te dis vous* by Patricia Kaas.
4. *War* by U2.
5. *Promises and Lies* by UB40.
6. *Chronologie* by Jean Michel Jarre.
7. *The Bodyguard* by Whitney Houston.

---

[1]These titles were in fact number 2 and number 9 respectively but were selected because *River of Dreams* by Billy Joel was number 1 and *Zooropa* by U2 number 10.

8. *Hélène* by Hélène.
9. *Medley 60's* by Magazine 60.
10. *Carcassonne* by Stephan Eicher.

Germany
1. *Bigger, Better, Faster, More!* by 4 Non Blondes.
2. *Keep The Faith* by Bon Jovi.
3. *Happy Nation* by Ace Of Base.
4. *Promises and Lies* by UB40.
5. *Seiltänzertraum* by Pur.
6. *River of Dreams* by Billy Joel.
7. *Pocket Full Of Kryptonite* by Spin Doctors.
8. *Gute Zeiten Schlechte Zeiten 2*—Soundtrack.
9. *Zooropa* by U2.
10. *Serenity* by Culture Beat.

Denmark
1. *Absolute Majic 3*—Various artists
2. *Absolute Let's Dance 2*—Various artists
3. *When* by Thomas Helmig
4. *Unplugged* by Rod Stewart
5. *The Bodyguard*—Soundtrack
6. *Gold* by Vikingarna
7. *Turn Up The Base 2*—Various artists
8. *Tutte Starle* by Eros Ramazzotti
9. *Pocket Full Of Kryptonite* by Spin Doctors
10. *Sunshine Dance*—Various artists

Exchange rates

53. The exchange rates used to convert price to sterling and their sources are detailed below:

Country	Exchange rate	Date
USA	1.50 US$	1 July to 31 December 1993 average
France	8.72 FFr	1 July to 31 December 1993 average
Germany	2.52 DM	1 July to 31 December 1993 average
Denmark	10.05 Dkr	1 July to 31 December 1993 average

Tax rate

54. The tax rates applicable to retail sales were as follows:

Country	Tax rate	
UK	17.5%	%
USA	Varies by city and state:	
	Seattle, Washington	6.50
	Washington DC	6.00
	San Francisco, California	8.00
	Los Angeles, California	8.25
	Phoenix, Arizona	5.00
	Dallas, Texas	8.25
	Des Moines, Iowa	4.00
	New Orleans, Louisiana	4.00
	Nashville, Tennessee	8.25
	Detroit, Michigan	4.00
	Miami, Florida	6.00
	Philadelphia, Pennsylvania	7.00
	Columbus, Ohio	5.75
	Boston, Massachusettes	5.00
	Atlanta, Georgia	4.00
	Albany, New York	8.00
	New York, New York	8.25
	Raleigh, North Carolina	5.00
	Denver, Colorado	3.00
	Salt Lake City, Utah	6.25
	Chicago, Illinois	6.25
France	18.6%	
Germany	15%	
Denmark	25% on cassettes.	
	25% VAT + 3/23 of the value as a luxury tax on CDs.	

USA—sampling, fieldwork and market profile

55. Given the size of the US market a number of major cities were selected in order to obtain a nationally representative sample. For each city urban and suburban areas were covered. The following cities were sampled:

Seattle, Washington	Philadelphia, Pennsylvania
Washington DC	Columbus, Ohio
San Francisco, California	Boston, Massachusetts
Los Angeles, California	Atlanta, Georgia
Phoenix, Arizona	Albany, New York
Dallas, Texas	New York, New York
Des Moines, Iowa	Raleigh, North Carolina
New Orleans, Louisiana	Denver, Colorado
Nashville, Tennessee	Salt Lake City, Utah
Detroit, Michigan	Chicago, Illinois
Miami, Florida	

56. Interviewers in these areas were contacted and given quotas for the different retail outlets which were to be sampled in that area. In each market 12 'interviews' were completed and the quotas by retailer type were as follows:

— one-third multiple: retailers which have several branches and sell other goods as well as recorded music (principally mass merchandise or general merchandise chains such as Woolworths, K-Mart, Caldor and other department stores or discount stores with a music department);

— one-third specialist: retailers which have several branches and specialize in recorded music, eg Tower Records, Sam Goody, HMV, Coconuts; and

— one-third independent: independent outlets (ie not chains) which specialize in recorded music excluding very specialized independents, eg those stores which only have, say, world music or jazz and second-hand record stores.

314

Fieldwork details

57. In the USA the survey was conducted by Goldstein Krall Marketing Resources. A total of 250 price checks was carried out between 8 and 11 September 1993.

Market profile

58. The US market profile was reported in the music magazine *Billboard* as comprising the following approximate numbers of outlets:

	Outlets
Independents	5,000– 6,000 (24%)
Specialists	4,000– 5,000 (20%)
Multiples	10,000–15,000 (56%)

Source: *Billboard*.

France—sampling, fieldwork and market profile

Sampling

59. Two or three cities/towns were selected in each Nielsen region and the number of outlets to be sampled in each city/town was allocated depending on their regional importance.

Region	City/town	Number of outlets
Paris		18
	Paris	18
Nord 2		11
	Lille	6
	Roubaix	3
	Villeneuve d'Ascq	2
Nord 3		10
	Rennes	7
	Fougères	1
	Redon	1
	Saint Gregoire	1
Est 2		10
	Nancy	5
	Metz	4
	Pont à Mousson	1
Est 4		10
	Lyon	7
	Tassin la demi-Lune	1
	Caluire	1
	Francheville	1
Est 5		9
	Aix en Provence	5
	Marseille	4
West 5		10
	Toulouse	6
	Montauban	4
South 3		11
	Nantes	6
	Cholet	5
Centre 4		11
	Bourges	4
	Châteauroux	4
	Nevers	2
	Vierzon	1

Stores within each of the principal retail type categories were then selected from *Yellow Pages* in each of the above centres. The quotas set aimed to cover a sufficient number of outlets for each type of

315

retail outlet. Independents, however, were over-sampled in order to cover the widest price variations. The sample was composed as follows:

	%
Independents	39
Specialists	23
Multiples	38

Fieldwork details

60. In France the survey was conducted by CSA. A total of 97 price checks was carried out between 6 and 13 September 1993. A number of problems were experienced by interviewers:

— the selected titles were frequently unavailable (even some mainstream titles such as *Diva* by Annie Lennox)—this problem was greater in the South, where national titles appear to be more popular than international ones;

— cassettes are becoming increasingly difficult to find; and

— more often than not, upon attempting to order a title the shop assistants could not supply the interviewers with a price.

Overall, the interviewer's task was more difficult in smaller towns and in small independent stores. In multiple stores it was difficult to find a wide range of titles and cassettes were virtually unavailable. For the purposes of the research the best outlets were specialists in Paris.

Market profile

61. The details of market profile were as follows:

	per cent	
	Sales	Outlets
Independent	10	18
Specialists	35	15
— FNAC	23	3
— Virgin	5	-
— other	6	11
Multiples	55	67
— hypermarkets	50	
— other	4	

Source: SNEP (Syndicat National des Editeurs Phonographiques).

Germany—sampling, fieldwork and market profile

Sampling

62. The following cities/towns were selected as being representative of the five Nielsen areas and covering a variety of community sizes:

Nielsen I:	Kiel
	Flensburg
	Hamburg
	Hannover
	Celle
	Bremen
	Gottingen

Nielsen II:	Essen
	Gelsenkirchen
	Köln
	Bielefeld
	Paderborn

Nielsen IIIa:	Saarbrücken
	Kassel

Nielsen IIIb:	Freiburg
	Heidelberg

Nielsen IV:	Würzburg
	Nürnberg
	München
	Regensburg

Nielsen Va:	Berlin (West)

Interviewers in these areas were contacted and given quotas for the different retail outlets which were to be sampled in that area. The quotas set were as follows:

— one-third multiple: retailers which have several branches and sell other goods as well as recorded music, including hi-fi stores;

— one-third specialist: retailers which have several branches and specialize in recorded music, eg WOM, Pro Markt, Montanus; and

— one-third independent: independent outlets (ie not chains) which specialize in recorded music excluding very specialized independents, eg those stores which only have, say, world music or jazz and second-hand record stores.

Fieldwork details

63. In Germany the survey was conducted by Basis Research. A total of 111 price checks was carried out between 6 and 13 September 1993. No major problems were experienced by interviewers except that:

— the collection of data in the smaller outlets was more difficult that in larger ones;

— the selected titles were not always available;

— cassettes are becoming increasingly difficult to find; and

— more often than not, upon ordering the title the shop assistants could not supply the interviewers with a price.

Market profile

64. The details for market profile were as follows:

248336   X2

| | per cent | |
	Sales	Outlets
Independent	50	39
Specialists	4	26
Multiples	46	34
— supermarkets/discount stores	14	9
— department stores	2	14
— radio/hi-fi stores	30	11

Source: Nielsen.

Denmark—sampling, fieldwork and market profile

Sampling

65. In order to obtain a regionally representative sample the four largest towns and their suburbs and 12 smaller towns were selected as sampling points. More specifically the following towns were selected:

Region	City/town	Number of outlets
Copenhagen	Copenhagen	10
	Tåstrup	3
Frederiksborg	Hillerød/Allerød/Birkerød	5
	Helsingør	5
Århus	Århus	7
	Brabrand	2
	Silkeborg	5
North Jutland	Ålborg	7
	Nørresundby	2
Fyn	Odense	7
	Blommenslyst	2
	Bogense/Middelfart	5
	Fåborg/Svendborg	5
Roskilde	Roskilde	5
West Zeeland	Slagelse/Høng/Dianaland	5
Viborg	Viborg	5
Vejle	Vejle	5
Ringkøbing	Herning	5
Ribe	Ribe/Vejen	5
South Jutland	Åbenrå	5

In order to set quotas according to retailer type, the following categories from the Dun & Bradstreet database were used as a sampling frame:

— varehuse (the equivalent of large supermarkets);
— department stores; and
— radio/television shops.

These categories were used as there was no separate section for outlets selling recorded music.

66. A nationally representative sample of 300 outlets was screened in order to identify the relevant shops and estimate the number of outlets within each main retailer type. A sample of 300 was deemed

sufficient since the total number of interviews required was 100. Out of those stores selling recorded music the distribution according to retailer type was as follows:

	%
Independents	10
Specialists	2
Radio/hi-fi stores	64
(independents	12)
(chains	52)
supermarkets/department stores	24

It appears therefore that there are very few outlets which only sell recorded music, and by far the most popular outlets are radio/hi-fi stores. The quotas set were broadly representative of the distribution by retailer type outlined above, except that independents and specialists were supplemented with names from *Yellow Pages* so that one specialist and two independents were visited in each sampling point if they existed.

Fieldwork details

67. In Denmark the survey was conducted by GFK Denmark. A total of 100 price checks was carried out between 6 and 11 September 1993. No major problems were experienced by interviewers except that:

— the collection of data in the smaller outlets was more difficult that in larger ones;

— the selected titles were not always available, particularly classical albums in smaller stores;

— cassettes are becoming increasingly difficult to find; and

— more often than not, upon ordering the title the shop assistants would not supply the interviewers with a price.

Market profile

68. The details of market profile were as follows:

	Outlets %
Independents/specialists	12
— independents	10
— specialist	2
Multiples	88
— radio/hi-fi stores	64
(independents	12)
(chains	52)
— supermarkets/department stores	24

Source: GFK screening of Dun & Bradstreet database.

BMRB International survey of retail prices, November 1993

Introduction

Background

1. BMRB International carried out a second price survey between 17 and 23 November 1993 in Great Britain and the USA only. For comparison purposes we have again used the average exchange rate for the period July to December 1993 ($1.50=£1).

The sample

2. The sample for the first survey comprised 250 outlets, drawn from *Yellow Pages*. A representative sample of 75 local expenditure zones (LEZs) was picked and within each a cluster of three to four outlets was selected. The sample used is representative of urban, suburban and regional retail locations and represents the types of retailer equally, and thus is not truly representative of the total market. All data are unweighted. Interviewers were provided with specific outlets and addresses at which to record prices, so that the structure of the sample might be maintained. In Great Britain the principal retailer types are:

specialist	— chains specializing in music (eg HMV, Our Price, Virgin);
independent	— specializing in music, but not part of a chain; and
multiple	— non-specialist in music (eg W H Smith, Woolworths).

3. For the second price survey a random 1 in 5 sample was drawn from the original 250 outlets, giving a total of 50 stores in Great Britain and in the USA, stratified by region and store type. However, due to operational reasons, three of the stores visited at the second stage in the USA were not part of the first survey.

Method

4. Fieldwork for the second survey was conducted between 17 and 23 November 1993. Interviewers visited the outlets selected and recorded the prices of 14 titles on both CD and cassette. Of the 14 pieces of music, 11 were pre-selected by the MMC with the other three being numbers 1, 5 and 10 in the national album chart in each country. As noted in paragraph 8 in Appendix 7.2, problems arose with the three classical titles included in the 11 mentioned above. Analyses of the results for these classical titles have therefore been omitted in the report below. If interviewers were unable to find the price of a title they were instructed to ask the price of the title if it was to be ordered.

Results

Pre-selected popular titles

5. For each title in the survey the price was recorded for both CD and cassette formats.

6. As noted in paragraph 14 of Appendix 7.2, the pre-selected titles were chosen by the MMC from short lists provided by the major record companies. This section covers the eight pre-selected popular titles. These titles were consistent between first and second price survey. We begin by commenting on the availability of each title.

Availability of pre-selected popular titles

7. One of the criteria on which pre-selected titles were chosen was that they were widely available in the countries surveyed. Although this was largely the case, there were still instances where a title was often not available, and it was rare for a title to be available at every store surveyed. If a title was not on the shelves, interviewers were instructed to ask store staff whether the title was in stock, or if not, whether it could be ordered. As in the first survey this gives us three measures of availability:

 (a) available from stock;

 (b) available to order; and

 (c) not available.

Table 1 lists the overall availability (ie *(a)* or *(b)*) of each pre-selected popular title in both of the countries surveyed.

TABLE 1 **Availability of pre-selected popular titles**

Base: All stores

| | Great Britain | | USA | |
	Survey 1	Survey 2	Survey 1	Survey 2
Number of stores in sample	249	50	250	50
				per cent
Diva—Annie Lennox				
CD	96	100	78	88
Cassette	96	98	81	86
Soul Dancing—Taylor Dayne				
CD	76	80	85	94
Cassette	75	78	86	90
Zooropa—U2				
CD	98	96	90	94
Cassette	97	96	91	94
Keep the Faith—Bon Jovi				
CD	98	98	88	90
Cassette	98	96	86	88
River of Dreams—Bill Joel				
CD	99	100	91	96
Cassette	89	100	89	96
Timeless—Michael Bolton				
CD	98	100	89	90
Cassette	97	100	88	96
Tubular Bells II—Mike Oldfield				
CD	97	98	60	72
Cassette	96	98	56	68
What's Love Got To Do With It?— *Tina Turner*				
CD	98	100	90	86
Cassette	98	100	87	90

Source: BMRB survey.

8. Overall, most titles were widely available in both surveys and were generally to be found in at least four-fifths of the stores surveyed. Where titles were available they were largely available from stock, a pattern consistent across surveys. However, at both stages, *Tubular Bells II* was noticeably less widely available in the USA than other pre-selected titles, and considerably less widely available than the same title in Britain.

9. Generally both formats for each title had similar availability. Cassettes were often less widely available in the first survey due to poor availability in Denmark and Germany, countries which were not surveyed in the second survey.

Prices of pre-selected popular titles

10. Table 2 shows the unweighted average price obtained for each of the pre-selected popular titles on both CD and cassette format at both waves of research. This figure is based on the number of stores where a price was obtained. The base therefore excludes stores where the title was unavailable. However, it varied from store to store as to whether store staff could give a price for a title that was only available to order. Therefore this has also depressed some base sizes.

TABLE 2 **Average prices of pre-selected popular titles***

Base: All stores where obtained a price

£ sterling

| | Great Britain | | | | USA | | | |
| | Without tax | | With tax | | Without tax | | With tax | |
	Survey 1	Survey 2	Survey 1	Survey 2	Survey 1	Survey 2	Survey 1	Survey 2
Diva—Annie Lennox								
CD	11.78	11.81	13.85	13.89	10.21	10.06	10.83	10.68
Cassette	8.11	8.28	9.53	9.73	6.79	6.81	7.19	7.23
Soul Dancing—Taylor Dayne								
CD	11.25	11.32	13.23	13.31	9.83	9.99	10.42	10.59
Cassette	7.91	8.04	9.29	9.45	6.67	6.85	7.06	7.28
Zooropa—U2								
CD	10.22	10.96	12.02	12.88	9.85	9.90	10.44	10.50
Cassette	7.07	7.47	8.31	8.78	6.39	6.57	6.77	6.97
Keep the Faith—Bon Jovi								
CD	10.56	10.99	12.42	12.92	10.53	10.25	11.15	10.87
Cassette	7.30	7.46	8.58	8.77	6.80	6.77	7.21	7.17
River of Dreams—Bill Joel								
CD	10.33	9.77	12.14	11.48	9.45	9.62	10.01	10.21
Cassette	7.12	6.72	8.37	7.91	6.17	6.24	6.53	6.61
Timeless—Michael Bolton								
CD	11.26	11.52	13.23	13.54	10.45	10.11	11.07	10.74
Cassette	7.76	8.01	9.13	9.41	6.79	6.69	7.19	7.10
Tubular Bells II—Mike Oldfield								
CD	11.71	12.02	13.76	14.13	10.21	9.99	10.81	10.60
Cassette	8.13	8.45	9.56	9.94	6.80	6.91	7.20	7.34
What's Love Got To Do With It?— Tina Turner								
CD	10.06	10.35	11.83	12.17	9.67	9.91	10.25	10.53
Cassette	7.24	7.31	8.51	8.59	6.42	6.77	6.80	7.19

Source: BMRB survey.

*Using average exchange rates for July to December 1993 ($1.50=£1).

11. The tables show prices with and without tax for Great Britain and the USA. The varying tax levels are detailed in paragraph 27. Each pair of prices (ie with and without tax) are calculated on individual bases, which vary as described above. All prices are in sterling.

12. The pattern of results is very consistent across the two surveys. The USA is cheaper than Britain for all eight titles on both formats across both surveys. This applies to prices both with and without tax. Thus the same overall conclusion can be drawn about the relative prices of these pre-selected titles in Great Britain and the USA as was apparent in the first survey. However, within

this overall framework the prices of some individual titles have changed significantly. For example, there has been a significant increase in the without-tax price of the U2 title in Great Britain, whereas the Billy Joel title has seen a significant drop in price. This will to some extent be a 'life-cycle' effect.

13. However, generally prices are more likely to have risen between surveys, particularly in Great Britain. This increase may reflect the timing of the two surveys, the second survey data suggesting a pre-Christmas retail price increase.

14. Another consideration is the extent to which titles were discounted via a sale or special offer. There was an option on the questionnaire for the interviewer to record whether a title was on special offer or in a sale. The responses are tabulated below for the second survey. However, it should be noted that this method will only record whether a title has been conspicuously discounted via a sticker or display. Also tabulated is a coefficient of variation for each title. This is calculated by dividing the standard deviation (SD) by the mean and multiplying by 100. This gives a measure of how widely distributed the recorded prices of each title are.

TABLE 3 **Comparison of coefficients of variation (without tax): second survey (November 1993)**

Base: All stores where obtained a price

£ sterling

	Great Britain				USA			
	Average	SD	Coeff of var	% special offer/sale	Average	SD	Coeff of var	% special offer/sale
Diva—Annie Lennox								
CD	11.81	0.96	8.13	4	10.06	1.02	10.14	7
Cassette	8.28	0.83	10.02	10	6.81	0.75	11.06	5
Soul Dancing—Taylor Dayne								
CD	11.32	0.73	6.45	-	9.99	1.03	10.35	13
Cassette	8.04	0.59	7.34	3	6.85	0.64	9.34	5
Zooropa—U2								
CD	10.96	0.86	7.85	6	9.90	1.49	15.02	20
Cassette	7.47	0.62	8.30	8	6.57	0.91	13.89	22
Keep the Faith—Bon Jovi								
CD	10.99	0.95	8.64	9	10.25	1.21	11.83	7
Cassette	7.46	0.66	8.85	9	6.77	0.77	11.33	5
River of Dreams—Bill Joel								
CD	9.77	1.13	11.57	21	9.62	1.27	13.24	38
Cassette	6.72	0.72	10.71	20	6.24	0.88	14.10	44
Timeless—Michael Bolton								
CD	11.52	1.33	11.55	4	10.11	1.55	15.36	12
Cassette	8.01	1.54	19.23	6	6.69	0.79	11.85	9
Tubular Bells II—Mike Oldfield								
CD	12.02	0.87	7.24	6	9.99	1.00	10.01	3
Cassette	8.45	1.02	12.07	4	6.91	0.66	9.55	-
What's Love Got To Do With It?— Tina Turner								
CD	10.35	1.62	15.65	17	9.91	1.00	10.09	9
Cassette	7.31	0.53	7.25	10	6.77	0.63	9.25	5

Source: BMRB survey.

15. As can be seen, and as was noted in Appendix 7.2, the practice of discounting appears to be more widespread in the USA. Clearly this in part explains why in all but 3 of the 16 cases the coefficient of variation is greater in the USA than in Great Britain. For the sake of comparison, the same measures are tabulated below for the first survey (September 1993).

TABLE 4 Comparison of coefficients of variation (without tax): first survey (September 1993)

Base: All stores where obtained a price

£ sterling

	Great Britain				USA			
	Average	SD	Coeff of var	% special offer/sale	Average	SD	Coeff of var	% special offer/sale
Diva—Annie Lennox								
CD	11.78	1.02	8.66	3	10.21	1.13	11.10	6
Cassette	8.11	0.64	7.89	3	6.79	0.87	12.86	4
Soul Dancing—Taylor Dayne								
CD	11.25	0.72	6.40	1	9.83	1.33	13.50	19
Cassette	7.91	0.89	11.25	1	6.67	0.99	14.89	15
Zooropa—U2								
CD	10.22	0.64	6.26	7	9.85	1.36	13.81	39
Cassette	7.07	0.48	6.79	6	6.39	0.92	14.40	40
Keep the Faith—Bon Jovi								
CD	10.55	0.84	7.95	8	10.53	1.34	12.73	9
Cassette	7.30	0.41	5.62	7	6.80	0.84	12.35	12
River of Dreams—Bill Joel								
CD	10.33	0.66	6.39	7	9.45	1.25	13.19	52
Cassette	7.12	0.43	6.04	7	6.17	0.91	14.80	49
Timeless—Michael Bolton								
CD	11.26	1.55	13.77	7	10.45	1.31	12.57	10
Cassette	7.76	1.03	13.27	5	6.79	0.81	11.98	8
Tubular Bells II—Mike Oldfield								
CD	11.71	1.05	8.97	1	10.21	1.09	10.64	5
Cassette	8.13	0.88	10.82	4	6.80	0.95	14.02	6
What's Love Got To Do With It?— Tina Turner								
CD	10.06	1.10	10.93	7	9.67	1.36	14.06	29
Cassette	7.24	0.79	10.91	17	6.42	1.09	17.03	29

Source: BMRB survey.

The chart titles

16. This section covers the three titles taken from the album chart in each country. It was decided to select numbers 1, 5 and 10 from the chart unless one of the preselected titles occupied one of these positions. In this eventuality the next position up (or down if number 1) was used. Full details of the titles selected are given in paragraph 24.

Availability of the chart titles

17. As would be expected for chart titles, availability was high with all titles being available in at least eight out of ten stores and most in nine out of ten with some reaching 100 per cent. Table 5 illustrates the availability of the three chart titles at both waves of research in Britain and the USA.

TABLE 5 **Availability of chart titles**

Base: All stores

	Great Britain		USA	
	Survey 1	Survey 2	Survey 1	Survey 2
Number of stores	249	50	250	50
				per cent
Number 1				
CD	99	100	90	98
Cassette	98	100	87	96
Number 5				
CD	83	100	80	98
Cassette	81	100	77	96
Number 10				
CD	99	98	92	86
Cassette	98	98	90	86

Source: BMRB survey.

Stocking levels were higher than for the eight pre-selected popular titles.

Prices of the chart titles

18. This section deals with the prices of widely demanded music in each of the countries represented in this research. Demand patterns for the pre-selected titles vary from country to country, while it is known that demand for the chart titles is high in each country. These data should be less title-sensitive. Table 6 shows the average price obtained for each of the chart titles at each survey.

TABLE 6 **Average prices of chart titles (sterling)**

Base: All stores where obtained a price

£ sterling

	Great Britain				USA			
	Without tax		With tax		Without tax		With tax	
	Survey 1	Survey 2	Survey 1	Survey 2	Survey 1	Survey 2	Survey 1	Survey 2
Number 1								
CD	10.34	10.16	12.15	11.94	9.69	9.45	10.27	10.02
Cassette	7.03	6.97	8.27	8.19	6.31	6.03	6.68	6.39
Number 5								
CD	10.15	10.40	11.93	12.22	9.49	9.29	10.06	9.86
Cassette	6.56	7.12	7.72	8.37	6.34	6.15	6.72	6.53
Number 10								
CD	10.43	10.36	12.26	12.18	9.65	9.69	10.22	10.29
Cassette	7.27	7.20	8.54	8.47	6.51	6.21	6.89	6.59

Source: BMRB survey.

19. There is a clear pattern that is consistent across both surveys. The USA is consistently cheaper for chart material than Britain, with prices without tax generally up to £1 less in the USA. This gap widens when we consider prices with tax since the taxes imposed in the USA are generally substantially lower than the 17.5 per cent VAT applied in Britain. The absolute differentials vary little by format, and so relatively the gap is greater for cassettes due to their cheaper price.

20. The coefficients of variation for each title in the second survey are shown in Table 7.

TABLE 7 Comparison of coefficients of variation (sterling without tax): second survey

Base: All stores where obtained a price

| | Great Britain | | | | USA | | | |
	Average	SD	Coeff of var	% special offer/sale	Average	SD	Coeff of var	% special offer/sale
Number 1								
CD	10.16	0.87	8.56	20	9.45	1.13	11.93	50
Cassette	6.97	0.38	5.45	18	6.03	0.79	13.16	57
Number 5								
CD	10.40	0.91	8.75	14	9.29	1.34	14.42	55
Cassette	7.12	0.59	8.29	16	6.15	0.90	14.63	52
Number 10								
CD	10.36	0.73	7.05	14	9.69	1.13	11.62	40
Cassette	7.20	0.44	6.11	10	6.21	0.75	12.12	48

Source: BMRB survey.

21. The coefficients of variation are higher in the USA for all three titles on both formats, indicating a greater variation in the range of prices observed. Undoubtedly this is driven to some extent by the apparently wider practice of discounting chart material in the USA. Approximately half of the prices collected for chart material in the USA for the second survey were known to be discounted. In Great Britain the highest incidence of discounting observed was 20 per cent for the number 1 CD. However, as previously noted, it is possible that discounting is less conspicuous in Britain than in the USA, and so would not have been recorded when the price was collected.

22. The equivalent figures for the first survey are tabulated below. Although levels may differ slightly, the same pattern of results is apparent, and so the same conclusions may be drawn.

TABLE 8 Comparison of coefficients of variation (without tax): first survey

Base: All stores where obtained a price

£ sterling

| | Great Britain | | | | USA | | | |
	Average	SD	Coeff of var	% special offer/sale	Average	SD	Coeff of var	% special offer/sale
Number 1								
CD	10.34	0.89	8.61	8	9.69	1.29	13.28	43
Cassette	7.03	0.47	6.69	8	6.31	0.88	13.95	43
Number 5								
CD	10.15	0.52	5.12	8	9.49	1.27	13.34	35
Cassette	6.56	0.56	8.54	7	6.34	0.98	15.46	32
Number 10								
CD	10.43	0.93	8.92	7	9.65	1.36	14.10	28
Cassette	7.27	0.52	7.15	6	6.51	0.99	15.15	28

Source: BMRB survey.

The titles researched

23. The eight pre-selected titles were as for the first survey. (See Appendix 7.2, paragraph 49.)

The three chart titles

24. As in the first survey, prices were collected for the albums positioned at numbers 1, 5 and 10 in the album chart of each of the countries. Details of the titles picked for the second survey were as follows:

UK

No 1   *Both Sides* by Phil Collins.
No 5   *One Woman: The Ultimate Collection* by Diana Ross.
No 10 *So Close* by Dina Carroll.

US

No 1   *Vs.* by Pearl Jam.
No 5   *Music Box* by Mariah Carey.
No 10 *In Utero* by Nirvana.

Exchange rate

25. The same exchange rate of $1.50 = £1 (the average for the period July to December 1993) has been used in the analyses of both surveys for the sake of comparability.

Tax rates

26. Tax rates during the second survey were as follows:

Country	Tax rate	
UK	17.5%	
USA	Varies by city and state:	%
	Seattle, Washington	6.50
	Washington DC	6.00
	San Francisco, California	8.00
	Los Angeles, California	8.25
	Phoenix, Arizona	5.00
	Dallas, Texas	8.25
	Des Moines, Iowa	4.00
	New Orleans, Louisiana	4.00
	Nashville, Tennessee	8.25
	Detroit, Michigan	4.00
	Miami, Florida	6.00
	Philadelphia, Pennsylvania	7.00
	Columbus, Ohio	5.75
	Boston, Massachusetts	5.00
	Atlanta, Georgia	4.00
	Albany, New York	8.00
	New York, New York	8.25
	Raleigh, North Carolina	5.00
	Denver, Colorado	3.00
	Salt Lake City, Utah	6.25
	Chicago, Illinois	6.25

27. A brief summary of sampling and fieldwork details for the USA survey is given below.

Sampling

28. Fifty out of the 250 stores surveyed in the first survey were revisited. The sample was still as geographically scattered as in the first survey and the following markets were covered:

Seattle, Washington	Philadelphia, Pennsylvania
Washington DC	Columbus, Ohio
San Francisco, California	Boston, Massachusetts
Los Angeles, California	Atlanta, Georgia
Phoenix, Arizona	Albany, New York
Dallas, Texas	New York, New York
Des Moines, Iowa	Raleigh, North Carolina
New Orleans, Louisiana	Denver, Colorado
Nashville, Tennessee	Salt Lake City, Utah
Detroit, Michigan	Chicago, Illinois
Miami, Florida	

327

Interviewers in these areas were contacted and instructed to revisit two to three of the 12 stores they had visited in the first survey. As before, interviewers were given quotas for the different retail outlets which were to be sampled in that area. In each market two to three 'interviews' were completed resulting in the following overall distribution:

— one-third multiple: retailers which have several branches and sell other goods as well as recorded music (principally mass merchandise or general merchandise chains such as Woolworths, K-Mart, Caldor and other department stores or discount stores with a music department);

— one-third specialist: retailers which have several branches and specialize in recorded music, eg Tower Records, Sam Goody, HMV, Coconuts; and

— one-third independent: independent outlets (ie not chains) which specialize in recorded music excluding very specialized independents, eg those stores which only have, say, world music or jazz and second-hand record stores.

Fieldwork details

29. In the USA the survey was conducted by Goldstein Krall Marketing Resources. A total of 50 price checks was carried out between 17 and 22 November 1993.

Average UK/US retail prices for full-price classical albums

	UK cat no	US cat no	Average UK £	Average US £	US/UK index (UK = 100)
Polygram					
Glass/Low Symphony/Brooklyn PO	4381502	As UK	12.33	9.44	77
Górecki/Beatus Vir/Totus Tuus/Nelson	4368352	As UK	12.54	9.88	79
Bernstein/'On the Town'/Tilson Thomas	4375162	As UK	12.37	9.22	75
Lemper, Ute/Illusions: Piaf & Dietrich	4367202	As UK	12.47	9.88	79
Bartoli, Cecilia/Love songs (Arie Antiche)/Fischer	4362672	As UK	12.33	9.88	80
Pavarotti, Luciano/& Friends	4401002	As UK	12.19	10.10	83
Bartoli, Cecilia/Song Recital/Schiff	4402972	As UK	12.33	9.44	77
Lemper, Ute/Sings Kurt Weill Vol2	4364172	As UK	12.47	9.88	79
Puccini: La Bohème Highlights/von Karajan	4212452	As UK	12.47	N/A	N/A
Puccini: Butterfly Highlights/von Karajan	4212472	As UK	12.47	N/A	N/A
Ti Amo-Puccini's Love Songs/Pavarotti		4250992	N/A	8.55	N/A
Rossini Arias/Bartoli, Cecilia/Patanè		4254302	N/A	9.88	N/A
EMI					
Kennedy, Nigel: Beethoven Violin Concerto	CDC 7545742	CD54574	12.47	9.88	79
Kennedy, Nigel: Vivaldi Four Seasons	CDC 7495572	CD49557	12.47	9.88	79
Te Kanawa, Dame Kiri: Best of	CDC 7545302	CD54530	12.47	9.88	79
Various Artists: Gershwin Crazy	CDC 7546182	CD54618	12.47	9.88	79
Te Kanawa, Dame Kiri: Kern Album	CDC 7545272	CD54527	12.42	9.88	70
Kennedy/Tortelier: Tchaikovsky Violin Concerto	CDC 7548902		12.47	N/A	N/A
Kennedy, Nigel: Brahms Violin Concerto	CDC 7541872		12.42	N/A	N/A
Various Artists: Classic Experience Vol 2	CDS 7944312		14.39	N/A	N/A
Kennedy/Rattle/Kamu: Tchaikovsky/Sibelius: Violin		CD54559	N/A	9.88	N/A
Perlman: Brahms Violin Concerto in D		CD54580	N/A	9.88	N/A
Hampson: American Dreamer		CD54621	N/A	9.88	N/A
Sony					
Christmas in Vienna: Carreras/Domingo/Ross	SK53358		12.04	9.44	78
The Seville Concert: John Williams	SK53359		12.09	N/A	N/A
Verdi: Ballet Music: Levine/Metropolitan	SK52489		12.17	N/A	N/A
Baroque Duet: Wynton Marsalis/Kathleen Battle	CD46672		12.13	N/A	N/A
Night and Day: Williams, John/Boston		SK67235	N/A	9.44	N/A
Tchaikovsky: Nutcracker: Ormandy, Eugene		MK06621	N/A	9.16	N/A
Live in Concert: Battle, Kathleen/Rampal		SK53106	N/A	9.44	N/A
Warner					
Górecki Symphony No 3: Upshaw/LS/Zinman	755979282	79282	12.18	9.33	77
With A Song in My Heart: Jose Carreras	450992369	92369	12.18	9.22	76
Sensual Classics: Various	450990055	90055	12.26	9.99	81
Ultimate Opera Collection: Various	229245797	45797	12.18	9.99	82
Satie Piano Music: Michel Legrand	450992857	92857	12.18	9.22	76
Short Stories: Kronos Quartet	755979310	79310	12.09	9.99	83
Górecki String Quartets: Kronos Quartet	755979319	79319	12.18	9.99	82
Opera Duets: Hampson & Hadley	903173283	73283	12.18	9.22	76
BMG					
Harnoy, Ofra: Vivaldi Concertos Vol 3	9026615782	As UK	12.27	9.88	81
Galway, James: Italian Flute Concerto	9026611642	As UK	12.37	9.88	80
Zukerman, Pinchas: Elgar Violin Con/Slatkin	9026616722	As UK	12.37	9.88	80
De Larrocha, Alicia: Ravel Concertos/Slatkin	9026609852	As UK	12.37	9.88	80
Ludwig, Christa: Farewell Recital	9026615472	As UK	12.30	9.88	80
Galway, James: Concerto! Mozart Flute and harp	9026617892		12.30	N/A	N/A
Douglas, Barry: Concerto! Rach: Piano Con No 2	9026616792		12.30	N/A	N/A
Kissin/Spivakov: Rachmaninov Piano Con No 3	9026615482		12.37	N/A	N/A
Lanza, Mario: The Legendary Tenor	RD86218		12.37	N/A	N/A
Takezawa Kyoko: Concerto! Bartok Violin Con No 2	9026616752		12.37	N/A	N/A
Galway, James: Mercadante Concertos		09026614472	N/A	9.88	N/A
Rubinstein: Last Recital for Israel		09026616602	N/A	9.88	N/A
Cliburn, Van: Tchaikovsky & Rachmaninov Cons		07863559122	N/A	9.88	N/A
Home—Von Stade: Duets		09026616812	N/A	9.88	N/A
Meyer: Mendelssohn Violin Concerto		09026617002	N/A	9.88	N/A

	UK cat no	US cat no	Average UK £	Average US £	US/UK index (UK = 100)
Average at prices shown (40 items in each country)			12.37	9.71	78
Average—items available in both UK and US (27 items)			12.32	9.74	79

Source: MMC from information provided by the UK retailers listed below.

Notes:

1. Prices are without tax.
2. US prices have been converted at £1 = $1.50 (the average exchange rate for the period July to December 1993).
3. The prices are the averages of those in force in the stores of the chains listed below:

Average UK price of:	*Average US price of:*
HMV (inc campaign offers)	HMV
W H Smith	The Wall
Our Price	
Virgin	
TMG (Sam Goody)	
Tower Records	Tower Records

Sony retail price survey

1. Sony carried out a survey of the retail prices of 85 of its titles across all price bands in the UK and the USA in October and December 1993. On the basis of the survey Sony calculated an average selling price weighted by sales volume to obtain an indication of the average price paid for recorded music by consumers in the two countries. The survey covered only the prices of Sony's records and therefore may not be representative of the overall market.

2. At our request Sony provided average prices for full-price pop titles. We refined the list of full-price titles further by removing any title that appeared to be priced at lower than full-price in the UK or the USA. This had the effect of reducing the difference in average prices for full-price titles compared with the original Sony result. Sony did not provide average prices for full-price classical titles. We have calculated averages of CD and cassette prices for full-price classical titles by selecting the full-price titles from the original sample.

3. The summary results of the Sony survey are presented in Table 1 for the same exchange rate as that used for the BMRB results (£1 = $1.50).

TABLE 1 **Summary results of Sony Music UK price surveys**

	UK average price (£)		US average price (£)*		Difference US/UK		Percentage difference US/UK	
	Full-price only	*All price categories*	*Full-price only*	*All price categories*	*Full-price only*	*All price categories*	*Full-price only*	*All price categories*
Non-classical								
CDs	10.53	10.32	9.92	9.73	0.61	0.58	-5.8	-5.6
Cassettes	7.25	7.09	6.45	6.32	0.80	0.77	-11.0	-10.9
Classical								
CDs	11.32	10.38	9.86	9.65	1.46	0.73	-12.9	-7.0
Cassettes	7.87	6.81	6.43	5.86	1.44	0.95	-18.3	-14.0

Source: Sony Music UK.

*Based on the average exchange rate for the period July to December 1993.

4. Sony also found, from an analysis of the average retail prices (unweighted) of Sony CDs in 13 US cities, that the range of prices to be found in the USA was greater than the differences between the UK and the USA.

Management Horizons UK/US price comparison survey
for leisure goods

Background

1. In parallel with the BMRB survey of recorded music pricing the MMC commissioned a separate study into the pricing of other leisure-related products in the UK and the USA. The purpose of this study was to establish whether CD price differentials between the two countries deviated substantially from the differentials found in other leisure product groups. Management Horizons has undertaken a price audit of a pre-defined basket of leisure goods in both countries. A summary of the results of the survey is given below.

Survey specification

2. The survey was designed so as to be sufficiently robust to draw reasonable conclusions. The objective was to obtain representative prices and not just anecdotal samples. To this end it was agreed that a large number of products would be surveyed, across a broad range of stores, but that the survey should be limited to one city in each country. We were advised by our consultants that greater price variations are found to occur between different products and between different stores than between different cities, because the overwhelming majority of store chains operate national pricing policies. Hence the inclusion of additional cities would have added substantially to the survey costs, without yielding proportionate benefits in terms of the results.

Survey cities

3. The cities selected for the survey were chosen to be as representative of each country as possible, in order to avoid introducing any unnecessary bias.

4. The following criteria were used to screen for suitable candidate cities:

(a) Wealth indicators to be representative of the national norm.

(b) Age profile to be representative of the national norm.

(c) Ethnic mix to be representative of the national norm (especially in the USA).

(d) Household composition/family composition to be representative of the national norm.

(e) Location of city not geographically isolated (ie no undue distribution costs).

(f) City sufficiently large to have a good representation of retailers.

5. The cities selected for the surveys were:

UK: Bristol
USA: Kansas City, Missouri

Stores audited

6. Rather than specifying a predetermined list of stores or channels to be surveyed for each product category, all of the stores within designated areas were audited in order to cover a more representative cross-section of retailers.

7. In the case of Bristol the designated areas were:

(a) the city centre (Broadmead); and

(b) Cribbs Causeway (the largest retail warehouse park in the Bristol area).

In the case of Kansas City the designated areas were:

(a) Metro North Mall (1.09 million square feet, North Kansas City); and

(b) Bannister Mall (1.15 million square feet, South Kansas City).

The malls chosen in Kansas City were both of modern build, with a diverse tenant mix, and were amongst the top three malls (by retail sales area) in the Kansas City area. The 'downtown' area of Kansas City was not included.

8. In addition the following important retailers or retail channels were specified for inclusion in the audit:

— a large supermarket (USA and UK);
— Toys 'R' Us (USA and UK);
— a large hardware/DIY store (USA and UK); and
— K-Mart (USA).

Products audited

9. The basket of products was selected to reflect the diversity of leisure-related products available in the USA and the UK. The following criteria were used to screen the products chosen:

— identical specification of products in both countries;

— principal price focus under £30, with a selection of more expensive items for comparison purposes;

— similar maturity of product category (and product) in both countries;

— similar mass-market positioning in both countries; and

— wide availability of products in both countries.

10. Of the total universe of leisure products in the USA and the UK only a small percentage was available with identical specifications in both countries, hence the breadth and depth of product category coverage was largely dictated by availability. However, this factor was not believed to introduce any systematic skew or to compromise the survey's objectivity.

11. In some instances the requirement for exact specification matches was relaxed:

(a) to accommodate differences in pack sizes on otherwise identical products; and

(b) to accommodate differences in product nomenclature on otherwise identical products.

12. Where pack sizes were different in each country adjustments were made during the analysis in order to make valid comparisons.

13. In addition to the core leisure-related products a number of consumable items were included within the survey for comparison purposes. These included batteries, toiletry items and some motoring items.

248336 Y2

14. The product categories included within the survey were:

Blank tapes	Electronic goods	Sports footwear
Books	Motoring	Stationery
Calculators	Personal electrics	Toiletries
DIY	Photographic goods	Toys and games
Electronic games	Sports equipment	

15. Products that were excluded on the basis of the criteria above include:

Watches
Golf clubs
PC software
Luggage/bags
Home security

In the case of watches the US assortment was generally more up-scale than the UK assortment, suggesting that the market positioning in the two countries was not comparable.

16. In the case of PC software the pricing of products was not transparent, with introductory offers and upgrade prices confusing the picture. In the case of golf clubs, luggage and home security very few identical products could be identified in both countries.

Auditing procedure

17. The audit was undertaken by Management Horizons personnel, using the same auditors in both countries for consistency of approach. The US audit was undertaken between 25 November and 4 December and the UK audit was undertaken in the period 6 to 11 December.

18. All stores were visited within the designated areas and any occurrences of the specified products were recorded. The price recorded was the price that the customer would actually pay (exclusive of sales tax in the USA) rather than the 'full price'. Hence the survey reflects the availability of special offers, promotions and sale prices; however, 'happy hour pricing' and 'privilege customer prices' were excluded.

19. Details of the date, location, store type, store name and any other pertinent information for each observation were recorded on pre-prepared audit sheets in the store. In particular a note was made where a particular item was being sold at a discount price. A score was also given to each store in order to record the relative importance of that store for the product in question.

Audit notes

20. The pricing survey was conducted after the American Thanksgiving holiday which marks the beginning of the Christmas shopping season. In recent years the major stores have tended to hold pre-Christmas sales timed to start on the day after Thanksgiving. In practice, although the sales generate a lot of publicity, they are very limited in scope offering deep discounts on a limited number of special purchase lines, plus smaller discounts on clothing. The special offers are generally 'stage-managed' and do not necessarily relate to products previously sold in the store. In addition the offers are generally confined to non-branded items to avoid an adverse impact on gross margins.

21. Amongst the basket of items audited within the survey very little seasonal discounting was observed in either the USA or the UK and Management Horizons concluded that the impact of seasonal factors on the study was minimal.

22. The range of stores included within the audit was believed to represent a good cross-section of the market in each country. Management Horizons concluded that no particular bias had been introduced into the survey on the basis of the coverage of stores.

Analysis of results

Sales tax and VAT

23. Prices recorded excluded sales tax in the USA, but included VAT in the UK. In order to make valid comparison all prices were analysed exclusive of tax. It should be noted that books and disposable nappies were zero rated for VAT.

Multipacks

24. Certain products are sold in a number of different multipack sizes. This is particularly true, for example, in the case of blank audio and video tapes. Given that the number of units per multipack can vary by store Management Horizons recorded the price for all available multipack variants in each store for the following products:

Post-It Notes	Tennis balls
Bic ball-point pens	Blank audio tape
Crayola crayons	Blank video tape
Golf balls	

25. In practice the distribution of multipack sizes was found to be very similar in the UK and the USA for all product categories, hence no skew to the results should be introduced by the inclusion of these categories. For the purpose of the analysis comparisons were made on the calculated price of a single unit, whether sold singly or in multipacks.

26. For the following products Management Horizons recorded prices for the standard multipack variant:

PC disks	Boxes of 10
Heated hair stylers	24 styler set
Heater hair rollers	20 roller set
Spark plugs	Pack of 4
Disposable razors	Pack of 10
Disposable nappies	24 pack
Polaroid film	2 x 10 exposures

27. The prices for these items were compared on a per-pack basis rather than on a single item basis. All other items were compared on a single item basis, including batteries even though these had been audited in packs of four.

Exchange rates

28. Prices reported were converted to pounds sterling. The exchange rate used to convert dollar prices to sterling was £1 = $1.50 for consistency with the BMRB survey.

Analysis table

29. The analysis table shown below covers four types of comparison:

(a) standard analysis: average price comparisons;

(b) store-weighted average price comparisons;

(c) average price comparisons (£5 to £20 price range); and

(d) 'bargain hunter' price comparisons.

The basis of each category of analysis is given below.

Standard analysis: average price comparisons

30. For each product audited, the arithmetical mean of all price observations has been calculated for the UK and for the USA. In order to standardize the price comparisons a price index has been calculated for each product. An index of 100 indicates an identical average price in the two countries, whilst an index of 90 indicates that the average price in the USA is 10 per cent lower than the average price in the UK.

31. In addition, summary indices have been calculated for each product category, these being the arithmetical mean of the individual indices of each product within the category.

Store-weighted average price comparisons

32. For each price recorded during the audit a score was assigned to the store in order to reflect the relative importance of that store for the product in question. The scoring system was structured as follows:

Score 1: Store is a much less important outlet than average for the given product (eg drugstore selling a small range of board games).

Score 2: Store is an outlet of average importance for the given product (the majority of observations would fall into this category).

Score 3: Store is a dominant outlet for the given product (eg Toys 'R' Us for board games).

33. The store-weighted average price comparisons were based upon a revised average price for each product which was a weighted average reflecting the importance of the store in each observation. The weightings used to calculate the revised average prices were.

Score	Weighting
1	0.5
2	1.0
3	2.0

Average price comparisons (£5 to £20 price range)

34. The analysis was limited only to those products with an arithmetic mean price in the UK range of £5 to £20.

'Bargain hunter' price comparisons

35. The 'bargain hunter' price comparison was based upon the lowest price found for each item in each country from which a 'bargain hunter index' has been calculated.

Audit sample size

36. Number of products audited   119
       Number of observations in UK   454
       Number of observations in USA   440
       Number of products priced £5 to £20[1]   33

Summary of findings

37. Table 1 summarizes the findings of the audit. The overall price index shown is the average of the without tax product category price indices, weighted by the national market sizes of each category in the UK.

Observations—general

38. Of the 119 products audited only 31 (26 per cent) were cheaper on average in the UK.

39. US prices were found to be 8 per cent lower than UK prices on the basis of the standard analysis of average prices.

40. An overall weighted index of 91.7 was recorded for the store-weighted price analysis. This index matches the index of 91.7 for the standard analysis reflecting the fact that relatively few stores were deemed to be considerably more or less dominant within the market for particular products.

41. When a filter is applied to include only those products with a UK average price of £5 to £20, even though the individual product category indices are found to vary from the standard analysis, nevertheless the overall weighted index is 91.4. The greater variation in individual product category indices is to be expected due to the smaller sample size of £5 to £20 items; however, the consistency of the overall weighted index provides some evidence that the findings are robust.

42. The overall weighted index for the 'bargain hunter' price comparison, where only the lowest prices for each product are compared, is rather lower at 88.5. This indicates that on average the differentials on lowest available prices are greater, and probably reflects the fact that the discount sector is a much more established part of US retailing than British retailing. For example, no direct equivalent of K-Mart or Wal-Mart, which are national chains of discount variety stores, exists in the UK.

43. The price index frequency distribution graphs show a very similar morphology for the following analyses:

     Standard analysis: average price comparisons
     Store-weighted price comparisons
     'Bargain hunter' price comparisons

In each case the highest frequency of observations is recorded for the interval 86 to 100, the second highest frequency being the interval 71 to 85.

44. The frequency distribution of average price indices for items between £5 and £20 is less well-clustered. The mode for this distribution is 76 to 85.

---

[1]Excludes products where single item prices were calculated from multipack prices. Price interval based upon average price (unweighted) in the UK.

TABLE 1   US/UK price indices (on a without-tax basis); end November 1993

Product category	Market size £m	Standard analysis average price index	Store-weighted average price index	Average price index (£5 to £20 only)	'Bargain hunter' price index
Books	1,500	93	93	122	93
Calculators	50	92	92	75	89
DIY (tools and equipment only)	470	81	81	79	81
Electrical (batteries and personal electricals only)	525	89	88	106	91
Electronic games	750	86	85	79	82
Electronics (personal stereo and keyboards only)	75	88	88	86	85
Motoring	120*	47	44	52	36
Photographic (film and equipment only)	970	91	91	84	86
Sports equipment	400	63	65	-	61
Sports footwear	1,100	97	98	-	95
Stationery	300†	99	97	78	93
Tapes (blank video and audio tape)	270	86	86	-	85
Toiletries (hair care, oral hygiene, razors and disposable nappies only)	1,500	120	120	-	109
Toys and games	800	91	91	-	90
Overall weighted index ‡		**91.7**	**91.7**	**91.4**	**88.5**

Source: Management Horizons.

*Consumable car cleaning products and spark plugs only.
†Writing instruments and PC discs only.
‡Weighted by UK market size.

Notes on product category specific observations

— *Books:* Book prices are relatively constant between stores. In the UK this is as a result of retail price maintenance through the net book agreement. In the USA the prices are also printed on the majority of books. Little discounting was found, and that was restricted to hardback books only. The average price index varied from 76 to 133, but for paperbacks the index ranged from 80 to 93.

— *Calculators:* Prices of calculators are relatively constant between stores in the UK, but a larger spread of prices was recorded in the USA. Considerable variability was found in the average price indices, which ranged from 51 to 141. A systematic difference was found by manufacturer.

— *DIY/household:* All DIY tools were found to be more expensive in the UK.

— *Electrical:* The majority of products were more expensive in the UK. All electrical items were chosen with care to avoid specification differences. Dual-voltage or battery models were selected where possible. The only minor difference between countries is the two-pin plug fitted.

— *Electronic games:* All hardware items were found to be more expensive in the UK. However, two of the software items were cheaper on average in the UK. Prices between stores were found to be very consistent, and only rarely was a substantially discounted price found. The distribution channels were similar in both countries and ranged from specialists, to electrical stores, variety stores and toy stores.

— *Electronics:* The item list was restricted to battery-powered items (personal stereos/headphones and keyboards) to avoid problems of specification mismatches, and no reception equipment was included for similar reasons. All but one of the items were found to be more expensive in the UK with the average price index ranging from 72 to 102. Item prices were found to be very consistent between stores.

— *Motoring:* The motoring category which included car care, additives and spark plugs showed far larger price differentials than other categories. In particular the petrol additive index was 28. (Anecdotal evidence suggests that across the spectrum motoring costs in the USA are cheaper with automobiles (although not directly comparable) being very competitively priced, and with unleaded gasoline still available for under $1.00 per gallon due to much lower duty.)

— *Photographic:* Relatively few low-priced camera models were found to be available in both countries, and in the case of the US audit each camera was only found in one store.

— *Sports equipment:* Few identical items could be found in both countries. The overall index of 63 for the category was strongly influenced by the very low indices for the selected tennis balls which were very much more expensive in the UK.

— *Sports footwear:* Care was taken to avoid auditing different items with the same model name (eg ranges from previous seasons).

— *Stationery:* Considerable variation existed between the average price indices for individual products, which ranged from 67 to 238. In addition the category was subject to a large variability in prices between stores.

— *Blank tapes:* Prices for both audio and video tape were more expensive in the UK. The distribution channels were broadly similar in both countries. Slight product differences existed for video tape between the countries. A T120 tape in the USA has a tape length of 247 metres whilst an E180 tape in the UK is 258 metres long, but in all other respects the products are identical.

— *Toiletries:* This category was the only one to be cheaper overall in the UK. Considerable variation in price differentials existed with indices ranging from 78 to 222.

— *Toys and games:* Whilst overall, prices were more expensive in the UK, nevertheless there were individual exceptions. Price indices ran from 75 to 133.

PolyGram's realized dealer prices

TABLE 1   **PolyGram: average realized dealer prices of popular CDs**

£ sterling equivalent*

	Full-price	Mid-price	Budget	Overall
UK	[			
USA				
Germany				
France				
Italy				
Spain				
Netherlands	*Figures omitted. See note on page iv.*			
Switzerland				
Belgium				
Sweden				
Denmark				
Japan				
Canada			]	

Indices of average realized dealer prices of popular CDs

UK	[			
USA				
Germany				
France				
Italy				
Spain				
Netherlands	*Figures omitted. See note on page iv.*			
Switzerland				
Belgium				
Sweden				
Denmark				
Japan				
Canada			]	

Source: MMC based on company information.

---

*Reconverted from Dutch guilder equivalents to sterling equivalent (July to December 1993 average rates). Prices have only been converted from Dutch guilders into pounds sterling for 13 of the 20 countries in the PolyGram study.

TABLE 2 PolyGram: average realized dealer prices of classical CDs

| | £ sterling equivalent* | | | |
	Full-price	Mid-price	Budget	Overall
UK	[			
USA				
Germany				
France				
Italy				
Spain				
Netherlands	*Figures omitted. See note on page iv.*			
Switzerland				
Belgium				
Sweden				
Denmark				
Japan				
Canada			]	

Indices of average realized dealer prices of popular CDs

UK	[			
USA				
Germany				
France				
Italy				
Spain				
Netherlands	*Figures omitted. See note on page iv.*			
Switzerland				
Belgium				
Sweden				
Denmark				
Japan				
Canada			]	

Source: MMC based on company information.

*Reconverted from Dutch guilder equivalents to sterling equivalent (July to December 1993 average rates). Prices have only been converted from Dutch guilders into pounds sterling for 13 of the 20 countries in the PolyGram study.

The core business results of each of the major record companies

[

Details omitted. See note on page iv.

]

[

Details omitted. See note on page iv.

]

[

Details omitted. See note on page iv.

]

[

Details omitted. See note on page iv.

]

[

Details omitted. See note on page iv.

]

[

Details omitted. See note on page iv.

]

248336   Z

[

Details omitted. See note on page iv.

]

[

]

Details omitted. See note on page iv.

248336   Z2

[

Details omitted. See note on page iv.

]

[

Details omitted. See note on page iv.

]

Extract from KPMG Peat Marwick's report on business valuations

1   Introduction and background

2   Methodologies

3   Calculation of turnover multiple

4   Adjustments to the Companies' financial statements

Appendices

1   **Introduction and background**

1.1   As part of the Monopolies and Mergers Commission's ('MMC') inquiry into the recorded music industry, this paper sets out possible methodologies for evaluating profits and assets not recorded in the accounts of the UK recorded music businesses of the major recorded music companies (the 'Companies').

1.2   Having recommended the most appropriate valuation method based on the information available, this paper provides a rough gauge estimate of corresponding adjustments over three years to the underlying profitability and build-up of value in respect of each company's operating results and provides calculations of the return on turnover and on capital employed which reflect these adjustments, together with any qualifications on their usefulness.

1.3   In the initial brief prepared by the MMC in connection with this exercise the MMC noted that:

'the effect of the companies' prudent accounting policies was that their profits do not reflect any change in the value of their copyrights.'

1.4   There have been a number of major international acquisitions of music businesses in recent years. In all cases the acquiring company was prepared to pay a significant amount in excess of the acquired company's assets. Inter alia, this excess represents the value of the copyrights of recorded music which is not reflected on the balance sheet.

1.5   [Not reproduced].

1.6   **It must be emphasised that the methodologies, and therefore any calculations, are limited by the extent of the information provided to us and by what is possible within any desk top exercise.** In order to perform a more detailed and more rigorous evaluation of the underlying profits and assets of the Companies, we would require access to the financial records and catalogues of the Companies.

1.7   In particular we would seek to obtain from the Companies projections of the future earnings of individual copyrights, together with their revenue history. Having established future earnings of the catalogue as a whole, its value would be calculated by discounting the future net earnings stream to obtain its net present value.

1.8   However, given the inherent uncertainty in any projections of future earnings, particularly in respect of popular recorded music, a desk top exercise based on appropriate assumptions can provide a workable solution.

1.9   We have not independently verified any of the information included within this report and express no opinion on its accuracy. Where appropriate we have included an indication of the source of information provided.

2   Methodologies

2.1   Based on available information, possible methodologies for valuing the underlying assets not currently shown in the accounts of the Companies are as follows:

(1)   Obtain information on recent acquisitions of recorded music businesses and establish a 'rule of thumb' multiple, or range of multiples, of the purchase price compared to historic turnover ('turnover multiple'). The turnover multiple could then be applied to each of the Company's trading results to establish underlying economic asset value,

(2)   As for (1) above but based on earnings ('earnings multiple') rather than turnover.

(3)   Establish a market average historic price earnings ratio ('PE basis') based on US and UK stock market information. Having established a PE ratio for each year, this could then be applied to each of the Company's results to establish underlying economic asset values.

(4)   Establish an accounting policy for expensing artist and repertoire ('A&R') expenditure to ensure that the annual charge to the profit and loss account matches the income stream to which it relates ('A & R capitalisation'). Having established the accounting policy, each of the Company's results could be amended to reflect the new policy.

2.2   Having established the economic asset value of each of the Companies at various period ends, the economic profitability for the period since the last economic value was established, is the movement less the effects of acquisitions. We will refer to this movement as the economic profitability and it represents a combination of profits recorded in the companies' profit and loss accounts and the unrealised economic profit arising as a result of the increase in the value of copyrights.

Turnover multiple

2.3   The turnover multiple basis is relatively straight forward to calculate and can be supported by a significant number of relevant transactions. As the multiple is based on completed sale and purchase transactions, it will reflect market values of recorded music businesses at the time of the transaction.

2.4   This basis has been applied to other industries. For example it was a common 'rule of thumb' for advertising agencies during the 1980s to be bought and sold at 1.5 times prior period's billings. Similar bench marks also developed in the publishing industry. In addition it has been estimated that the remaining value of a mature television film library will approximate to 4 or 5 times the estimated earnings in the following 12 month period.

2.5   This basis of valuation is limited to the extent that the price paid on acquisition may reflect other factors in addition to the underlying value of the business. For example, as the ownership of the 'majors' has concentrated, the value of any remaining quality 'independent' has increased.

2.6   Furthermore the excess of the purchase price over the net assets will not only reflect the value of the catalogue of copyrights but will also include other components which contribute to goodwill. For example, the purchaser's evaluation of the management team and the extent to which they can be 'tied in' to the enlarged group. Another factor is the quality of the company's distribution network or its perceived ability to attract new artists. For the purposes of this paper, we will refer to these other components as 'trademarks'.

Earnings multiple

2.7 The earnings multiple basis of calculating the underlying value is similar to that of the turnover multiple. It has the advantage over the turnover basis of incorporating the cost of exploiting the copyrights but is more likely to be distorted by non-recurring or unusual items.

2.8 For example, earnings will be affected by the level of A & R expenditure. As has already been discussed above the level of A & R expenditure charged to any individual year's profit and loss account is not necessarily matched against the anticipated revenue flow.

2.9 The international and diversified nature of the Companies' businesses means their earnings could be affected by inter-group charges and transfer prices outside of normal commercial terms.

PE Basis

2.10 The PE basis would require calculating an average price earnings ratio for any recorded music business. This method is similar to the previous two methodologies but would exclude any bid premium which would be inherent on valuations based on completed acquisitions. It could also be calculated at the date the shares of a recorded music business became publicly traded. There have been three flotations of music businesses over the last ten years, Chrysalis, Virgin and PolyGram.

2.11 Given that there are now few, if any, pure recorded music businesses whose shares are quoted on a recognised stock exchange it would be necessary to use businesses with more than one significant earnings stream. Accordingly, any valuation basis would have to eliminate the non-recorded music business income. This would require assumptions which might reduce the underlying accuracy of the valuation.

2.12 As the PE basis will be directly related to the market capitalisations of the individual companies they will be affected by general market confidence and perception over and above the underlying businesses value.

2.13 Further, the PE basis will be affected by the accuracy of stockbrokers' estimates of future earnings.

A & R capitalisation basis

2.14 The A & R capitalisation basis of calculating the underlying value is based on the assumption that expenditure on A & R is not matched to the relevant earnings stream.

2.15 A & R expenditure is a recorded music businesses' investment in copyright. Copyrights, if owned outright rather than licensed, have a life of 50 years and therefore can potentially earn revenues for 50 years.

2.16 The earning cycle of any copyright is directly related to the nature and success of the artist and related recording. Further earnings also arise as new formats (CD, CDi, etc) are established. Whilst successful recordings work in the 1960s are still earning revenues for the copyright owners, many others fail to recoup the initial A & R expenditure.

2.17 The A & R capitalisation basis of valuation assumes that for any major recorded music business there is a sufficient portfolio of copyrights to pool the A & R costs and establish an average period over which earnings will be generated. This period would be used as the basis of amortisation.

2.18   The information provided to the MMC by the Companies would provide some information as to the appropriate amortisation period which could be combined with more general market information. In addition sufficient information has been provided in respect of A & R expenditure since 1989. Together with underlying assumptions, a basis would need to be established for determining the brought forward capitalised A & R balance for 1989.

2.19   The A & R capitalisation basis would be an appropriate basis if the purpose of this exercise was to establish a methodology which was supportable under generally acceptable accounting principles. However such methodology would not incorporate any increase in the economic value of the underlying goodwill as a result of a copyright being more successful than the average. Accordingly it would not reflect the speculative nature of some A & R expenditure.

Conclusion

2.20   Based on available information it is considered that the most appropriate desk top valuation method for the Companies would be the application of the turnover multiple basis.

2.21   This conclusion is based on the following matters discussed earlier:

- An earnings basis would be corrupted by unusual transactions and any inter-group charges and transfer pricing issues.

- Stock market valuations are affected by forces in addition to the underlying value of a business and are likely to be difficult to obtain for pure recorded music businesses. Fair valuations are probably only available at the date of flotation, information on which is probably too old.

- The A & R capitalisation basis does not reflect any increase in economic value of the related business.

3   **Calculation of turnover multiple**

3.1   The turnover multiple has been calculated using historic information collected on 15 of the largest acquisitions in the music industry since 1986. The sources of this information are contained in the glossary included at Appendix I.

3.2   An estimation of the turnover multiple of 1.2 has been calculated and the detailed calculations are included at Appendix II. The general principles applied to each acquisition are summarised below.

Translation to sterling

3.3   All transactions are in or converted to pounds sterling. Where applicable, the US dollar value of the acquisition has been translated into sterling using the exchange rate at the date of the acquisition. Additionally, the US dollar value of the target company's turnover for the accounting period preceding the acquisition has also been translated into sterling using the exchange rate at the date of acquisition.

Turnover adjustment

3.4   Where applicable, the sterling turnover figure detailed in paragraph 3.3 has been adjusted to reflect the percentage of the target company acquired. This adjustment has been calculated by reducing the sterling turnover figure to the percentage of the share capital of the target company acquired.

Simple turnover multiple

3.5   A simple turnover multiple has then been calculated by dividing the sterling acquisition value by the sterling value of the turnover acquired.

3.6   It is apparent that the simple turnover multiple derived from the PolyGram acquisition of 30% of the share capital of Really Useful Holdings is significantly different from the other 14 turnover multiples calculated.

[Not reproduced]

... and consequently this acquisition has been excluded from the final turnover multiple calculation.

Bid premium and trademark adjustment

3.7   The simple turnover multiple has then been adjusted to remove the effect of a premium paid on acquisition ('bid premium') and for the value of the target company's trademarks ('trademark adjustment').

3.8   It is a 'rule of thumb' in the City that if a serious bid is to be made by an acquiring company for a target company, the initial offer should be in the order of 25% above the current market capitalisation of the target company. This reflects the premium on control compared to the value of small shareholdings. Consequently the simple turnover multiple has been adjusted to remove this bid premium.

3.9   Our knowledge of the music industry indicates that the value of a trademark of a record company represents of the order of 10% of the purchase price required to acquire that company. Therefore we have adjusted the simple turnover multiple for this trademark adjustment.

Adjusted turnover multiple

3.10   The adjusted turnover multiple for each of the individual acquisitions, excluding the PolyGram acquisition of Really Useful Holdings, have been summed and the result divided by 14. This calculation produced a simple average for the adjusted turnover multiple of 1.2. A weighted average multiple would have produced a similar result.

4   Adjustments to the Companies' financial statements

4.1   Based on the assumption that the underlying value of a recorded music business represents 1.2 times prior year turnover, set out below is an aggregation of the Companies' profit and loss accounts for 1991, 1992 and 1993, together with aggregated balance sheets for 1990, 1991, 1992 and 1993 after making any adjustments considered appropriate. Appendix III sets out this information in respect of each of the individual Companies.

Figure 4.1: Aggregation of profit and loss accounts

	1989 £'000	1990 £'000	1991 £'000	1992 £'000	1993 £'000
Turnover					
Net sales of records	382,054	441,462	454,611	471,410	497,696
Royalties, licence fees etc	182,072	204,412	235,940	346,455	344,596
Joint venture revenue	14,829	16,605	11,101	17,474	21,477
Third party label distribution	11,175	13,418	12,087	14,619	15,874
Other activities	21,912	19,310	15,142	18,261	18,236
Total	**612,042**	**695,207**	**728,881**	**868,219**	**897,879**
Contribution before A&R expenses, interest and tax					
Record sales			26,219	(6,960)	855
Royalties, licence fees etc			90,663	138,902	144,063
Joint ventures			(412)	989	1,726
Third party label distribution			4,928	4,969	4,100
Other activities			832	160	668
Total			**122,230**	**138,060**	**151,412**
A&R expenses					
Gross expenditure			(164,160)	(218,249)	(183,150)
Recoupment, capitalisations and movements in provisions			74,788	109,485	87,657
Written off to profit and loss account			**(89,372)**	**(108,764)**	**(95,493)**
Profit before interest and tax as reflected in the Companies' financial statements			**32,858**	**29,296**	**55,919**
Adjustment			**23,420**	**(13,855)**	**32,318**
Economic profit (see fig 4.5)			**56,278**	**15,441**	**88,237**

Source: MMC/KPMG calculation

4.2 It should be noted that the balance sheets of the Companies reflect only the recorded music businesses and that financial information for 1993 is estimated. Furthermore the financial results of Sony for 1992 represent a fourteen month period. We have only sought to adjust this for the purposes of calculating the underlying value.

Figure 4.2: Aggregation of balance sheets

[Not reproduced]

Figure 4.3: Note to the aggregation of balance sheets

	1990 £'000	1991 £'000	1992 £'000	1993 £'000
Prior year turnover multiplied by 1.2	734,450	834,248	874,657	1,041,863
Adjustment to reflect full years turnover	21,387	2.012	(22,956)	
Valuation of business	755,837	836,260	851,701	1,041,863

Source: MMC/KPMG calculation

4.3 The adjustments set out in the above table are to reflect the effects of acquisitions. For the purposes of calculating the underlying value of a business, the full year's turnover of an acquired company has been included in the calculation for the year of acquisition.

4.4 The difference between the underlying value of the recorded music businesses as calculated by the turnover multiple, and their net asset value including any investment in artists already included on the balance sheet, is assumed to represent the value of the Companies' catalogue of copyrights.

4.5 **Figure 4.4: Underlying value not currently reflected in the balance sheets**

[Not reproduced]

4.6 The increase in the underlying value, not recorded in the Companies' balance sheets, comprises the effects of acquisitions together with any organic movement in the economic value of the businesses. Our estimate of this is as follows:

Figure 4.5: Increase in the underlying value

	1991 £'000	1992 £'000	1993 £'000
Increase due to acquisitions	24,145	-	101,925
Organic movement in the value of underlying businesses (Economic profitability)	56,278	15,441	88,237
Total increase	80,423	15,441	190,162

Source: MMC/KPMG calculation

4.7 The resulting return on turnover and capital employed is as follows:

Figure 4.7: Return on turnover and capital employed

Return on turnover

	1991 %	1992 %	1993 %	Average %
Total	7.7	1.8	9.8	6.4

Return on capital employed

	1991 %	1992 %	1993 %	Average %
Total	6.7	1.8	8.5	5.7

Source: MMC/KPMG calculation

4.8 The effect of the basis of the adjustment to profitability is that the Companies' earnings are dependent upon the increase or decrease in turnover between the year immediately prior to the year in question, and the year before that. Accordingly as turnover remained relatively flat in 1991 but showed increases of 14% in 1990 and 19% in 1992, economic profitability for 1992 is significantly lower than other periods. Therefore, the adjusted profitability is more sensitive to general economic pressures than that calculated under generally accepted accounting principles. Accordingly, the returns for any one year should be viewed with caution.

4.9 As a result of the methodology for calculating economic profit and economic values of the businesses we do not consider that the return on capital employed ratios provided above to be meaningful as they are circular.

4.10 Due to the available information and the basis of calculation it has only been possible to provide three years of adjusted profits. In order to provide an indication of the movement over time we recommend that this exercise should be extended to earlier years.

Appendix II

Calculation of turnover multiple

Acquiror	Target	Date	Currency Value in millions	£:$ rate	Value in sterling in millions	Total turnover of target in currency in millions	$:£ rate	Turnover adjustment	Acquired turnover in sterling in millions	Simple turnover multiple	Bid Premium and Trademark adjustment of 35%*	Adjusted turnover multiple
Bertelsmann	RCA (75%)	1986	$300	1:1.48	£202.7	$850	1:1.48	0.75	£430.70	0.47	0.74	0.35
Sony	CBS Records	1987	$2,000	1:1.77	£1,129.9	$1490	1:1.77		£841.80	1.34	0.74	0.99
Fujisankei	Virgin Music Group (25%)	1989	$150	1:1.56	£96.0	£239.00	1	0.25	£59.75	1.61	0.74	1.19
PolyGram	A&M Records	1989	$500	1:1.62	£308.6	$250	1:1.62		£154.32	2.00	0.74	1.48
PolyGram	Island Records	1989	$322	1:1.57	£205.1	$200	1:1.57		£127.40	1.61	0.74	1.19
Thorn EMI	Chrysalis (50%)	1989	$96.6	1:1.55	£62.3	$44.40	1	0.50	£22.20	2.81	0.74	2.08
Matsushita	MCA (NB not just music)	1990	$6,600	1:1.93	£3,419.7	$3300	1:1.93		£1,709.80	2.00	0.74	1.48
MCA	Geffen Records	1990	$550	1:1.64	£335.4	$275	1:1.64		£167.70	2.00	0.74	1.48
Thorn EMI	Filmtrax	1990	£48.20	1	£48.2	£19.41	1		£19.41	2.48	0.74	1.84
PolyGram	Really Useful Holdings (30%)	1991	£78.00	1	£78.0	£54.30	1	0.30	£16.29	4.79	0.74	3.55
Thorn EMI	Virgin Music Group	1992	$957	1:1.61	£593.0	£330.00	1		£330.00	1.80	0.74	1.33
Warner Music Finland	Fazer Musiikki	1993	£16.50	1	£16.5	£31.70	1		£31.70	0.52	0.74	0.39
PolyGram	Motown	1993	$300	1:1.49	£201.3	$133.3	1:1.49		£89.47	2.25	0.74	1.67
[†]												
[†]												
								Total		27.44		20.33
								Less: Really Useful Holdings		4.79		3.55
								Adjusted total		22.65		16.78
								Simple average		1.62		1.20

*Turnover multiple/(Turnover multiple + bid premium + trademark adjustment) = 100/(100 + 25 + 10) = 100/135 = 0.74
†Information on two transactions is not reproduced in this appendix.

Source: KPMG from information within the public domain.

**The major record companies: reconciliation of results shown
in Table 8.10 with the results shown in Table 8.5**

[

Details omitted. See note on page iv.

]

Discounts and other allowances from record companies to their customers

[

Details omitted. See note on page iv.

]

[

Details omitted. See note on page iv.

]

248336 2A

[

Details omitted. See note on page iv.

]

[

Details omitted. See note on page iv.

]

Products and services bought-in from connected companies and divisions

1. In addition to royalty payments to connected companies overseas for licensed-in repertoire, all the majors' recorded music businesses buy in cassettes, or CDs or products in other formats from connected companies or divisions. Also in some cases distribution is undertaken by connected self-accounting units. So as to illustrate the range of such transactions, we set out in Table 1 the majors' recorded music businesses expenditures in 1992 (our aggregate year—see paragraph 8.12) with connected companies and divisions in the UK and overseas.

TABLE 1 **The majors' recorded music businesses: expenditure on manufacturing, distribution and other activities bought-in from connected companies and divisions, 1992**

£ million

Year ended	BMG June 1992	EMI March 1993	PolyGram Dec 1992	Sony March 1993	Warner Nov 1992	Total
Connected businesses in the UK						
Manufacturing*		[¤	[¤]	[¤]		43.3
Distribution†		¤				23.8
Other‡		]				1.5
Connected businesses outside the UK						
Manufacturing§	[		¤		]	41.0
Other¶					[¤]	2.8

Source: MMC from companies' data.

---

*Manufacturing
EMI: CD Swindon £[¤]m; EMI Music Services £[¤]m
PolyGram: Philips, Blackburn £[¤]m
Sony: Sony Music Operations £[¤]m

†*Distribution*
EMI: EMI Music Services £[¤]m
PolyGram: PRO, Chadwell Heath £[¤]m
Sony: Sony Music Operations £[¤]m

‡*Other*
EMI: EMI Recording £[¤]m

§*Manufacturing*
BMG: Sonopress £[¤]m; Other £[¤]m
PolyGram: Amersfoort (Holland) £[¤]m; ISC (Germany) £[¤]m; Louviers (France) £[¤]m; Other £[¤]m
Sony: ISC (Holland) £[¤]m; DADC (Austria) £[¤]m
Warner: Warner Music Manufacturing Europe £[¤]m

¶*Other*
Warner: WMIS—Video clip costs £[¤] m; Tour support £[¤]m; Management fee £[¤]m;
            Time Warner—Miscellaneous £[¤]m; US product distribution £[¤]m

2. The basis of transfer pricing between the majors' recorded music businesses and their principal connected suppliers of products and services is set out below.

BMG

3. Albums are manufactured through BMG's associated Central Manufacturing Group (CMG) in Germany. Manufacturing contracts are arranged by CMG with Sonopress, a subsidiary of BMG's parent company Bertelsmann AG, and with other suppliers. Prices are negotiated centrally with CMG

¤Figures omitted. See note on page iv.

for all BMG record companies within Europe. CMG guarantees a set 'standard' price irrespective of order size with additional costs for variable finishes. The price is negotiated annually on an arm's length basis and reflects the range of anticipated orders and reorders from all group companies in Europe. BMG's singles are manufactured outside the BMG group and are purchased on an arm's length basis.

EMI

4. The basis for transfer pricing of recording at EMI's recording studios is arm's length and reflects market prices. All EMI artists have a choice of where to record their music which includes the UK studios owned by EMI. A price list is available for all users of EMI recording studios and discounts can be negotiated depending on such factors as time purchased and equipment used. In 1992/93 just under half the revenues of EMI recording studios were provided by EMI record companies but these received no preferential discounts because of their membership of the EMI group.

5. Manufacturing prices vary according to the product specification and, with rare exceptions, EMI Manufacturing charges the same price per unit irrespective of order size for an identical specification. The basis of pricing is to recover costs and, for simplicity, costs are averaged over all production for all sites. Comparisons between this 'blended' or average price and market rates are made and negotiations take place annually between management at EMI Marketing and EMI Manufacturing before prices are agreed. The market rates are those that would be payable to a reliable supplier for a large-volume, year-long flexible contract that ensures sufficient capacity at all times including the (pre-Christmas) busy season and which meets EMI's service requirements. For distribution services the basis of transfer pricing is estimated cost of the service provided plus a small fixed profit percentage.

PolyGram

6. PolyGram in the UK is a member of the PolyGram International Group. With the exception of manufacturing products and associated finished artwork, all activities are dealt with by each local PolyGram company on a self-contained basis. In the case of PolyGram UK the majority of new popular releases are obtained on an arm's length basis from Philips Blackburn which is owned by Philips, PolyGram UK's ultimate parent company. In 1992 Philips Blackburn supplied [*] per cent of its CD requirements. A further [*] per cent of PolyGram's CD requirement—for classical and catalogue product—was met by the Supply Centre in Hanover, Germany, which is part of the PolyGram International Group. The balance of CDs is supplied from PolyGram International Group's plant in Louviers, France. Cassette products are supplied from local plants in the UK (eg Ablex and TDC) and from PolyGram International Group's plant at Amersfoort, in the Netherlands. Singles are obtained from local third party manufacturers except for CD singles which are supplied by Philips Blackburn.

7. For PolyGram UK's purchases of records from within the PolyGram International Group it pays a Factory Standard Price for all products supplied. The prices charged by Philips Blackburn are negotiated on a group-wide arm's length basis between Philips UK and PolyGram International Music BV. These prices are calculated by reference to the fixed and variable costs of manufacture and overhead. Prices charged by Hanover and Louviers are based on factors combining costs of both manufacture and distribution and include the costs of keeping the entire catalogue available, inventory obsolescence, and storage and distribution costs (including costs associated with holding 15,000 line items available in small quantities at short notice). However, prices quoted vary according to order run, quantity, packaging and other special features. Cassette prices, including supplies from Amersfoort, are all at arm's length as are singles prices and supplies of vinyl records (from COPS, an unconnected third party supplier).

---

*Figures omitted. See note on page iv.

Sony

8. The Sony recorded music business is charged a 'manufacturing cost' for each unit supplied by Sony manufacturing divisions. For products manufactured in the UK ie cassette product, manufacturing cost is fixed at the start of each financial year and equates to the fully absorbed cost (termed the 'standard cost') incurred by the manufacturing centre. The overriding principle is that the price charged by the manufacturing division should fully absorb all costs of manufacture. For products manufactured overseas, ie CDs and vinyl, the manufacturing cost is negotiated annually having regard to open market prices and, as with products manufactured in the UK, is fixed at the start of the financial year. However, overseas supplies are charged in the currency of the supplying plant. The same principles apply to distribution as to manufacture, ie fees are fixed at the start of the financial year so as to absorb fully the costs of the distribution centre.

Warner

9. Most CD albums sold by Warner in the UK are manufactured by Warner's affiliate in Alsdorf, Germany—Warner Music Manufacturing Europe GmbH (WMME). Manufacturing at Alsdorf is almost solely for Warner companies in Europe. Prices charged by WMME are based on a standard price list with adjustments for special requirements. This standard price list is calculated on an arm's length basis which reflects the level of service WMME provides. Other format supplies are from third party manufacturers in the UK at arm's length prices. Prices vary from list for a number of reasons including delivery times, mastering, coding, artwork and so on. Warner UK distributes all its own product through its distribution centre and also acts as distributor for three other record labels (PWLI, Beggars Banquet and Solid).

10. For the principal connected companies and divisions in the UK, the results of their business with the majors' UK recorded music businesses are summarized in Tables 2 to 6 and paragraph 11.

TABLE 2   **EMI: manufacturing companies' transactions with the recorded music business**

					£ million
	Year to 31 March				
	1990	*1991*	*1992*	*1993*	*1994 estimated*
Sales to recorded music business					
EMI Music Services	[				
CD Swindon					
EMI Music Services					
Sales to recorded music business (A)					
Operating profit (B)					
Average capital employed (C)					
Return on sales (%) (B/A)					
Return on capital employed (%) (B/C)	*Figures omitted. See note on page iv.*				
CD Swindon					
Sales to recorded music business (A)					
Operating profit (B)					
Average capital employed (C)†					
Return on sales (%) (B/A)					
Return on capital employed (%) (B/C)†					]

Source: EMI.

[*Details omitted. See note on page iv.*]

†Total capital employed pro-rated on basis of sales to connected companies in UK and sales to all other connected companies.

Note: Percentages may not correspond exactly to the figures shown because of rounding.

TABLE 3   PolyGram: manufacturing company's transactions with the recorded music business*

		Year to 31 December			£ million	
	1989	1990	1991	1992	1993 estimated
Philips Blackburn					
Sales to recorded music business (A)	[				
Operating profit (B)					
Return on sales (%) (B/A)		*Figures omitted. See note on page iv.*			
Return on capital employed (%)†					]

Source: PolyGram.

---

*Philips Blackburn was unable to supply information on its sales and results with its connected companies in the UK for 1989.

†Philips Blackburn was unable to identify capital employed on its business with PolyGram UK. The ROCE figures in percentages for its business as a whole are 1990—[‡]; 1991—[‡]; 1992—[‡] and 1993 (estimated)—[‡].

Note: Percentages may not correspond exactly to the figures shown because of rounding.

TABLE 4   Sony: manufacturing companies' transactions with the recorded music business*

					£ million	
	1990	1991	1992	1993	1994 estimated
Sony Music Operations (division)					
Sales to recorded music business (A)	[				
Operating profits (B)					
Average capital employed (C)		*Figures omitted. See note on page iv.*			
Return on sales (%) (B/A)					
Return on capital employed (%) (B/C)					]

Source: Sony.

---

*For 1990 and 1991—year to 31 January; for 1992—14 months to 31 March; for 1993 and 1994—year to 31 March.

[*Details omitted. See note on page iv.*
                    ]

Note: Percentages may not correspond exactly to the figures shown because of rounding.

EMI

TABLE 5   EMI: distribution company's transactions with the recorded music business

		Year to 31 March			£ million	
	1990	1991	1992	1993	1994 estimated
EMI Music Services					
Sales to recorded music business (A)	[				
Operating profit (B)		*Figures omitted. See note on page iv.*			
Return on sales (%) (B/A)					]

Source: EMI.

Note: Percentages may not correspond exactly to the figures shown because of rounding.

PolyGram

11. PolyGram's distribution division, PRO, Chadwell Heath, receives fees for the products it distributes for the recorded music business. In its recorded music business results, PolyGram reported

---

‡Figures omitted. See note on page iv.

PRO, Chadwell Heath's actual costs of distribution rather than the fees paid to it. Table 8.5 includes this cost for Chadwell Heath, so that neither profits nor losses arise in the figures reported to us for distribution through this division.

Sony

TABLE 6 **Sony: distribution division's transactions with the recorded music business***

					£ million
	1990	1991	1992	1993	1994 estimated
Sony Music Operations (division)					
Sales to recorded music business (A)	[				
Operating profits (B)			*Figures omitted. See note on page iv.*		
Return on sales (%) (B/A)					]
Source: Sony.					

*For 1990 and 1991—year to 31 January; for 1992—14 months to 31 March; for 1993 and 1994—year to 31 March.
Note: Percentages may not correspond exactly to the figures shown because of rounding.

Results of the major retailers

[

Details omitted. See note on page iv.

]

[

Details omitted. See note on page iv.

]

[

Details omitted. See note on page iv.

]

[

Details omitted. See note on page iv.

]

[

Details omitted. See note on page iv.

]

248336 2C

[

Details omitted. See note on page iv.

]

List of the independent record companies which submitted views to the inquiry

Abstract Sounds Ltd
Academy Sound and Vision Ltd
Ace Records Ltd
Big Bear Records
Black Mountain Records
Chandos Records Ltd
Chaos Records Ltd (Cha'os)
China Records Ltd
Circle Sound Services
Collegium Records
Collins Classics
Conifer Records Ltd
Cooking Vinyl Ltd
Demon Records Ltd
Dino Entertainment Ltd
Disc Imports Ltd (DI Music)
Electronical Dreams
Exallshow Ltd (First Night Records)
FM-Revolver Records Ltd
Food (Records) Ltd
Gimell Records Limited
Graduate Music Ltd (Graduate Records & Music)
HTD Records Ltd
Harmonia Mundi UK Ltd
Horatio Nelson Records & Tapes Ltd
Hot House Records Ltd
Ice Records Ltd
Klub Records Limited
Look Good Products
Lyrita Recorded Edition
M&R Records Ltd
Mute Records Ltd
New Leaf Records
NMC Recordings Ltd
Olympia Compact Discs Ltd
Park Records
Pavilion Records Ltd
Plaza Records Ltd
Pulse 8 Records Ltd
PWL International Ltd
REL Records Ltd
Rumour Records Ltd
See for Miles Records Ltd
Serengeti Records
Soliton Records Ltd
Sound Solutions Ltd
Strange Fruit Records
Tema Records Ltd
Temple Records
The Abbey Recording Company Ltd
The Flying Record Company Ltd

248336   2C2

The Magnum Music Group
Toff Records (Pendragon)
Unicorn Records Limited (Unicorn-Kanchana Records)
Zomba Records Limited

One other company wished to remain anonymous.

Glossary

In this report the expressions and abbreviations listed have the meanings given below: in other contexts they may have different meanings.

1988 Copyright Act	The Copyright, Designs and Patents Act 1988, which consolidated UK copyright legislation and repealed earlier legislation, *inter alia*, the Copyright Act 1956.
A&R	Artist & Repertoire. The activity in a record company whose functions are to discover new talent, to sign artists and to develop the company's musical repertoire. The record industry regards it as the equivalent of research and development.
Album	A double-sided long-playing **(LP)** 10" or 12" **vinyl** disc which is designed to be played at 33 rpm and the equivalent full-length **cassette** and **CD**. To be eligible for the album **charts**, albums must consist of at least four **tracks**. **CD** albums are capable of containing nearly 80 minutes of music.
APRS	Association of Professional Recording Services Limited. The trade association for the professional sound industry of the UK.
BARD	British Association of Record Dealers. A body representing retailers of recorded music.
BBC AI	BBC Audio International. A joint venture between BBC Enterprises (a subsidiary of the BBC) and Monty Lewis Associates Ltd, established to make the BBC's classical sound recordings, recorded for broadcast purposes, available to the public on a commercial basis.
BCC	British Copyright Council. A body representing the interests of copyright owners of virtually all categories of works and products eligible for protection under the UK copyright laws, except sound recordings and films.
BEUC	The Bureau of European Consumer Unions. The body representing 23 national consumer organizations from all EC member states.
BIEM	The international organization managing the registration of mechanical reproduction rights.
BMG	BMG Records (UK) Limited. One of the **majors**.
BMRB	BMRB International, a company which conducted a survey for the MMC into price comparisons of recorded music in Europe and the USA.
Bootlegging	The unauthorized recording of a performance broadcast on radio or television, or of a live concert—one form of **illegal copying**.
BPI	The British Phonographic Industry Ltd. The leading UK trade association representing manufacturers, producers and sellers of recorded music.
Breaking an artist	A term of art in the industry. An artist is said to be 'broken' when he or she has achieved a significant degree of public recognition.
BREMA	British Radio and Electrical Manufacturers' Association.

Budget-price record	A **record** offered to dealers typically at a price below one-half that of a full-price **record**.
Cassette	An analogue tape record format. Also referred to as **music cassette** or MC.
Catalogue	The total number of recorded music titles offered by a record company for commercial exploitation.
CD-I	CD-interactive. A hardware system using discs with the same physical properties as a **CD** which allows a two-way flow of information between it and a user, responding immediately to the latter's input.
Charts	Lists of recordings showing on a historic (or, in the case of some retailers' charts, predictive) basis the top-selling 20, 40, 75 (or other) **singles** or **albums** in any one week.
CIN	Chart Information Network. The company which commissions and is the copyright holder of the official UK music and video **charts**.
Collective licensing body	A body which acts on behalf of individual and corporate holders of intellectual property rights, with a view to facilitating the licensing of such rights and collection of revenue from their exploitation.
Compact disc (CD)	A digital **format** used for the carriage and reproduction of music. Its music signals are read by a laser beam.
Counterfeiting	A form of **illegal copying** of sound recordings where unauthorized reproductions of an authorized recording are made and packaged to sound and look identical to the original.
DAT	Digital audio tape. A high-quality tape used in the industry to produce master recordings; it is no longer sold as a commercial format.
DCC	Digital compact cassette—a new record **format** in the form of a digitally encoded tape **cassette**.
Dealer price	The price at which a record company or its distributor sells records to retailers or wholesalers (see **PPD**).
EC	The European Community.
EMI	The EMI Music record companies in the UK including EMI Records Limited, Virgin Records Ltd and their subsidiaries. One of the **majors**.
EPOS	Electronic point of sale. A system connected to shop tills which records sales and can assist in sales analysis and stock control.
EROS	An electronic ordering system operated jointly by the distribution companies of **EMI**, **PolyGram** and **BMG**, which allows a retailer to place an order with any of these companies at any time.
EUK	Entertainment UK Ltd, the wholly-owned wholesaler and rack-jobber subsidiary of Kingfisher plc.
Format	The physical form in which recordings are sold: for example, a **single** or **album** on **vinyl**, **cassette**, **CD**, **MiniDisc** or **DCC**.
GATT	General Agreement on Tariffs and Trade.

Gig	A live show or concert by a pop artist.
HHI	Herfindahl Hirschmann Index of industry concentration.
Home taping	The taping by individuals on to blank audio tape of recorded music from commercial **records** or from the radio.
IBA	Independent Broadcasting Authority.
IFPI	The International Federation of the Phonographic Industry, the body which represents the world-wide recording industry, especially in the area of copyright protection.
Illegal copying	Illegal copying falls broadly into the following areas: **piracy** (which includes **bootlegging** and **counterfeiting**) and **home taping**.
IMF	International Managers' Forum. A forum for managers of popular music artists and producers.
Independent	An independent **label** or a record company not owned by a **major**. The term used in this report to refer to any record company other than one of the five **majors**.
Indie music	A genre of music recorded by and particularly associated with some **independents**, but also sometimes recorded by the **majors**.
KPMG	KPMG Peat Marwick, the firm of accountants which conducted a study for the MMC to evaluate the **majors'** profits and assets, taking into account the value of copyrights. See Appendix 8.2.
Label	The trading name under which the **catalogue** (or a portion of it) is marketed and managed. Often the term is synonymous with a record company, particularly small **independent** companies. Larger record companies may have many labels.
Leisure Goods Survey	A survey conducted by Management Horizons Europe for the MMC comparing the retail prices of a variety of leisure-related products valued at under £30 in the USA and the UK.
Line item	A particular title in a particular **format**; so that if a title is available in three **formats**, there will be three separate line items.
LP	Long-playing **record** or **album**. The term LP has traditionally been applied to **vinyl** albums.
Major(s)	(One of) the five record companies which are part of international groups and which have wholly-owned distribution operations in the UK: ie **BMG**, **EMI**, **PolyGram**, **Sony** and **Warner**.
Master	A two-track stereo recording fully edited, equalized and leadered, or metal parts created from such a tape, suitable for the manufacture of **CDs**, **vinyl** records or **cassettes**.
MCPS	Mechanical Copyright Protection Society Ltd. One of the UK **collective licensing bodies**.

MEA	Matrix Exchange Agreement. Each of the **majors** has an MEA which specifies the licence and royalty payments to be made by an affiliate in another territory who owns the copyright in that territory, in return for the exclusive licence to sell a recording there.
Mid-price record	A **record** offered to dealers typically at a price between one-half and two-thirds that of a full-price **record**.
MiniDisc	A new digital record **format** which is similar to a small **CD**.
MPA	Music Publishers Association. The trade association for the UK music publishing businesses.
MU	Musicians' Union. The main trade body representing musicians in the UK.
Music cassette (MC)	See **cassette**.
NHC	The National Heritage Committee of the House of Commons. It published a report, *The Price of Compact Discs*, on 6 May 1993.
Parallel imports	Imports, other than through the record companies' normal distribution channels, of **records** which have been lawfully put on the market overseas. For example, in the case of UK-sourced copyright material, the **records** might be produced under licence in the USA for sale there and then imported into the UK by a retailer or intermediary.
PBIT	Profit before interest and tax.
Piracy	A generic term used to describe the commercial exploitation of unauthorized sound recordings. The most common forms of piracy are **bootlegging** and **counterfeiting**.
PolyGram	PolyGram UK Holdings Plc and its record company subsidiaries in the UK. One of the **majors**.
PPD	The published price to dealer, before discount (see **dealer price**).
PPL	Phonographic Performance Ltd. One of the UK **collective licensing bodies**.
PRS	Performing Right Society Ltd. One of the UK **collective licensing bodies**.
PSA	The Prices Surveillance Authority in Australia. It produced a report on Australian record prices in 1990.
Record	A physical item of recorded music offered for sale, whether in the form of a **vinyl** disc, a **cassette** or a **CD** (or one of the newer **formats**).
Recording	The term used in this report to denote a musical work sold commercially in one or more **formats**.
Rental Directive	The EC Council Directive 92/100/EEC of 19 November 1992 which requires member states to provide a right for copyright holders to control the rental and lending of copyright works and also a right to control the first distribution of certain products within the **EC**.
Re-Pro	The Guild of Recording Producers, Directors and Engineers. A division of the **APRS**, representing record producers.

ROCE	Return on capital employed.
ROR	Return on revenue.
Royalty	In general, the term is used to refer to the payment made for the right to use copyright works for gain. In particular, it is used to describe the payment made by a record company to an artist out of the proceeds of sale of the recordings of his or her performance.
Single	A 7", 10" or 12" **vinyl** disc and the corresponding **cassette** and **CD** equivalent, embodying no more than four musical tracks.
Sony	Sony Music Entertainment (UK) Limited. One of the **majors**.
TMPDF	Trademarks Patents and Designs Federation. A body representing the interests of owners of intellectual property.
Track	The term used to describe a discrete item of music included on a **record**, for example one of the songs on a pop album or one of the movements of a classical work.
TRIPS	Agreement on trade-related aspects of intellectual property rights, including trade in counterfeit goods, concluded within the Uraguay Round of the **GATT**.
Umbrella	The Umbrella Organization Ltd. A body representing a number of small independent record companies.
Vinyl	An analogue **format** which consists of a 7", 10" or 12" plastic disc on which the music is recorded in grooves. It may be a **single** or an **album**. Vinyl albums are often referred to as **LPs**.
VPL	Video Performance Ltd. One of the UK **collective licensing bodies**.
Warner	Warner Music UK Limited. One of the **majors**.
WIPO	World Intellectual Property Organization. An international body responsible for promoting the protection of intellectual property throughout the world.

Index

Printed in the United Kingdom by HMSO
Dd 0402599   C16   6/94   3248336   19542